Excel 2000 Expert Course

Brian Favro

Russel Stolins

Developmental Editor: Brian Favro
Marketing Director: David Gauny
Production Management, Design and
   Publishing Consultation: The Cowans
Copy Editing: Nick Murray

Composition: The Cowans
Index: Bayside Indexing Service
Proofreading: Laura Lionello
Manufacturing Coordinator: The Cowans
Printer and Binder: Courier, Kendallville

LABYRINTH
PUBLICATIONS®

3314 Morningside Drive, El Sobrante, California   94803
(800) 522-9746   www.labyrinth-pub.com

Contents

From the Keyboard Summary Sheet—Excel 2000 Expert Course

NAVIGATION

Beginning of row	HOME
Down one screen	PGDN
End of row	CTRL+→
Go To specific cell	CTRL+G
Home cell (A1)	CTRL+HOME
Last cell in active part of worksheet	CTRL+END
Left one screen	ALT+PGUP
Right one screen	ALT+PGDN
Up one screen	PGUP

SELECTING

Block	SHIFT while clicking last cell in block
Current column	CTRL+SPACE BAR
Current row	SHIFT+SPACE BAR
Entire worksheet	CTRL+A
Extend selection	SHIFT+Arrow Key
Multiple objects	SHIFT while clicking objects
Multiple ranges	CTRL while selecting ranges
Multiple worksheets	CTRL while clicking sheets
Range of worksheets	SHIFT while clicking last sheet in range

EDITING

Cancel entry	ESC
Complete entry	ENTER
Copy while dragging	CTRL
Copy	CTRL+C
Cut	CTRL+X
Delete cell contents	DELETE
Delete text to end of line	CTRL+DELETE
Hard Carriage Return	ALT+ENTER
Paste	CTRL+V
Redo	CTRL+Y
Repeat	CTRL+Y
Undo	CTRL+Z

TEXT AND NUMBER FORMATS

Bold	CTRL+B
Comma style	CTRL+SHIFT+!
Currency style	CTRL+SHIFT+$
Format cells dialog box	CTRL+1
General style	CTRL+SHIFT+~
Italics	CTRL+I
Percent style	CTRL+SHIFT+%
Underline	CTRL+U

FORMULAS AND DIALOG BOXES

Absolute cell reference	F4
AutoSum	ALT+=
Find dialog box	CTRL+F4
Hyperlink dialog box	CTRL+K
Office Assistant (displaying)	F1
Office Assistant (hiding speech balloon)	ESC
Open dialog box	CTRL+O
Print dialog box	CTRL+P
Replace dialog box	CTRL+H
Save	CTRL+S
Display or hide formulas	CTRL+~

DRAWING OBJECTS

Draw circle	SHIFT while drawing new oval
Draw lines at 15-degree increments	SHIFT while drawing new line
Draw square	SHIFT while drawing new rectangle
Maintain proportions of existing oval	SHIFT while sizing existing oval
Maintain proportions of existing rectangle	SHIFT while sizing existing rectangle
Size object while maintaining proportions	SHIFT while sizing object

Quick Reference Index

Visual Conventions

This book uses many visual and typographic cues to guide you through the lessons. This page provides examples and describes the function of each.

Typographic Cue	What It Indicates
Ⓐ Ⓑ Ⓒ	These characters indicate the order in which tasks should be performed in a Hands-On exercise.
Type this text	Anything you should type at the keyboard is printed in this typeface.
TIP!	This is an important tip which usually contains shortcuts or reminders.
Note!	This contains information that will help you understand a concept or a feature.
Warning!	Read and consider each warning before continuing with the lesson.
Command→Command	Indicates multiple selections to be made from a menu bar. For example: **File→Save** means you should click the **File** command in the menu bar, then click the **Save** command from the drop-down menu.
From the Keyboard **From the Keyboard** CTRL+S to Save	These margin notes indicate shortcut keys for executing a task described in the text. For example, CTRL+S to save your work in an application program.

Special Section	Purpose
Quick Reference **Quick Reference**	These sections contain generic procedures you can use to accomplish a task at any time. *Note: As you work through a lesson, you should not perform instructions in Quick Reference sections unless you are told to do so in a Hands-On exercise instruction.*
Hands-On Exercise	This section contains specific instructions for the exercise you are working on. You should always work through the Hands-On exercises. These exercises will guide you step-by-step through the topics. You will be told exactly what to do, which keys to press, and other steps to try out a new skill or feature.
Concepts Review	This section contains questions that help you gauge your mastery of the concepts covered in the lesson.
Skill Builders	This section contains additional exercises that provide opportunities for review.
Assessment	This section contains a test on the material covered in the lesson.
Critical Thinking	Critical Thinking exercises give you the opportunity to apply your knowledge to solve a realistic problem with minimal guidance. Some of these exercises are performed on your own, others are performed in groups.

LESSON 1

Creating and Editing a Simple Worksheet

In this lesson, you will develop fundamental Excel 2000 skills. This lesson will provide you with a solid foundation of skills so that you are prepared to master the advanced features introduced in later lessons. For example, you will learn basic skills, including selecting cells, entering and editing text and numbers, and aligning cell entries. In addition, you will use Excel's powerful yet easy-to-use AutoSum tool to sum rows and columns of numbers.

In This Lesson

Case Study

Susan Lee is a student intern at Computer Depot, a discount retailer of computers and computer accessories. Joel Williams, the buyer for Computer Depot, has asked Susan to report the number of PCs, laptop computers, printers, and monitors sold during a five-day period. Joel has instructed Susan to report the data on a daily basis and to include the number of units sold by each manufacturer. After analyzing Joel's request, Susan decides that Excel 2000 is the right tool for the job. She organizes the data in an Excel worksheet and uses Excel's AutoSum feature to compute the necessary totals.

	A	B	C	D	E	F	G	H
1	Computer Depot Weekly Sales Data							
2								
3			Wednesday	Thursday	Friday	Saturday	Sunday	
4	PCs							Totals
5		Compaq	3	10	12	15	16	56
6		IBM	4	8	10	13	14	49
7		Acer	6	13	15	18	19	71
8		Total	13	31	37	46	49	176
9								
10	Laptops							
11		IBM	2	5	4	10	8	29
12		Apple PowerBook	3	7	5	12	10	37
13		Compaq	4	8	11	14	14	51
14		Toshiba	2	3	5	5	3	18
15		Total	11	23	25	41	35	135
16								
17	Printers							
18		IBM	3	5	5	6	8	27
19		HP	6	1	2	3	7	19
20		Canon	8	2	3	4	5	22
21		Total	17	8	10	13	20	68
22								
23	Monitors							
24		NEC	3	6	8	7	2	26
25		Sony	5	3	2	2	1	13
26		Compaq	2	2	6	8	3	21
27		Total	10	11	16	17	6	60

What Is Microsoft Excel?

Microsoft Excel is an electronic spreadsheet (also known as a worksheet) program that makes working with numbers a pleasure instead of a chore. Excel provides tools to assist you in virtually every aspect of worksheet creation and analysis. Whether you are creating dynamic charts for a presentation or interactive worksheets for group collaboration, Excel has the right tool for the job. For these and many other reasons, Excel is the most widely used worksheet program in both homes and businesses.

Why Use Excel?

Excel provides a number of important features and benefits that make it a smart choice.

1. **IntelliSense technology**—Excel's IntelliSense technology includes automated tools to assist you in entering, editing, and analyzing data. This speeds up the process of creating worksheets so that you can focus on analysis and other tasks.

2. **GUI**—Excel's Graphical User Interface is so easy to use that even beginning computer users find it simple. The interface reduces the need to memorize commands, and it will make you more productive.

3. **Charting**—Have you heard the expression, "One picture is worth a thousand words?" This is especially true with financial or numeric data. Excel's powerful charting and formatting features let you display your data in a powerful and convincing graphic format.

4. **Widely used**—Excel is the most widely used worksheet software. Excel is the right choice if you are trying to develop marketable skills and find employment.

5. **Integration with other Office programs**—Excel 2000 is part of the Microsoft Office 2000 suite of programs, which also includes Word, Access, PowerPoint, Outlook, PhotoDraw, and others. The ability to exchange data with these programs is one of the most powerful and attractive features of Excel.

6. **Web integration**—Excel 2000 lets you easily publish your worksheets to Web sites on the World Wide Web or to your company Intranet.

It's Time to Learn Excel!

It's time to put your fears behind and learn this wonderful program. You will be amazed at the power and simplicity of Excel and how easy it is to learn. The knowledge you are about to gain will give you a marketable skill and make you an Excel master.

Starting Excel

The method you use to start Excel and other Office programs depends in large part upon whether you intend to create a new workbook or open an existing workbook. A workbook is a file containing one or more worksheets. If you intend to create a new workbook, then use one of the following methods to start Excel. Once the Excel program has started, you can begin working in the new workbook that appears.

- Click the **Start** button, and choose Microsoft Excel from the Programs menu.

- Click the Microsoft Excel button on the Quick Launch toolbar (located near the Taskbar).

- Click the Start button, choose New Office Document, choose the General tab, and double-click the Blank Workbook icon.

Use one of the following methods if you intend to open an existing Excel workbook. Once the Excel program has started, the desired workbook will open in an Excel window.

■ Navigate to the desired document using Windows Explorer or My Computer, and double-click the workbook.

■ Click the **Start** button and point to Documents. You can choose the desired workbook from the Documents list. The Documents list displays the most recently used Office documents.

Hands-On 1.1 Start Excel

In this exercise, you will start the Excel program.

1. Start your computer, and the Windows desktop will be displayed.

2. Click the **Start** button and choose Programs.

3. Choose Microsoft Excel from the Programs menu.
   The Excel program will load, and the Excel window will appear. Don't be concerned if your window appears different from the example shown in the following illustration.

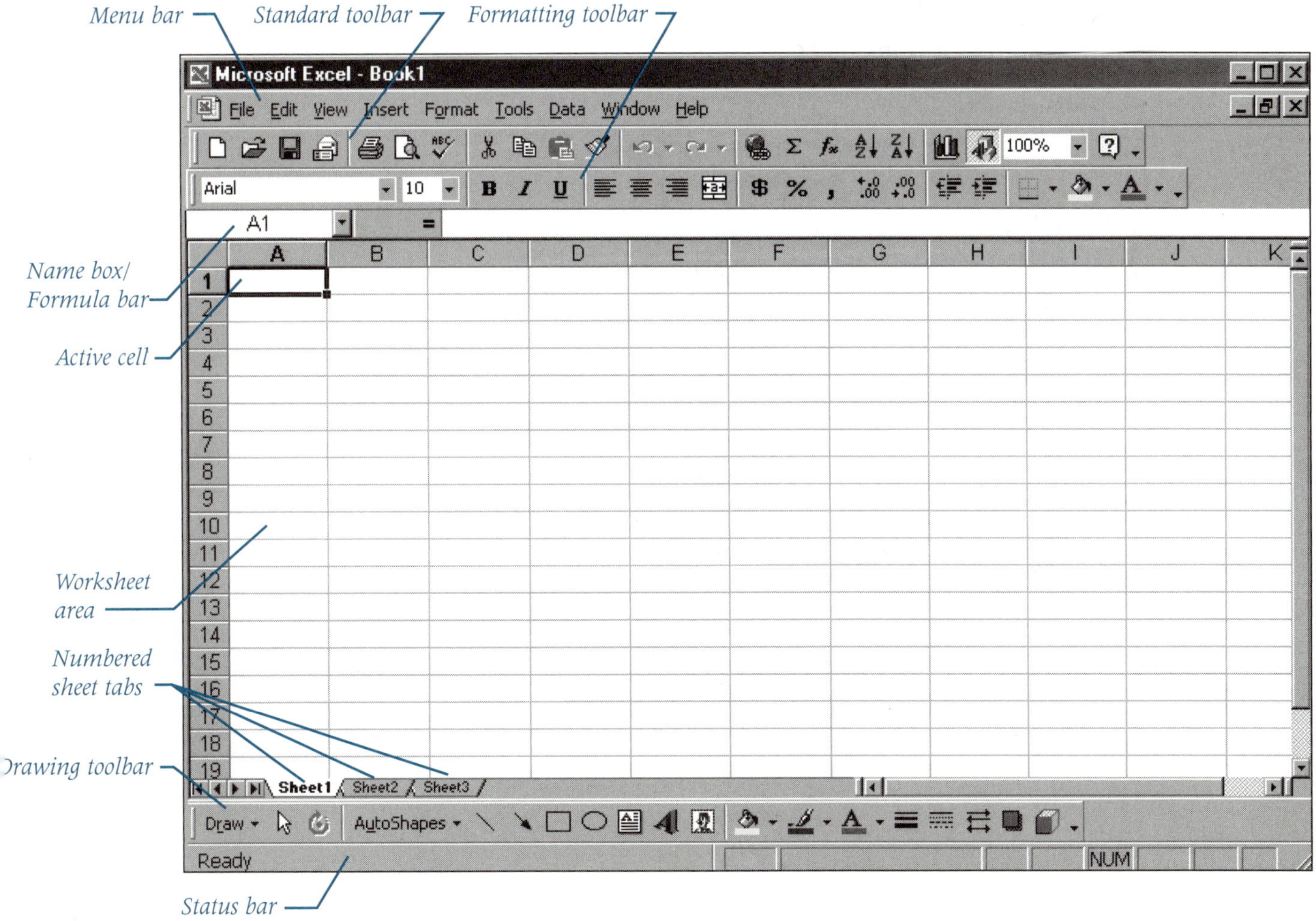

Menu bar — Standard toolbar — Formatting toolbar

Name box/
Formula bar

Active cell

Worksheet
area

Numbered
sheet tabs

Drawing toolbar

Status bar

Worksheets and Workbooks

Excel displays a blank **workbook** the moment you start the program. A workbook is composed of **worksheets.** This is similar to a paper notebook with many sheets of paper. You enter text, numbers, formulas, charts, and other objects in worksheets. Excel displays three worksheets in a new workbook. You can insert new worksheets, up to a maximum of 255 worksheets per workbook.

A worksheet has a grid structure with horizontal rows and vertical columns. A new worksheet has 256 columns and 65,536 rows. However, at any given time, only a small number of the rows and columns are visible in the worksheet window. The intersection of each row and column is a **cell.** Each cell is identified by a **reference.** The reference is the column letter followed by the row number. For example, A1 is the reference of the cell in the top–left corner of the worksheet. So, we refer to this cell as Cell A1.

The Highlight

The **highlight** is a thick line surrounding the active cell. You can move the highlight by clicking in a cell or by using the keyboard. Moving the highlight is important because data is entered into the active cell. The vertical and horizontal scroll bars let you scroll through a worksheet. However, scrolling does not move the highlight. You must position the highlight in the desired cell after scrolling. The following table lists important keystrokes that move the highlight.

Quick Reference

NAVIGATING A WORKSHEET

Keystroke(s)	How the Highlight Is Moved
→ ← ↑ ↓	One cell to the right, left, up, or down
(HOME)	To the beginning of current row
(CTRL)+→	End of current row
(CTRL)+(HOME)	Home cell, usually Cell A1
(CTRL)+(END)	Last cell in active part of worksheet
(PGDN)	Down one screen
(PGUP)	Up one screen
(ALT)+(PGDN)	One screen to the right
(ALT)+(PGUP)	One screen to the left
(CTRL)+G	Displays Go To dialog box. Enter cell reference and click OK to go to that cell.

1. Slide the mouse, and the pointer will have a thick cross ✛ shape when it is in the worksheet area.

2. Click the pointer on any cell, and the highlight will move to that cell.

3. Move the highlight five times by clicking in various cells.

Use the Keyboard to Move the Highlight

In the next few steps, you will move the highlight with the keyboard. You can use the keys on the main part of your keyboard or on the Numeric keypad at the bottom right corner of your keyboard. Keep in mind, however, that you must have the (NUM LOCK) *key turned off if you want to move the highlight with the Numeric keypad. The word NUM will disappear from the Status bar when Num Lock is turned off.*

4. Use the arrow → ← ↑ ↓ keys to position the highlight in Cell F10.

5. Tap the (HOME) key, and the highlight will move to Cell A10.
   The (HOME) *key always moves the highlight to Column A in the active row.*

6. Press (CTRL)+(HOME) to move the highlight to Cell A1.

7. Tap the (PGDN) key two or three times.
   Notice that Excel displays the next twenty or so rows each time you tap (PGDN).

8. Press and hold the ↑ key until the highlight is in Cell A1.

Use the Scroll Bars

9. Click the Scroll Right ▶ button on the horizontal scroll bar until Columns AA and AB are visible.
   Excel labels the first 26 columns A–Z and the next 26 columns AA–AZ. A similar labeling scheme is used for the remaining columns.

10. Take a few minutes to practice scrolling and moving the highlight.

(Continued on the next page)

Explore the Excel Window

11. Follow these steps to explore the Excel window.

Ⓐ *Notice the Name box on the Formula bar. Don't worry if your Formula bar is not displayed. You will learn to display and hide the Formula bar soon. The Name box displays the name or reference of the active cell.*

Ⓑ *Click the Sheet2 tab, and another blank worksheet will be displayed. A workbook can have up to 255 worksheets.*

Ⓒ *Click the Sheet1 tab.*

12. Press CTRL+HOME to move the highlight to Cell A1.

Entering Data

You can begin entering data the moment Excel is started. Data is entered into the active cell (the cell with the highlight). You can enter text, numbers, or formulas into cells. Text and numbers are used for different purposes in a worksheet. Text is used for descriptive headings and entries that require alphabetic characters or a combination of alphabetic and numeric characters. Numbers can be calculated using formulas. Excel recognizes the data you enter and decides whether the entry is text, a number, or a formula.

Long Text Entries

Text entries are often too long to fit in a cell. These entries are known as **long entries.** Excel uses the following rules when deciding how to display long entries.

- If the cell to the right of the long entry is empty, then the long entry displays over the adjacent cell.

- If the cell to the right of the long entry contains an entry, then Excel shortens, or **truncates,** the display of the long entry.

Keep in mind that Excel does not actually change the long entry, it simply truncates the display of the entry. You can always widen a column to accommodate a long entry.

The entry, Computer Depot Weekly Sales *is a long entry. The entire phrase is entered in Cell A1 although it displays over Cells B1 and C1.*

	A	B	C
1	Computer Depot Weekly Sales		
2			
3			Wednesday
4	PCs		

Completing Cell Entries

Enter text or numbers by positioning the highlight in the desired cell, typing the desired text or number, and completing the entry. You can use (ENTER) and any of the arrow → ← ↑ ↓ keys to complete an entry. When you complete an entry with (ENTER), the text or number is entered in the cell, and the highlight moves down to the next cell. When you complete an entry with an arrow key, the text or number is entered in the cell, and the highlight moves to the next cell in the direction of the arrow key. If you are entering text or numbers and change your mind prior to completing the entry, you can press (ESC) to cancel the entry.

The Enter and Cancel Buttons

The Enter ☑ button and Cancel ☒ button appear on the Formula bar whenever you are entering or editing an entry. The Enter button completes the entry, and the highlight remains in the current cell. The Cancel button cancels the entry, as does the (ESC) key.

The Cancel button and Enter button appear when an entry is being entered or edited.

| A1 | ▾ | ✗ ✓ | = | Computer Depot Weekly Sales |

	A	B	C	D	E
1	Computer Depot Weekly Sales				
2					

Deleting and Replacing Entries

You can delete an entry after it has been completed by clicking in the cell and tapping (DELETE). Likewise, you can replace an entry by clicking in the cell and typing a new entry. The new entry will replace the original entry.

Undo and Redo

Excel's Undo ↰ button lets you reverse your last 16 action(s). You can reverse simple actions such as accidentally deleting a cell's content, or you can reverse more complex actions such as deleting an entire row. Most actions can be undone. Actions that can't be undone include commands such as printing workbooks and saving workbooks.

From the Keyboard

(CTRL)+Z for undo

(CTRL)+Y for redo

The Redo ↱ button reverses Undo. Use Redo when you Undo an action but decide to go through with that action after all.

Undoing and Redoing Multiple Actions

The arrows ▾ on the Undo and Redo buttons display lists of actions that can be undone or redone. You can undo or redo multiple actions by dragging the mouse over the desired actions. You can undo or redo up to 16 actions using this method. However, you must undo or redo actions in the order in which they appear on the drop-down list.

Repeat

The **Edit→Repeat** command lets you repeat your last action. For example, imagine you want to change the font size for several cells in a worksheet. To accomplish this, you could change the font size in one cell, reposition the highlight, and then issue the Repeat command. The Repeat command will set the font size for the new cell to the same size you set in the previous cell. You can repeat an action as many times as desired. However, the Repeat command is only available when the Redo button is unavailable. The **Edit→Repeat** command changes to **Edit→Redo** as soon as you undo an action.

From the Keyboard

(CTRL)+Y for repeat

Hands-On 1.3 Entering Text

Type a Long Entry

1. Make Cell A1 active by clicking the mouse pointer ✛ in it.

2. Type **Computer Depot Weekly Sales**, and tap (ENTER).
   The text should be entered in the cell, and the highlight should move down to Cell A2. Excel moves the highlight down when you tap (ENTER) because most people enter data column by column. Notice that the entry displays over Cells B1 and C1. The long entry would not display over these cells if they contained data.

3. Click in Cell A1, and note the appearance of the Formula bar.

| A1 | ▾ | = | Computer Depot Weekly Sales |

Notice that the Formula bar displays the name of the active Cell (A1) and the cell's content. In this example, the cell's content is the title Computer Depot Weekly Sales. The title is a long entry because it is wider than Cell A1. Cells B1 and C1 are empty, so the long entry is displayed over them. Keep in mind; however, that the entire entry belongs to Cell A1. This concept will be demonstrated in the next few steps.

Delete the Entry and Use Undo and Redo

4. Tap (DELETE) and the entire entry is deleted.

   Notice that the entire entry was deleted because it belonged to Cell A1.

5. Click Undo [↶] to restore the entry.

6. Click Redo [↷], and the entry will be deleted again.

   Redo always reverses Undo.

7. Click Undo [↶] again to restore the entry.

Verify That the Entry Belongs to Cell A1

8. Tap the → key to make Cell B1 active.

9. Look at the Formula bar, and notice that Cell B1 is empty.

   Once again, the long entry belongs to Cell A1 even though it is displayed over Cells B1 and C1.

Type Additional Text Entries

10. Use the → and ↓ keys to position the highlight in Cell C3.

11. Type **Wednesday**, and tap → once.

    Notice that the entry is completed and the highlight moves to Cell D3. You can always use the arrow keys to complete an entry and move the highlight in the desired direction.

12. Type **Thursday** in Cell D3, and tap →.

    Notice that the display of Wednesday is shortened or truncated. A long entry is always truncated when the cell to the right contains text or a number.

13. Enter the remaining text entries as shown in the illustration on the following page.

    Use Undo if you make a mistake. Also, you can change any entry by clicking in the desired cell and retyping the entry.

(Continued on the next page)

	A	B	C	D	E	F	G
1	Computer Depot Weekly Sales						
2							
3			Wednesda	Thursday	Friday	Saturday	Sunday
4	PCs						
5		Compaq					
6		IBM					
7		Acer					
8		Total					
9							
10	Laptops						
11		IBM					
12		Apple					
13		Empower					
14		Toshiba					
15		Total					
16							
17	Printers						
18		IBM					
19		HP					
20		Canon					
21		Total					
22							
23	Monitors						
24		NEC					
25		Sony					
26		Compaq					
27		Total					

You will continue to enhance your worksheet in the next exercise.

Number Entries

Numbers can only contain the digits 0–9 and a few other characters. Excel initially right-aligns numbers in cells, although you can change the alignment. The following table lists characters Excel will accept as part of a number entry.

Valid Characters in Number Entries

Digits 0–9

The following characters: + – ( ) , / $ % .

Number Formats

It isn't necessary to type commas, dollar signs, or other number formats when entering numbers. It is easier to just enter the numbers and then use Excel's formatting commands to add the desired number format(s). You will learn how to format numbers soon.

Decimals and Negative Numbers

You should always type a decimal point if the number you are entering requires one. Likewise, you should precede a negative number entry with a minus sign or enclose it in parenthesis ( ).

Hands-On 1.4 Enter Numbers

Use the Enter Button

1. Position the highlight in Cell C5.

2. Type **3**, but don't complete the entry.

3. Look at the Formula bar, and notice the Cancel ☒ and Enter ☑ buttons.
   These buttons appear whenever you begin entering or editing data in a cell.

4. Click the Enter ☑ button to complete the entry.
   Notice that the highlight remains in Cell C5. You can use the Enter button to complete entries; however, it is more efficient to complete entries with the keyboard when building a worksheet. This is because the highlight automatically moves to the next cell. The Enter button is most useful when editing entries.

Use the Cancel Button and the (ESC) Key

5. Position the highlight in Cell C6 and type **4**, but don't complete the entry.

6. Click the Cancel ☒ button on the Formula bar to cancel the entry.

7. Type **4** again, but this time tap (ESC) on the keyboard.
   (ESC) has the same effect as the Cancel button.

8. Type **4** once again, and tap ↓.
   Notice that Excel right-aligns the number in the cell.

9. Enter the remaining numbers as shown in the illustration on the following page.
   Keep in mind that some of the numbers you enter will cause entries in Column B to be truncated. You will solve this problem by widening Column B later in this exercise.

(Continued on the next page)

	A	B	C	D	E	F	G
1	Computer Depot Weekly Sales						
2							
3			Wednesda	Thursday	Friday	Saturday	Sunday
4	PCs						
5		Compaq	3	10	12	15	16
6		IBM	4	8	10	13	14
7		Acer	6	13	15	18	19
8		Total					
9							
10	Laptops						
11		IBM	2	5	4	10	8
12		Apple	3	7	5	12	10
13		Empower	4	8	11	14	14
14		Toshiba	2	3	5	5	3
15		Total					
16							
17	Printers						
18		IBM	3	5	5	6	8
19		HP	6	1	2	3	7
20		Canon	8	2	3	4	5
21		Total					
22							
23	Monitors						
24		NEC	3	6	8	7	2
25		Sony	5	3	2	2	1
26		Compaq	2	2	6	8	3
27		Total					

10. Take a moment to check the accuracy of your text and numbers.

    It is very important to be accurate when entering data in worksheets. Excel's formulas, charts, and other features are of little use unless your data is accurate. You will learn how to save the workbook in the next topic.

Save Concepts

One important lesson to learn is to save your workbooks frequently! Power outages and careless accidents can result in lost data. The best protection is to save your workbooks every 10 or 15 minutes, or after making significant changes. Workbooks are saved to storage locations such as floppy disks, hard disks, or to Web sites on the World Wide Web.

Save Command

From the Keyboard

CTRL+S for Save

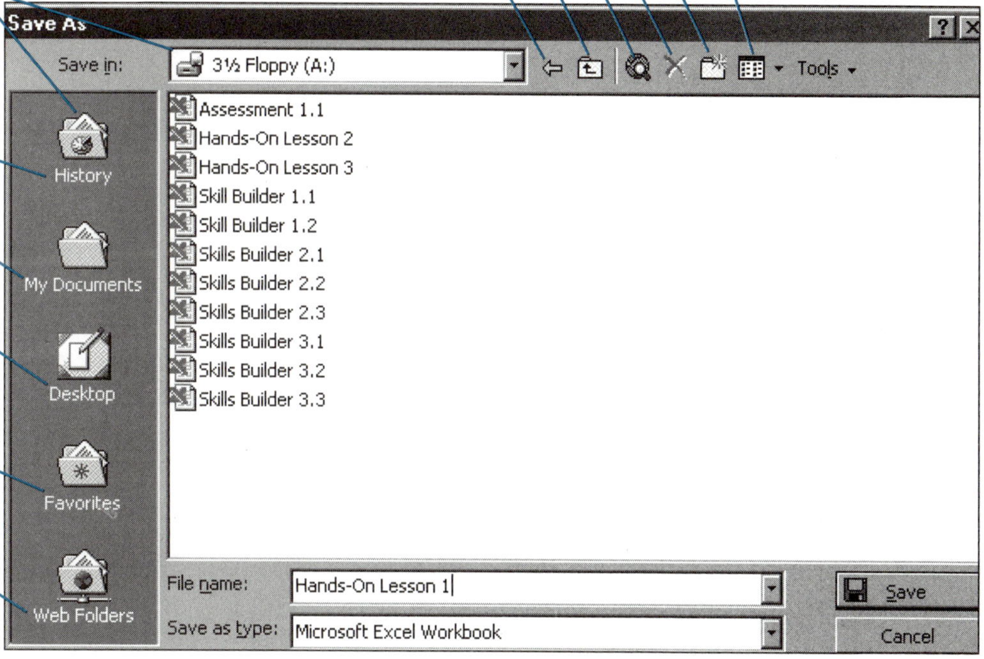

The Save 🖫 button on the Standard toolbar and **File→Save** initiate the Save command. If a document has previously been saved, Excel then replaces the original version with the new edited version. If a document has never been saved, Excel then displays the **Save As** dialog box. The Save As dialog box has been significantly enhanced in Excel 2000. The Save As dialog box lets you specify the name and storage location of the document. You can also use the Save As dialog box to make a copy of a document by saving it under a new name or to a different location. You can use filenames containing as many as 255 characters. The following illustration outlines the Save As dialog box functions.

Search the Web displays a list of Web search engines. —

— Delete the selected file(s) or folder(s).

Move up one level in the storage hierarchy. —

— Create a new folder.

Go to previous storage location. —

— Change the view.

You can choose a storage location from the **Save In** list or click a button on the Places bar.

The **History** button on the Places bar displays the last 20 to 50 documents and folders accessed. —

My Documents is the default storage location in Office programs. —

The **Desktop** lists storage locations in the Windows desktop. —

Favorites is a folder to which you can add frequently used files and folders. —

Web folders is a location to which you can save Web pages for publication on the Internet or an Intranet. —

In this exercise, you will save the workbook created in the previous exercises. Your instructor will most likely want you to save your workbooks onto the exercise diskette that is provided with this book. You will most likely be saving workbooks onto the A: disk drive.

1. Click the Save ⊞ button, and the Save As dialog box will appear.

2. Follow these steps to save the workbook.
   Keep in mind that your dialog box will contain more files than shown here.

Ⓐ *Click here, and choose the disk drive with your exercise diskette. It is most likely 3½ Floppy (A:).*

Ⓑ *Notice that Excel proposes the filename* Book1 *in the File name box.*

Ⓒ *Type the name* **Hands-On Lesson 1***, and it will replace the proposed name. (If you switched disk drives, then you may need to click in the* File name *box, delete the proposed name with the* (DELETE) *and/or* (BACKSPACE) *keys, and then type the new name.)*

Ⓓ *Click the* **Save** *button.*

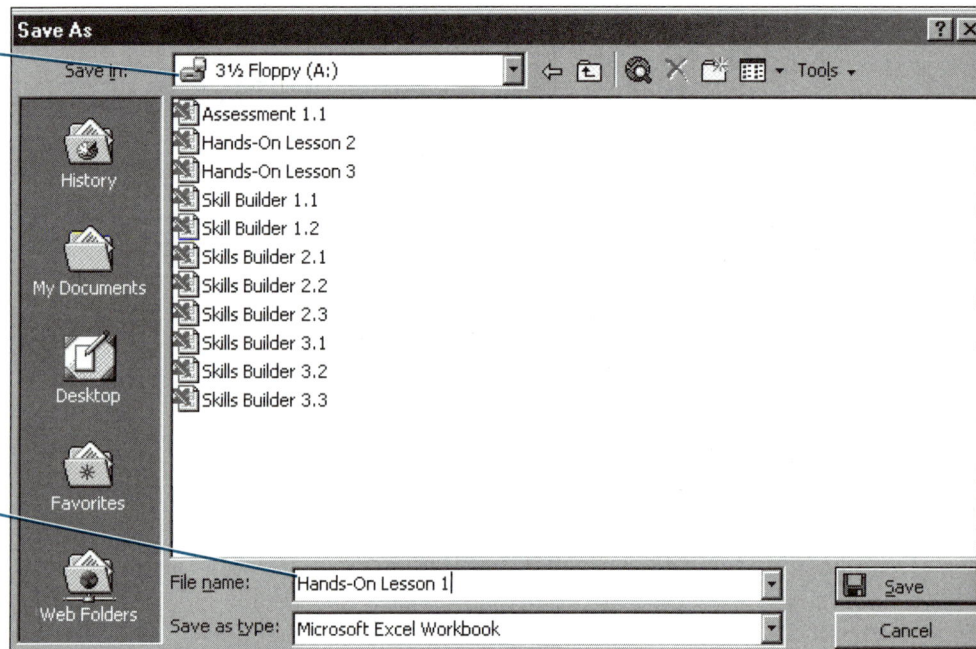

Save As		? X
Save in:	3½ Floppy (A:)	⇐ 🔼 🔍 ✕ 📁 ▦ ▾ Tools ▾

Assessment 1.1
Hands-On Lesson 2
Hands-On Lesson 3
Skill Builder 1.1
Skill Builder 1.2
Skills Builder 2.1
Skills Builder 2.2
Skills Builder 2.3
Skills Builder 3.1
Skills Builder 3.2
Skills Builder 3.3

History
My Documents
Desktop
Favorites
Web Folders

File name:	Hands-On Lesson 1		🖫 Save
Save as type:	Microsoft Excel Workbook		Cancel

Notice that the workbook was saved and remains on the screen. You will continue to use this workbook throughout the lesson.

Editing Entries

You can edit the active cell by clicking in the Formula bar and making the desired changes. You can also double-click a cell and then edit the contents directly in the cell. This technique is known as **in-cell editing.**

Replacing Entries

Editing an entry is efficient if the entry is long enough that retyping it would be time-consuming. Editing can also be efficient with complex formulas and other functions that are difficult to recreate. If the entry requires little typing, however, it is usually easier to just replace it.

Deleting Characters

From the Keyboard

(CTRL)+(DELETE) to delete text to end of line

Use the (DELETE) and (BACKSPACE) keys to edit entries in the Formula bar or within a cell. The (DELETE) key removes the character to the right of the insertion point, while the (BACKSPACE) key removes the character to the left of the insertion point.

Hands-On 1.6 Edit Entries

The Hands-On Lesson 1 workbook should be open from the previous exercise.

Edit in the Formula Bar

1. Click Cell A1.

2. Follow these steps to edit Cell A1 using the Formula bar.

Ⓐ *Click in the Formula bar just to the right of the word* Sales. Ⓑ *Tap the* (SPACE BAR)*, and type the word* **Data**.

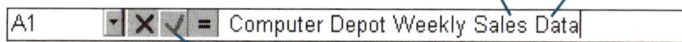

| A1 | ▾ | X | √ | = | Computer Depot Weekly Sales Data |

Ⓒ *Click the* (ENTER) *button.*

Replace an Entry

3. Click Cell B13.

4. Type **Compaq**, and tap (ENTER).
   The entry Compaq will replace Empower.

Use In-Cell Editing

5. *Double-click* Cell B12 (the cell with the word *Apple*).

6. Use the mouse or the → key to position the flashing insertion point to the right of the word *Apple*.

7. Tap the (SPACE BAR) once, and type **PowerBook**.

8. Tap (ENTER) or click Enter ☑ to complete the change.
   The entry should now read Apple PowerBook (although the entry will be slightly truncated). You will fix the truncation by widening the column later in this lesson.

9. Click the Save 🖫 button to update the changes.
   The Save button automatically saves changes to a workbook that has previously been saved.

Selecting Cells

In Excel, you can select cells using both the mouse and the keyboard. You can perform a variety of actions on selected cells, including moving, copying, deleting, and formatting.

A **range** is a rectangular group of cells. Earlier in this lesson, you learned that each cell has a reference. For example, A1 refers to the first cell in a worksheet. Likewise, a range reference specifies the cells that are included within a range. The range reference includes the first and last cells in the range separated by a colon (:). For example, the Range C3:G3 includes all cells between C3 and G3. The following illustration highlights several ranges and their corresponding range references.

The Range C3:G3 —

The Range B5:B8 —

The Range B11:C14 —

	A	B	C	D	E	F	G
1	Computer Depot Weekly Sales Data						
2							
3			Wednesda	Thursday	Friday	Saturday	Sunday
4	PCs						
5		Compaq	3	10	12	15	16
6		IBM	4	8	10	13	14
7		Acer	6	13	15	18	19
8		Total					
9							
10	Laptops						
11		IBM	2	5	4	10	8
12		Apple Pow	3	7	5	12	10
13		Compaq	4	8	11	14	14
14		Toshiba	2	3	5	5	3

The following Quick Reference table describes selection techniques in Excel.

Quick Reference

SELECTION TECHNIQUES

Technique	How to Do It
Select a range.	Drag the mouse pointer over the desired cells.
Select several ranges.	Select a range; then press (CTRL) while selecting additional range(s).
Select an entire column.	Click a column heading, or press (CTRL)+(SPACE BAR).
Select an entire row.	Click a row heading, or press (SHIFT)+(SPACE BAR).
Select multiple columns or rows.	Drag the mouse pointer over the desired column or row headings.
Select an entire worksheet.	Click the Select All button at the top–left corner of the worksheet, or press (CTRL)+A.
Select a range using the (SHIFT) key.	Position the highlight in the first cell you wish to select, press (SHIFT), and click the last cell in the range.
Extend a selection with the (SHIFT) key.	Press (SHIFT) while tapping any arrow key.

1. Position the mouse pointer ⊕ over Cell C3.

2. Press and hold the left mouse button while dragging the mouse to the right until the range C3:G3 is selected.

3. Deselect the cells by clicking anywhere in the worksheet.

Select Multiple Ranges

4. Select the range C3:G3 as you did in steps 1 and 2.

5. Press and hold (CTRL) while you select the range B5:B8, as shown to the right.
   Both the C3:G3 and B5:B8 ranges should be selected. The (CTRL) key lets you select more than one range at the same time.

5		Compaq
6		IBM
7		Acer
8		Total

6. Press and hold (CTRL) while you select another range.
   There should now be three ranges selected.

7. Deselect the ranges by releasing (CTRL) and clicking anywhere in the worksheet.

Select Entire Rows and Columns

8. Follow these steps to select various rows and columns.

Ⓐ *Click on the **Column A** heading to select the entire column.*

Ⓑ *Position the mouse pointer on the **Column C** heading, then drag to the right until **Columns C, D,** and **E** are selected. **Column A** will be deselected.*

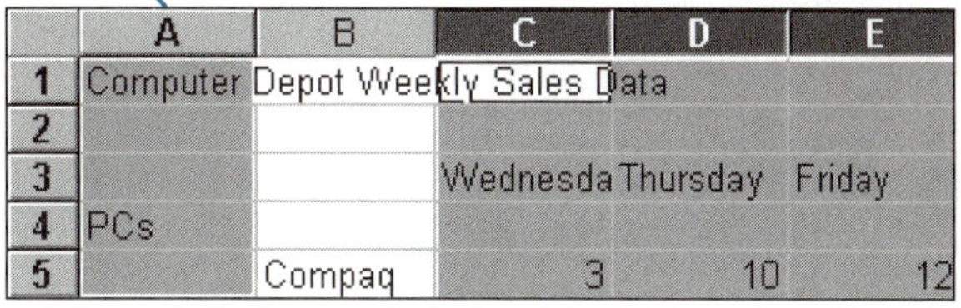

	A	B	C	D	E
1	Computer	Depot Weekly Sales Data			
2					
3			Wednesda	Thursday	Friday
4	PCs				
5		Compaq	3	10	12

Ⓐ *Click the Select All button to select the entire worksheet.*

Ⓑ *Click the Row 1 heading to select Row 1.*

Ⓒ *Drag the mouse pointer down over the headings to Rows 5–8 to select them.*

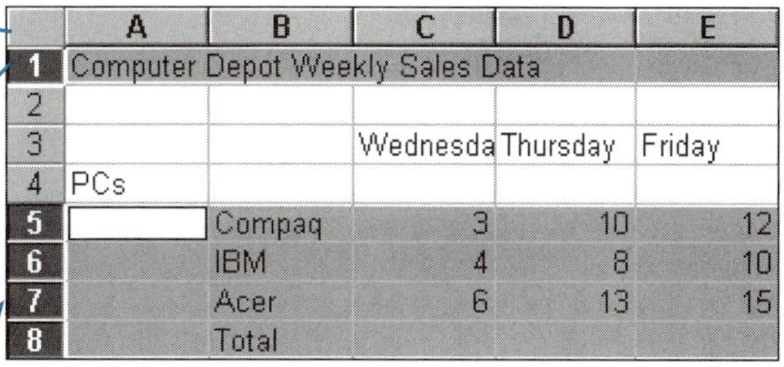

	A	B	C	D	E
1	Computer Depot Weekly Sales Data				
2					
3			Wednesda	Thursday	Friday
4	PCs				
5		Compaq	3	10	12
6		IBM	4	8	10
7		Acer	6	13	15
8		Total			

(Continued on the next page)

Use Keyboard Techniques

9. Click Cell B5.

10. Press and hold (SHIFT); then click Cell G8 to select the range B5:G8.

11. Click Cell B11.

12. Press and hold (SHIFT) then tap → five times, and ↓ four times.
    The range B11:G15 should be selected. Notice that the (SHIFT) key techniques give you precise control when selecting. You should use the (SHIFT) key techniques if you find it difficult to select with the mouse.

13. Take a moment to practice selection techniques.

Aligning Cell Entries

The Align Left, Center, and Align Right buttons on the Formatting toolbar let you align entries within cells. By default, text entries are left-aligned and numbers are right-aligned. To change alignment, select the cell(s) and click the desired alignment button.

Hands-On 1.8 Align Text Entries and Widen Columns

In this exercise, you will align the entries in Row 3. You will also widen Columns B and C.

1. Select the range C3:G3.

   | Wednesda | Thursday | Friday | Saturday | Sunday |

2. Click the Align Right button on the Formatting toolbar.
   Each entry in the range (except Wednesday) should appear right-aligned. Wednesday does not appear right aligned because it is too wide for the cell. You will change the width of Column C in a moment.

Adjust Column Widths

In the next few steps, you will adjust the width of Columns B and C. This exercise provides a brief introduction to adjusting column widths. A complete discussion of adjusting column widths is given in a later lesson.

3. Follow these steps to adjust the width of Column B.

Ⓐ Position the mouse pointer on the border between Columns B and C, and the Adjust pointer will appear.

Ⓑ Drag the border to the right until Column B is wide enough to display all entries in the column.

	A	B	C	D
1	Computer Depot Weekly Sales Data			
2				
3			Wednesda	Thursday

4. Widen Column C until the word *Wednesday* is completely visible in Cell C3. *You will need to drag the border between the column headings C and D.*

5. Click the Save 🖫 button to save the changes.

AutoSum

The power of Excel becomes apparent when you begin using formulas and functions. The most common type of calculation is when a column or row of numbers is summed. In fact, this type of calculation is so common that Excel provides the AutoSum function specifically for this purpose.

From the Keyboard
`ALT`+= for
AutoSum

The AutoSum Σ button on the Standard toolbar automatically sums a column or row of numbers. When you click AutoSum, Excel proposes a range of numbers. You can accept the proposed range or drag in the worksheet to select a different range. When you complete the entry, Excel inserts a SUM function in the worksheet, which adds the numbers in the range.

Hands-On 1.9 Use AutoSum

In this exercise, you will use AutoSum to compute several totals. Keep in mind that this section provides an introduction to formulas. You will learn more about formulas as you progress through this course.

Compute One Column Total

1. Click Cell C8.

2. Click the AutoSum Σ button.

3. Follow these steps to review the formula and complete the entry.

	SUM	▾	✕ ✓ = =SUM(C5:C7)

	A	B	C	D
1	Computer Depot Weekly Sales Data			
2				
3			Wednesda	Thursd
4	PCs			
5		Compaq	3	
6		IBM	4	
7		Acer	6	
8		Total	=SUM(C5:C7)	

Ⓐ *Notice that Excel proposes the formula =SUM(C5:C7) in Cell 8 and in the Formula bar. All formulas begin with an equal (=) sign. SUM is a built-in function that adds the numbers in a range (in this example the range is C5:C7).*

Ⓑ *Notice the flashing marquee surrounding the range C5:C7. AutoSum assumes you want to add together all cells above C8 until the first empty cell is reached. The marquee identifies this range of cells.*

Ⓒ *Click the Enter ✓ button on the Formula bar to complete the entry. The total should be 13.*

4. Click Cell D8.

5. Click AutoSum Σ and complete ✓ the entry.

6. Use the preceding technique to compute the column totals in Cells E8, F8, and G8.

(Continued on the next page)

Compute Several Totals With One Command

7. Select the Range C15:G15.

| 15 | | Total | |

8. Click the AutoSum Σ button.

   The column totals for Cells C15, D15, E15, F15, and G15 should automatically be computed. AutoSum displays the marquee and requires confirmation only when you are computing a single total.

9. Use the preceding steps to compute the column totals in Rows 21 and 27.

Make Column H a Totals Column

10. Click Cell H4, type the word **Totals**, and complete the entry.

11. Use the Align Right ▤ button to right-align the entry in Cell H4.

12. Click Cell H5.

13. Click AutoSum Σ and Excel will propose the Range C5:G5, which includes all numbers in Row 5.

14. Complete ☑ the entry and the row sum should total 56.

15. Use the preceding steps to compute the row total in Cell H6.

Override the Range AutoSum Proposes

16. Click Cell H7, and then click AutoSum Σ.

    Notice that Excel assumes you want to sum the Cells H5 and H6, above H7. This assumption is incorrect. Excel made this assumption because there were two cells above H7, which is enough to make a range. Excel will always propose a column summation if it has a choice between a column and row summation.

17. Follow these steps to override the proposed range.

Ⓐ *Position the mouse pointer in Cell C7, and then drag to the right until the range C7:G7 is selected.* ——

Ⓑ *Notice that the new range C7:G7 appears in the formula.* ——

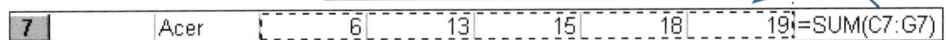

| 7 | | Acer | 6 | 13 | 15 | 18 | 19 | =SUM(C7:G7) |

18. Complete the entry, and the row sum should total 71.

19. Use the preceding technique to compute the row total in Cell H8 (the total should equal 176).

    Actually, you could have accepted the formula that AutoSum proposed for Cell H8. In this case, the column and row summations would have been the same.

Compute Several Totals with One Command

You can eliminate the problem of AutoSum proposing the wrong formula by summing a range of row totals with one command. This is the same technique you used to sum the column totals.

20. Select the range H11:H15 as shown in the following illustration.

	A	B	C	D	E	F	G	H
9								
10	Laptops							
11		IBM	2	5	4	10	8	
12		Apple PowerBook	3	7	5	12	10	
13		Compaq	4	8	11	14	14	
14		Toshiba	2	3	5	5	3	
15		Total	11	23	25	41	35	

21. Click the AutoSum Σ button.

The five row totals should be computed.

22. Use the preceding steps to compute the row totals for the ranges H18:H21 and H24:H27.

Your completed worksheet should match the worksheet shown in the Case Study at the start of this lesson.

AutoCalculate

The AutoCalculate box on the Status bar lets you view the sum of a range of numbers without actually inserting a SUM function in the worksheet. You can also right-click on the AutoCalculate box to see the average, minimum, or maximum of the selected range. The following illustration highlights these concepts.

To use AutoCalculate, first select a range. Excel displays the sum in the AutoCalculate box on the Status bar.

If desired, you can right-click the AutoCalculate box and choose another function from the pop-up menu.

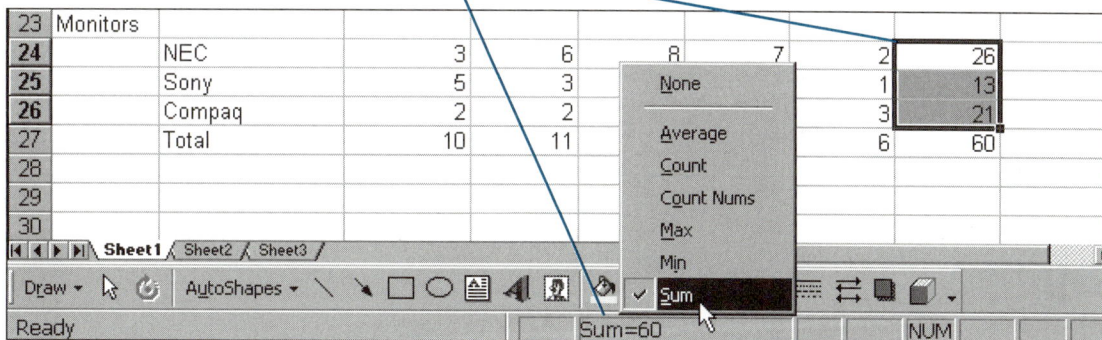

Hands-On 1.10 Use AutoCalculate

1. Select any range of numbers in your worksheet.

2. Locate the AutoCalculate box on the Status bar. The sum of the selected numbers should be displayed.

3. *Right-click* the AutoCalculate box, and the pop-up menu will appear.

4. Choose **Average** from the pop-up menu to display the average of the numbers in the AutoCalculate box.

5. Select another range to display the average in the AutoCalculate box.

6. *Right-click* the AutoCalculate box, and choose **Sum** from the pop-up menu.

Print Preview

The Print Preview button on the Standard toolbar displays the Print Preview window. Print Preview lets you see exactly how a worksheet will look when it is printed. Print Preview can save time, paper, and wear-and-tear on your printer. Print Preview is especially useful when printing large worksheets, or with worksheets containing charts and intricate formatting. It is always wise to preview a large or complex worksheet before sending it to the printer. When you display the Print Preview window, the standard toolbars are replaced by the Print Preview toolbar.

Hands-On 1.11 Use Print Preview

1. Click the Print Preview button on the Standard toolbar.

2. Zoom in by clicking anywhere on the worksheet.

3. Zoom out by clicking anywhere on the worksheet.

4. Click the **Close** button on the Print Preview toolbar to exit without printing.

Printing

The Print button on the Standard toolbar sends the entire worksheet to the current printer. You must display the Print dialog box if you want to change printers, adjust the number of copies to be printed, or set other printing options. Display the Print dialog box with the **File→Print** command. The illustration on the following page explains the most important options available in the Print dialog box.

From the Keyboard

(CTRL)+P to display Print dialog box

Choose a printer from this drop-down list.

Specify the number of copies here. The Collate option is useful when you are printing more than one copy of a multiple page worksheet. If the Collate box is checked, the first copy is printed before the second copy begins printing, etc.

Choose to print all pages or a range of pages.

Choose to print only selected cells, the active sheet(s), or the entire workbook here.

Print

Printer
Name: HP LaserJet 6P | Properties...
Status: Idle
Type: HP LaserJet 6P
Where: LPT1:
Comment: ☐ Print to file

Print range
◉ All
○ Page(s) From: ☐ To: ☐

Print what
○ Selection ○ Entire workbook
◉ Active sheet(s)

Copies
Number of copies: 1
☑ Collate

Hands-On 1.12 Print the Worksheet

1. Choose **File→Print** to display the Print dialog box.

2. Take a few moments to review the dialog box options.

3. When you are ready to print, make sure the options are set as shown in the preceding illustration, then click the **OK** button.
   Keep in mind that your printer will probably be different than the printer shown in the illustration.

4. Retrieve your worksheet from the printer.

Closing Workbooks

The **File→Close** command is used to close an open workbook. When you close a workbook, Excel prompts you to save the changes. If you choose *Yes* at the prompt and the workbook has previously been saved, then Excel saves the changes. If the workbook is new, Excel displays the Save As dialog box, allowing you to assign a name and storage location to the workbook.

Hands-On 1.13 Close the Workbook

1. Choose **File→Close** from the menu bar.

2. Click the **Yes** button if Excel asks you to save the changes.
   Notice that there is no workbook in the Excel window. The Excel window always has this appearance when all workbooks have been closed.

Opening Workbooks

The Open ⌐ button on the Standard toolbar and the **File→Open** command display the Open dialog box. The Open dialog box lets you navigate to any storage location and open previously saved workbooks. Once a workbook is open, you can browse it, print it, or even make editing changes. The organization and layout of the Open dialog box are similar to the Save dialog box discussed earlier in this lesson.

From the Keyboard

(CTRL)+O to Open

Hands-On 1.14 Open the Workbook

1. Click Open ⌐ on the Standard toolbar.

2. Follow these steps to open the Hands-On Lesson 1 workbook.
   Keep in mind that your dialog box will contain more files than shown here.

Ⓐ *Choose the disk drive containing your exercise diskette. It is most likely in 3½ Floppy (A:).*

Ⓑ *Choose Hands-On Lesson 1.*

Ⓒ *Click the Open button.*

TIP!

You can also double-click a document on the list.

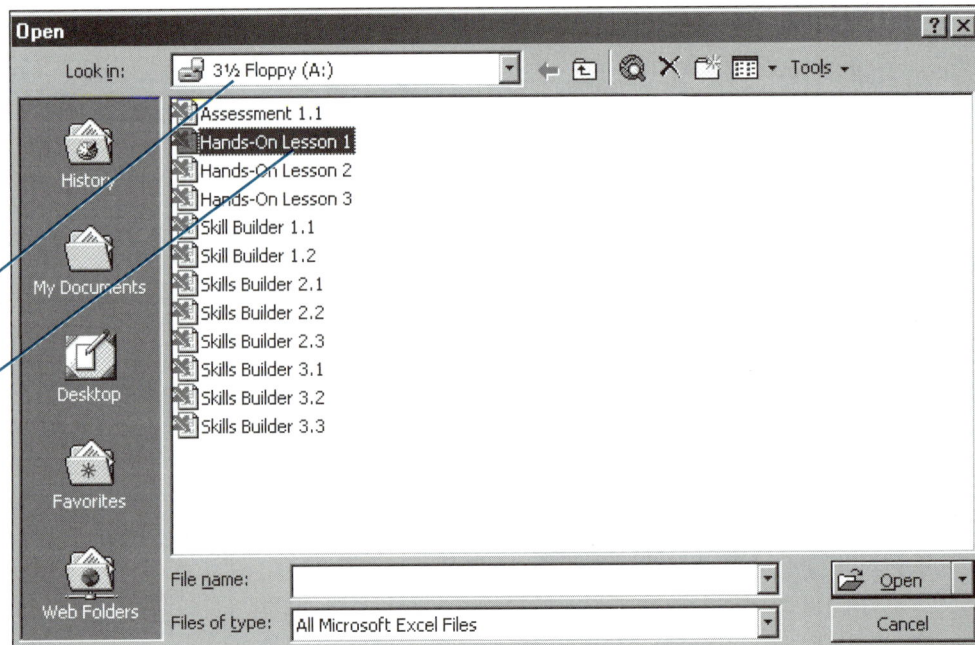

Notice that the worksheet is exactly as it was before it was closed.

Exiting from Excel

The **File→Exit** command is used to close the Excel program. You should close Excel and other programs if you are certain you won't be using them for some time. This will free up memory for other programs. When you close Excel, you will be prompted to save any workbooks that have unsaved edits.

Hands-On 1.15 Exit from Excel

1. Choose **File→Exit** from the menu bar.

   Excel will close without prompting you to save the workbook because you have not changed the workbook since it was opened last.

Concepts Review

True/False Questions

1. Each workbook can have a maximum of one worksheet.   TRUE   FALSE

2. A worksheet is composed of horizontal rows and vertical columns.   TRUE   FALSE

3. Text entries can contain spaces.   TRUE   FALSE

4. Numbers can only contain the digits 0–9. No other characters are permitted.   TRUE   FALSE

5. The Undo button lets you reverse up to the last 16 actions.   TRUE   FALSE

6. A colon (:) is used to separate the beginning and ending cells in a range reference.   TRUE   FALSE

7. You can select an entire row by clicking the row header.   TRUE   FALSE

8. When given a choice, AutoSum will always sum the numbers to the left of the active cell instead of summing the numbers above the active cell.   TRUE   FALSE

Multiple-Choice Questions

1. Which of the following keystrokes moves the highlight to Cell A1?
   a. HOME
   b. CTRL + PGUP
   c. CTRL + HOME
   d. CTRL + INS

2. What happens when you enter text in a cell that already contains an entry?
   a. The text replaces the original entry.
   b. Excel rejects the new entry, keeping the original entry intact.
   c. The cell contains both the original entry and the new entry.
   d. None of the above

3. What happens when you insert an entry in the cell to the **right** of a long text entry?
   a. The display of the long entry is truncated.
   b. The long entry is replaced by the entry in the cell to the right.
   c. It has no effect on the long entry.
   d. None of the above

4. What happens when you insert an entry in the cell to the **left** of a long text entry?
   a. The display of the long entry is truncated.
   b. The long entry is permanently truncated.
   c. It has no effect on the long entry.
   d. None of the above

Skill Builders

Skill Builder 1.1 Edit a Worksheet

In this exercise, you will edit a worksheet. This exercise demonstrates that sometimes it is easier to replace entries, and at other times it is easier to edit them.

Replace Several Entries

1. Start Excel and click the Open ![Open] button on the Standard toolbar.

2. Navigate to your exercise diskette, and double-click the workbook named **Skill Builder 1.1.**

3. Click Cell A4.

4. Type **Ralph**, and tap (ENTER).
   Notice that it was easy to replace the entry because the name Ralph is easy to retype.

5. Replace the name Calvin in Cell A6 with the name **Steven**.

Edit Using the Formula Bar

6. Click Cell C4.

7. Click in the Formula bar just in front of the telephone prefix 222.

8. Tap (DELETE) three times to remove the prefix.

9. Type **333** and complete ![checkmark] the entry.

10. Change the area code in Cell C8 from 714 to **814**.

Use In-Cell Editing

11. Double-click Cell D4.
    The flashing insertion point should appear in the cell.

12. Use → or ← to position the insertion point in front of the word *Lane*.

13. Use (DELETE) to remove the word *Lane*.

14. Type **Reservoir**, and complete the entry.

(Continued on the next page)

15. Edit the next five addresses using either the Formula bar or in-cell editing. The required changes appear bold in the following table.

Cell	Make These Changes
D5	2900 **Carlton** Drive, San Mateo, CA 94401
D6	**2300** Palm Drive, Miami, FL 33147
D7	888 Wilson Street, **Concord**, CA **94518**
D8	320 Main Street, **Pittsburgh**, PA 17951
D9	132nd Street, Los Angeles, CA **90045**

16. When you have finished, choose **File→Close** from the menu bar, and click the **Yes** button when Excel asks if you wish to save the changes.

Skill Builder 1.2 Use AutoSum and Align Entries

In this exercise, you will edit a worksheet. You will use AutoSum to compute totals, and the alignment buttons to align entries.

Compute Totals

1. Click the Open 📁 button on the Standard toolbar.

2. Navigate to your exercise diskette, and double-click the workbook named **Skill Builder 1.2.**

3. Click Cell C10, and then click AutoSum Σ.
   Notice that Excel proposes the formula =SUM(C8:C9). Excel proposes this incorrect formula because there are empty cells in the range you are to sum.

4. Drag the mouse pointer over the range C5:C9. The flashing marquee will surround the range C5:C9, as shown to the right.

5. Complete the entry; the total should equal 650.

6. Use the preceding steps to compute the totals in Cells E10, G10, and I10.
   You may need to scroll to the right to see Column I.

Amount
100
350
200
=SUM(C5:C9)

Align the Entries

7. Follow these steps to align the cell entries for Q1.

	A	B	C
1	Employee Benefits Plan Quarterly Participati		
2			
3		Q1	
4	Employee	Participated?	Amount
5	Jackson	Y	100
6	Chang	N	
7	Phillips	N	
8	Nguyen	Y	350
9	Watson	Y	200
10	Totals		650

Ⓐ *Select this range, and click the Center button to align the highlighted entries here.*

Ⓑ *Click Cell C4, and click the Align Right button to align the highlighted entry here.*

8. Align the entries for Q2, Q3, and Q4 as you just did for Q1. You can do this quickly by using the CTRL key to select all three ranges and aligning them with a single click of the Center button.

9. Right-align the word *Amount* in Cells E4, G4, and I4. Once again, you can use CTRL to select all three cells and then issue the command.

10. Save the changes to your workbook, and then close the workbook.

Skill Builder 1.3 Create a Worksheet with Decimal Numbers

In this exercise, you will create the worksheet shown on the following page. You will enter numbers containing two decimal places. You will also use the alignment buttons to align the text and numbers.

Enter Text and Widen Columns

1. Click the New button on the Standard toolbar.
   You can always use the New button to display a new workbook.

2. Enter text in Rows 1–3 as shown in the following illustration.
   *Make sure you enter the entire phrase **Order Tracking Sheet** into Cell D1. Also, the entries in Cells A3, B3, and E3 will be truncated. You will correct this by widening the columns in the following steps.*

	A	B	C	D	E	F	G
1				Order Tracking Sheet			
2							
3	Customer ID	Order Status	Item #	In Stock?	Order Total	Shipping Address	

(Continued on the next page)

3. Position the mouse pointer on the border between the column headings A and B, and the Adjust pointer will appear.

4. Drag the border to the right until Column A is wide enough for the Customer ID entry.

5. Widen Columns B and E until the entries in those columns are completely visible.

Enter Numbers with Decimals

6. Click Cell E4.

7. Type **100.91**, and tap (ENTER).
You should always type a decimal point if the number requires one.

8. Type **45.87**, and tap (ENTER).

9. Enter the numbers shown below in Cells E6, E7, and E8 (don't type the total 292.38 in Cell E9).

Use AutoSum

10. Click Cell E9.

11. Click AutoSum $\boxed{\Sigma}$, and then complete the entry.
The total should be 292.38 as shown below.

12. Complete the worksheet as shown below. You will need to enter the numbers and text shown. Make sure you enter each shipping address into a single cell. For example, the address **1603 Catalina** . . . should be entered in Cell F4. Also, you will need to select the range A3:D8 and use the Center button to center the entries. Align all other entries as shown below.

13. When you have finished, click the Save 🖫 button, and save the workbook as **Skill Builder 1.3**. Close the workbook after it has been saved.

	A	B	C	D	E	F	G	H	I	J
1				Order Tracking Sheet						
2										
3	Customer ID	Order Status	Item #	In Stock?	Order Total	Shipping Address				
4	341	S	A423	Y	100.91	1603 Catalina Avenue, Redondo Beach, CA 90277				
5	234	S	A321	Y	45.87	Will Pickup				
6	567	I	S345	N	43.23	450 Terrace Drive, Santa Clara, CA 95050				
7	879	H	D567	N	78.92	No address at this point				
8	233	I	S230	Y	23.45	23 Maple Lane, Crawfordsville, IN 47933				
9	Total Orders				292.38					

Assessments

Assessment 1.1

1. Open the workbook named **Assessment 1.1** on your exercise diskette.

2. Edit the title in Cell A1 to read **Computer Depot Sales Bonuses**.

3. Widen Column A until all names in the column are visible.

4. Right-align the headings in Row 3.

5. Use AutoSum to compute the totals in Row 9.

6. Change the name Mary Johnson in Cell A5 to **Sally Adams**.
   Your completed worksheet should match the worksheet below.

7. Print the completed worksheet, save the changes, and then close the workbook.

	A	B	C	D	E	F	G
1	Computer Depot Sales Bonuses						
2							
3		January	February	March	April	May	June
4	Employee						
5	Sally Adams	100	125	300	235	125	300
6	Cliff Packard	200	200	200	210	210	250
7	Helen Martinez	200	350	250	120	230	225
8	Sarah Stonestown	150	125	235	250	135	175
9	Total	650	800	985	815	700	950

Assessment 1.2

1. Click the New ▢ button to open a new workbook.

2. Use the following guidelines to create the following worksheet.

   ▪ Widen the columns as necessary to prevent long entries from being truncated.

   ▪ Use AutoSum to compute the totals. Be careful, as certain rows and columns contain blank cells. You will need to manually override the ranges proposed by AutoSum.

   ▪ Align the text entries in Row 3 as shown.

3. When you have finished, click the Print ▢ button on the Standard toolbar to print the worksheet.

4. Save the workbook as **Assessment 1.2,** and then close the workbook.

	A	B	C	D	E	F	G
1	Computer Depot Employee Time Log						
2							
3	Employee	Wednesday	Thursday	Friday	Saturday	Sunday	Totals
4	Mary Johnson	6.5		5	6.5	4	22
5	Cliff Packard	4	6	6.5	6.5	4	27
6	Helen Martinez	4	6	6.5	6.5		23
7	Sarah Stonestown		4	4	4		12
8	Totals	14.5	16	22	23.5	8	84

Assessment 1.3

1. Open a New ▢ workbook.

2. Create the worksheet shown in the following illustration. Make sure the numbers and totals match the worksheet. Widen columns and align entries as shown.

3. Print the workbook when you have finished.

4. Save the workbook as **Assessment 1.3,** and then close the workbook.

	A	B	C	D	E	F
1	Big City Diner Q1 Expenses					
2						
3	Item		January	February	March	Q1 Totals
4	Rent and Utilities	Rent	800	800	800	2400
5		Utilities	340	400	250	990
6		Phone	250	200	300	750
7		Insurance	350			350
8		Total	1740	1400	1350	4490
9						
10	Cost of goods sold	Produce	2500	2320	1700	6520
11		Meat	4000	3400	3700	11100
12		Grains	1000	1200	890	3090
13		Total	7500	6920	6290	20710
14						
15	Salaries	Simmons	800	780	800	2380
16		Swanson	750	650	870	2270
17		Martinez	900	780	680	2360
18		Richardson	1200	1000	990	3190
19		Total	3650	3210	3340	10200
20						
21	Other	Advertising	500	300		800
22		Uniforms		340		340
23		Janitorial	200	200	200	600
24		Miscellaneous	100	2000		2100
25		Total	800	2840	200	3840

Critical Thinking

Critical Thinking 1.1 On Your Own

Mary Kelley is a math teacher at Washington High School. Mary wants an Excel workbook that tracks student test scores for her Trigonometry class. Students receive a final letter grade for the course that is determined by the total number of points they accumulate throughout the course. They are given four-hour tests, a mid term, a final, and four extra-credit homework assignments. They can receive a maximum of 100 points for each of the four tests, 200 points for the mid term, 300 points for the final exam, and 25 points for each extra-credit homework assignment. Thus, the total number of possible points for the course is 1,000. Letter grades are assigned as follows:

A 900 or more points

B 800-899 points

C 700-799 points

D 600-699 points

E less than 600 points

You have been assigned the task of setting up a worksheet for Mary. The worksheet should list the points received by each student for the four-hour tests, the mid term, final, and four homework assignments. Use AutoSum to calculate the total points for each student. In addition, assign a letter grade to each student using the scale shown above. Include scores for the following four students: Jack Simmons, Samantha Torres, Elaine Wilkins, and Tonya Robertson. Assign points to the students as you deem appropriate. Save your workbook as **Critical Thinking 1.1.**

Critical Thinking 1.2 On Your Own

Tanisha Jones is running for President of the Westmont Community College Student Association. Westmont College regulates student campaigns in various ways. In particular, the college imposes a maximum fund raising limit of $1,500 on each candidate who is running for office. In addition, there are strict reporting requirements for campaign contributions. Each contribution must be reported and must include the date of the contribution, the individual or organization making the contribution, and the amount of the contribution. The reports are made available to the public in print and on the college's Web site. You have been assigned the task of setting up a worksheet to track Tanisha's campaign contributions. List five contributions in your worksheet from the following individuals and organizations: Cindy Thomas; Richardson Vending Services; Campus Computer Equipment; Elaine Wilson; and Party Time Music and Video. You determine the contribution amounts and the dates. Include a total cell that calculates the total contributions. Make sure the total contributions do not exceed $1,500. Save your workbook as **Critical Thinking 1.2.**

Critical Thinking 1.3 On Your Own

Big Slice Pizza is a rapidly growing pizza chain that serves the best deep-dish pizza in town. An important part of Big Slice's growth strategy is the development of a franchise network using independent franchise owners. Recently, Big Slice launched a West Coast advertising campaign to attract new franchise owners. You have been assigned the task of collecting the franchise applications and creating a worksheet that summarizes the application information. Your worksheet should include each prospective franchise owner's name, city and state, investment amount, telephone number, and whether or not the prospect has previous franchise experience. Include information for the following prospects: Ben Barksdale; Sylvia Ramirez; Bill Chin; Wanda Stone; and Terry Collins. You determine the remaining information for each prospective owner. Save your workbook as **Critical Thinking 1.3**.

Critical Thinking 1.4 Web Research

Alexia Williams is the Information Systems Manager of Bellmont Health Care. Bellmont is a rapidly growing health care concern with over one billion dollars is in FY 2000 revenues. Alexia has mandated that, beginning in FY 2001, at least 50% of Bellmont's technology purchases will be made using online purchasing systems. Alexia believes this strategy will reduce costs and increase the efficiency of the procurement process. As a student intern working under the direction of Alexia, you have been assigned the task of locating five vendors that allow personal computers and accessories to be purchased online. Alexia has asked you to construct a worksheet that includes the vendor's name, Web site URL, and their customer service telephone number. Use Internet Explorer and a search engine of your choice to conduct your research. Record your results in a worksheet as **Critical Thinking 1.4**.

Critical Thinking 1.5 Web Research

George Miller is the Operations Manager of Speedy Package Delivery Service. Speedy is in the business of same-day package delivery. Speedy is located in the heart of Silicon Valley. They have grown rapidly as Silicon Valley has become a driving force in the U.S. economy. George has been instructed to purchase six new mini vans to be used for package delivery. George has assigned you the task of locating three Web sites where vehicle information can be located and where vehicles can be purchased. Use Internet Explorer and a search engine of your choice to locate three Web sites that specialize in vehicle sales. Set up a worksheet that lists the Web site name and URL of three such Web sites. For each Web site, include the posted retail price range and the dealer invoice price for Ford Windstar, Chevrolet Astro, and Dodge Caravan mini vans. Use a consistent vehicle configuration from each Web site so that the pricing comparisons are valid. Include any additional vehicle information that you think would be useful to George. Save your workbook as **Critical Thinking 1.5**.

Critical Thinking 1.6 With a Group

Set up a worksheet to record whether or not your classmates have used Windows, Outlook, Word, Excel, Access, PowerPoint, and Internet Explorer in a business environment. Survey five of your classmates and record the results of your survey in the worksheet. Use a 1 to indicate that a classmate has experience with a particular program and a 0 to indicate no experience. Use AutoSum to sum the totals for each program. The totals should give you some idea of how much each program is used in business. Save your workbook as **Critical Thinking 1.6**.

LESSON 2

Expanding on the Basics

In this lesson, you will expand upon the basic skills you learned in the previous lesson. You will use several types of formulas to create totals, calculate profits, and determine financial ratios. You will also learn powerful tools and techniques such as the fill handle and the Format Painter. When you have finished this lesson, you will have developed the skills necessary to produce more sophisticated worksheets.

In This Lesson

Case Study

Donna Prusko is an entrepreneur and the founder of Donna's Deli. Donna recently resigned from her corporate position to pursue her dream and passion—a deli that serves delicious, healthy food at reasonable prices. Donna also realizes that the health of her business is just as important as the health of her customers. For this reason, she wants to develop a worksheet to track her income and expenses. The worksheet will use formulas to determine gross profits, net profits, and important financial ratios. Microsoft Excel is an important tool for any entrepreneur in today's highly competitive business world.

	A	B	C	D	E
1	**Donna's Deli - Income and Expense Worksheet**				
2					
3			**Quarterly Income**		
4	Food Sales	**Q1**	**Q2**	**Q3**	**Q4**
5	Dine-in Sales	21,000	23,000	28,000	42,000
6	Takeout Sales	12,000	16,000	25,000	56,000
7	Subtotal	**$33,000**	**$39,000**	**$53,000**	**$98,000**
8	Other Income				
9	Tips	2,500	2,700	3,000	4,500
10	Sublease	500	500	500	500
11	Subtotal	**$3,000**	**$3,200**	**$3,500**	**$5,000**
12	Total Income	**$36,000**	**$42,200**	**$56,500**	**$103,000**
13					
14			**Quarterly Expenses**		
15	Expenses	**Q1**	**Q2**	**Q3**	**Q4**
16	Rent	3,000	3,000	3,000	3,000
17	Utilities	400	310	290	380
18	Marketing	800	800	800	800
19	Salaries	12,000	12,000	14,000	14,000
20	Supplies	15,000	15,500	18,000	24,000
21	Equipment	6,000	2,000	1,000	-
22	Total Expenses	**$37,200**	**$33,610**	**$37,090**	**$42,180**
23					
24	Gross Profit	**($1,200)**	**$8,590**	**$19,410**	**$60,820**
25	Net Profit	**($1,200)**	**$8,590**	**$16,499**	**$45,615**
26	Gross Profit vs. Income	**-3%**	**20%**	**34%**	**59%**

Adaptive Menus

Excel's menus now consist of a short section containing the commands you use most frequently and an expanded section containing commands that are rarely used. These adaptive menus reduce the number of commands on the main (short) menu, thereby reducing screen clutter. The following illustrations define the adaptive menus in Excel 2000.

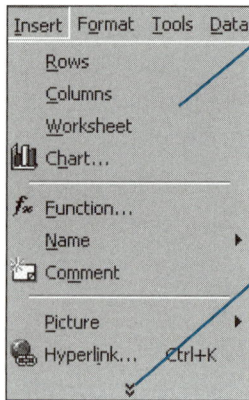

The short menu contains only commands that are frequently used.

When you point at the Expand button, the menu expands to show all commands.

On the expanded menu, commands from the short menu appear in a dark shade of gray, while infrequently used commands appear in a light shade of gray. When you choose a command from the expanded menu, it moves up to the short menu.

Working with Toolbars

In Excel 2000, the Standard toolbar and Formatting toolbar are placed side by side on a single row just below the menu bar. This is a change from earlier versions of Excel where the Formatting toolbar was positioned below the Standard toolbar. In addition to the Standard toolbar and Formatting toolbar, Excel has approximately 15 additional toolbars that are used with various program features.

Adaptive Toolbars

Like adaptive menus, adaptive toolbars may change depending upon how you use Excel. Buttons may automatically be added to or removed from these toolbars. The right end of each Excel toolbar now contains a button named More Buttons. Use this button to display buttons not currently visible on the toolbar, and to add or remove buttons from a toolbar. The following illustration uses the Formatting toolbar to outline adaptive toolbars in Excel 2000.

A right-pointing arrow indicates the toolbar has additional buttons that are not currently displayed. Clicking the button displays the additional buttons.

You can click the additional buttons as you would if they were displayed.

When you choose Add or Remove Buttons, the Buttons palette is displayed.

Buttons can be added to the toolbar by checking them, or removed by unchecking them on the Buttons palette. If you don't use a button for a long time, Excel will remove it from the toolbar and place it on the Buttons palette.

Displaying and Hiding Toolbars

You can display and hide toolbars by choosing **View→Toolbars** from the menu bar and checking or unchecking the desired toolbars. You can also display or hide toolbars by right-clicking any toolbar on the screen and checking or unchecking the desired toolbar.

Moving Toolbars

You can move a toolbar to any screen location. For example, many users prefer to move the Formatting toolbar below the Standard toolbar, as in previous versions of Excel. Move toolbars by dragging the Move handle located on the left end of the toolbar.

The Move pointer appears when you point to a Move handle. You can move a toolbar to any screen location by dragging the Move handle.

Displaying the Formatting Toolbar On a Separate Row

Dragging the Formatting toolbar below the Standard toolbar can be tricky. Fortunately, Excel provides an easier way to display the Standard and Formatting toolbars on separate rows. This technique is explained in the following Quick Reference table.

Quick Reference

DISPLAYING THE STANDARD AND FORMATTING TOOLBARS ON SEPARATE ROWS

■ Choose View→Toolbars→Customize from the menu bar.

■ Click the Options tab in the Customize dialog box.

■ Uncheck the *Standard and Formatting toolbars share one row* checkbox.

Hands-On 2.1 Display the Formatting Toolbar on a Separate Row

1. Start Excel and choose **View→Toolbars→Customize** from the menu bar.

2. Click the Options tab in the Customize dialog box.

3. Uncheck the **Standard and Formatting toolbars share one row** checkbox.

4. Click the **Close** button. The Formatting toolbar should be positioned below the Standard toolbar.

IMPORTANT! *From this point forward, the instructions in this text will assume the Standard and Formatting toolbars are displayed on separate rows. This will make it easier for you to locate buttons when instructed to do so.*

The Fill Handle

The fill handle is a small black square visible at the bottom right corner of the active cell. A black cross appears when you position the mouse pointer on the fill handle. You can drag the fill handle to fill adjacent cells as described below:

- **Copying an entry**—If the entry in the active cell is a number, a formula, or a typical text entry, the fill handle copies the entry to adjacent cells.

- **Expanding a repeating series of numbers**—If you select two or more cells containing numbers, Excel assumes you want to expand a repeating series. For example, if you select two cells containing the numbers 5 and 10 and drag the fill handle, Excel will fill the adjacent cells with the numbers 15, 20, 25, etc.

- **AutoFill of date entries**—If the active cell contains a date entry, then Excel will increment the date value filling in the adjacent cells. For example, if the current cell contains the entry Q1 and you drag the fill handle, AutoFill will insert the entries Q2, Q3, and Q4 in the adjacent cells.

The fill handle is located at the bottom right corner of the active cell.

If the active cell contains a date entry such as Q1, AutoFill automatically fills the adjacent cell with the next item in the series (Q2).

The completed series.

Hands-On 2.2 Use the Fill Handle

1. Open the workbook named **Hands-On Lesson 2** from your exercise diskette.

Use AutoFill to Expand the Q1 Series

2. Click Cell B4.
   Notice that Cell B4 contains the heading Q1. Excel recognizes Q1 as the beginning of the series Q1, Q2, Q3, and Q4.

3. Follow these steps to fill the adjacent cells.

A *Position the mouse pointer on the bottom right corner of the active cell, and a black cross will appear.*

B *Drag to the right over the next three cells, and a shaded rectangle will appear.*

| 4 | Food Sales | Q1 | | | |
| 5 | Dine-in Sales | 21000 | 23000 | 28000 | Q4 |

C *Release the mouse button to fill the adjacent cells.*

Excel recognizes Q1, days of the week (Sunday), months (January), and other date values as the beginning of a series. You can expand any of these series with the fill handle.

4. Click Cell B15, and use the fill handle to expand Q1 to Q1–Q4, as you did in the previous step.

5. Click Cell B7.

6. Click AutoSum $\boxed{\Sigma}$, and complete the entry.
The subtotal should equal 33000.

7. Make sure Cell B7 is active; then drag the fill handle ✛ to the right until the shaded rectangle is over Cells C7, D7, and E7.

8. Release the mouse button. The formula should be copied to those cells.
Excel determines whether it should copy the cell or expand a series.

9. Click Cell B11, and use AutoSum to compute the subtotal.

10. Use the fill handle to copy the formula in Cell B11 to Cells C11, D11, and E11.

11. Use these techniques to compute the total expenses in Row 22 (not total income in Row 12).
It actually would have been easier to select the four cells in these examples and use AutoSum to compute the totals. However, there are times when it is easier to copy cells with the fill handle, as you will see in the next topic.

Formulas

You have already learned how to compute totals with AutoSum. AutoSum provides a convenient method for summing a range of numbers. However, you will need to use many other types of formulas in Excel. In fact, many worksheets, such as financial models, require hundreds or even thousands of complex formulas.

Beginning Character in Formulas

If you are typing a formula in a cell, it is recommended that you always begin the formula with an equal (=) sign. You can also begin formulas with a plus (+) or minus (–) sign; however; it is better to adopt one method in order to create consistency.

Cell and Range References

Formulas derive their power from the use of cell and range references. For example, in the previous exercise, you used AutoSum to insert the formula =SUM(B16:B21) in Cell B22. Because the range reference (B16:B21) was used in the formula, you were able to copy the formula across the row using the fill handle. There are two important benefits to using references in formulas.

- When references are used, formulas can be copied to other cells.

- Since a reference refers to a cell or a range of cells, the formula results are automatically recalculated when the data is changed in the referenced cell(s).

Arithmetic Operators and Spaces

Formulas can include the standard arithmetic operators shown in the following table. You can also use spaces within formulas to improve their appearance and readability. Notice that each formula in the table begins with an equal (=) sign. Also, keep in mind that each formula is entered into the same cell that displays the resulting calculation.

Quick Reference

ARITHMETIC OPERATORS IN FORMULAS

Operator	Example	Comments
+ (addition)	=B7+B11	Adds the values in B7 and B11.
– (subtraction)	=B7–B11	Subtracts the value in B11 from B7.
* (multiplication)	=B7*B11	Multiplies the values in B7 and B11.
/ (division)	=B7/B11	Divides the value in B7 by the value in B11.
^ (exponentiation)	=B7^3	Raises the value in B7 to the third power (B7*B7*B7).
% (percent)	=B7*10%	Multiplies the value in B7 by 10% (.10).
( ) (calculations)	=B7/(C4–C2)	Parentheses change the order of calculations. In this example, C2 would be subtracted from C4, and then B7 would be divided by the result. Order of calculations is discussed in detail in a later lesson.

Hands-On 2.3 Use the Keyboard to Enter Formulas

1. Click Cell B12.

2. Type **=B7+B11**, and complete the entry.
   The result should be 36000. This is the summation of the two subtotals in Cells B7 and B11.

3. Click Cell C12.

4. Type **=C7+C11**, and complete the entry.
   The result should be 42200.

Relative Cell References

All formulas use relative cell references unless you specifically instruct Excel to use an absolute reference. Relative references make it easy to copy formulas to other cells. For example, in the Hands-On Lesson 2 worksheet, Cell C12 contains the formula =C7+C11. If this formula is copied to Cell D12, then the formula in D12 will become =D7+D11. The references to Cells C7 and C11 are updated to reflect the new location of the formula.

Point Mode

One potential danger that can occur when typing formulas is that you will accidentally type the wrong cell reference. This is easy to do, especially if the worksheet is complex and contains large numbers of cells. Point mode can help you avoid this problem. With point mode, you can insert a cell reference in a formula by clicking the desired cell as you are typing the formula. Likewise, you can insert a range reference in a formula by dragging over the desired cells. You will use point mode in the following exercise.

Hands-On 2.4 Use Point Mode

1. Click Cell D12.

2. Type an equal (=) sign.
   Notice that Excel begins building the formula by entering the equal = sign in the Formula bar.

3. Click Cell D7.
   Notice that Excel adds the reference D7 to the formula in the Formula bar.

4. Type a plus (+) sign (try tapping the plus (+) key on the numeric keypad).

5. Click Cell D11.
   The Formula bar should contain the formula =D7+D11.

6. Complete the entry. The total should be 56500.

7. Make sure the highlight is in Cell D12, and then drag the fill handle one cell to the right.
   The formula should be copied to Cell E12, and the result should be 103000.

8. Click Cell E12, and notice the formula in the Formula bar.
   The formula should be =E7+E11. The references were updated to reflect the new formula location.

Using the Formula Bar to Enter Formulas

You can enter a formula by first clicking the Edit Formula ▣ button on the Formula bar. When you click this button, the Formula bar expands to include a function box containing a list of recently used functions, an area that displays the formula results as the formula is constructed, an OK button, and a Cancel button. You may want to use this technique because it is often helpful to view the formula results as the formula is constructed.

IF	▼	✕	✓	=	=B12-B22

?	Formula result =-1200		OK	Cancel

Hands-On 2.5 Enter Formulas with the Formula Bar

Calculate the Gross Profit

1. If necessary, scroll down until Rows 12–26 are visible.

2. Click Cell B24.
   Cell B24 will contain the gross profit. The gross profit is calculated as the total income in Cell B12 minus the total expenses in Cell B22.

3. Click the Edit Formula ▣ button on the Formula bar.
   Excel will enter an equal (=) sign in the Formula bar, and the Formula bar will expand. Also, the Office Assistant may pop up. The Office Assistant is an interactive Help tool that monitors your activities and provides suggestions whenever it assumes you need assistance. For now, ignore the Office Assistant and continue with the next step.

(Continued on the next page)

4. Click Cell B12, and the Formula bar will indicate a result of 36000.

5. Type a minus (−) sign, then click Cell B22.

6. Complete the formula by clicking the OK button on the Formula bar.
   The gross profit should equal −1200. As you can see, Donna's Deli is not profitable in the first quarter.

7. Copy the formula to the next three cells by dragging the fill handle to the right.

Calculate the Net Profit

*You will calculate the net profit in the next few steps. You will use a simplified net profit calculation: that is, the gross profit minus income taxes. We will make the assumption that Donna will pay no taxes in Q1 and Q2. This is because she lost money in Q1, and her gross profit was only $8,590 in Q2. Furthermore, we will assume that Donna's tax rate will be 15% for Q3 and 25% for Q4. The formula is, Net Profit = Gross Profit * (1−Taxrate). For example, if the tax rate is 15%, then Donna will keep 85% of her gross profit. So the Net Profit = Gross Profit * 0.85.*

8. Click Cell B24.
   Look at the Formula bar and notice the gross profit is calculated as B12−B22. In the next few steps, you will attempt to copy the gross profit formula from Cell B24 to Cell B25.

9. Follow this step to copy the formula from Cell B24 to B25.

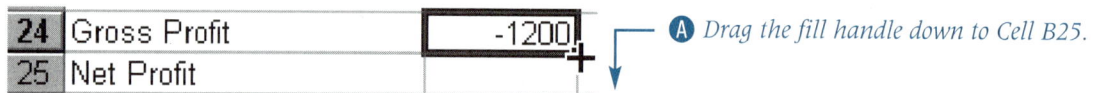

24	Gross Profit		-1200
25	Net Profit		

Ⓐ *Drag the fill handle down to Cell B25.*

10. Click Cell B24, and notice that the gross profit formula in the Formula bar is =B12−B22.

11. Click Cell B25, and notice that the net profit formula is =B13−B23.

12. Look at Cells B13 and B23 in the worksheet, and you will see they are empty.
    The formula result is 0 because Cells B13 and B23 are empty. This example demonstrates that you must be careful when copying formulas. Excel updated the cell references when you copied the formula. This produced an incorrect result because the formula is referencing incorrect cells.

13. Click Undo ⟲ to reverse the copy procedure.

14. Click Cell B25, type the formula **=B24**, and complete the entry.
    This simple formula makes Cell B25 equal to Cell B24.

15. Click Cell C25, type the formula **=C24**, and complete the entry.
    Once again, the net profit and gross profit should be equal in Q2 because Donna has no tax liability in the second quarter.

16. Click Cell D25, and enter the formula **=D24*85%.**
    The result should be 16498.5. We are assuming a tax rate of 15% in Q3, so Donna gets to keep 85% of her gross profit.

17. Click Cell E25, and enter the formula **=E24*75%.**
    The result should be 45615. Keep in mind that you can either type the formulas or use point mode and the Formula bar. From this point forward, you will simply be instructed to enter a formula. You should use whichever method works best for you.

Calculate the Ratios

Donna wants to determine the ratio of gross profit to total income, or GP/TI. This ratio is important in determining the health of a business. This ratio is one indicator that will show Donna how fast she can grow her business by reinvesting the money she earns. This ratio will show Donna the amount of profit she will earn from each dollar of product she sells.

18. Click Cell B26, and enter the formula **=B24/B12**.
    The result should be –0.03333. You will convert this number to a percentage later in this lesson.

19. Use the fill handle to copy the formula to Cells C26, D26, and E26.
    The results should match the following example.

26	Gross Profit vs. Income	-0.03333	0.203555	0.34354	0.590485

20. Click Cell C26, and notice the formula =C24/C12.
    Once again, Excel updated the cell references when the formula was copied. In this case, it is good that the references were updated because the formula now refers to the correct gross profit and total income in cells C24 and C12.

21. Click the Save 🖫 button to save the changes.

Number Formats

Excel lets you format numbers in a variety of ways. Number formats change the way numbers are displayed; however, they do not change the actual numbers. The following Quick Reference table describes the most common number formats.

Quick Reference

NUMBER FORMATS	
Number Format	**Description**
General	Numbers have a General format when they are first entered. The General format does not apply any special formats to the numbers.
Comma	The Comma format inserts a comma between every third digit in the number. An optional decimal point with decimal places can also be displayed.
Currency	The Currency format is the same as the Comma format, except a dollar $ sign is placed in front of the number.
Percent	A percent % sign is inserted to the right of the number. The number is multiplied by 100, and the resulting percentage is displayed in the cell.

The following table provides several examples of formatted numbers.

Number Entered	Format	How the Number Is Displayed
1000.984	General	1000.984
1000.984	Comma with 0 decimal places	1,000
	Comma with 2 decimal places	1,000.98
1000.984	Currency with 0 decimal places	$1,000
	Currency with 2 decimal places	$1,000.98
.5366	Percent with 0 decimal places	54%
	Percent with 2 decimal places	53.66%

Applying Number Styles with the Formatting Toolbar

From the Keyboard

CTRL+SHIFT+$ for Currency style
CTRL+SHIFT+% for Percent style
CTRL+SHIFT+! for Comma style
CTRL+SHIFT+~ for General style

The Formatting toolbar contains buttons that allow you to apply the Currency, Comma, and Percent number styles. These are the most common types of number styles. The Formatting toolbar also includes buttons that allow you to increase or decrease the number of displayed decimals. The following illustration displays the number formatting buttons on the Formatting toolbar.

Changing the Number of Displayed Decimals

The Increase Decimals and Decrease Decimals buttons change the number of displayed decimal places. For example, you could enter the number 100.37 and then decrease the decimals to 0. The number would then be displayed as 100. However, the actual number would remain 100.37. The number 100.37 would be used in any calculations referencing the cell.

Hands-On 2.6 Format Numbers

In this exercise, you will format numbers using buttons on the Formatting toolbar.

Apply the Currency Style

1. Scroll up until the top row of the worksheet is visible.

2. Select the four subtotals in Row 7 (be careful not to drag the fill handle).
   The fill handle is not used to select cells. It is only used to copy cells or to expand a series. Make sure your pointer has the thick white cross shape whenever you wish to select cells.

3. Click the Currency Style $ button, and the cells should be formatted as shown below.

7	Subtotal	$33,000.00	$39,000.00	$53,000.00	$98,000.00

Notice that the Currency style adds a dollar sign in front of the number and a comma between every third digit. It also adds a decimal point with two decimal places. Excel should also have widened the columns to accommodate the additional characters and numbers.

Decrease the Decimals

4. Make sure the four cells you just formatted are selected.

5. Click the Decrease Decimal button twice to remove the displayed decimals.
   Notice that the dollar signs $ are positioned on the left side of the cells. You will adjust this alignment later in the lesson.

6. Select the subtotal and total income cells in Rows 11 and 12, as shown below.

| 11 | Subtotal | 3000 | 3200 | 3500 | 5000 |
| 12 | Total Income | 36000 | 42200 | 56500 | 103000 |

7. Click the Currency Style [$] button; then decrease the decimals [.00→.0] to 0.

8. Format the numbers in Rows 22, 24, and 25 as currency with 0 decimals.

Apply the Comma Style

9. Select the numbers in Rows 5 and 6.

10. Click the Comma Style [,] button, and then decrease the decimals [.00→.0] to 0.
    Notice that the Comma style is similar to the Currency style, except a dollar sign is not displayed. Also notice that the numbers now line up with the currency formatted numbers in the subtotal row.

11. Format the numbers in the ranges B9:E10 and B16:E21 as Comma style with 0 decimals.

Apply the Percent Style

12. Select the numbers in the last row of the worksheet.

13. Click the Percent Style [%] button.
    The numbers should be formatted as percent with 0 decimal places. The Percent style does not display decimals; however, you can always use the Increase Decimal button to display decimals.

Setting Number Styles with the Format Cells Dialog Box

rom the Keyboard

(CTRL)+1 to display
Format Cells dialog box

The **Format→Cells** command displays the Format Cells dialog box. This dialog box provides additional built-in number styles that are not available on the Formatting toolbar. You can format numbers with one of the built-in styles by displaying the dialog box and choosing the desired style. You can even create your own customized number styles to suit your needs.

Accounting and Currency Styles

The dollar signs $ in the Hands-On Lesson 2 worksheet currently have a fixed format. In other words, they are fixed on the left side of the cells. You can use the Format Cells dialog box to choose a number style that floats the dollar signs next to the numbers. There are two number styles that apply currency symbols (such as dollar signs) to numbers, as discussed below.

- **Accounting style**—The Currency Style [$] button on the Formatting toolbar actually applies an Accounting style to numbers. The Accounting style lines up dollar signs and decimal points in columns. The dollar signs appear fixed at the left edges of the cells.

- **Currency style**—The Currency style floats dollar signs next to the numbers. Like the Accounting style, the Currency style displays a comma between every third digit, and it displays decimals and a decimal point.

Displaying Negative Numbers

Negative numbers can be displayed either preceded by a minus sign or surrounded by parentheses. You can also display negative numbers in red. The Currency option and Number option in the Format Cells dialog box let you choose the format for negative numbers.

The negative numbers format you choose affects the alignment of numbers in cells. If the format displays negative numbers in parentheses, then a small space equal to the width of a closing parenthesis appears on the right edge of cells containing positive numbers. Excel does this so that decimal points are aligned in columns containing both positive and negative numbers. These concepts are described in the following illustration.

15	Expenses		Q1
16	Rent		3,000
17	Utilities		400
18	Marketing		800
19	Salaries		12,000
20	Supplies		15,000
21	Equipment		6,000
22	Total Expenses	$	37,200
23			
24	Gross Profit	$	(1,200)
25	Net Profit	$	(1,200)

Notice the slight space between positive numbers and the right edge of the cells.

Notice that the closing parenthesis of negative numbers is flush with the right edge of the cell.

15	Expenses	Q1
16	Rent	3,000.00
17	Utilities	400.00
18	Marketing	800.00
19	Salaries	12,000.00
20	Supplies	15,000.00
21	Equipment	6,000.00
22	Total Expenses	37,200.00
23		
24	Gross Profit	(1,200.00)
25	Net Profit	(1,200.00)

When the numbers are displayed with decimals, this slight shift of the positive numbers lines up the decimal points of both the positive and negative numbers.

Hands-On 2.7 Use the Format Cells Dialog Box

1. Select the numbers with the Currency style in Row 7.

2. Choose **Format**→**Cells** from the menu bar.

3. Make sure the Number tab is active at the top of the dialog box.

4. Notice that the Custom option is chosen at the bottom of the Category list.
   The Custom option is chosen because you modified the number style when you decreased the decimal places in the previous exercises, creating a custom number format.

5. Follow these steps to format the numbers with floating dollar ($) signs.

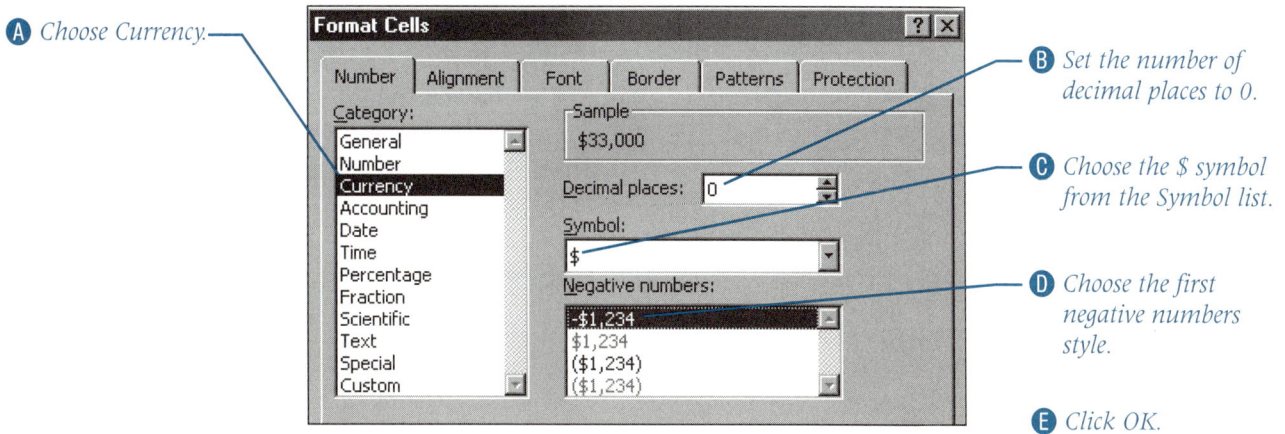

Ⓐ *Choose Currency.*

Format Cells

| Number | Alignment | Font | Border | Patterns | Protection |

Category:
General
Number
Currency
Accounting
Date
Time
Percentage
Fraction
Scientific
Text
Special
Custom

Sample
$33,000

Decimal places: 0

Symbol:
$

Negative numbers:
-$1,234
$1,234
($1,234)
($1,234)

Ⓑ *Set the number of decimal places to 0.*

Ⓒ *Choose the $ symbol from the Symbol list.*

Ⓓ *Choose the first negative numbers style.*

Ⓔ *Click OK.*

Notice that the dollar signs are now floating just in front of the numbers. Also, notice that the numbers are now shifted slightly to the right, and that they no longer line up with the numbers above them. This is because of the Negative Numbers option you set. You will adjust the Negative Numbers option in the next step.

Adjust the Negative Numbers Option

6. Make sure Cells B7:E7 are still selected, and choose **Format→Cells** from the menu bar.

7. Notice the various negative numbers formats.
Formats that are red display negative numbers in red. Also notice that some of the formats are surrounded with parentheses. Formats with parentheses cause positive numbers to shift slightly to the left. as discussed earlier.

8. Choose the third Negative Numbers format ($1,234), and click **OK.**
The numbers should now be right-aligned with the numbers in Rows 5 and 6. The numbers in Rows 5 and 6 are formatted with the Comma style. The Comma style displays negative numbers in parentheses. This is why the positive numbers in Rows 5 and 6 are shifted slightly to the left.

Check Out the Accounting Style

9. Make sure Cells B7:E7 are still selected, and choose **Format→Cells** from the menu bar.

10. Choose the Accounting category.

11. Make sure the symbol type is set to $ and the decimal places are set to 0.

12. Click **OK,** and the dollar ($) signs will once again have a fixed placement on the left side of the cells.
Notice that this was how the numbers were formatted when you first clicked the Currency Style button in an earlier exercise. The Currency Style button actually applies the Accounting style to numbers.

13. Click Undo 🔙 to restore the Currency style.

(Continued on the next page)

14. Choose **Format→Cells** from the menu bar.

15. Take a few minutes to browse through the various number styles in the Category list.
    Feel free to choose a style, and then read the description that appears at the bottom of the dialog box.

16. Click the **Cancel** button when you have finished exploring.
    You will continue to format numbers in a later exercise.

17. Save the changes, and continue with the next topic.

Merging Cells

Excel's merge cells option lets you merge cells together. Merged cells behave as one large cell. You can merge cells vertically or horizontally. The merge cells option is useful if you want to place a large block of text (such as a paragraph) in the worksheet. You merge cells by selecting the desired cells, issuing the **Format→Cells** command, and checking the Merge Cells box on the Alignment tab. Likewise, you can split a merged cell into the original cell configuration by removing the check from the Merge Cells box.

The Merge and Center Button

The Merge and Center ⊞ button merges selected cells and changes the alignment of the merged cell to center. This technique is often used to center a heading across columns. Keep in mind that the Merge and Center button has the same effect as merging cells, and then changing the alignment of the merged cell to center. You can split a merged and centered cell the same way you would split any other merged cell. The following example shows a heading centered across Columns B through E.

The Quarterly Income heading is centered above Columns B–E.

	A	B	C	D	E
2					
3			Quarterly Income		
4	Food Sales	Q1	Q2	Q3	Q4

Hands-On 2.8 Use Merge and Center

1. Select the range B3:E3, as shown to the right.
   Notice that this range includes the heading you wish to center

	A	B	C	D	E
1	Donna's Deli - Income and Expense Worksheet				
2					
3		Quarterly Income			

   (Quarterly Income) and the range of cells you wish to center this heading across (B3:E3).

2. Click the Merge and Center 🔲 button (near the middle of the Formatting toolbar).
   Notice that the cells have been merged together and the Center button on the Formatting toolbar is pushed in.

3. Click the Align Left 🔲 button and the entry will move to the left side of the merged cell.

4. Click the Center 🔲 button to center the entry in the merged cell.

5. Choose **Format→Cells** from the menu bar.

6. Click the Alignment tab on the Format Cells dialog box.
   Notice that the Merge Cells box is checked. This box is checked whenever cells are merged.

7. Remove the check from the Merge Cells box and click **OK.**

8. Click anywhere to deselect the cells, and notice that they are no longer merged.
   You use this technique to split merged cells.

9. Click Undo 🔲 to restore the merged cell.

10. Select the range B14:E14.

11. Click the Merge and Center 🔲 button to center the Quarterly Expenses heading.

Indenting Entries

The Increase Indent 🔲 button and Decrease Indent 🔲 button on the Formatting toolbar let you offset entries from the left edges of cells. Indenting is useful in conveying the hierarchy of entries. The following illustration shows indented cells.

These cells are indented to show their subordination to the Food Sales heading.

	A
3	
4	Food Sales
5	Dine-in Sales
6	Takeout Sales
7	Subtotal

Hands-On 2.9 Indent Entries

1. Click Cell A5.

2. Click the Increase Indent 🔲 button twice.
   Notice that the entry is indented slightly each time you click the button.

3. Click the Decrease Indent 🔲 button once.

4. Click Cell A6, and increase the indent 🔲 once.

5. Select Cells A9 and A10.

6. Press and hold the (CTRL) key while you select the range A16:A21.
   The range A16:A21 contains the Rent, Utilities, etc. subheadings below the Expenses heading in Column A.

7. Increase the indent 🔲 once.

Formatting Entries

From the Keyboard

CTRL +B for Bold
CTRL +U for Underline
CTRL +I for Italics

In Excel and other Office programs, you can format text by changing the font, font size, and color. You can also apply various font formats, including bold, italics, and underline. To format cells, select the desired cells and apply formats using buttons on the Formatting toolbar. You can also choose formats from the Font tab of the Format Cells dialog box.

You can choose a font from the font list. You can also click the drop-down button and type the desired font name to rapidly scroll the list.

The Font Color button is on the right end of the Formatting toolbar. The color palette appears when you click the drop-down button. Once you choose a color, the color is displayed on the button. From that point forward, you can rapidly apply the color by clicking the button.

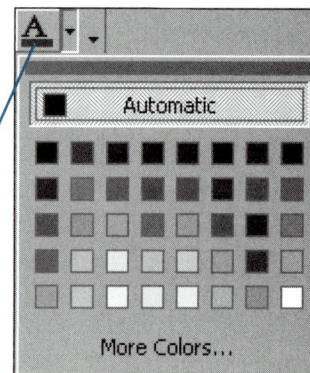

Font size

Bold, italics, and underline

Hands-On 2.10 Format Entries

1. Click Cell A1.

2. Click the Font Size button on the Formatting toolbar, and choose **14.**

3. Click the Bold **B** button on the Formatting toolbar.
   Notice that the entire title is formatted. Once again, the entire title belongs to Cell A1, even though it is displayed over the adjacent cells.

4. Click the drop-down button on the Font Color button located at the right end of the Formatting toolbar.

5. Choose one of the dark blue shades from the color palette.
   Notice that the color you chose is now displayed on the Font Color button. You can now apply the same color to other cells by selecting the cells and then clicking the button.

6. Click Cell B3.
   Cell B3 is now part of the large merged cell in the range B3:E3.

7. Click the Font Color **A** button, and the same color will be applied to the Quarterly Income cell.

8. Increase the size of the Quarterly Income cell to **12,** and apply **bold** formatting.

9. Select the Q1–Q4 headings in Row 4.

10. Apply bold formatting, and then choose a different color from the Font Color button's color palette.
    In the next exercise, you will use the Format Painter to copy font and number formats to other cells.

The Format Painter

The Format Painter [icon] lets you copy text and number formats from one cell to another. The Format Painter copies all text and number formats from the source cell to the target cell(s). The Format Painter saves time and helps create consistent formatting throughout a workbook.

USING THE FORMAT PAINTER

- Click on the cell with the format(s) you wish to copy.

- Click the Format Painter once if you want to copy formats to one other cell or range. Double-click if you want to copy to multiple cell(s) or range(s).

- Select the cells to which you want to copy the format(s). If you double-clicked in the previous step, the Format Painter will remain active, allowing you to select cells at multiple locations. You can even scroll through the workbook to reach the desired location(s).

- If you double-clicked in the first step, then click the Format Painter when you have finished. This will turn off the Format Painter.

Hands-On 2.11 Use the Format Painter

Copy Text Formats

1. Click Cell B3 (the merged cell with the Quarterly Income heading).

2. Click the Format Painter [icon] on the Standard toolbar, and an animated paintbrush icon will be attached to the mouse pointer.

3. Click Cell B14 (the merged cell with the Quarterly Expenses heading).
   The text formats should be copied to that heading. The animated paintbrush icon also vanished because you clicked the Format Painter button just once in the previous step. If you want to copy formats to multiple locations, you must double-click the Format Painter.

4. Click Cell B4.
   This cell should contain the heading Q1.

5. Click the Format Painter [icon].

6. Select the range B15:E15 to copy the formats to those cells, as shown below.

15	Expenses	Q1	Q2	Q3	Q4

Copy Number Formats

7. Select the cells containing numbers in Row 7, and apply bold formatting to the numbers.
   Notice that the numbers in Row 7 have a Currency style with a floating dollar sign. In the next few steps, you will use the Format Painter to copy both the number and text formats to the numbers in Rows 11, 12, and 22–25. Notice that these rows currently have fixed dollar signs on the left edges of the cells.

(Continued on the next page)

8. Click Cell B7.

9. *Double-click* the Format Painter [icon].

10. Select the range B11:E12 to copy the formats to those cells, as shown below.

| 11 | Subtotal | $3,000 | $3,200 | $3,500 | $5,000 |
| 12 | Total Income | $36,000 | $42,200 | $56,500 | $103,000 |

11. Select the range B22:E26 to copy the formats to those cells, as shown below.

22	Total Expenses	$37,200	$33,610	$37,090	$42,180
23					
24	Gross Profit	($1,200)	$8,590	$19,410	$60,820
25	Net Profit	($1,200)	$8,590	$16,499	$45,615
26	Gross Profit vs. Income	($0)	$0	$0	$1

12. Click the Format Painter [icon] to turn it off.
Notice that you had to turn the Format Painter off this time because you double-clicked it initially. Also, notice the Percent number style in Row 26 has been removed. Be careful when you are trying to copy text formats but not number formats. In this example, you wanted to copy the bold text style to Row 26 but not the Currency style. Keep in mind that the Format Painter copies both text formats and number formats.

13. Select the numbers in Row 26 and use the Percent Style [%] button to reapply the Percent style

14. Save the changes, and continue with the next topic.

Clearing Cell Contents and Formats

The **Edit→Clear** command displays a submenu that lets you clear the content, formats, or comments from cells. The submenu also contains an All option that clears all of these items from the selected cells. Each of these items is defined below.

- **Content**—Clearing the content has the same effect as tapping the (DELETE) key. This deletes a cell's contents, but any format applied to the cell will still be in effect if new data is entered in the cell.

- **Formats**—The Formats option removes all text and number formats, leaving unformatted entries in the cell(s).

- **Comments**—You can insert comments in cells to document your worksheet. The Comments option removes comments from the selected cells.

Hands-On 2.12 Clear Formats

1. Notice the formatting applied to the Q1–Q4 headings in Rows 4 and 15.

   These headings will probably look better if they have simple bold formatting like the numbers in the sub-total and total rows.

2. Select the Q1–Q4 headings in Row 4 and choose **Edit→Clear→Formats.**

   Excel will remove all formats, including the right alignment.

3. Click the Align Right ⊞ button, and then apply bold formatting to the cells.

4. Clear the formats from the Q1–Q4 headings in Row 15.

5. Right-align the Q1–Q4 headings in Row 15, and apply bold formatting to the headings.

   Your completed worksheet should match the worksheet shown in the case study at the start of this lesson.

6. Save the changes to your workbook.

7. Feel free to experiment with the **Edit→Clear** command.

8. When you have finished experimenting, close the workbook without saving the changes.

   Continue with the end-of-lesson questions and exercises.

Concepts Review

True/False Questions

1. The fill handle cannot be used to copy formulas.   TRUE   FALSE

2. The Merge and Center button can only be used with numbers.   TRUE   FALSE

3. Formulas must always begin with an open parenthesis (.   TRUE   FALSE

4. Formulas can include both cell and range references.   TRUE   FALSE

5. The asterisk * is used to represent multiplication in formulas.   TRUE   FALSE

6. Point mode can be used to insert cell references in formulas.   TRUE   FALSE

7. The Comma number style inserts a dollar sign in front of the number.   TRUE   FALSE

8. The Format Painter copies text formats, but not number formats.   TRUE   FALSE

Multiple-Choice Questions

1. What should you do before clicking the Merge and Center button?
   a. Click the cell that contains the entry you wish to center.
   b. Select the cells you wish to center the entry across, while making sure the entry is included in the selection.
   c. Select the entire row that contains the entry you wish to center.
   d. None of the above

2. Which of the following symbols can be used to begin a formula?
   a. +
   b. −
   c. =
   d. All of the above

3. How would the number 10000.367 be displayed if you format it as comma with 2 decimals?
   a. 10,000.38
   b. $10,000.38
   c. 10,000
   d. None of the above

4. How is the dollar sign positioned with the Accounting number style?
   a. Floats to the immediate left of the number
   b. Fixed on the left edge of the cell
   c. The Accounting style does not place a dollar sign in front of the number.
   d. The answer depends on whether the number has a decimal point.

Skill Builders

Skill Builder 2.1 Formatting and Formulas

In this exercise, you will open a home budget worksheet on your exercise diskette. You will format the worksheet using the skills you have learned in this lesson.

1. Open the workbook named **Skill Builder 2.1** on your exercise diskette.

2. Widen Column A until the text entries in that column are visible.

3. Select the range A1:G1, as shown below.

	A	B	C	D	E	F	G
1	1999 Home Budget						
2							

4. Click the Merge and Center ⊞ button to center 1999 Home Budget above the worksheet.

Use AutoFill

5. Follow these steps to AutoFill the headings in Row 3.

	A	B	C	D	E	F	G
1	1999 Home Budget						
2							
3		January					

Ⓐ *Select Cells B3 and C3, and release the mouse button.*

Ⓑ *Drag the fill handle four cells to the right as shown here, and release the mouse button.*

Excel assumes you want the series January–March with an empty cell between each month. This is a correct assumption, and the resulting cells are shown below.

3	January	February	March

6. Select Cells B4 and C4 (the Budget and Spent cells).

7. Drag the fill handle over the next four cells to the right, and Excel will copy Cells B4 and C4 to those cells.
   You should now have three sets of Budget and Spent cells. As you can see, the fill handle is used for a variety of purposes.

(Continued on the next page)

Use Merge and Center

8. Select Cells B3 and C3 (the January cell and the blank cell to the right of it).

9. Click Merge and Center ⊞ to center the January heading over the Budget and Spent columns.

10. Merge and center the February and March headings over their Budget and Spent columns.

11. Select Row 4, and right-align ▤ the Budget and Spent headings.

Calculate the Subtotals

12. Select the range B9:G9 (the subtotal cells in Row 9).

13. Press and hold the (CTRL) key while you select the subtotal ranges B14:G14 and B19:G19.
    All three of the subtotal ranges should be selected.

14. Click AutoSum Σ to calculate all subtotals with a single command.

Calculate the Totals and Differences

15. Click Cell B21.

16. Enter the formula **=B9+B14+B19.**

17. Use the fill handle to copy the formula across the row.

18. Click Cell B22.
    This cell will contain the difference between the January budget and January spent in Row 21.

19. Enter the formula **=B21−C21**.
    The result should equal 158.

20. Calculate the differences in Cells D22 and F22. You may want to use some shortcut to enter these formulas. For example, you could use the fill handle to copy the formula in Cell B22 across and then delete the formulas in Cells C22, E22 and G22.
    The results should equal 118 and −739.

Copy Number Formats

21. Select the subtotal numbers in Row 9.

22. Click the Currency Style $ button.

23. Click the Decrease Decimal button twice to reduce the decimals to 0.
    If you want the dollar ($) signs to float next to the numbers, make sure the cells are selected, and use the Format→Cells command. Choose the Currency style and set the number of decimal places and other options as desired.

24. Click Cell B9.

25. *Double-click* the Format Painter ![icon].

26. Drag the animated paintbrush over the subtotal numbers in Rows 14 and 19, and then drag over the totals and differences in Rows 21 and 22.
The Currency format will be copied to the numbers in those rows.

27. Click the Format Painter ![icon] to turn it off.

Format Text Entries

28. Click Cell A1 (the large merged cell).

29. Set the font size to 16, apply bold formatting, and choose a color ![icon].

30. Apply bold formatting to the headings in Row 3, and apply the same color you used for the title in Cell A1.

31. Format the headings in Row 4 with the same color you used in Row 3.

32. Apply bold formatting to the subtotals in Rows 9, 14, and 19.

33. Format the totals and differences rows with the same color you used in Rows 3 and 4.

Recalculate Formulas

34. Click Cell G5.
Imagine you have an adjustable rate mortgage, and the monthly payment just went up. In the next step, you will change the number in Cell G5. Keep an eye on the totals and differences formulas at the bottom of the worksheet when you change the number. The formulas will automatically recalculate the numbers.

35. Type **1075**, and complete the entry.
The new total in Cell G21 should equal 2879, and the new difference in Cell F22 should equal –814.

36. Save the changes to the workbook, and then close the workbook.

Skill Builder 2.2 Formatting Practice

In this exercise, you will open a workbook on your exercise diskette. You will format the worksheet until it closely matches the completed worksheet shown below.

1. Open the workbook named **Skill Builder 2.2.**

2. Merge and Center ▦ the title, Corporate Budget, across Columns A–E.

3. Use the fill handle to expand the series Q1 to Q1–Q4.

4. Right-align the headings Q1–Q4.

5. Calculate the subtotals and totals.

6. Widen Column A until the entries in the column are visible.

7. Format the numbers as shown below.

8. Format the title and headings with text formats of your choice.

9. Format the subtotal rows with italics as shown.

10. Format the total row with bold and italics as shown.

11. When you have finished, save the changes, and then close the workbook.

	A	B	C	D	E
1			Corporate Budget		
2					
3		Q1	Q2	Q3	Q4
4	Marketing	1,234,890	2,346,890	2,156,580	1,900,890
5	Sales	2,316,780	2,145,670	2,134,670	2,145,760
6	*Subtotal*	$ *3,551,670*	$ *4,492,560*	$ *4,291,250*	$ *4,046,650*
7					
8	Manufacturing	8,909,800	8,769,870	7,869,870	9,878,760
9	Distribution	3,456,570	3,245,670	2,314,560	3,897,860
10	*Subtotal*	$ *12,366,370*	$ *12,015,540*	$ *10,184,430*	$ *13,776,620*
11					
12	Customer Support	93,450	72,150	63,670	93,670
13	Human Resources	65,640	87,890	65,670	86,780
14	*Subtotal*	$ *159,090*	$ *160,040*	$ *129,340*	$ *180,450*
15					
16	*Total*	$ *16,077,130*	$ *16,668,140*	$ *14,605,020*	$ *18,003,720*

Skill Builder 2.3 Formatting and Formulas

In this exercise, you will open a workbook on your exercise diskette. You will format the worksheet until it closely matches the completed worksheet shown below.

1. Open the workbook named **Skill Builder 2.3.**

2. Merge and Center 🔲 the title Q2 Sales Volume Comparison across Columns A–E.

3. Use the fill handle to expand the series Store 1 to Store 1–Store 4 in Rows 3, 8, and 13.

4. Right-align the headings Store 1–Store 4.

5. Left-align all dates in Column A.

6. Widen Column A until the Percentage Increase entries fit within the column.

7. Format the numbers in Rows 4, 5, 9, 10, 14, and 15 as Comma style with 0 decimals.

8. Click Cell B6.
   In the next step, you will enter a formula that calculates the percentage increase. This formula uses parenthesis to change the order of calculations. The percentage increase is calculated as the April 99 sales minus April 98 sales. This difference is then divided by the April 98 sales. The formula is (B5–B4)/B4.

9. Enter the formula **=(B5–B4)/B4**.

10. Use the fill handle to copy the formula across the row.

11. Enter similar formulas in Cells B11 and B16, and then copy the formulas across the rows.

12. Format the numbers in the Percentage Increase rows with the Percent style 🔲 with 2 decimals.

13. Increase the font size of the title in Row 1 to 12, and apply bold formatting.

14. Apply the color of your choice to the title in Row 1, and then apply the same color to the percentage increases in Rows 6, 11, and 16.
    The completed worksheet should closely match the worksheet shown below.

15. When you have finished, save the changes, and then close the workbook.

	A	B	C	D	E
1	Q2 Sales Volume Comparison				
2					
3		Store 1	Store 2	Store 3	Store 4
4	April-98	13,234,657	34,789,564	23,000,908	65,908,456
5	April-99	14,456,900	40,987,560	28,546,905	70,987,235
6	Percentage Increase	9.24%	17.82%	24.11%	7.71%
7					
8		Store 1	Store 2	Store 3	Store 4
9	May-98	18,985,342	40,234,908	24,234,908	45,003,345
10	May-99	19,234,987	41,210,908	24,400,098	46,989,456
11	Percentage Increase	1.31%	2.43%	0.68%	4.41%
12					
13		Store 1	Store 2	Store 3	Store 4
14	Jun-98	24,234,980	65,230,980	18,230,350	51,006,983
15	Jun-99	25,235,908	66,234,908	27,908,990	58,231,900
16	Percentage Increase	4.13%	1.54%	53.09%	14.16%

Assessments

Assessment 2.1

In this assessment, you will create the completed worksheet shown below. Excel has a feature called AutoComplete that can assist you in entering data. As you are entering data in Column A, AutoComplete may propose entries in the current cell. These entries will be derived from cells that you have already typed in Column A. Just ignore this and continue typing your entries. You will learn more about AutoComplete in the next lesson.

1. Click the New [ ] button to start a new workbook.

2. Use the following guidelines to create the worksheet shown below.

   ■ Enter the data as shown in the completed worksheet. You must create formulas in Columns D and F and in Rows 10, 12, and 13. The completed worksheet shows the cells requiring formulas in bold. The following table lists the formulas you will need to begin.

Cell	Use this Formula
D4	=C4/B4
F4	=D4*E4
Row 10	Column summations (use AutoSum)
B12	=E10/B10
B13	=F10/C10

   ■ Format the numbers with currency formats and percent formats as shown. Make sure you use the same number of decimals as shown.

   ■ Widen the columns, and align the text entries as necessary.

   ■ Indent the items in Column A as shown.

   ■ Add bold as shown, and enhance the worksheet in any other way you choose.

3. Use Print Preview when you have finished, and then print the worksheet.

4. Save your workbook as **Assessment 2.1,** and then close the workbook.

	A	B	C	D	E	F
1	Donna's Deli - Produce Wastage Tracking Sheet (October)					
2						
3	Item	Pounds Purchased	Total Purchase $	Cost per Lb.	Pounds Wasted	Total Wastage $
4	Sweet Potatoes	350	$101.50	0.29	52	$15.08
5	Corn	220	$85.80	0.39	34	$13.26
6	Greens	180	$124.20	0.69	23	$15.87
7	Bean Sprouts	120	$22.80	0.19	34	$6.46
8	Tomatoes	290	$258.10	0.89	80	$71.20
9	Zucchini	90	$38.70	0.43	23	$9.89
10	Totals	1250	$631.10		246	$131.76
11						
12	Waste % (Lbs.)	19.68%				
13	Waste % ($)	20.88%				

Assessment 2.2

In this assessment, you will develop the completed worksheet shown below.

1. Click the New [□] button to start a new workbook.

2. Create the completed worksheet shown at the below. You must use formulas in Columns D and F and Row 11. Make sure the formula results match the completed worksheet. Format the numbers and text as shown.

3. Use print preview when you have finished, and then print the worksheet.

4. Save your workbook as **Assessment 2.2,** and then close the workbook.

	A	B	C	D	E	F
1	Donna's Deli - Customer Credit Lines					
2						
3	Customer	Previous Balance	New Charges	Subtotal	Payment Amount	New Balance
4	George Lopke	100	50	150	150	0
5	Wanda Watson	230	85	315	315	0
6	Alicia Thomas	58	100	158	100	58
7	Bill Barton	60	35	95	0	95
8	Latisha Robertson	140	80	220	0	220
9	Amy Chang	200	150	350	350	0
10	Dan Long	90	65	155	100	55
11	Total Credit	$878	$565	$1,443	$1,015	$428

Assessment 2.3

1. Create the following worksheet, formatting the cells as shown.

2. Print the worksheet, save the workbook as **Assessment 2.3,** and then close the workbook.

	A	B	C	D
1	Donna's Deli - Customer Survey Results			
2				
3	Category	January	February	March
4	Flavor	4.80	4.75	4.80
5	Service	4.60	4.50	4.70
6	Nutritional Value	4.95	4.95	4.83
7	Presentation	4.20	4.35	4.30
8	Price	4.20	4.20	4.45
9	Convenience	4.30	4.40	4.20
10	Total	27.05	27.15	27.28

Critical Thinking

Critical Thinking 2.1 On Your Own

Fred Watson is the owner of Fred's Quality Lawn Care service. Fred has provided high-quality lawn care and landscaping services for over 25 years. Recently, Fred purchased a personal computer with Office 2000 preinstalled. He intends to use his new computer and Office 2000 to improve his customer service, conduct mailings, computerize his billing processes, and increase his profits. He recently took an Excel class at a local community college. Fred wants to use Excel to track his activities and help maximize his profits. You have been assigned the task of setting up a job log for Fred. The worksheet should assign a job number to each job. It should include the customer name, day of the week, type of work performed, the number of hours required to complete the activity, and the total dollar amount billed for the job. Use a formula to calculate the effective hourly rate for each job. This calculation will allow Fred to determine the types of work that yield the highest hourly rates. Include enough jobs to account for an entire week of activity with perhaps one or two jobs per day. Use the following categories of work performed:

Mowing	Irrigation system installation
Tree trimming	General maintenance

Save your workbook as **Critical Thinking 2.1.**

Critical Thinking 2.2 On Your Own

Cathy Adams works for George Miller at Speedy Package Delivery Service. Cathy has assigned you the task of setting up a worksheet to record mileage, gasoline usage, and other expenses for Speedy drivers. Cathy provides you with the following information for the month of March.

Driver	Miles Driven	Gasoline Used (gallons)	Gasoline Expense	Tolls
Harold Robinson	4,850	202	$267	$152
Jane Allen	5,232	194	$256	$165
Bill Peterson	4,100	158	$208	$ 90
Janine Rockwell	5,050	240	$317	$158

Use formulas to calculate the miles/gallon for each driver. Also, calculate the total expenses for each driver from as the gasoline expense plus tolls. Format the entries as shown in the table above. Use the Format Painter to apply the same format to the total Expense cells that is used in the Tolls cells. Use the Merge and Center tool to center a descriptive title above the worksheet data. Apply indents and any types of formats that you think are appropriate. Save your workbook as **Critical Thinking 2.2.**

Critical Thinking 2.3 On Your Own

Cindy Johnson conducts tests of PC hard drives at Data Storage Incorporated. Cindy has asked you to construct an Excel workbook to help her quantify her test results. Cindy provides you with the following data to get you started.

Unit Type	Total Produced	Passed Test	Failed but Repaired	Destroyed
CX4-4 Gigabyte	9,500	9,200	240	60
CX8-8 Gigabyte	8,000	7,450	350	200
CX16-16 Gigabyte	7,000	6,910	25	65

Use formulas to calculate the percentage of each drive type that passed the test, failed but were prepared, and were destroyed. Now use formulas to calculate totals for the columns shown in the preceding table, then calculate percentages for that total row as you did for the other rows. Format the entries as shown in the table above. Format the cells containing the percentage calculations as Percent style with two decimals. Use the Merge and Center tool to center a descriptive title above the worksheet data. Apply any types of formats that you think are appropriate. Save your workbook as **Critical Thinking 2.3.**

Critical Thinking 2.4 **Web Research**

Dominique Aguyo is a senior at West Side high school. Dominique is quite certain that she wants to major in Chemical Engineering when she attends college in the fall. Your task is to help Dominique identify schools that offer Chemical Engineering as a major. Use Internet Explorer and a search engine of your choice to locate at least five universities that offer Chemical Engineering majors. Record your results in an Excel spreadsheet. Include the school, city and state, size of the student population, and other information that you think would help Dominique make her decision. Save your workbook as **Critical Thinking 2.4.**

Critical Thinking 2.5 **Web Research**

Vivian Chu is a history major at San Francisco State University. Vivian is taking a demographics class in order to fulfill the requirements of her major. Part of the course requirements is a research paper on the effects of population growth in the next millennium. Use Internet Explorer and a search engine of your choice to help Vivian find the following population statistics for the United States, China, India, Brazil, and Germany.

Current population	Overall population growth rate
Birth rate	Estimated population in 2050
Death rate	

Use Excel to enter and organize the data. Format all cells containing rate information in Percent style with two decimals. Format cells with population numbers in Comma style with zero decimals. Center a descriptive title over the worksheet cells. Save your workbook as **Critical Thinking 2.5.**

Critical Thinking 2.6 **With a Group**

Work with a classmate to develop a revenue and expense worksheet for a new business venture. You can base your worksheet on the worksheet developed in the Hands-On exercises in this lesson. Decide what type of business you would like to model, what the potential revenue sources might be, and what the potential expenses might be. Include as many potential revenue sources and expense details as possible. Use formulas to determine whether or not the business can be profitable based on the model you set up. Format your worksheet as necessary, and save it as **Critical Thinking 2.6.**

Powerful Features and Automated Tools

In this lesson, you will be introduced to Excel functions. Excel has hundreds of built-in functions including the AVERAGE, MIN, MAX, and COUNT functions which are introduced in this lesson. This lesson will also give you the skills necessary to move and copy cells. You will learn the Cut, Copy, and Paste techniques as well as Drag and Drop. Finally, you will learn how to apply borders and fill colors to cells and use Excel's powerful AutoFormat command.

In This Lesson

Case Study

Lisa Wilkins is the National Sales Manager for Centron Cellular—a nationwide distributor of cellular telephone equipment. Lisa has instructed her assistant, Carl Jenkins, to provide her with a commission report for her sales force. Lisa wants the report separated into two regions. She wants to know the monthly sales and commissions for each sales rep. She also wants the total, average, minimum, and maximum sales of the reps in each region on a monthly basis. This would be a formidable task for most people, but Carl Jenkins is not concerned. Carl has expert knowledge of Excel 2000. With a little planning and the power of Excel 2000, Carl will produce this worksheet with ease.

	A	B	C	D	E	F	G
1	Centron Cellular						
2							
3	Region 1						
4	Sales Rep	Jan Sales	Jan Comm	Feb Sales	Feb Comm	Mar Sales	Mar Comm
5	Branston	32000	4800	32000	4800	23000	3450
6	Barton	15000	2250	32000	4800	23890	3583.5
7	Alexander	45000	6750	8900	1335	43000	6450
8	Alioto	23000	3450	19000	2850	10900	1635
9	Chin	34000	5100	34000	5100	32000	4800
10	Total		22350		18885		19918.5
11	Average		4470		3777		3983.7
12	Maximum		6750		5100		6450
13	Minimum		2250		1335		1635
14							
15							
16	Region 2						
17	Sales Rep	Jan Sales	Jan Comm	Feb Sales	Feb Comm	Mar Sales	Mar Comm
18	Richardson	18000	2700	54000	8100	36790	5518.5
19	Thomas	12000	1800	35900	5385	45678	6851.7
20	Carter	56000	8400	34900	5235	72490	10873.5
21	Williams	39000	5850	54000	8100	21000	3150
22	Jones	23000	3450	89000	13350	38900	5835
23	Total		22200		40170		32228.7
24	Average		4440		8034		6445.74
25	Maximum		8400		13350		10873.5
26	Minimum		1800		5235		3150

The Office Assistant

The Office Assistant is an interactive Help tool available in all Office 2000 applications. The Assistant monitors your activities and provides tips, suggestions, and alert messages whenever it assumes you need assistance. For example, the Assistant displays a **speech balloon** when it recognizes certain actions such as clicking the Edit Formula button on the Formula bar. You can use the speech balloon to get help with the action.

Office Assistant

Would you like help with this feature?

● Yes, please provide help

● No, don't provide help now

The Office Assistant

Using the Assistant to Get Help

The Assistant's speech balloon contains a search box where you can enter phrases and questions. When you click the Search button, the Assistant interprets the phrase or question in the search box and displays a list of topics relating to the search box text. When you click a topic, Excel displays a Help window providing you with detailed help information.

Controlling the Assistant

You can control all aspects of the Assistant. For example, you may not want the Assistant to display a tip of the day, or you may want to turn the Assistant off. You set options for the Assistant in the Office Assistant dialog box. The following Quick Reference table describes various methods of controlling the Assistant.

Quick Reference

CONTROLLING THE OFFICE ASSISTANT

Task	Procedure
Display the Assistant's speech balloon. (four different methods)	■ Click anywhere on the Assistant.
	■ Press F1.
	■ Click the Help button on the Standard toolbar.
	■ Choose Microsoft Excel Help from the Help menu.
Close the speech balloon.	Click anywhere in the worksheet, or tap ESC.
Display Office Assistant dialog box.	Display the speech balloon, and click the Options button.
Change animated character.	Display the Office Assistant dialog box, click the Gallery tab, use the Next button to browse the available characters, choose a character, and click OK.
Temporarily hide the Assistant.	Choose Help→Hide the Office Assistant, or right-click the Assistant, and choose Hide from the pop-up menu.
Turn Assistant off completely.	Display the Office Assistant dialog box, and uncheck the Use the Office Assistant box.
Unhide the Assistant or turn the Assistant back on.	Choose Help→Show the Office Assistant

In this exercise, you will use the Assistant to learn about functions.

Display the Speech Balloon

1. Start Excel, and the Assistant should appear.

2. If the Assistant is not visible on your screen, choose Help→Show the Office Assistant.
   This text shows the default Assistant character known as "Clippit." The Assistant on your machine may be different.

3. Click the Assistant, and the speech balloon will pop up.

4. Click anywhere in the worksheet to close the speech balloon.
   You can always close the speech balloon by clicking in the worksheet or by tapping (ESC).

5. Position the mouse pointer on the Assistant and drag it to a new screen location.
   You can always reposition the Assistant, even if the speech balloon is displayed.

Get Help

6. Click the Assistant to display the speech balloon.

7. Follow these steps to get help with functions.

Ⓐ *Type the phrase* **Tell me about functions** *in the Search box.*

Ⓑ *Click the Search button to display a list of Help topics.*

> **What would you like to do?**
> ● About nesting functions within functions
> ● About calculating a value based on a condition
> ● About using functions to calculate values
> ● Enter a formula to calculate a value
> ● RECEIVED worksheet function
> ▼ See more...
>
> Tell me about functions
>
> Options   Search

Ⓒ *Choose the* About using functions to calculate values *topic. If this topic did not display, then check the search phrase you entered, and search again.*

Excel will display a Help window relating to functions. The Help window will most likely appear beside the Excel document window. As you can see, the Assistant can be used to display Help windows. You will learn more about functions and online Help in a moment.

(Continued on the next page)

8. For now, click the Close ☒ button at the top-right corner of the Help window.
   The Help window should close, and the Excel window will return to its original size.

9. Type the word **functions** in the Assistant's search box.

10. Click the **Search** button, and a list of topics will appear.
    Notice that About using functions to calculate values is one of the topics. This is the same topic you searched for previously when you entered the search phrase "Tell me about functions." This example shows that it isn't always necessary to type long phrases in the search box. Often, a single word is enough to locate a desired topic.

Check Out the Options

11. Click the Options button on the speech balloon.

12. If necessary, click the Options tab in the dialog box that appears.

13. Click the Question Mark ❓ button at the top-right corner of the dialog box, and then click on any option check box.
    Excel will provide a ScreenTip describing the purpose of the option.

14. Tap the (ESC) key to close the ScreenTip.

15. Feel free to get help on the various Office Assistant options. You may also want to click the Gallery tab in the dialog box to check out the other Assistant characters. If you are studying in a computer lab, it is recommended that you not change any options.

16. Close the Office Assistant dialog box when you have finished.

Online Help

Excel's online Help puts a complete reference book at your fingertips. Help is available for just about any topic you can imagine. Online Help is important because Microsoft does not provide reference manuals with Office 2000. The reference manuals are now integrated into online Help.

Locating Help Topics

Your goal when using online Help is to locate Help topics. There are several different search methods you can use to locate topics. All Help topics have key words that identify them. For example, a Help topic that discusses printing workbooks can probably be located by including the key word *printing* in your search method. Regardless of which search method you use, the goal is to locate a topic. Once you locate the desired topic, you can display it and follow the instructions in the topic.

When Help Is Available

In Excel 2000, you can display the Help window directly only when the Office Assistant is turned off. You learned how to turn off the Office Assistant in the previous topic. When the Office Assistant is turned off, the Help window can be displayed using any of the following methods:

- Click the Help [?] button on the Standard toolbar.

- Press (F1).

- Choose Help→Microsoft Word Help from the menu bar.

The following Quick Reference table describes the various methods for locating Help topics.

LOCATING HELP TOPICS

Search Method	Procedure
Contents	The Contents method is useful if you are trying to locate a topic but you aren't really sure how to describe it. The Contents method lets you navigate through a series of categories until the desired topic is located.
Answer Wizard	The Answer Wizard lets you find topics the same way that you find them with the Office Assistant. You type a phrase into a search box and execute a search.
Index	The Index method lets you locate a topic by typing key words. An alphabetically indexed list of topics is displayed from which you can choose the desired topic. This method is most useful if you know the name of the topic or feature for which you need assistance.

The Help Window Toolbar

The Help window contains a toolbar to assist you with online Help. The following illustration describes the buttons on the Help toolbar.

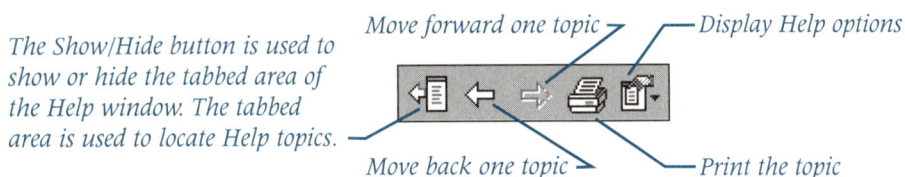

The Show/Hide button is used to show or hide the tabbed area of the Help window. The tabbed area is used to locate Help topics.

Move forward one topic — *Display Help options*

Move back one topic — *Print the topic*

Hands-On 3.2 Use Online Help

Turn Off the Office Assistant

1. Click the Office Assistant, and then click the Options button.

2. Make sure the Options tab is active, and remove the check from the **Use the Office Assistant** box.

3. Click **OK,** and the Office Assistant will vanish.
   Once the Office Assistant is turned off, commands that would normally display the Office Assistant display the Help window instead.

(Continued on the next page)

4. Choose **Help→Microsoft Excel Help** from the menu bar.
   The Help window will be displayed beside the Excel window. If the Office Assistant had been active, this command would have popped up the Assistant's speech balloon.

5. If the tabbed area of the Help window is not displayed, then click the Show 🔲 button on the Help toolbar.

6. Click the **Index** tab.

7. Type the word **function** in the Type keywords box, and click the **Search** button.
   A list of Help topics is displayed in the bottom section of the Help window. The About using functions to calculate values *topic should be the third one on the list.*

8. Click the **About Using Functions to Calculate Values** topic to display the topic in the right side of the Help window.
   This is the same Help topic you located earlier with the Office Assistant.

9. Take a moment to read the help information. Notice the blue phrases such as **cell references** that are scattered throughout the topic.

10. Click the **cell references** phrase, and a definition will pop up.

11. Tap ⌨ESC to close the definition.

Experiment with Help

12. Try using the Index method to locate additional Help topics. You can type keywords in the Keyword box, click the Search button, and click the desired topic. Try locating Help topics for Excel features you have already learned or for new features to be covered in this lesson.

13. Try using the Contents tab to locate topics. You must double-click closed books in the Contents tab to locate topics.

14. When you have finished, click the Close ❎ button on the Help window.

15. Finally, turn the Office Assistant back on with the **Help→Show the Office Assistant** command. If necessary, close the Assistant's speech balloon.

AutoCorrect

Excel's AutoCorrect feature can improve the speed and accuracy of entering text. AutoCorrect is most useful for replacing abbreviations with a full phrase. For example, you could set up AutoCorrect to substitute *as soon as possible* whenever you type *asap.* AutoCorrect also automatically corrects common spelling errors. For example, the word *the* is often misspelled as *teh* and the word *and* is often misspelled as *adn.* These and other common spelling mistakes are built into AutoCorrect, so they are fixed automatically. AutoCorrect also automatically capitalizes the first letter of a day if you type the day in lowercase. For example, if you type *sunday* and complete the entry, AutoCorrect will enter *Sunday* in the cell. Finally, AutoCorrect fixes words that have two initial capital letters by switching the second letter to lowercase.

Expanding AutoCorrect Entries

AutoCorrect goes into action when you type a word in a text entry and tap (SPACE BAR) or when you complete a text entry. The word or entry is compared to all entries in the AutoCorrect table. The AutoCorrect table contains a list of words and their replacement phrases. If the word you type matches an entry in the AutoCorrect table, then a phrase from the table is substituted for the word. This is known as expanding the AutoCorrect entry.

Creating and Editing AutoCorrect Entries

The **Tools→AutoCorrect** command displays the AutoCorrect dialog box. You use the AutoCorrect dialog box to add entries to the AutoCorrect table, to delete entries from the table, and to set other AutoCorrect options. To add an entry, you type the desired abbreviation in the Replace box and the desired expansion for the abbreviation in the With box.

AutoComplete

The AutoComplete feature is useful if you want the same entry repeated more than once in a column. If the first few characters you type match another entry in the column, then AutoComplete will offer to complete the entry for you. You can accept the offer by completing the entry or you can reject the offer by typing the remainder of the entry yourself.

Hands-On 3.3 Use AutoCorrect and AutoComplete

In this exercise, you will open a workbook from your exercise diskette. You will experiment with AutoCorrect and AutoComplete, and create a new AutoCorrect entry.

Use AutoCorrect

1. Open the workbook named **Hands-On Lesson 3.**

2. Type **adn** (that's adn, not and) in Cell A1, and tap (ENTER).
   Excel should correct the misspelling and enter the word and *in the cell.*

3. Click Cell A1, and type **This adn that**, but don't complete the entry.
   Notice that AutoCorrect fixes the typo immediately after you tap (SPACE BAR).

4. Tap (ESC) to cancel the entry.

(Continued on the next page)

Create a New AutoCorrect Entry

5. Choose **Tools→AutoCorrect** from the menu bar.

6. Follow these steps to create a new AutoCorrect entry.

Ⓐ *Notice these check boxes. They instruct AutoCorrect to automatically make the specified corrections in your worksheets.*

Ⓑ *Type* **cc** *in the Replace box.*

Ⓒ *Type* **Centron Cellular** *in the With box.*

Ⓓ *Click the* **Add** *button to add the entry to the list.*

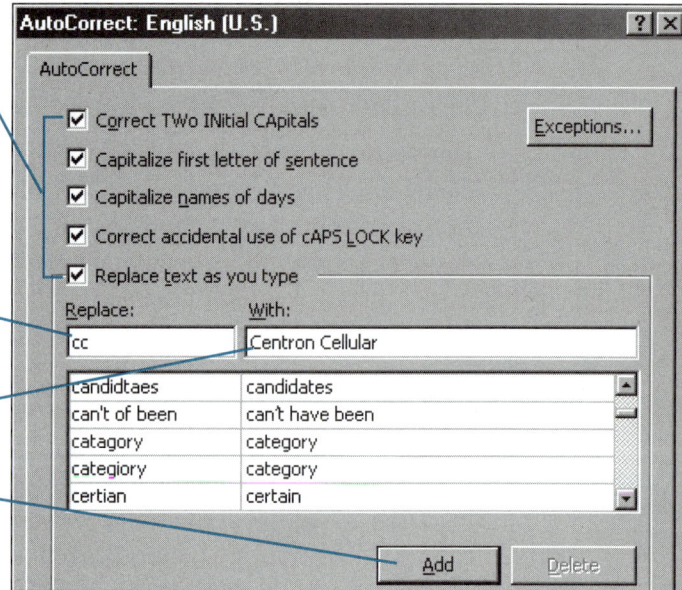

AutoCorrect: English (U.S.)

AutoCorrect

- ☑ Correct TWo INitial CApitals
- ☑ Capitalize first letter of sentence
- ☑ Capitalize names of days
- ☑ Correct accidental use of cAPS LOCK key
- ☑ Replace text as you type

Exceptions...

Replace:	With:
cc	Centron Cellular
candidtaes	candidates
can't of been	can't have been
catagory	category
categiory	category
certian	certain

Add   Delete

Ⓔ *Feel free to scroll through the list. You will see hundreds of AutoCorrect entries. All Office 2000 programs share the same AutoCorrect entries.*

Ⓕ *Click OK.*

7. Click Cell A1, type **cc**, and tap (ENTER).
AutoCorrect should replace cc with Centron Cellular. Notice that you can use AutoCorrect as a type of shorthand. AutoCorrect can replace abbreviations with phrases you use often such as your company name or address.

Delete the AutoCorrect Entry

8. Choose **Tools→AutoCorrect** from the menu bar.

9. Scroll through the list of AutoCorrect entries and choose the **cc, Centron Cellular** entry.

10. Click the **Delete** button below the AutoCorrect table, and then click **OK.**
The entry is deleted from the AutoCorrect table, but the phrase Centron Cellular will remain in Cell A1.

Use AutoComplete

11. Click Cell A5, type **Branston**, and then tap (ENTER).

12. Type the letter **B** in Cell A6 and AutoComplete will display the word Branston in the cell.
You could accept this proposal by completing the entry; however, you will continue to type in the next step thus typing over the proposed entry.

13. Type **arton** (to make the entry Barton), and tap (ENTER).
AutoComplete will constantly try to assist you in completing entries. You can either ignore AutoComplete and continue typing your entries or complete the entries that AutoComplete proposes.

14. Enter the following sales rep names into the next three cells.

7	Alexander
8	Alioto
9	Chin

You will continue to enhance the worksheet throughout this lesson.

Functions

Excel has over 400 built-in functions. Functions are predefined formulas that perform calculations. Functions must be constructed using a set of basic rules known as **syntax.** Fortunately, most functions use the same or similar syntax. The following illustration defines the syntax of the SUM function. This syntax also applies to the MIN, MAX, AVERAGE, and COUNT functions, which are discussed in the Quick Reference table following the illustration.

Always begin formulas containing functions with an equal (=) sign.

The function name always follows the equal (=) sign.

If an argument has more than one parameter, then commas must separate the parameters. In this example, Cells A5 and A10 would be added to the range B5:B9.

=SUM(B5:B9)   =SUM(A5,A10,B5:B9)

A set of parentheses always surrounds the argument. The argument is usually a range of cells.

Quick Reference

COMMON FUNCTIONS

Function	What It Does	Syntax Example
MIN	Returns the minimum value of a range	=MIN(B5:B9)
MAX	Returns the maximum value of a range	=MAX(B5:B9)
AVERAGE	Returns the average of values in a range	=AVERAGE(B5:B9)
COUNT	Determines how many cells in a range contain numbers, dates, or formulas	=COUNT(B5:B9)

Entering Functions with the Keyboard

You can type a function and its argument(s) directly in the desired cell. You can also click in the desired cell and type the function in the Formula bar. If you choose to type a function, you can use point mode to assist you in entering the function arguments.

Do a Little Detective Work and Use AutoSum

1. Notice that the Hands-On Lesson 3 worksheet has a January Commissions column (Jan Comm).
   The commissions in Column C are calculated with a simple formula.

2. What commission rate is being used to calculate the sales rep's commissions?
   You can find this out by clicking a commission cell in Column C and reviewing the formula in the Formula bar.

3. Click Cell C10, click AutoSum $\boxed{\Sigma}$, and complete the entry.
   The total commissions for January should equal 20550.

4. Look at the Formula bar and notice the function =SUM(C5:C9) that AutoSum has placed in the cell.
   The SUM function uses the standard function syntax discussed at the beginning of this topic.

Type the AVERAGE Function

5. Click Cell C11, type the function **=AVERAGE(C5:C9)**, and complete the entry.
   The result should equal 4110. This is the average of the values in the range C5:C9. Notice that the syntax is the same as the SUM function syntax, except you used the function name AVERAGE instead of SUM.

Pasting Functions

The Paste Function $\boxed{f_\pi}$ button on the Standard toolbar displays the Paste Function box. The Paste Function box provides access to all built-in functions in Excel. The Paste Function box organizes functions into various categories to help you easily locate the desired function. When you choose a function and click OK, Excel displays the Formula Palette below the Formula bar. The Formula Palette can assist you in constructing the function by helping you enter the arguments. The Paste Function box and the Formula Palette are shown in the following illustrations.

*The **Paste Function** box organizes functions into categories. This example shows some of the functions in the Statistical category.*

The Formula Palette appears below the Formula bar when you choose a function and click OK.

As you build the formula, Excel displays it in the Formula bar.

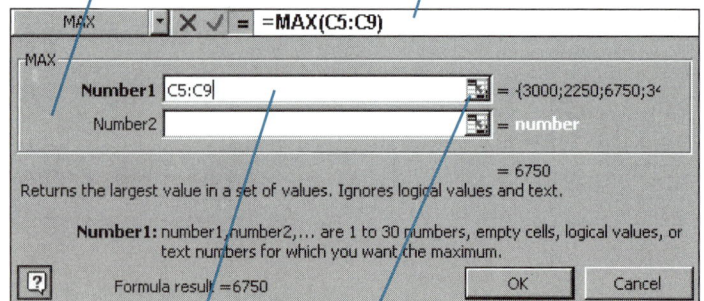

You can type the argument (typically a range) in this box or select the desired range in the worksheet.

The Collapse button can be used to collapse the Formula Palette while you select the desired range in the worksheet.

The Function Box

When you click the Edit Formula ▣ button, the Function box appears on the left end of the Formula bar. The Function box has a drop-down button containing a list of the 10 most recently used functions. When you choose a function from the list, the Formula Palette appears below the Formula bar. This technique has the same result as displaying the Paste Function box; however, it is more efficient if you are pasting a function that has recently been used.

The Function box also has a More Functions choice at the bottom of the drop-down menu that displays the Paste Function dialog box. This is convenient if the function you desire is not on the 10 most recently used functions list.

Clicking the Function box drop-down button displays the 10 most recently used functions.

Clicking the Edit Formula button displays the Function box.

Hands-On 3.5 Paste a Function and Use Point Mode

In this exercise, you will insert the MAX and MIN functions in your worksheet.

Paste the MAX Function

1. Click Cell C12, and then click the Edit Formula ▣ button on the Formula bar.

2. Follow these steps to explore the Function box.

A *Click the Function box drop-down button. The list shows the 10 most recently used functions on your computer.*

B *Notice that the most recently used function (in this case, AVERAGE) appears on the button and at the top of the list.*

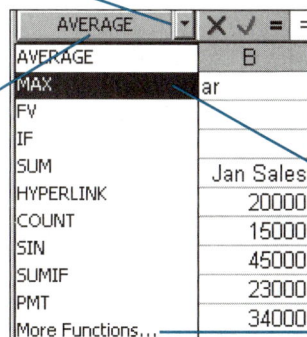

C *The MAX function will probably appear on your list. You could choose MAX at this point; however, you will choose the MAX function in the next step using the Paste Function box.*

D *Choose More Functions to display the Paste Function box.*

(Continued on the next page)

3. Follow these steps to choose the MAX function.

Ⓐ *Notice that the functions are organized by categories. The functions for the highlighted category are displayed to the right.*

Ⓑ *Choose the Statistical category.*

Ⓒ *Scroll down through the list of functions and choose MAX.*

Ⓓ *Click* **OK.**

Paste Function	? ☒
Function category:	Function name:
Most Recently Used	HYPGEOMDIST
All	INTERCEPT
Financial	KURT
Date & Time	LARGE
Math & Trig	LINEST
Statistical	LOGEST
Lookup & Reference	LOGINV
Database	LOGNORMDIST
Text	MAX
Logical	MAXA
Information	MEDIAN

Notice the MAX(C11) function appears in the Formula bar. This is the correct function; however, the range C11 is incorrect. You could type the correct range, C5:C9, in the Formula Palette or the Formula bar; however, you will insert the range by dragging in the worksheet in the following steps.

4. Follow this step to collapse the Formula Palette.

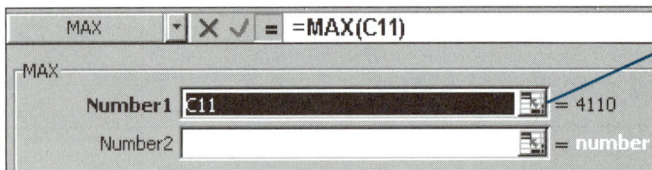

MAX	▾ ✗ ✓ =	=MAX(C11)

MAX
Number1 C11 = 4110
Number2 = number

Ⓐ *Click the Collapse button on the Formula Palette.*

5. Follow these steps to select the appropriate range of cells and restore the Formula Palette.

Ⓐ *Drag the mouse over the range C5:C9, as shown here.*

MAX	▾ ✗ ✓ =	=MAX(C5:C9)

C5:C9

		Jan Sales	Jan Comm	Feb Sales	Feb Comm	Mar Sales
1	Centron Cellular					
2						
3	Region 1					
4	Sales Rep	Jan Sales	Jan Comm	Feb Sales	Feb Comm	Mar Sales
5	Branston	20000	3000	32000		23000
6	Barton	15000	2250	32000		23890
7	Alexander	45000	6750	8900		43000
8	Alioto	23000	3450	19000		10900
9	Chin	34000	5100	34000		32000
10	Total		20550			
11	Average		4110			
12	Maximum					

Ⓑ *Click the Collapse button to restore the Formula Palette.*

Take a moment to equal the formula in the Formula bar. It should be =MAX(C5:C9).

6. Complete the function by clicking **OK** on the Formula palette (the result should equal 6750).

Use Point Mode to Enter the MIN Function

7. Click Cell C13 and type **=min(**.

   If you type a function in lowercase, Excel will convert it to uppercase when you complete the entry. Remember, you must always type the opening parenthesis when entering a function in point mode.

8. Drag the mouse down the range **C5:C9.**

9. Type a closing parenthesis **)**, and your formula should be =min(C5:C9).

10. Complete the entry. The result should equal 2250.

    In this exercise, you used two different methods to create functions. You can also insert functions by typing them directly into the cell or Formula bar. In the future, use whichever method you prefer.

Change the Values

You may be wondering why you used the MIN and MAX functions in this worksheet when it is relatively easy to see which sales reps had the minimum and maximum commissions. The benefit of using the functions becomes apparent when the values change or when there are a large number of rows. The functions automatically recalculate the SUM, AVERAGE, MAX, and MIN values when other values in the worksheet change.

11. Click Cell B5, change the sales number from 20000 to 32000, and complete the entry.

    Notice how the functions in Cells C10 and C11 recalculate the sum and average.

12. Click Undo [↶] to change the number back to 20000.

Cut, Copy, and Paste

Cut, Copy, and Paste are available in all Office 2000 applications. With Cut, Copy, and Paste you can move or copy cells within a worksheet, between worksheets, or between different Office applications. For example, you could use the Copy command to copy a range from one worksheet and the Paste command to paste the range into another worksheet. Cut, Copy, and Paste are most efficient for moving or copying cells a long distance within a worksheet or between worksheets. Cut, Copy, and Paste are easy to use if you remember the following concepts.

- You must select cells before issuing a Cut or Copy command.

- You must position the highlight at the desired location before issuing the Paste command. This is important because the range you paste will overwrite any cells in the paste area.

Command	Discussion	Procedure
Cut	The Cut command removes entries from selected cells and places them on the Windows clipboard.	Click the Cut button, or press CTRL+X.
Copy	The Copy command also places entries on the Windows clipboard, but it leaves a copy of the entries in the original cells.	Click the Copy button, or press CTRL+C.
Paste	The Paste command pastes entries from the Windows clipboard to worksheet cells beginning at the highlight location.	Click the Paste button, or press CTRL+V.

The Office 2000 Clipboard

Office 2000 introduces a new clipboard that can hold up to 12 cut or copied items. The Clipboard toolbar appears once you have cut or copied two or more items. The Clipboard toolbar displays an icon representing each cut or copied item. You can paste any item by choosing it from the Clipboard toolbar. You can paste all items from the toolbar by clicking the Paste All button. The items are pasted in the order in which they were cut or copied to the toolbar.

This Clipboard has had two items copied to it. The Clipboard can hold items from all Office programs.

This button pastes all items into the worksheet.

When you point at an item, a ScreenTip pops up. When you click an item, it is pasted into the worksheet.

This button clears the Clipboard contents.

Hands-On 3.6 Use Copy and Paste

Copy the Commission Formula to Cell E5

1. Click Cell C5, and take a moment to review the formula in the Formula bar.
   Your objective is to copy this formula to the February and March commission columns. This cannot be done with the fill handle because those cells are not adjacent to Cell C5.

2. Click the Copy button on the Standard toolbar.
   Notice the flashing marquee in Cell C5. This indicates that the sales commission formula is on the clipboard and ready to be pasted.

3. Click Cell E5, and then click the Paste button.
   The formula will be pasted, and it will calculate the commission as 4800. The flashing marquee in Cell C5 indicates the formula is still available for pasting into other cells.

Paste to a Range

4. Select the range E6:E9.

5. Click the Paste button to paste the formula.
   You can always copy a single cell and paste it into a range of cells.

6. Select the range G5:G9 and paste the formula into those cells.
   You can continue to paste as long as the marquee is flashing.

7. Tap (ESC) on the keyboard, and the marquee will stop flashing.
   You can always turn off the flashing marquee with the (ESC) key.

8. Click any cell that you just pasted into, and review the formula in the Formula bar.
   Excel updates the references in the formulas to reflect the new formula locations.

9. Click Cell C10, and click the Copy 🖹 button.

10. Click Cell E10.

11. Press and hold the (CTRL) key, and click Cell G10.
   Both Cells E10 and G10 should be selected.

12. Click the Paste 🖹 button to paste the formula into both cells.

13. Use the preceding techniques to copy the AVERAGE, MAX, and MIN functions from Column C to Columns E and G. You can copy the functions one at a time, or you can select all three functions, and copy and paste them simultaneously.

Copy the Heading Rows

14. Select all entries in Rows 3 and 4 by dragging over the cells.

15. Click the Copy 🖹 button, and then click Cell A16.
   In the next step, you will paste the range to Cell A16. You should always paste a large range like this to one cell (A16 in this case). Excel will use Cell A16 as the starting location of the pasted range. However, you must be careful when using this technique because Excel will overwrite any cells in the pasted range.

16. Click the Paste 🖹 button.
   In the next exercise, you will continue to copy cells with the drag-and-drop technique. For now, continue with the data entry task in the next step.

17. Enter the following names into the range A18:A22.

18	Richardson
19	Thomas
20	Carter
21	Williams
22	Jones

18. Change the heading in Cell A16 from Region 1 to Region 2.

Drag and Drop

Drag and Drop produces the same results as Cut, Copy, and Paste. However, Drag and Drop is usually more efficient if you are moving or copying entries a short distance within the same worksheet. If the original location and destination are both visible in the current window, then it is usually easier to use Drag and Drop. With Drag and Drop, you select the cells you wish to move or copy and release the mouse button. Then you point to the edge of the selected range and drag the range to the desired destination. If you press the (CTRL) key while releasing the mouse button, the cells are copied to the destination.

Right Dragging

Right dragging is a variation of the drag and drop technique. Many beginners find Drag and Drop difficult to use because they have difficulty controlling the mouse. This difficulty is compounded if they are trying to copy entries using drag and drop. This is because copying requires the (CTRL) key to be held while the selected range is dragged. With the Right-Drag method, the right mouse button is used when dragging. When the right mouse button is released at the destination, a pop-up menu appears. The pop-up menu allows you to choose Move, Copy, or Cancel. This provides more control because there is no need to use the (CTRL) key when copying, and you have the option of canceling the move or copy.

Hands-On 3.7 Use Drag and Drop

In this exercise, you will use Drag and Drop to move and copy text and formulas in the worksheet.

Move Entries

1. Follow these steps to drag and drop text entries.

Ⓐ *Select the range A10:A13.*

Ⓑ *Point to the bottom border of the range, and the pointer will become an arrow. (You can actually point to any border when using Drag and Drop.)*

Ⓒ *Drag the mouse down until the shaded box is positioned just below the names in Region 2.*

Ⓓ *Release the mouse button to move the range.*

Notice how easy it was to move the cells using Drag and Drop. You should focus on using Drag and Drop if the move is a short distance within the same worksheet. Unfortunately, you should have copied the cells instead of moving them. You will correct this in the next few steps.

2. Click Undo 🔙 to reverse the move.

Use Right Drag

3. Make sure the range A10:A13 is still selected.

4. Position the mouse pointer on the bottom edge of the selected range and press and hold the **right** mouse button.

5. Drag the mouse down until the range A23:A26 is highlighted as in the previous steps, and release the right mouse button.

A pop-up menu will appear with several choices.

6. Choose **Copy Here** from the pop-up menu.

The selected range will be copied.

Use Right Drag to Copy Formulas

7. Follow these steps to copy the January commission formulas to Region 2.

Ⓐ *Select the range C5:C13.*

Ⓑ *Point to the bottom edge of the range, and press and hold the right mouse button.*

Ⓒ *Drag the mouse down until the shaded rectangle is positioned just below the* Jan Comm *heading in Cell C17.*

Ⓓ *Release the mouse button, and choose* Copy Here *from the pop-up menu.*

Jan Comm
3000
2250
6750
3450
5100
20550
4110
6750
2250

Jan Comm

(Continued on the next page)

8. Use the right-drag method to copy the February and March commission formulas to Region 2.

9. Save the changes to your workbook.
   At this point, your worksheet should match the following worksheet.

	A	B	C	D	E	F	G
1	Centron Cellular						
2							
3	Region 1						
4	Sales Rep	Jan Sales	Jan Comm	Feb Sales	Feb Comm	Mar Sales	Mar Comm
5	Branston	20000	3000	32000	4800	23000	3450
6	Barton	15000	2250	32000	4800	23890	3583.5
7	Alexander	45000	6750	8900	1335	43000	6450
8	Alioto	23000	3450	19000	2850	10900	1635
9	Chin	34000	5100	34000	5100	32000	4800
10	Total		20550		18885		19918.5
11	Average		4110		3777		3983.7
12	Maximum		6750		5100		6450
13	Minimum		2250		1335		1635
14							
15							
16	Region 2						
17	Sales Rep	Jan Sales	Jan Comm	Feb Sales	Feb Comm	Mar Sales	Mar Comm
18	Richardson	18000	2700	54000	8100	36790	5518.5
19	Thomas	12000	1800	35900	5385	45678	6851.7
20	Carter	56000	8400	34900	5235	72490	10873.5
21	Williams	39000	5850	54000	8100	21000	3150
22	Jones	23000	3450	89000	13350	38900	5835
23	Total		22200		40170		32228.7
24	Average		4440		8034		6445.74
25	Maximum		8400		13350		10873.5
26	Minimum		1800		5235		3150

Cell Borders

The Borders [⊞▾] button on the Formatting toolbar lets you add borders to cell edges. When you click the Borders drop-down button, a tear-off palette of popular border styles appears. You can apply a style to all selected cells by choosing it from the palette. You can also use the **Format→Cells** command to display the Format Cells dialog box. The Borders tab on the dialog box lets you apply additional border combinations. You can also choose a color from the dialog box to apply colored borders.

The Borders drop-down button displays a tear-off palette.

The most recently applied border style appears on the Borders button.

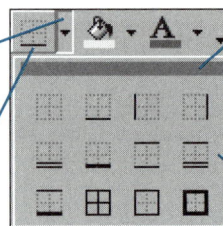

You can drag this bar to "tear off" the palette and place a copy of it anywhere on the screen.

The border style you choose is applied to all selected cells.

Fill Colors and Patterns

The Fill Color [icon] button on the Formatting toolbar lets you fill selected cells with color. When you click the Fill Color drop-down button, a tear-off palette of colors appears. You can apply a color to all selected cells by choosing it from the palette. The fill color is independent of the font color used to format text and numbers. You can also use the Format→Cells command to display the Format Cells dialog box. The Patterns tab on the dialog box lets you apply fill colors and a variety of patterns.

Hands-On 3.8 Add Borders and Fill Colors

Format the Title Cells

1. Select the range A1:G1 in Row 1, and click the Merge and Center [icon] button.

2. Make sure the range is selected, and click the Borders drop-down [icon] button.

3. Follow these steps to put a thick border around the range.

A *Take a moment to review the various border styles. The first style removes all borders from the selected cells. Notice the other styles place thin, thick, or double lines on various borders.*

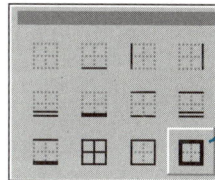

B *Choose this option to apply the Thick Box Border style to the selected cells.*

4. Make sure the range is selected, click the Fill Color drop-down [icon] button, and choose any color.

5. Make sure the range is selected, and click the Font Color drop-down [icon] button.

6. Choose a color that will provide adequate contrast to the fill color you chose.

7. Click outside the range, and you will be able to see the formats.
   The lines on the top and left sides of the range may not be visible because the column and row headings are blocking them. Notice the fill color fills the range, while the font color only affects the text. Also notice that the colors and line style you chose now appear on the buttons. If desired, you could apply these same colors and line style to other selected cells by clicking the buttons.

8. Click the Print Preview [icon] button.

9. Click anywhere on the worksheet to zoom in.
   The lines on the top and left sides of the range should now be visible. However, the colors will not be visible if you have a black-and-white printer. Print Preview displays colors in gray shades, as they will appear on the printed page.

   (Continued on the next page)

Add Additional Borders

10. Click the **Close** button to exit from Print Preview.

11. Select the range A2:G26.
    This range includes all cells in the active worksheet area except for the title row.

12. Click the Borders drop-down ▣▾ button.

13. Choose the All Borders ⊞ style (second style on the bottom row).

14. Click the Print Preview 🔍 button.
    Notice that the lines on every border of every cell appear too busy. You will change the borders in the next few steps.

Remove Borders and Reapply Borders

15. Close the Print Preview window.

16. Make sure the range A2:G26 is still selected.

17. Click the Borders drop-down ⊞▾ button, and choose Thick Box Border ▣ style.

18. Click Print Preview 🔍 and notice that a thick border has been applied to the outside of the range but the inside borders have not been removed.

19. Close the Print Preview window.

20. Click the Borders drop-down ▣▾ button, and choose No Borders ▢ style (first button).
    This will remove the borders from the selected range.

21. Click the Borders drop-down ▦▾ button, and choose Thick Box Border ▣ style.

22. Click Print Preview 🔍, review the results, and then close Print Preview.

Apply Fill Color and Font Color

23. Select the range A10:G13.
    This range includes all cells containing entries in Rows 10, 11, 12, and 13.

24. Click the Fill Color 🖍 button (not the drop-down button) to apply the same fill color that was applied to the large merged cell at the top of the worksheet.

25. Click the Font Color 🅰 button (not the drop-down button) to apply the same font color that was applied to the merged cell.

26. Apply the same fill color and font color to the range A23:G26.

27. Save the changes to your workbook.

28. Take a few moments to experiment with borders and fill colors. Use Undo to reverse any changes you make.

AutoFormat

NOTE!

You must select a range before applying an AutoFormat.

The **Format→AutoFormat** command lets you choose from a variety of predefined formats. The predefined formats automatically apply number formats, borders, fill colors, font colors, font sizes, and other formats to a selected range. You may be pleasantly surprised when you see the professional formatting that AutoFormat can apply.

The AutoFormat box shows previews of the available formats.

You can scroll through the list to view additional formats. The last format on the list is the None format, which removes all formats.

Hands-On 3.9 Use AutoFormat

Use AutoFormat on Region 1

1. Select the range A3:G13, which includes all cells for Region 1.

2. Choose **Format→AutoFormat** from the menu bar.

3. Click the Options button just below the Cancel button on the right side of the box.
   Check boxes will appear at the bottom of the dialog box. These boxes determine the formats that AutoFormat will apply. Make sure all of the boxes are checked.

4. Scroll through the list and notice the various formats.

5. Scroll to the top of the list and choose **Classic 3** style.

6. Click **OK,** and then click anywhere in the worksheet to view the formats.
   Notice that AutoFormat detected rows containing formulas and formatted those rows in a different manner than the body and header rows. AutoFormat makes its formatting decisions by determining which rows and columns have text, numbers, and formulas.

(Continued on the next page)

Remove the AutoFormats

7. Select the range A3:G13 (the range you just formatted).

8. Choose **Format→AutoFormat** from the menu bar.

9. Scroll to the bottom of the list and choose the **None** format.

10. Click **OK,** and the formats will be removed.
    You can use this technique to remove all formats, whether or not they were applied with AutoFormat.

Format Other Ranges

11. Click Undo ⟲ to restore the AutoFormats to Region 1.

12. Select the range A16:G26, which includes all cells for Region 2.

13. Choose **Format→AutoFormat,** and apply the **Classic 3** style.

14. Click in the large merged cell at the top of the worksheet.

15. Apply the Classic 3 AutoFormat to the merged cell.

16. Increase the font size of the merged cell to 12, and remove italics.

17. Save the changes to your workbook.

18. Feel free to experiment with AutoFormat, and then continue with the next topic.

Zooming

The Zoom Control lets you "zoom in" to get a close-up view of a worksheet or "zoom out" to see the full view. Zooming changes the size of the onscreen worksheet but has no effect on the printed worksheet. You can zoom from 10% to 400%.

Notice how large the onscreen worksheet appears. However, it will print in the normal size.

You can type a zoom percentage in the Zoom box and tap (ENTER) *or . . .*

. . . you can click the drop-down button and choose an option from the list.

	A	B	C		E
1			**Centron Cellular**		
2					
3			**Region 1**		
4	**Sales Rep**	*Jan Sales*	*Jan Comm*	*Feb Sales*	*Feb Comm*
5	**Branston**	20000	3000	32000	4800
6	**Barton**	15000	2250	32000	4800
7	**Alexander**	45000	6750	8900	1335
8	**Alioto**	23000	3450	19000	2850
9	**Chin**	34000	5100	34000	5100
10	**Total**		20550		18885

Hands-On 3.10 Use the Zoom Control

1. Follow these steps to adjust the zoom percentage.

   A *Click in the Zoom box, type* **150**, *and tap* (ENTER).

   B *Click the Zoom drop-down button, and choose 200%.*

   C *Zoom to 100%.*

2. Select the range A4:C13.
   Imagine that you want to analyze just the January sales numbers. You can zoom in to get a close-up view of just this range.

3. Click the Zoom drop-down button, and choose **Selection.**
   Excel will zoom to the maximum percentage possible for that selection.

4. Zoom to 100%, and continue with the next topic.

Hiding Rows and Columns

You can hide selected rows and columns with the **Format→Row→Hide** command and the **Format→Column→Hide** command. Hidden rows and columns are not visible in the worksheet, and they are not printed when the worksheet is printed. However, hidden rows and columns are still part of the worksheet. Their values and formulas can be referenced by other formulas in the visible rows and columns. Hiding rows and columns can be useful if you are trying to focus attention on other parts of the worksheet.

Notice that Columns B, D, and F have been hidden. These columns are hidden to draw attention to the commission columns.

	A	C	E	G
1	Centron Cellular			
2				
3	Region 1			
4	Sales Rep	Jan Comm	Feb Comm	Mar Comm
5	Branston	3000	4800	3450
6	Barton	2250	4800	3583.5
7	Alexander	6750	1335	6450

Unhiding Rows and Columns

You can unhide rows and columns with the **Format→Row→Unhide** command and the **Format→Row→Unhide** command. Before unhiding rows, you must select row(s) above and below the hidden rows. Likewise, you must select column(s) on the left and right of hidden columns before issuing the Unhide command.

To unhide Column D, you must first select Columns C and E.

	A	C	E	G
1	Centron Cellular			
2				
3	Region 1			
4	Sales Rep	Jan Comm	Feb Comm	Mar Comm
5	Branston	3000	4800	3450
6	Barton	2250	4800	3583.5
7	Alexander	6750	1335	6450

You could unhide Columns B, D, and F with a single command by selecting Columns A–G and then issuing the Unhide command.

1. Follow these steps to hide Columns B, D, and F.

Ⓐ *Click the Column B heading to select that column.*

Ⓑ *Press and hold* CTRL *while you click the Column D and F headings.*

Ⓒ *Choose Format→ Column→Hide from the menu bar.*

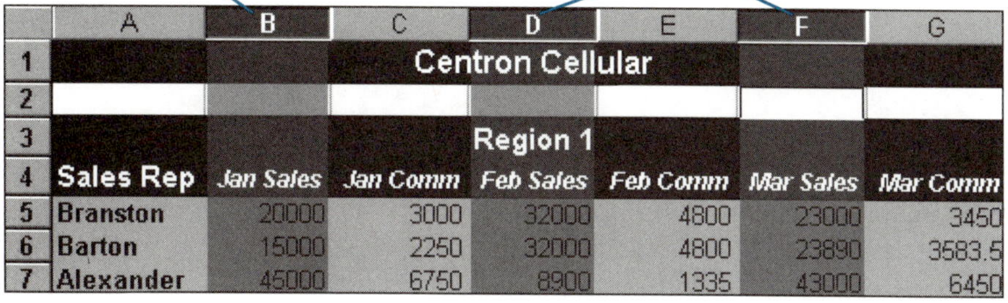

	A	B	C	D	E	F	G
1				Centron Cellular			
2							
3				Region 1			
4	Sales Rep	Jan Sales	Jan Comm	Feb Sales	Feb Comm	Mar Sales	Mar Comm
5	Branston	20000	3000	32000	4800	23000	3450
6	Barton	15000	2250	32000	4800	23890	3583.5
7	Alexander	45000	6750	8900	1335	43000	6450

2. Follow these steps to unhide Columns B, D, and F.

Ⓐ *Position the mouse pointer on the Column A heading and drag to the right until Columns A–G are selected, as shown here.*

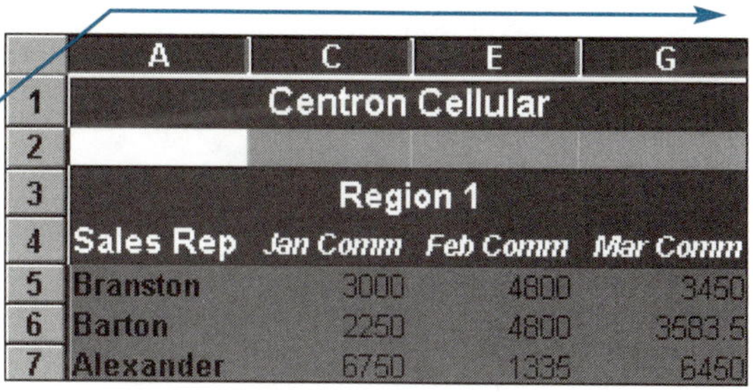

	A	C	E	G
1		Centron Cellular		
2				
3		Region 1		
4	Sales Rep	Jan Comm	Feb Comm	Mar Comm
5	Branston	3000	4800	3450
6	Barton	2250	4800	3583.5
7	Alexander	6750	1335	6450

Ⓑ *Choose Format→Column→ Unhide from the menu bar.*

3. Click Undo 🔙 to hide the columns again.
   Imagine that you are only interested in the overall results of the Centron Cellular sales force—not the performance of the individual sales reps.

4. Select Rows 5–9 by dragging the mouse down over the row headings.

5. Choose **Format→Row→Hide** to hide the rows.

6. Hide the rows for the individual sales reps in Region 2.

7. Feel free to experiment with any of the topics you have learned in this lesson.

8. Save the workbook when you have finished experimenting, and then close the workbook.

Concepts Review

True/False Questions

1. The Office Assistant's speech balloon has a Search box that lets you search for Help topics. TRUE FALSE

2. AutoCorrect entries are expanded when (SPACE BAR) is tapped or when the entry is completed. TRUE FALSE

3. You must accept an AutoComplete entry that Excel proposes. TRUE FALSE

4. MIN and MAX are examples of functions. TRUE FALSE

5. A function's arguments are always surrounded by quotation marks " ". TRUE FALSE

6. You can paste a copied formula into multiple cells with one Paste command. TRUE FALSE

7. The maximum zoom percentage is 200%. TRUE FALSE

8. Values in hidden rows and columns cannot be referenced by formulas in visible rows and columns. TRUE FALSE

Multiple-Choice Questions

1. Which command displays the AutoCorrect dialog box?
   a. Format→AutoCorrect
   b. Tools→AutoCorrect
   c. Edit→AutoCorrect
   d. None of the above

2. Which command is used to display the AutoFormat dialog box?
   a. Tools→AutoFormat
   b. Format→AutoFormat
   c. Format→Cells
   d. None of the above

3. What is the maximum number of cut or copied items that can be placed on the Office Clipboard?
   a. 3
   b. 6
   c. 12
   d. 18

4. Which of the following methods of moving entries displays a pop-up menu when the mouse button is released?
   a. Cut and Paste
   b. Drag and Drop
   c. Right Drag and Drop
   d. All of these

Skill Builders

Skill Builder 3.1 **Use Copy and Paste**

1. Open the workbook named **Skill Builder 3.1**.

2. Select the range A1:E2.

3. Click the Copy [icon] button.

4. Click Cell A10, and click the Paste [icon] button.

5. Change the year 1999 in the pasted heading to 1998.

6. Select the city names and the Total and Average headings in the range A3:A8.

7. Click Copy [icon], click Cell A12, and then click Paste [icon].

8. Use AutoSum [icon] to compute the totals in Rows 7 and 16.

9. Click Cell B8, and enter the function **=AVERAGE(B3:B6)**.

10. Use Copy [icon] and Paste [icon] to copy the formula with the AVERAGE function across Rows 8 and 17.

    You can safely copy this formula to both Rows 8 and 17 because the range in the function includes four cells (B3:B6). The formulas in Rows 8 and 17 both require AVERAGE functions that average four cells.

11. Click Cell B20, and enter the formula **=B7−B16**.

12. Copy this formula across Row 20.

13. Enter a formula in Cell B21 that computes the difference between the averages for 1999 and 1998, and then copy the formula across Row 21.

    Your completed worksheet should match the following example.

14. Save the changes to the workbook, and then close the workbook.

	A	B	C	D	E
1	Quality Greeting Cards - 1999 Customer Complaints				
2		Christmas	Easter	Valentines	Thanksgiving
3	Boston	27	43	14	34
4	Los Angeles	31	47	19	39
5	New York	35	51	24	44
6	St. Louis	39	55	29	49
7	Total	132	196	86	166
8	Average	33	49	21.5	41.5
9					
10	Quality Greeting Cards - 1998 Customer Complaints				
11		Christmas	Easter	Valentines	Thanksgiving
12	Boston	19	31	16	24
13	Los Angeles	22	34	18	26
14	New York	25	37	20	28
15	St. Louis	28	40	22	30
16	Total	94	142	76	108
17	Average	23.5	35.5	19	27
18					
19	Differences Between 1999 and 1998				
20	Totals	38	54	10	58
21	Averages	9.5	13.5	2.5	14.5

Skill Builder 3.2 Use AutoFormat

In this exercise, you will open a workbook on your exercise diskette. You will use AutoFormat to apply an attractive format to the worksheet.

Use AutoFormat

1. Open the workbook named **Skill Builder 3.2.**

2. Select the range A1:E16, which includes all active cells in the worksheet.

3. Choose **Format→AutoFormat** from the menu bar.

4. Scroll through the list, choose the **List 2** style, and click **OK.**

5. Click outside the worksheet, and you will be able to see the format.
   The format looks good, although it may be nice to have a slightly larger title.

6. Click Cell A1, and increase the size to 12.
   You can always add your own formatting enhancements to a worksheet after AutoFormat has been used.

7. Save the changes to the workbook, and then close the workbook.

Skill Builder 3.3 Use Copy and Paste

1. Open the workbook named **Skill Builder 3.3.**

2. Select the range A3:E4, which includes all the text entries in Rows 3 and 4.

3. Click the Copy [icon] button.

4. Click Cell A10, and Paste [icon] the entries above the second set of numbers.
   Notice that the text formats (including the coloring) were copied with the text.

5. Click Cell A17 and Paste [icon] the entries above the third set of numbers.

6. Change the headings to **February** and **March** for the second and third sets of numbers.

7. Select the range A5:A8, which includes the names and Totals heading in Column A.

8. Copy [icon] the selection, and then Paste [icon] it to Cells A12 and A19.

9. Copy [icon] the formulas from the totals row below the first set of numbers, and Paste [icon] them below the second and third sets of numbers.

10. Save the changes to the workbook, and then close the workbook.

Skill Builder 3.4 Use the AVERAGE Function

In this exercise, you will open a workbook on your exercise diskette and calculate averages using three methods. First, you will use a formula with parentheses that change the order of calculations. Then, you will enter AVERAGE functions using the keyboard and point mode.

Use a Formula with Parentheses

1. Open the workbook named **Skill Builder 3.4.**

2. Click Cell B18.

3. Type the formula **=(B4+B9+B14)/3**, and complete the entry.
   The result should equal 193.333 . . . Notice that the formula you entered includes parentheses ( ). The parentheses change the order of calculations. They instruct Excel to add Cells B4, B9, and B14 and then divide the result of that summation by 3. Without the parentheses, Excel would first divide Cell B14 by 3 and then add the result to B4 + B9. This would produce a very different result, and you would not receive the average you are trying to achieve. Keep in mind that the AVERAGE function does this work for you. This formula was used to demonstrate the way an average is calculated and to show how parentheses are used to change the order of calculations.

4. Use the fill handle to copy the formula across Row 18.

Type the AVERAGE Function

5. Click Cell B19.

6. Type the function **=average(b5,b10,b15)**, and complete the entry.
   The result should equal 23.3333. Once again, you can type the function name and arguments in lowercase and Excel will convert them to uppercase. Notice that the function you entered has three parameters within the argument. In this function, the parameters are cell references separated by commas. Most functions let you have multiple arguments within the parentheses. Commas always separate the arguments. In this example, the function calculates the average of Cells B5, B10, and B15.

7. Use the fill handle to copy the formula across Row 19.

(Continued on the next page)

Use Point Mode

8. Click Cell B20.

9. Type **=average(**.

10. Click Cell B6.
The reference B6 will be added to the function in the Formula bar.

11. Type a comma **,** and click Cell B11.

12. Type a comma **,** and click Cell B16.

13. Type a closing parenthesis **)**, and complete the entry.
The result should equal 8.3333. Once again, point mode is helpful in preventing typing errors.

14. Use the fill handle to copy the formula across Row 20.

15. Select the cells in Rows 18, 19, and 20, and decrease the decimals [icon] to 2.

16. Save the changes to the workbook, and then close the workbook.

Assessments

Assessment 3.1

1. Use the following guidelines to create the worksheet shown below.

   ▪ The beginning balance, purchases, and payments numbers in the range B5:D9 should be typed into the cells. Don't type the numbers shown in Rows 10, 11, and 12 or Columns E and F. In a moment, you will be instructed to create those formulas.

   ▪ Use formulas to calculate the interest charge in Column E and the new balance in Column F. The formulas are as follows:

   Interest Charge = 1.5% * (Beginning Balance – Payments)

   New Balance = Beginning Balance + Purchases – Payments + Interest Charge

   Notice that you must use parentheses in the Interest Charge formula to change the order of calculations. You want Excel to subtract the payments from the beginning balance and then multiply the result by 1.5%. Also, don't type the words *Beginning Balance,* etc. in the formulas. You should use the appropriate cell references in the formulas.

   ▪ Format Rows 5, 10, 11, and 12 with the Currency formatting shown below.

   ▪ Format the title row and header rows as shown.

   ▪ Calculate the totals in Row 10.

   ▪ Use the MAX and MIN functions to calculate the highest and lowest numbers in Rows 11 and 12.

   ▪ Print the worksheet when you have finished.

   ▪ Save the workbook as **Assessment 3.1,** and then close the workbook.

	A	B	C	D	E	F
1	Bill's Hot Tubs - Accounts Receivable Report					
2						
3		Beginning			Interest	
4	Customer	Balance	Purchases	Payments	Charge	New Balance
5	Zelton	$2,000	$2,300	$1,000	$15	$3,315
6	Ranier	2450	1000	2450	0	1000
7	Worthington	5400	2190	3000	36	4626
8	Alonzo	3400	500	3400	0	500
9	Barton	100	3400	100	0	3400
10	Totals	$13,350	$9,390	$9,950	$51	$12,841
11	Highest	$5,400	$3,400	$3,400	$36	$4,626
12	Lowest	$100	$500	$100	$0	$500

Assessment 3.2

1. Use the following guidelines to create the worksheet shown below.

   ■ Enter all the numbers and text as shown. Use the Copy and Paste or Drag and Drop techniques to copy the text or numbers whenever possible. For example, all three of the Wilson family children were given the same allowances in all four years. Therefore, you can enter the data in Row 5 and then copy Row 5 to Rows 10 and 15.

   ■ Use Increase Indent [image] to indent the allowance, saved, and interest earned entries in Column A, as shown.

   ■ Calculate the interest earned with the formula **Interest Earned = Saved * Interest Rate.** Use the interest rates shown in the following rate table. You will notice that the interest rates change from year to year.

1996	1997	1998	1999
3.5%	4.5%	6.5%	6.5%

   ■ Widen the columns as necessary, and format the worksheet with bold, italics, and the Currency format as shown.

2. Your completed worksheet should match the example shown below.

3. Print the workbook, save it as **Assessment 3.2,** and then close it.

	A	B	C	D	E	F
1	Wilson Family Allowances					
2						
3		1996	1997	1998	1999	Total Interest
4	Jason					
5	Allowance	260	300	300	340	
6	Saved	120	110	200	220	
7	*Interest Earned*	$ 4.20	$ 4.95	$ 13.00	$ 14.30	$ 36.45
8						
9	Cindy					
10	Allowance	260	300	300	340	
11	Saved	120	110	200	220	
12	*Interest Earned*	$ 4.20	$ 4.95	$ 13.00	$ 14.30	$ 36.45
13						
14	Betty					
15	Allowance	260	300	300	340	
16	Saved	130	290	280	310	
17	*Interest Earned*	$ 4.55	$ 13.05	$ 18.20	$ 20.15	$ 55.95
18						
19	Total Family Interest 1996 - 1999				$	128.85

Assessment 3.3

1. Open the workbook named **Assessment 3.3.**

2. Use the **Classic 3** AutoFormat style to format the worksheet as shown below.

3. Print the workbook, save the changes, and then close the workbook.

	A	B	C	D	E	F	G
1	Diane's Café - Employee Hourly Time Log						
2							
3	Employee	Wednesday	Thursday	Friday	Saturday	Sunday	Totals
4	Mary Johnson	6.5		5	6.5	4	22
5	Cliff Packard	4	6	6.5	6.5	4	27
6	Helen Martinez	4	6	6.5	6.5		23
7	Sarah Stonestown		4	4	4		12
8	Totals	14.5	16	22	23.5	8	84

Critical Thinking

Critical Thinking 3.1 On Your Own

Stacy Sanchez is a freelance graphic designer and Web site developer. Stacy specializes in helping small businesses establish corporate identities. Stacy's mastery of the computer allows her to transform creative ideas into stunning visual designs that win over customers and provide her with lucrative contracts. She wants to focus her energies on the types of customers that produce the highest rates of return. Stacy has asked you to set up a worksheet to help her analyze her customer base. She provides you with the following initial data.

Company Type	Number of Projects	Total Billings	Total Hours
Consulting	14	$25,900	235
Technology	23	$81,420	679
Manufacturing	6	$16,200	171
Food Service	8	$15,200	179
Retail Sales	12	$30,480	311

Calculate the average billings per project for each company type. Calculate the average hourly billing rate for each company type. Use the AVERAGE function to calculate the average total billings and the average hourly rate for all company types combined. Use AutoFormat to apply attractive formats to the worksheet. Save the workbook as **Critical Thinking 3.1.**

Critical Thinking 3.2 On Your Own

Marina Berkman is a manager in the research department of CTA, Inc. CTA prepares studies on consumer buying habits for companies and organizations throughout the United States. Marina has asked you to prepare a worksheet that will record the food-buying habits of consumers. The worksheet must record on a daily basis the amount of money spent on groceries, breakfast out, lunch out, dinner out, and snacks out. The worksheet should record the information for one person for an entire week. Enter the data you desire and include totals of all expenditures for each day of the week and for each expenditure type. Use the AVERAGE function to calculate the average daily expenditures for each expenditure type. Format all numbers in the worksheet as Currency style with two decimals, and apply formats of your choice using the Formatting toolbar. Save your workbook as **Critical Thinking 3.2.**

Critical Thinking 3.3 On Your Own

Mary Perkins is the Customer Service Manager at a large retail store that sells everything from potato chips to televisions sets. Mary has instructed you to set up a worksheet to track customer returns. The worksheet should include the customer name, item name, SKU code, purchase price, purchase date, return date, and reason for return. Enter five items into your worksheet using your imagination to determine the product names, SKU codes, price, dates, etc. Organize the worksheet rows by customer name in alphabetical order. Save your workbook as **Critical Thinking 3.3.**

Critical Thinking 3.4 Web Research

You have been assigned the task of setting up a worksheet that tracks and analyzes an investment portfolio of publicly traded stocks. You have been given the following information as a starting point.

Symbol	Purchase Price	Shares Purchased
CORL	6	500
ORCL	25	100
LU	54	200
MSFT	70	300
GLC	45	60
HAL	25	250

Use Internet Explorer and a search engine of your choice to locate a Web site that offers free stock quotes. Use the site you locate and the symbols shown in the preceding table to determine the current price at which the stocks are trading and the company names associated with the symbols. Set up a worksheet that contains the information shown in the preceding table. Also, include the company name and current price of each stock in the worksheet. Use formulas to calculate the initial value of each investment and the current value based upon the quotes you receive. Calculate the gain or loss of each stock in dollars. Calculate the percentage gain or loss of each stock. Use the SUM function to calculate the total value of the initial portfolio and the total current portfolio value. Calculate the total gain or loss for the portfolio. Use the AVERAGE function to calculate the average gain or loss percentage of the entire portfolio. Rearrange the worksheet rows until they are sorted in alphabetical order based upon the symbols. Format the worksheet using the Autoformat of your choice. Save your workbook as **Critical Thinking 3.4.**

Critical Thinking 3.5 Web Research

Use Internet Explorer and a search engine of your choice to locate five Web sites that sell music CD's. Choose five of your favorite CD's, and set up a worksheet to categorize and analyze the information you find. In particular, include the name of the company Web site, the URL, the CD title, the artist, the price of the CD, and the freight costs. Gather this information for all five CD's from all five Web sites. Use formulas to calculate the total cost of each CD from each Web site. Use the MIN and MAX functions to determine the least expensive site and the most expensive site for each CD. Format your worksheet as desired. Save your workbook as **Critical Thinking 3.5.**

LESSON 4

Dates, Text Features, and Restructuring Worksheets

In this lesson, you will learn fundamental concepts and techniques for working with dates. You will insert dates in worksheets and use formulas to perform calculations using dates. You will explore several new formatting techniques including multiline text entries and additional cell alignment options. Finally, you will learn how to restructure a worksheet by inserting and deleting cells, rows, and columns.

In This Lesson

Case Study

Tamika Jones is the proud owner of her own home-based business—Tamika's Jewelry Exchange. Tamika wants to record her checking transactions electronically, to help her manage her money more effectively. Tamika has considered purchasing a program such as Microsoft Money to manage her checkbook and finances. However, at this point, Tamika doesn't have the time to learn another program. She decides to set up a simple checkbook register using Excel.

	A	B	C	D	E	F	G
1	Tamika's Jewelry Exchange - Checkbook Register						
2	Today's Date		June 21, 1999				
3							
4	Date	Check Number	Transaction Description	P/B	Amount of Payment (-)	Amount of Deposit (+)	Balance Forward
5	1/1/99		Opening Balance				2000
6	1/1/99	100	Payment to Barbara Jennings for 5 pound supply of jade	B	-400		-400
7							1600
8	1/3/99		Sales from Berkeley, Telegraph Avenue	B		700	700
9							2300
10	1/3/99		Sale to Donna Brown of Taylor's Emporium	B		250	250
11							2550
12	1/7/99	101	Abalone shells from Pacific Abalone Supply	B	-175		-175
13							2375
14	1/9/99	102	Gold from the San Francisco Diamond and Jewelry Exchange	B	-850		-850
15							1525
16	1/14/99		Check from Mom for Christmas	P		350	350
17							1875
18	1/18/99	103	Purchased 100 jewelry boxes from Acme Packaging	B	-57		-57
19							1818
20							
21	Total days in use		171				

Working with Dates

There are two ways in which dates are used in workbooks. First, dates are simply displayed in cells using various formats. For example, a date can be displayed as 12/25/99, December 25, 1999, or 25-Dec-99. Second, dates can be used in formulas. For example, you may want to compute the number of days that an invoice is past due. This would be calculated as the difference between the current date and the original invoice date.

Serial Numbers

When you enter a date in a cell, Excel converts the date to a **serial number** between 1 and 2,958,525. These numbers correspond to the 10-millenium period from January 1, 1900 through December 31, 9999. The date January 1, 1900 is assigned the serial number 1, January 2, 1900 is assigned the serial number 2 . . . and December 31, 9999 is assigned the serial number 2,958,525. Converting dates to numbers enables you to use the numbers/dates in calculations.

Entering Dates

Excel performs the following steps when you enter a date in a cell.

- Excel recognizes the entry as a date if you enter it using a standard date format, such as 12/25/99, December 25, 1999, or 25-Dec-99.

- Excel converts the date to a serial number between 1 and 2,958,525.

- Excel formats the serial number entry with the same date format you used when you entered the date.

This roundabout process is transparent to you. However, the benefit of converting dates to numbers and then formatting them with a date format is that the dates can then be used in calculations.

Hands-On 4.1 Enter Dates

In this exercise, you will begin developing a checkbook register. You will enter dates in Column A of the register.

Start Excel and Enter a Date

1. Start Excel, and enter the following text entries. Type the phrase Today's Date in Cell A2 (not the actual date).

	A	B	C	D	E
1	Tamika's Jewelry Exchange - Checkbook Register				
2	Today's Date				
3					
4	Date				

2. Click Cell A5.

3. Type **1/1/99**, and complete the entry.
   Notice that Excel right-aligns the entry in the cell. This occurred because Excel recognized your entry as a date and converted the date to a number. Excel always right-aligns numbers.

Verify that the Entry Is a Number

4. Click Cell A5, and choose **Format→Cells** from the menu bar.

5. Make sure the Number tab is active; then choose the General category, and click **OK.**
   The number 36161 should be displayed in the cell. This is the serial number for the date January 1, 1999. This number will be used in any formulas that reference Cell A5. Notice that the General format displays the number with no commas, currency symbols, or other special formats.

Experiment with the Various Date Formats

6. Choose **Format→Cells** from the menu bar, and choose the **Date** category.
   A variety of date formats will be displayed in the Type list. You can format a date (or any number for that matter) by choosing a format from the list. This list also shows you the types of formats Excel recognizes as dates. Excel won't recognize your entry as a date if you use a format other than the formats shown in this list.

7. Choose the fifth format on the list (it should be 14-Mar-98), and click **OK.**
   Your date should now be formatted with the new format.

8. Use the **Format→Cells** command to change the format back to **1/1/99.** You will need to choose the second format from the Type list.

9. Enter the following dates into Column A.

	A	B	C	D	E
1	Tamika's Jewelry Exchange - Checkbook Register				
2	Today's Date				
3					
4	Date				
5	1/1/99				
6					
7	1/3/99				
8					
9	1/3/99				
10					
11	1/7/99				
12					
13	1/9/99				

10. Select all of the dates and click the Align Left ▤ button.

11. Save the checkbook register with the name **Hands-On Lesson 4.**
    You will continue to develop the checkbook register as you progress through this lesson.

Date and Time Functions

Excel provides a number of date and time functions. The following Quick Reference table discusses three of the most common date and time functions.

Quick Reference

DATE AND TIME FUNCTIONS	
Function	**Description**
TODAY( )	Returns the serial number of the current date and formats the cell with a date format.
NOW( )	Returns the serial number of the current date and time and formats the cell with a date and time format.
DATE(year,month,day)	Returns the serial number of the date entered as the argument and formats the cell with a date format.

Hands-On 4.2 Use the TODAY Function

The current date is often required in worksheets. This may be necessary to show the date the worksheet was created or printed. In this exercise, you will use the TODAY function to display the current date at the top of the checkbook register.

Use the Paste Function Box

1. Click Cell C2.

2. Click the Paste Function button on the Standard toolbar.
   Excel inserts an = sign in the Formula bar and displays the Paste Function box.

3. Click the **Date & Time** category.

4. Click the various date functions in the Function name list and read the descriptions at the bottom of the dialog box.

5. Scroll down, and choose the TODAY function; then click **OK.**
   The Formula Palette and the =TODAY( ) function will appear. The syntax =TODAY( ) is the complete syntax because the TODAY function requires no argument within the parenthesis.

6. Click **OK** on the Formula Palette.
   Today's date should be inserted in Cell C2.

Change the Date Format

7. Make sure Cell C2 is active and choose **Format→Cells** from the menu bar.

8. Scroll through the list, and choose the ninth date type (March 14, 1998).

9. Click **OK,** and the new format will be applied to the date.
   Notice how you can change the appearance of a date by applying a date format. If you are entering a large number of dates, it is easiest to enter the dates in a simple format such as 1/1/99. After entering the dates, you can format them using whichever format you desire.

In the next few steps, you will use a formula that subtracts the first date the checkbook register was used (January 1, 1999) from today's date. This will tell you the total number of days that the checkbook register has been in use.

10. Click Cell A16, and enter the phrase **Total days in use**.

11. Click Cell C16, and type the formula **=C2-A5**.

12. Complete the entry, and Excel will calculate the difference between the two serial numbers that represent the dates in Cells C2 and A5.
    The result in Cell C16 will be formatted as a date and time. In the next step, you will use the Format Painter to copy the General format from any blank cell in the workbook to Cell C16. All cells in a new workbook are formatted as General. The General format will let you see the number of days the checkbook has been in use.

13. Click any blank cell in the workbook.

14. Click the Format Painter 🖌, and then click Cell C16.
    The General format should be copied to the cell. Let's assume your checkbook register has been in use from January 1, 1999 until today. How many days has your register been in use? The answer is in Cell C16.

15. Save the changes, and continue with the next topic.

Line Breaks

There are two techniques you can use to insert multiple lines within a cell.

Hard Carriage Returns

Use the keystroke combination (ALT)+(ENTER) to insert a hard carriage return. You use this technique when you want to force a line break within a cell. The line break remains in place unless you decide to delete it by clicking in the Formula bar and using the (DELETE) key.

A line break was inserted in this cell. To remove the break, click to the right of the first line, and tap (DELETE).

Wrap Text Option

The Wrap Text option on the Alignment tab of the Format Cells dialog box forces text to wrap within a cell as it would in a word processing document. You can turn the Wrap Text option on an off by selecting the desired cell(s), choosing Format→Cells, clicking the Alignment tab, and checking or unchecking the Wrap Text box.

Hands-On 4.3 Create Multiple-Line Text Entries

Force a Line Break

1. Click Cell B4.

2. Type **Check**, and press (ALT)+(ENTER).

3. Type **Number**, and click the Enter ☑ button to complete the entry.
   Notice that Excel displays the multiple line entry in the Formula bar.

4. Click Cell C4, and type **Transaction**.

5. Press (ALT)+(ENTER) to insert a line break.

6. Type **Description**, and tap → to complete the entry.

Use the Wrap Text Option

7. Click Cell B5.

8. Type the number **100**, and tap → to complete the entry.

9. Choose **Format→Cells** from the menu bar.

10. Choose the Alignment tab at the top of the dialog box.
    You will use the various alignment options as you progress through this lesson.

11. Click the **Wrap text** check box (it should now be checked), and click **OK.**

12. Type the three-line paragraph shown to the right **without** pressing
    (ENTER) or (ALT)+(ENTER), and complete the entry when you have finished.
    *Keep in mind that the text may wrap differently in your cell because the column
    width may be different than shown here.*

    > Payment to Barbara
    > Jennings for 5 pound
    > supply of jade

13. Widen Column C until the text in Cell C5 wraps as shown in the preceding illustration.
    *Don't be concerned if the height of Row 5 is higher than the text. You will learn how to adjust the row
    height later in this lesson.*

Have Excel Automatically Check the Wrap Text Box

14. Click Cell D4.

15. Choose **Format→Cells** from the menu bar, and make sure the Alignment tab is chosen.
    *Notice that the Wrap text box is not checked. This box must be checked if you want text to automatically
    wrap within cells.*

16. Click the **Cancel** button without checking the box.

17. Type **Amount of**, and press (ALT)+(ENTER).

18. Type **Payment (-)** on the second line, and tap (ENTER) to complete the entry.
    The Payment (-) *line should be too wide to fit in the cell so Excel will wrap the line. Excel turns
    the Wrap Text option on whenever you insert a line break in a cell and then type a line that is too wide
    for the cell.*

19. Click Cell D4, choose **Format→Cells,** and notice that the Wrap text box is checked.

20. Click the **Cancel** button.

21. Make sure the highlight is in Cell D4 (the Amount of Payment cell).

22. Try to position the mouse pointer on the column heading, and you will notice that it is blocked by the two-line display in the Formula bar.

23. Click Cell D3 (which has no entry), and the column headings will be visible.

24. Widen Column D until the Payment (-) line no longer wraps.
The first and second lines in Cell D4 will remain as two lines no matter how wide the column is. This is because you inserted a line break, thus forcing the second line down.

25. Click cell E4 and use the (ALT)+(ENTER) keystroke to create the entry shown to the right. You will need to widen Column E slightly after completing the entry to prevent the second line from wrapping.

> Amount of
> Deposit (+)

26. Enter the phrase **Balance Forward** in Cell F4 **without** inserting a line break.
Excel will automatically format the entry to fit on two lines. Excel recognized that you were consistently using two-line entries, so it formatted the entry accordingly. Excel did this by turning on the Wrap text option. At this point, Rows 1 through 5 of your worksheet should match the following example (although the date will be different).

	A	B	C	D	E	F
1	Tamika's Jewelry Exchange - Checkbook Register					
2	Today's Date		June 21, 1999			
3						
4	Date	Check Number	Transaction Description	Amount of Payment (-)	Amount of Deposit (+)	Balance Forward
5	1/1/99	100	Payments to Barbara Jennings for 5 pound supply of jade			

Vertical Alignment

The Vertical Alignment option lets you change the vertical positioning of text within a cell. You can set the vertical alignment to top, bottom, center, or justify. The default alignment is bottom. The Justify option is useful with multiple-line entries. For example, the Justify option evenly distributes unused space between the lines in a multiline entry. You set the vertical alignment by choosing **Format→Cells,** clicking the Alignment tab, and choosing the desired alignment from the Vertical box.

Hands-On 4.4 Use the Alignment Options

1. Click Cell A4.
   Notice that the text is currently aligned with the bottom of the cell.

2. Choose **Format→Cells,** and click the Alignment tab.

3. Set the Vertical Alignment to **Top,** and click **OK.**
   The entry should now be aligned with the top of the cell.

Rotating Text

You can rotate text from 0 to 90 degrees using the orientation option on the Alignment tab of the Format Cells dialog box. When you rotate text, Excel automatically increases the row height to accommodate the rotated text. You change the orientation by choosing **Format→Cells,** clicking the Alignment tab, and setting the orientation as desired.

Hands-On 4.5 Rotate Text

1. Make sure the insertion point is in Cell A4, and choose **Format→Cells** from the menu bar.

2. Follow these steps to rotate the Date entry in Cell A4.

Ⓐ *Notice the* **Vertical** *option. This option positions the text vertically in the cell.*

Ⓑ *Click here to set the* **Orientation** *to 45 degrees. You can also set the orientation by dragging the pointer to the desired position.*

Ⓒ *Notice the other options in this dialog box. You have already used most of them. The only one you have not used is* **Shrink to fit,** *which reduces the font size of an entry until it fits in the cell.*

Ⓓ *Click* **OK,** *and the entry should be at a 45-degree angle.*

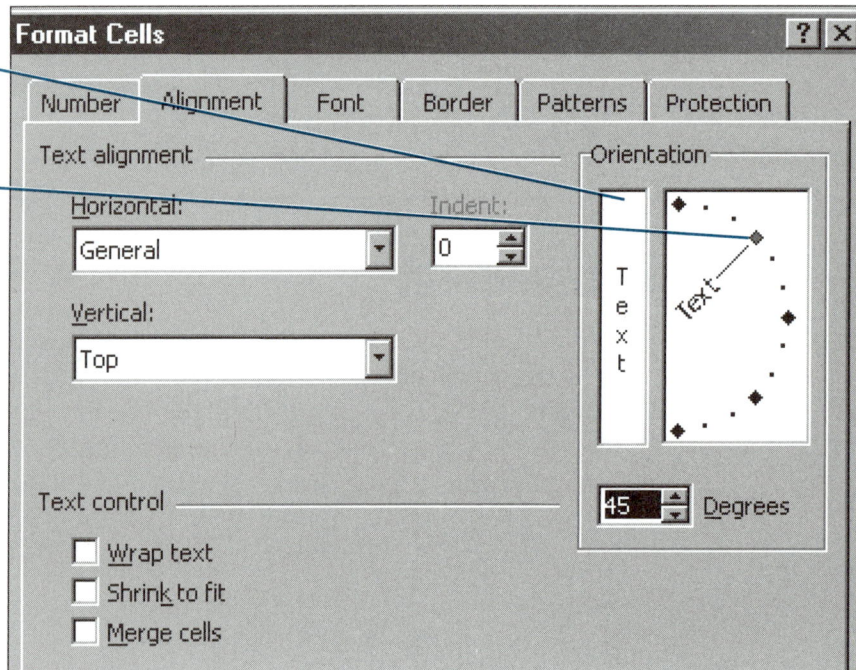

Hands-On 4.6 Enter Text and Formulas

Enter a Negative Number and a Formula

1. Click Cell D5, type **–400**, and complete the entry.
   This entry will eventually be subtracted from the Balance Forward, so it is entered as a negative number. You must precede numbers with minus signs (hyphens) if you want Excel to recognize them as negatives.

2. Click Cell F5, and enter the formula **=D5+E5**.
   The result should equal –400. This formula carries the payment or deposit into the Balance Forward column, so it can be used in a Balance Forward formula.

Use the Format Painter

3. Click Cell C7.

4. Type **Sales from Berkeley, Telegraph Avenue**, and complete the entry.

5. Click Cell C5; then click the Format Painter [icon].

6. Click Cell C7, and the Wrap Text formatting will be copied to that cell.
   Remember that you can use the Format Painter to copy any type of text, number, or cell formats.

Copy the Formula

7. Click Cell F5; then click the Copy [icon] button.

8. Click Cell F7, and then press the (CTRL) key while you click Cells F9, F11, and F13.
   All four cells should be selected.

9. Click the Paste [icon] button to copy the formulas to the selected cells.
   The results should be 0 in each cell.

10. Enter the number **700** into Cell E7.

(Continued on the next page)

11. Enter the text and numbers shown in Rows 9, 11, and 13 in the following illustration. However, do not enter the numbers shown in column F. These numbers will be automatically calculated by the formulas you just copied to the cells in Column F. Also, use the Format Painter to copy the Wrap Text format from Cell C7 to Cells C9, C11, and C13. Your completed worksheet should match the following example.

	A	B	C	D	E	F
1	Tamika's Jewelry Exchange - Checkbook Register					
2	Today's Date		June 21, 1999			
3						
4	Date	Check Number	Transaction Description	Amount of Payment (-)	Amount of Deposit (+)	Balance Forward
5	1/1/99	100	Payment to Barbara Jennings for 5 pound supply of jade	-400		-400
6						
7	1/3/99		Sales from Berkeley Telegraph Avenue		700	700
8						
9	1/3/99		Sale to Donna Brown of Taylor's Emporium		250	250
10						
11	1/7/99	101	Abalone shells from Pacific Abalone Supply	-175		-175
12						
13	1/9/99	102	Silver from the San Francisco Diamond and Jewelry Exchange	-850		-850
14						
15						
16	Total days in use		171			

Column Widths and Row Heights

Thus far, you have adjusted column widths by dragging column headings. This basic method is often the most efficient way to adjust column widths. The height of rows can also be adjusted by dragging the row headings. Besides these basic methods, Excel provides additional methods of adjusting column widths and row heights.

AutoFit

Both column widths and row heights can be adjusted with the AutoFit command. AutoFit adjusts column widths to fit the widest entry in the column. Likewise, AutoFit adjusts row heights to accommodate the tallest entry in the row. The following table discusses the AutoFit options and other commands for setting column widths and row heights. Keep in mind that you should select the desired columns or rows before using these commands.

COLUMN WIDTHS AND ROW HEIGHTS

Technique	Procedure
Set a precise column width.	Choose **Format→Column→Width,** and enter the desired width.
Set column widths with AutoFit.	Choose **Format→Column→AutoFit Selection**, or double-click the right edge of the column heading. You can also select multiple columns and double-click between any two selected column headings. This will AutoFit all selected columns.
Set a precise row height.	Choose **Format→Row→Height.**
Set row heights with AutoFit.	Choose **Format→Row→AutoFit**, or double-click the bottom edge of the row heading. You can also select multiple rows and double-click between any two selected row headings. This will AutoFit all selected rows.
Manually adjust column widths and row heights.	Select the desired columns or rows and drag the column or row headings.

Standard Column Widths and Row Heights

Each column in a new worksheet has a standard width of 8.43 characters, where the default character is Arial 10pt. Each row has a standard height of 12.75 points, which is approximately equal to 1/6th inch. You can change the standard width of all columns in a worksheet with the **Format→Column→Standard Width** command. There is no such command for changing the standard row height.

Hands-On 4.7 Change Column Widths and Row Heights

Adjust Column Widths

1. Select the range A1:F16, which includes all active cells in the worksheet.

2. Choose **Format→Column→AutoFit Selection** from the menu bar.
   Excel will widen each column to fit the largest entry in the column. Column A should be very wide because the entry in Cell A1 is quite wide. Also, notice that AutoFit had no impact on the cells in Column C, which have the Wrap Text option turned on.

3. Undo ⟲ the AutoFit; then select all cells in the range A2:F16.
   Notice that this range does not include the wide entry in Cell A1.

4. Choose **Format→Column→AutoFit Selection** from the menu bar.

5. Click anywhere in the worksheet to deselect, and notice that AutoFit did a better job this time.

6. Drag the border between Columns C and D to the right until each entry in Column C has a maximum height of two lines.

7. Click anywhere in Column C, and choose **Format→Column→Width** from the menu bar.

8. Enter **28** in the width box, and click **OK.**
   This will size Column C to just the right width.

9. Follow these steps to adjust the height of Row 5.

Ⓐ *Position the mouse pointer on the border between Row Headings 5 and 6, and drag the border up slightly.*

Ⓑ *Now double-click the border between Row Headings 5 and 6 to AutoFit the height of Row 5.*

| | 1/1/99 | | 100 | Payment to Barbara Jennings for 5 pound supply of jade |

10. Use the double-click technique to AutoFit Rows 9, 11, and 13.

11. Take a few minutes to experiment with the various column width and row height options. *Try using the double-click AutoFit technique on columns. However, you will need to widen the columns first, since they have already been AutoFit.*

12. Save the changes to your workbook, and continue with the next topic.

Inserting and Deleting Rows and Columns

Excel lets you insert and delete rows and columns. This gives you the flexibility to restructure your worksheets after they have been set up. The following table discusses the various procedures that are used to insert and delete rows and columns.

Quick Reference

INSERTING AND DELETING ROWS AND COLUMNS

Task	Procedure
Insert rows.	■ Select the number of rows you wish to insert. When you issue the Insert command, the same number of new rows will be inserted above the selected rows. ■ Choose **Insert→Rows,** or right-click the selected rows, and choose **Insert** from the pop-up menu.
Insert columns.	■ Select the number of columns you wish to insert. When you issue the Insert command, the same number of new columns will be inserted to the left of the selected columns. ■ Choose **Insert→Columns,** or right-click the selected columns, and choose **Insert** from the pop-up menu.
Delete rows.	■ Select the desired rows and choose **Edit→Delete,** or right-click the selected rows, and choose **Delete** from the pop-up menu.
Delete columns.	■ Select the desired columns, and choose **Edit→Delete,** or right-click the selected columns, and choose **Delete** from the pop-up menu.

Impact on Cell References in Formulas

One advantage to using cell references in formulas is that the references are updated when rows and columns are inserted or deleted. For example, a SUM formula such as =SUM(A1:A5) would become =SUM(A1:A7) if two rows were inserted between Rows 1 and 5. This makes the formulas dynamic and allows you to restructure your worksheets as needed.

An Important Exception to the Automatic Updating Rule

Cell references in formulas are not updated if you try to insert rows directly above a row containing a formula. For example, imagine that Ccll B6 contains the formula =SUM(B2:B5). If you insert a row directly above B6, then the references in the formula will not be updated.

Notice that the formula in Cell B6 references Cells B2:B5.

B6	▼	=	=SUM(B2:B5)
	A	B	C
1	Item	Q1	
2	Copiers	2,300	
3	Printers	1,600	
4	Computers	3,200	
5	Fax Machines	1,200	
6	Total	$ 8,300	

B7	▼	=	=SUM(B2:B5)
	A	B	C
1	Item	Q1	
2	Copiers	2,300	
3	Printers	1,600	
4	Computers	3,200	
5	Fax Machines	1,200	
6			
7	Total	$ 8,300	

If a row is inserted directly above Row 6, the formula continues to reference Cells B2:B5. This would most likely be incorrect, because you would want Cell B6 to be included in the reference.

Inserting and Deleting Cells

You can also insert and delete selected cells. However, this will shift the position of other cells in the rows or columns where the cells are inserted or deleted. This may cause problems because it alters the structure of your entire worksheet. For this reason, it is recommended that you avoid inserting or deleting cells and stick to inserting and deleting entire rows and columns.

Quick Reference

INSERTING AND DELETING SELECTED CELLS

Task	Procedure
Insert cells.	■ Select cells in the worksheet where you want the inserted cells to appear.
	■ Choose Insert→Cells from the menu bar.
	■ Choose the desired Shift Cells option. Other worksheet cells will shift position to make room for the inserted cells.
Delete cells.	■ Select the cells you wish to delete.
	■ Choose Edit→Delete from the menu bar.
	■ Choose the desired Shift Cells option. The cells will be deleted and other worksheet cells will shift position to fill in the space.

Hands-On 4.8 Insert Rows and Columns

Insert a Row for the Opening Balance

1. Click Cell F5, and notice the formula in the Formula bar.
   The formula should be =D5+E5. This formula will be updated when you insert a row for the opening balance.

2. Choose **Insert→Rows** from the menu bar, and a new row will be inserted above Row 5.

3. Click Cell F6, and notice that the formula has been updated to =D6+E6.

4. Click Cell F5, and enter the number **2000**.
   2000 represents Tamika's opening checkbook balance.

(Continued on the next page)

5. Enter the date **1/1/99** in Cell A5.
   Excel will format the cell with the same orientation used in Cell A4. When you insert a row, the cells in the new row will have the same formatting as the row above.

6. Click Cell A6, and then click the Format Painter ⬚.

7. Click Cell A5 to copy the date format from Cell A6 to Cell A5.

8. Enter the phrase **Opening Balance** in Cell C5.

Insert a Column to Differentiate Personal and Business Expenses

Imagine that Tamika has decided to combine her personal and business expenses in one checking account. You will add a column to track whether an expense is personal or business.

9. Click anywhere in Column D.

10. Choose **Insert→Columns,** and a new column will be inserted to the left of Column D.
    Notice that the new column has the same width as Column C. The cells in this new column will also have the same text and number formats as the cells to the left of them in Column C.

11. Click Cell D4, and enter **P/B** for Personal or Business.

12. At this point, all of the expenses are business-related, so enter the letter **B** in Cells D6, D8, D10, D12, and D14.

13. AutoFit Column D by double-clicking the border between Column Headings D and E.
    Column D should be just wide enough to fit the P/B entry.

14. Select Column D, and Center Align ⬚ the entries.

Add Formulas to Calculate the Balance

15. Click Cell G7, and enter the formula **=G5+G6**.
    The result should be 1600. Notice that Excel subtracted the number 400 in Cell G6 because it was preceded by a minus sign.

16. Copy the formula from Cell G7 to Cells G9, G11, G13, and G15.
    The balance in Cell G15 should be 1525.

Format the Worksheet

17. Select the range A4:G4, which includes all the headings in Row 4.

18. Use the Fill Color ⬚ button to apply a medium weight color or shade.

19. Click Cell G7, and apply a light fill color to that cell.

20. Use the Format Painter ⬚ to copy the format from Cell G7 to Cells G9, G11, G13, and G15.
    This will highlight every balance line with a color.

Insert Rows for New Transactions

21. Select Rows 16 through 19 by dragging the mouse down the row headings.

22. Choose **Insert→Rows** from the menu bar.

Notice that Excel inserts the same number of rows as you selected.

23. Click anywhere in the worksheet to deselect the rows.

Notice that Excel formatted the new rows with the same format as the row above them. In particular, the color from Cell G15 should have been copied to the Column G cells in the new rows.

Remove Color from Cells

24. Click Cell G16.

25. Press and hold the (CTRL) key while you click Cell G18.

26. Click the Fill Color ⬛ drop-down button, and choose No Fill from the top of the color palette.

27. Enter the data shown below into Rows 16 and 18. However, do not enter the numbers shown in Column G. Copy the balance forward formulas from previous rows to the cells in Column G. Also, use the Format Painter as necessary to copy formats (such as the Wrap Text format) from the other rows.

	A	B	C	D	E	F	G
16	1/14/99		Check from Mom for Christmas	P		350	350
17							1875
18	1/18/99	103	Purchased 100 jewelry boxes from Acme Packaging	B	-57		-57
19							1818

28. Your completed worksheet should match the worksheet shown in the case study at the beginning of this lesson.

29. Feel free to format and enhance the worksheet as desired.

30. Continue with next topic, where you will spell-check your worksheet.

Spell Checking

The Spelling button on the Standard toolbar is used to spell-check the current worksheet. The spell checker checks the spelling of all text entries in a worksheet. The spell checker functions much like the spell checker in Microsoft Word. Excel's spell checker also uses the same main dictionary and custom dictionaries as Word.

Hands-On 4.9 Spell Check the Worksheet

1. Click Cell A1.
   This will force the spell checker to begin checking at the top of the worksheet.

2. Click the Spelling button on the Standard toolbar.
   The Spelling dialog box will appear, and the word Tamika's *will be marked as Not in Dictionary.*

3. Take a moment to study the Spelling dialog box options discussed in the following Quick Reference table.

Quick Reference

THE SPELLING DIALOG BOX

Button	Function
Ignore	Ignores the misspelled word this time only. The speller will prompt you the next time it encounters the same misspelling.
Ignore All	Ignores the misspelled word now and for all spell checks during this Excel session.
Change	Replaces the misspelled word with the word in the Change to box.
Change All	Replaces all occurrences of the misspelled word in this worksheet with the word in the Change to box.
Add	Adds the misspelled word to a custom dictionary.
Suggest	Displays a full list of suggested replacement words.

4. Click the **Ignore** button to skip over the word *Tamika's*.
   Tamika's name may not be in the spell checker's dictionary, but her name is spelled correctly. At this point, the spell checker may finish, or it may find additional misspelled words if you made typing errors.

5. Continue to spell check the worksheet, using your best judgment to complete the spell check.

Find and Replace

From the Keyboard

CTRL+F4 for Find
CTRL+H for Replace

Excel's Find command lets you search a worksheet for a particular word, cell reference, formula, or other item. Find is often the quickest way to locate an item in a worksheet. The Find dialog box is displayed with the **Edit→Find** command. The Replace dialog box lets you find an item and replace it with a different item. The Replace dialog box is displayed with the **Edit→Replace** command.

Hands-On 4.10 Use Find and Replace

Find a Word

Imagine that Tamika is trying to locate a checkbook register transaction involving the purchase of jade.

1. Choose **Edit→Find** from the menu bar.

2. Follow these steps to search for the word *jade*.

Ⓐ *Click in this box, and type* **jade***.*

Ⓑ *Notice the find options. These options let you refine the search. The options in the* **Search** *box are designed to speed up a search. However, the speed of a search is only a factor in very large worksheets.*

Ⓒ *Click the* **Find Next** *button, and the highlight should move to Cell C6.*

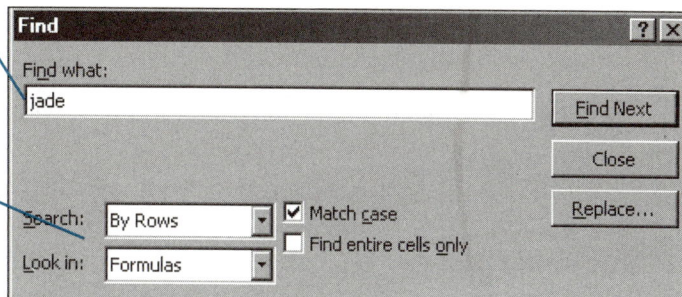

Find	? X
Find what: jade	Find Next
	Close
Search: By Rows ▼ ☑ Match case	Replace...
Look in: Formulas ▼ ☐ Find entire cells only	

Use Replace

3. Click the **Replace** button on the dialog box.
   The Replace with box and two Replace buttons will appear.

4. Delete the entry in the Find what box, and type **Silver**.

5. Type **Gold** in the Replace with box. Make sure you capitalize the word.

6. Click the **Find Next** button, and the highlight will move to Cell C14.
   Notice that this cell contains the word silver.

7. Click the **Replace** button to replace silver with gold.

8. Click the **Close** button to close the Replace dialog box.

9. Feel free to experiment with any of the topics you have learned in this lesson.

10. Save the workbook, close it, and continue with the end-of-lesson questions and exercises.

Concepts Review

True/False Questions

1. When you enter a date, Excel converts it to a number.   TRUE   FALSE

2. Excel applies a date format to dates after it converts them to numbers.   TRUE   FALSE

3. You cannot combine a manually inserted line break and automatic text wrapping in the same cell.   TRUE   FALSE

4. The AutoFit command changes the column width to fit the narrowest entry in the column.   TRUE   FALSE

5. Row heights cannot be changed.   TRUE   FALSE

6. Row heights cannot be AutoFit.   TRUE   FALSE

7. New columns arc inserted to the left of selected columns.   TRUE   FALSE

8. New rows are inserted above selected rows.   TRUE   FALSE

Multiple-Choice Questions

1. Which keystroke combination inserts a manual line break?
   a. (SHIFT)+(ENTER)
   b. (SHIFT)+(TAB)
   c. (ALT)+(ENTER)
   d. (CTRL)+(ENTER)

2. Which command displays a dialog box that can be used to set the Wrap Text option?
   a. Format→Cells
   b. Edit→Cells
   c. Format→Alignment
   d. None of the above

3. Which statement most accurately describes the effect that inserting a row directly above a formula would have on the formula?
   a. The formula would continue to reference the same cells.
   b. The formula references would change to include the new row.
   c. A row cannot be inserted directly above a formula.
   d. None of the above

4. How many columns would be inserted if you had three columns selected and you issued the Insert→Columns command?
   a. 1
   b. 3
   c. 0
   d. None of the above

Skill Builders

Skill Builder 4.1 Restructure a Worksheet

In this exercise, you will open a worksheet and you will modify it until it matches the worksheet on the following page.

Add Two New Columns

1. Open the workbook named **Skill Builder 4.1.**
   Look at the worksheet on the following page and notice that it contains two additional columns with the headings Extra Small and Extra Large.

2. Click Cell E4, and notice that the formula is =SUM(B4:D4).

3. Click anywhere in Column B.

4. Choose **Insert→Columns** from the menu bar.

5. Now click in Column F (the totals column), and insert a column.

6. Click Cell G4, and notice that the formula has changed to =SUM(C4:E4).
   The formula should be =SUM(B4:F4). The cell references changed to reflect the new location of Cells B4:D4, which were the cells originally referenced in the formula. However, the references did not expand to include the new columns. Be careful when inserting rows and columns because Excel will not always expand the references, as you desire. In this example, you inserted columns outside the range that was referenced in the original formula, so Excel did not update the formula references. Excel only updates the references if you insert columns inside the range that is referenced in the formula. You will repair the Total column formulas later in this exercise.

7. Type the headings **Extra Small** and **Extra Large** in the new columns as shown on the following page.
   Notice that both headings have the formatting of the cell to the left of them. The formatting from the column to the left was copied to the inserted columns.

8. Use the Format Painter [icon] to copy the formatting from the Small heading to the headings you just typed.

Use AutoFit to Adjust the Column Widths

9. Select the range A3:G14, which includes all cells in the main part of the worksheet.

10. Choose **Format→Column→AutoFit Selection.**

Insert Subtotal Rows and Blank Rows

Look at the worksheet on the following page, and notice that it contains a Subtotal row and a blank row after each clothing group.

11. Click Cell G14, and notice the formula =SUM(G4:G13) in the Formula bar.

12. Click anywhere in Row 6 and use the **Insert→Rows** command to insert a blank row.

(Continued on the next page)

13. Click Cell G15, and notice that the formula reference has been expanded to =SUM(G4:G14). *This formula reference was expanded because you inserted a row inside the range G4:G13, which was the original range referenced by the formula.*

14. Insert a blank row above Row 11.

15. Click Cell G16, and the formula should now be =SUM(G4:G15). *In the next few steps, you will insert two blank rows above Row 16. The formula reference will not expand when you do this, because you will insert directly above the row containing the formula.*

16. Select Rows 16 and 17 by dragging the mouse over the row headings.

17. Choose **Insert→Rows**, and two blank rows will be inserted.

18. Click Cell G18, and notice that the formula reference has not expanded. *Excel does not expand formula references when you insert rows directly above the formulas. You must be aware of this unusual convention and either design your worksheets to accommodate this or manually adjust the formulas after inserting. Notice that this was the same situation that occurred when you inserted columns earlier in this exercise.*

Add Headings, Numbers, and Subtotal Formulas

19. Enter the numbers shown in Columns B and F and the Subtotal headings and Subtotal formulas shown in Rows 6, 11, 16, and 18 below. The formulas in Row 18 should add up the subtotals in each column. Also, you will need to redo all the formulas in Column G. These formulas are no longer correct because you inserted Columns B and F, which were outside of the columns originally referenced by the total formulas.

20. Take a few minutes to carefully check over your worksheet when you have finished. In particular, make sure all of the formulas are calculating correctly. Your completed worksheet should match the following worksheet.

	A	B	C	D	E	F	G
1	Ricky's Clothing Store - Defective Items						
2							
3	**Shirts**	Extra Small	Small	Medium	Large	Extra Large	Total
4	Long sleeve	13	12	13	9	11	58
5	Short sleeve	8	9	8	9	8	42
6	Subtotal	21	21	21	18	19	100
7							
8	**Pants**						
9	Blue	6	5	6	4	3	24
10	Khaki	8	7	8	9	4	36
11	Subtotal	14	12	14	13	7	60
12							
13	**Shorts**						
14	White	2	3	2	4	3	14
15	Red	9	1	9	7	6	32
16	Subtotal	11	4	11	11	9	46
17							
18	Total	46	37	46	42	35	206

21. Save the changes to the workbook, and then close the workbook.

Skill Builder 4.2 Set Up an Accounts Receivable Report

In this exercise, you will create an accounts receivable aging report that calculates the number of days accounts are past due.

Set Up the Worksheet

1. Click the New Workbook ⬜ button to open a new workbook.

2. Set up the worksheet by typing the headings and numbers shown below. Use the (ALT)+(ENTER) keystroke combination to create the multiline headings in Columns C through F. You will need to widen the columns after typing the headings. Also, you may need to AutoFit Row 4 to reduce the row height.

	A	B	C	D	E	F
1	Accounts Receivable Aging Report					
2	Report Date					
3						
4	Customer	Invoice #	Invoice Date	Invoice Amount	# of days since invoice was issued	# of days past due
5	Wilson	345		123		
6	Arthur	367		980		
7	Bellmont	456		345		
8	Alexander	478		234		
9	Wilmont	489		765		
10	Barton	505		469		

Change the Computer's Date

Later in this exercise, you will use the NOW function to determine the number of days that the invoices are past due. In the next few steps, you will change your computer's internal clock so that the NOW function returns the same current date (6/8/99) as shown later in this exercise.

3. Double-click the clock on the Taskbar at the bottom right corner of your screen (if it is displayed). If the clock isn't displayed on the Taskbar, then click the Start button, choose Settings, choose Control Panel, and double-click the Date and Time icon in the Control Panel.
   The Date/Time Properties dialog box should be displayed.

4. Use the dialog box controls to set the date to June 8, 1999, and click **OK.**
   There is no need to set the time.

Insert the Current Date and Invoice Dates

5. Click cell C2, and enter the function **=NOW( )**.
   The date 6/8/99 and the current time should be displayed in the cell. Notice that the NOW function inserts the date and time, whereas the TODAY function that you used earlier in this lesson inserts only the date.

6. Make sure the highlight is in Cell C2, and choose **Format→Cells** from the menu bar.

7. Click the Number tab, and choose the Date category.

(Continued on the next page)

8. Scroll to the top of the list, choose the second date format (3/14/98), and click **OK.**
The format will display only the date (not the time).

9. Enter the invoice dates shown below into Column C.

	A	B	C
1	Accounts Receivable Aging Report		
2	Report Date		6/8/99
3			
4	Customer	Invoice #	Invoice Date
5	Wilson	345	1/20/99
6	Arthur	367	3/12/99
7	Bellmont	456	3/28/99
8	Alexander	478	4/4/99
9	Wilmont	489	4/8/99
10	Barton	505	4/20/99

Calculate the Number of Days Since the Invoices Were Issued

10. Click Cell E5, and enter the formula **=TODAY( )-C5**.
Enter the formula exactly as shown. Excel will format the result as a date.

11. Click any blank cell in the worksheet; then click the Format Painter .

12. Click Cell E5, and the General number format will be copied to that cell.
The result will be either 139 or 140 (depending upon the time of day). This is the difference between June 8, 1999 (today's date in this exercise) and the date the invoice was issued.

13. Use the fill handle to copy the formula down the column to Cell E10.

14. Click Cell F5, and enter the formula **=E5-30**.
The result will be either 109 or 110. This number represents the number of days the invoice is past due assuming the terms are Net 30 days.

15. Copy the formula down the column. The worksheet should match the following worksheet.

	A	B	C	D	E	F
1	Accounts Receivable Aging Report					
2	Report Date		6/8/99			
3						
4	Customer	Invoice #	Invoice Date	Invoice Amount	# of days since invoice was issued	# of days past due
5	Wilson	345	1/20/99	123	139	109
6	Arthur	367	3/12/99	980	88	58
7	Bellmont	456	3/28/99	345	72	42
8	Alexander	478	4/4/99	234	65	35
9	Wilmont	489	4/8/99	765	61	31
10	Barton	505	4/20/99	469	49	19

Change the System Date Back to Today's Date

16. Use the technique discussed in Steps 3 and 4 of this exercise to change the system date back to today's date.

    Notice that the NOW function does not display today's date in Cell C2, and the dates do not change in the days past due calculations. This is because the NOW and TODAY functions are refreshed only when the workbook is closed and then reopened.

17. Save the workbook with the name **Skill Builder 4.2,** and close the workbook.

18. Choose **File** from the menu bar, and Skill Builder 4.2 will be displayed at the bottom of the menu.

    You can open the most recently used workbooks by choosing them from the menu.

19. Choose **Skill Builder 4.2** from the File menu, and the workbook will open.

    Take a moment to check out the worksheet, and notice that the date in Cell C2 is now set to today's date. The numbers in Column E should also be significantly larger, because they are now measuring the number of days past due from today's date. The formula results in Column F should also reflect significantly larger numbers.

20. Close the workbook, and continue with the next exercise.

Skill Builder 4.3 Insert and Delete Rows

In this exercise, you will open an order entry worksheet from your exercise diskette. You will modify the worksheet by removing and inserting new line items.

Open the Workbook and Create the Formulas

1. Open the workbook named **Skill Builder 4.3.**

2. Click Cell D4, and enter a formula that calculates the extended price as the quantity multiplied by the unit price.

   The result should be 239.7.

3. Copy the Extended Price formula down to Rows 5 through 8.

4. Use AutoSum to compute the subtotal for the extended prices in Column D.

5. Calculate the sales tax as the subtotal multiplied by 7.75%.

6. Calculate the total as the subtotal plus the sales tax.

7. Select all the numbers in Columns C and D, and increase the decimals to 2.

(Continued on the next page)

Delete a Row, and Then Insert a Row

Imagine the customer has decided to cancel his order for electric pencil sharpeners. He also wants to add toner cartridges to his order.

8. Select Row 5 by clicking the row heading, and choose Edit→Delete.
   The subtotal, sales tax, and total should be recalculated.

9. Click anywhere in Row 7 and choose Insert→Rows.

10. Add the following item, but make sure you use a formula in Cell D7.

7	Toner cartridge	10	89.95	899.50

Insert a Row

11. Click anywhere in Row 9, and insert a row above the subtotal row.

12. Add the following item to the new row, but make sure you use a formula in Cell D9.

9	Two-line telephone	5	145.00	725.00

13. Click Cell D10, and notice that Excel has adjusted the formula reference to accommodate the new row.
    Excel adjusted the formula reference because the Subtotal heading and structure of the worksheet gave it enough information to make this decision. The total in Cell D12 should be 3158.91.

14. Use the TODAY function to insert the current date in Cell E1.

15. Format the date with the date format of your choice.

16. Select the range A3:D12, and use the AutoFit command to adjust the column widths.

17. Save the changes to your workbook when you have finished, then close the workbook.

Skill Builder 4.4 Insert and Delete Cells

In this skill builder, you will open a workbook on your exercise diskette. You will experiment with inserting and deleting cells.

1. Open the workbook named **Skill Builder 4.4.**

Insert a Single Cell

2. Click Cell A6.
   Imagine you want to add a new sales rep to the report. You will attempt to use the Insert→Cells command to accomplish this.

3. Choose **Insert→Cells** from the menu bar.

4. Follow these steps to insert a cell and explore the dialog box options.

Ⓐ *Make sure the **Shift cells down** option is chosen. The first two options determine the way that other worksheet cells are moved when you insert one or more cells.*

Ⓑ *The last two options give you another way to insert entire rows and columns.*

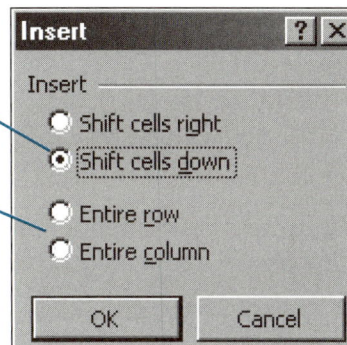

5. Click **OK** to insert a single cell.
Notice how the three entries below the inserted cell moved down. The entries in Columns B and C did not move. One of the potential problems with inserting cells is that some cells in the worksheet will move, while others won't. This changes the structure of the entire worksheet.

6. Click Undo 🔄 to reverse the insertion.

Delete a Single Cell

7. Make sure the highlight is in Cell A6, and choose **Edit→Delete** from the menu bar.

8. Make sure the **Shift cells up** option is chosen, and click **OK.**
The cells below the deleted cell shift up, while all other worksheet cells remain as they were.

9. Click Undo 🔄 to reverse the deletion.

Insert Multiple Cells

10. Select the range A6:B7, and choose **Insert→Cells** from the menu bar.

11. Choose the **Shift cells right** option, and click **OK.**
Notice how this command destroyed the structure of your worksheet.

12. Click Undo 🔄 to reverse the insertion.

Use the DATE Function

13. Click Cell C2.

14. Type **=DATE(99,12,25)**, and tap (ENTER) to complete the entry.
The date 12/25/99 should be displayed in the cell. The DATE function converts the year, month, and day that you use as arguments into a serial date. The serial date is then formatted with the date format displayed in Cell C2. You probably won't use the DATE function much in your day-to-day work. This function is most often used by programmers.

15. Close the workbook without saving the changes.

Assessments

Assessment 4.1 **Restructure an Accounts Receivable Report**

1. Open the workbook named **Assessment 4.1.**

2. Use the TODAY function to insert the current date in Cell C2.

3. Insert and move rows as necessary until the customer Rows 5-10 are reorganized in alphabetical order. You learned how to move rows in the previous lesson, and you learned how to insert rows in this lesson.

4. Insert a column between Columns A and B, and enter the invoice numbers shown in the illustration below. Also, enter the heading shown in Cell B4 below.

5. Use a formula in Column F to calculate the number of days past due. Assume the terms are net 30, which means the invoice is supposed to be paid within 30 days. Your formula should subtract 30 from the number of days since the invoice was issued. Your numbers will be different from the numbers shown below because your current date will be different. Your numbers should be much larger.

6. Use AutoFormat to format the worksheet. The example shown below uses the Classic 2 format.

7. Your completed worksheet should match the worksheet shown below. However, the # of days since invoices were issued and # of days past due will be different.

8. Print the worksheet, save the changes, and then close the workbook.

	A	B	C	D	E	F
1	Accounts Receivable Aging Report					
2	Report Date			6/8/99		
3						
4	Customer	Invoice Number	Invoice Date	Invoice amount	# of days since invoice was issued	# of days past due
5	Alexander	210	4/4/99	234	65	35
6	Arthur	155	3/12/99	980	88	58
7	Barton	246	4/20/99	469	49	19
8	Bellmont	189	3/28/99	345	72	42
9	Wilmont	228	4/8/99	765	61	31
10	Wilson	130	1/20/99	123	139	109

Assessment 4.2 Create a Worksheet with Averages

In this assessment, you will create the worksheet shown below. This worksheet calculates the number of days between two test dates, the point increase in test scores, the percentage increase in test scores, the average number of days, and the average percentage increase.

1. Enter all text, numbers, and dates into the worksheet as shown below, except for the numbers and percentages in Columns F, G, and H. Use the following guidelines to create the large paragraph shown near the top of the worksheet.

   - Use the Merge and Center button to merge Cells A2:C2.

   - Turn the Wrap Text option on.

   - Increase the height of Row 2 as shown.

   - Type the text in the large merged cell.

2. Use formulas in Column F to calculate the number of days between the two tests.

3. Use formulas in Column G to calculate the point increase between the two tests.

4. Use formulas to calculate the percentage increase in Column H. The percentage increase is calculated as the point increase in Column G divided by the first test score in Column C.

5. Use the AVERAGE function to compute the averages in Cells F12 and H13.

6. Format all numbers, dates, and text as shown. Adjust row heights and column widths as shown.

7. Print the worksheet when you have finished.

8. Save the workbook as **Assessment 4.2,** and close the workbook.

	A	B	C	D	E	F	G	H
1	**Grade 10 Performance Evaluations**							
2	This worksheet computes the percentage increase in test scores for students who have been receiving special assistance. The average number of days required to achieve the results is also shown.							
3								
4		First Test		Second Test				
5	Student	Date	Score	Date	Score	Number of Days Between Tests	Point Increase	Percentage Increase
6	Lisa Evans	2/3/99	78	4/30/99	87	86	9	12%
7	Clara Johnson	2/5/99	77	4/28/99	82	82	5	6%
8	Ted Thomas	2/5/99	65	5/5/99	80	89	15	23%
9	Brian Wilson	3/10/99	64	6/1/99	72	83	8	13%
10	Elizabeth Crawford	3/12/99	68	5/2/99	78	51	10	15%
11	Bernice Barton	4/1/99	72	7/10/99	88	100	16	22%
12	Average Days					81.83		
13	Average Increase							15%

Critical Thinking

Critical Thinking 4.1 On Your Own

Open the **Critical Thinking 3.3** workbook that you created in Critical Thinking Exercise 3.3. Insert a column immediately to the right of the return date column. Use a formula to calculate the number of days between the return date and purchase date. Format the cells in the "number of days" column so that a number is displayed with 0 decimal places. Reorganize the columns so that the purchase price column is to the right of the "number of days" column. Calculate the total value of the returns. Adjust all column widths to fit the widest entries in the columns. Save the modified workbook as **Critical Thinking 4.1.**

Critical Thinking 4.2 On Your Own

Open the **Critical Thinking 3.4** workbook that you created in Critical Thinking Exercise 3.4. Assume that the stocks in the portfolio were purchased on the following dates.

Stock Symbol	Date Purchased
CORL	3/5/98
GLC	11/5/99
HAL	11/6/99
LU	8/5/99
MSFT	9/1/99
ORCL	4/25/98

Insert a column to the left of the purchase price column, and enter the Date Purchased information shown in the preceding table. Make sure you associate the correct purchase date with the correct stock symbol. Format the dates in the Purchase Date column with a date format. Add another column to the worksheet that calculates the Number of Days the investment has been held as of today's date. The formula should automatically recalculate the number of days whenever the workbook is opened. Format all cells in the Number of Days column so that they display a number with zero decimals. Add another column to calculate the Average Daily Dollar Gain for each stock since the purchase date. Use AutoFormat to apply the AutoFormat of your choice to the worksheet. Save the workbook as **Critical Thinking 4.2.**

Critical Thinking 4.3 On Your Own

Janine Carmichael works in the Accounts Payable Department of Data Storage, Inc. Data Storage, Inc. is in the data warehousing business. With the emergence of the Internet, Data Storage's business has grown rapidly as many hot new Internet companies have turned to Data Storage to assist them with their data warehousing needs. As with any rapidly growing business, cash flow is important to Data Storage. Janine is responsible for tracking the accounts of delinquent customers and initiating collection activities. Janine has asked you to prepare a worksheet that tracks delinquent accounts.

Prepare a worksheet that includes the customer name, invoice number, invoice date, and invoice amount. Include five fictitious customer accounts in the worksheet. Use a formula to calculate the number of days each account is past due. The formula should count from today's date. And it should be dynamic, recalculating the number of days past due each time the workbook is opened. Format the Number of Days Past Due cells with the General number format. Calculate an interest charge for each past-due account. Assume an annual interest rate of 18%. Assume that an interest rate of 18% / 365 is charged each day since there are 365 days in a year and 18% is an annualized rate. Calculate the total amount due as the invoice amount plus interest. Use formulas to sum the total invoice amounts, total interest, and total amounts due for all accounts. Use the AVERAGE function to calculate the average days past due for all accounts. Save the workbook as **Critical Thinking 4.3.**

Critical Thinking 4.4 Web Research

Open the **Critical Thinking 4.3** workbook that you created in the previous exercise. Save the workbook as **Critical Thinking 4.4.** Use Internet Explorer and a search engine of your choice to locate three companies on the World Wide Web that provide collection services. Add the names of these companies, their Web site URL's, and telephone numbers to the second worksheet tab in the workbook.

Critical Thinking 4.5 Web Research

Open the **Critical Thinking 4.2** workbook that you created in Critical Thinking Exercise 4.2. Use Internet Explorer and a search engine to locate a Web site that gives free stock quotes. Get quotes on stocks with the symbols CSCO, INTC, and PAYX. Add the stock symbols, company names, and date purchased to the worksheet. Insert this new information so that the rows are in alphabetical order by stock symbol. Assume that you are buying 100 shares of each company. Also assume that the purchase price and current price are the same. If necessary, copy formulas from other cells to the empty cells in the new rows. Format all cells as necessary. Save the workbook as **Critical Thinking 4.5.**

Critical Thinking 4.6 As a Group

Choose four classmates and form an investment club. Set up a worksheet to track stock purchases. You can use your **Critical Thinking 4.5** workbook as the basis for your new workbook. Name the new workbook **Critical Thinking 4.6.** Have each classmate contribute three stocks to the portfolio. Include the name of the classmate (or your name) with each stock. This will identify the person who chose the stock. Use a Web site that gives free stock quotations to determine the initial purchase price of your investments. Assume that you are buying 100 shares of each company. If possible, find a Web site that offers free company research and stock tips to help make your investment decisions. One example is www.cnbc.com. Format the worksheet as desired.

Working with Large Worksheets

In this lesson, you will work with a large worksheet that tracks a personal budget and expenditures. You will sort the worksheet rows using various techniques. You will also learn commands that are particularly useful with large worksheets, including freezing rows and columns, splitting window panes, printing techniques, and page breaks.

In This Lesson

Case Study

Carla Adams has recently purchased a computer for home use. Carla has a flexible occupation that allows her to work out of her home two days per week. With her new Pentium computer, a high-speed Internet connection, and Office 2000, Carla can work as efficiently from home as she can in the office. Carla also uses Office 2000 for personal projects. Her most recent endeavor is to create a personal budget using Excel 2000. Carla likes the flexibility of Excel and the sophisticated tools she can use with large worksheets like her home budget.

	A	B	C	D	E	F	G	H	I	J	K
1	1999 Home Budget										
2											
3		January		February		March		April		May	
4		Budget	Spent	Budget	Spent	Budget	Spent	Budget	Spent	Budget	Spent
5	Utilities	100	78	100	120	100	95	100	78	100	120
6	Phone	60	75	60	80	60	145	60	75	60	80
7	Mortgage	1000	1000	1000	1000	1000	1075	1075	1075	1075	1075
8	Insurance	200	200	0	0	0	0	200	200	0	0
9	Subtotal	$1,360	$1,353	$1,160	$1,200	$1,160	$1,315	$1,435	$1,428	$1,235	$1,275
10											
11	Food	235	220	235	190	235	250	235	220	235	190
12	Entertainment	120	80	120	90	120	245	120	80	120	90
13	Clothing	100	54	100	0	100	234	100	54	100	0
14	Subtotal	$455	$354	$455	$280	$455	$729	$455	$354	$455	$280
15											
16	Car Payment	400	400	400	400	400	400	400	400	400	400
17	Car Maintenance	50	0	50	67	50	435	50	0	50	67
18	Car Insurance	180	180	0	0	0	0	180	180	0	0
19	Subtotal	$630	$580	$450	$467	$450	$835	$630	$580	$450	$467
20											
21	Grand Total	$2,445	$2,287	$2,065	$1,947	$2,065	$2,879	$2,520	$2,362	$2,140	$2,022
22	Differences	$158		$118		-$814		$158		$118	

Sorting

Excel has powerful sorting capabilities that let you sort worksheet rows or columns. The most common type of sort is when entire rows are sorted based upon the text or values in a column.

Sort Keys

When sorting rows, Excel must know which rows you want to sort and which column to use as the sort key. Excel uses the sort key to decide how to arrange the rows. For example, imagine a worksheet has a list of names in Column A. If you wanted to sort the rows according to the names, then you would specify Column A as the sort key by clicking in the column.

The Sort Buttons

The Sort Ascending [A/Z↓] and Sort Descending [Z/A↓] buttons let you rapidly sort lists. A list is a group of rows that are isolated from other rows in the worksheet. Being isolated means there is at least one empty row above and below the list. Because a list is isolated from other rows, Excel can easily determine which rows to sort when you click the Sort Ascending or Sort Descending buttons. Excel sorts all rows in the list unless it determines that the list has a header row. A header row is the row at the top of a list containing column headings. To sort a list, click within the list in the column that you want to use as the sort key, then click either the Sort Ascending or Sort Descending button.

Selecting Rows Before Sorting

You can always select the rows in a list before clicking the Sort Ascending and Sort Descending buttons. This may be necessary if the list contains rows that you do not want included in the sort. By selecting the rows, you are instructing Excel to sort only those rows. Excel will sort only the selected rows, and it will use Column A as the sort key.

Dangers of Sorting

Sorting mistakes can easily render a worksheet useless. For this reason, always save your worksheet prior to sorting. If a problem arises and you forget to use Undo, then you can close the worksheet without saving it. When you reopen the worksheet, it will be in the state it was in prior to sorting.

Hands-On 5.1 Use the Sort Buttons

In this exercise, you will open a workbook on your exercise diskette. You will use the sort buttons to sort several lists.

Sort the Lists

1. Open the workbook named **Hands-On Lesson 5.**

2. Take a few moments to browse through this worksheet.
   Notice that this worksheet is very large and contains budgetary data for all 12 months of the year. You will use this worksheet throughout this lesson.

3. Scroll to the top of the worksheet and click Cell A5.

   In the next few steps, you will sort Rows 5–8. When you do this, Excel will sort the entire rows. The rows will be sorted according to the text entries in Column A. Keep in mind, however, that the entire rows will be sorted. Before you begin, notice that Row 5 (the Utilities row) has the values 100, 78, 100, 120, etc., and Row 6 (the Mortgage row) has 1000 or 1075 in each column. Also notice that the rows are not in alphabetical order at this point.

4. Click the Sort Ascending ⬇ button.

   Notice that the Insurance row is now on top because it is the first row in alphabetical order. Also notice that the entire rows were rearranged. For example, the Utilities row is now at the bottom of the list, and the values 100, 78, 100, 120 are still part of that row. Finally, notice that the Header rows 3 and 4 were not included in the sort.

5. Click the Sort Descending ⬇ button to reverse the sort order.

6. Click Cell B5.

7. Click the Sort Ascending ⬇ button, and the rows will now be sorted based upon the numbers in Column B.

   The Sort Ascending and Sort Descending buttons always sort rows based upon the column that contains the highlight.

8. Click the Sort Descending ⬇ button to sort in descending order based upon the numbers in Column B.

9. Click Cell A5, and click the Sort Ascending ⬇ button.

10. Click Cell A11, and click the Sort Ascending ⬇ button.

    The rows in the second list should now be in ascending order.

11. Sort the third list (Rows 16–18) in ascending order based upon Column A.

Add Subtotal Rows, and Sort the Lists

12. Click Cell A9, and enter the word **Subtotal** in the cell.

13. Enter the word **Subtotal** in Cells A14 and A19.

14. Click Cell A5 and click the Sort Descending ⬇ button.

    Notice that Excel includes the Subtotal row in the sort. Excel usually does not include header rows and total rows in a sort. In this case, it could not determine that this was a subtotal row because formulas had not yet been used to compute the subtotals.

15. Click Undo ↺ to reverse the sort.

16. Select Rows 5–8 by dragging the mouse over the row headings.

    If you need to select rows before sorting, then make sure you select entire rows. If you select only certain cells in the rows, then Excel will only sort those cells. This may render the entire worksheet useless. By dragging the row headings, you can be certain that you have selected entire rows.

17. Click the Sort Descending ⬇ button.

    Excel should leave the Subtotal row out of the sort. Notice that Excel used Column A as the sort key. Excel always uses Column A as the sort key if you select rows prior to using the sort buttons.

18. Sort Rows 11–13 and 16–18 in Descending order (you need to select the rows before sorting).

19. Save the workbook, and continue with the next topic.

Multilevel Sorts

The Sort dialog box is used to specify more than one sort key for multilevel sorts. For example, imagine you had a worksheet with last names in Column A and first names in Column B. Using the Sort dialog box, you would instruct Excel to first sort the rows by last name and then by first name. This way, all rows with the same last name would be grouped together. Then the rows would be sorted by first name within each group. You display the Sort dialog box with the **Data→Sort** command. You will use the Sort dialog box to perform multilevel sorts in the end-of-lesson exercises.

Freezing Header Rows and Columns

The **Window→Freeze Panes** command lets you keep header rows and columns in view while you scroll through a worksheet. The Freeze Panes command is quite useful with large worksheets. When you issue this command, Excel freezes all rows above the highlight and all columns to the left of the highlight. For this reason, you must click the correct cell before issuing the command. You can unfreeze the frozen rows and columns with the **Window→Unfreeze Panes** command.

If Column A is frozen, you can scroll to the right, and Column A will remain in view.

In this example, the worksheet has been scrolled all the way to Column J, but Column A is still visible.

	A	J	K	L
1	1999 Home			
2				
3			May	Ju
4		Budget	Spent	Budget
5	Utilities	100	120	100
6	Phone	60	80	60
7	Mortgage	1075	1075	1075
8	Insurance	0	0	0
9	**Subtotal**			

Hands-On 5.2 Freeze and Unfreeze Rows and Columns

Freeze Panes

1. Scroll through the worksheet until Column Y is visible.

2. Scroll down until Row 25 is visible.
   Notice that the row and column headings have scrolled out of view. This makes it difficult to edit or understand the worksheet data.

3. Press (CTRL)+(HOME) to move the highlight to Cell A1.
   You learned this keystroke combination from the Quick Reference table on page 6 of Lesson 1. This keystroke combination is quite useful when working with large worksheets.

4. Click Cell B5.

5. Choose **Window→Freeze Panes** from the menu bar.

6. Scroll to Column Y; then scroll down to Row 25.
   Notice that the headings in Column A and Rows 1–4 remain visible, allowing you to identify the contents of the worksheet cells.

7. Press (CTRL)+(HOME), and notice that the highlight moves to Cell B5 instead of A1.
   Cell B5 is now the "home" cell, since you froze the window panes at that location.

8. Click Cell A5, and notice that you could edit this cell if desired.
   Frozen columns and rows are still available for editing.

9. Choose **Window→Unfreeze Panes** from the menu bar.

10. Feel free to experiment with freezing and unfreezing panes, then continue with the next topic.

Splitting Window Panes

The **Window→Split** command lets you view two sections of a worksheet at the same time. This can be useful for comparing data in two different sections of a large worksheet. As with the Freeze Panes command, you should position the highlight in the desired cell before issuing the command. You can remove the split with the **Window→Remove Split** command.

*The **Split** command lets you view two different parts of the worksheet. In this example, the January and February numbers are compared to the October and November numbers.*

	B	C	D	E	T	U	V	W
1	Budget							
2								
3	January		February		October		November	
4	Budget	Spent	Budget	Spent	Budget	Spent	Budget	Spent
5	100	78	100	120	100	78	100	120
6	60	75	60	80	60	75	60	80
7	1000	1000	1000	1000	1075	1075	1075	1075
8	200	200	0	0	200	200	0	0

Hands-On 5.3 Split Window Panes

1. Click Cell B5.

2. Choose the **Window→Split** command.
   Notice the thick border separating the window into four panes.

3. Tap the ↑ key **four** times.
   Notice that the header rows are displayed in both the top and bottom panes. You can view any section of the worksheet in any pane. You can even view the same section in two or more panes.

(Continued on the next page)

4. Follow this step to adjust the vertical split bar.

A *Position the mouse pointer on the vertical split bar, and drag it to the right until it is in the middle of the window.*

Notice that this increases the amount of available space in the left panes. This allows you to compare two sections of the worksheet using the left and right panes.

5. Use the scroll bar at the bottom of the fourth pane (the bottom right pane) to scroll to the right until December is visible.
Notice the left panes remain stationery as you scroll through the right panes. You can now compare the data for January and December.

6. Use the scroll bar below the left panes to scroll until December is visible in the left panes.

7. Scroll through the right panes until January is visible in the right panes.

8. Take a few minutes to experiment with the **Window→Split** and **Window→Freeze Panes** commands. You may want to try splitting and freezing at the same time.

9. When you have finished experimenting, use the **Window→Remove Split** command to remove the split from the panes.

10. Click Cell B5 and use the **Window→Freeze Panes** command to freeze the panes.

Hands-On 5.4 Insert Formulas

Practice Navigation Techniques

1. Follow this step to scroll to the right one screen at a time.

A *Click in an open part of the horizontal scroll bar to scroll one screen.*

2. Use the preceding technique to scroll one screen to the left.

3. Choose **Edit→Go To** from the menu bar.

4. Type **Y9** in the reference box, and click **OK.**
Excel will move the highlight to Cell Y9. The Go To command was introduced in Lesson 1. You can always use the Go To command to rapidly move to a specific cell.

5. Press (CTRL)+(HOME) to move the highlight to Cell B5.

Create Subtotal Formulas

6. Click Cell B9.

7. Scroll to the right (using the mouse and the scroll bar) until Cell Y9 is visible.

8. Press the (SHIFT) key while you click Cell Y9.
   This should select the range B9:Y9, which includes all the subtotal cells in Row 9. You learned this "Shift and click" technique in Lesson 1. This technique works well in large worksheets. In large worksheets, you may want to use this selection technique instead of the drag technique.

9. Click AutoSum Σ to calculate the Subtotals.

10. Use the preceding techniques to calculate the subtotals in Rows 14 and 19.

Create Grand Total Formulas

11. Click Cell B21.

12. Type the formula **=B9+B14+B19**, and click the Enter ☑ button to complete the entry.

13. Click the Copy 🗐 button to copy the formula to the clipboard.

14. Click Cell C21.

15. Use the mouse and the horizontal scroll bar (not the keyboard) to scroll to the right until Cell Y21 is visible.

16. Press the (SHIFT) key while you click Cell Y21.

17. Click the Paste 📋 button.
    The formula should be copied across the row.

Create Difference Formulas

18. Click Cell B22.

19. Enter the formula **=B21-C21**, and click the Enter ☑ button to complete the entry.

20. Select Cells B22 and C22, and Copy 🗐 them to the clipboard.

21. Click Cell D22.

22. Scroll to the right until Cell Y22 is visible.

23. Press the (SHIFT) key while you click Cell Y22.

24. Click the Paste 📋 button.
    The Differences formula and the blank cell to the right of it should be copied across the row.

25. Press (CTRL)+(HOME) to move to Cell B5, and tap the (ESC) key to turn off the flashing marquee.

26. Save the changes to your workbook, and continue with the next topic.

Printing Large Worksheets

Excel has a number of options to help you print large worksheets. Most print options are accessed through the Page Setup dialog box. Using the Page Setup dialog box, you can adjust the page orientation, margins, headers and footers, and many other options. The Page Setup dialog box is displayed with the **File→Page Setup** command.

Page Setup—Page Options

The Page tab of the Page Setup dialog box lets you set various page options. For example, you can choose Portrait or Landscape orientations to print your pages vertically or horizontally. Landscape orientation is useful with wide worksheets like the 1999 Home Budget. The Page options also provide automated scaling options to let you easily print large worksheets.

You can choose an orientation.

*The **Adjust to** option compresses or expands all worksheet elements by the percentage you specify.*

*The **Fit to** option is most convenient when you have a few rows or columns spilling over to an extra page. You can specify the number of pages you want, and Excel will make the worksheet fit.*

*You can choose the **Paper size** and set the **Print quality**. Lowering the print quality can speed up printing and possibly save toner or ink.*

*You can change the starting **First page number**.*

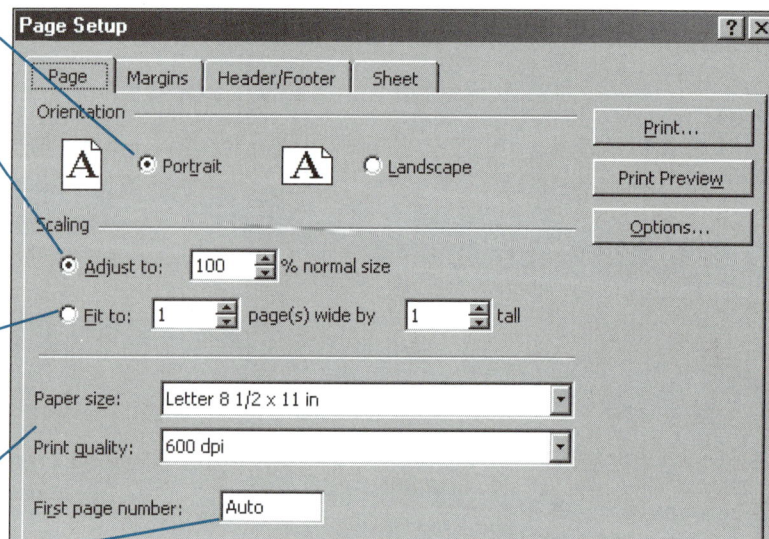

Hands-On 5.5 Use the Page Options

Use Print Preview

1. Click the Print Preview button.

2. If necessary, zoom in by clicking anywhere on the worksheet until the entire page is visible.
   Notice that Excel can only fit a portion of the worksheet on the page. Excel breaks the worksheet up over multiple pages if it is too large to fit on a single page. Also notice the header (Sheet1) at the top of the page and the footer (Page 1) at the bottom of the page. You will work with headers and footers later in this lesson.

3. Use the **Next** button on the Print Preview toolbar to view the next two pages.
   Your worksheet should have three pages.

4. Use the **Previous** button to move back to Page 1.

5. Click the **Close** button to exit from Print Preview.

6. Scroll to the right, and you will notice vertical dashed lines near Columns I and R.
   These lines represent the page breaks. They indicate where one page ends and another begins.

Switch to Landscape Orientation

7. Choose **File→Page Setup** from the menu bar.

8. Make sure the Page tab is active, and then choose **Landscape** orientation.

9. Click the **Print Preview** button on the right side of the dialog box.

10. If necessary, zoom in by clicking on the worksheet until the entire page is visible.
    Print Preview and Page Setup are designed to work together, so Excel lets you access Print Preview from Page Setup and vice versa. Notice the Landscape (horizontal) orientation of the page.

11. Use the **Next** button to view the second page.
    Your worksheet should now fit on two pages.

Use the Scaling Options

12. Click the **Setup** button to display the Page Setup dialog box.

13. Choose the **Fit to** option and make sure the pages are set to 1 page wide by 1 page tall as shown to the right.

14. Click **OK,** and Excel will compress the worksheet to fit on one page.
    As you can see, it wasn't such a good idea to compress a two-page worksheet onto one page. The printed worksheet will be so small that it will be unreadable. The Fit To option is most convenient when you have a few columns or rows that are spilling over to an extra page. Compressing a few rows or columns will have little impact on the font sizes and other worksheet elements. The Fit to option is also convenient if you have a long worksheet that is just slightly wider than the page. You can specify the pages wide as 1 and then specify a pages tall setting of 100 or some other number that is larger than the number of pages you will actually have. Excel will reduce the width of the worksheet to fit on the page, and then it will print as many pages as necessary to complete the worksheet.

15. Click the **Setup** button.

16. Choose the Adjust to option button and set the percentage to 100% as shown to the right.
    Setting the Adjust to percentage back to 100% effectively turns off the Fit to option.

17. Click **OK** to display the worksheet in Print Preview.
    Continue with the next topic, where you will work with margin options.

Page Setup—Margin Options

The Margins tab of the Page Setup dialog box lets you adjust the margins and the header and footer position. You can also use the Margins tab to center the worksheet horizontally or vertically on the page.

*The **Top, Left, Bottom,** and **Right** margins determine the distance from the edges of the page to the worksheet. You can set all four margins independently. The default margin settings for new workbooks are shown here.*

*The **Center on Page** options let you center the worksheet horizontally or vertically on the page.*

*The **Header** and **Footer** settings determine the distance of the header and footer from the top and bottom edges of the page. They should always be smaller than the top and bottom margins, or the header and footer may print on top of the worksheet data.*

Page Setup

| Page | Margins | Header/Footer | Sheet |

Top: 1
Header: 0.5

Left: 0.75
Right: 0.75

Options...

Bottom: 1
Footer: 0.5

Center on page
☐ Horizontally   ☐ Vertically

Hands-On 5.6 Use the Margin Options

The worksheet should still be in Print Preview mode from the previous exercise.

Set the Margins with Page Setup

1. If necessary, use the **Previous** button to move back to Page 1.
   The last visible column on your worksheet will most likely be the June Budget column. The June Spent column will most likely be on the second page, and the word June may be cut off and split between the two pages. You can bring the June Spent column back to the first page by reducing the left and right margins. This will create more room on the page.

2. Click the **Setup** button.

3. Click the **Margins** tab in the Page Setup dialog box.

4. Set the left and right margins to **0.5** (that's 0.5 not 5).

5. Click the **Vertically** check box at the bottom of the dialog box.

6. Click **OK** to complete the changes.
   The June Spent column should be on the first page. The worksheet should also be centered vertically between the top and bottom margins.

7. Click the **Setup** button.

8. Remove the check from the **Vertically** check box.

9. Change the **Header** and **Footer** settings to **1**, and click **OK.**
   Now both the worksheet and the header (Sheet 1) are positioned 1" down from the top of the page. You should always make the header and footer settings smaller than the top and bottom margins. This forces the header and footer to print in the margin area.

10. Click the **Setup** button.

11. Change the Header and Footer settings to **0.5**, and click **OK.**

Page Setup—Header/Footer Options

Headers print at the top of every page, while footers print at the bottom of every page. You can include page numbers, dates, the workbook name, and any text in a header or footer. Excel provides a variety of built-in headers and footers from which you can choose. You can also create customized headers and footers to suit your particular needs.

Header and Footer Sections

Excel divides headers and footers into left, center, and right sections. The left section prints on the left side of the page, the center section prints in the center, and the right section prints on the right side of the page. You can instruct Excel to insert the current date, page number, or time in any section. You can also format customized headers and footers by changing the font size and typeface.

You can choose built-in headers and footers from the drop-down lists. The footer shown here displays the word Page *followed by the current page number.*

*You use the **Custom Header** and **Custom Footer** buttons to create custom headers and footers. Custom headers and footers appear on the same drop-down lists as the built-in headers and footers.*

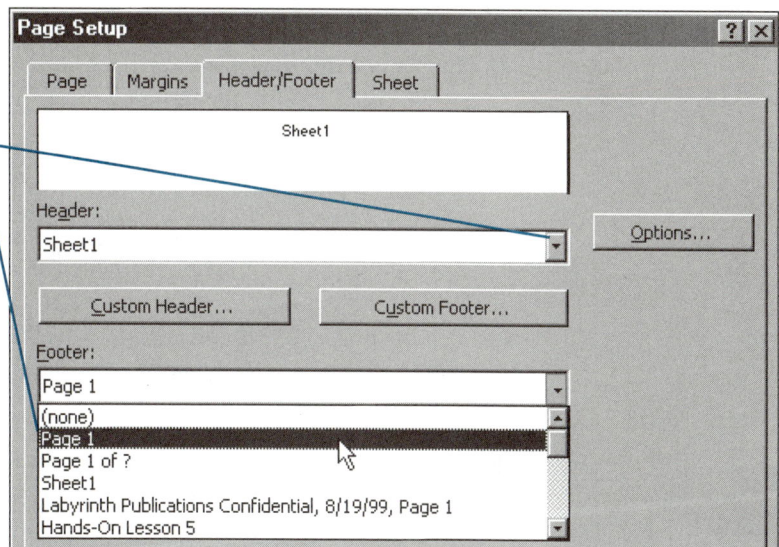

*The **Left section** of this customized header has a simple text label.*

*The **Center section** contains text and fields. The fields are preceded by & symbols. The &[Page] field inserts the current page number, and the &[Pages] field inserts the total number of pages in the worksheet.*

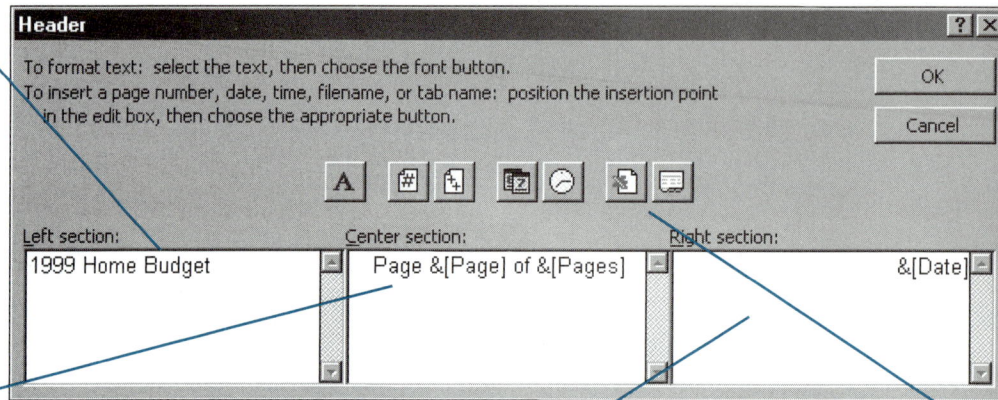

Header

To format text: select the text, then choose the font button.
To insert a page number, date, time, filename, or tab name: position the insertion point in the edit box, then choose the appropriate button.

OK

Cancel

Left section:
1999 Home Budget

Center section:
Page &[Page] of &[Pages]

Right section:
&[Date]

*The &[Date] field in the **Right section** inserts the current date.*

Use these buttons to insert fields.

Hands-On 5.7 Headers and Footers

The worksheet should still be displayed in Print Preview from the previous exercise.

Use Built-In Headers and Footers

1. Click the **Setup** button, and then click the **Header/Footer** tab.
   Notice that the header is currently set to Sheet1, and the footer is set to Page 1. These are built-in headers and footers. The header and footer will print at the top and bottom of every page. The sheet number and page number are updated on every page. For example, the footer will appear as Page 2 on the second page.

2. Follow these steps to remove the header and choose a different footer.

   A *Click the **Header** drop-down button to display a list of built-in headers.*

   B *Scroll through the list, and notice the various headers. Commas within a header or footer indicate a section change. For example, text or codes to the right of a comma will be in the center section or right section.*

   C *Scroll to the top of the list and choose (none). You can always remove a header or footer by choosing (none).*

   D *Click the **Footer** button and choose the footer, Hands-On Lesson 5, Page 1. Excel always displays built-in headers and footers that reflect the workbook name, company name, etc.*

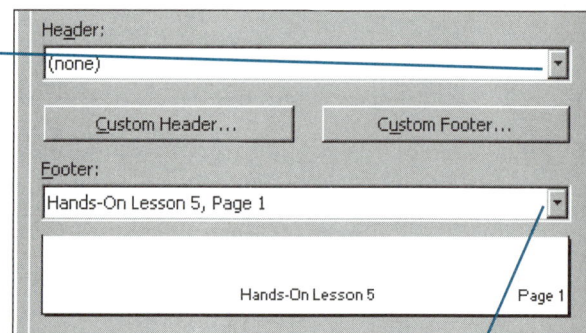

   Header:
   (none)

   Custom Header...   Custom Footer...

   Footer:
   Hands-On Lesson 5, Page 1

   Hands-On Lesson 5   Page 1

3. Click **OK,** and the new footer will appear in Print Preview.
   The header will not be displayed, because you chose (none).

4. Take a few minutes to experiment with different built-in headers and footers. You will need to click the Setup button to return to the Page Setup dialog box. Be adventurous and choose any built-in headers or footers you desire. You will create a customized header and footer in the remainder of this exercise.

Use Customized Headers and Footers

5. Display the Page Setup dialog box, and make sure the Header/Footer tab is active.

6. Click the **Custom Header** button.

7. Follow these steps to begin creating a custom header.

A *Click the **Question Mark** button.*

B *Click the **Page** button to get help on how the button is used. Help will inform you that this button inserts the current page number into the header.*

C *Continue to use the **Question Mark** button to get help on all seven customizing buttons*

D *Type **1999 Home Budget** here. You can type any text in a header or footer.*

Header ? X

To format text: select the text, then choose the font button.
To insert a page number, date, time, filename, or tab name: position the insertion point in the edit box, then choose the appropriate button.

OK

Cancel

Left section:
1999 Home Budget

Center section:
Page &[Page] of &[Pages]

Right section:
&[Date]

E *Click in the center section, type the word **Page**, and tap the (SPACE BAR). You will complete the center section and right section in the following steps.*

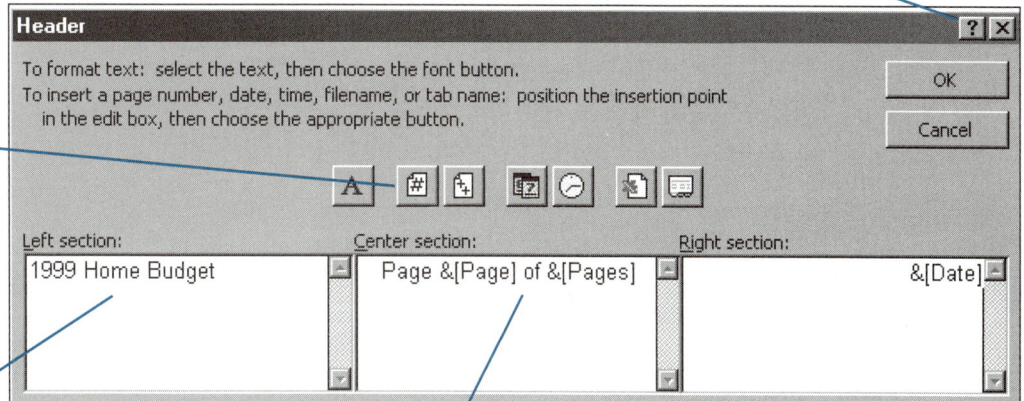

8. Follow these steps to complete the center section.

- Click the Page Number [#] button to insert the &[Page] code.

- Tap the (SPACE BAR), type the word **of**, and tap the (SPACE BAR) again.

- Click the Total Pages [+] button to insert the &[Pages] code.

9. Click in the right section, and then click the Date [z] button to insert the &[Date] code.

10. Take a few moments to study the header you just created. Your header should match the header shown in the above illustration. Try to understand the significance of the text and codes. If necessary, use the Question Mark button again to get help on the various buttons. The descriptions that appear will discuss the codes and how the buttons function.

11. Click **OK,** and the customized header will be displayed in the Page Setup dialog box.

12. Click the Footer drop-down button, scroll to the top of the list, and choose **(none).**

13. Click **OK** on the Page Setup dialog box, and the new header will be displayed in Print Preview.

14. Click the **Next** button, and notice that the header is also displayed on Page 2.

15. Take a few minutes to experiment with the header and footer options.

Page Setup—Sheet Options

The Sheet tab of the Page Setup dialog box contains options that affect all pages in the worksheet. For example, the gridlines option lets you turn gridlines on and off. Gridlines are dotted lines that surround every cell in a printed worksheet.

*The **Print area** option lets you specify a range of cells to print.*

*Print titles with these options. The **Print titles** option is discussed in detail in the next topic.*

*You can turn these **Print options** on and off.*

Change the order in which pages are printed in a multiple-page worksheet.

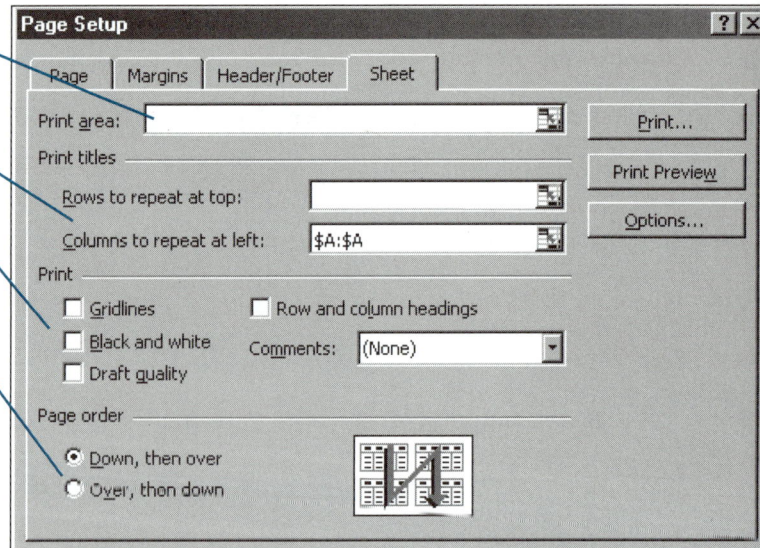

Title Rows and Columns

You can specify one or more rows as title rows and one or more columns as title columns. Title rows and title columns are printed as titles on every page of a worksheet. For example, the 1999 Budget worksheet will print on two pages. It may be difficult to understand the data on the second page because Column A contains the headings that describe the content of the various rows. This can be resolved by specifying Column A as a title column. Column A will then print on both pages.

Availability of Title Rows and Title Columns Option

The title rows and title columns options are not available if you display the Page Setup dialog box from the Print Preview window. To use these options, you must display the Page Setup dialog box from the worksheet with the **File→Page Setup** command.

Hands-On 5.8 Use the Sheet Options

Use Print Options

1. Display the Page Setup dialog box from Print Preview, and click the **Sheet** tab.

2. Follow these steps to set the Gridlines and the Row and Column Headings options.

A *Notice that the **Print area** and **Print titles** options are not available if you display the **Page Setup** dialog box from the **Print Preview** window.*

B *Check the **Gridlines, Black and white,** and **Row and column headings** boxes.*

Page Setup

| Page | Margins | Header/Footer | Sheet |

Print area:

Print titles

  Rows to repeat at top:

  Columns to repeat at left:

Print

☑ Gridlines   ☑ Row and column headings
☑ Black and white   Comments: (None)
☐ Draft quality

3. Click **OK,** and then examine the results in the Print Preview window.

4. Click the **Close** button to exit from Print Preview.

Set a Title Column

5. Choose **Window→Unfreeze Panes** to unfreeze the panes.

6. Use the Zoom Control to zoom to 75%.

7. If necessary, scroll up or down until Cells A1:A22 (all active cells in Column A) are visible.

8. Choose **File→Page Setup** from the menu bar.

9. Make sure the Sheet tab is active.

10. If necessary, drag the Page Setup dialog box to the side until Column A is visible.

(Continued on the next page)

11. Follow these steps to set the title column and adjust other options.

Ⓐ *Click in the **Columns to repeat at left** box.*

Ⓑ *Click the Column A heading in the worksheet. Notice that the symbols $A:$A appear in the **Columns to repeat at left** box. If you had selected Columns A and B, the symbols would read $A:$B, etc.*

Ⓒ *Uncheck the **Gridlines, Black and white,** and **Row and column headings** options.*

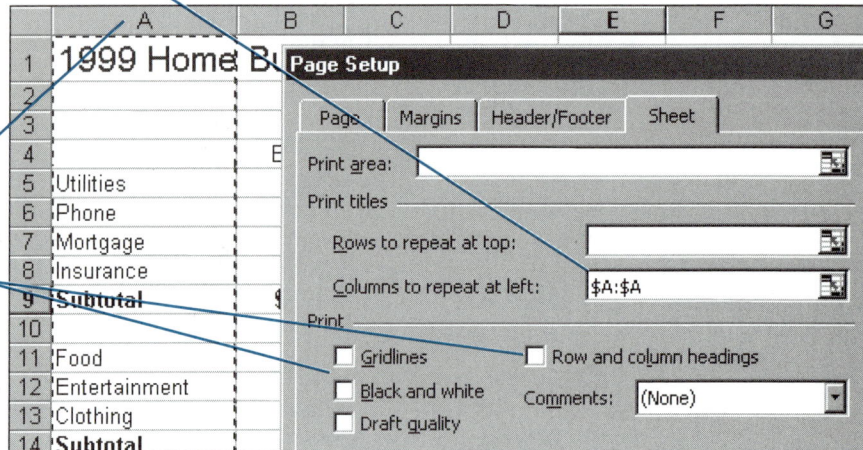

12. Click the **Print Preview** button, and notice Column A on the left side of the page.

13. Click the **Next** button, and Column A will be repeated on the second page.
It is now easy to identify the rows on both the first and second pages.

14. Click the **Setup** button, and notice that the Print titles section is unavailable.
Once again, you must display the Page Setup dialog box from the worksheet if you want to set print titles.

15. Click **OK** to close the **Page Setup** dialog box.

16. Take a few minutes to experiment with the Page Setup options.

17. Close Print Preview when you have finished experimenting.

Inserting Page Breaks

Excel satisfactorily formats most printed worksheets by inserting automatic page breaks when necessary. However, there are times where you may want to force a page break to occur. For example, in the budget worksheet, Excel may split a month by printing the budget column on the first page and the spent column on the second page. This is undesirable because the budget and spent columns for a given month should be printed side-by-side. You insert manual Page breaks with the **Insert→Page Break** command. Manual page breaks appear as dashed lines with slightly longer dashes than automatic page breaks.

Location of Manual Page Breaks

The **Insert→Page Break** command inserts page breaks to the left of the highlight and above the highlight. For this reason, you must position the highlight in the desired cell before issuing the command.

Removing Page Breaks

To remove a page break, position the highlight just below or to the left of the desired break. The **Insert→Remove Page Break** command will then remove the desired page break(s). If necessary, Excel will insert automatic page breaks after you remove manual page breaks.

Hands-On 5.9 Experiment with Page Breaks

Restore Print Options

1. Choose **File→Page Setup** from the menu bar.

2. Click the Margins tab, and set all four margins to 1".

3. Click the Sheet tab, and delete any codes or text in the Columns to repeat at left box.

4. Click **OK** to return to the worksheet.

Insert and Remove a Page Break

5. Notice the vertical dashed line between Columns L and M.
   This automatic page break "breaks the page" after the June Budget column.

6. Click Cell L1.
   In the next step, you will insert a manual page break. This will cause the automatic page break between Columns L and M to vanish. The automatic page break will be replaced by the manual page break. Also, the page break will be inserted to the left of the column with the highlight. The highlight is positioned in Row 1 because you only need to break the page horizontally. If the highlight is in Row 1, no page break will be inserted above the highlight (only to the left of the highlight). Your worksheet would print on several pages if you inserted the break further down the column.

7. Choose **Insert→Page Break** from the menu bar.
   The vertical dashed line should now be to the left of Column L.

8. Now choose **Insert→Remove Page Break.**
   The automatic page break should return between Columns L and M.

Page Break Preview

Page Break Preview shows where page breaks occur on a worksheet and which part of the worksheet will be printed. In Page Break Preview, areas of the worksheet that will be printed appear in white. Areas that will not print are shown in gray. You can also adjust the location of page breaks by dragging them in Page Break Preview. When you adjust page breaks using Page Break Preview, Excel automatically sets the Scaling percentage in the Page Setup dialog box to fit the worksheet within the page break boundaries you specify. You use the **View→Page Break Preview** command to switch to Page Break Preview. You return to the normal view mode with the **View→Normal** command.

*In **Page Break Preview**, you can drag the page break lines to change the page breaks. Excel scales the worksheet to fit within the boundaries you specify.*

Hands-On 5.10 Use Page Break Preview

1. Choose **View→Page Break Preview** from the menu bar.

2. If the Welcome to Page Break Preview dialog box appears, then click the **OK** button to close the dialog box.
   You should see a vertical, dark blue page break line near the middle of the worksheet.

3. Try dragging the blue page break line to the left or right.
   Notice that Excel shows you exactly which part of the worksheet will be printed on Page 1 and Page 2.

4. Drag the blue page break line until it is positioned between Columns O and P.

5. Click anywhere on Page 1, and then click the Print Preview button.
   Notice that the worksheet has been scaled to fit within the page break boundaries you specified.

6. Click the **Setup** button on the Print Preview toolbar, and then click the **Page** tab in the Page Setup dialog box.
   Notice that the Adjust to percentage has been reduced to make the page fit within the boundaries you specified.

7. Click **Cancel** to close the Page Setup dialog box.

8. Close the Print Preview window, and then choose **View**→**Normal** to return to the normal view.

9. Scroll to the right in your worksheet, and notice that a page break is positioned between Columns O and P.
   This is the page break you inserted by dragging the page break in Page Break Preview.

10. Click in Column P, and choose **Insert**→**Remove Page Break.**

11. Save the changes to your workbook, close the workbook, and continue with the end-of-lesson questions and exercises.

Concepts Review

True/False Questions

1. Sorting has the potential to damage worksheets, so you should always save before sorting.   TRUE   FALSE

2. The Sort Ascending ![button] button can only be used if you first select the desired rows.   TRUE   FALSE

3. The Sort dialog box lets you specify more than one sort key.   TRUE   FALSE

4. The Window→Freeze Panes command lets you view two sections of the worksheet at the same time.   TRUE   FALSE

5. Freezing the panes makes it easier to identify data in large worksheets.   TRUE   FALSE

6. The Page Setup dialog box provides access to many features that are useful when printing large worksheets.   TRUE   FALSE

7. Headers and footers have three sections.   TRUE   FALSE

8. Page Break Preview can be used to view page breaks, but you cannot change page breaks in this view.   TRUE   FALSE

Multiple-Choice Questions

1. Which columns and rows are frozen when the Window→Freeze Panes command is issued?
   a. Columns to the left of the highlight and rows above the highlight
   b. Columns to the left of the highlight and rows below the highlight
   c. Columns to the right of the highlight and rows below the highlight
   d. Columns to the right of the highlight and rows above the highlight

2. Which tab in the Page Setup dialog box lets you set the Landscape orientation?
   a. Page
   b. Margins
   c. Header/Footer
   d. Sheet

3. Assuming the current page is 1, how will the header Page &[Page] be printed?
   a. Page 1 of 1
   b. Page 1 of 2
   c. Page 1
   d. Page 1, Current Date

4. Which command is used to insert a manual page break?
   a. Format→Page Break
   b. Insert→Page Break
   c. CTRL + ENTER
   d. None of the above

Skill Builders

Skill Builder 5.1 Insert Formulas and Sort Rows

In this exercise, you will open a workbook that contains an accounts receivable aging report. You will use a formula to calculate the number of days the accounts are past due, and you will sort the rows. You will also use the TODAY function.

Create the Formulas

1. Open the workbook named **Skill Builder 5.1.**

2. Use the TODAY function to insert the current date in Cell C2.

3. Click Cell E5, and enter the formula **=TODAY()-C5**.

4. Use the Format Painter 🖌 to copy the General number format from a blank cell to Cell E5. *A whole number should be displayed in the cell.*

5. Use the fill handle to copy the formula down the column.

6. Click Cell F5, and enter the formula **=E5-30**.

7. Use the fill handle to copy the formula down the column.

Sort the Rows

8. Notice that the rows are currently sorted by invoice number in Column B.

9. Click Cell A5.

10. Click the Sort Ascending ⬇ button to sort the rows by the names in Column A.

11. Click Cell B5, and click the Sort Descending ⬇ button.

    The rows should be sorted in descending order by invoice number.

12. Sort the rows in descending order by the invoice amount. When you have finished, the largest invoice amount should be at the top of the list.

13. Save the changes, and then close the workbook.

Skill Builder 5.2 Use Multiple Sort Keys

In this exercise, you will use the Sort dialog box to sort worksheet rows using two sort keys.

1. Open the workbook named **Skill Builder 5.2.**

2. Click anywhere in the list of names, and choose **Data→Sort** from the menu bar.
   Excel will identify the list and select the correct rows. The header row will not be selected.

3. Set the Sort by key to **Lastname** in **Ascending** order.

4. Set the first Then by key to **Firstname** in **Ascending** order and click **OK.**
   Take a moment to study the results. Notice the rows with the same last names are grouped together. Those groups are then sorted by the first names.

(Continued on the next page)

5. Choose **Data→Sort** from the menu bar.

6. Make sure the Sort by key is set to Lastname in Ascending order.

7. Change the first Then by key to **Outstanding Balance** (it will appear as Outstanding once you choose it), and click **OK.**
   Notice that the rows are still grouped by last name, but the groups are now sorted according to the Outstanding Balance code in Column D.

8. Sort the rows in ascending order using the Outstanding Balance in Column D as the only sort key.
   There is no need to use the Sort dialog box because you are using just one sort key. Just click in Column D, and use the Sort Ascending button. All rows with an Outstanding Balance code of N should move to the top.

9. Save the changes, and then close the workbook.

Skill Builder 5.3 Create a Customized Footer

1. Open the **Hands-On Lesson 5** workbook that you used throughout the Hands-On exercises in this lesson.

2. Choose **File→Page Setup,** and click the Header/Footer tab.

3. Remove the header by clicking the header drop-down button and choosing **(none)** from the top of the list.

4. Click the **Custom Footer** button.

5. Follow these steps to create a customized footer and format the footer.

Ⓐ *Enter the text and codes in the left, center, and right sections as shown here. You will need to use the toolbar buttons to enter the codes.*

Ⓑ *Select the* Page &[Page] *text and code in the **Left section** by dragging the mouse over it.*

Left section:	Center section:	Right section:
Page &[Page]	Skill Builder 5.3	&[Date]

Ⓒ *Click the **Font** button, choose **Bold Italic** from the **Font** style list, and click **OK.***

Ⓓ *Apply bold and italics formatting to the **Center section** and the **Right section.***

6. Click **OK,** and the customized footer should be displayed in the Page Setup dialog box.

7. Click the **Print Preview** button on the dialog box.

8. Use the **Next** button to browse though the worksheet and check out the footer.

9. Close Print Preview, save the changes, and then close the workbook.

Skill Builder 5.4 Print a Large Worksheet on One Page

In this exercise, you will open a workbook on your exercise diskette. Your objective is to get the worksheet to print on a single page. You will accomplish this by using the Landscape orientation and Fit to options in Page Setup. You will also add a header and footer.

1. Open the workbook named **Skill Builder 5.4.**

2. Click the Print Preview ⬚ button.
   Notice that the worksheet currently is in a Portrait (vertical) orientation.

3. Use the **Next** button to browse though the pages, and you will notice there are three pages.
   In the remainder of this exercise, you will adjust settings in the Page Setup dialog box until this worksheet prints on a single page.

4. Use the **Previous** button to go back to Page 1.

5. Click the **Setup** button on the Print Preview toolbar.

6. Make sure the Page tab is active, and set the orientation to **Landscape.**

7. Click the **Fit to** button, and make sure the **Fit to** option is set to 1 pages wide by 1 pages tall.

8. Click the **Header/Footer** tab.

9. Choose the built-in header **Skill Builder 5.4.**

10. Choose the built-in footer **Page 1 of ?**

11. Click **OK,** and the worksheet should fit on one page.

12. Close Print Preview, save the changes, and then close the workbook.

Assessments

Assessment 5.1 Use Multiple Sort Keys

In this assessment, you will sort the rows in a worksheet using three sort keys.

1. Open the workbook named **Assessment 5.1.**

2. Use the Zoom Control to zoom to 75% of normal.
   This will allow you to see all the worksheet rows at the same time. Notice that the rows are currently sorted by 1999 Sales Volume in Column D.

3. Use the Sort dialog box to sort the rows using three sort keys as follows.

   ■ Key 1—Customer in Ascending order

   ■ Key 2—Division in Ascending order

   ■ Key 3—Key Contact in Ascending order

4. Format the numbers in Column D as Comma style with no decimals.

5. AutoFit all column widths.
   Your completed worksheet should match the following example.

6. Print the worksheet, save the changes, and then close the workbook.

	A	B	C	D
1	**1999 Orders**			
2				
3	**Customer**	**Division**	**Key Contact**	**1999 Sales Volume**
4	Alexis	Battery Division	Frank Jordan	3,303,336
5	Alexis	Battery Division	Richard Warren	1,605,476
6	Alexis	Battery Division	Susan Christopher	1,775,262
7	Alexis	Battery Division	William J. Pinckerton	4,831,410
8	Dimension Systems	Automotive	Michael Chricton	2,624,192
9	Dimension Systems	Automotive	Michael Wilson	3,473,122
10	Dimension Systems	Automotive	Stephen Crane	2,963,764
11	Dimension Systems	Large Vehicle	Bill Clayton	2,114,834
12	Dimension Systems	Large Vehicle	Carl Bartholomew	4,152,266
13	Dimension Systems	Large Vehicle	Larry Alexander	4,661,624
14	Qualtron	Computer Technology	Bill Thompson	2,454,406
15	Qualtron	Computer Technology	Dick Morris	1,435,690
16	Qualtron	Computer Technology	Sandy Princeton	2,793,978
17	Qualtron	Medical Techologies	Joe Gecko	3,133,550
18	Qualtron	Space Systems	Bill Rogers	1,945,048
19	Qualtron	Space Systems	Stacey Crawford	4,322,052
20	Qualtron	Space Systems	Stan Barnes	1,265,904
21	Qualtron	Space Systems	Wanda Wilson	3,812,694
22	Zenex	CAD	Alice Senton	4,491,838
23	Zenex	CAD	Joseph Harding	3,982,480
24	Zenex	Semiconductor	Ben Warren	3,642,908
25	Zenex	Semiconductor	Lois Lane	2,284,620

Assessment 5.2 Print a Large Worksheet on One Page

In this assessment, you will open a workbook from your exercise diskette. You will use the Page Setup dialog box to format the worksheet to print on one page. You will also include a header and footer in the printed worksheet.

1. Open the workbook named **Assessment 5.2.**

2. Use the Page Setup dialog box to format the worksheet to print on one page as shown below. You will need to change the orientation, add a header and footer, and change the margins or use the Fit to option.

3. Use Print Preview to check out the worksheet prior to printing.

4. Print the worksheet, save the changes, and then close the workbook.

Mary Cook 1999 Expenses

1999 Expenses for Mary Cook

	January	February	March	April	May	June	July	August	September	October	November	December
Cell Phone	245	270	295	320	345	370	205	220	235	250	265	280
Automobile	325	345	365	385	405	425	205	240	275	310	345	380
Entertainment	150	170	190	210	230	250	15	70	125	180	235	290
Miscellaneous	105	115	125	135	145	160	165	170	175	180	185	190

Selmar Systems   Pages 1 of 1   8/20/99

Critical Thinking

Critical Thinking 5.1 On Your Own

Carmen Brandow is an Administrative Assistant at Fremont Pet Supplies. Fremont is a whole-sale distributor of Pet Supplies to companies in Northern California. Carmen has asked you to set up a worksheet to track the number of orders and the total dollar value of those orders for Fremont's six largest customers. You have been instructed to record the information on a monthly basis for each month of the year. Carmen provides you with the following data to help you get started.

		January
Customer	**# of Orders**	**Total Dollar Value**
Northern California Pet Care	12	$ 2,568
My Pet Stores	16	$ 4,568
John Adams Pet Stores	23	$ 6,870
Pinnacle Pet Care	10	$ 1,250
West Side Pet Care	6	$ 5,900
Perfect Pets	52	$19,900

Set up a worksheet using the data shown above. Format the entries using the formats shown above. Set up the worksheet for all twelve months but only add numeric data for January, February, and March. You determine the numbers used for February and March. Center the headings January, February, etc. above the # of Orders and Total Dollar Value columns as shown above. Save the workbook as **Critical Thinking 5.1.**

Critical Thinking 5.2 On Your Own

Open the **Critical Thinking 5.1** workbook and save it as **Critical Thinking 5.2.** Insert a row above the row with the months. Use the Merge and Center option to center the headings Quarter 1, Quarter 2, Quarter 3, and Quarter 4 above the corresponding months. For example, the heading Quarter 1 should be centered above the January-March headings. If your worksheet doesn't have data for Quarters 2, 3, and 4, then add it now. You can copy the data from another quarter and paste the duplicate data into the new quarters. Add a totals row that calculates the total # of Orders and the Total Dollar Value of orders for each month. Set up the worksheet to print on four pages in portrait orientation. Each page should include the headings and data for one quarter. For example, all of the Quarter 1 information will print on the first page, Quarter 2 will print on the second page, etc. Make sure that the Customer names in Column A are repeated on every printed page. Format the worksheet as desired.

Critical Thinking 5.3 On Your Own

Brittany Johnson is the manager of the accounting department of Kids in Cloth. Kids in Cloth is a provider of reusable cloth baby diapers. Some aspects of Kids in Cloth's business can be quite messy, but not Brittany's Accounting Department. Brittany has asked you to prepare a work-sheet that lists each customer account and the number of diapers used on a weekly basis. Set up a worksheet to track the information requested by Brittany. Use customer numbers beginning with the number 100 and continuing sequentially through 200. Use the headings Week 1, Week 2, etc. through Week 52. This may seem like a lot of data entry but you can do this very rapidly using the fill handle. Also, enter a number in the first cell requiring a number and then copy the number to all other cells in the worksheet. Each cell will have the same number, but this is a qiuck way to fill the sheet with data. Set up the worksheet to print in portrait orientation two pages high by five pages wide. Make sure the customer numbers and the weeks are printed on every page. Don't print the worksheet, just use Print Preview to preview your work. Save the workbook as **Critical Thinking 5.3.**

Critical Thinking 5.4 Web Research

Open the **Critical Thinking 5.2** workbook and save it as **Critical Thinking 5.4.** Use Internet Explorer and a search engine of your choice to locate potential customers for Fremont Pet Supplies in Northern California. Enter the customer names, location (city), Web site URLs, and telephone numbers in Sheet 2 of the workbook. Also include any information that may be useful to the sales force at Fremont Pet Supplies, such as the size of the potential customer and the types of pets to which they cater. Include as many potential customers as you can find. When you have finished, format the worksheet to print on a single page. You can use either portrait or landscape orientations.

Critical Thinking 5.5 Web Research

Martha Robinson is the owner of Martha's books. In recent years, Martha's business has come under intense competitive pressure from online booksellers. Martha has hired you to conduct a research project to help her analyze the threat posed by her deep-pocketed competitors. Locate three online booksellers and visit their Web sites to get pricing information on six different book titles. You choose the book titles or use titles you find on the sites. Set up a worksheet with the three online bookseller's names and URL's, the six titles you have chosen, the ISBN's of the titles, the suggested retail price, actual selling price, freight charges, and Martha's price for the same titles (you determine Martha's prices). Use a formula to calculate the total price of the online sellers books, which includes the selling price plus freight. Format all total cells with a blue color. For each title, use a formula to calculate the difference between Martha's price and the average price of the three online booksellers. Format all different cells with a distinctive color. Set up the worksheet to print on a single page in landscape orientation. Save the workbook as **Critical Thinking 5.5.**

Critical Thinking 5.6 As a Group

Exchange your Critical Thinking 5.5 data with three classmates. Add their data to your workbook. You should have approximately 24 titles in your workbook when finished. If you do this in the most efficient manner possible, you won't need to type a single character of data. Keep in mind that you may need to rearrange their worksheets before adding the data to your worksheet. Save your updated workbook as **Critical Thinking 5.6.**

LESSON 6

Creating an Impact with Charts

In this lesson, you will use Excel's Chart Wizard to create various types of charts. Charting is an important skill to have when using worksheets because comparisons, trends, and other relationships are often conveyed more effectively with charts. You will use the Chart Wizard to create bar charts, column charts, line charts, and pie charts. In addition, you will learn how to edit and format chart objects.

In This Lesson

Case Study

Cynthia Robbins is the founder and CEO of AutoSoft—a rapidly growing software development company. Cynthia has asked her sales manager, Gary Roberts, to prepare several charts depicting revenue for the 1999 fiscal year. Cynthia wants charts that compare sales in the various quarters, the growth trend throughout the year, and the contributions of each sales rep to the total company sales. Gary uses Excel's Chart Wizard to produce impressive charts that meet Cynthia's high standards.

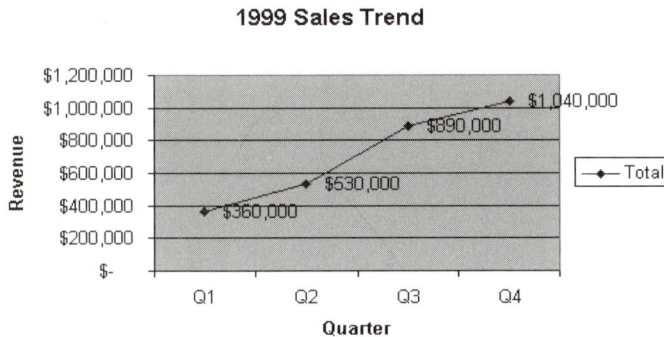

A column chart

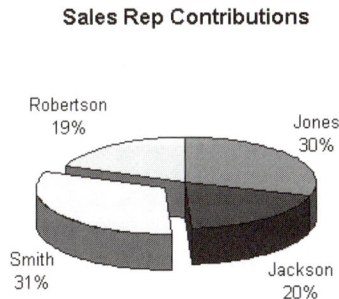

A line chart

A pie chart

Managing Worksheets

Excel displays three worksheets in a new workbook. You can insert new worksheets up to a maximum of 255 sheets per workbook. Each worksheet is identified by a tab located at the bottom of the sheet. You can rename, insert, delete, move, and copy worksheets.

Quick Reference

MANAGING WORKSHEETS

Task	Procedure
Activate worksheet.	Click the desired worksheet tab.
Rename worksheet.	Double-click the worksheet tab, type a new name, and tap (ENTER).
Insert worksheet.	Click anywhere in the desired worksheet and choose **Insert→Worksheet**. The new worksheet is inserted to the left of the current sheet.
Delete worksheet.	Click anywhere in the desired worksheet, choose **Edit→Delete Sheet**, and click **OK**.
Move worksheet.	Drag the worksheet tab to the desired position in the worksheet order.
Copy worksheet.	Choose **Edit→Move** or **Copy Sheet**, choose the desired position in the Before sheet box, click the **Create a copy box**, and click **OK**.

Hands-On 6.1 Experiment with Worksheets

1. Open the workbook named **Hands-On Lesson 6**.

2. Follow these steps to rename Sheet1.

Ⓐ *Double-click the* Sheet1 *tab at the bottom of the worksheet. The name* Sheet1 *will become selected.*

Ⓑ *Type the name* **Sales** *as shown here.*

Ⓒ *Tap* (ENTER) *to complete the name change.*

3. Follow these steps to move the sheet.

Ⓐ *Position the mouse pointer on the* Sales *sheet tab.*

Ⓑ *Drag the tab to the right of the* Sheet3 *tab, as shown here.*

Ⓒ *Release the mouse button to complete the move.*

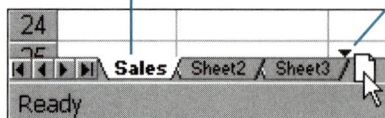

4. Now drag the Sales sheet back to the first position in the sheet order.

5. Click the Sheet3 tab and choose **Edit→Delete Sheet** from the menu bar.

6. Click **OK** to complete the deletion.

7. Try clicking Undo ⟲, and notice that the sheet cannot be restored.
   *Worksheets are permanently deleted when you issue the **Edit→Delete Sheet** command. The only way to recover a deleted sheet is to close the workbook without saving, and then reopen the workbook.*

8. Choose **Insert→Worksheet** from the menu bar.
   A new sheet will be inserted to the left of the current sheet.

9. Drag the new sheet to the right of Sheet2, and rename it Sheet3.

10. Click the **Sales** sheet tab, and continue with the next topic.

Chart Concepts

It is often easier to interpret numerical data if it is presented in a chart. Excel lets you create and modify a variety of charts. Excel provides 14 major chart types. Each chart type also has several subtypes from which you can choose. Excel literally has a chart for every occasion.

Chart Placement

You can embed a chart in a worksheet so that it appears alongside the worksheet data. You can also place a chart on a separate worksheet. This prevents the chart from cluttering the worksheet containing the data. Regardless of their placement, charts are always linked to the data from which they were created. Charts are automatically updated when worksheet data changes.

Chart Types

Each chart type represents data in a different manner. You can present the same data in completely different ways by changing the chart type. For this reason, you should always use the chart type that most effectively represents your data.

User-Defined Charts

Excel lets you create and save customized charts to meet your particular needs. For example, you could create a customized chart containing the name of your company and your company color(s) in the background. You could save the chart and then use it as the basis for all new charts of that type.

Creating Charts with the Chart Wizard

Excel's Chart Wizard 📊 guides you through each step of chart creation. You can also edit and enhance a chart after it has been created. The first, and arguably the most important step in creating a chart, is to select the data you want included in the chart. Many beginners find this step to be the most difficult because they are unsure how Excel will interpret the selected data. You will receive plenty of practice selecting data in this lesson.

Column Charts and Bar Charts

Column charts compare values (numbers) using vertical bars. Bar charts compare values using horizontal bars. Each column or bar represents a value from the worksheet. Column charts and bar charts are most useful for comparing sets of values.

Category Axis and Value Axis

The horizontal line that forms the base of a column chart or bar chart is called the *category axis*. The category axis typically measures units of time such as days, months, or quarters. The vertical line on the left side of a column chart or bar chart is known as the *value axis*. The value axis typically measures values such as dollars. Most chart types (including column charts and bar charts) have a category and value axis. The following illustrations show the column chart you will create in the next few exercises. The illustrations show the objects that are present on most column charts and the corresponding data that was used to create the chart. Take a few minutes to study these illustrations carefully.

The chart below was created using the selected data shown here. Notice the Total *row was not included in the selection. The column chart compares the sales numbers for the individual quarters, but it does not include the total sales from Row 9.*

	A	B	C	D	E
1	Autosoft 1999 Quarterly Sales				
2					
3		Q1	Q2	Q3	Q4
4	Jones	100,000	230,000	280,000	230,000
5	Jackson	50,000	130,000	170,000	200,000
6	Smith	120,000	120,000	320,000	340,000
7	Robertson	90,000	50,000	120,000	270,000
8					
9	Total	$ 360,000	$ 530,000	$ 890,000	$ 1,040,000

This is the vertical value axis. The numbering scale (0–350,000) was created by Excel after it determined the range of values that were included in the chart.

Notice the chart includes a chart title (Sales Performance), a value axis title (Sales), and a category axis title (Quarter). The Chart Wizard lets you specify the titles when you create the chart.

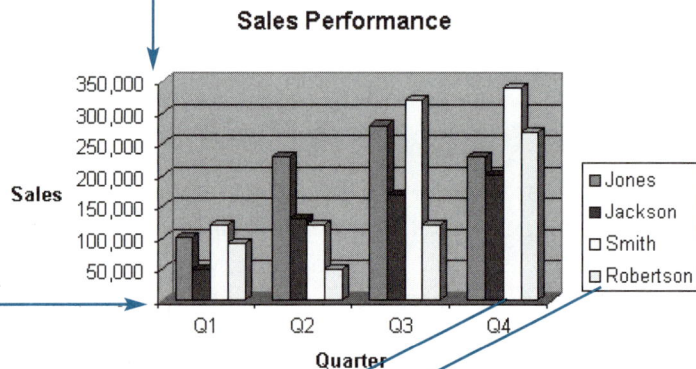

Sales Performance

This is the horizontal category axis. Notice the category axis labels (Q1, Q2, Q3, and Q4) were taken from Row 3 of the selected worksheet cells.

Notice the chart columns. The columns represent values from the various data series. The first data series is the Jones' numbers in Row 4. The first column in each quarter represents the Jones' numbers.

This is a legend that identifies the various columns. Notice that the legend text (Jones, Jackson, Smith, and Robertson) was taken from the first column of the selected worksheet cells.

The Hands-On Lesson 6 workbook should still be open from the previous exercise.

Create a Column Chart on a Separate Chart Sheet

1. Select the range **A3:E7** as shown on the previous page.

2. Click the **Chart Wizard** 📊 button on the Standard toolbar.
   The Chart Wizard dialog box will appear.

3. Follow these steps to explore the dialog box.

Ⓐ *Click the **Custom Types** tab. This tab displays built-in chart types that can be modified and saved as customized charts.*

Ⓑ *Click the **Standard Types** tab, and check out the various chart types by clicking them on this list.*

Ⓒ *Choose the* Column *type when you have finished exploring. Also, make sure the first subtype is chosen on the right side of the dialog box.*

Ⓓ *Press and hold the mouse pointer on this button to see a sample of your chart.*

Ⓔ *Click the **Next** button.*

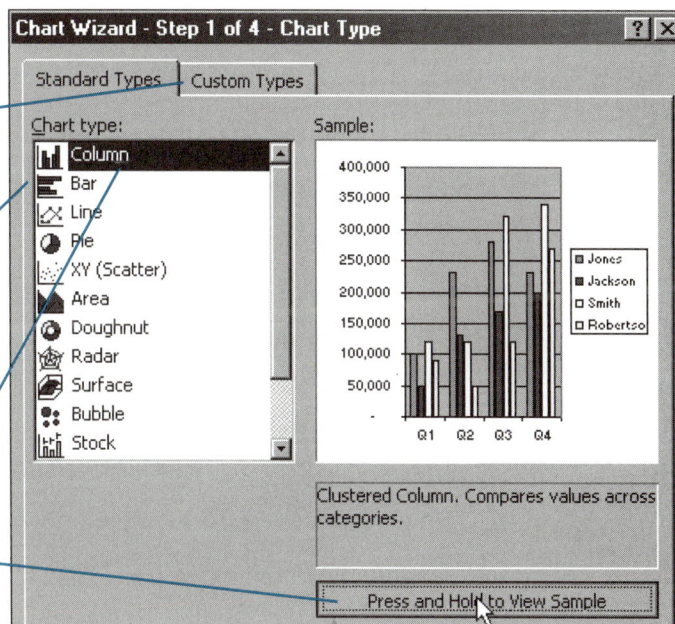

The Chart Wizard—Step 2 of 4 *box will appear. This box lets you choose a different range of cells. Notice that the range in the dialog box is =Sales!$A$3:$E$7. Sales is the worksheet name, and the dollar signs indicate that these are absolute cell references. For now, just ignore the dollar signs, and think of the range as A3:E7.*

4. The range Sales!$A$3:$E$7 is correct, so click the **Next** button.
   The Step 3 box contains 6 tabs that let you set various chart options. You will explore these options in the next few steps.

5. Click the **Titles** tab and note the three available titles.
   You will add titles to a chart in the next exercise.

6. Click the **Axes** tab.
   The options on the Axes tab let you hide the labels on the category axis and value axis. You will almost always want to leave these options set to the default settings.

7. Click the **Gridlines** tab.
   Gridlines help identify the values in the chart. Your chart should have major gridlines for the value axis displayed. The gridlines are the horizontal lines across the chart.

8. Feel free to click the various gridlines boxes and notice how they appear in the Preview window.

9. Click the **Legend** tab.

Notice the legend on the right side of the Preview window. The legend identifies the various columns. For example, the columns for Jones are identified by a color that also appears in the legend.

10. Remove the check from the Show legend box, and the legend will vanish.

11. Click the **Show legend** box to redisplay the legend.

12. Click the **Data Labels** tab.

Data labels display the values from the worksheet on top of the columns.

13. Click the **Show value** option to display values at the top of each column.

The numbers will be very crowded in the Preview window.

14. Click the **Show Label** option, and then click the **None** option to remove the data labels.

15. Click the **Data Table** tab.

16. Click the **Show data table** check box, and a table will appear below the Preview chart.

17. Take a moment to check out the data table, then remove the check from the Show data table box.

18. Click the **Next** button, and the Step 4 of 4 box will appear.

19. Click the **As new sheet** option.

This option instructs Excel to create the chart on a separate chart sheet.

20. Click the **Finish** button.

Look at the sheet tabs, and notice that the chart has been created on a new sheet named Chart1.

21. Double-click the **Chart1** sheet tab.

22. Type the new name **Column Chart**, and tap (ENTER) to complete the name change.

Create an Embedded 3-D Column Chart

23. Click the **Sales** sheet tab. The range A3:E7 should still be selected.

24. Click the **Chart Wizard** button.

25. Choose the fourth column chart subtype, as shown to the right.

This subtype is known as a clustered column with a 3-D visual effect.

26. Click the **Next** button, then click **Next** again on the Step 2 of 4 box.

27. Click the **Titles** tab, and follow these steps in the Step 3 of 4 box.

Ⓐ *Enter the titles shown here.*

Ⓑ *Notice the position of the various titles in the Preview window.*

28. Click the **Next** button.

29. Leave the chart location set to **As object in** on the Step 4 of 4 box and click **Finish.**
Excel will embed the chart in your worksheet. The Chart toolbar will most likely appear as well.

Previewing and Printing Charts

You can use the Print Preview 🔍 and Print 🖨 buttons to preview or print charts. If a chart is on a separate chart sheet, you must first activate it by clicking the sheet tab. If a chart is embedded, you must first select the chart before clicking the Print Preview or Print buttons.

Hands-On 6.3 Use Print Preview and Print a Chart

1. Click anywhere in the worksheet to deselect the chart.

2. Click the Print Preview 🔍 button.
Notice that both the worksheet and part or all of the embedded chart are displayed.

3. Click the **Close** button on the Print Preview toolbar.

4. Click in the blank area near one of the corners of the chart.
Black squares known as sizing handles should appear on the corners and edges of the chart. Sizing handles indicate that the chart or one of the chart objects is selected.

5. Click the Print Preview 🔍 button, and only the chart should be displayed.
At this point, you could print the chart by using the Print button on the Print Preview toolbar. However, you will close the chart and then print it on the separate chart sheet.

6. Click the **Close** button on the Print Preview toolbar.

7. Click the **Column Chart** worksheet tab to activate that worksheet.

8. Click the Print Preview 🔍 button, and notice that the chart is displayed.
You don't need to select a chart prior to printing if it is on a separate chart sheet.

(Continued on the next page)

9. Close the Print Preview window, and then click the Print 🖶 button.

10. Retrieve your printout from the printer.
    Your chart will be printed in shades of gray unless you have a color printer.

Moving and Sizing Embedded Charts

You can easily move and size embedded charts and other objects. You must select a chart or other object before you can move, size, or modify the object. To select a chart, you click anywhere in the Chart Area. The Chart Area is the blank area just inside the border of the chart where no other objects are present. Small squares called sizing handles appear on the corners and four sides of a selected chart.

Task	Procedure
Move an embedded chart.	Drag the selected chart to a new location.
Change the chart size.	Drag any sizing handle.
Change the size while maintaining original proportions.	Press (SHIFT) while dragging a corner-sizing handle.

Hands-On 6.4 Move and Size the Embedded Chart

1. Click the **Sales** worksheet tab to activate that worksheet.

2. Click anywhere outside of the chart to deselect the chart.
   The sizing handles will vanish.

3. Use the Zoom Control to zoom to 50% of normal.
   This will give you plenty of room to move and size the chart.

4. Follow these steps to move and size the chart.

Ⓐ *Click in the Chart Area (the blank area inside of the chart border), and the sizing handles will reappear.*

Ⓑ *Position the mouse pointer in the Chart Area, and drag the chart to a new location.*

Ⓒ *Point to a corner-sizing-handle, and the Adjust pointer will appear.*

Ⓓ *Press the (SHIFT) key while you drag the sizing handle to change both the width and height proportionally.*

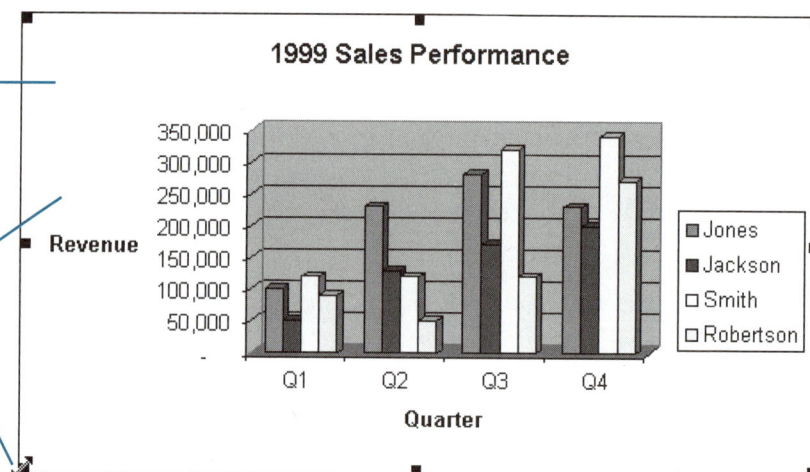

Ⓔ *Move the chart below the worksheet data, and adjust the size until the chart has the same width as the data.*

1999 Sales Performance

Revenue — 350,000 / 300,000 / 250,000 / 200,000 / 150,000 / 100,000 / 50,000 / -

Quarter — Q1, Q2, Q3, Q4

Legend: Jones, Jackson, Smith, Robertson

5. Click anywhere outside of the chart to deselect it, then zoom to 100%.

6. Take a moment to study your chart and the worksheet data that was used to create it.
   Make sure you understand the relationship between the columns and the worksheet data.

7. Click Cell **B4.**

8. Enter the number **300000** (five zeros) and watch the first column in the chart rise.
   Charts are linked to the worksheet data. They always reflect changes in the data even if they are placed in a separate chart sheet.

9. Click Cell **B4** again, and enter the number **1000000** (six zeros).
   Notice that 1000000 is much larger than the other numbers in the worksheet. Notice how the other columns are very small, and it is difficult to determine their values in the chart. The large number changes the scale of the value axis so much that it makes the chart difficult to interpret.

10. Click Cell **B4** again, and enter the number **100000** (five zeros).

11. Save the changes, and continue with the next topic.

Line Charts

Line charts are most useful for comparing trends over a period of time. For example, line charts are often used to show stock market activity where the upward or downward trend is important. Like column charts, line charts also have a category axis and value axis. Line charts also use the same or similar objects as column charts. The illustration below shows a line chart depicting the trend in quarterly sales throughout the year. Take a moment to study the illustration and the accompanying worksheet.

The chart below was created using the selected data shown here. Notice that the data is in two separate ranges. You will use the (CTRL) *key to select these non-contiguous ranges. This will let you chart just the totals for each quarter, and the Q1–Q4 labels.*

3		Q1	Q2	Q3	Q4
4	Jones	100,000	230,000	280,000	230,000
5	Jackson	50,000	130,000	170,000	200,000
6	Smith	120,000	120,000	320,000	340,000
7	Robertson	90,000	50,000	120,000	270,000
8					
9	Total	$ 360,000	$ 530,000	$ 890,000	$ 1,040,000

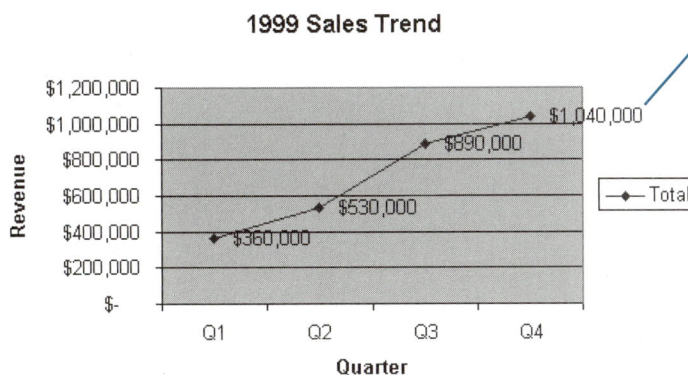

1999 Sales Trend

This is a data label. Data labels show the precise value of the various data points. You can use data labels with any chart type.

The line chart clearly depicts the upward trend in sales volume.

In this exercise, you will create a line chart in the Sales sheet. When you are finished, the Sales sheet will contain the data and both the column and line charts.

Shrink and Move the Column Chart

1. Click in the chart area of the column chart, and sizing handles will appear on the chart border.

2. Press the (SHIFT) key while dragging a corner-sizing handle until the chart is very small (approximately 1″ high).
   Pressing (SHIFT) *while sizing the chart maintains the proportions. You will increase the size of the chart later in this exercise.*

3. Position the mouse pointer in the chart area, and drag the chart to the top-right corner of the screen (just to the right of the worksheet data).

4. Click outside the chart to deselect it.

Create the Line Chart

5. Follow these steps to select the data for the line chart.

3		Q1	Q2	Q3	Q4
4	Jones	100,000	230,000	280,000	230,000
5	Jackson	50,000	130,000	170,000	200,000
6	Smith	120,000	120,000	320,000	340,000
7	Robertson	90,000	50,000	120,000	270,000
8					
9	Total	$ 360,000	$ 530,000	$ 890,000	$ 1,040,000

Ⓐ *Select the range A3:E3.*

Ⓑ *Press the* (CTRL) *key while you select the range A9:E9. Both ranges should be selected.*

6. Click the Chart Wizard 📊 button.

7. Choose Line from the Chart type list, and choose the fourth subtype, as shown to the right.

8. Click **Next** twice to display the Step 3 of 4 box.

9. If necessary, click the **Titles** tab on the Step 3 of 4 box.

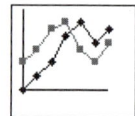

10. Enter the titles in the Step 3 of 4 box as shown below.

When you have completed entering the titles, your sample chart should match the chart shown in the following illustration.

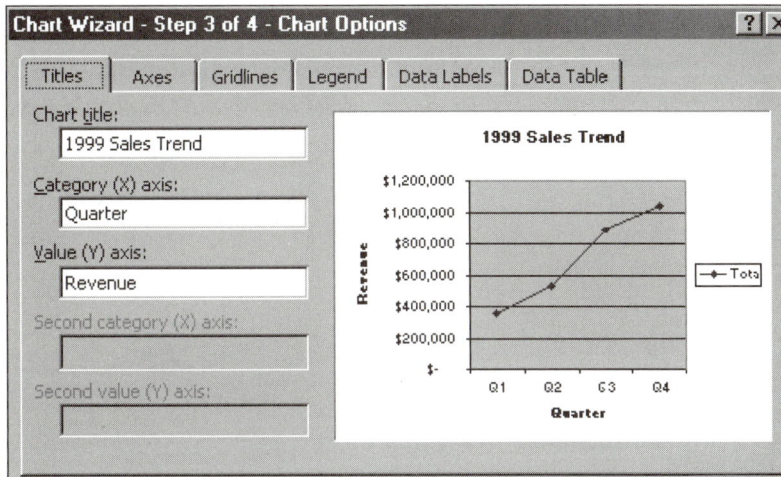

11. Click the **Finish** button.

There was no need to click Next on the Step 4 of 4 box because we want the chart embedded in the current worksheet. You can click Finish at any step in the Chart Wizard.

12. Take a few moments to examine your chart. In particular, notice the relationship between the data and the points on the line.

Pie Charts

Pie charts are useful for comparing parts of a whole. For example, pie charts are often used in budgets to show how the budget is allocated. You typically select two sets of data when creating a pie chart. You select the values to be represented by the pie slices and labels to identify the slices. The following illustration shows a worksheet and accompanying 3-D pie chart. Notice that the worksheet has a total column. You will create the total column in the next exercise.

3		Q1	Q2	Q3	Q4	Total
4	Jones	100,000	230,000	280,000	230,000	840,000
5	Jackson	50,000	130,000	170,000	200,000	550,000
6	Smith	120,000	120,000	320,000	340,000	900,000
7	Robertson	90,000	50,000	120,000	270,000	530,000

The names in Column A will become labels on the pie slices. The numbers in Column F will determine the size of the slices.

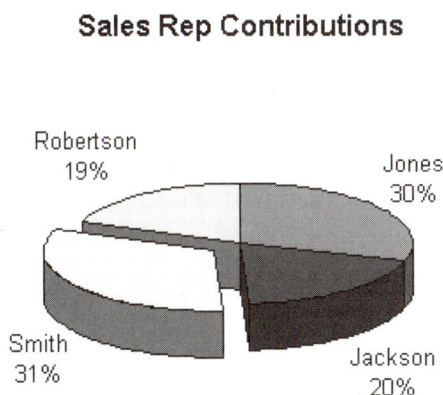

Sales Rep Contributions

Excel calculates the percentages based upon the numbers you select. Notice that the Smith slice is "exploded" out from the pie.

1. Click Cell **F3,** and enter the word **Total** (you may need to move the column chart or line chart).

2. Select the range F4:F7, and use AutoSum $\boxed{\Sigma}$ to compute the totals for Column F.
   The totals calculate the total annual sales for each sales rep. Your totals should match those shown in the preceding illustration.

3. Select the ranges A4:A7 and F4:F7 as shown in the preceding illustration (you will need to use the (CTRL) key when selecting the second range).

4. Click the Chart Wizard 📊 button.

5. Choose Pie from the Chart type list, and choose the second subtype as shown to the right.

6. Click **Next** twice to display the Step 3 of 4 box.

7. If necessary, click the *Titles* tab on the Step 3 of 4 box.

8. Type **Sales Rep Contributions** as the Chart title.

9. Click the *Legend* tab, and remove the check from the Show legend box.
   The legend won't be needed because you will add data labels in the next step.

10. Click the *Data Labels* tab, and choose the **Show label and percent** option.
    Each pie slice should have the sales rep name and percentage of the total sales displayed.

11. Click **Next** to display the Step 4 of 4 box.

12. Choose the **As new sheet** option, and type the name **Pie Chart** in the As new sheet box.

13. Click the **Finish** button.
    Notice that the chart has been created on a separate sheet, and that the name Pie Chart has been assigned to the new sheet. The sheet was named Pie Chart because you typed this name in the As new sheet box in Step 12.

14. Save the changes to your workbook, and continue with the next topic.

Modifying Charts

You can modify any chart object after the chart has been created. For example, you can add or remove objects, such as legends or data labels. You can change the size, font, and color of titles. You can even move an embedded chart to a separate chart sheet and vice versa.

Using the Chart Wizard to Modify Charts

You can change the setup of a chart using the Chart Wizard. Simply click the desired embedded chart, or click a separate chart sheet, and then click the Chart Wizard button. You can move through all four screens in the Chart Wizard, choosing options as you do when a chart is first created.

The Chart Menu

When you activate a separate chart sheet or click an embedded chart, a Chart option appears on the menu bar. The first four options on the Chart menu display the same screens that appear in the Chart Wizard. You can add, remove, or modify chart objects using the desired screen(s) and change the chart location from embedded to separate sheet and vice versa. The 3-D View option on the Chart menu is useful for changing the elevation and rotation of pie charts.

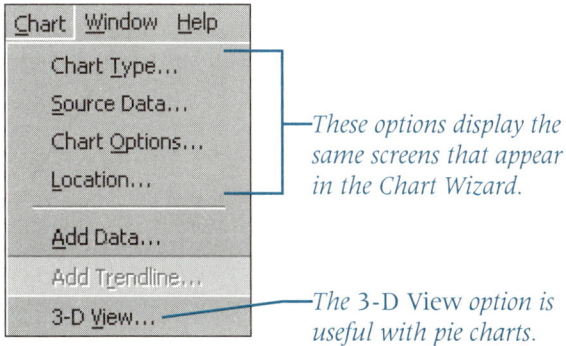

These options display the same screens that appear in the Chart Wizard.

The 3-D View option is useful with pie charts.

Hands-On 6.7 Use the Chart Wizard and the Chart Menu

Move the Line Chart to a Separate Sheet

1. Click the **Sales** sheet tab.

2. Click in the chart area of the line chart, and sizing handles should appear on the chart borders.
   Notice that the Chart option now appears on the menu bar because a chart is selected.

3. Choose **Chart→Location** from the menu bar.
   Notice that the dialog box that appears is the same dialog box that appears in the fourth step of the Chart Wizard.

4. Choose the **As new sheet** option, and type **Line Chart** in the As new sheet box.

5. Click **OK** to move the chart to a separate chart sheet.
   Notice that the Chart option is available on the menu bar even though the chart is not selected. The Chart option is always available in chart sheets.

6. Choose **Chart→Location** from the menu bar.

7. Choose the **As object in** option and choose **Sales** from the drop-down list of sheet names.

8. Click **OK** to move the chart back into the Sales sheet as an embedded chart.

9. Now move the chart back to a separate chart sheet named Line Chart as you did in steps 2 through 5.

Add Data Labels to the Column Chart

10. Click the **Sales** sheet tab.

11. Click in the chart area of the column chart to select the chart.

12. Now drag the chart below the worksheet data.

(Continued on the next page)

13. Press the (SHIFT) key while dragging a corner-sizing handle until the chart is as wide as the worksheet data. If necessary, adjust the chart position until it is just below the data.

14. Click the Chart Wizard 📊 button.

15. Click **Next** twice, and then click the **Data Labels** tab.
    Notice that the same screens appear as when you created a new chart.

16. Choose the **Show value** option, and click the **Finish** button.
    Excel displays data labels at the top of each column. The data labels display the actual values from the worksheet. Notice, however, that the data labels are too crowded. Data labels aren't really appropriate in this column chart because they crowd the chart.

17. Make sure the chart is still selected, and choose **Chart→Chart Options** from the menu bar.
    Notice that this is the same screen that appears in Step 3 of the Chart Wizard.

18. Choose **None** on the Data Labels tab, and click **OK** to remove the data labels.

19. Feel free to experiment with the Chart menu and the Chart Wizard, and then continue with the next topic.

Chart Objects

Charts are composed of various objects. For example, the legends, titles, and columns are all types of objects. You must select an object before you can perform an action on that object. You can select an object by clicking it with the mouse. Once an object is selected, you can delete, move, size, and format the object. You delete a selected object by tapping the (DELETE) key. You move a selected object by dragging it with the mouse. You change the size of a selected object by dragging a sizing handle.

Formatting Chart Objects

You can use buttons on the Formatting toolbar to format titles and other objects containing text. You can also use the Fill Color button on the Formatting toolbar to apply fill colors and fill effects to selected objects.

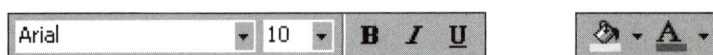

These buttons on the Formatting toolbar can be used to format text objects and add fill colors to objects.

Hands-On 6.8 Format Titles, and Fill the Chart Area

Change Text in the Titles

1. Click the chart title in the column chart, and it will become selected.

2. Click the mouse pointer I just in front of the word Performance in the title.
   The flashing insertion point should be just in front of the word Performance.

3. Type the word **Rep** and tap the (SPACE BAR) to make the title "1999 Sales Rep Performance."

4. Click the "Revenue" title (the title on the left side of the chart), and it will become selected.

5. Now select the word **Revenue** within the title box by double-clicking the word.

6. Type the replacement word `Sales`.

Format the Titles

7. Click the **Chart Title** ("1999 Sales Rep Performance").

8. Click the Font Color ![A] drop-down button on the Formatting toolbar, and choose a blue color.

9. Format the "Sales" and "Quarter" titles with the same blue color.

Apply a Fill Color to the Chart Area

10. Click the chart area to select the entire chart.

11. Click the Fill Color ![fill] drop-down button on the Formatting toolbar, and choose a light fill color.
    The entire chart area should be filled.

12. Feel free to experiment with the formatting techniques discussed in this exercise.

The Chart Toolbar

The Chart toolbar appears when a chart sheet is active, or when an embedded chart is selected. The Chart toolbar is used primarily for formatting chart objects. You can use the **View→Toolbars→Chart** command to display the Chart toolbar if it does not automatically appear.

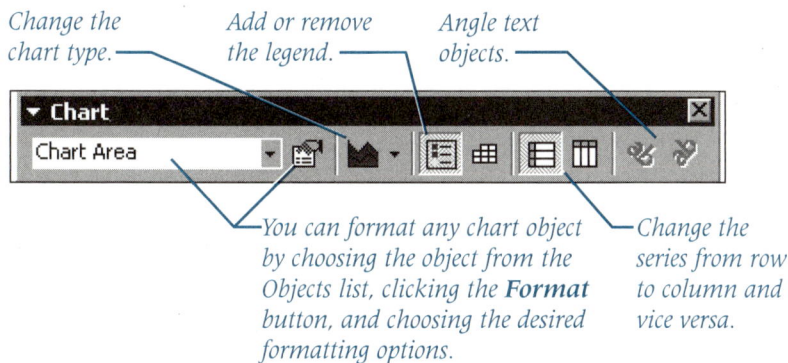

Change the chart type.

Add or remove the legend.

Angle text objects.

*You can format any chart object by choosing the object from the Objects list, clicking the **Format** button, and choosing the desired formatting options.*

Change the series from row to column and vice versa.

Hands-On 6.9 Use the Chart Toolbar

Change the Orientation of the Sales Title

1. Choose **View→Toolbars** from the menu bar.

2. If the Chart option is already checked, close the menu by clicking in the worksheet. Otherwise, choose Chart and the Chart toolbar will appear.
   The Chart toolbar may be anchored above the worksheet, or it may float in the worksheet area.

3. Click the "Sales" title on the left side of the chart.
   All of the buttons on the Chart toolbar should now be available.

(Continued on the next page)

4. Follow these steps to display a formatting box for the title.

Ⓐ *Notice that* Value Axis Title *is displayed in the Chart Objects box. The Chart Objects box always displays the name of the selected object. You can also choose the object you wish to format from the drop down list.*

▾ **Chart** ✕
Value Axis Title ▾

Ⓑ *Click the* **Format** *button to display the* Format Axis Title *dialog box.*

5. Click the various dialog box tabs, and notice that you can format the title text, apply a font color, and set other formatting options.

6. Click the **Alignment** tab.

7. Follow these steps to change the orientation to vertical.

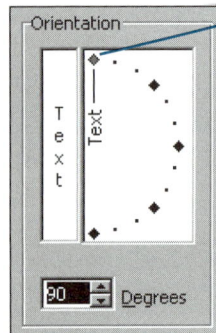

Orientation

Ⓐ *Click here to set the orientation to 90 degrees.*

Ⓑ *Click* **OK** *and the title will have a vertical orientation.*

90 Degrees

Experiment with the Chart Toolbar

8. Click in the chart area to select the entire chart.

9. Follow these steps to explore the Chart toolbar.

Ⓐ *Click the* **Chart Type** *drop down button and choose a chart type such as 3-D Cylinder from the bottom row of the list.*

▾ **Chart** ✕
Legend ▾

Ⓑ *Click* **Undo** *to reverse the change.*

Ⓒ *Click the* **Legend** *button to remove the legend and then click the button again to reapply the legend.*

10. Feel free to experiment with the options on the Chart toolbar.

Exploding Pie Slices

You can make a pie slice stand out from the rest of a pic chart by *exploding* the slice. An exploded slice is pulled out from the rest of the pie. You can also explode all pie slices, thus breaking the pie into individual pieces.

EXPLODING PIE CHARTS

Explode one slice.	■ Click once to select the entire pie.
	■ Click the slice you wish to explode.
	■ Drag the slice out from the pie.
Explode all slices.	■ Click once to select the pie.
	■ Drag any slice (without clicking first), and all slices will separate.
Restore an exploded slice or an exploded pie.	■ Select the entire pie, and drag any exploded slice back into the pie.

Hands-On 6.10 Explode Pie Slices

Explode the Smith Slice

1. Click the **Pie Chart** worksheet tab to activate the sheet.

2. Click in the chart area to make sure the pie is not selected.

3. Click anywhere on the pie, and the entire pie will become selected.

4. Now click once on the Smith slice to select just that slice.

5. Follow this step to explode the Smith slice.

Ⓐ *Position the mouse pointer on the* Smith *slice and drag it out of the pie, as shown here.*

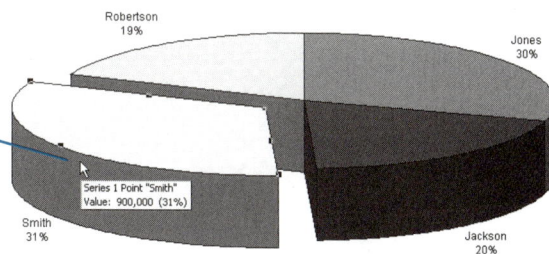

Robertson 19%
Jones 30%
Series 1 Point "Smith"
Value: 900,000 (31%)
Smith 31%
Jackson 20%

Explode All Slices

6. Drag the Smith slice back until the pie is whole again.

7. Click outside of the pie to deselect it.

8. Click anywhere on the pie, and the entire pie will become selected.

9. Drag any slice out of the pie, and all of the slices will explode.

10. Reverse the explosion by dragging any slice back to the center of the pie.

11. Now explode just the Smith slice again.

Changing the Rotation and Elevation of Pie Charts

You can rotate a pie chart to bring an important slice into view. Likewise, you can change the elevation to make an important slice more noticeable. You change the rotation and elevation using options on the 3-D View dialog box. The 3-D View dialog box is displayed with the **Chart→3-D View** command.

Hands-On 6.11 Change the Rotation and Elevation

1. Click outside of the pie, and then click the pie to make sure the entire pie is selected.

2. Choose **Chart→3-D View** from the menu bar.

3. Follow these steps to adjust the rotation and elevation.

Ⓐ *Click this button until the elevation is set to 25 in the **Elevation** box.*

Ⓑ *Click this button until the rotation is set to 320 in the **Rotation** box.*

Ⓒ *Click **OK**, and notice how the rotation and elevation change the view.*

4. Feel free to experiment with any of the topics you have learned in this lesson.

5. Save your workbook when you have finished, close the workbook, and continue with the end-of-lesson questions and exercises.

Concepts Review

True/False Questions

1. You can rename a worksheet by double-clicking the sheet tab and typing the new name. TRUE FALSE

2. Embedded charts are updated when the worksheet data changes. TRUE FALSE

3. Charts on separate chart sheets are not updated when the worksheet data changes. TRUE FALSE

4. Column charts are most useful for comparing the parts of a whole. TRUE FALSE

5. Column charts have a category and value axis. TRUE FALSE

6. The Chart Wizard can only be used to create embedded charts. TRUE FALSE

7. The Chart Wizard is used to explode pie slices. TRUE FALSE

8. You must select a chart before you can move or resize it. TRUE FALSE

Multiple-Choice Questions

1. Which procedure would you use to change the position of a worksheet in the sheet order?
   a. Double-click the sheet tab, and drag the tab to the desired location.
   b. Click the sheet tab, and choose Edit→Move sheet from the menu bar.
   c. Drag the sheet tab to the desired location.
   d. None of the above

2. Which command would you use to move an embedded chart to a separate sheet?
   a. Edit→Move chart
   b. Chart→Location
   c. Chart→Move
   d. This cannot be done.

3. Which chart would be best for showing a trend over a period of time?
   a. Line
   b. Bar
   c. Column
   d. Pie

4. Which technique can be used to insert data labels after a chart has been created?
   a. Select the chart, and click the Data Labels button on the Chart toolbar.
   b. Select the chart, and choose the Insert→Data Labels command.
   c. Select the chart, choose Chart→Chart Options, click the Data Labels tab, and choose the desired data labels format.
   d. Data labels cannot be inserted after a chart has been created.

Skill Builders

Skill Builder 6.1 Use Help

In this exercise, you will use Excel's Help feature to get a description of the various chart types.

1. Start a New Workbook ☐.

2. Use the Office Assistant to search for the phrase *chart types*.

3. Choose **Examples of chart types** from the Assistant's search results.

4. Click the graphic that appears in the Help window to display a help topic on Examples of chart types.

5. Click the various chart types on the left side of the dialog box to see a detailed description in the right side of the dialog box.

6. Close all Help windows when you have finished.

7. Click in the worksheet to dismiss the Assistant's speech balloon.

Skill Builder 6.2 Create a Column Chart

In this exercise, you will create a column chart to display student enrollments at a university.

Expand a Series

1. Open the workbook named **Skill Builder 6.2.**
   Notice that the enrollment data has been completed in Column B, but the years have not been completed in Column A. Notice the first two years (1983 and 1984) form the beginning of the series 1983–1999. The best way to expand this series is with the fill handle.

2. Select Cells A4 and A5.

3. Drag the fill handle down to Row 20 to expand the series.

4. Left align ▤ the years in Column A.

Create the Chart

5. Select the range A3:B20.
   This range includes the enrollment data, and the Year and Total Enrollment headings.

6. Click the Chart Wizard ▥ button.

7. Choose the Column chart type and the first subtype.

8. Click **Next** to display the Step 2 of 4 box.
   Take a moment to study the Step 2 dialog box, and you will notice a problem. Excel is interpreting the years 1983–1999 as numbers. The numbers are appearing as a data series in the chart. The years are the short columns to the left of the tall, thin enrollment data columns. The years should actually be displayed as labels on the horizontal category axis. You will correct this in the next few steps.

9. Click the **Series** tab on the dialog box.
   The Series tab lets you modify the data series that are plotted in the chart.

10. Follow these steps to remove the years from the series and to add the years as Category (X) axis labels.

Ⓐ *Choose* Year *from the* **Series** *list and click the* **Remove** *button.*

Ⓑ *Click in the* **Category (X) axis labels** *box (the box will be empty).*

Ⓒ *Select the years 1983–1999 in the worksheet (the Source Data box will temporarily close as you select the data). When you release the mouse button, the range shown in this illustration should appear in the* **Category (X) axis labels** *box.*

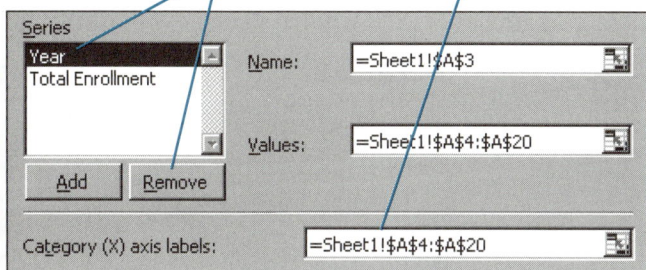

4	1983
5	1984
6	1985
7	1986
8	1987
9	1988
10	1989
11	1990
12	1991
13	1992
14	1993
15	1994
16	1995
17	1996
18	1997
19	1998
20	1999

Series
Year
Total Enrollment

Name: =Sheet1!$A$3

Values: =Sheet1!$A$4:$A$20

Add   Remove

Category (X) axis labels: =Sheet1!$A$4:$A$20

Notice that the dates are now displayed in an angled fashion on the Category axis.

11. Click **Next** to continue with Step 3 of 4.

12. Click the **Titles** tab, and type the title **Student Enrollments** in the Chart title box.

13. Click the **Legend** tab, and remove the legend.

14. Click **Finish** to complete the chart.
Take a few moments to study your worksheet and chart. Make sure you understand the relationship between the worksheet data and the chart.

Convert the Chart to a Line Chart

Suppose you are interested in seeing only the trend in enrollments as opposed to the enrollments in individual years. You can easily convert this chart to a line chart.

15. Make sure the chart is selected.

16. Choose **Chart→Chart Type** from the menu bar.

17. Choose Line as the Chart type, and choose the fourth subtype.

18. Click **OK** to convert the chart to a line chart with data markers.

Format the Chart Title

19. Click the Student Enrollments chart title.

20. Use the Font Color [A▾] button to format the title with a color.

21. Feel free to format the chart and title in any other way you desire.

22. Save the changes, and then close the workbook.

Skill Builder 6.3 Create a Doughnut Chart

In this exercise, you will create a chart for Holy Doughnuts. The chart will show the contributions of various types of doughnuts to the total sales volume for two different years. What type of chart will you use? Why, a doughnut chart, what else! Like pie charts, doughnut charts are useful for comparing parts of a whole. However, doughnut charts can contain more than one data series. Each ring in a doughnut chart represents a data series.

Set Up the Worksheet

1. If necessary, start a New Workbook [icon], and create the worksheet shown below. Format the numbers in Column C as Comma style with 0 decimals. Also, merge and center the Units Sold heading over Cells B3 and C3 and AutoFit Columns B and C.

	A	B	C	D	E
1	Holy Doughnuts Volume Comparison				
2					
3		Units Sold			
4	Type of Doughnut	1998	1999		
5	Creme Filled	12,000	14,500		
6	Frosted	10,500	9,000		
7	Nut Covered	2,300	2,500		
8	Glazed	7,000	8,200		
9	Old Fashioned	4,500	4,300		

Create the Chart

Doughnut charts function much like pie charts because they are used to compare parts of a whole. Therefore, the data is selected in a manner similar to pie charts.

2. Select the data in the range A4:C9.

3. Click the Chart Wizard [icon] button.

4. Choose Doughnut as the Chart type, and choose the first subtype.

5. Click **Next** twice to display the Step 3 of 4 box.

6. Click the **Titles** tab, and enter the Chart title **Doughnut Sales: 1998 vs. 1999**.

7. Click the **Data Labels** tab, and choose the Show percent option.

8. Click the **Finish** button to create an embedded chart.

Format the Percent Labels

9. Click any of the percent labels in the outer ring of the doughnut, and all percentages for the series will be selected.

10. Use the Font Color ![A button] button on the Formatting toolbar to choose a high-contrast color such as red or white.

    This will differentiate the numbers in the outer ring from those in the inner ring. Notice that the doughnut chart does not provide a title or label to identify the rings as 1998 or 1999. This is a deficiency that can only be overcome by using a textbox and arrows or lines to label the rings.

11. Save the workbook with the name **Skill Builder 6.3**, and then close the workbook.

Skill Builder 6.4 Create Pie Charts

In this exercise, you will create four pie charts to illustrate employee expenses for Hollywood Productions—a motion-picture production company. The pie charts will show how employee costs are divided between departments, and how each department's employee costs are allocated. You will create each chart on a separate chart sheet.

Create the Company Chart

1. Open the workbook named **Skill Builder 6.4.**

2. Follow these steps to select the required data.

3		Marketing	Production	Finance
4	Salaries	3,400,000	4,500,000	1,200,000
5	Benefits	1,292,000	1,980,000	336,000
6	Travel	1,700,000	1,500,000	120,000
7	**Total**	**$ 6,392,000**	**$ 7,980,000**	**$ 1,656,000**

Ⓐ *Use the mouse to select the range B3:D3, as shown here.*

Ⓑ *Press the (CTRL) key while you select the range B7:D7.*

3. Click the Chart Wizard ![chart button] button, and create the pie chart shown to the right on a separate chart sheet.
   Make sure the chart type, title, and labels match the chart shown here. Also, notice that the chart does not include a legend.

Hollywood Employee Expenses

Finance 10%
Marketing 40%
Production 50%

4. Double-click the Chart1 sheet tab, and change the sheet name to **Hollywood Chart.**
   Notice that you can use long names when naming sheets.

5. Rename Sheet1 as **Employee Expense Data.**

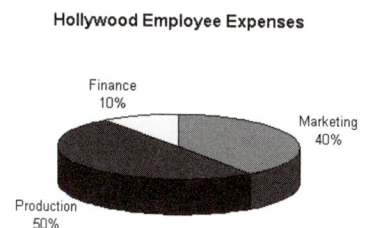

(Continued on the next page)

Create a Pie Chart for the Marketing Department

6. Select the range shown below.

3		Marketing	Production	Finance
4	Salaries	3,400,000	4,500,000	1,200,000
5	Benefits	1,292,000	1,980,000	336,000
6	Travel	1,700,000	1,500,000	120,000
7	Total	$ 6,392,000	$ 7,980,000	$ 1,656,000

7. Click the Chart Wizard ▥ button, and create a pie chart on a separate chart sheet. Use the same chart type and labels as in the previous chart, but use the title "Marketing Employee Costs."

8. Rename the sheet as **Marketing Chart**.

9. Click the Employee Expense Data sheet tab to return to that sheet.

Create Pie Charts for the Production and Finance Departments

10. Use the techniques in this exercise to create the same style pie charts for the Production and Finance departments. Create each chart on a separate chart sheet. Use the chart titles and sheet names shown in the table below. Select data for the Production department chart as shown to the right. You will need to decide how to select the data for the Finance department (although that should be an easy decision to make).

3		Marketing	Production	Finance
4	Salaries	3,400,000	4,500,000	1,200,000
5	Benefits	1,292,000	1,980,000	336,000
6	Travel	1,700,000	1,500,000	120,000
7	Total	$ 6,392,000	$ 7,980,000	$ 1,656,000

Chart	Use This Title	Use This Sheet Name
Production	Production Employee Costs	Production Chart
Finance	Finance Employee Costs	Finance Chart

11. Follow these steps to move the Employee Expense Data sheet tab.

Ⓐ *If necessary, scroll to the right using the tab scrolling buttons until the* **Employee Expense Data** *tab is visible.*

|◀ ◀ ▶ ▶| ⊞ Hollywood Chart ╱ Marketing Chart ╱ Production Chart ╱ Finance Chart ╲ **Employee Expense Data** ╱

Ready

Ⓑ *Drag the* **Employee Expense Data** *tab to the left until it is in front of the* **Hollywood Chart** *tab. You may need to drag part way, use the left tab-scrolling button, and then continue dragging.*

Explode Pie Slices and Increase Elevation

12. Click the Hollywood Chart tab to activate it.

13. Click once on the pie, pause, and then click the Production slice (the largest slice).

14. Drag the slice out slightly to explode it.

15. Choose **Chart→3-D View** from the menu bar.

16. Increase the Elevation ⬆ to 25, and click **OK.**

17. Click the **Marketing Chart** sheet tab.

18. Explode the Salaries slice (the largest slice), and increase the Elevation to 25.

19. Explode the largest slice, and increase the Elevation to 25 for the Production and Finance charts.
    Take a few moments to click the various sheet tabs and check out your charts. Feel free to format and enhance your charts in any way.

20. Save the changes, and then close the workbook.

Skill Builder 6.5 **Create a Pie Chart**

In this exercise, you will create a pie chart that shows the budget allocation for a school district.

1. Open the workbook named **Skill Builder 6.5.**

2. Select the data shown below.

4	Facilities	3,500,000
5	Employee Costs	4,500,000
6	Transportation	540,000
7	Students	2,300,000
8	Equipment	1,200,000

3. Use the Chart Wizard 📊 to create the embedded pie chart shown to the right. Make sure to include the chart title and data labels, remove the legend, and increase the elevation as shown.

4. Save the changes, and then close the workbook.

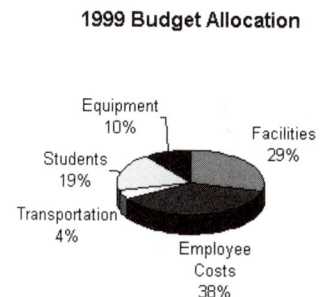

1999 Budget Allocation

Equipment 10%
Facilities 29%
Students 19%
Transportation 4%
Employee Costs 38%

Skill Builder 6.6 Create a Line Chart

In this exercise, you will create a worksheet and line chart to track the trends in a stock portfolio.

1. Start a New Workbook 🗋.

2. Follow these guidelines to create the worksheet shown to the right:

	A	B	C	D
1	Stock Portfolio Trends			
2				
3		Silicon Technology	Dakota Mining	Anderson Diesel
4	9/6/99	58 1/2	32	45
5	9/13/99	59	31	43
6	9/20/99	56	28	45
7	9/27/99	59	30 1/8	48
8	10/4/99	63	33	49
9	10/11/99	68	34	47
10	10/18/99	70	34	42
11	10/25/99	69	36 1/2	38

   - ▪ Notice that the dates in Cells A4 and A5 form the beginning of a series. You can enter these dates, select them, and then drag the fill handle down to Cell A11 to complete the series.

   - ▪ Columns B–D contain mixed numbers (whole numbers and fractions). Just type the numbers exactly as shown with a space between the whole numbers and the fractions.

   - ▪ AutoFit Columns B–D.

3. Select the range A3:D11 (all active cells except for the title).

4. Use the **Chart Wizard** 📊 to create the line chart shown below. Use the first line chart subtype, and place the chart on a separate chart sheet named Line Chart. Make sure you use the same titles and legend as shown.

Stock Portfolio Trends

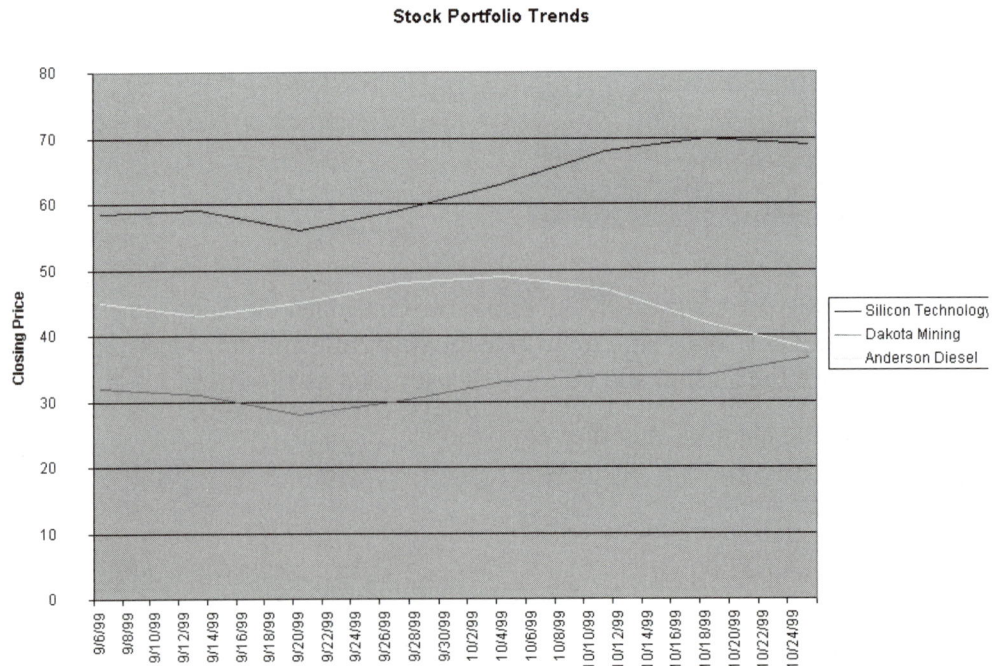

5. Save the workbook with the name **Skill Builder 6.6,** then close the workbook.

Assessments

Assessment 6.1 Create a Line Chart

1. Start a New Workbook, and create the following worksheet.

	A	B	C	D
1	SysTech Stock Performance			
2	March 1998 Through February 1999			
3				
4	Date	Stock Price		
5	3/1/98	78		
6	4/1/98	82.6		
7	5/1/98	83		
8	6/1/98	78.6		
9	7/1/98	72		
10	8/1/98	62		
11	9/1/98	65.8		
12	10/1/98	72.6		
13	11/1/98	85		
14	12/1/98	86		
15	1/1/98	90		
16	2/1/98	92		

2. Use the worksheet data to create the following chart on a separate chart sheet. Make sure you set up the data labels and title as shown.

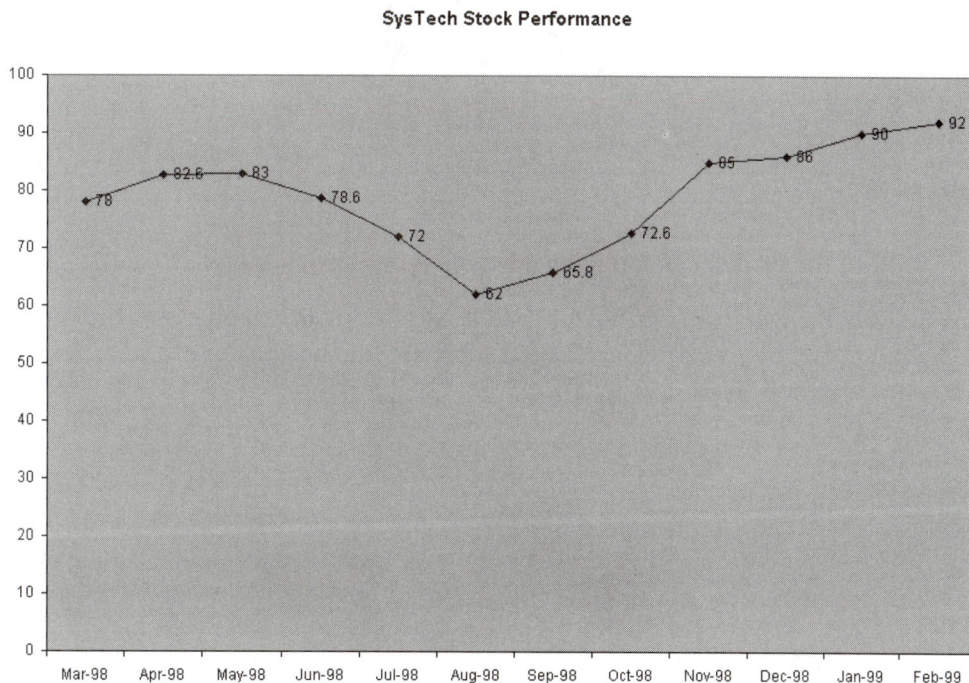

SysTech Stock Performance

3. Rename the Chart1 sheet as **Stock Performance**.

4. Rename the Sheet1 sheet as **Supporting Data**.

5. Print both the worksheet and chart.

6. Save the workbook with the name **Assessment 6.1,** then close the workbook.

Assessment 6.2 Create an Embedded Column Chart

1. Create the worksheet and embedded column chart shown below. Notice the column chart is two-dimensional. The differences in Row 6 are simply the budget numbers minus the spent numbers. Notice that the negative differences dip below the X-axis in the chart. Adjust the position and size of the embedded chart as shown.

	A	B	C	D	E	F	G	H
1	Personal Budget Analysis (January 99 - June 99)							
2								
3		Jan	Feb	Mar	Apr	May	Jun	
4	Budget	5000	5500	5000	5300	5300	5500	
5	Spent	4500	6000	4750	6200	4900	5500	
6	Difference	500	-500	250	-900	400	0	
7								

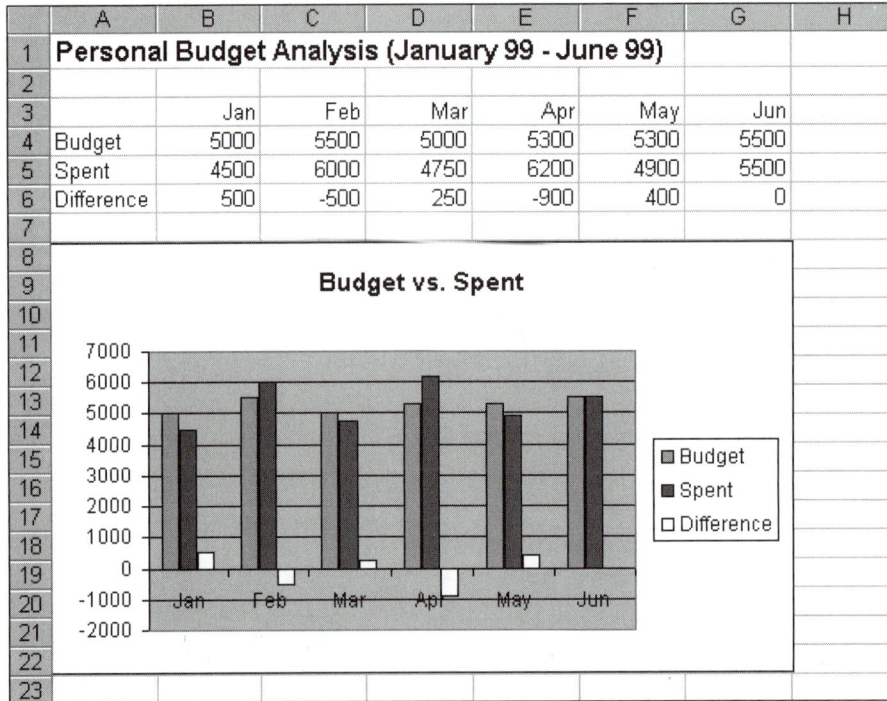

Budget vs. Spent

2. Print the worksheet and embedded chart on a single page.

3. Save the workbook with the name **Assessment 6.2,** then close the workbook.

Assessment 6.3 Create a Worksheet and Pie Chart

1. Follow these guidelines to create the following worksheet and chart.

■ Type all of the numbers and text entries as shown, but use formulas to calculate the New Balance in Column E and the Totals, Highest, and Lowest in Rows 9–11. The formula for New Balance is **New Balance = Beginning Balance + Purchases – Payments.** The Totals in Row 9 can be calculated with AutoSum. The Highest and Lowest calculations in Rows 10 and 11 can be accomplished with the MIN and MAX functions.

■ Format the worksheet with the AutoFormat Classic 2 style.

■ Create the embedded 3-D pie chart shown in the illustration. The pie chart slices represent the new balance percentages of each customer. The pie chart does not represent any of the data in Rows 9–11.

■ Adjust the position and size of the embedded chart as shown in the illustration.

■ Explode the Bishop slice, and adjust the chart rotation and elevation.

■ Bold all of the pie slice labels.

■ Format the chart title with bold and italics.

2. Print the worksheet and embedded chart on a single page.

3. Save the workbook as **Assessment 6.3,** then close the workbook.

	A	B	C	D	E	F
1	Mary's Imported Rugs: Accounts Receivable Report					
2						
3	Customer	Beginning Balance	Purchases	Payments	New Balance	
4	Allison	$4,000	$2,300	$2,000	$4,300	
5	Washington	3450	1000	2450	$2,000	
6	Bishop	6500	2190	3000	$5,690	
7	Worthington	3400	500	3400	$500	
8	Cosby	3000	3400	5000	$1,400	
9	Totals	$20,350	$9,390	$15,850	$13,890	
10	Highest	$6,500	$3,400	$5,000	$5,690	
11	Lowest	$3,000	$500	$2,000	$500	
12						

Customer's With Outstanding Balances

Cosby 10%
Allison 31%
Worthington 4%
Bishop 41%
Washington 14%

Critical Thinking

Critical Thinking 6.1 On Your Own

Open the workbook named **Critical Thinking 2.2.** You will need to complete Critical Thinking 2.2 if this workbook is not on your diskette. Create an embedded column chart that displays the miles driven by each driver. Use the chart title: Miles Driven. The name of each driver should be displayed at the base of the columns. Use data labels to display the precise number of miles driven at the top of each column.

Create another embedded column chart that displays the total expenses of each driver. Use the chart title: Total Expenses. The name of each driver should be displayed at the base of the columns. Use data labels to display the total expenses at the top of each column.

Adjust the size and position of the column charts so that they are side by side and positioned below the worksheet data. Format the worksheet to print on a single page in landscape orientation. Save the completed workbook as **Critical Thinking 6.1.**

Critical Thinking 6.2 On Your Own

Open the workbook named **Critical Thinking 2.3.** You will need to complete Critical Thinking 2.3 if this workbook is not on your diskette. Change the worksheet name to Test Results. Create a 3-D pie chart on a separate chart sheet that shows the percentage each Unit Type contributes to the total units produced. Include data labels that show the percentage and unit type label of each unit type. Do not display a legend. Use the chart title Percent of Unit Types Produced. Rotate the chart so that the largest slice is in the front of the chart. Increase the elevation of the chart and explode the largest slice. Change the sheet name to Pie Chart.

Insert a new column to the right of the Passed Test column. Use a formula in the new column to calculate the number of units that did not pass the test. Create a stacked column chart on a separate chart sheet that compares the units produced to the units that did not pass the test. Display a chart legend but no data labels. Use the title: Total Produced vs. Did Not Pass. Change the sheet name to Stacked Column Chart. Reorganize the sheets so that Test Results is first in the sheet order, Pie Chart second, and Stacked Column Chart third. Save the workbook as **Critical Thinking 6.2.**

Critical Thinking 6.3 On Your Own

Open the workbook named **Critical Thinking 3.1.** You will need to complete Critical Thinking 3.1 if this workbook is not on your diskette. Create an embedded pie chart that shows the contribution of each company type to the total billings. Include data labels that show only the company types. Do not display a legend. Use the chart title: Billing Breakdown. Position the chart below the data. Save the workbook as **Critical Thinking 6.3.**

Critical Thinking 6.4 Web Research

Use Internet Explorer and a search engine of your choice to locate a Web site that offers free stock quotations and charts. Search for the symbols CSCO, IBM, and ORCL, and display charts for each of the stocks. Set up an Excel workbook that includes a row for each stock and columns for each of the past 12 months. View the chart for one of the stocks and enter the approximate value of the stock into your worksheet for each of the past 12 months. Create a line chart on a separate chart sheet that includes all three stocks on the same chart. The chart should show the stock trends over the past 12 months. Use the chart title: 12 Month Stock Trends. Change the name of the chart sheet to 12-Month Trends Chart. Save the workbook as **Critical Thinking 6.4.**

Critical Thinking 6.5 Web Research

Use Internet Explorer and a search engine of your choice to find the Gross Domestic Product of the G7 industrial nations in any given year. The G7 nations include the United States, Germany, Japan, Great Britain, France, Italy, and Canada. Set up a worksheet that lists the nations in order by largest GDP. The GDP numbers will be measured in trillions of dollars. You can eliminate the 12 zeros from the numbers and just include the multiples. For example, if a nation has a GDP of 1.4 trillion dollars then use the number 1.4 in the worksheet. Create an embedded column chart to compare the various GDPs. Include data labels in the chart and a descriptive title. Save the workbook as **Critical Thinking 6.5.**

Critical Thinking 6.6 As a Group

Open the workbook named **Critical Thinking 4.6.** You will need to complete Critical Thinking 4.6 if this workbook is not on your diskette. Create a column chart on a separate chart sheet. The column chart should include columns for the purchase price and current price of each stock. Make sure that each pair of columns is identified by the appropriate stock symbol. Use the chart title: Gains and Losses. Include a legend that identifies the columns as either Purchase Price or Current Price. Name the chart sheet Gains and Losses Chart. Save the workbook as **Critical Thinking 6.6.**

Internet Integration: Online Collaboration

Collaborative projects are becoming a typical business activity. The Internet makes it easy to exchange documents and other types of information to coordinate geographically diverse activities. However, the lack of face-to-face contact also places a premium on sharing information efficiently. In this lesson, you will learn how to participate in an online collaboration. You will set up folders for project files, receive and send workbook files as attachments to email messages, and place comments into an Excel workbook.

In This Lesson

Case Study

Grace works at the grant office of her local college. She administers grant funds that are awarded the college to support various educational activities. One of her responsibilities is the filing of quarterly financial reports to the agencies that pay the grant awards. These reports are sent along with a brief narrative of how the grant funds were spent.

One of the grants Grace administers involves another college as well as her own. They applied for the grant as a consortium. Grace must assemble financial data from both colleges each quarter and submit it by email to the granting agency. Since the collaborating colleges are about 100 miles apart, Grace and her colleagues use email to transmit information back and forth in the form of messages and Excel workbooks.

A grant administrator from another college attached an Excel workbook to an email message. Grace can open the workbook with a double-click and read it like any other Excel workbook.

From:	Terry Sanchez	Sent: Fri 11/12/1999 5:04 PM
To:	Grace Barry	
Cc:		
Subject:	Re: Grant budget	

Hi Grace:

Here is the Southern College Connections grant budget report. I hope this includes everything you need. If not, please call me right away.

Yours,

Southern College ...

In order to clarify how some funds are spent, or their source in the case of matching funds, Grace and her colleagues use comments to document various notes and facts. Comments help everyone involved in the project understand any special formulas or values contained in worksheet cells.

The triangle at the top-right corner of this cell indicates that there is a comment embedded in the cell.

1,462   600
284   120

Terry Sanchez:
Grace, am I correct that the formula for this cell is the salary * 20% ?

1,010

When Grace points at the comment marker, she sees a question from Terry about a formula in the draft budget report.

Organizing a Project

When you work on a project, it is usually a good idea to create one or more folders on the computer to store the documents and other types of files you will work with. This topic will give you practice in creating folders and teach techniques to access the new folders quickly.

Project Folders

Depending on the size of the project and the number of files you must organize, you may need to create more than one folder. Windows lets you create folders inside of other folders, so you can have one folder for the project, and then create subfolders inside it for major types of documents or major sections of the project. The following diagram displays an example of project folders.

This My Computer window displays the folder that Grace created for the Connections grant.

Grace creates a folder for each quarterly report.

Various files that apply to the entire grant project are kept in the main folder.

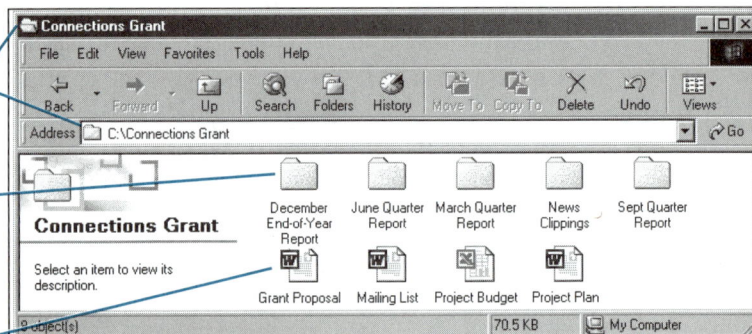

Example

Grace sets up a Connections Grant folder in the My Documents folder on her hard drive. She also creates folders for each quarterly report. This keeps the list of files in any one folder from becoming too long. Now Grace can quickly find and open the files for any quarterly report.

Hands-On 7.1 Create Project Folders

1. Double-click the My Computer 🖳 icon near the top-left corner of the Desktop. If necessary, maximize the window.
   Some computers may be set to display a new window for each new drive or folder that you browse. You will set the My Computer window to display just a single window as you browse—to avoid cluttering the Desktop with too many windows.

2. Follow the instructions below for your version of windows.

Windows 98

- Choose **View→Folder Options** from the menu bar.

- Click the **Settings** button.

- Make sure that the Browse folders option is set to *same window* as shown at right.

- Click **OK;** then click the **Close** button to close the dialog box.

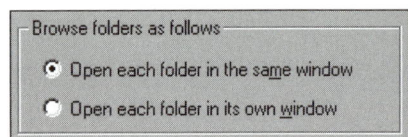

Windows 95 and Windows NT

- Click **View** on the menu bar. Follow the instructions in the *Windows 98* section above if the last item in the view menu reads: *Folder Options.* Otherwise, click **Options** in the View menu.

- Make sure that the Folders option is set to *single window* as shown at right

- Click **OK** to close the dialog box.

Windows 2000

- Choose **Tools→Folder Options** from the menu bar.

- Make sure that the Browse folders option is set to *same window* as shown at right.

- Click **OK** to close the dialog box.

3. Make sure your exercise diskette is in the floppy drive.

4. Double-click the *3½ Floppy (A:)* icon to view the exercise diskette.

5. Choose **View→Large Icons** from the menu bar.

6. Follow these steps to create a new folder on your floppy disk.

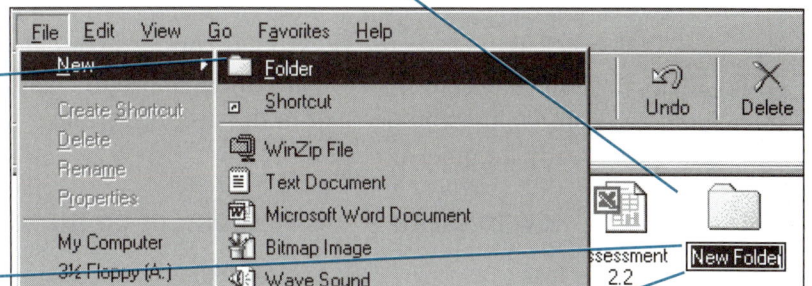

A *Click once on a clear portion of the My Computer window.*

B *Choose File→New→Folder from the menu bar.*

C *Notice how a new folder icon appears. The name is selected (shaded), so you can type the new name for the folder immediately.*

D *Type the name **Connections Grant**, and tap the* (ENTER) *key.*

7. Double-click the *Connections Grant* folder icon to navigate to your new folder.
   Notice that the name of the folder is displayed in the Address bar near the top of the My Computer window and also in the Title bar.

Create Subfolders

Now that you have created a new project folder, you can add the two subfolders to it. Any new folders you create will be added inside the Connections Grant folder, since this is where you are currently navigated.

8. Choose **File→New→Folder** from the menu bar. Type **First Quarter Report** as the name for the new folder, and tap the (ENTER) key.

9. Choose **File→New→Folder** from the menu bar. The **New** command may appear further down the menu than it did previously. Type **Second Quarter Report** as the name for the new folder, and tap the (ENTER) key.
   There should now be two folders displayed in the Connections Grant folder.

10. Minimize the My Computer window.

Placing a Shortcut on the Desktop

A shortcut is a type of file that points to some other file, folder, or drive on your system. You can recognize a shortcut by the small arrow in the lower left corner of its icon.

When to Use a Shortcut

You should use a shortcut if you want to access a file, folder, or drive from more than one location. For example, you might keep a file named *First Quarter Report* in a folder named *Connections Grant*, but you also want to access the file from another folder named *Current Work*. A shortcut to the First Quarter Report file inside the Current Work folder makes it easy to access the file, while keeping it in its proper location inside the Connections Grant folder.

The Benefits of Shortcuts

A shortcut occupies less storage space (about one kilobyte) than making another copy of the same file. You could make copies of a file or folder and place them at different locations on your system. However, this would have two disadvantages:

- Each copy of the file would occupy additional storage space on a drive. Since shortcuts are just one kilobyte in size, they take up very little space compared to the file they point to.

- If you wanted to change the file, you would have to change each copy of the file individually. This could become very confusing and time-consuming. With a shortcut to the single file or folder, only one file needs to be modified.

Placing Shortcuts to Folders on the Desktop

TIP!

Avoid placing folders on the Desktop. Place shortcuts to folders on the Desktop instead.

You can easily open a folder by placing a shortcut to it on the Desktop. It is a bad idea to place the actual folder on the Desktop. If you move a folder to the Desktop, it loses its place in the hierarchy on your floppy disk or hard drive. Shortcuts help you work around this problem. The actual folder can be in its proper spot in the disk drive/folder hierarchy, while the shortcut sits on the Desktop ready for quick access.

Quick Reference

HOW TO CREATE A FOLDER SHORTCUT ON THE DESKTOP

Task	Procedure
Create a shortcut to a folder on the Desktop.	■ Open a My Computer or Exploring window, and restore the window so part of the Desktop is visible.
	■ Navigate to the item for which you are creating a shortcut.
	■ Drag the folder with the right (not the left) mouse button from the My Computer window to a spot over the Desktop; then release the mouse button.
	■ Choose Create Shortcut(s) here from the pop-up menu.

Example

Since she will be working with files for this project a great deal during the coming week, Grace places a shortcut to the First Quarter Report folder on the Desktop. This makes it easy to open the folder quickly, while keeping it in its proper location on her hard drive (or on your floppy disk).

Using Favorites for Folders

A Favorite works like a command that points to a specific folder or file on a disk drive. There may be some folders on your system that you will want to jump to frequently. Although you could create shortcuts to these folders, a Favorite may be a better choice. You can access Favorites from the Favorites menu in a My Computer or Exploring window or in the Open and Save dialog boxes in Office 2000 application programs such as Excel. Because you access Favorites from a menu, they are often more convenient than shortcuts, which must always reside on the Desktop or in a specific location on a hard drive or floppy disk.

Uses for Favorites

You can use Favorites to quickly navigate to three different types of locations:

- Folders on the computer system or on a network

- Disk drives on your computer or on a network

- Web pages

Creating Favorites

You can create a new favorite whenever you need one. You create favorites in My Computer and Exploring windows, in Internet Explorer, or in the *Open* and *Save* dialog boxes of Office 2000 applications such as Word, Excel, and Outlook.

Quick Reference

WORKING WITH FAVORITES TO FOLDERS AND FILES

Task	Procedure
Create a Favorite to a folder from a My Computer or Exploring window.	■ Display the icon for the target folder in a My Computer or Exploring window. ■ Click to select the target folder; then choose **Favorites→Add to Favorites** from the menu bar. ■ Revise the name for the Favorite if necessary; then click **OK.** *Note: Some versions of Windows 95 and NT 4.0 do not support this method.*
Create a Favorite to a folder from an Open or Save dialog box.	■ Use **File→Save As** or **File→Open** to display a dialog box. ■ Click to select the disk drive, folder, or file for which to create a Favorite. ■ Click the **Tools** button in the dialog box; then choose **Add to Favorites** from the drop-down menu.
Access a Favorite from an Office 2000 Open or Save dialog box.	■ Use **File→Save As** or **File→Open** to display a dialog box. ■ Click the **Favorites** button to view all of your Favorites. ■ Double-click on the **Favorite** to which you wish to navigate.
Access a Favorite from a My Computer or Exploring window.	■ Open a *My Computer, Exploring,* or *Internet Explorer* window. ■ Click Favorites on the menu bar, and select the Favorite to which you wish to navigate. *Note: Some versions of Windows 95 and NT 4.0 do not support this method.*

In this exercise, you will create a Favorite that opens the First Quarter Report folder on your floppy disk. You will also create a shortcut on the Desktop to this folder.

Create a Favorite

1. Start Microsoft Excel; then click the Open 📂 button on the toolbar.

2. Follow these steps to create the Favorite.

Ⓐ *Choose the 3½ Floppy (A:) drive in the* **Look in** *box.*

Ⓑ *Double-click to open the Connections Grant folder.*

Ⓒ *Click once to select the First Quarter Report folder.*

Ⓓ *Click the* **Tools** *button; then choose* **Add to Favorites.**

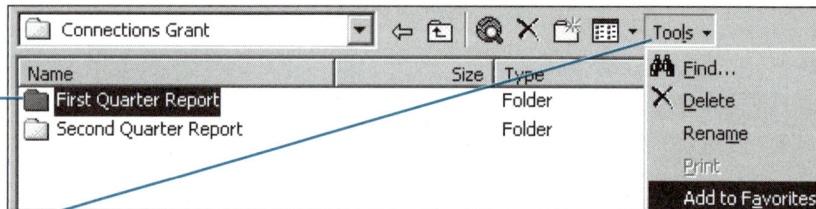

Open

Look in:	3½ Floppy (A:)
History	Connections Grant

Connections Grant		
Name	Size	Type
First Quarter Report		Folder
Second Quarter Report		Folder

Tools ▾
- 🔍 Find...
- ✕ Delete
- Rename
- Print
- Add to Favorites

3. Click the **Favorites** button on the left side of the dialog box.
The dialog box will display a list of all of the Favorites defined for your log-on name. Each log-on name can maintain a custom list of Favorites.

4. Tap the letter **F** on the keyboard until you see a Favorite named *First Quarter Report* or *First Quarter Report folder.*

5. If you see a Favorite named *First Quarter Report folder,* click the **icon** (not the name) to select the Favorite; then tap the (DELETE) key. Click **Yes** if you are asked to confirm the deletion.
Another student created this Favorite previously. There is no need to have more than one Favorite to this folder.

6. Follow these steps to rename the Favorite.

   You can use this technique to rename any file or folder that you view in an Open or Save As dialog box.

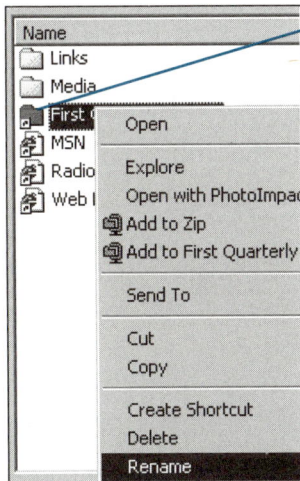

Ⓐ Right-click *on the* First Quarter Report *favorite; then choose* **Rename** *from the pop-up menu.*

```
Name
  Links
  Media
  First Q     Open
  MSN
  Radio       Explore
  Web I       Open with PhotoImpac
           📋 Add to Zip
           📋 Add to First Quarterly

              Send To

              Cut
              Copy

              Create Shortcut
              Delete
              Rename
```

Ⓑ *Tap the* (END) *key, tap the* (SPACE BAR), *and type* **folder** *at the end of the Favorite name; then tap the* (ENTER) *key.*

`First Quarter Report folder`

7. Click the **Cancel** button to close the dialog box

   The Cancel button cancels the Open File command, not the creation of the Favorite. The Favorite you created in this dialog box will remain after you give the Cancel command.

8. Minimize ▬ the Excel window.

Create a Shortcut to the Folder

9. If you see a folder on the Desktop named *Shortcut to First Quarter Report,* drag it to the *Recycle Bin.* Click **Yes** if you are asked to confirm the deletion.

10. Click the **Connections Grant** button on the Windows Taskbar to make the window active.

11. Click the Restore 🗗 button at the top-right corner of the My Computer window. If necessary, *drag* on the borders of the window to make a portion of the Desktop visible.

12. Follow these steps to create the shortcut.

Ⓐ *Point at the* First Quarter Report *folder; then start to drag with the* **right** *(not left) mouse button.*

Ⓑ *Release the mouse button anywhere over the Desktop.*

Ⓒ *Choose* **Create Shortcut(s)** *Here on the pop-up menu.*

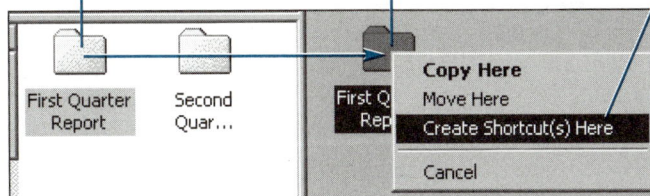

```
  📁            📁            📁
First Quarter  Second      First Q     Copy Here
  Report       Quar...       Rep       Move Here
                                        Create Shortcut(s) Here

                                        Cancel
```

Now a shortcut to the folder will appear on the Desktop. Notice the small arrow on the icon that identifies it as a shortcut.

```
   📁
   🔗
Shortcut t
First Quart
  Report
```

13. Close ☒ the My Computer window.

(Continued on the next page)

14. Double-click on the *Shortcut to First Quarter Report* that you just created.
    A new My Computer window will open to display the folder.

15. Close ☒ the My Computer window.

16. Double-click the My Computer 🖥 icon to open a new My Computer window.

17. Choose **Favorites→First Quarter Report folder** from the menu bar. If you do not see
    Favorites on the menu bar, skip to Step 18—your version of Windows does not support this
    menu command in the My Computer window.
    *The First Quarter Report folder is displayed immediately. You can access this folder from any window that
    features the* Favorites *command. You will use the* Favorites *command in Excel's* Open *dialog box later in
    this lesson, which even works with versions of Windows that do not have a Favorites command on the My
    Computer window menu bar.*

18. Close ☒ the My Computer window.

Sending an Email Message

Outlook is a program for managing email, your calendar, names and addresses of contacts, and task
lists. The Outlook program has a flexible interface that lets you shift among these various functions. This topic will only cover the basic knowledge required to send and receive email messages
with Outlook. For a more complete treatment of this program, see the Labyrinth Publications Office
2000 Essentials Course and Outlook 2000 Essentials Course in the Off to Work series.

Hands-On 7.3 Start Outlook

In this exercise, you will start the Outlook program and browse views of some program features.

1. Choose **Start→Programs→Microsoft Outlook** from the Start menu.

2. Make sure that the Outlook window is Maximized ☐.

3. Follow these steps to open the Inbox view in Outlook.

    Ⓐ *Click the* **Outlook Shortcuts** *button
    to make sure the primary buttons are
    displayed on the Outlook bar.*

    Ⓑ *Click the* **Inbox** *shortcut to
    display a view of incoming
    email messages.*

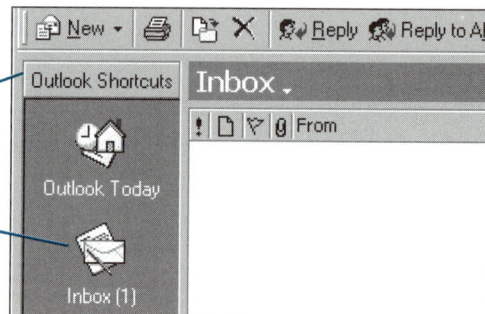

This view displays incoming email messages.

About Electronic Mail

Along with the Web, *electronic mail (email)* is the most popular of all Internet services. Email is simply the capability to send an electronic message to a specific individual's email address anywhere in the world. An email message can also have one or more computer files (attachments) sent along with it. With email you can send and receive messages, send one message to more than one recipient, and exchange documents and images.

Sending an Email Message

Sending an email message is easy. If you know how to use a word processor, you know more than enough to create and send an email message. This topic will take you through the steps of sending an email message with Outlook 2000. To start an email message, you simply choose **File→New→Mail Message,** or you can click the *New Message* button on the toolbar while the Inbox view is displayed.

Email Addresses

You send and receive email with email addresses. An email address uniquely identifies your email account and where the mail server system that serves your account is located on the Internet. An email address looks similar to, and functions much like, the URL for a Web page. The diagram below shows the parts of a typical email address.

rsmith@offtowork.com

Account   *Separator*   *Domain*
name   *name*

RULES FOR EMAIL ADDRESSES

■ Email addresses *always* contain the @ symbol to separate the account name from the domain name.

■ An email address *cannot* contain space characters.

■ An email address *can* contain certain punctuation characters, such as a dash and periods.

Hands-On 7.4 Create and Send an Email Message

In this exercise, you will create a new email message and send it to an email address at offtowork.com. This email address will automatically send a message back to you.

Before you begin: If you do not have access to email in your computer lab, skip this exercise, continue with the next topic, and then start with Step 6 *in* Hands-On Exercise 7.5.

Compose an Email Message

1. Click the New Mail Message [New] button at the left side of the Outlook toolbar.
   A new email message window will appear on the screen. Outlook always gives you a separate window to compose email messages.

2. Follow these steps to start composing the first email message.

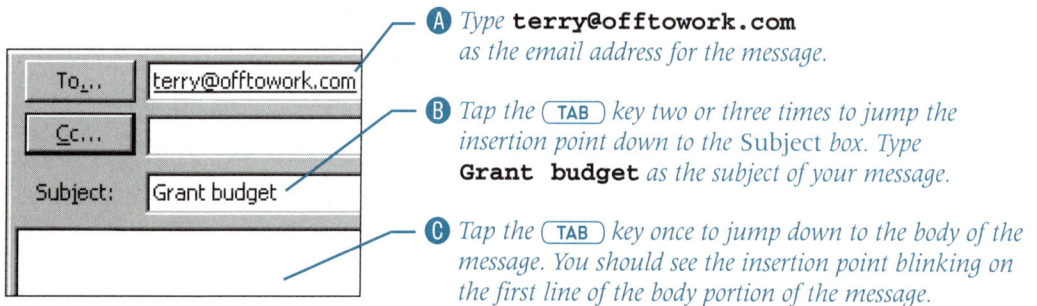

   A *Type* **terry@offtowork.com** *as the email address for the message.*

   B *Tap the* (TAB) *key two or three times to jump the insertion point down to the Subject box. Type* **Grant budget** *as the subject of your message.*

   C *Tap the* (TAB) *key once to jump down to the body of the message. You should see the insertion point blinking on the first line of the body portion of the message.*

3. Follow these guidelines as you type the message that appears below:

   - Don't worry about the message lines wrapping around exactly as they appear below. When you type to the end of the message box, a new line will be started for you automatically.

   - You only need to tap (ENTER) when you want to start a new line at the end of a paragraph or insert a blank line in the message.

   - If you tap (ENTER) at the end of each line, your message will be difficult for the addressee to read.

   > Hello Terry,
   >
   > Please send me this quarter's budget figures for the Connections grant. I need to send off a quarterly report to the grant manager by tomorrow.
   >
   > Regards,
   >
   > Grace

Send the Message

4. Look over the message and fix any typographic errors you may have made. If you see an error, click just to the right of the error, then tap the (BACKSPACE) key to delete the error. You can then retype the word and it will be inserted into the message. After you've made any necessary corrections, go on to the next step.

Many users make typos in their email messages. It's a good idea to scan your messages for typos before you send them off. You should use the same level of care with business correspondence via email as you would use in a standard business letter.

5. Click the ☐ Send button on the message toolbar to send your message.
   Depending on how Outlook is configured, this command may not actually send the message over the Internet just yet. The message may be held in Outlook's Outbox, ready to transmit when you give the Send/Receive command in the next step.

6. Click the ☐ Send/Receive button on the Outlook toolbar.

7. Follow these steps if you are asked to enter a password.

   Ⓐ *Click in the* Password *box; then type your password. Notice how the password is displayed as a series of asterisks. This helps protect the confidentiality of your password from passers-by.*

   Ⓑ *Make sure that the* Remember Password *box is not checked. If you tell Outlook to remember your password, anyone can send and receive email on your account.*

   Ⓒ *Click OK.*

   Logon
   Server: pop.mindspring.com
   User Name: student 10
   Password: *****
   ☐ Remember Password
   OK

Outlook will usually display a window that shows the progress of sending and receiving messages. Since your message is very short, this window may only appear for a few seconds. A portion of the window is displayed below.

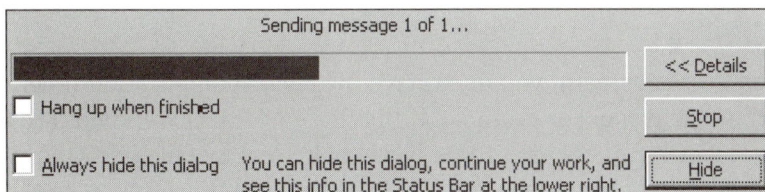

Sending message 1 of 1...
[progress bar]   << Details
☐ Hang up when finished   Stop
☐ Always hide this dialog   You can hide this dialog, continue your work, and   Hide
                            see this info in the Status Bar at the lower right.

If the progress window is not visible, you should see a display at the bottom-right *corner of the Outlook window in the* Status bar. *The Status bar can display information about making a connection to the mail server and the delivery of email messages.*

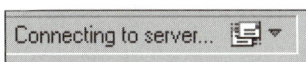

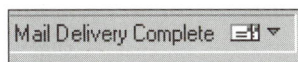

Connecting to server... ☐ ▼   Mail Delivery Complete ☐ ▼

Email Attachments

An *attachment* is a file you include with an email message. Some types of information are not as easy to work with in the form of an email message. For example, an Excel workbook transmitted as an email message would not have any functioning formulas (the data would be transmitted as values). If the recipient needs to edit the workbook, it is better sent as an attachment. You will have the opportunity to send a worksheet and workbook as an email message and an attachment at the end of this lesson. Here are some examples of attachments:

Project Budget   Project Plan Presentation   Project Status Report

- An Excel workbook, a Word document, or a PowerPoint presentation

- A photograph (converted to an image file)

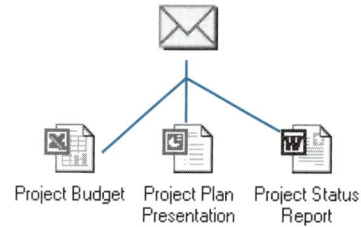

Receiving and Opening Attachments

When you receive a file that has an attachment, Outlook will indicate that the file has an attachment by displaying a small paper clip next to the message name. As you view the message in Outlook's preview pane of the Inbox view, you will also see a paper clip at the top-right corner of the Preview pane. Clicking on the paper clip will display the names of all the attachments. If you double-click to open an email message, any attachments are displayed as icons at the bottom of the message window.

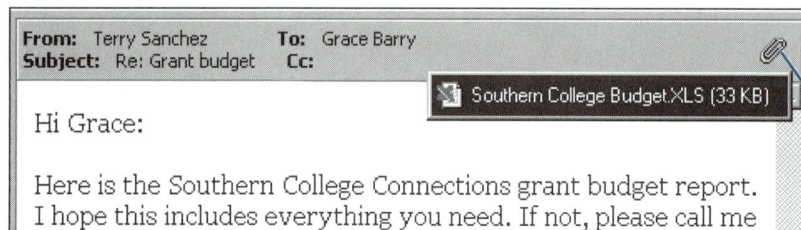

From: Terry Sanchez   **To:** Grace Barry
Subject: Re: Grant budget   **Cc:**

Southern College Budget.XLS (33 KB)

Hi Grace:

Here is the Southern College Connections grant budget report. I hope this includes everything you need. If not, please call me

When you click the paper clip icon in the message preview window, a menu displays the available attachments.

File Compatibility

In order to open an attachment, you must have installed an application program that is capable of opening the attachment file. For example, if the file is an Excel workbook, you must have Excel (or another program capable of opening Excel workbook files) installed on your computer. If Windows cannot find a program that can open the file, it will ask you to select an application program. Fortunately, most attachments you receive will probably be word processing and workbook files, so file compatibility will rarely be an issue.

Quick Reference

OPENING ATTACHMENTS IN OUTLOOK

Task	Procedure
Open an attachment from the *Inbox* view.	■ Click to select the message with the attachment.
	■ Click the **paper clip icon** on the right corner of the Preview pane; then select the attachment you wish to open.
Open an attachment from a *message* window.	■ Double-click to *open* the message in a message window.
	■ *Double-click* the **icon** for the attachment, or *right-click* on the icon; then choose **Open** from the pop-up menu.

Saving Attachments

After you receive an attachment, you may wish to store it with related files somewhere else on the hard drive or a floppy disk. Outlook stores attachments as a part of the email message. In order to work with the attachment apart from the email message it was attached to, you must save the attachment file(s). One way to save an attachment is to open it in an application program, then use the programs' *Save As* command. You can also right-click on an attachment in a message window; then give the *Save As* command.

TIP!

When you delete *a message that has attachments, the* attachment *files are deleted as well—unless you have already saved the attachments.*

Example

When Grace gets the email message from Terry with the quarterly budget workbook attached, she saves it into the *First Quarter Report* folder she set up earlier. Otherwise, it could be difficult to locate the document later unless she went back into her email program to look up the email message that had the attachment. By saving the attachment, Grace places the workbook in a location where she can find it easily.

Attachments and Computer Viruses

Remember that attachments may contain a computer virus. This will probably be rare, but you should always be cautious when handling attachments from users you do not know well. Even co-workers can unknowingly transmit a virus through a *macro virus* in a workbook file. (A macro is a small program you can create in Excel. You will learn how to create Excel macros in Lesson 14.)

Quick Reference

SAVING ATTACHMENTS IN OUTLOOK

Task	Procedure
Save an attachment in a *message* window.	■ Double-click to *open* the message with the attachment. ■ *Right-click* on the attachment file icon at the bottom of the message window; then choose **File→Save As** from the pop-up menu.

In this exercise, you will save an attachment to an email message in the First Quarter Report folder.

Before you begin: *If you do not have access to email in the computer lab, you should skip directly to the* Move the Attachment File into the First Quarter Report Folder *section (*Step 6*) near the end of this exercise.*

1. Click the 🖳 Send/Receive button on the Outlook toolbar, and look at the top of the Inbox message list for a reply to the message you sent in the previous exercise. The reply will have an attachment. If you do not receive a reply, keep clicking the **Send/Receive** button on the toolbar about twice a minute until a reply arrives.
   Notice the small paper clip for the message in the message list. This indicates that the message contains an attachment.   ✉️   📎 **Terry Sanchez   Re: Grant budget**

2. Double-click on the message in the Inbox view to open it in its own message window. *The attachment will appear at the bottom of the message.*

3. Follow these steps to save the attachment to your floppy disk.

Ⓐ Right-click *on the attachment document at the bottom of the message; then choose* **Save As** *from the pop-up menu.*

Terry
📧
Open
South   Print
Colleg   Save As...

Ⓑ *Click the* **Desktop** *button.*

Ⓒ *Double-click to open the Shortcut to First Quarter Report.*

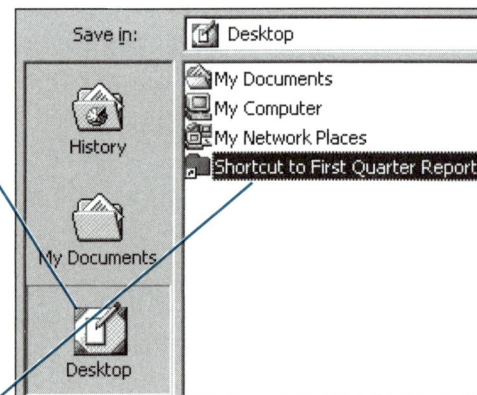

Save in:	📁 Desktop
History	📄 My Documents
	💻 My Computer
	🖧 My Network Places
My Documents	Shortcut to First Quarter Report
Desktop	

Ⓓ *Click the* **Save** *button.*

4. Close ✖ the message window; then minimize ▬ the Outlook window.

5. Double-click the *Shortcut to First Quarter Report* icon on the Desktop.
   You should skip the next section of this exercise and continue with Step 13 *at the end of this exercise.*

Copy the Attachment File into the First Quarter Report Folder

If you do not have access to email in the computer lab, you should move the attachment file on your exercise diskette to the First Quarter Report *folder.*

6. Double-click the My Computer 🖥️ icon near the top-left corner of the Desktop. If necessary, maximize ▢ the window.

7. Double-click the 3½ Floppy (A:) 💾 icon to view the exercise diskette.

8. **Right-click** on the *Hands-On Lesson 7b* file on the exercise diskette; then choose **Copy** from the pop-up menu.

9. Double-click to open the *Connections Grant* folder; then double-click to open the *First Quarter Report* folder.

10. Use (CTRL)+V to paste the file into the *First Quarter Report* folder.

11. *Right-click* on the Excel workbook file; then choose **Rename** from the pop-up menu. Change the name of the file to **Southern College Budget**, and tap the (ENTER) key.

12. Use the command **Start→Programs→Microsoft Outlook** to start the *Outlook 2000* application; then minimize ▭ the Outlook window.
This step ensures that your Windows Taskbar matches the instructions later in this exercise.

Open the Workbook

13. Double-click to open the *Southern College Budget* workbook file.

14. *Right-click* the *First Quarter Report* button on the Windows taskbar; then choose **Close** from the pop-up menu.

Sending Workbook Attachments

Nearly all email programs have a command for attaching a file to a message. You can also attach a workbook or worksheet as an attachment directly from the Excel Program window. You will learn how to do this later in the lesson in the *Emailing the Workbook* topic on page 220.

Working with Comments

Excel's Comments feature is a great tool for online collaboration. A **comment** is a text note that you can embed inside a workbook cell, without cluttering the normal view of the workbook. When someone inserts a comment, Excel places a small red triangle at the top-right corner of the cell. When you point over the red triangle, Excel displays the name of the author and the text of the comment. You can also display all of the comments on a worksheet, and even print them out. The illustration below shows a cell and its associated comment.

The red triangle indicates that there is a comment embedded in this cell.

When Grace points at this cell, Excel displays a comment from Terry, asking about the figure in that cell.

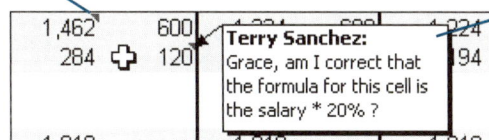

When to Use a Comment

Comments are an excellent way to handle situations such as the examples below:

- When you want to document the formula or value in a cell

- To record a question about the worksheet data to be followed-up later

- To ask a question of an online collaborator without placing it into the normally printed page of the workbook

Viewing Comments

To view a comment, simply place the cell pointer over any cell with a red triangle in the upper-right corner. You can also view comments with the **View→Comments** command to open the Reviewing toolbar. The Reviewing toolbar lets you navigate through comments in the workbook and control the display of comments. It is also possible to print out comments by setting an option in Excel's *Page Setup* dialog box.

Navigating Comments

You can jump from one comment to the next with the Reviewing toolbar. When you reach the last comment in the workbook, the Reviewing toolbar starts over with the first comment in the workbook. The figure below displays the primary features of the Reviewing toolbar.

These buttons navigate you forward and backward through the comments.

This button lets you edit a comment.

This button deletes the currently selected comment.

This button switches the display of a single comment on and off.

This button switches the display of all comments on and off.

Hands-On 7.6 Review Comments

In this exercise, you will review comments inserted into the workbook previously by Terry Sanchez.

1. Follow these steps to display some comments on the worksheet.

Ⓐ *Point at this cell with a comment triangle. This window contains the text of a comment from Terry Sanchez.*

EXPENSES							
PROJECT STAFF							
Salaries		1,462	600	1,224	600	1,224	600
Benefits		284	120	194	120	194	120
OPERATING COSTS							
Curriculum development		1,010		1,010		1,010	
Faculty/staff development						216	
Industry contributions				400			8,000
Publicity and Outreach				40			

Ⓑ *Point at the other two cells with comment triangles, and read the comments.*

2. Choose **View→Comments** from the menu bar.
The Reviewing toolbar will appear. All of the comments on the worksheet are also displayed when you choose this command.

3. Click the **Hide All Comments** button to toggle off the display of the comments.

4. Click the **Next Comment** button on the Reviewing bar.
This button is a useful way to go one-by-one through the comments.

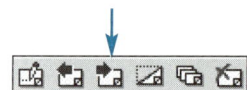

5. Click the **Next Comment** button on the Reviewing bar again.

6. Click the **Previous Comment** button on the Reviewing bar.

7. Close ☒ the Reviewing toolbar.

Inserting Comments

You can insert comments into any cell of an Excel worksheet with the **Insert→Comment** command. This command is also available when you *right-click* on a worksheet cell. A comment is specific to a cell—you cannot assign a comment to a *range* of cells. After you give the **Insert→Comment** command, a comment box will appear where you can type the text of the comment; then click anywhere else to close the comment box. You can also change the dimensions of any comment box by dragging on any of the eight small squares (handles) that appear around its edge.

Grace Barry:
The small squares around the outside of this comment box are called "handles".

Setting the User Name

Before you insert comments, you should set the *user name* to identify that the comment came from you. You make this setting in Excel's **Tools→Options** window, under the *General* tab. Once you set the user name, Excel will keep this setting until someone else changes it again.

User name: Grace Stanton

Example

Grace shares her computer with a co-worker who comes into the office part-time. Before she starts working on the draft project budget workbook, Grace checks to make sure her own name is set in the *user name* box of the General options tab.

Editing Comments

You can edit a comment at any time. You can even edit or add to comments made by other authors. Simply *right-click* on the existing comment, and then choose **Edit Comment** from the pop-up menu. When you edit a comment made by another author, that author's name remains with the comment. You edit comments in the same comments box that displays the comment. You can also change the dimensions of the comment box when you edit a comment.

Example

As she reads comments inserted by her counterpart at the other college, Grace notices one that requests her opinion. Rather than insert a new comment, Grace decides to add her answer by editing the existing comment. Grace also applies a different text color to this edit, so that the other readers can readily distinguish her addition from the original comment.

WORKING WITH COMMENTS IN EXCEL

Task	Procedure
Insert a comment.	■ **Right-click** on the desired cell; then choose **Insert→Comment** from the pop-up menu.
	■ Type the text of your comment.
	■ Click anywhere else to make the comment box disappear.
Associate your name with comments.	■ Choose **Tools→Options** from the menu bar.
	■ Click the **General** tab.
	■ Enter your name in the *User Name* box; then click **OK.**
View a comment in a worksheet cell.	■ *Point* on the cell with the comment triangle for about 1 second to make the comment box pop up.
View all of the comments in a workbook.	■ Choose **View→Comments** from the menu bar.
	■ Use the buttons on the Reviewing toolbar to navigate to specific comments and to display all comments.
Edit a comment.	■ *Right-click* on the cell with the comment; then choose **Edit Comment** from the pop-up menu.
	■ Edit the comment text normally. You can change the text color if you like.
	■ Click anywhere else to make the comment box disappear.
Change the dimensions of a comment box.	■ While creating or editing a comment, drag on any of the eight *handles* (small squares) around the outside edge of the comment box.
Delete a comment.	■ *Right-click* on the cell with the comment; then choose **Delete Comment** from the pop-up menu.

Hands-On 7.7 Insert and Edit Comments

In this exercise, you will insert a new comment into a cell and edit an existing comment with Grace's answer to a question.

Set the User Name

1. Choose **Tools→Options** from the menu bar; then click the *General* tab.

2. Enter your **first** and **last** name in the *User Name* box; then click **OK** to save the change.

Insert a Comment

3. *Right-click* on Cell **G20;** then choose **Insert Comment** from the pop-up menu.
   A comment box will appear. Notice that your name is spelled out as you entered it in the User Name *box.*

4. Type the following comment in the comment box.

   Participation in the League for Innovation conference.

5. Click on Cell **G20** to close the edit comment box and display your comment.

Edit a Comment

6. *Right-click* on Cell **D12;** then choose **Edit Comment** from the pop-up menu.
   The insert comment box will appear to display the text of the comment you selected to edit. Notice the small boxes around the edge of the comment box. These are called handles.

7. Follow these steps to edit the comment.

Ⓐ *Click at the end of the comment line; then tap the* (ENTER) *key.*

Ⓑ *Click the drop-down portion of the* **Font Color** *button on the toolbar; then choose a new text color such as blue.*

Ⓒ *Type the comment as shown here. Notice as you type that text scrolls off the top of the comment box to make room for the new lines you are typing.*

Ⓓ *Point at this handle until you see a* double-arrow; *then* drag down *until all of the comment text is visible again.*

8. Click on Cell **D12** to close the edit comment box and view your editing.
   Notice that the blue font color you used in the comment is visible. This will help other readers notice that the comment has been edited.

9. *Right-click* on Cell **H17;** then choose **Edit Comment** from the pop-up menu.
   Notice how this comment covers some of the data. You will move the comment off the data portion of the workbook.

10. Follow these steps to change the location of a comment on the worksheet.

Ⓐ *Point at the border of the comment box until you see the four-pointed arrow; then drag the comment box to the right.*

Ⓑ *Release the mouse button here where the comment box is clear of the data.*

A line still connects the comment to its cell, so you can move a comment box to most any location on the worksheet where it is out of the way of any important data. This may be important when you print the comments on the worksheet, as you will learn to do in the next topic.

(Continued on the next page)

11. *Right-click* on Cell **C11;** then choose **Delete Comment** from the pop-up menu.

12. Save 🖫 the workbook.

Printing Comments

Excel's default setting is to suppress the printing of comments. To print the comments in a workbook, you choose a comments printing mode in Excel's *Page Setup* dialog box. Excel gives you the option of printing each currently displayed comment where it appears on the worksheet or printing all of the comments (displayed or not) on a separate sheet.

PRINTING COMMENTS IN EXCEL

Task	Procedure
Print the comments in a workbook.	■ If you are going to print comments as they appear on the worksheets, display all of the comments you want printed.
	■ Choose **File→Page Setup** from the menu bar.
	■ Click the **Sheet** tab.
	■ Choose a print mode from the *Comments* box; then click **OK.**

Note: To stop printing comments, choose (None) in the Comments box.

Hands-On 7.8 Print Comments

1. Choose **View→Comments** from the menu bar.
   Notice that all of the comments on the worksheet are displayed. One of the options will only print comments as they are currently displayed on the worksheet.

2. Choose **File→Page Setup** from the menu bar; then click the *Sheet* tab.

3. Choose **As displayed on sheet** in the Comments box; then click **Print Preview.**
   Excel displays the print preview window. Notice that some comments interfere with data cells in this printout.

4. Click near a comment in the print preview window to zoom in to a closer view.
   The comments will print exactly as shown here. Notice that some of the data is covered by the comments boxes and would be hidden in the printout.

5. Click the Close button at the top-right side of the Print Preview window.

6. Choose **File→Page Setup** from the menu bar.

7. Choose **At end of sheet** in the Comments box; then click **Print Preview.**
   Now the display of comments over your data in the printout is suppressed.

8. Click the **Next** button at the top-left corner of the Print Preview window.
   A second sheet has been added to the printout. This prints the comments along with their cell references. Since the comments print on a separate sheet, they will not cover any of the data as they did with the As displayed on sheet option.

9. Click the **Print** button at the top-center of the Print Preview window; then click **OK** to print the worksheet with a separate comments page. Retrieve the printout from the printer.

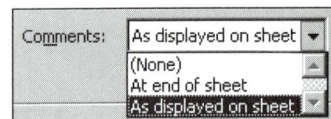

10. Choose **File→Page Setup** from the menu bar.

11. Choose *(None)* from the comments option list; then click **OK.**

12. Close ☒ the Reviewing toolbar.

    Now the printing of comments is suppressed until you switch this option on again.

13. Choose **View→Comments** from the menu bar.

The Paste Special Command

In previous lessons, you have used the copy and paste commands to paste information from one place to another within the same workbook. The information you work with in various Windows applications such as Excel can be pasted in a variety of formats. Each format has features that may make it well or ill suited for pasting into a document.

Paste Special Command

Excel's Paste Special command lets you choose the format for the content you paste into any cell. When you give the Paste Special command, Excel displays a dialog box with all of the available formats you can choose.

The following table lists examples of commonly used formats.

Format Name	Description
All	This command pastes any and all contents of the source cell(s) into the target cell(s), including any cell formatting.
Formulas	This command pastes any formulas in the selected cells, without pasting the cell formatting.
Values	This command pastes only the value in the target cells, rather than any formula or cell formatting from the source cell.
Formats	This command pastes only cell formatting, such as font and color, rather than any formulas or values that might also be in the source cell.
Comments	This command pastes a copy of the comment from the source cell.
Validation	This command pastes a copy of the validation rules from the source cell.
All except borders	This command pastes any values, formulas, and cell formatting with the exception of border formatting.
Column widths	This command sets the column width of the target cell to match the source cell.
Operation	Lets you specify that the copied data should be used in a mathematical operation with any value currently in the cell you are pasting to.

Example

As she prepares a workbook for submission to the grant agency, Grace chooses to send only the values from her budget worksheets, excluding the formulas used to calculate some amounts. Rather than retype the data to enter values from cells with formulas, Grace uses the *Paste Special* command to paste the values into a fresh workbook page.

Hands-On 7.9 Use the Paste Special Command

In this exercise, you will copy and paste data from the Southern College budget worksheet to a consortium workbook. You will also create a new version of the quarterly grant budget in a new workbook. This version will contain the formatting of the original workbook, but not the formulas. Instead you will paste the values from all calculated cells into this version of the workbook.

1. Drag to select Cells **C11** to **J22**; then click the Copy ⬚ button on the toolbar.
   Notice that there are no color fills on any of the cells you copied.

2. Click the Open ⬚ button on the toolbar. Choose the **3½ Floppy (A:)** drive in the *Look in* box; then double-click to open the *Hands-On Lesson 7a* workbook file.
   This workbook has a yellow fill on many of the rows to aid readability.

3. Make sure that the *Southern College* tab is selected; then click on Cell **C11**.

4. If you cannot see most of the worksheet in the window, set the zoom level to **75%.**

5. Click the Paste ⬚ button on the toolbar; then click on a cell outside the pasted data to dismiss the selection so you can view the worksheet clearly.
   Notice that the color background of the worksheet has disappeared. The normal paste command overwrote the yellow fills. Notice that the comments were also copied.

6. Click the Undo ⬚ button on the toolbar to reverse the Paste command.

7. Click in Cell **C11,** and choose **Edit→Paste Special** from the menu bar; then click to choose the *Values* option, and click **OK.**
   Now the yellow fills are preserved, since you pasted only values into the cells.

8. Choose **Edit→Paste Special** from the menu bar; then click to choose the *Comments* option, and click **OK.**
   Now the comments are pasted as well. The Paste Special command lets you selectively paste just what you need.

Paste Formats and Values

Now you will create a new workbook that contains the budget information from both colleges, without the breakdown by individual college.

9. Click the *Quarterly Budget Report* worksheet tab.

10. Click on Cell **C11.**
    Notice that this cell contains a formula that sums the cells on the other two worksheets. If you were to paste this formula into a new worksheet, the formula would be linked to this workbook, and would only work if the both workbooks were in the same folder.

11. Drag to select Cells **A1** to **J26**; then click the Copy ⬚ button on the toolbar.

12. Click the New ⬚ button on the toolbar to create a new workbook.

13. Make sure that the highlight is on Cell **A1;** then choose **Edit→Paste Special** from the menu bar, click to choose the *Values* option, and click **OK.**
    The values of the cells are pasted; however, the formatting has been left behind.

14. Choose **Edit→Paste Special** from the menu bar; then click to choose the *Formats* option, and click **OK.**

    Now the formatting has been transferred to the new page, but the column widths need to be adjusted. If this were a large worksheet, this process could be tedious, but you are going to accomplish it with a single command.

15. Choose **Edit→Paste Special** from the menu bar; then click to choose the *Column Widths* option, and click **OK.**

    As you can see, the Paste Special command can save you a great deal of time.

16. Click on Cell **C11,** and look at the contents of this cell.

    Notice that there is no formula in the cell. In the Consortium Budget Report worksheet, the contents of this cell read: =SUM('Columbia State College:Southern College'!C8)

17. Choose **File→Save As** from the menu bar.

18. Click the **Favorites** button on the left side of the *Save As* dialog box, and double-click to open the *First Quarter Report folder* Favorite. Save this new workbook with the name **Consortium Budget Report** into the *First Quarter Report* folder.

    The Favorite made it easy to navigate to the appropriate folder during the Save command. It's a good idea to create Favorites for folders or files that you expect to use frequently.

19. Choose **Window→Hands-On Lesson 7a** from the menu bar.

Creating Hyperlinks

A hyperlink is a piece of text or a graphic that jumps the user to another location when clicked. Web pages use hyperlinks to let you jump from one Web page to another. You can create hyperlinks on Excel worksheets that work just like the ones on Web pages. This makes it easy for others to navigate to important items of data that you wish to highlight. You create links with the **Insert→Hyperlink** command, or by clicking the **Insert Hyperlink** button.

From the Keyboard

(CTRL)+K to insert a hyperlink.

Types of Hyperlinks

There are three types of links you can create on a worksheet.

- **To cells in a workbook**—a hyperlink can point to another *named range* of cells in the workbook.

- **To another file**—a hyperlink can open a related file. For example, a hyperlink can open a Word document associated with a workbook. A hyperlink can also point to another Excel workbook.

- **To a web page**—a hyperlink can point to a page on the Web or on a corporate intranet. You will learn how to create a hyperlink to a Web page in Lesson 13.

NOTE!

For more details on naming cells, see the "Cell Names and Range Names" *topic in Lesson 9.*

Quick Reference

Naming Worksheet Cells

Excel lets you give a name to a cell or range of cells. After you have named a cell or range, you can refer to it by the name rather than a cell reference. For example, you can refer to a cell by its name in a formula. Naming cells can make it easier and more intuitive to refer to them in formulas and other types of references. You will learn about using named cells in formulas in a later lesson in this course. Since a named cell is required to create a hyperlink to a cell, you will name a cell in the following Hands-On Exercise.

HOW TO CREATE A HYPERLINK

Task	Procedure
Insert a hyperlink to another cell on a worksheet.	■ Create a *name* for the cell or range of cells that the hyperlink will point to.
	■ Click on the cell(s) that will contain the hyperlink.
	■ Click the **Insert Hyperlink** button on the toolbar or use (CTRL)+K from the keyboard.
	■ Click the **Bookmark** button on the dialog box; then choose the name of the target cell in the *Defined Names* list and click **OK**.
	■ Click **OK** again to finish the command.
Insert a hyperlink to a file.	■ Click on the *cell* that will contain the hyperlink.
	■ Click the **Insert Hyperlink** button on the toolbar.
	■ Click the **File** button on the dialog box. Navigate to the desired file; then click **OK**.
	■ Click **OK** again to finish the command.
Remove a hyperlink.	■ *Right-click* on the cell with the hyperlink; then choose **Link→Remove Hyperlink** from the pop-up menu.

Hands-On 7.10 Create Hyperlinks

Create a Hyperlink to a Cell

In this portion of the exercise, you will name a cell on a worksheet and then create a hyperlink to this cell from another worksheet.

1. Click the *Southern College* worksheet tab; then click on Cell **H17**.

2. Click in the *Name* box; then type the cell name **Internships**, and tap (ENTER).

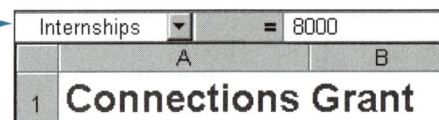

3. Click the **Quarterly Budget Report** worksheet tab; then click on Cell **H17**.

4. Click the Insert Hyperlink button on the toolbar.

5. Click the **Bookmark** button in the dialog box.

6. Follow these steps to select the named cell as the target for the hyperlink.

Ⓐ *If you see a* plus *sign (+) here, click on the plus sign to expand the* Defined Names *list.*

Ⓑ *Click the name* Internships; *then click* **OK** *to close the dialog box.*

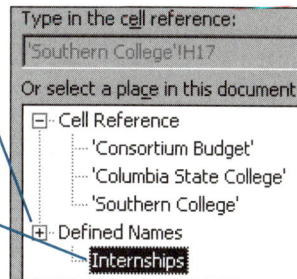

> Type in the cell reference:
> 'Southern College'!H17
>
> Or select a place in this document:
> ⊟ Cell Reference
>   'Consortium Budget'
>   'Columbia State College'
>   'Southern College'
> ⊞ Defined Names
>   Internships

7. Click **OK** to close the *Insert Hyperlink* dialog box.

Navigate with the Hyperlink

8. Click on Cell **G17** to make Cell H17 more visible.   16,120
Notice that the cell has an <u>underscore</u> *beneath the value. This tells you that the cell is a hyperlink.*

9. Point (don't click) on Cell **H17.**
Notice that the cell pointer changes shape to a hand 🖑 *. This also indicates you are pointing at a hyperlink. Notice also that a ScreenTip pops up to display the target of the hyperlink.*

10. Click on Cell **H17.**
You have immediately jumped to the target cell for the hyperlink. If you were viewing the workbook for the first time, you would probably notice that there is a comment in this cell, and you could proceed to display the comment.

Navigate with the Web Toolbar

11. *Right-click* on the toolbar; then choose **Web** from the pop-up toolbar list.
The Web toolbar appears beneath the existing toolbars near the top of the window. This toolbar has navigation buttons that let you navigate among hyperlinks that you have visited previously.

12. Click the Back ⟵ button on the left side of the Web toolbar.
This jumps you back to the Consortium Budget *worksheet and the hyperlink cell.*

13. *Right-click* on the toolbar; then choose **Web** from the pop-up toolbar list to dismiss the Web toolbar.

Create a Hyperlink to a File

Now you will create a hyperlink to a Word file that contains a narrative of the quarter's Connections Grant activities.

14. Choose **Window→Consortium Budget Report** from the menu bar. Click on Cell **E2;** then type the following text, and tap (ENTER).

    Click here to view the Narrative Activities Report

This creates a text label for the hyperlink you are about to create.

15. *Drag* to select Cells **E2:F2;** then use (CTRL)+K to issue the *Insert Hyperlink* command.

.(Continued on the next page)

16. Click the **File** button. Click the Up ⬆ button twice; then double-click on the *Hands-On Lesson 7c* file on your exercise diskette to create a hyperlink to this file.
    Notice that the filename is now listed as the target for the hyperlink.

Text to display:	Click here to view the Narr
Type the file or Web page name:	
Hands-on Lesson 7c.doc	
e or	Or select from list:

17. Click **OK** to complete the command.
    Notice that the text you typed in the cell is underscored to indicate that this is a hyperlink.

18. Point over the word *Report* at the end of the hyperlink text.
    *Notice that the pointer does not turn into a hand 👆. This is because the text is outside of cells **E2:F2** that you selected before you gave the Insert Hyperlink command. Links apply only to cells, not labels that extend outside the selected cells.*

19. Move the cell pointer anywhere on Cells **E2** and **F2** to display the pointer hand; then click to navigate with the hyperlink.
    The Word program will immediately start to display the narrative document. Notice that there is also a Web toolbar near the top of the Word window.

20. Click the Back ⬅ button on the left side of the Web toolbar.
    Now you have returned to the Excel workbook.

21. Right-click on the Excel toolbar; then choose Web from the pop-up toolbar list.

22. Click the Forward ➡ button on the left side of the Web toolbar.
    This returns you to the Word document. The Web toolbar helps you navigate among linked workbook pages, other linked files, and Web pages (as you will see in Lesson 13).

23. Close ☒ the Word window. Click the **Consortium Budget Report** button on the Windows taskbar.

24. Save 💾 the workbook.

25. Choose **Window→Southern College Budget** from the menu bar.

26. Close ☒ the *Southern College* Excel workbook. Click **No** if you are asked to save changes to the workbook.
    The Consortium Budget Report workbook window should now be the active window.

27. *Right-click* on the Excel toolbar; then choose **Web** from the pop-up menu to dismiss the Web toolbar.

Emailing the Workbook

When you want to send an Excel workbook to someone by email, you have two choices. You can send the entire workbook as an *attachment* similar to the one you received earlier in this lesson. Or you can send a single worksheet as the *body* of the email message. Each method has its uses. Sending a worksheet as an email message may cause some formatting to be lost. However, if you just need to transmit a single worksheet, sending it as the body of an email message may be more convenient for the recipient to quickly view and print.

TIP!

If you need to send a multi-worksheet workbook, you must use the attachment method.

The Send To Command

Excel's *Send To* command lets you choose whether the document should be sent as an email message or as an attachment. You simply choose **File→Send To** from the menu bar, and then choose the method of transmission. If you want to send a single worksheet as an email message, Excel offers an even faster way to give this command.

The E-mail Button

The Excel toolbar contains an **E-mail** button that gives the command to send the currently displayed worksheet as a message. When you click the **E-mail** button, Excel immediately displays boxes for you to fill in email addresses, a subject for the message, and a *Send* button to send the message.

TIP!

*If you click the **E-mail** button by mistake, just click it again to dismiss the command.*

Quick Reference

SENDING A WORKBOOK VIA EMAIL

Task	Procedure
Send a single worksheet as an email message.	■ Display the worksheet you wish to send by email.
	■ Click the **E-mail** button on the Excel toolbar.
	■ *Address* the message, and accept or revise the default *subject* for the message (the document name).
	■ Click the **Send a Copy** button on the Excel toolbar.
Send an entire workbook as an attachment to an email message.	■ Open the workbook file you wish to send by email.
	■ Choose **File→Send To→Mail Recipient as Attachment** from the menu bar. A new email message will be created in a normal Outlook (Or Outlook Express) message window.
	■ *Address* the message, and accept or revise the default *subject* for the message (the document name).
	■ Click the **Send** button on the message toolbar.

In this exercise, you will send the Consortium Budget workbook twice: once with the E-mail button and once as an attachment.

Use the Email Message Command

1. Click the E-mail [icon] button on the Excel toolbar.

2. Click **Send the current sheet as the message body** if an Office Assistant speech balloon appears asking how you wish to send the workbook or worksheet.
   A new toolbar will appear at the top of the Excel window. It has boxes that let you address the message and enter a subject just like the Outlook message window. Your Excel workbook has become the "body" of the message.

3. Address the message to **rsmith@offtowork.com**

4. Change the subject line to read: **Quarterly Report**
   Although you could type in the body of the message, in this case it is unnecessary. Your correspondent will recognize the worksheet immediately.

5. Click the [Send this Sheet] button on the Excel toolbar.
   The message with the worksheet is placed into Outlook's Outbox view for delivery. It will be sent the next time Outlook sends and receives email.

Send the Document as an Attachment

6. Choose **File→Send To→Mail Recipient (as Attachment)** from the Excel menu bar.
   A new message will be created in a normal Outlook message window. Notice that the Excel workbook is already attached—its icon is visible in the bottom section of the message window.

7. Address the message to **rsmith@offtowork.com**
   rsmith@offtowork.com *is the email address of a fictitious email correspondent with the name Robert Smith.*

8. Change the message subject to: **Quarterly Report**, then tap (TAB).

9. Type the body of the message as shown below. Don't worry about the workbook icon at the bottom of the message window. It will move down as you type the body of the message.

```
Hello Robert,

Attached is the Quarterly Budget Report for our
consortium. Please let me know if you have any
questions about our expenditures.

Regards,

Grace
```

10. Click the Send [Send] button on the message window toolbar.
    The message is sent to the Outlook outbox for delivery with the next Send/Receive command.

11. Close [X] the Excel window. Click **Yes to all** if you are asked to save any changes to the workbooks.

Read the Documents in Email

12. Make the Outlook window active; then click the ⬚ Send/Receive button on the Outlook toolbar to send any outgoing messages and receive incoming messages.

13. Continue to click the **Send/Receive button** until you receive two replies from Robert Smith. Double-click on the first reply in the Inbox to view the message.

Inbox ▾	
! ▯ ∇ ▯ From	Subject
✉ rsmith@offtowo...	**RE: Quarterly Report**
✉ rsmith@offtowo...	**RE: Quarterly Report**

14. Close ☒ the message window.
The second reply is identical to the first, so there is no need to open it.

15. Follow these steps to view the message you sent with a worksheet in the body.

Ⓐ *Click the **My Shortcuts** button at the bottom of the Outlook bar.*

Outlook Shortcuts

Drafts (13)

Outbox

Sent Items

My Shortcuts

Other Shortcuts

Sent Items ▾

! ▯ ∇ ▯ To	Subject	Sent △
Robert Smith	Quarterly Report	Tue 11/23/1999 3:58 PM
Robert Smith	Quarterly Report	Tue 11/23/1999 3:50 PM

From: Russ Stolins **To:** Robert Smith
Subject: Quarterly Report **Cc:**

Connections Grant
Quarterly Report for 1st Quarter 2000

	Authorized Budget	October grant	October match	N
INCOME	290,000			

Ⓑ *Click the **Sent Items** button on the Outlook bar.*

Ⓒ *Double-click to open the second Quarterly Report message to Robert Smith. This should be the message with the worksheet.*

This is how Robert Smith would receive your worksheet email message. The worksheet is faithfully reproduced in the message. However, notice that there are no working formulas on the worksheet. Robert Smith could not edit this worksheet. All he can do is view and print it

16. Close ☒ the message window; then close ☒ the Outlook window.

17. Drag the **Shortcut to First Quarter Report** shortcut on the Desktop to the Recycle Bin. Click **Yes** if you are asked to confirm the deletion.

Concepts Review

True/False Questions

1. Windows lets you create folders inside of other folders.   TRUE   FALSE

2. A shortcut lets you access a folder from the Desktop.   TRUE   FALSE

3. An attachment is a file that is sent along with an email message.   TRUE   FALSE

4. Excel always automatically prints the comments in any document.   TRUE   FALSE

5. Once a comment has been created, you cannot change it.   TRUE   FALSE

6. A hyperlink in an Excel workbook works just like a hyperlink on a typical Web page.   TRUE   FALSE

7. It doesn't matter which format you select when you use the Paste Special command.   TRUE   FALSE

8. Excel's **E-mail** button on the toolbar sends the workbook as an attachment.   TRUE   FALSE

9. To view comments on a worksheet, you must point at each cell individually.   TRUE   FALSE

10. A Favorite can help you navigate quickly to a folder or disk drive.   TRUE   FALSE

Multiple-Choice Questions

1. Which statement about email message attachments is true?

   a. An attachment can be any type of file.

   b. An attachment must be an Excel workbook file.

   c. An attachment is a second email message attached to the first one.

   d. None of the above

2. What controls the name that identifies a comment?

   a. The name is set up in the Comments window.

   b. You must reinstall Excel in order to change the name.

   c. The name is set in Excel's Options window.

   d. Excel sets the name according to your log-on name.

3. Which description of a hyperlink in Exel is true?

   a. A hyperlink can point to another cell in a workbook.

   b. A hyperlink can point to another file on a disk drive.

   c. A link can point to a Web page.

   d. Only a and c

   e. a, b, and c

4. Which statement best describes how the Paste Special command differs from an ordinary Paste command?

   a. Paste Special can only be used to paste values, not formulas.

   b. Paste Special lets you select the format of the data you paste.

   c. Paste Special works exactly like the Paste command.

   d. Paste Special never pastes formatting.

Financial Modeling and Absolute Cell References

Excel lets you reference cells in several ways. Thus far, you have used relative cell references. In this lesson, you will use a new type of referencing known as absolute cell referencing. Absolute cell references are useful in financial models and a variety of other worksheets. You will learn important financial modeling techniques in this lesson, as well as several new printing techniques.

In This Lesson

Case Study

In his spare time, Martin Johnson has developed a fun new board game to help both children and adults develop language skills. Martin decides to set up a new business venture to market his Crazy Words board game. You will develop a financial model to help Martin plan the growth and profitability of his business. You will use absolute cell references when setting up the model.

The model will be set up to allow Martin to change variables such as the selling price of the game, manufacturing costs, and the commission rates of sales people. Whenever a variable is changed, the model will recalculate important financial information, such as the gross profit. This powerful capability will let Martin perform "what-if" analysis. For example, the model will provide answers to questions such as "What will my gross profit be if I lower my manufacturing cost to $9 per unit?" The completed model is shown below.

	A	B	C	D	E	F
1	**Crazy Words Financial Model**					
2						
3	Projected Units Sold	$10,000	$50,000	$100,000	$500,000	$1,000,000
4	Revenue	$150,000	$750,000	$1,200,000	$4,875,000	$7,500,000
5	Manufacturing Cost	$100,000	$415,000	$730,000	$2,260,000	$3,160,000
6	Marketing	$3,000	$15,000	$24,000	$97,500	$150,000
7	Commissions	$15,000	$75,000	$120,000	$487,500	$750,000
8	Office Expenses	$750	$3,750	$6,000	$24,375	$37,500
9	Rent	$12,000	$12,000	$12,000	$36,000	$36,000
10	Consulting Fees	$5,000	$5,000	$5,000	$15,000	$15,000
11						
12	Total Costs	$135,750	$525,750	$897,000	$2,920,375	$4,148,500
13	Gross Profit	$14,250	$224,250	$303,000	$1,954,625	$3,351,500
14	Net Profit	$9,263	$145,763	$196,950	$1,270,506	$2,178,475
15	Gross Profit vs. Revenue	10%	30%	25%	40%	45%
16						
17	Initial Selling Price	$15		Commission Rate		10%
18	Manufacturing Setup Cost	$10,000		Tax Rate		35%
19	Initial Manufacturing Unit Cost	$9		Office Expenses		0.50%

Absolute Cell References

Excel lets you use **relative, absolute,** and **mixed** cell references in formulas. You have been using relative references thus far in this course. Relative references are convenient because they are updated when formulas are moved or copied. However, you will encounter situations where you may not want references updated when a formula is moved or copied. You must use absolute or mixed references in these situations. Absolute references always refer to the same cell regardless of which cell the formula is moved to or copied to.

Creating Absolute References

You create absolute references by placing dollar signs in front of the column and row components of the reference. For example, the reference $C$1 is absolute because it has a dollar sign in front of both the column and row components. You can type the dollar signs as you enter a formula, or you can add the dollar signs later by editing the formula. The following illustration shows an example of how absolute references are used in formulas.

C4	▼	=	=B4*$C$1

	A	B	C
1	Commission Rate		10%
2			
3		Total Sales	Commission
4	John	$ 8,500	850
5	Ned	$ 10,000	
6	Ellen	$ 18,000	

Cell C4 contains the formula =B4*$C$1, *as shown in the Formula bar.*

The formula becomes =B5*$C$1 *when it is copied down to Cell C5. The relative reference B4 is updated to B5 in the new formula, but the absolute reference $C$1 continues to refer to the Commission Rate in Cell C1.*

The formula becomes =B6*$C$1 *when it is copied to this cell.*

Mixed References

You can mix a relative reference and an absolute reference within a reference. For example, the reference $C1 is a combination of an absolute reference to Column C and a relative reference to Row 1. Mixed references are useful when copying many types of formulas.

Using the (F4) Key

You can make a reference absolute or mixed by typing dollar signs while entering the reference. You can also click in front of a reference in the Formula bar and use the (F4) key to insert the dollar signs. The first time you tap (F4), dollar signs are placed in front of both the column and row components of the reference. If you tap (F4) again, the dollar sign is removed from the column component, thus creating a mixed reference. If you tap (F4) a third time, a dollar sign is placed in front of just the column component.

Revising Formulas

You can revise any formula by editing the formula directly in the cell, or you can click in the Formula bar and make the desired editing changes. You can complete an edited formula by tapping the (ENTER) key or clicking the Enter button on the Formula bar.

Hands-On 8.1 Use Absolute Cell References and Edit Formulas

In this exercise, you will open the Crazy Words workbook from your exercise diskette. You will enter formulas using absolute cell references. You will also copy formulas.

Enter a Formula with Relative References

1. Start Excel, and open the workbook named **Hands-On Lesson 8.**

   Take a few moments to study the workbook. In particular, notice that Rows 4 through 15 will contain formulas. Many of the formulas require absolute references. The absolute references will refer to the variables in Rows 17 through 19. When this project is finished, you will be able to apply what-if analyses by quickly changing the Initial Selling Price, Manufacturing Setup Cost, and other variables. The model will be recalculated each time you change a variable.

2. Click Cell B4.

   The Revenue in Cell B4 is equal to the Projected Units Sold in B3 multiplied by the Initial Selling Price in B17. In the next step, you will enter a formula that uses relative references.

3. Type the formula **=B3*B17**, and complete the entry.

   The result should be 150,000. This is the correct number.

4. Use the fill handle to copy the formula one cell to the right.

   Cell C4 should display a blank result.

5. Click Cell C4, and notice the formula =C3*C17 in the Formula bar.

   Notice that Cell C17 is empty. The formula in Cell B4 uses relative references, so Excel updated the references in Cell C4 when you copied the formula. This is incorrect because you want Cell C4 to continue to refer to the Initial Selling Price in Cell B17. In the next few steps, you will convert the reference in Cell B4 to an absolute reference.

6. Click Undo [↺] to reverse the copy.

Edit and Copy the Formula

7. Click Cell B4 and follow these steps to convert the B17 reference to absolute:

   Ⓐ *Click in the Formula bar just in front of the B17 reference.*

   ✕ ✓ = =B3*B17

   Ⓑ *Tap the F4 key, and Excel will insert dollar signs in front of the B and the 17.*

8. Complete the entry, and the result should still be 150,000.

9. Use the fill handle to copy the formula one cell to the right.

   Cell C4 should now have the correct result of 750,000.

10. Click Cell C4, and notice the formula =C3*$B$17 in the Formula bar.

    Notice that the relative reference B3 was updated to C3. This is correct because the formula should refer to the Projected Units Sold in Cell C3. The absolute reference $B$17, however, continues to refer to the Initial Selling Price in Cell B17. This is also correct.

11. Use the fill handle to copy the formula in Cell C4 across the row to Cells D4, E4 and F4.

(Continued on the next page)

Apply a Discount Percentage to Cells D4, E4, and F4

This model assumes that the selling price decreases as the Number of Units Sold increases. This is because Martin will need to depend upon large distributors to sell large numbers of games. Initially, he will sell his game through small outlets at $15 per copy. However, he will need large distributors if he ever wants to sell 1,000,000 games. These distributors will demand large discounts.

12. Click Cell D4.

13. Click in the Formula bar just to the right of the formula.
Notice that Excel changes the color of the cell references and the corresponding worksheet cells. This makes it easy for you to identify which cells the formula is referencing.

14. Type ***80%** to make the formula =D3*$B$17*80%.
The new formula will reduce the selling price to 80% of the Initial Selling Price.

15. Complete the entry, and the result should be 1,200,000.

16. Click Cell E4, and use the technique in the preceding steps to multiply that formula by 65%.
The result should be 4,875,000.

17. Multiply the formula in Cell F4 by 50%.
The result should equal 7,500,000. Fifty percent is the maximum discount that Martin will give.

Experiment with What-If Analysis

In the next few steps, you will adjust the Initial Selling Price in Cell B17. When you do this, the formulas will be recalculated in Row 4. Financial models are usually set up with variables that can be adjusted. This allows you to apply what-if analyses and determine the outcome of various variable combinations.

18. Click Cell B17.

19. Type **20**, and complete the entry.
Notice how the numbers in Row 4 have been recalculated. The number displayed in Cell B4 should be 200,000, B5 should be 1,000,000, etc.

20. Change the number in B17 to **10**, and watch the numbers recalculate again.
Notice that this lets you determine the impact of the Initial Selling Price on the revenue.

21. Change the number in B17 back to **15**.

Calculate the Manufacturing Costs in Row 5

The manufacturing cost of the Crazy Words game is composed of an initial setup cost and a per unit cost for each additional game manufactured. The setup cost is fixed unless Martin can find another manufacturer with lower setup fees. The per-unit cost decreases as the volume increases. For example, Martin can expect to have much lower per-unit manufacturing costs at 1,000,000 units sold than at 10,000 units sold. In the next few steps, you will enter the formulas to model this situation.

22. Click Cell B5.

23. Type **=$B$18+B3*$B$19** exactly as shown, including the dollar signs.

24. Complete the entry, and the result should be 130,000.

25. Take a few moments to study the formula you just entered.

Notice that it adds the Manufacturing Setup Cost in Cell B18 to the product (multiplication) of the Units Sold in B3 and the Initial Manufacturing Unit Cost in B19. Notice that both the B18 and B19 references are absolute, because you will copy the formula across the row in the next few steps. You will want the copied formulas to continue to refer to those same cells.

26. Use the fill handle to copy the formula across the row to Cells C5 through F5.

27. Take a moment to study the results.

Notice that Martin's Manufacturing costs are greater than his revenue when the Projected Units Sold reaches 500,000 in Column E. This is because the Manufacturing Cost needs to decrease as the Projected Units Sold increases. You will apply the necessary discount percentages in the next few steps. We will assume that Martin's Initial Manufacturing Unit Cost will be reduced by 65% when the Projected Units Sold reaches 1,000,000.

Apply the Discount Percentages

28. Click Cell C5.

29. Click in the formula bar, and type ***90%** at the end of the formula.

*The new formula =$B$18+C3*$B$19*90% will reduce the manufacturing cost of each unit to 90% of the initial manufacturing cost.*

30. Complete the entry, and the result should be 480,000.

31. Click Cell D5, and use the technique in the preceding steps to multiply that formula by 80%.

The result should be 830,000.

32. Multiply the formula in Cell E5 by 50%, and multiply the formula in Cell F5 by 35%.

Calculate the Marketing Costs in Row 6

The Marketing Costs in Row 6 will include a $100,000 charge for developing an infomercial to promote Martin's game. The Marketing Costs will also include a component that is equal to 3% of the revenue. This 3% will cover the cost of running the infomercial, and developing and mailing product literature.

33. Click Cell B6.

34. Enter the formula **=100000+B4*3%** (five zeros).

The result should be 104,500. Notice that there is no need to use absolute references in this formula, because you are not referencing the variables in Rows 17, 18, and 19. In fact, you want B4 to be a relative reference, because you will want it to change to B5, B6, etc. when you copy the formula across the row.

35. Use the fill handle to copy the formula to Cells C6 through F6.

Calculate the Commissions in Row 7

36. Click Cell B7.

37. Enter the formula **=B4*$F$17**.

The result should be 21,000.

38. Use the fill handle to copy the formula to Cells C7 through F7.

39. Click in each cell in Row 7 and notice the formulas in the Formula bar.

Notice how Excel updates the relative reference B4 but leaves the absolute reference $F$17 as it is.

(Continued on the next page)

Calculate the Office Expenses in Row 8

The Office Expenses use the same type of formula as the commissions. They are calculated as 1/2% of the revenue. Once again, these are approximations. You will apply what-if analysis with these percentages later in this lesson.

40. Click Cell B8.

41. Enter the formula **=B4*$F$19**.

42. Copy the formula across the row to Cells C8 through F8.

Enter the Rent and Consulting Fees in Rows 9 and 10

Martin is starting his Crazy Words business out of his home and garage. He believes he can achieve a unit volume of 100,000 before opening an office and warehouse. His rent payment is $12,000 per year ($1,000 per month). He assumes an office and warehouse will cost $36,000 per year. Likewise, he expects to spend $5,000 on consulting fees when his unit sales are below 100,000 and $15,000 when sales are above 100,000. In the next step, you will enter these numbers into Rows 9 and 10 of the model. There is no need to use formulas in Rows 9 and 10.

43. Enter the numbers shown below into Rows 9 and 10.

9	Rent	12,000	12,000	12,000	36,000	36,000
10	Consulting Fees	5,000	5,000	5,000	15,000	15,000

Calculate the Total Costs in Row 12

44. Click Cell B12.

45. Click the AutoSum Σ button, and Excel will propose the incorrect formula =SUM(B3:B11). *This formula includes the Projected Units Sold and Revenue in Rows 3 and 4, which is incorrect.*

46. Select the range B5:B11, and complete the entry. *The result should be 273,250.*

47. Use the fill handle to copy the formula across the row.

Calculate the Gross Profit in Row 13

The Gross Profit is the Revenue in Row 4 minus the Total Costs in Row 12.

48. Click Cell B13 and enter the formula **=B4−B12**. *The result should be −123,250 or (123,250). As you can see, the model shows us that Martin won't do well if he sells only 10,000 units.*

49. Use the fill handle to copy the formula across the row.

Calculate the Net Profit in Row 14

*The Net Profit is equal to the Gross Profit minus taxes. In this model, we will assume a flat tax rate of 35%, as shown in Cell F18. The Net Profit formula is Net Profit = Gross Profit * (1−TaxRate). For example, if the tax rate is 35%, then (1−TaxRate) = 65%. Martin will retain 65% of the profit and 35% will be paid in taxes. You will use absolute references in the Net Profit formula when referencing the Tax Rate in Cell F18. You will also use parentheses to change the order of calculations.*

50. Click Cell B14, and enter the formula **=B13*(1–$F$18)** exactly as shown.

The result should be –80,113 or (80,113). This result makes no sense, because Martin won't pay taxes if he loses money. However, we will leave it as it is for now. Notice that parentheses were required in the formula you just entered. You want Excel to subtract the Tax Rate in F18 from the number 1 first, then multiply the result by Cell B13. The parentheses instruct Excel to perform the subtraction calculation first.

51. Use the fill handle to copy the formula across the row.

Calculate the Gross Profit vs. Revenue in Row 15

In a previous lesson, you learned that the Gross Profit vs. Revenue ratio can be an important ratio in determining the health of a business. You will calculate this ratio in the following steps.

52. Click Cell B15, and enter the formula **=B13/B4**.

The result should be –1 or (1). Notice there is no need to use absolute references in this formula.

53. Use the fill handle to copy the formula across the row.

Cells C15 through F15 should contain zeros. This is because the ratio returns a number between 0 and 1. You must format the cells with the Percent style in order to see the correct percentage.

54. Select Cells B15:F15.

55. Use the Percent Style % button to format the numbers.

56. Save the changes to your workbook.

At this point, your worksheet should match the following example.

	A	B	C	D	E	F
1	**Crazy Words Financial Model**					
2						
3	Projected Units Sold	10,000	50,000	100,000	500,000	1,000,000
4	Revenue	150,000	750,000	1,200,000	4,875,000	7,500,000
5	Manufacturing Cost	130,000	480,000	830,000	2,530,000	3,530,000
6	Marketing	104,500	122,500	136,000	246,250	325,000
7	Commissions	21,000	105,000	168,000	682,500	1,050,000
8	Office Expenses	750	3,750	6,000	24,375	37,500
9	Rent	12,000	12,000	12,000	36,000	36,000
10	Consulting Fees	5,000	5,000	5,000	15,000	15,000
11						
12	Total Costs	273,250	728,250	1,157,000	3,534,125	4,993,500
13	Gross Profit	(123,250)	21,750	43,000	1,340,875	2,506,500
14	Net Profit	(80,113)	14,138	27,950	871,569	1,629,225
15	Gross Profit vs. Revenue	-82%	3%	4%	28%	33%
16						
17	Initial Selling Price	$15		Commission Rate		14%
18	Manufacturing Setup Cost	$30,000		Tax Rate		35%
19	Initial Manufacturing Unit Cost	$10		Office Expenses		0.50%

Custom Number Formats

Thus far, you have used buttons on the Formatting toolbar to apply formatting styles to numbers. For example, the Comma button applies the Comma style, and the Currency button applies the Currency style. You have also applied number formats using the Number tab on the Format Cells dialog box. The Number tab also has a Custom option that lets you create your own custom number formats if the built-in formats do not meet your needs.

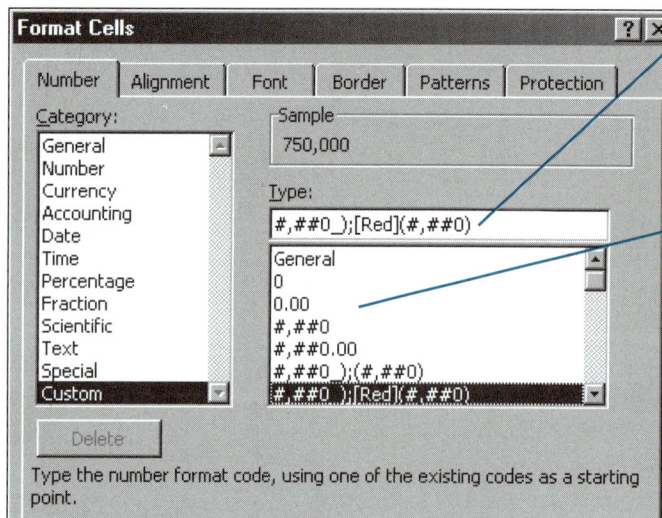

*You can create a custom number format by typing a sequence of formatting symbols in the **Type** box.*

*You can also choose one of Excel's built-in custom formats from this list and then modify the format in the **Type** box.*

Custom Number Format Sections

Custom number formats can have up to four sections. Each section contains formatting symbols. The formatting symbols determine how an entry is formatted if it meets the criteria of that section. The sections are positive format, negative format, zero format, and text-value format. For example, if a number entry is positive, then the formatting symbols from the positive section are used to format the number. If the number entry is negative, then the formatting symbols from the negative section are used to format the number. The following illustration shows a typical custom number format. Notice the formatting symbols in each section. Semicolons are used to separate the sections.

Postive format *Zero format*

\#,##0.00_);[Red](\#,##0.00); _(* "-"??_);_(@_)

Negative format *Text-value format*

Formatting Symbols

The formatting symbols in custom number formats determine how Excel formats an entry. The following table describes the most common symbols.

CUSTOM NUMBER FORMAT SYMBOLS

Symbol	Description
Decimal point (.)	Symbols to the left of the decimal format the integer portion of the number. Symbols to the right of the decimal format the decimal portion of the number.
Zero (0)	The zero symbol acts as a placeholder. Excel will display as many digits as there are zeros in a particular part of a formatting code. For example, in the preceding illustration, there are two zeros to the right of the decimal point in the positive format section. This instructs Excel to format positive numbers by displaying two digits to the right of the decimal point.
Number sign (#)	The number sign symbol behaves like the zero symbol. However, if the number sign symbol is used, then Excel will only display as many digits as there are in the actual number. For example, if two number signs ## were used to the right of the decimal point but the number only had one decimal digit, then Excel would only display one digit to the right of the decimal. In this same example, if two zeros (00) had been used in the formatting code, then Excel would display the decimal digit plus one additional zero to the right of the decimal point.
Thousands separator (,)	The comma is used as a thousands separator. For example, the format symbol sequence #,### instructs Excel to place a comma between every third digit.
Color [Red]	You can change the color of an entry by inserting square brackets with the name of a color at the front of a custom number format section. For example, the preceding illustration shows the formatting code [Red](#,##0.00) for the negative number format. This instructs Excel to format negative numbers with red. You can use the colors Black, Blue, Cyan, Green, Magenta, Red, White, and Yellow.
Underscore (_)	The underscore inserts space equal to the width of the next character. For example, the preceding illustration shows the formatting code #,##0.00_) for the positive format code. The _) combination instructs Excel to insert space equal to the width of the) character.

Use Online Help

1. Click the Office Assistant or choose **Help→Microsoft Excel Help** if the Office Assistant is not visible.

2. Type the phrase **custom number formats** in the Assistant's speech balloon, and click the Search button.

3. Choose the **Create a custom number format** topic.

4. Take a moment to read the Help topic, and then click the *number* hyperlink in the last paragraph of text.

5. Read through the Help topic until you are confident that you understand the concepts presented thus far.

   Custom number formatting is a rather difficult topic for most beginners to understand. Fortunately, you probably won't need to use it often, since most of the necessary number formatting styles are built into Excel.

6. Close the Help screen when you have finished.

Create the Custom Number Format

7. Select the range B4:F14.

   This range includes all numbers from the Revenue row down to the Net Profit row.

8. Choose **Format→Cells** and make sure the Number tab is active.

9. Follow these steps to create the custom format:

Ⓐ *Choose* Custom, *and then choose this number format from the list of built-in custom formats. It should be the seventh format on the list.*

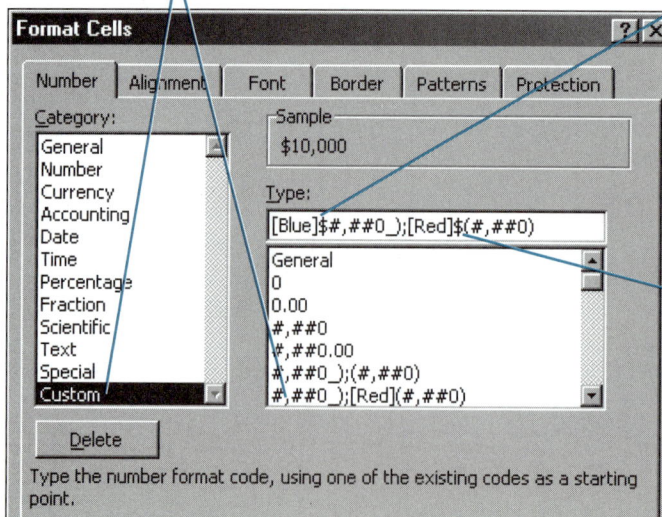

Ⓑ *Click in the* **Type** *box in front of the first # character in the format.*

Ⓒ *Type* **[Blue]$**, *making sure to include the square brackets and the dollar sign.*

Ⓓ *Click just in front of the left parenthesis (in the negative format section), and type a dollar sign* **$**. *Your new custom format should match the format shown here.*

Ⓔ *Click* **OK** *to apply the format to the selected cells.*

Format Cells   ? ×

| Number | Alignment | Font | Border | Patterns | Protection |

Category:

- General
- Number
- Currency
- Accounting
- Date
- Time
- Percentage
- Fraction
- Scientific
- Text
- Special
- Custom

Sample
$10,000

Type:
[Blue]$#,##0_);[Red]$(#,##0)

- General
- 0
- 0.00
- #,##0
- #,##0.00
- #,##0_);(#,##0)
- #,##0_);[Red](#,##0)

Delete

Type the number format code, using one of the existing codes as a starting point.

---

10. Click anywhere in the worksheet to deselect the cells.

    All positive numbers in the range B4:F14 should now be formatted with blue, while negative numbers will be in red. Also, all numbers should be preceded by dollar signs. As you can see from this exercise, often the best way to create a custom format is to modify one of Excel's built-in custom formats. The new format you just created has been added to the end of the list of custom formats. The built-in custom format you modified has been preserved in its original format.

11. Save the changes to your workbook.

    The custom number format is only available in this workbook. If you wanted to use it in another workbook, then you could use Copy and Paste to copy a cell containing the format to the new workbook.

Displaying Formulas

CTRL +~ to display or hide formulas

Excel normally displays the results of formulas in worksheet cells. However, you may need to display the actual formulas from time to time. Displaying the formulas can be helpful, especially in complex worksheets like the Crazy Words financial model. Displaying the formulas can help you understand how a worksheet functions. It can also be used to "debug" the worksheet to locate potential problems. To display formulas, you use the **Tools→Options** command to display the Options dialog box. The Options dialog box contains a View tab with a Formulas check box. Checking the Formulas box will cause formulas to be displayed in all worksheet cells. The Options dialog box can be used to set numerous other global options.

Hands-On 8.3 Display Formulas and Perform What-If Analyses

1. Choose **Tools→Options,** and make sure that the View tab is active.

2. Check the Formulas box, and click **OK.**
   Excel will widen the worksheet columns to display the formulas.

3. Feel free to browse through the worksheet and review the formulas.
   Notice how useful this technique could be if you wanted to understand how a worksheet functions. This technique is also useful for locating problems in formulas.

4. Click the Print Preview ⬛ button.

5. Feel free to use the Next and Previous buttons to browse through the pages.
   Notice that you could print the formulas if desired.

6. Click the **Close** button to exit from Print Preview.

7. Choose **Tools→Options** from the menu bar.

8. Uncheck the Formulas box, and click **OK** to remove the formulas display.

(Continued on the next page)

9. Take a close look at the Gross Profit in Row 13 and the Gross Profit vs. Revenue in Row 15. Can you draw any conclusions from the numbers? Will Martin's business be healthy if Projected Units Sold is less than 100,000?

   After analyzing the model, Martin realizes he will be quite wealthy if everything goes right and he sells 500,000 units or more. However, he also realizes this may not happen. He needs to make the business profitable even if only 10,000 units are sold. His goal is a Gross Profit vs. Revenue ratio of 10% at 10,000 units sold, and 20% at 50,000 units and above.

10. Click Cell B6.

    Look at the Formula bar, and notice the 100,000 cost for developing the infomercial. Martin realizes the $100,000 infomercial is a bad idea. He decides to cancel the infomercial and concentrate on hiring sales people. You will make the necessary adjustments in the next few steps.

11. Enter the new formula **=B4*2%** in Cell B6.

    The result should be 3,000. You reduced the percentage from 3% to 2%, because Martin no longer needs to air the infomercial.

12. Use the fill handle to copy the formula across the row.

    Notice that eliminating the $100,000 infomercial has a huge impact on the Gross Profit and Gross Profit vs. Revenue. This is especially true when the units sold are 100,000 or less. However, the Gross Profit vs. Revenue is still less than 20% when the units sold are less than 100,000. Martin realizes that the Manufacturing Setup Cost in Cell B18 is prohibitively high. Also, the initial Manufacturing Unit Cost of $10 is high, especially when the Units Sold are small. Martin decides to locate another manufacturer to help reduce these costs.

13. Click Cell B18.

14. Enter the number **15000**, and watch the impact this change has on the model.

    Notice that the entire model is recalculated. Pay close attention to the numbers in Rows 13 and 15.

15. Now enter the number **10000**, and notice the impact this change has.

16. Change the Initial Manufacturing Cost in Cell B19 from $10 to **$9**.

    This should have a huge impact on the profitability of the business. As you can see, the model has shown us that keeping the manufacturing cost low is extremely important. Also, notice that there are no longer any negative numbers in the worksheet. Excel automatically formats the new positive numbers with blue, using the custom number format you set up in the previous exercise.

17. Click Cell F17, and change the commission rate from 14% to **10%**.

    What kind of impact does this change have? Will reducing the commission rate have an impact on the number of units sold? As you can see, many of the variables are interdependent. However, the model shows us the impact of changing one or more variables.

18. Take a few minutes to experiment with the model.

    Feel free to change any of the variables in Rows 17 through 19.

Printing Selections

There are times that you may want to print only a range of cells. You can do this by selecting the desired cells, choosing **File→Print,** clicking the Selection button, and clicking **OK.**

Hands-On 8.4 Print a Selection

1. Select the range A1:F15.
   This selection will allow you to print the main part of the model without the variables.

2. Choose **File→Print** from the menu bar.

3. Choose the Selection option button, and then click the **Preview** button at the bottom left corner of the dialog box.
   Notice that only the selected cells are visible in Print Preview.

4. Click the **Close** button to exit from Print Preview.

Print Areas

A print area is a range of cells that are marked for printing. When you set a print area, only that area is printed. This has the same effect as printing a selection; however, a print area remains in effect until you reset it. Print areas are convenient if you intend to print the same area more than once. For example, you may have a report that you print on a weekly or monthly basis.

Quick Reference

SETTING, PRINTING, AND CLEARING PRINT AREAS	
Set a print area.	Select the desired cells, and choose File→Print Area→Set Print Area
Print a print area.	Click the Print button.
Clear a print area.	Choose File→Print Area→Clear Print Area.

1. Select the same range, Cells A1:F15, as you selected in the previous exercise.

2. Choose **File→Print Area→Set Print Area** from the menu bar.

3. Click in the worksheet to deselect the cells.
   Notice that a dashed line surrounds the range A1:F15. This line shows you the current print area.

4. Click the Print Preview [icon] button.
   Notice that only Cells A1:F15 are visible in Print Preview, even though they are no longer selected in the worksheet. A print area remains in effect until you clear it or reset it.

5. Close Print Preview, and choose **File→Print Area→Clear Print Area** from the menu bar.

6. Click the Print Preview [icon] button, and notice the variable rows are now displayed at the bottom of the worksheet.

7. Close Print Preview, and save the changes to your workbook.

Auditing Tools

Excel's auditing tools are useful for analyzing and debugging worksheets. These tools are particularly useful in worksheets with complex formulas that are dependent upon other formulas. The auditing tools are also quite useful for locating errors in formulas.

The Auditing Toolbar

The **Tools→Auditing→Show Auditing Toolbar** command displays the Auditing toolbar. The Auditing toolbar is used primarily for displaying and hiding **cell tracers.** Cell tracers are arrows that identify precedent and dependent cells. You will learn about precedents and dependents in a moment. The following illustration describes the buttons on the Auditing toolbar.

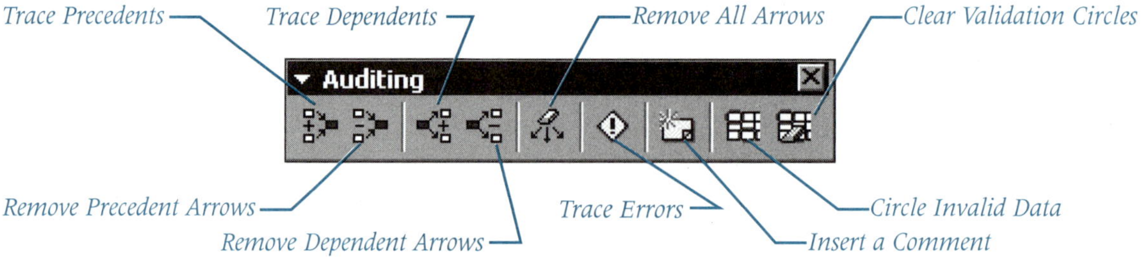

Trace Precedents — Trace Dependents — Remove All Arrows — Clear Validation Circles

▼ Auditing ✕

Remove Precedent Arrows — Trace Errors — Circle Invalid Data
Remove Dependent Arrows — Insert a Comment

Tracing Precedents

The Trace Precedents ![button] button on the Auditing toolbar lets you see the precedent cells of a cell containing a formula. Precedents are cells that are referenced by a formula. A formula can reference cells with values or it can reference cells that contain formulas. Thus, a formula can have several levels of precedents. The Trace Precedents button displays arrows that point from the precedent cells to the cell with the formula. The arrows show you the cells the formula is dependent upon. The first time you click the Trace Precedents button, the first level of precedent arrows is displayed. If there are two or more levels of precedent cells, you can continue to click the Trace Precedents button to display the additional levels. The following illustration shows the Hands-On Lesson 8 workbook with the precedent cell tracers (arrows) displayed.

*Cell B4 contains the revenue formula =B3*$B$17. Cells B3 and B17 are the precedent cells because the formula is dependent upon them.*

	A	B	C
1	**Crazy Words Financial Model**		
2			
3	Projected Units Sold	10,000	50,000
4	Revenue	$150,000	$750,000
5	Manufacturing Cost	$100,000	$415,000
6	Marketing	$3,000	$15,000
7	Commissions	$15,000	$75,000
8	Office Expenses	$750	$3,750
9	Rent	$12,000	$12,000
10	Consulting Fees	$5,000	$5,000
11			
12	Total Costs	$135,750	$525,750
13	Gross Profit	$14,250	$224,250
14	Net Profit	$9,263	$145,763
15	Gross Profit vs. Revenue	10%	30%
16			
17	Initial Selling Price	$15	
18	Manufacturing Setup Cost	$10,000	
19	Initial Manufacturing Unit Cost	$9	

When Trace Precedents is activated, arrows point from the precedent cells to the cell with the formula. The arrows begin in the precedent cells with a large dot and terminate with an arrowhead in the cell containing the formula.

1. Click Cell B4 and choose **Tools→Auditing→Show Auditing Toolbar** from the menu bar.

2. Click the Trace Precedents ⬚ button on the Auditing toolbar.
   Excel should display arrows pointing from the precedent cells B3 and B17 to Cell B4. The arrows indicate that cell B4 is dependent upon these cells.

3. Click the Clear Precedent Arrows ⬚ button on the Auditing toolbar.

4. Click cell B15 and click the Trace Precedents ⬚ button.
   Excel displays the first level of precedent arrows.

5. Click the Trace Precedents ⬚ button three more times.
   Each time you click the Trace Precedents button, Excel displays the next level of precedent arrows. There are several levels of precedent cells because the formula in cell B15 refers to cells B13 and B4, which also contain formulas, etc. The precedent arrows should clearly show you the cells that Cell B15 is dependent upon.

6. Now click the Remove All Arrows ⬚ button to remove all precedent arrows.
   You must use the Remove All Arrows button to remove arrows if multiple precedent levels are displayed.

Tracing Dependents

The Trace Dependents ⊞ button on the Auditing toolbar lets you see the dependent cells of a cell containing a value. Dependents are cells with formulas that reference the cell with the value. The Trace Dependents button displays a new set of arrows each time you click the button until all dependent cells are identified.

Hands-On 8.7 Trace Dependents

1. Click Cell B17.
   There are several cells with formulas that depend upon the Initial Selling Price in Cell B17.

2. Click the Trace Dependents ⊞ button on the Auditing toolbar.
   Arrows should point to Cells B4:F4. These cells have formulas that reference Cell B17.

3. Click the Trace Dependents ⊞ button again.
   A new set of arrows appears. The arrows point to cells that are dependent upon Cells B4:F4.

4. Click the Trace Dependents ⊞ button two more times until all dependent arrows are displayed.

5. Click the Remove All Arrows ⊞ button.

Tracing Errors

The Trace Error ⬦ button can help you identify cells that are causing an error to occur in a formula. Often, cells with formulas will display error messages such as #VALUE!, #NAME!, or #DIV/0!. Errors such as these are caused by incorrect values or errors in formulas in precedent cells (cells the formula is dependent upon). The Tracing Errors button displays arrows that point from the cell(s) causing the problem to the cell with the formula.

Hands-On 8.8 Trace Errors

1. Click Cell B15.
   Notice the formula =B13/B4 is entered in the cell. Excel displays a #DIV/0! message whenever a formula references a cell that causes division by 0. For example, in the next step, you will enter 0 into Cell B4. This will cause the formula to divide by 0, which will produce an error.

2. Click Cell B4 and enter **0** in the cell.

3. Click Cell B15 and then click the Trace Error ⬦ button.
   Excel displays an arrow pointing from Cell B4 to Cell B13 and then to Cell B15. Notice that the Trace Error feature does not tell you what the error is. It simply identifies the cell or cells where the error is located.

4. Click Cell B4 and enter the formula **=B3*$B$17**.

5. Click the Remove All Arrows ⬦ button.

6. Feel free to experiment with the auditing tools.

7. Close the Auditing toolbar when you have finished.

8. Save the changes to the workbook, and then close the workbook.

Concepts Review

True/False Questions

1. Absolute references continue to refer to the same cell even if a formula that contains them is moved.   TRUE   FALSE

2. Formulas containing absolute references cannot be copied.   TRUE   FALSE

3. Absolute references are identified by dollar signs.   TRUE   FALSE

4. Absolute references and relative references can be combined in the same formula.   TRUE   FALSE

5. Custom number formats can have up to three different sections.   TRUE   FALSE

6. You can apply colors to numbers using custom number formats.   TRUE   FALSE

7. The comma symbol (,) is used as a thousands separator in custom number formats.   TRUE   FALSE

8. A print area is automatically cleared immediately after you print a worksheet.   TRUE   FALSE

Multiple-Choice Questions

1. Which keystroke is used to convert a relative reference to an absolute reference?
   a. F1
   b. F2
   c. F4
   d. F8

2. Which cell reference is a mixed reference?
   a. $B$6
   b. $B6
   c. B$6
   d. Both B and C

3. Which command is used to turn on the display of formulas?
   a. Format→Cells
   b. Tools→Options
   c. File→Page Setup
   d. Format→Borders and Shading

4. Which of the following can be included in a custom number format?
   a. Color
   b. Thousands separators
   c. Dollar signs
   d. All of these

Skill Builders

Skill Builder 8.1 Use Absolute References

In this exercise, you will create a worksheet that calculates commissions as Total Sales * Commission Rate. You will change the Commission Rate to see the impact this change has on the Total Sales. You will use an absolute reference when referencing the commission rate.

1. Start a new workbook, and set up the worksheet shown below. Type all numbers in the worksheet as shown.

	A	B	C
1	January Commission Report		
2			
3	Commission Rate		10%
4			
5		Total Sales	Commission
6	John	42000	
7	Ned	38000	
8	Ellen	65000	
9	Hellen	18000	
10	Bill	29000	

2. Click Cell C6, and enter the formula **=B6*$C$3**.
   The result should be 4200. Cell C3 must be referenced with an absolute reference. This is because you will copy the formula down the column, and the new formulas must also reference Cell C3.

3. Use the fill handle to copy the formula down the column to Cells C7 through C10.

4. Click Cell C3, and change the percentage to 15%.
   By this time, you should see the benefit of setting up variables (such as the commission rate) and then referencing them in formulas. This gives you the ability to perform what-if analyses. Keep in mind that you will almost always need to use absolute references when referencing variables in this manner. Absolute references are necessary whenever you copy a formula that references a variable in a fixed location.

5. Change the commission percentage back to 10%.

6. Save the workbook with the name **Skill Builder 8.1,** and then close the workbook.

Skill Builder 8.2 **Use Mixed References**

In this exercise, you will open a workbook from your exercise diskette. You will create a formula that uses a mixed cell reference. The column component of the reference will be relative, but the row component will be absolute.

Enter the Initial Formula

1. Open the workbook named **Skill Builder 8.2.**

2. Take a moment to study the worksheet.
   The goal of this exercise is to create a formula in Cell B6 that can be copied across Rows 6, 9, 12, and 15. The formula in Cell B6 will divide the Eastern Region's Q1 sales in Cell B5 by the Q1 goal in Cell B3. The general form of the formula will be =B5/B3. However, a mixed reference will be needed to allow you to copy the formula.

3. Click Cell B6, and enter the formula **=B5/B3.**
   The result should be 75%. The formula returned the correct result. However, you won't be able to copy the formula to other rows, as you will see in the next few steps. Also notice that Cell B6 (and the other cells) have already been formatted with the proper currency and percent formats.

Try Copying the Formula

4. Make sure the highlight is in Cell B6, and click the Copy 📋 button.

5. Click Cell B9, and click the Paste 📋 button.
   The result should be a very large percentage. This is obviously an incorrect result.

6. Look at the Formula bar, and notice that the formula in Cell B9 is =B8/B6.
   Look at Cells B8 and B6, and you will notice that B8 is the correct reference, but B6 is incorrect. You must use a mixed reference if you want to copy the formula from Cell B6.

7. Click Undo ↩ to reverse the paste.

Convert the Reference to a Mixed Reference

8. Click Cell B6.

9. Click in the Formula bar just in front of the B3 reference.

10. Tap the (F4) key **twice** to convert the reference to the mixed reference B$3.
    The formula should now be =B5/B$3. The F4 key converts a reference to absolute the first time you tap it. When you tap it a second and third time, it converts the reference to mixed.

11. Complete the entry by clicking the Enter ☑ button on the Formula bar.
    When you copy this formula across the row or to other rows, the reference to Column B will be updated to C, D, etc. This way, the formula will refer to the correct goal in Row 3. The absolute reference to Row 3, however, will not change because you used the dollar sign. This way, you can copy the formula to any row, and the reference will refer to the correct cell in Row 3.

(Continued on the next page)

Copy the Formula

12. Make sure the highlight is in Cell B6, and click the Copy [icon] button.

13. Select Cells C6 through E6 in Row 6.

14. Click the Paste [icon] button.

15. Notice that the marquee is still flashing in Cell B6.
    You can continue to paste the formula as long as the marquee is flashing.

16. Select Cells B9:E9 in Row 9.

17. Click the Paste [icon] button.

18. Paste [icon] the formula into the cells in Rows 12 and 15.
    To accomplish this, simply select the cells, and click the Paste button.

19. Tap the ⟨ESC⟩ key to turn off the flashing marquee.

20. The completed worksheet is shown below.

	A	B	C	D	E
1	Regional Sales Results				
2		Q1	Q2	Q3	Q4
3	Goal	$1,000,000	$1,250,000	$1,500,000	$2,000,000
4					
5	Eastern Region	$750,000	$825,000	$1,400,000	$1,800,000
6	Percent of Goal	75%	66%	93%	90%
7					
8	Southern Region	$900,000	$1,100,000	$1,600,000	$1,950,000
9	Percent of Goal	90%	88%	107%	98%
10					
11	Central Region	$1,200,000	$1,300,000	$2,300,000	$1,800,000
12	Percent of Goal	120%	104%	153%	90%
13					
14	Western Region	$500,000	$1,250,000	$2,200,000	$3,000,000
15	Percent of Goal	50%	100%	147%	150%

Analyze the Worksheet

21. Take a moment to study the percentages shown in the preceding illustration. Notice that they reflect the percentage of the goal (in Row 3) that each region achieved.

22. Click Cell C9, and the formula =C8/C$3 should appear in the Formula bar.
    Notice that the C8 reference refers to the cell immediately above the formula. The C$3 reference is mixed. The C component refers to Column C, and the $3 component is absolute, so it will always refer to Row 3. This mixed reference lets you copy the formula to any row and still have the reference refer to the proper goal in Row 3.

23. Take as much time as necessary to study the worksheet and understand the importance of the mixed cell references.

24. Save the changes to the workbook, and then close the workbook.

Skill Builder 8.3 Use Absolute References and Create a Pie Chart

In this exercise, you will create a worksheet that calculates interest payments on a loan. You will set up the interest rate and loan amount as variables. This will allow you to easily adapt the worksheet for use with various loans. You will also create a pie chart to show the percentage of the payments that are applied to interest and the percentages that are applied to principal.

Set Up the Worksheet

1. Start a new workbook, and set up the worksheet shown below.

   Enter the opening balance and interest rate as shown. Use the (ALT)+(ENTER) keystroke combination to create the two line entries in Cells B6 and C6. Widen the columns as needed.

	A	B	C	D
1	**Loan Analysis**			
2				
3	Opening Balance		10000	
4	Interest Rate		10%	
5				
6	Payment	Interest Paid	Principal Paid	Balance

2. Click Cell D7 and enter the formula **=C3**.

   This assignment formula sets up the opening balance for the loan. This way, you can change the opening balance in Cell C3 and create a whole new loan scenario.

3. Click Cell A8, and enter **500** as the first payment.

4. Click Cell B8.

5. Enter the formula **=D7*$C$4/12**.

   The result should be 83.33333. Notice that this formula calculates the interest. It multiplies the opening balance in Cell D7 by the interest rate in Cell C4. The result is divided by 12 because Cell C4 contains an annual rate, and the payments are monthly. Once again, the reference to Cell C4 is absolute because you want the formula to continue to refer to this cell when it is copied down the column.

6. Click Cell C8, and enter the formula **=A8−B8**.

   The result should be 416.6667.

7. Click Cell D8, and enter the formula **=D7−C8**.

   The result should be 9583.333. Notice that this formula deducts the current payment's principle from the previous balance.

8. Use the Comma Style [,] button to format Cells D7, B8, C8, and D8 as Comma style with two decimals.

   (Continued on the next page)

Copy the Formulas and Create Totals

9. Set the zoom control percentage to 75%.
If necessary, adjust the zoom control to an even smaller percentage until 25 or more rows are visible.

10. Click Cell A8, and use the fill handle to copy the number 500 down to Row 20.
Cells A8 through A20 should now contain the number 500.

11. Use the fill handle to copy the formulas in Cells B8, C8, and D8 down to Row 20.
You will need to complete all three columns before the formulas will calculate correctly.

12. Click Cell A22, and enter the word **Totals**.

13. Click Cell B22, and use AutoSum Σ to calculate the total Interest Paid.
Row 21 will remain a blank row. The result should be 804.05.

14. Use AutoSum Σ to calculate the total Principal Paid in Cell C22.
The result should be 5,695.95.

15. Format Cells B22 and C22 as Currency style with 2 decimals.

Create an Embedded Pie Chart

16. Select the Interest Paid and Principal Paid headings in Cells B6 and C6.

17. Press the (CTRL) key while you select the total interest and principle in Cells B22 and C22.

18. Click the Chart Wizard 📊 button.

19. Choose the Pie chart type and the 3-D subtype (the second subtype).

20. Click the **Next** button twice to display the Step 3 of 4 box.

21. If necessary, click the Titles tab, and enter the chart title **Interest vs. Principal**.

22. Click the Legend tab, and remove the check from the Show legend box.
The legend won't be needed, because you will add data labels in the next step.

23. Click the Data Labels tab, and choose the Show label and percent option.

24. Click the **Finish** button.
The Interest should equal 12% of the pie. This represents 12% of the total payments.

Perform What-If Analyses

25. Click Cell C4, and enter **15%** as the interest rate.
Notice how the model recalculates the interest, principal, and balance. The chart is also updated to reflect the new worksheet data.

26. Click Cell C3, and enter **20000** as the opening balance.

27. Take a few minutes to experiment with your loan worksheet.
Try changing the opening balance in Cell C3 and the interest rate in Cell C4. Try entering new payment amounts in Column A.

28. Save the workbook with the name **Skill Builder 8.3,** and then close the workbook.

Assessments

Assessment 8.1 Use Absolute References

1. Follow these guidelines to create the worksheet shown below.

   ▪ Enter the text entries as shown in the worksheet. Enter the numbers in Column B and the percentage in Cell B3.

   ▪ Use a formula to calculate the discounted price in Cell C6. Use an absolute reference when referring to the discount rate in Cell B3. Remember that you are trying to calculate the discounted price. This means your formula must subtract the discount rate in B3 from 1. The generic formula is Discounted Price = Original Price * (1 – Discount Rate).

   ▪ Copy the formula in Cell C6 down the column.

2. Format the Cells with the Currency format shown.

3. Sort the worksheet rows so they are in ascending order by Column A.

4. Change the percentage in Cell B3 to 10%, and watch the worksheet recalculate.

5. Change the percentage in Cell B3 to 15%, and watch the worksheet recalculate.

6. Save the workbook with the name **Assessment 8.1,** and then close the workbook.

	A	B	C
1	**January Price Change Worksheet**		
2			
3	January Discount Rate	**20%**	
4			
5	Item	Original Price	Discounted Price
6	Track and Walk Footwear	$34.50	$27.60
7	Action Aerobics Wear	$19.00	$15.20
8	Designer Jeans	$50.00	$40.00
9	Sherman Cowboy Boots	$67.95	$54.36
10	Jensen Back Packs	$34.55	$27.64
11	Rain or Shine Coats	$45.00	$36.00
12	Diamond Back Socks	$2.95	$2.36
13	Steck-Harman Shirts	$19.95	$15.96
14	Back Country Jeans	$24.95	$19.96

Assessment 8.2 Use Mixed References

1. Open the workbook named **Assessment 8.2.**

2. Follow these guidelines to calculate the compensation in Rows 9, 13, 17, and 21.

   ■ Create the compensation formula **=B8*B4+B5** in Cell B9. Notice that the compensation is calculated as the Sales * Commission Rate + Bonus.

   ■ Take a few minutes to study the formula, and predict what will happen when you copy the formula to another row or cell. The references are relative, so they will continue to refer to cells in the same location relative to the original formula.

   ■ Edit the formula in the Formula bar, and insert dollar signs in front of the row components of both the B4 and B5 references. This will convert the references to mixed references as you did in Skill Builder 8.2.

   ■ Copy the formula across Rows 9, 13, 17, and 21. The results are shown in the worksheet below.

3. Create the Total Sales and Total Compensation rows shown in the worksheet below.

4. Format all cells as shown.

5. Save the changes to the workbook, and then close the workbook.

	A	B	C	D	E
1	Sales Rep Compensation Worksheet - 1999				
2					
3		Q1	Q2	Q3	Q4
4	Commission Rates	8%	10%	12%	15%
5	Bonuses	$2,000	$3,000	$5,000	$10,000
6					
7	**Bev Hart**				
8	Sales	$85,000	$56,000	$35,000	$127,000
9	Compensation	$8,800	$8,600	$9,200	$29,050
10					
11	**Liz Davidson**				
12	Sales	$45,000	$67,000	$87,000	$34,000
13	Compensation	$5,600	$9,700	$15,440	$15,100
14					
15	**Milton Jones**				
16	Sales	$56,000	$23,000	$87,900	$65,780
17	Compensation	$6,480	$5,300	$15,548	$19,867
18					
19	**Alex Sheraton**				
20	Sales	$45,000	$78,000	$62,890	$65,900
21	Compensation	$5,600	$10,800	$12,547	$19,885
22					
23	**Total Sales**	$231,000	$224,000	$272,790	$292,680
24	**Total Compensation**	$26,480	$34,400	$52,735	$83,902

Assessment 8.3 **Create a Financial Model**

1. Follow these guidelines to create the financial model shown below.

   ■ Type the headings, labels, and numbers shown in Column A, and Rows 1 through 4.

   ■ Use formulas to calculate the numbers in Rows 6 through 9. The formulas should multiply the revenue in Row 4 by the variables in Rows 15 through 19. For example, the employee costs in Cell B6 are calculated as the revenue in Cell B4 multiplied by the percentage in Cell B15. Use absolute references in these formulas when referring to the variables, so that you can copy the formulas across the rows. You must use absolute references in order to get full credit for this assessment!

   ■ Use AutoSum to calculate the Total Costs in Row 10.

   ■ Calculate the Gross Profit in Row 12 as the Revenue minus Total Costs.

   ■ Calculate the Net Profit in Row 13 as the Gross Profit * (1 – Tax Rate). Once again, use absolute references when referring to the Tax Rate in Cell B19.

   ■ Format the numbers and text entries as shown below.

2. Apply what-if analyses to your model by changing the variable percentages in Rows 15–19. You may want to demonstrate this to your instructor. Make sure the model recalculates correctly when the variables are changed.

3. Print the worksheet.

4. Set a print area for the range A1:E13, and then print just that area.

5. Save your model with the name **Assessment 8.3,** and then close the workbook.

	A	B	C	D	E
1	**1999 Projected Income**				
2					
3		Q1	Q2	Q3	Q4
4	Revenue	$345,000	$390,000	$480,000	$500,000
5					
6	Employee Costs	62,100	70,200	86,400	90,000
7	Capital Expenditures	75,900	85,800	105,600	110,000
8	Manufacturing	58,650	66,300	81,600	85,000
9	Marketing & Sales	55,200	62,400	76,800	80,000
10	Total Costs	$251,850	$284,700	$350,400	$365,000
11					
12	Gross Profit	$93,150	$105,300	$129,600	$135,000
13	**Net Profit**	**$55,890**	**$63,180**	**$77,760**	**$81,000**
14					
15	Employee Costs	18%			
16	Capital Expenditures	22%			
17	Manufacturing	17%			
18	Marketing & Sales	16%			
19	Tax Rate	40%			

Critical Thinking

Critical Thinking 8.1 On Your Own

John Jennings is the founder and owner of Crispy Crust Pizza. He started Crispy Crust in a stall in the local shopping mall and has had so much success that he wants to expand by opening three more stores over the next 18 months. John thinks he can increase the profit margin of Crispy Crust by opening new stores. He figures that the combined sales volume of the four stores will allow him to lower his food costs and packaging costs. In addition, he will now be able to amortize his advertising, management, and overhead costs over the four stores. John has hired you to prepare an income and expense model.

Use Excel to set up a financial model for Crispy Crust Pizza using the following information for the original (first) store. In addition, calculate the pretax profit and the profit vs. revenue for the original store. The pretax profit is simply the revenue minus total costs and expenses.

First Store Forecasted Revenue	$200,000
Food costs as a percentage of revenue	12%
Packaging costs as a percentage of revenue	2%
Advertising expenses as a percentage of revenue	14%
Management expenses as a percentage of revenue	13%
Overhead costs as a percentage of revenue	22%

Set up a variable section in the model that has the following initial percentages.

Per store sales increase	10%	Advertising savings	38%
Food cost savings	4%	Management cost savings	23%
Packaging savings	16%	Overhead savings	12%

Calculate the revenue, expenses, pretax profit, and pretax profit vs. revenue for two, three, and four stores. Assume that the revenue and expenses are equal to the original store revenue and expenses multiplied by the number of stores. You will also need to adjust the revenue and expenses using the percentages in the variable section. For example, imagine John has three stores. The revenue would be equal to the revenue of the original store multiplied by three (three stores) plus an additional 10% of the three stores' revenue. John assumes the additional revenue will result from cross over traffic between stores. Use absolute references in formulas that refer to the variable section of the model. You should copy formulas whenever possible and use absolute references where necessary to allow the formulas to be copied. Save your completed worksheet with a descriptive name.

Critical Thinking 8.2 Web Research

David is a junior in high school with a 4.0 GPA and a bright future. David's parents want him to attend Harvard University. You have been asked to set up an expense worksheet for a four-year stay at Harvard. Use Internet Explorer and a search engine of your choice to locate the Web site of Harvard University. Determine the approximate tuition, fees, room, board, and personal expenses for a full time undergraduate student. The purpose of your model is to determine the out-of-pocket expenses for which David's parents must plan. Use the following payment sources for the first year of attendance.

David's contribution (first year)	$3,500
Scholarship contribution (first year)	$12,500
Student loans (first year)	$5,700

Use formulas to calculate the amount that David's parents will need to contribute for each of the next four years. Use formulas to adjust the expenses and payment sources for David's sophomore, junior, and senior years as shown below. When you have finished, save your workbook with a descriptive name.

Tuition, fees, room, board, and personal expenses	5% annual increase
David's contribution	15% annual increase
Scholarships	No change ($12,500 each year)
Student loans	10% annual increase

Critical Thinking 8.3 As a Group

Use Excel to create an important event calculator. Your calculator should calculate the number of days until important events occur. Important events can be dates such as birthdays, the arrival of a new baby, or the number of shopping days remaining until Christmas. Ask five of your classmates for their birth dates, and include their names and birth dates in the worksheet. The calculator should automatically recalculate the number of days whenever the worksheet is opened. To accomplish this, insert the TODAY function in one cell, and then reference that cell in the formulas that calculate the number of days to the event(s). Use an absolute reference when referencing the TODAY function so that you can copy the formula to other cells.

Working with Multiple-Sheet Workbooks

As you continue to work with Excel, you may find your worksheets growing in size and complexity. Often it is better to break a worksheet up into several smaller worksheets. For example, many Excel workbooks are organized with a master sheet and two or more detail sheets. Summary information from the detail sheets is often reflected on the master sheet. In this lesson, you will learn various techniques for working with multiple-sheet workbooks. You will set up a workbook with a master sheet and detail sheets. You will also learn how to efficiently print multiple-sheet workbooks, copy worksheets, and protect workbooks.

In This Lesson

Case Study

Folsom Technical College has just received its 1999 Federal grant. Janice Milton, the Budgeting Department's Director, needs to allocate the grant to various budget categories. Janice needs a workbook that tracks the year-to-date expenditures and consolidates the information on a master worksheet. The master sheet will provide summary information and give Janice an instant overview of how their expenditures compare to their budget allocations. The workbook will be dynamic. The master sheet will be linked to detail sheets where all the necessary detail information will be stored. This illustration shows the master sheet and three detail sheets that you will create in this lesson.

	A	B	C
1	**Postage Tracking Sheet**		
2			
3		**Amount Spent**	
4	September	300	
5	October	350	
6	November	325	
7	December	400	
8	January		
9	February		
10	March		
11	April		
12	May		
13	June		
14	July		
15	August		
16	**Total**	**$1,375**	

	A	B	C
1	**Equipment Tracking Sheet**		
2			
3		**Amount Spent**	
4	September	3,000	
5	October	2,500	
6	November	4,000	
7	December	1,000	
8	January		
9	February		
10	March		
11	April		
12	May		
13	June		
14	July		
15	August		
16	**Total**	**$10,500**	

	A	B	C	D
1	**Folsom Technical College**			
2	**1999 - 2000 Federal Grant and Budget Tracking**			
3				
4	**Grant Amount**	$300,000		
5	**Today's Date**	10/11/99		
6				
7	**Category**	**Budget Allocation**	**Year-to-Date Spent**	
8	Postage	5,000	1,375	
9	Equipment	40,000	10,500	
10	Instructional Materials	50,000	40,500	

	A	B	C
1	**Instructional Materials Trackir**		
2			
3		**Amount Spent**	
4	September	25,000	
5	October	10,000	
6	November	5,000	
7	December	500	
8	January		
9	February		
10	March		
11	April		
12	May		
13	June		
14	July		
15	August		
16	**Total**	**$40,500**	

Linking Cells

Excel lets you link cells between different worksheets and between different workbooks. Linking lets you reflect values from a "source" worksheet into a "destination" worksheet. This powerful capability is the glue that binds worksheets together.

Summary Sheets and Detail Sheets

Linking is often used to make totals from detail worksheets appear in a summary or master worksheet. This lets you keep detailed information in the detail sheets and see the totals or the "big picture" in the summary sheet. This capability reflects the needs of many organizations. For example, top-level managers are usually interested in seeing the "big picture," whereas detailed information is needed at the departmental level. The illustration on the previous page shows data from three detail sheets appearing in a master sheet. Notice that the totals on the detail sheets are also visible in the master sheet.

Linking Formulas

You link cells by inserting linking formulas in the destination worksheet. Linking formulas specify the cells in the source worksheet from which the data originates. You must use the correct syntax when creating linking formulas. The following illustrations show examples of linking formulas between cells in the same workbook and between cells in different workbooks.

This formula is inserted into a cell in a destination worksheet. The exclamation point separates the sheet name Postage from the cell name B16. The number in Cell B16 of the Postage Sheet will appear in the cell in the destination sheet that contains this formula.

This formula also specifies a filename (which is surrounded by square brackets). This type of formula lets you link cells between different workbooks.

=Postage!B16

='[Federal Grant – 99.xls]Postage'!B16

Creating Linking Formulas

The syntax of linking formulas is quite simple. A linking formula specifies the sheet name and cell name of the source cell. Like all formulas, you begin a linking formula with an equal sign. Then, you include the sheet name of the source cell followed by an exclamation mark. Finally, you include the cell reference of the source cell. If the source cell is in a different workbook, then you must include the workbook name as shown in the second example of the preceding illustration. You can type linking formulas or use the mouse to create them in point mode. You will use both of these techniques in this lesson.

Check Out the Workbook

1. Open the workbook named Hands-On Lesson 9.

2. Click Cell B4, and notice that this cell contains the number $300,000.
   This is the amount of the Federal grant that Folsom Technical College was awarded for the 1999–2000 school year. Their objective is to allocate this grant to several budget categories and then track their actual expenditures throughout the year. Janice Milton wants up-to-date information on how their expenditures compare to their budget forecasts.

3. Click Cell B5, and notice that this cell contains the TODAY function.
   This cell will always display the current date.

4. Notice the categories in Column A and the budget allocations in Column B.
   The budget allocations add up to $300,000 as shown in Cell B19. As you can see, the budgets are equal to the total grant of $300,000.

5. Notice that the cells in Column C will contain the Year-to-Date Spent numbers.
   The detail sheets will track the year-to-date expenditures for each category. The cells in Column C will be linked to the year-to-date expenditure totals in the detail sheets.

6. Notice Column D.
   The Available Balance in Column D will be the difference between the Budget Allocation in Column B and the Year-to-Date Spent numbers in Column C. Column D will show how much of the budget remains for each category.

7. Click the Postage sheet tab.
   Each month the total amount spent on postage will be entered into a cell in Column B. Cell B16 will contain a SUM function that will sum up all cells in the column. Cell B16 will be linked to Cell C8 in the Master sheet.

8. Click the Master sheet tab.
   Notice that Cell C8 will contain the Year-to-Date Spent amount for postage. Once again, this cell will be linked to Cell B16 in the Postage sheet.

Create a Link to the Postage Sheet

9. Click the Postage sheet tab.

10. Enter the three numbers shown below into Column B.

	A	B
1	Postage Tracking Sheet	
2		
3		Amount Spent
4	September	300
5	October	350
6	November	325

(Continued on the next page)

11. Click Cell B16, and use AutoSum Σ to calculate the column total.

    The total should be 975. Notice that AutoSum summed the entire range B4:B15. This is desirable, because AutoSum will keep a running total as you enter data throughout the year.

12. Click the Master sheet tab.

13. Click Cell C8, and enter the formula **=Postage!B16**.

    Make sure that you type the formula exactly as shown, including the exclamation mark. The number 975 should appear in Cell C8. Notice that the formula instructs Excel to link to Cell B16 in the Postage sheet. The exclamation mark separates the two arguments.

14. Click the Postage sheet tab.

15. Click Cell B7, and enter the number **400**.

    The SUM formula in Cell B16 should display the number 1,375.

16. Click the Master sheet tab, and Cell C8 should now display 1,375.

    This link is dynamic, always reflecting the current value in the source cell.

Delete the Link, and Recreate It Using Point Mode

17. Click Cell C8, and tap the (DELETE) key to remove the linking formula.

    You can delete linking formulas just as you delete any other formula.

18. Make sure the highlight is in Cell C8, and type an equal sign.

    Excel will display the equal sign in the Formula bar.

19. Click the Postage sheet tab.

    Excel will display the Postage sheet. The sheet name Postage will appear in the Formula bar followed by an exclamation point.

20. Click Cell B16, and the linking formula =Postage!B16 will appear in the Formula bar.

21. Complete the formula by clicking the Enter ✔ button on the Formula bar.

    Excel will display the Master sheet with the completed link in Cell C8. Once again, the result should be 1375. Notice that point mode works the same with linking formulas as it does with other formulas.

Calculate the Available Balance in Cell D8

22. Click Cell D8, and enter the formula **=B8-C8**.

    The result should be 3,625.

23. Click Cell B8, and use the Format Painter 🖌 to copy the Comma style to Cell C8.

24. Save the changes and continue with the next topic.

Copying Worksheets

The Folsom grant and budget workbook will eventually contain several worksheets with the same structure as the Postage sheet. For example, each sheet will have a title in Cell A1, and monthly totals for September through August will be entered in Column B. Rather than recreate each sheet, you can use the **Edit→Move or Copy Sheet** command to copy the desired sheet. A new sheet created with the Move or Copy Sheet command is an exact duplicate of the original sheet. The data, structure, print settings, and page setup settings are all identical to the original sheet.

*The **Edit→Move or Copy sheet** command displays this dialog box.* ⎯⎯

The active sheet can be moved or copied to any position in the sheet order. ⎯⎯

Check this box to create a copy. Otherwise, the sheet is just moved. ⎯⎯

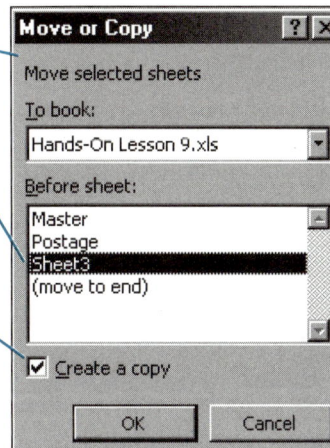

Hands-On 9.2 Make Two Copies of the Postage Sheet

In this exercise, you will make two copies of the Postage worksheet. The copies will become two new sheets named Equipment and Instructional Materials.

Create the Equipment Sheet

1. Click the Postage sheet tab.
   The active sheet is always the sheet that is copied.

2. Choose **Edit→Move or Copy Sheet** from the menu bar.

3. Choose Sheet3 from the Before sheet list.

4. Check the *Create a copy* box, and click **OK.**
   Excel positions the new sheet before Sheet3 and names it Postage (2).

5. Double-click the Postage (2) worksheet tab.

6. Type the new name **Equipment**, and tap ⟨ENTER⟩ to rename the sheet.

Edit the Title and Number Entries in the Equipment sheet

7. Double-click Cell A1 to position the insertion point in the cell.
   You learned how to do in-cell editing in an earlier lesson.

8. Use the (DELETE) and/or (BACKSPACE) keys to remove the word Postage.

9. Type the word **Equipment**, and complete the entry.
   The title should now read Equipment Tracking Sheet.

10. Change the numbers in the range B4:B7 as shown below.

	A	B
1	Equipment Tracking Sheet	
2		
3		Amount Spent
4	September	3,000
5	October	2,500
6	November	4,000
7	December	1,000

Create the Instructional Materials Sheet

11. Click the Postage sheet tab.

12. Use the technique in the previous steps to create a copy of the Postage sheet. Position the new sheet before Sheet3.

13. Change the name of the new sheet to **Instructional Materials**.

14. Edit the title in Cell A1 of the new sheet, and change the numbers in the B4:B7 range as shown below.

	A	B	C
1	Instructional Materials Tracking Sheet		
2			
3		Amount Spent	
4	September	25,000	
5	October	10,000	
6	November	5,000	
7	December	500	

15. Save the changes to your workbook, and continue with the next topic.

A Quick Copying Technique

The Select All [ ] button is located at the top-left corner of the worksheet area. You can use the Select All button and the Copy and Paste technique to copy the data and structure of a worksheet to another worksheet. This technique is a fast way to copy a worksheet without inserting a new sheet into the workbook. This technique produces a duplicate worksheet, except that the Page Setup settings are not copied to the new sheet.

From the Keyboard

(CTRL)+A to select all

Hands-On 9.3 Create a Mileage Tracking Sheet

1. Click the Postage sheet tab.

2. Click the Select All ⬜ button on the Postage sheet.

3. Click the Copy 📋 button on the Standard toolbar.

4. Click the Sheet3 sheet tab.

5. Make sure the highlight is in Cell A1, and click the Paste 📋 button.

6. Click anywhere in the worksheet to deselect.
   Notice that the data, column widths, and other formats were copied.

7. Change the name of the new sheet to **Mileage**.

8. Edit the title in Cell A1 of the new sheet, and change the numbers in the B4:B7 range as shown below.

	A	B
1	Mileage Tracking Sheet	
2		
3		Amount Spent
4	September	2,000
5	October	1,700
6	November	1,280
7	December	1,000

9. Save the changes to your workbook, and continue with the next topic.

Copying Formats Between Worksheets

The Format Painter 🖌 can be used to copy text and number formats between worksheets. This technique can help you create consistent formatting between worksheets. You can copy the formats from one cell, or a range of cells. You can also use the Select All button to copy the formats of an entire worksheet. This technique is useful, provided that the sheets have the same structure.

Hands-On 9.4 Copy Formats

In this exercise, you will format the text and number entries in the Postage sheet. You will use the Format Painter to copy the formats to the three worksheets you just created.

Copy Formats from the Master Sheet to the Postage Sheet

1. Click the Master sheet tab, and click Cell A2.
   You will copy the text formats from this subheading to the heading in the Postage sheet.

2. Click the Format Painter 🖌.

3. Click the Postage sheet tab.

(Continued on the next page)

4. Click Cell A1, and the formats will be copied to that cell.
   Cell A1 should have the same dark blue color and size as the subheading in the Master sheet. Notice that you can switch to any sheet after the Format Painter has been activated.

5. Click the Master sheet tab, and click Cell A4.

6. Click the Format Painter 🖌, then click the Postage sheet tab.

7. Click Cell B3 to copy the formats to that cell.

8. Click the Master sheet tab, and select Cells A19 and B19 (the cells in the total row).

9. Click the Format Painter 🖌.

10. Click the Postage sheet tab, and select Cells A16 and B16 (the cells in the total row).
    The bold formatting and the Currency number format should be copied to the cells.

Copy All Formats from One Sheet to Another

The Postage, Equipment, Instructional Materials, and Mileage sheets all have identical structure and format. This common structure enables you to use the Format Painter to copy all formats from one sheet to another. The Format Painter will copy all text and number formats, and it will even copy column widths and row heights, to the other sheets.

11. Make sure the Postage sheet is active, and click the Select All ▭ button.
    The entire Postage sheet should be selected.

12. Click the Format Painter 🖌, and then click the Equipment sheet tab.

13. Click the Select All ▭ button.

14. Click anywhere in the worksheet to deselect.
    The entire sheet should have the same formatting as the Postage sheet. Notice how this technique creates consistent formatting between worksheets (provided they have an identical structure).

15. Click the Select All ▭ button on the Equipment sheet.

16. Double-click the Format Painter 🖌.
    Double-clicking the Format Painter lets you copy the formats as many times as desired.

17. Click the Instructional Materials sheet tab, then click the Select All ▭ button.
    Notice that the Format Painter is still active.

18. Click the Mileage sheet tab, then click the Select All ▭ button.

19. Click the Format Painter 🖌 to deactivate it.

20. Click anywhere in the worksheet to deselect.
    Take a few moments to review the various sheets. The formatting should be consistent.

Edit the Mileage Sheet

21. Click the Mileage sheet tab.

22. Click Cell B3, change the heading to **Mileage**, and then click the Align Right ▤ button.
    The numbers in Column B are the number of miles that have been driven in a given month. You will add another column to calculate the actual Mileage Expense. The Mileage Expense is calculated as the number of miles multiplied by a cost of 32 cents per mile.

23. Click Cell C3, and type the heading **Mileage Expense**.

24. Click Cell C4, and enter the formula **=B4*.32**.
   The result should be 640.

25. Use the fill handle to copy the formula down the column as far as Row 15.
   Some of the cells will display zeros because Column B is not yet complete.

26. Use AutoSum Σ to calculate the total mileage expense in Cell C16.

Format the Mileage Sheet

27. Use the Format Painter to copy the formats from Cell B3 to C3, and from B16 to C16.

28. Autofit Column C to make the heading in Cell C3 visible.

29. Use the Format Painter to copy the Comma format from Cell B4 to Cell B16.
   The Total Mileage should not have a Currency format.

30. Now apply Bold **B** formatting to Cell B16.
   Your next task will be to link the Master sheet with the three worksheets you just created. First, you will learn how to name cells. You will use the names to simplify the linking formulas.

Cell Names and Range Names

You can assign a name to any cell or range of cells. You can use cell names and range names in formulas in place of cell references. For example, Cell C8 in the Master sheet contains the linking formula =Postage!B16, where Postage is the sheet name, and B16 is the cell reference. If you assigned the name PostageTotal to Cell B16 in the Postage sheet, then you could use the linking formula =PostageTotal in the Master sheet instead of the more abstract formula =Postage!B16. Cell names and range names are available throughout a workbook. This is convenient because you can assign a name in one sheet and then reference the name in any other sheet.

Creating Names with the Name Box

The Name box is located on the left end of the Formula bar. The Name box usually displays the reference of the active cell or range. When a cell or range has been assigned a name, however, the name is displayed in the Name box. You can easily name a cell by clicking in the Name box and typing the desired name. The name is assigned when you tap (ENTER). To name a range, you select the desired range, click in the name box, type the desired name, and tap (ENTER).

PostageTotal ▾		= =SUM(B4:B15)
A	**B**	**C**
1	**Postage Tracking Sheet**	
2		
3		**Amount Spent**	
4 September	300	
5 October	350	
6 November	325	
7 December	400	
8 January		
9 February		
10 March		
11 April		
12 May		
13 June		
14 July		
15 August		
16 **Total**	**$1,375**	

Name box with the Postage Total *name*

Rules for Creating Names

Cell and range names can have up to 255 characters (although you should keep names much shorter than this). Also, names cannot contain spaces. If necessary, use the underscore _ character as a substitute for spaces. For example, use the name Instructional_Materials instead of Instructional Materials.

Hands-On 9.5 Create Cell Names

In this exercise, you will create descriptive names for the totals in the detail sheets.

Name the Total Cell in the Equipment Sheet

1. Click the Equipment sheet tab, then click Cell B16.

2. Follow these steps to name the cell.

Ⓐ *Click in the **Name** box at the left end of the Formula bar and the B16 reference will become selected.*

| B16 | ▾ | = | =SUM(B4:B15) |

Ⓑ *Type the name **Equipment** (it will replace B16), and tap* (ENTER).

3. Click anywhere in the worksheet (other than Cell B16).

4. Click Cell B16, and the name Equipment will appear in the Name box.
   The Name box displays the cell name or reference of the current cell.

Name the Total Cells in the Instructional Materials and Mileage Sheets

5. Click the Instructional Materials sheet tab, then click Cell B16.

6. Click in the Name box.

7. Type **Instructional_Materials** (be careful not to use a space), and tap (ENTER).
   The underscore character is inserted by pressing (SHIFT) *and tapping the hyphen key. Don't use a blank space, because Excel won't accept it.*

8. Click the Mileage sheet tab, then click Cell C16.

9. Click in the Name box, and enter the name **Mileage**.

Using the Name List

The drop-down ▪ button on the right side of the Name box displays the Name list. The Name list displays all cell and range names in the workbook. You can rapidly move the highlight to a named cell or range by choosing it from the list.

1. Follow these steps to go to the cell named Equipment.

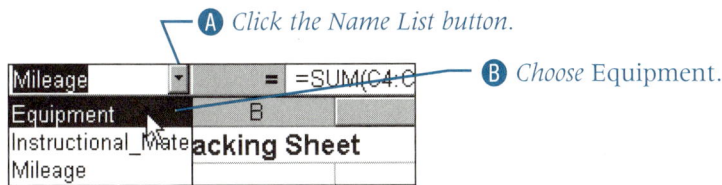

Ⓐ *Click the Name List button.*

Ⓑ *Choose Equipment.*

Mileage ▾	= =SUM(C4:C	
Equipment	B	
Instructional_Mate	**acking Sheet**	
Mileage		

Notice that Excel displays the Equipment sheet, and positions the highlight in the Equipment cell.

2. Follow the preceding steps to go to the cell named Instructional_Materials.

Create a Linking Formula by Typing a Cell Name

3. Click the Master sheet tab, and then click Cell C8.
   Notice that this cell contains the linking formula =Postage!B16. You created this link in an earlier exercise. In the remainder of this exercise, you will create links to the totals in the other three sheets. However, you will use cell names in the linking formulas instead of using sheet names and cell references as you did in Cell C8.

4. Click Cell C9, and enter the linking formula **=Equipment**.
   The number 10500 should appear. This is the total from Cell B16 of the Equipment sheet.

5. Click the Name List ▾ button, and choose Equipment.
   Excel will position the highlight in Cell B16 of the Equipment sheet. Notice that the total is 10500.

Create a Linking Formula Using Point Mode

6. Click the Master sheet tab, and then click Cell C10.

7. Type an equal **=** sign.

8. Click the Instructional Materials sheet tab.

9. Click Cell B16, and click the Enter ☑ button to complete the entry.
   The formula =Instructional_Materials appears in the Formula bar. The result should be 40500.

Create the Last Linking Formula, Format Cells, and Copy a Formula

10. Click Cell C11.

11. Type **=Mileage**, and complete the entry.
    The result should be 1913.6. Keep in mind that these links are dynamic. If the totals change in the detail sheets, then the Master sheet will change as well.

12. Click Cell C8, then click the Format Painter 🖌.

13. Select Cells C9:C11 to copy the Comma style to those cells.

14. Use the fill handle to copy the Available Balance formula from Cell D8 to Cells D9:D11.

15. Save the changes to your workbook, and continue with the next topic.

Changing and Deleting Cell Names and Range Names

You can change and delete cell names and range names after they have been created. However, formulas that use the names will not work after the names have been changed or deleted. You will need to recreate any linking formulas that used the changed or deleted names. For this reason, you should choose names carefully when you create them. Names are changed and deleted with the **Insert→Name→Define** command.

Hands-On 9.7 Change the Instructional_Materials Name

In this exercise, you will change the Instructional_Materials cell name to Instructional. You will also recreate the linking formula that used the Instructional_Materials cell name.

Rename the Instructional_Materials Cell

1. Click the Name List ▾ button, and choose Instructional_Materials.

2. Choose **Insert→Name→Define** from the menu bar.

3. Follow these steps to add the name Instructional and delete the name Instructional_Materials.

Ⓐ *Click in this box and type the name* **Instructional**.

Ⓑ *Click the* **Add** *button to add Instructional to the list.*

Ⓒ *Choose Instructional_Materials from the list, and click the* **Delete** *button.*

Ⓓ *Click OK, and notice that the name* Instructional *is now assigned to Cell B16*

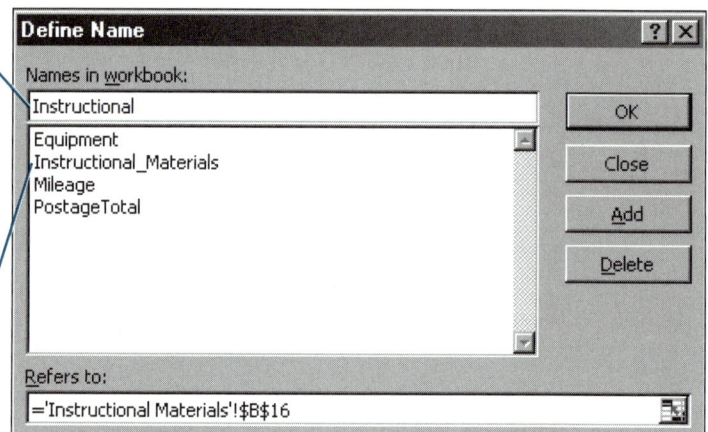

Define Name	? ✕
Names in workbook:	
Instructional	OK
Equipment	Close
Instructional_Materials	
Mileage	Add
PostageTotal	Delete
Refers to:	
='Instructional Materials'!$B$16	

4. Click the Name List ▾ button, and notice that the name Instructional_Materials is no longer available.

Repair the Formula in the Master Sheet

5. Tap the (ESC) key, and click the Master sheet tab.
   Notice that a #NAME? message appears in Cells C10 and D10. This message indicates that a formula is referencing a cell name that no longer exists. You will correct this by replacing the formula in Cell C10.

6. Click Cell C10, and enter the formula **=Instructional**.
   The result should once again be 40500. The formula in D10 is dependent on C10, so it will return the correct result (9500) once the formula in C10 is corrected.

Create a Salaries Sheet

7. Choose **Insert→Worksheet** from the menu bar.
A new worksheet will be inserted to the left of the current sheet.

8. Drag the new worksheet tab to the right until the new sheet is last in the sheet order.

9. Double-click the new sheet tab, and change the sheet name to **Salaries**.

10. Click the Postage sheet tab.
In the next few steps, you will copy the data and structure of the Postage sheet to the Salaries sheet.

11. If necessary, click the Select All ⬜ button to select the Postage sheet.

12. Click the Copy 📋 button.

13. Click the Salaries sheet tab, and make sure the highlight is in Cell A1.
The highlight must be in Cell A1 if you wish to paste an entire sheet.

14. Click the Paste 📋 button to paste the Postage sheet.

15. Click anywhere in the sheet to deselect.

16. Follow these steps to edit the Salaries sheet as shown below.

▪ Add the names and numbers shown in Columns B through F. Also, edit the title in Cell A1 as shown below.

▪ Copy the SUM formula from Cell B16 across the row to Cells C16:F16.

▪ Use the **Format→Column→Width** command to widen Columns B through F to 10.

▪ Use the Format Painter to copy the text and comma formats from Column B to Columns C through F.

	A	B	C	D	E	F
1	Salaries Tracking Sheet					
2						
3		Connie	Alicia	Thomas	Mildred	Burt
4	September	3,500	2,750	3,400	4,250	4,200
5	October	3,750	3,250	3,450	3,850	3,450
6	November	4,200	3,800	3,400	2,900	3,480
7	December	4,000	3,750	3,400	3,450	3,490
8	January					
9	February					
10	March					
11	April					
12	May					
13	June					
14	July					
15	August					
16	Total	$15,450	$13,550	$13,650	$14,450	$14,620

(Continued on the next page)

Name the Cells in the Salaries Sheet

17. Make sure the Salaries sheet is active, and click Cell B16.

18. Follow these steps to name Cell B16.

Ⓐ *Click in the **Name** box to select the B16 reference currently in the box.*

| B16 | ▾ | = | =SUM(B4:B15) |

Ⓑ *Type the name* **Connie_Salary**, *and tap* ⏎(ENTER).

19. Name Cells C16 through F16 as shown in the following table.

Cell	Use this name
C16	Alicia_Salary
D16	Thomas_Salary
E16	Mildred_Salary
F16	Burt_Salary

Create Links in the Master Sheet

20. Click the Master sheet tab, then click Cell C14.
Cell C14 needs to be linked to the Connie_Salary cell.

21. Enter the formula **=Connie_Salary**, and the result should be 15450.

22. Use the names you just created to link Cells C15, C16, C17, and C18 to the Salaries sheet.

23. Use the Format Painter 🖌 to copy the Comma style format from Cell C11 to Cells C14 through C18.

Copy the Available Balance Formula to Rows 14–18

24. Click Cell D11, and click the Copy 📋 button.

25. Select Cells D14–D18, and click the Paste 📋 button.

26. Now use the fill handle to copy the total formula from Cell B19 to Cells C19 and D19.
The completed Master sheet should match the example on the top of page 271 (except for the date).

	A	B	C	D
1	**Folsom Technical College**			
2	**1999 - 2000 Federal Grant and Budget Tracking**			
3				
4	Grant Amount	$300,000		
5	Today's Date	10/11/99		
6				
7	Category	**Budget Allocation**	**Year-to-Date Spent**	**Available Balance**
8	Postage	5,000	1,375	3,625
9	Equipment	40,000	10,500	29,500
10	Instructional Materials	50,000	40,500	9,500
11	Mileage	5,000	1,914	3,086
12				
13	**Salaries**			
14	Connie	42,000	15,450	26,550
15	Alicia	40,000	13,550	26,450
16	Thomas	40,000	13,650	26,350
17	Mildred	38,000	14,450	23,550
18	Burt	40,000	14,620	25,380
19	**Total**	**$300,000**	**$126,009**	**$173,991**

Take a few minutes to study the work you have completed thus far in this lesson. In particular, try to understand how the Master sheet functions. The number in Cell C19 reflects the total year-to-date expenditures. The number in Cell D19 shows how much of the $300,000 grant is still available. All of the numbers in the Year-to-Date Spent column are linked to the detail sheets.

Using Row and Column Titles to Create Cell Names

You can rapidly name a group of cells using existing row and/or column titles as the names. You accomplish this by selecting both the titles and the cells to which you wish to assign the names. These cells will normally be adjacent to the title cells. You then use the **Insert→Names→Create** command to create the names.

Hands-On 9.8 Assign Names Using Column Titles

In this exercise, you will assign names to each of the budgeted amounts for the employees in Column B of the Master sheet. You will use these names to create linking formulas in the Salaries sheet. The linking formulas will reflect the budgets from Column B of the Master sheet.

Create Names for the Employee Budgets

1. Make sure the Master sheet is active.

2. Select the range A14:B18, as shown to the right.
   You will use the Name Create command to assign the employee names to Cells B14:B18.

14	Connie	42,000
15	Alicia	40,000
16	Thomas	40,000
17	Mildred	38,000
18	Burt	40,000

3. Choose **Insert→Name→Create** from the menu bar.
   The Create Names dialog box appears. The check boxes let you specify which cells should be used for the names. In this example, the cells in the left column (Column A) will be used to name the cells in Column B. For this reason, the Left Column box should be checked.

(Continued on the next page)

4. Make sure the Left Column box is checked, and click **OK.**

5. Click Cell B14, and notice that the word Connie appears in the Name box.
   This cell was assigned the name Connie.

6. Click the Name List ▪ button, and scroll up and down the list of names. Notice that the names Connie, Alicia, Thomas, Mildred, and Burt now appear on the list.

7. Click Cell B15, and notice that this cell has been assigned the name Alicia.

Insert Links in the Salaries Sheet

8. Click the Salaries sheet tab.

9. Click Cell A17, and enter the word **Budget**.

10. Click Cell B17, and enter the formula **=Connie**.
    The number 42000 should appear. This is the budget amount for Connie from the Master sheet.

11. Enter the formula **=Alicia** in Cell C17.

12. Create the same type of linking formulas in Cells D17, E17, and F17.

13. Save the changes, and continue with the next topic.

Protection Options

Excel lets you protect the structure of workbooks and the contents of worksheets. The protection options prevent your workbooks and worksheets from being accidentally or intentionally modified. Protection is often used to prevent inexperienced users from damaging workbooks.

Protecting Workbooks

Protecting a workbook prevents structural changes from being made to the workbook. For example, you cannot delete, rename, or move worksheets in a protected workbook. You can also protect the workbook window to prevent users from changing the appearance of the window. You use the **Tools→Protection→Protect Workbook** command to protect a workbook. You use the **Tools→Protection→Unprotect Workbook** command to unprotect a workbook. The following illustration highlights the options available in the Protect Workbook dialog box.

*Protect the workbook **Structure**.*

*Prevent a workbook's **Windows** from being moved, resized, or hidden.*

*Assign a **Password** to prevent unauthorized users from removing workbook protection.*

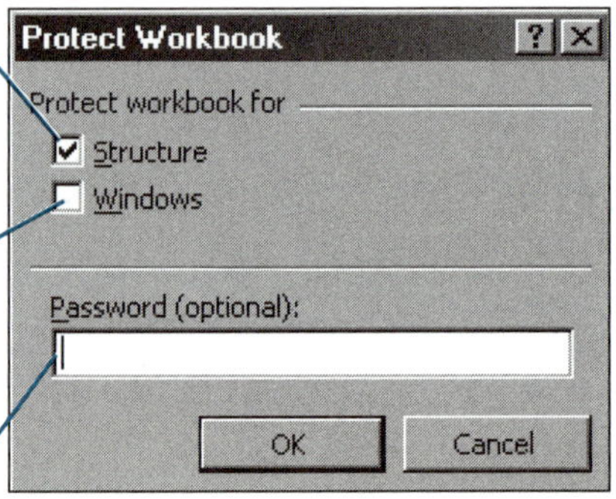

Protect Workbook dialog box:
Protect workbook for
☑ Structure
☐ Windows

Password (optional):

OK   Cancel

Protecting Worksheets

The **Tools→Protection→Protect Sheet** command lets you protect individual worksheets within a workbook. You can specify the types of items you wish to protect. Protected items cannot be modified or deleted. You use the **Tools→Protection→Unprotect Sheet** command to unprotect a protected sheet. The following illustration highlights the options available in the Protect Sheet dialog box.

*Protect the **Contents** of cells.*

*Protect graphic **Objects,** such as charts and pictures.*

*Protect **Scenarios.***

*Assign a **Password** to prevent unauthorized users from removing protection from this worksheet.*

Hands-On 9.9 Protect the Workbook and the Master sheet

In this exercise, you will protect the workbook and the Master sheet. The Master sheet can be protected because there is no need to modify it or enter data into it. The Master sheet also contains important data and formulas, such as the grant numbers and the budget numbers. This data should be protected to prevent unauthorized users from modifying it.

Protect the Workbook

1. Make sure the Excel window is maximized.

2. Notice the two sets of quick sizing buttons [_][a][X] at the top-right corner of the Excel window.
   The top buttons size the program window, and the bottom buttons size the worksheets within the program window. The bottom buttons will disappear once you protect the Windows on the sheet.

3. Choose **Tools→Protection→Protect Workbook** from the menu bar.

4. Check both the Structure and Windows boxes, and click **OK.**
   Notice that the bottom set of quick sizing buttons has been removed from the window. The Windows protection option prevents you from sizing or moving the worksheet windows within the program window. If desired, you can still size and move the program window.

5. Try dragging the Master sheet tab to a different position in the worksheet order.
   An icon will appear indicating that you cannot change the worksheet position.

6. Double-click the Master worksheet tab, and Excel will display a warning box indicating that the workbook is protected.

7. Click **OK** to close the message box.
   At this point, you are prevented from modifying the workbook structure, but you can still work normally within the worksheets.

8. Choose **Tools→Protection→Unprotect Workbook** from the menu bar.

(Continued on the next page)

9. Double-click the Master worksheet tab, and notice that you could change the name if desired.

10. Click anywhere in the worksheet to cancel the action.

Protect the Master Sheet

11. Choose **Tools→Protection→Protect Sheet** from the menu bar.

12. Take a moment to browse the Protect Sheet dialog box.

13. Leave all three boxes checked, and click **OK.**

14. Click any cell in the worksheet, and try entering new text or a new number.
    Excel will display a message box indicating that the cell cannot be changed.

15. Click **OK** to close the message box.

Unprotect the Sheet

16. Choose **Tools→Protection→Unprotect Sheet** from the menu bar.

17. Click any empty cell in the worksheet, and enter any number or text.

18. Click Undo 🔄 to reverse the editing change.

19. Use the **Tools→Protection→Protect Sheet** command to reprotect the sheet.

20. Save the changes to your workbook, and continue with the next topic.

Unlocking Cells in Protected Worksheets

Excel lets you unlock specific cells within a protected worksheet. Unlocked cells can be edited even though the overall worksheet is protected. This way, you can protect important cells and important objects while allowing data entry in less important parts of the sheet. You must unlock the cells before protecting the worksheet.

Quick Reference

UNLOCKING CELLS

To Unlock Cells

- Select the cells you want to unlock.

- Choose Format→Cells, and click the Protection tab.

- Remove the check from the Locked box, and click OK.

- Use the Tools→Protection→Protect Sheet command to protect the worksheet.

Hands-On 9.10 Unlock Cells in the Postage and Salaries Sheets

In this exercise, you will unlock several cells in the Postage and Salaries sheets. You will then protect the sheets to prevent the formulas and overall structure from being changed.

Unlock Cells in the Postage Sheet

1. Click the Postage sheet tab, and select the range B4:B15.
   This range includes all cells in Column B between the Amount Spent heading and Cell B16.

2. Choose **Format→Cells** from the menu bar, and click the Protection tab.

3. Remove the check from the Locked box, and click **OK.**
   This action will have no effect on your sheet until you protect it in the next step.

Protect the Sheet and Enter Data

4. Use the **Tools→Protection→Protect Sheet** command to protect the sheet.

5. Click Cell B16, and try entering data in the cell.
   A message box will appear indicating that the cell is protected.

6. Click **OK** to close the message box.

7. Click Cell B8, and enter any number.
   Excel lets you enter the number because you unlocked the cell prior to protecting the sheet.

Unlock Cells and Protect the Salaries Sheet

8. Click the Salaries sheet tab, and select the range B4:F15.

9. Choose **Format→Cells** from the menu bar.

10. Remove the check from the Locked box, and click **OK.**

11. Protect the worksheet.
    All cells in this sheet will now be protected, except for the data entry cells in the range B4:F15.

12. Save the changes to your workbook, and continue with the next topic.

3-D Selecting and Formatting

You can use a variety of techniques to select and format several worksheets at the same time. These techniques are commonly known as 3-D techniques because worksheets have a 3-D (three dimensional) arrangement within workbooks. **3-D selecting and formatting** is most effective when all of the affected worksheets contain the same structure. For example, the Equipment, Instructional Materials, and Mileage worksheets all have the same structure. The critical step in using 3-D techniques is to first select all of the desired worksheets before issuing a command. This way, all of the selected worksheets are affected when the command is issued. You can select multiple worksheets by pressing the (CTRL) key and clicking the desired sheet tabs. You can select a range of sheets by clicking the first sheet in the desired range, pressing the (SHIFT) key, and clicking the last sheet in the range. All sheets between the first and last sheets are selected.

Hands-On 9.11 Unlock Cells in Multiple Sheets

1. Click the Equipment sheet tab.

2. Press the (CTRL) key while you click the Instructional_Materials sheet tab.
   Both the Equipment and Instructional Materials tabs will appear white in color.

3. Continue to hold (CTRL) while you click the Mileage sheet tab.
   Now all three tabs will be white, indicating that the sheets are selected. Any commands that you issue in the Equipment sheet will be applied to the same range of cells in the other two sheets.

4. Release the (CTRL) key, then select the range B4:B15 in the Equipment sheet.

5. Click the Instructional_Materials sheet tab, then click the Mileage sheet tab, and notice that the range B4:B15 is selected in those sheets as well.

(Continued on the next page)

6. Use the **Format→Cells** command to Unlock the cells.
   The three sheets should still be selected.

7. Choose **Tools→Protection** from the menu bar, and the Protect Sheet option will be ghosted out.
   The 3-D selection techniques let you issue commands that affect ranges of cells. However, some commands, such as Protect Sheet, are not available when multiple sheets are selected.

8. Click anywhere in the worksheet to close the menu.

9. Click the Postage sheet tab, and the three sheets will no longer be selected.

10. Click the Equipment sheet tab, and use the **Tools→Protection→Protect Sheet** command to protect just that sheet.

11. Protect the Instructional Materials sheet, and then protect the Mileage sheet.
    Now you can only enter data in the B4:B15 cell ranges of the Equipment, Instructional Materials, and Mileage sheets. All other cells in the sheets are locked.

12. Save the changes to your workbook, and continue with the next topic.

Printing Multiple-Sheet Workbooks

Excel prints the current worksheet when you click the Print button. If you are working with a multiple-sheet workbook, you can use a variety of techniques to set up and print multiple-sheets.

Applying Page Setup Options to Multiple Sheets

The Page Setup dialog box lets you adjust the margins, page orientation, headers and footers, and a variety of other settings that affect the printed worksheet. You can apply these settings to multiple worksheets by first selecting the desired sheets. You learned how to select multiple worksheets in the previous topic.

Printing All Sheets

You can print all sheets in a workbook by selecting the sheets, and clicking the Print button. You can also print all sheets by issuing the **File→Print** command and choosing the Entire workbook option. There is no need to select the sheets if you use the File→Print technique.

Printing and Previewing Selected Sheets

You can print selected sheets by selecting the desired sheets, and clicking the Print button. Selected sheets can also be printed by issuing the **File→Print** command, and choosing the Active sheets option. Print Preview can also be used to preview selected sheets.

Hands-On 9.12 **Preview and Print Selected Sheets**

1. Click the Master sheet tab.

2. Click the Print Preview ▣ button.
   Notice that the Next button is unavailable. Excel only displays the selected sheet(s) in Print Preview.

3. Close the Print Preview window.

4. Press the (SHIFT) key, and click the Salaries sheet tab.
   All sheets should be selected. The Shift key technique is useful for selecting a continuous range of sheets.

5. Click the Print Preview ▣ button.

6. Use the Next button to browse through the worksheets.
   Notice that all six sheets are available because you selected them prior to clicking Print Preview. These same sheets would have been printed if you had clicked the Print button instead of Print Preview.

7. Click the **Print** button on the Print Preview toolbar.
   Notice that the Active Sheets option is chosen. All six sheets are active and would print if you were to click OK. Notice the Entire Workbook option. This option can be used to print the entire workbook without having to first select the sheets.

8. Click the **Cancel** button to exit from the Print dialog box.

9. Save the changes to your workbook, close the workbook, and continue with the end-of-lesson questions and exercises.

Concepts Review

True/False Questions

1.	Linking formulas are inserted in the source worksheet.	TRUE	FALSE
2.	Linking formulas can be typed or created using point mode.	TRUE	FALSE
3.	The Format Painter can be used to copy formats between worksheets.	TRUE	FALSE
4.	The Select All ☐ button can be used to select an entire worksheet.	TRUE	FALSE
5.	It is OK to use spaces in cell names.	TRUE	FALSE
6.	Cell names can only be used within the worksheet in which they were created.	TRUE	FALSE
7.	You can move to a named cell by choosing the name from the Name list.	TRUE	FALSE
8.	You must unlock cells after a worksheet has been protected to be able to edit those cells.	TRUE	FALSE

Multiple-Choice Questions

1. Which of the following procedures can be used to create a cell name?
   a. Click the desired cell, click in the Name box, type the desired name, and tap **ENTER**.
   b. Click the desired cell, and type the desired name.
   c. Click the desired cell, click in the Name box, type the desired name, and click the Enter button on the Formula bar.
   d. None of the above

2. Which command is used to change or delete a cell name?
   a. Insert→Name→Create
   b. Tools→Name→Create
   c. Insert→Name→Define
   d. None of the above

3. Which command is used to create cell names from existing column or row titles?
   a. Insert→Name→Create
   b. Tools→Name→Create
   c. Insert→Name→Define
   d. None of the above

4. Which key can be used to select multiple worksheets?
   a. **SHIFT**
   b. **CTRL**
   c. **ALT**
   d. Both a and b

Skill Builders

Skill Builder 9.1 Copy and Format Worksheets

In this exercise, you will open a workbook that contains one worksheet. You will copy the worksheet twice to create three identical worksheets. You will then format the worksheets and use the Format Painter to ensure consistent formatting between the sheets. Finally, you will create a named range and use the range name in a formula.

Copy a Worksheet

1. Open the workbook named Skill Builder 9.1.

2. Click Cell B10, and follow these steps to calculate the average for Column B.

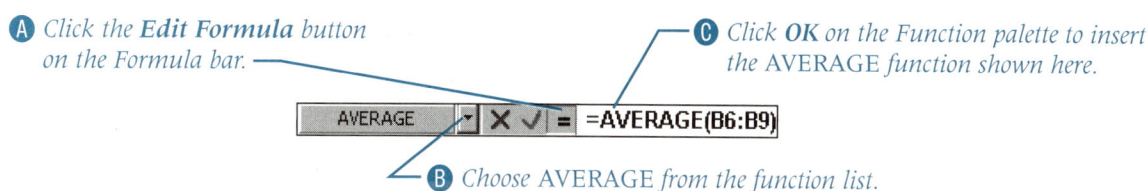

A *Click the **Edit Formula** button on the Formula bar.*

C *Click **OK** on the Function palette to insert the AVERAGE function shown here.*

AVERAGE ▾ | X ✓ = | =AVERAGE(B6:B9)

B *Choose AVERAGE from the function list.*

3. Copy the formula across the row.

4. Click the Select All [ ] button, then click the Copy [ ] button.

5. Click the Sheet2 tab, and Paste [ ] the sheet.

6. Paste the sheet into Sheet3.

7. Rename the sheets as Test1, Test2, and Test3.

8. Change the headings in Row 3 of the Test2 and Test3 sheets to Test 2 and Test 3.

9. Change a few of the numbers in the Test2 and Test3 sheets so the sheets contain different data.

Format the Test1 Sheet, and Copy the Formats

10. Click the Test1 tab, then click Cell A1.

11. Increase the font size to 14, and apply a color to the text.

12. Click Cell A3, increase the size to 12, and apply the same color as in the previous step.

13. Format the Average row in any way you desire.

14. Click the Select All [ ] button to select the entire sheet.

15. Double-click the Format Painter [ ].

16. Click the Test2 sheet tab.

17. Click the Select All [ ] button to copy the formats to that sheet.
    You were able to copy the formats in this manner because the sheets are identical.

18. Click the Test3 sheet tab, and click Select All [ ] to copy the formats to that sheet.

19. Click the Format Painter [ ] to turn it off.

(Continued on the next page)

Experiment with Range Names

20. Click the Test1 sheet tab.

21. Select Cells B10:D10, and tap (DELETE) to delete the average formulas.

22. Select the Ozone data in Cells B6:B9.

23. Click in the Name box, type the name **Ozone**, and tap (ENTER).

24. Click Cell B10, type the formula **=AVERAGE(Ozone)**, and tap (ENTER).
    The correct average, 18.5, should be displayed. You can assign names to any range and use the names in formulas.

25. Assign the name **CarbonMonoxide** to the range C6:C9.

26. Enter an average formula in Cell C10 that references the range name.

27. Assign the name **ParticulateMatter** to the range D6:D9.

28. Enter an average formula in Cell D10 that references the range name.

29. Save the changes to the workbook, and then close the workbook.

Skill Builder 9.2 Link Worksheets and Set Up Charts

In this exercise, you will create a workbook with four worksheets. The master sheet will be linked to three source sheets. You will also create two charts in the main sheet.

Create the Master Sheet

1. Start a new workbook, and set up the worksheet shown below. You will need to widen Columns A through E to 15. You can widen the columns by selecting them and then using the **Format→Column→Width** command.

	A	B	C	D	E
1	1999 Sales - Consolidated Systems, Inc.				
2					
3		Q1	Q2	Q3	Q4
4	Eastern Region				
5	Central Region				
6	Western Region				
7	Total Sales				

2. Change the name of the sheet to **National**.

Set Up the First Source Sheet

3. Change the name of Sheet2 to **Eastern Region**, and set up the worksheet shown below. Type the numbers shown in Rows 4 through 7, and use AutoSum to calculate the Total Sales in Row 8. Make sure you format the cells as shown, widening the columns to 15.

	A	B	C	D	E
1	1999 Eastern Region Sales				
2					
3		Q1	Q2	Q3	Q4
4	Boston	500,000	350,000	340,000	300,000
5	New York	560,000	450,000	280,000	700,000
6	Atlanta	700,000	325,000	450,000	650,000
7	Miami	650,000	600,000	200,000	230,000
8	Total Sales	$ 2,410,000	$ 1,725,000	$ 1,270,000	$ 1,880,000

4. Save the workbook as **Skill Builder 9.2**.

Copy the Eastern Region Sheet to Sheets 4 and 3

5. Click the Sheet3 tab, and choose **Insert→Worksheet** from the menu bar.
   A new worksheet named Sheet4 will appear.

6. Click the Eastern Region sheet tab.

7. Click the Select All ⬚ button, and click the Copy 📋 button.

8. Click the Sheet4 tab, and Paste 📋 the copied sheet.

9. Click the Sheet3 tab, and Paste 📋 the sheet again.

10. Rename Sheet4 as **Central Region**, and rename Sheet3 as **Western Region**.

Edit the New Sheets

11. Click the Central Region sheet tab.

12. Change the title to **1999 Central Region Sales**.

13. Change the city names to **Chicago, Dallas, St. Louis**, and **Denver**.

14. Change all the numbers in Row 4 to 500,000 by clicking in Cell B4 and dragging the fill handle three cells to the right.
    This will make the numbers slightly different from those in the Eastern Region sheet.

15. Click the Western Region sheet tab.

16. Change the title to **1999 Western Region Sales**, and change the city names to Los Angeles, San Francisco, Phoenix, and Seattle.

17. Enter the number **800,000** in Cell B4, then use the fill handle to copy the number to the next three cells to the right.

(Continued on the next page)

Name the Cells in the Detail Sheets

18. Click the Eastern Region sheet tab, then click Cell B8.

19. Click in the Name box on the left end of the Formula bar.

20. Type the name **Eastern_Q1**, and tap (ENTER).

21. Assign names to the Total Sales cells in the Eastern, Central, and Western sheets. Use the same naming convention as in the previous step. For example, use the names Eastern_Q2 for Cell C8 in the Eastern sheet, and Central_Q1 for Cell B8 in the Central sheet.

Create Linking Formulas in the National Sheet

22. Click the National sheet tab, then click Cell B4.

23. Enter the linking formula **=Eastern_Q1**.
    The number 2410000 should appear in Cell B4.

24. Create links in Rows 4, 5, and 6 to the three detail sheets. You may want to copy the formula in Cell B4 across the row and then edit the formula in each cell by simply changing the Q1 to Q2, etc. You may also want to enter the formulas using point mode. Point mode is much faster in some situations.

25. Use AutoSum ⟨Σ⟩ to calculate the Total Sales in Row 7 of the National sheet.

26. Format the numbers in Rows 4 through 6 as Comma style with 0 decimals, and format the totals in Row 7 as Currency style with 0 decimals. You may want to use the Format Painter to copy the formats from one of the detail sheets.

27. Create the column chart and pie chart shown in the following illustration.
    Notice that the column chart compares each region's numbers in the various quarters. The pie chart compares the contributions of each region to the total sales for the year. To create the pie chart, you will need to add Column F, as shown in the illustration.

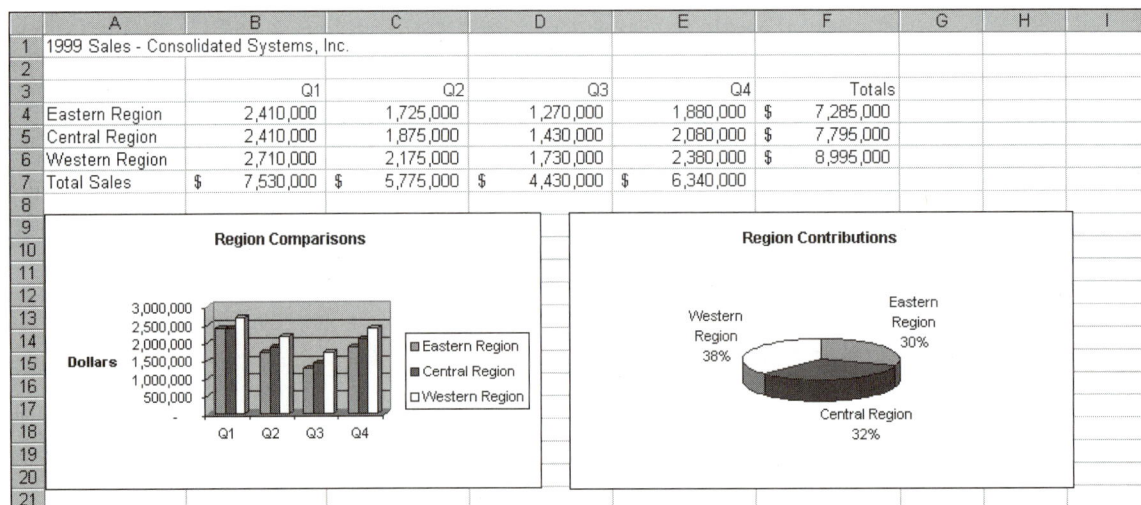

Edit the Eastern Region Numbers

Notice that the Eastern Region percentage in the pie chart is currently 30%. This number will change when you change numbers in the Eastern detail sheet in the next few steps.

28. Click the Eastern Region sheet tab, and click Cell B4.

29. Enter the number **1,000,000**, and copy it across the row.
This will make the Eastern numbers substantially larger than they were.

30. Click the National sheet tab and notice how the Eastern Region pie chart percentage is now 37%.

Format the Sheets

31. Format the title in Row 1, the headings in Row 3, and the total sales in Row 7 of the National sheet. Use whichever font sizes and colors you desire.

32. Select Rows 1 through 3 of the Master sheet by dragging the mouse pointer down the row headings.

33. Double-click the Format Painter [icon].

34. Click the Eastern Region sheet tab, then select Rows 1 through 3 by dragging the mouse pointer down the row headings.
The formats from the National sheet should be copied to Rows 1 through 3. Notice that you were able to copy the formats because Rows 1 through 3 have the same structure in both sheets.

35. Click the Central Region sheet tab, and paint the formats to Rows 1 through 3 of that sheet.

36. Paint the formats to Rows 1 through 3 of the Western Region sheet.

37. Use the Format Painter [icon] to paint the formats from Row 7 of the National sheet to Row 8 of the detail sheets.

Add a Header to All sheets

In the next few steps, you will create a header on all four sheets. You will display the Page Setup dialog box directly from the worksheet with the File→Page Setup command. You must display the Page Setup dialog box from the worksheet if you want the Page Setup options to take effect on all of the selected sheets. The Page Setup options will not affect all of the selected sheets if you display the dialog box from Print Preview.

38. Press the (CTRL) key, and click all four sheet tabs.

39. Choose **File→Page Setup** from the menu bar.

40. Click the Header/Footer tab, then click the Custom Header button.

41. Type the text **Folsom Technical College** in the Left Section box.

42. Click in the Center Section box, and click the Sheet Name [icon] button.
The &[Tab] code will appear. This code places the sheet name in the header.

(Continued on the next page)

43. Click in the Right Section box, and click the Date button.
The &[Date] code will appear. This code places the date in the header.

44. Click **OK** to complete the header, then click the **Print Preview** button on the dialog box.

45. Use the Next button to browse through the pages.
Notice that the National sheet is split by a page break. You will correct this soon. Also notice that the header appears on all pages.

46. Close the Print Preview window.

Switch the National Sheet to Landscape Orientation

47. Click the National sheet tab.
The other sheet tabs will be deselected.

48. Choose **File→Page Setup** from the menu bar.

49. Click the Page tab.

50. Set the orientation to Landscape, and click **OK.**

51. Select all four sheet tabs, and click the Print Preview button.

52. Use the Next button to browse through the pages.
The National sheet should be the only sheet with a Landscape orientation. This is because it was the only sheet tab selected when you set the Landscape orientation.

53. Close the Print Preview window.

54. Feel free to modify the worksheet in any way you desire. Try experimenting with the print options in the Page Setup dialog box.

55. Save the changes when you have finished, and then close the workbook.

Assessments

Assessment 9.1 Set Up Linked Worksheets

1. Follow these guidelines to create a new workbook with the three worksheets shown below.

   ▪ Enter the numbers and data shown into three separate sheets. However, do not enter the numbers in Rows 6 and 7 of the master sheet, because you will insert linking formulas in those cells. Use AutoSum to calculate the Totals in all three sheets.

   ▪ Name the master sheet **Both Stores**, and name the detail sheets **Eastside Store** and **Westside Store**.

   ▪ Create cell names for each total in Row 11 of the detail sheets. Name the Totals in the Eastside sheet **Eastside_January**, **Eastside_February**, and **Eastside_March**. Use a similar naming convention for the Westside sheet.

   ▪ Create links in Rows 6 and 7 of the master sheet to the Totals in the detail sheets.

   ▪ Format the titles, headings, and numbers as shown. Make sure you use consistent formatting across the worksheets. You can use the Format Painter to ensure consistent formatting. Use whichever font color you desire.

   ▪ Your completed worksheets should match the worksheets shown below.

	A	B	C	D
1	Jane's Collectibles			
2				
3	January - March Sales			
4				
5		January	February	March
6	Eastside Store	18,250	16,050	16,800
7	Westside Store	23,450	19,000	21,900
8	Totals	$ 41,700	$ 35,050	$ 38,700

	A	B	C	D	E
1	Jane's Collectibles - Eastside Store				
2					
3	January - March Sales				
4					
5		January	February	March	
6	Dolls	5000	3450	4500	
7	Spoons	1,500	3,400	3,700	
8	Figurines	2,750	2,000	2,300	
9	Antiques	5,600	4,500	3,400	
10	Crystal	3,400	2,700	2,900	
11	Totals	$ 18,250	$ 16,050	$ 16,800	

	A	B	C	D	E
1	Jane's Collectibles - Westside Store				
2					
3	January - March Sales				
4					
5		January	February	March	
6	Dolls	7,500	4,000	6,000	
7	Spoons	2,000	4,000	5,000	
8	Figurines	2,950	3,000	3,700	
9	Antiques	6,000	5,000	4,000	
10	Crystal	5,000	3,000	3,200	
11	Totals	$ 23,450	$ 19,000	$ 21,900	

2. You may want to demonstrate the linking formulas to your instructor by changing a number in one of the detail sheets and watching the numbers change in the master sheet.

3. Print all three sheets when you have finished.

4. Save the completed workbook as **Assessment 9.1,** and then close the workbook.

Assessment 9.2 Set Up Linked Worksheets

1. Follow these guidelines to create a new workbook with the four worksheets shown on the following page.

   ■ Enter the numbers and data shown into four separate sheets. You will need to insert one new worksheet. However, don't enter the transactions in Column D of the summary worksheet. These transaction numbers will be linked to the monthly transaction sheets.

   ■ Use AutoSum to calculate the Totals in all four sheets.

   ■ Name the master sheet **Transaction Summary**, and name the detail sheets **January**, **February**, and **March**.

   ■ Create cell names for each total in Cell C10 of the detail sheets. Name the total in Cell C10 of the January sheet **January_Total**. Likewise, name the totals in the February and March sheets **February_Total** and **March_Total**.

   ■ Create links in Column D of the summary sheet to the totals in the detail sheets. Use the cell names from the detail sheets in the linking formulas.

   ■ Format the titles, headings, and numbers as shown. Make sure you use consistent formatting across the detail worksheets. You can use the Format Painter to ensure consistent formatting. Use whichever font color you desire.

   ■ Your completed worksheets should match the worksheets shown on page 287.

	A	B	C	D
1	1999 Visa Card Transaction Summary			
2				
3	Month	Finance charge	Payment	Transactions
4	January	120	900	315.55
5	February	85	100	431.30
6	March	90	100	275.90
7	April			
8	May			
9	June			
10	July			
11	August			
12	September			
13	October			
14	November			
15	December			
16	Total	$295.00	$1,100.00	$1,022.75

	A	B	C
1	January Transactions		
2			
3	Date	Description	Amount
4	1/2/99	BayView Health Club	35.00
5	1/7/99	Bob's Pizza	14.90
6	1/9/99	Century Cinemas	34.90
7	1/4/99	William's AutoCare	230.75
8			
9			
10	Total		$315.55

	A	B	C
1	February Transactions		
2			
3	Date	Description	Amount
4	2/2/99	BayView Health Club	35.00
5	2/4/99	Southeast Airlines	230.00
6	2/8/99	Western Dental	120.50
7	2/16/99	Mel's Diner	45.80
8			
9			
10	Total		$431.30

	A	B	C
1	March Transactions		
2			
3	Date	Description	Amount
4	3/2/99	BayView Health Club	35.00
5	3/6/99	Home Depot	40.90
6	3/23/99	Aetna Insurance	200.00
7			
8			
9			
10	Total		$275.90

2. You may want to demonstrate the linking formulas to your instructor by changing a number in one of the detail sheets and watching the numbers change in the summary sheet.

3. Print all four sheets when you have finished.

4. Save the workbook as **Assessment 9.2,** and then close the workbook.

Critical Thinking

Critical Thinking 9.1 On Your Own

Set up a revenue and expense workbook for Berkeley Bicycles—a retailer of racing and mountain bicycles. Include four sheets in the workbook. The first sheet should be a summary sheet, and Sheets 2–4 should contain revenue and expense data for Store 1, Store 2, and Store 3. Include revenue and expense data for four quarters (Q1, Q2, Q3, and Q4). The expenses should include employee costs, lease costs, inventory, and overhead. Use whatever revenue and expense numbers you think would be appropriate for a small, bicycle retailer. Calculate the profit or loss of each store for each quarter by subtracting the expenses from the revenue.

Use linking formulas in the summary sheet to calculate the revenue and expenses for the combined stores for each quarter. This should be easy to do if the structure of your summary sheet is identical to the three source sheets.

Format the numbers with either Currency- or Comma-style number formats. Use AutoFormat to format all of the worksheets to be visually attractive. Save your workbook with a descriptive name when you have finished.

Critical Thinking 9.2 Web Research

Open the workbook that you set up in Critical Thinking 8.2. David's parents want to compare the costs of attending Yale and Princeton to the cost of attending Harvard. Copy the data and formatting from the Harvard sheet to the other two sheets in the workbook. Name the sheets Harvard, Yale, and Princeton. Use Internet Explorer and a search engine of your choice to locate the Web sites of Princeton University and Yale University. Determine the approximate tuition, fees, room, board, and personal expenses for a full-time, undergraduate student. Enter the expense number into the cell for the first year. The estimated expenses for the remaining years will be automatically calculated by the formulas you set up in the original Harvard sheet. Save the modified workbook with a descriptive name.

Critical Thinking 9.3 As a Group

Samantha is the owner of Samantha's used computer stores and has three store locations in various parts of the city. She has instructed each of her store managers to prepare an Excel worksheet that lists the number of computers, monitors, printers, scanners, and keyboards purchased by the stores in the past month. In addition, Samantha wants the items categorized as Poor Condition, Good Condition, and Excellent Condition. Samantha emails each store manager an Excel worksheet to use as a basis for the worksheets they submit. This way, each worksheet will have an identical format, and Samantha can easily summarize the data from the three stores.

Set up a worksheet using the criteria discussed above. Email the workbook to three classmates, instructing them to enter the data. One classmate should enter the data for Store 1, another for Store 2, and a third for Store 3. They should only enter the numeric data. You should set up the structure of the worksheet, including the headings.

Instruct your classmates to email the completed workbooks to you. Set up a workbook with a summary sheet that has the same structure as the sheets sent to your classmates. Copy and paste the data from your classmates' sheets into separate sheets in your workbook Use linking formulas to summarize the data from the various sheets on your summary sheet. Use AutoFormat to make all sheets visually attractive. Save the completed workbook with a descriptive name.

Templates and Graphics

As Excel becomes an integral part of your business toolkit, you may find a need to use certain workbooks over and over again. For example, many sales people need to fill out monthly expense reports, sales forecasts, and call reports. You can use Excel templates as the basis for these and other frequently used workbooks. You may also want to enhance your workbooks with pictures, drawing objects, and special effects, such as Office 2000's WordArt tool. This lesson will introduce you to templates and a variety of graphic tools.

In This Lesson

Case Study

Tom Davidson is the Manager of the Trade Winds Sailing Club. The sailing club sponsors frequent sailing events for club members. Tom is responsible for organizing the events and reporting the event results. He needs a report that calculates the average score of event participants and displays the results in a consistent manner. Tom decides that Excel is the right tool for the job. He sets up an Excel template that becomes the basis of new workbooks for reporting event results. Besides recording event results, the report also includes the club logo and other visual enhancements. In this lesson, you will create the template and workbook shown below.

	A	B	C	D	E
8	**Race Results**				
9	Gold Cup Fall Regatta				
10					
11	**Name**	Owner	Score		
12	Lucky Lady	Linda Burke	35		
13	Night Watch	Donna Billings	38		
14	Sandpiper	Jay Walton	42		
15	Donna Marie	Ben Prince	47		
16	Second Wind	Lisa Levine	50		
17	**Average**		**42.4**		

This is a four-point improvement over last year!

Clip Art and Pictures

You can dress up your worksheets using the professionally designed clip art provided with Office 2000. You can also insert your own graphics, such as a company logo or a scanned picture.

The Office 2000 Clip Gallery

The Insert Clip Art [icon] button on the Drawing toolbar displays the Clip Gallery. The Clip Gallery has been redesigned in Office 2000 to make it easier to locate and manage clip art and pictures. The Clip Gallery organizes clip art into categories such as business, animals, and Academic. The Clip Gallery can also be displayed with the **Insert→Picture→Clip Art** command.

*Displays all **Categories**, as shown in this illustration.*

Import your own clip art or pictures into the Clip Gallery.

Go online to Microsoft's ClipGallery Live site for access to thousands of additional clip art images and pictures.

Move backward and forward as you browse for images.

Search for clips using keywords.

*Clip art and pictures are organized into **Categories**. You can even add your own categories.*

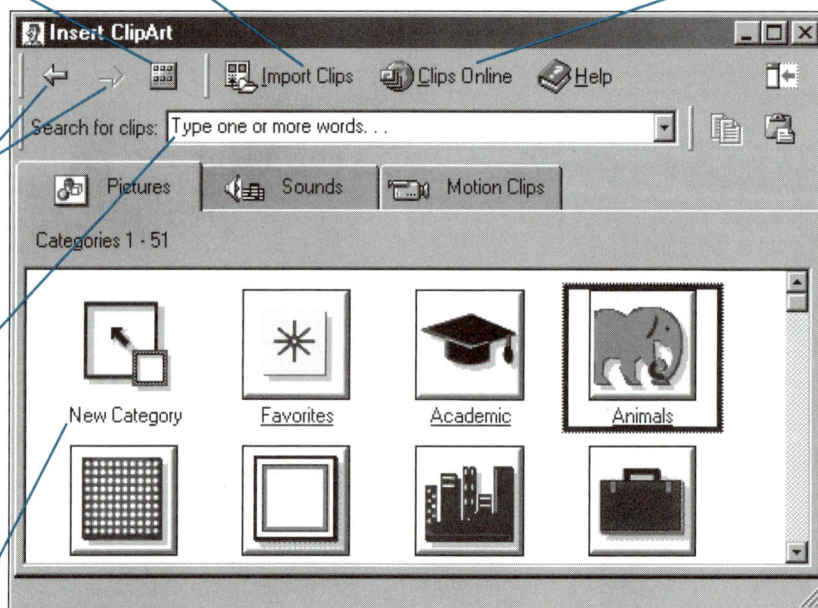

Hands-On 10.1 Use the Clip Gallery

In this exercise, you will explore the Clip Gallery and insert a picture.

Set Up the Worksheet

1. Start Excel, and a new workbook will be visible.

2. Click the Select All [button] button at the top left corner of the worksheet.

3. Use the **Format→Column→Width** command to set the width of all columns to 16.

4. Make sure the entire worksheet is still selected. Change the font to Bookman Old Style, and set the font size to 11. Use a Times New Roman font if Bookman Old Style is not available on your computer.
   These settings will provide a foundation for a new template that you will create later in this lesson.

5. Click anywhere in the worksheet to deselect.

Insert the Clip Art

6. Follow these steps to display the Clip Gallery.

Ⓐ *Locate the Drawing toolbar at the bottom of the Excel window. If the toolbar is not displayed, then use the View→Toolbars→Drawing command to display it.*

Ⓑ *Click the **Insert Clip Art** button.*

7. Click the Academic category to display clips related to academia.

8. Follow these steps to preview a clip.

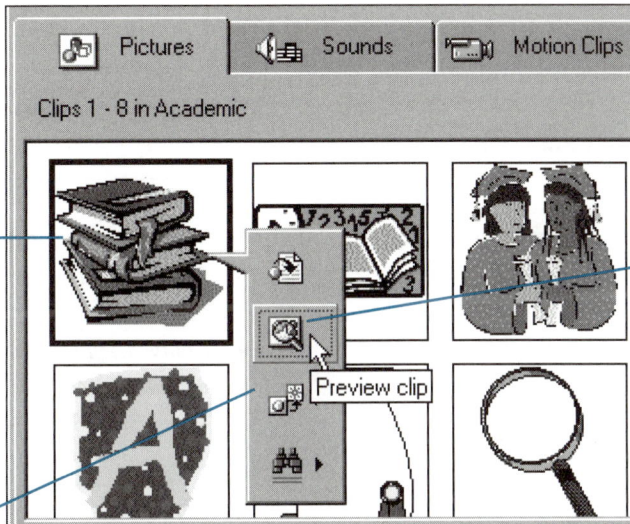

Ⓐ *Click the books clip.*

Ⓑ *Point (but don't click) at each button on the pop-up menu, and the button's function will appear in a ScreenTip.*

Ⓒ *Click the **Preview clip** option to display an enlarged preview of the clip.*

Ⓓ *Click the Close ☒ button on the Preview window.*

9. Follow these steps to navigate in the Clip Gallery and search for a clip.

Ⓐ *Click the **Back** button to move back one level. In this case, you are back at the All Categories (opening) screen.*

Ⓑ *Scroll down through the category list, click the Sports & Leisure category, and scroll through the available clips. In a moment, you will insert the boating clip.*

Ⓒ *Click the **All Categories** button to display the All Categories screen. You can always use this button to display the All Categories screen.*

Ⓓ *Click in the **Search for clips** box, type **boating**, and tap ENTER. Each clip has keywords associated with it. In this case, there are several clips associated with the keyword boating.*

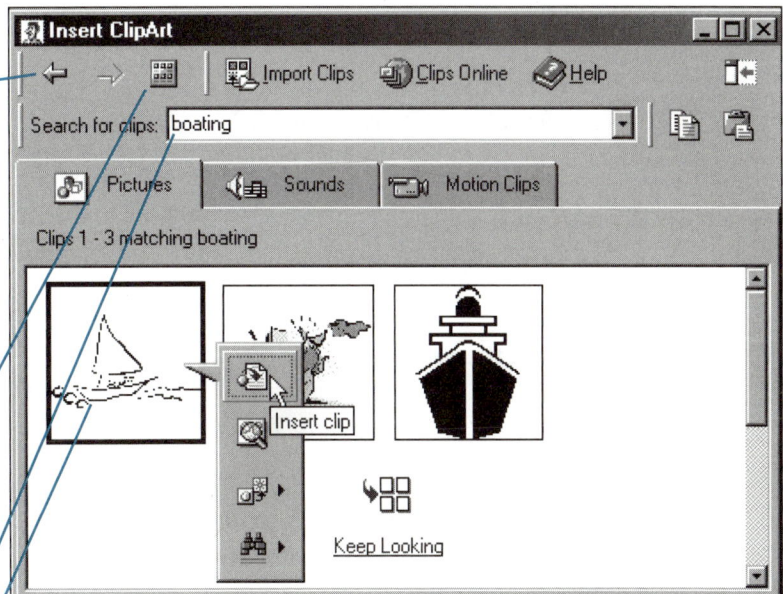

Ⓔ *Choose the boating clip shown here, and then click the **Insert clip** button.*

(Continued on the next page)

10. Click the Close ☒ button on the Clip Gallery.

   The boating picture will occupy a large portion of the worksheet. In the next exercise, you will position the picture and adjust its size.

Selecting, Moving, Sizing, and Deleting Objects

You must select pictures and other objects before you can move or size them. The easiest way to select an object is to click anywhere on the object. Small squares called sizing handles appear on the corners and four sides of a selected object. You can change the size of an object by dragging a sizing handle. If you drag a corner-sizing handle, then the height and width change proportionately, thus maintaining the original object proportions. You can delete a selected object by tapping the (DELETE) key on the keyboard.

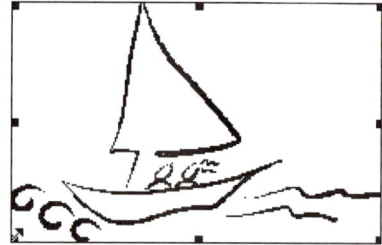

From the Keyboard

Tap arrow keys to move picture

Hands-On 10.2 Size and Move the Picture

1. Notice the sizing handles (small squares) on the corners and edges of the picture.
   You change the size of pictures by dragging sizing handles. This is the same technique you used to change the size of charts. Sizing handles appear whenever you click a picture or any other type of object. Also, a Picture toolbar may be visible in the Excel window. Excel displays the Picture toolbar when a picture is selected unless the Picture toolbar has been closed with the View→Toolbars→Picture command.

2. Follow these steps to reduce the picture size.

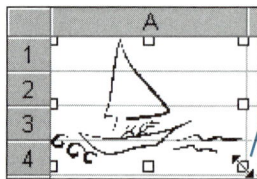

   Ⓐ *Drag this sizing handle up and left until the picture occupies a four-cell block (four cells high by one cell wide).*

   Ⓑ *Position the mouse pointer in the middle of the picture and drag it to the top corner of the worksheet so that it occupies the range A1:A4.*

3. Click outside the picture to deselect it.
   The Picture toolbar will close if it was displayed.

4. Click the picture, and the Picture toolbar will reappear.
   If the picture toolbar isn't visible, you can use the View→Toolbars→Picture command to display it. The Picture toolbar contains buttons that let you manipulate pictures.

Add a Fill Color to the Picture

5. Click the Fill Color 🖌 drop-down button (on either the Formatting toolbar or the Drawing toolbar), and choose any color.
   The color will fill the entire rectangular frame of the picture.

6. If necessary, adjust the size of the picture until it fills the A1:A4 range. You can first size it by dragging the corner-sizing handle. Then drag a sizing handle in the middle of the bottom or right edge to adjust the height or width.

7. Tap (DELETE) to delete the picture.
   You can delete any object by selecting it and clicking the (DELETE) button.

8. Click Undo ↶ to restore the picture.

9. Click anywhere in the worksheet to deselect the picture.

Drawing Object Concepts

Office 2000 has an excellent set of drawing tools that let you draw lines, arrows, rectangles, call-outs, WordArt, and many other objects. Drawing objects are easy to work with and a lot of fun! Lines and callouts are types of drawing objects that are particularly useful for emphasizing areas of interest on worksheets and charts. You insert a drawing object by choosing the desired object from the Drawing toolbar, and then dragging the mouse in the worksheet.

The Drawing ⬚ button on the Standard toolbar is used to display and hide the Drawing toolbar. The Drawing toolbar is usually located at the bottom of the Excel window. You can also display or hide the drawing toolbar with the **View→Toolbars→Drawing** command. The following illustration highlights the buttons on the Drawing toolbar.

Select objects.

Draw lines, arrows, rectangles, and ovals.

Text boxes let text float anywhere on a page.

Choose font colors, fill colors, line styles, and other settings.

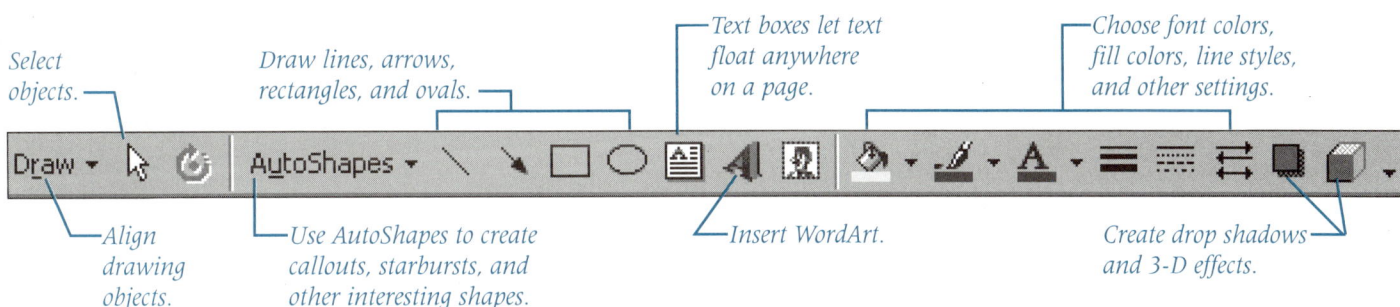

Align drawing objects.

Use AutoShapes to create callouts, starbursts, and other interesting shapes.

Insert WordArt.

Create drop shadows and 3-D effects.

WordArt

The WordArt ⬚ button on the Drawing toolbar displays the WordArt Gallery. You can add special effects to text by choosing a style from the gallery. Once you choose a style, Excel displays a dialog box where you enter the text and choose the font and font size for your stylized WordArt text. The WordArt gallery is shown below.

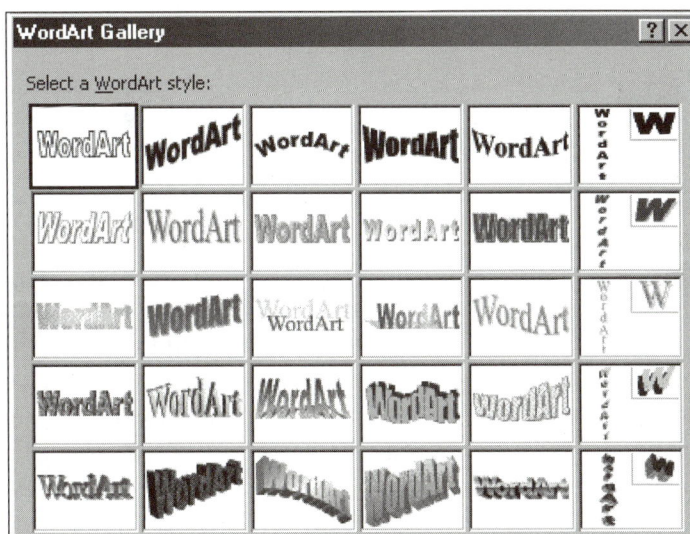

Insert and Edit a WordArt Object

1. Click the WordArt ![WordArt button] button on the Drawing toolbar.
   The WordArt Gallery appears.

2. Choose the style in the fourth row and fourth column, and click **OK.**
   The Edit WordArt Text box appears. This is where you enter your WordArt text.

3. Type the phrase **Tradewinds Sailing Club**.

4. If necessary, choose Impact from the font list, and set the font size to 24. Choose Arial as the font if Impact is not available.

5. Click **OK** to insert the WordArt object in the worksheet.
   The WordArt toolbar should have appeared. The WordArt toolbar lets you edit the text in the WordArt object and format the object.

6. Click the **Edit Text** button on the WordArt toolbar.

7. Edit the word Tradewinds by breaking it into the two words: **Trade Winds**.

8. Change the font size to 28, and click **OK.**

9. Follow these steps to reposition the WordArt object.

Ⓐ *Position the mouse pointer on the object, and a cross hair pointer will appear.* ——

Ⓑ *Drag the object to the right of the picture.*

Enter a Heading

10. Click Cell A8, and enter the heading **Race Results**.

11. Increase the font size of Cell A8 to 14, apply bold formatting, and apply a font color of your choice.
    You will save this workbook as a template in the next exercise.

Templates

You can use templates as the basis for new workbooks. Templates can include any type of cell entries, formatting, pictures, drawing objects, and any other objects or formats available in Excel. The benefit of templates is that they do not change when workbooks that are based upon them change. This lets you use templates over and over as the basis for new workbooks. Excel provides several ready-to-use templates known as spreadsheet solutions. You can use these templates as the starting point for new workbooks. However, you must run Office 2000's setup program and complete a custom setup to install the spreadsheet solutions.

Using Templates

You use the **File→New** command to display the New dialog box. You base a new workbook upon a template by choosing the desired template from the New dialog box and clicking OK. You then develop the workbook and eventually save it as you would save any other Excel workbook. The underlying template remains unchanged.

You can also base a workbook upon a template by navigating to the location where the template is stored and double-clicking the template. This is the technique you will use in the hands-on exercises in this lesson.

*Templates are organized into categories such as **General** and **Spreadsheet Solutions**.*

*The **General** category is the default category where custom templates are stored.*

*You base a new workbook on a template by double-clicking the template, or choosing it, and clicking the **OK** button.*

Template Organization

Templates are used with all Office 2000 applications. The New dialog box reflects the contents of the C:\Windows\Application Data\Microsoft\Templates folder. Any custom templates that you save in the Templates folder will appear under the General tab of the New dialog box when you issue the File→New command. Any folders that appear in the C:\Windows\Application Data\Microsoft\Templates folder will appear as tabs in the New dialog box. You may want to add tabs to the New dialog box to organize your custom templates. The quick reference table that follows will show you how to do this.

Creating Your Own Templates

The easiest way to create a template is to first create a workbook with the cell entries, formatting, graphics, and other settings you desire, then save the workbook as a template. The Quick Reference table on page 298 outlines three methods you can use to turn your workbooks into templates.

CREATING TEMPLATES

Save to the Default Template Location

■ Create the workbook, and choose File→Save As.

■ Choose Template from the Save as Type box.

■ Type a filename, and click the Save button. The template will appear in the General tab of the New dialog box whenever you issue the File→New command.

Save the Template to a Diskette or Other Location

■ Create the workbook, and choose File→Save As.

■ Choose Template from the Save as Type box.

■ Choose a storage location from the Save in box, type a filename, and click the Save button.

■ To use the template, use My Computer or Windows Explorer to navigate to the diskette or other storage location where the template is located.

■ Double-click the template, and a new workbook will appear that is based upon the template.

Create a New Tab in the New Dialog Box, and Save to That Tab

■ Create the workbook, and choose File→Save As.

■ Choose Template from the Save as Type box.

■ Click the New Folder 🖺 button on the Save As dialog box.

■ Type a name for the new folder, and click OK.

■ Type a name for the template, and click the Save button. The next time you issue the File→New command, a new tab will appear in the New box with the same name you assigned to the folder. Your template will appear in the new tab.

Hands-On 10.4 Create and Use a Template

In this exercise, you will be instructed to save your template to your exercise diskette. You won't save templates to the C: drive in this course. This is because many computer labs prevent students from accessing the C: drive. If you need to save templates to the default template folder and access them using the File→New command, then use the first method discussed in the Quick Reference table above.

Create the Template

1. Click the Save 🖫 button, and follow these steps to save the workbook as a template.

Ⓐ *Choose* Template *from the **Save as type** list at the bottom of the dialog box.*

Ⓑ *Choose 3½ Floppy (A:) from the **Save in** list at the top of the dialog box.*

Ⓒ *Type* **TradeWinds Race Results** *in the **File name** box.*

Ⓓ *Click the **Save** button.*

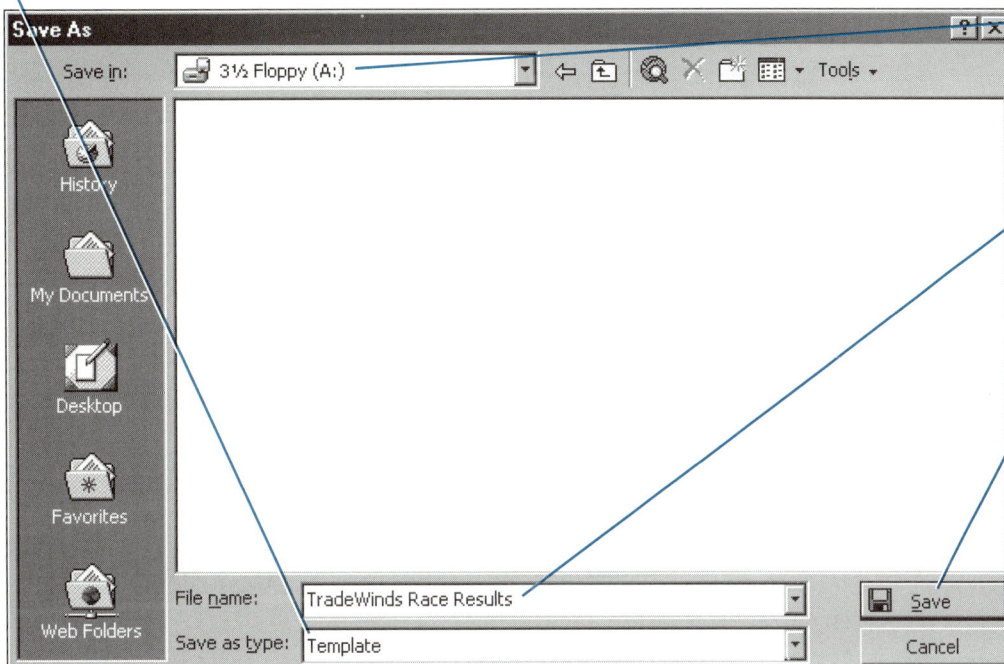

2. Choose File→Close from the menu bar to close the template.

Use the Template

In the next few steps, you will use Window's My Computer tool to display the contents of your exercise diskette. You will base a new workbook upon the TradeWinds Race Results template.

3. Click the Show Desktop 🖉 button on the Windows Taskbar to hide all program windows. If you don't have a Show Desktop button on your Taskbar, then right-click on an open part of the Taskbar and choose Minimize All Windows from the pop-up menu.

NOTE!

In steps 4 through 6, you can click once instead of double-clicking if you point to the objects and they appear as underlined hyperlinks.

4. Double-click the My Computer 🖳 icon on the Desktop.

5. Double-click the 3½ Floppy (A:) icon to display the contents of your exercise diskette.

6. Double-click the **TradeWinds Race Results** template.
A new workbook will appear with the same graphics and formatting as the template.

IMPORTANT!

Important: Use the previous steps to open templates that are stored in locations (such as a diskette) that prevent them from appearing in the New dialog box. Templates that appear in the New dialog box can be used by issuing the File→New command and double-clicking them in the New dialog box.

7. Now choose **File→Close** from the menu bar.
Notice that Excel did not ask you to save the workbook. This is because it is a new workbook that has not been changed in any way.

Modifying Custom Templates

You can easily modify a custom template after it has been created. The following Quick Reference table outlines the methods you can use to locate, modify, and save changes to templates.

MODIFYING CUSTOM TEMPLATES

To modify a template,

- Click the Open 📂 button, and choose Templates from the Files of Type list.
- Navigate to the location where the template is stored, choose the template, and click the Open button.
- Modify the template, save the changes, and then close the template.

Note: To modify a template, you must use the Open dialog box to open the template. If you use My Computer to navigate to the template and then double-click the template, you will create a new workbook.

Hands-On 10.5 Modify the Template

Open the Template

1. Click the Open 📂 button on Excel's Standard toolbar.

2. If necessary, choose Templates from the Files of Type list at the bottom of the dialog box, and choose 3½ Floppy (A:) from the Look in list at the top of the dialog box.

3. Choose the **TradeWinds Race Results** template, and click the Open button.
   Look at the title bar at the top of the Excel window, and notice the name TradeWinds Race Results. You are now working with the original TradeWinds Race Results template—not a workbook that is based on the template.

Modify the Template

4. Click Cell A11, and enter the word **Name**.

5. Enter the word **Owner** in Cell B11, and enter the word **Score** in Cell C11.

6. Right align the entry in Cell C11.

7. Apply bold formatting to all three entries, and apply the same color that you applied to the heading in Cell A8.

8. Click the Save 💾 button to save the changes to the template.

9. Choose **File→Close** to close the template.

Use the Modified Template

10. Click the 3½ Floppy (A:) button on the Windows Taskbar to switch to the My Computer window where your exercise diskette is displayed.

11. Double-click the TradeWinds Race Results template to base a new workbook upon the modified template.
    Notice that the changes you just made appear in the workbook.

12. Click the Save 💾 button, and save the new workbook to your exercise diskette with the name **Hands-On Lesson 10**.

13. Click the 3½ Floppy (A:) button on the Windows Taskbar, and then close the window.

14. Close any other My Computer windows that are open.

AutoShapes and Other Shapes

You can use AutoShapes to add a variety of fun shapes to your worksheets. AutoShapes are predefined shapes organized in categories such as stars and banners, callouts, and flowchart symbols. You choose AutoShapes with the AutoShapes button on the Drawing toolbar. You can also draw lines, arrows, rectangles, and ovals in your documents. To draw a shape, you click the desired button on the Drawing toolbar and then either click or drag in the document.

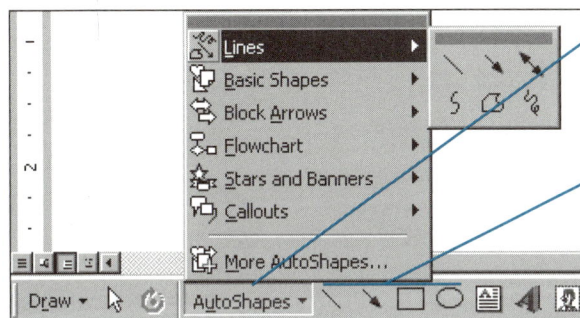

AutoShapes are organized in categories. Choose a shape from a category and drag in the document to draw the shape.

Use these tools to draw lines, arrows, rectangles, and ovals.

Formatting Buttons on the Drawing Toolbar

The Drawing toolbar has several buttons that let you format drawing objects. You can use the Drawing toolbar to format AutoShapes, rectangles, ovals, lines, text boxes, and other drawing objects. To format an object, you must select the object first and then apply the desired format(s). You can also select several objects and format them as a group. The following Quick Reference table discusses the formatting buttons on the Drawing toolbar.

Quick Reference

FORMATTING BUTTONS ON THE DRAWING TOOLBAR

Button	Function
Select Objects	Click this button and drag to enclose the desired objects in a selection box. You can also press (SHIFT) while clicking the desired objects.
Fill Color	Fills an object with a solid color, pattern, or gradient.
Line Color	Changes the color of lines or applies a line pattern.
Font Color	Changes the font color of text in a text box or other object.
Line Style	Changes thickness and style of lines and object borders.
Dash Style	Formats lines and borders with various dash styles.
Arrow Style	Applies arrowheads to lines or changes the arrowhead style of lines.
Shadow	Applies a shadow effect to objects.
3-D	Applies a 3-D effect to objects.

1. Enter the subtitle **Gold Cup Fall Regatta** in Cell A9. Add the text, numbers, and AVERAGE function (in Cell C17) shown to the right in Rows 12 through 17.
   Feel free to format the entries with the color and formatting options of your choice.

	A	B	C
7			
8	**Race Results**		
9	Gold Cup Fall Regatta		
10			
11	**Name**	Owner	Score
12	Lucky Lady	Linda Burke	35
13	Night Watch	Donna Billings	38
14	Sandpiper	Jay Walton	42
15	Donna Marie	Ben Prince	47
16	Second Wind	Lisa Levine	50
17	**Average**		42.4

Draw and Format an Oval

2. Click the Oval button on the Drawing toolbar.

3. Follow these steps to draw an oval in Cell C12.

Ⓐ *Position the mouse pointer slightly above and to the left of the number 35 and drag down and right.*

Ⓑ *Release the mouse button to position the oval over the cell. The entry will be hidden behind the oval.*

11	**Name**	Owner	Score
12	Lucky Lady	Linda Burke	35
13	Night Watch	Donna Billings	38

4. Make sure the oval is selected, and click the Fill Color drop-down button.
   You can use the Fill Color button on either the Formatting toolbar or the Drawing toolbar.

5. Choose **No Fill** from the top of the color palette.
   The oval should now have a transparent effect.

6. Use the Line Color button on the Drawing toolbar to change the line color of the oval. Use the same color that you used for the text entries.

7. Click the Line Style button on the Drawing toolbar and choose 1 1/2 pt.
   The oval line should now be much thicker.

Draw and Format a Callout AutoShape

8. Click the AutoShapes button on the Drawing toolbar.

9. Follow these steps to choose the Rounded Rectangular Callout shape.

Ⓐ *If necessary, click the Expand Menu button at the bottom of the AutoShapes menu to display the expanded menu. Slide the mouse pointer up and down the menu and notice the variety of AutoShapes.*

Ⓑ *Choose the **Callouts** category.*

Ⓒ *Choose the **Rounded Rectangular Callout** shape.*

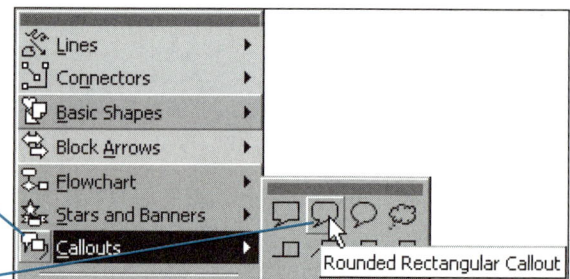

- Lines
- Connectors
- Basic Shapes
- Block Arrows
- Flowchart
- Stars and Banners
- Callouts

Rounded Rectangular Callout

10. Follow these steps to draw the callout.

11	Name	Owner	Score		
12	Lucky Lady	Linda Burke	35		
13	Night Watch	Donna Billings	38		
14	Sandpiper	Jay Walton	42		
15	Donna Marie	Ben Prince	47		
16	Second Wind	Lisa Levine	50		
17	Average		42.4		
18					

A *Position the mouse pointer to the right of the 42.4 average and drag up to the right until the callout has approximately this shape and size.*

B *Release the mouse button to complete the callout.*

11. Now type the text shown to the right into the callout. Don't be concerned if your text wraps in a location different than shown in the illustration.

This is a four-point improvement over last year!

12. Select the callout text by dragging the mouse over the text.

13. Format the text with a Bookman Old Style 11 point bold font.

14. Apply the same color to the text that you used for the cell entries and the oval border.

15. Click the Center button to center the lines within the callout.

16. Click anywhere in the worksheet to deselect the callout.

17. Follow these steps to select the callout.

A *Click anywhere on the callout, and a thick border will appear.*

B *Click the border, and the pattern will change to indicate that the callout is selected. (You must click the border before you can size, move, and format callouts.)*

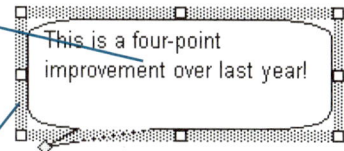

This is a four-point improvement over last year!

18. Use the Fill Color button on the Drawing toolbar to fill the callout with a light color.

19. Use the Line Color button on the Drawing toolbar to format the callout with the same line color you used for the text inside the callout.

20. Use the Line Style button on the Drawing toolbar to set the line weight to 1 1/2 pt.

(Continued on the next page)

21. Follow these steps to move and size the callout until it matches the example shown here.

Ⓐ *Adjust the callout size by dragging this sizing handle.*

Ⓑ *Move the callout by dragging any border.*

Ⓒ *Change the anchor position by dragging the yellow anchor point.*

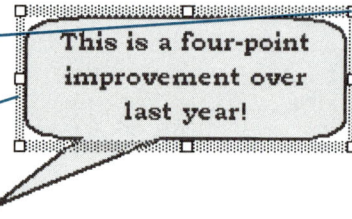

This is a four-point improvement over last year!

22. If necessary, continue to format your callout until it has the shape and position shown in the completed worksheet below.

	A	B	C	D	E
1					
2		Trade Winds Sailing Club			
3					
4					
5					
6					
7					
8	Race Results				
9	Gold Cup Fall Regatta				
10					
11	Name	Owner	Score		
12	Lucky Lady	Linda Burke	35		
13	Night Watch	Donna Billings	38		
14	Sandpiper	Jay Walton	42		
15	Donna Marie	Ben Prince	47		
16	Second Wind	Lisa Levine	50		
17	Average		42.4		

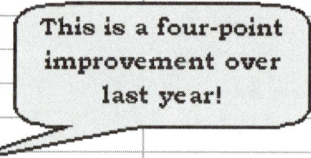

This is a four-point improvement over last year!

23. Save the changes to your workbook, and continue with the next topic.

Additional Drawing Object Techniques

Thus far, you have learned the basic techniques for working with drawing tools. A few of the other important drawing tools and drawing techniques are discussed in the following topics. Upon completion of this lesson, you should have enough knowledge to be able to use all of the drawing tools effectively.

Constraining Objects

You can constrain objects to specific shapes or angles as you draw. These techniques are outlined in the following Quick Reference table.

CONSTRAINING OBJECTS

Task	Procedure
Draw or insert squares.	Choose the Rectangle ▭ tool, and click in the worksheet. You can also draw a square by pressing the (SHIFT) key while drawing a new rectangle. If you press (SHIFT) while sizing an existing rectangle, then the original proportions of the rectangle are maintained.
Draw or insert circles.	Choose the Oval ⬭ tool, and click in the document. You can also draw a circle by pressing the (SHIFT) key while drawing a new oval. If you press (SHIFT) while sizing an existing oval, then the original proportions of the oval are maintained.
Draw lines at 15-degree increments.	Press the (SHIFT) key while drawing a line or arrow.

Layering Objects

Drawing objects reside on layers above the worksheet. Each time you draw an object, it is placed on a new layer. The layers are stacked on top of one another. You can change the layering of drawing objects by clicking the Draw button on the Drawing toolbar and choosing layering options from the Order menu.

The layering options appear on the Order *menu.*

Text Boxes

You use the Text Box 🖹 tool to draw text boxes. Text boxes are one of the most useful drawing objects. Text boxes look like rectangles when they are inserted; however, unlike rectangles, you can type text inside a text box. Text boxes let you position text anywhere on a worksheet. You can use text boxes to superimpose text on worksheet entries, pictures, and other graphics.

Draw Circles and a Square

1. Click the Sheet2 worksheet tab.
    You will experiment in this clean worksheet.

2. Click the Oval ⬭ button on the Drawing toolbar.

3. Click anywhere in the worksheet to create a perfect circle.

4. Click the Oval ⬭ button again.

5. Press the (SHIFT) key, and drag in the worksheet to create another perfect circle.

6. Use the Rectangle ⬜ tool and the (SHIFT) key technique to draw a square.

Experiment with Layers

7. Now drag the objects until they are positioned on top of one another. Adjust the object positions until you can see some part of each object.

8. Select the square by clicking anywhere on it.

9. Click the Draw button on the left end of the Drawing toolbar, and choose **Order→Send to Back.**
    The square should be behind the circles.

10. Now choose **Draw→Order→Bring to Front** to move the square to the front of the stack.

11. Take a few moments to experiment with the various Order options.

Use Other Tools

12. Experiment with the other tools on the Drawing toolbar. In particular, try drawing lines, arrows, and text boxes.

13. Try using the (SHIFT) key technique while you draw lines. You will notice the lines are constrained to 15-degree increments as they are drawn.

14. Save the changes to your workbook when you have finished experimenting.

15. Close the workbook, and continue with the end-of-lesson questions and exercises.

Concepts Review

True/False Questions

1. A template is updated each time you save a workbook that is based upon the template. TRUE FALSE

2. You can change the size of pictures after they have been inserted. TRUE FALSE

3. The Save As dialog box is used to save a workbook as a template. TRUE FALSE

4. The Drawing ⊞ button displays and hides the Drawing toolbar. TRUE FALSE

5. You cannot format text within a callout box. TRUE FALSE

6. The Select Objects ▨ tool is used to select multiple drawing objects. TRUE FALSE

7. You can press the CTRL key while using the Oval tool to draw a perfect circle. TRUE FALSE

8. The WordArt ◀ button displays the Clip Gallery. TRUE FALSE

Multiple-Choice Questions

1. Which command opens a template for use as a new workbook?
   a. Format→Template
   b. File→New
   c. Insert→Template
   d. None of the above

2. What happens if you use My Computer to navigate to a template and then double-click the template?
   a. Excel creates a new workbook that is based upon the template.
   b. The template is opened for editing.
   c. The New dialog box is displayed
   d. None of these

3. In which folder are Excel 2000 templates usually stored?
   a. C:\Windows\Application Data\Microsoft\Templates
   b. C:\Program Files\Templates\Microsoft Office\Excel
   c. C:\Windows\Microsoft Office\Templates
   d. C:\Excel\Templates

4. Which keyboard key is used to draw horizontal, vertical, or 45-degree lines?
   a. SHIFT
   b. ALT
   c. CTRL
   d. None of these

Skill Builders

Skill Builder 10.1 Modify a Template

In this exercise, you will modify the Tradewinds template.

Modify the Template

1. Click the Open 📂 button, and navigate to your exercise diskette.

2. Double-click the TradeWinds Race Results template.
   You should have created this template in the Hands-On exercises.

3. Change the text in Cell A8 from Race Results to **Regatta Results**.

4. Click the Save 💾 button to save the change.

5. Choose **File→Close** to close the template.

Use the Template

6. Click the Show Desktop 🖉 button on the Windows Taskbar to hide all program windows. If you don't have a Show Desktop button, then right-click on an open part of the Taskbar and choose Minimize All Windows from the pop-up menu.

7. Double-click the My Computer 🖥 icon on the Desktop.

8. Double-click the 3½ Floppy (A:) icon to display the contents of your exercise diskette.

9. Double-click the TradeWinds Race Results template.
   The new workbook should contain the modified text in Cell A8.

10. Close the new workbook without saving the changes.

11. Close all open My Computer windows.

Skill Builder 10.2 Draw and Copy Objects

In this exercise, you will insert a picture, use drawing objects, and then copy the objects.

Insert and Size a Picture

1. Start a new workbook, and click the Insert ClipArt 🖼 button.

2. Click the Animals category to display clips related to animals.

3. Choose any animal clip and insert the clip. The example in this exercise uses the bird clip as shown on the following page.

4. Close the Clip Gallery, and follow these steps to change the picture size.

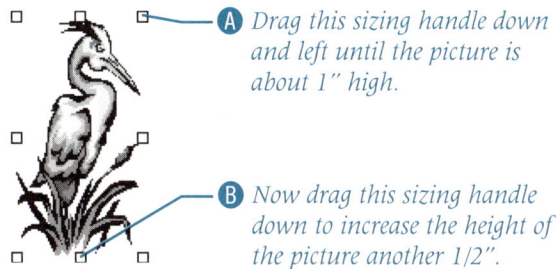

A *Drag this sizing handle down and left until the picture is about 1" high.*

B *Now drag this sizing handle down to increase the height of the picture another 1/2".*

Draw a Text Box and Arrow

5. Follow these steps to draw a text box and horizontal line.
Text boxes let you "float" text anywhere in a worksheet.

A *Click the Arrow button on the Drawing toolbar, then press the* (SHIFT) *key while your draw this arrow. When you have finished drawing, make sure you release the mouse button before releasing the* (SHIFT) *key.*

This is a tall bird

B *Click the Text Box button and drag to create this text box. Change the font size to 14, and type this text. Adjust the size and position of the box as necessary.*

Select and Copy the Objects

6. Click the Select Objects tool.

7. Drag the selection pointer to enclose all three objects in the selection box.

8. Release the mouse button, and all three objects will have sizing handles.

9. Position the mouse pointer anywhere on the selected objects, and it will have a four-headed arrow attached to it.
This is the move or copy pointer.

10. Press and hold the **right** mouse button as you drag the selected objects to a new location in the worksheet.

11. Release the mouse button, and choose **Copy Here** from the pop-up menu.
As you can see from this example, you can select groups of objects and move or copy the group.

12. Click the Select Objects tool to deactivate the selection pointer.

13. Feel free to experiment with drawing objects.

14. When you have finished, close the workbook without saving.

Skill Builder 10.3 Create a Template

In this exercise, you will create a template that will be used for quarterly forecasts at Zephron Industries. All Zephron sales reps will use the template as a basis for quarterly sales forecasts. The template will include three worksheets: a data sheet, a column chart sheet, and a pie chart sheet. You will create the charts and data worksheet as part of the template. This way, the charts will already be created for the sales reps.

Set Up the Worksheet Using Dummy Data

You will set up a worksheet in the next few steps. You will include dummy data in the worksheet to help you test the template. The data will be deleted prior to saving the template.

1. Start a new workbook, and click the Select All [ ] button.

2. Use the **Format→Column→Width** command to set the column widths to 12.

3. Follow these guidelines to set up the worksheet shown below.

   ■ Enter the data shown below. Use the Merge and Center [ ] button to center the title and subtitle in Rows 2 and 4 across Columns A through G. Also, you will need to use a SUM formula in Cell C14.

   ■ Apply a fill color and font color to the cells in Rows 1 through 5, 9, and 14. The example shown below uses a dark fill color and a white font color. This effect is known as reversing out.

   ■ Format the numbers with Comma style and Currency style as shown.

	A	B	C	D	E	F	G
1							
2			**Zephron Quarterly Sales Forecast**				
3							
4			**Sales Rep - Donna Wilson**				
5							
6							
7							
8							
9	**Product**	**Forecast Units**	**Forecast Dollars**				
10	Cell Phones	230	21,900				
11	Pagers	560	24,000				
12	GPS Systems	725	65,000				
13	PCs	120	190,000				
14	**Total**		**$ 300,900**				

4. Rename Sheet1 as **Data Sheet**.

Create a Bar Chart on a Separate Sheet

5. Use the (CTRL) key and the mouse to select the ranges A10:A13 and C10:C13, as shown to the right.

10	Cell Phones	230	21,900
11	Pagers	560	24,000
12	GPS Systems	725	65,000
13	PCs	120	190,000

6. Use the Chart Wizard to create the chart shown below on a separate chart sheet. The data is already selected, so you only need to be concerned with the various chart-formatting options.

Revenue Forecast

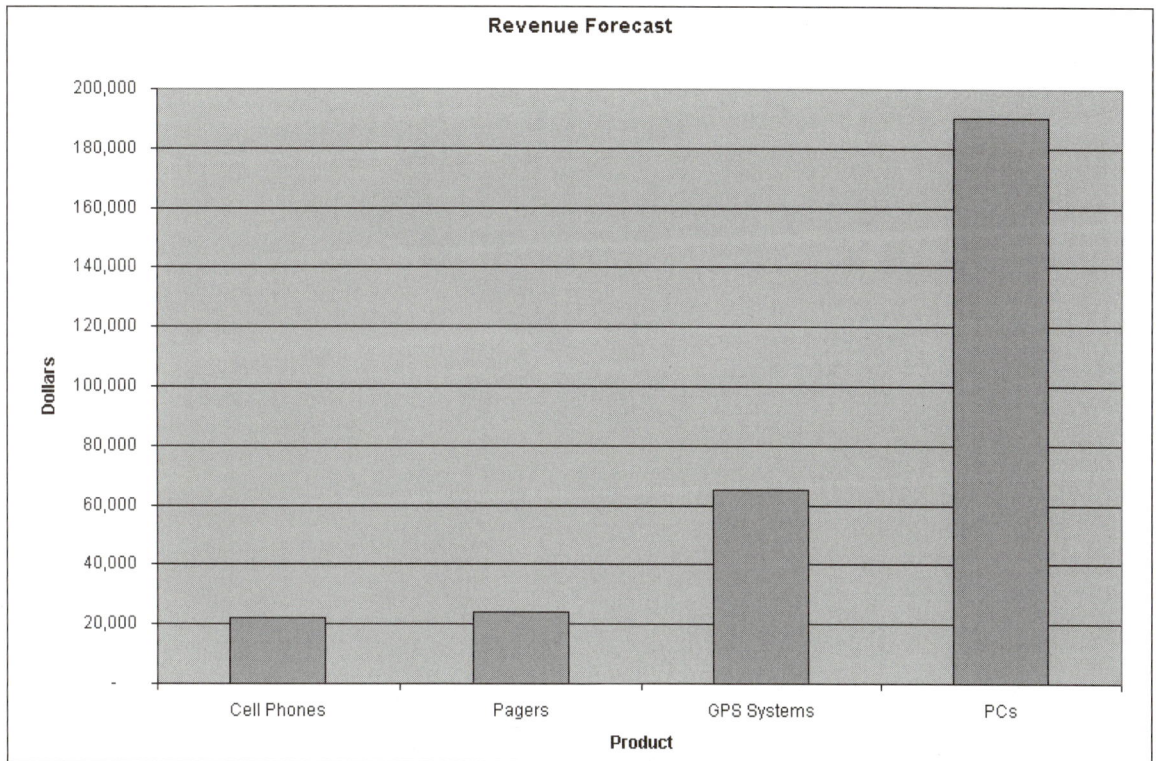

7. Rename the Chart1 sheet as **Revenue Forecast**.

(Continued on the next page)

Create a Pie Chart on a Separate Sheet

8. Insert the pie chart shown below on a separate chart sheet. You must decide which data to select, and determine the other chart options. Hint: Look at the pie chart, and notice the labels on the slices. Also notice that there are only four slices, so only four sets of data should be included in the selection.

Revenue Percentage by Product

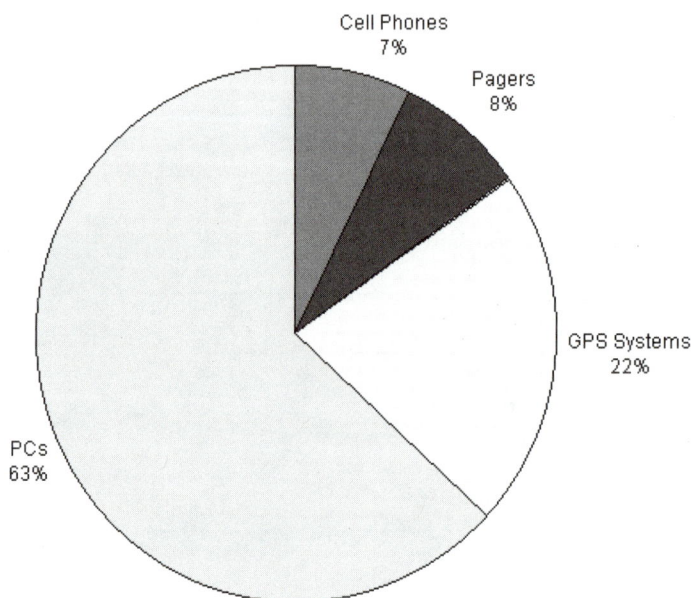

9. Rename the pie chart sheet as **Revenue Breakdown**.

10. Click the Data Sheet tab to activate it.

11. Change the order of the sheet tabs by dragging the Data Sheet tab to the left of the chart tabs.

Delete the Dummy Data, and Save the Workbook as a Template

12. Make sure the Data Sheet is active, and select the data in the range B10:C13, as shown to the right.

10	Cell Phones	230	21,900
11	Pagers	560	24,000
12	GPS Systems	725	65,000
13	PCs	120	190,000

13. Tap (DELETE) to delete the data.
    The total in Cell C14 will be zero (or a dashed line). However, the formula in Cell C14 is still intact, so the total will recalculate when new data is entered in the cells. The charts will be meaningless until data is entered into the Data Sheet.

14. Click the Save 💾 button, and set the Save as Type to Template.

15. Choose 3½ Floppy (A:) from the Save in list at the top of the dialog box.

16. Type the name **Zephron** in the File name box, and click the **Save** button.

17. Choose **File→Close** from the menu bar to close the template.
    You will use the template to create a new workbook in the next exercise.

Skill Builder 10.4 Use a Template

1. Click the Show Desktop [icon] button on the Windows Taskbar to hide all program windows. If you don't have a Show Desktop button, then right-click on an open part of the Taskbar, and choose Minimize All Windows from the pop-up menu.

2. Double-click the My Computer [icon] icon on the Desktop.

3. Double-click the 3½ Floppy (A:) icon to display the contents of your exercise diskette.

4. Double-click the **Zephron** template.
   This new workbook is based upon the template you set up in the previous exercise.

5. Enter the numbers shown to the right into Columns B and C of the Data Sheet. The text entries shown to the right should already be entered in Column A.

10	Cell Phones	100	12,500
11	Pagers	200	10,000
12	GPS Systems	450	85,000
13	PCs	250	350,000

   The Total should be calculated as $457,500. The data will also be formatted with the Comma and Currency style formats you set in the template.

6. Click the Revenue Forecast and Revenue Breakdown sheet tabs.
   Notice that these charts have been recreated.

7. Click the Save [icon] button to display the Save as dialog box.

8. Choose 3½ Floppy (A:) from the Save in list, and make sure the Save as Type option is set to Microsoft Excel Workbook.

9. Type the name **Skill Builder 10.4** in the File name box, and click the **Save** button.
   The workbook has been saved, and the template is ready to be used again.

Close the Workbook and Check Out the Template

10. Choose **File→Close** to close the workbook.

11. Click the My Computer button on the Windows Taskbar to switch to the My Computer window.

12. Double-click the **Zephron** template to create another workbook that is based upon the template.
    Notice that the template is unchanged. As you can see, this powerful template contains text, formatting, formulas, and charts. This type of template is especially useful when provided to inexperienced users who are interested only in entering data. You can also use the protection techniques discussed in the previous lesson to protect a template. This way, inexperienced users won't accidentally damage a workbook that is based upon the template.

13. Close the workbook without saving, and then close all open My Computer windows.

Assessments

Assessment 10.1 Use Drawing Objects

1. Create the workbook shown below. You will need to create the chart as shown and use the drawing tools to create the text box and arrow. Use the chart style shown here, and notice that the chart has data labels on top of each column. Also, draw the arrow as a perfect horizontal line.

2. Print the worksheet, chart, and drawing objects on a single page.

3. Save the workbook with the name **Assessment 10.1,** and then close the workbook.

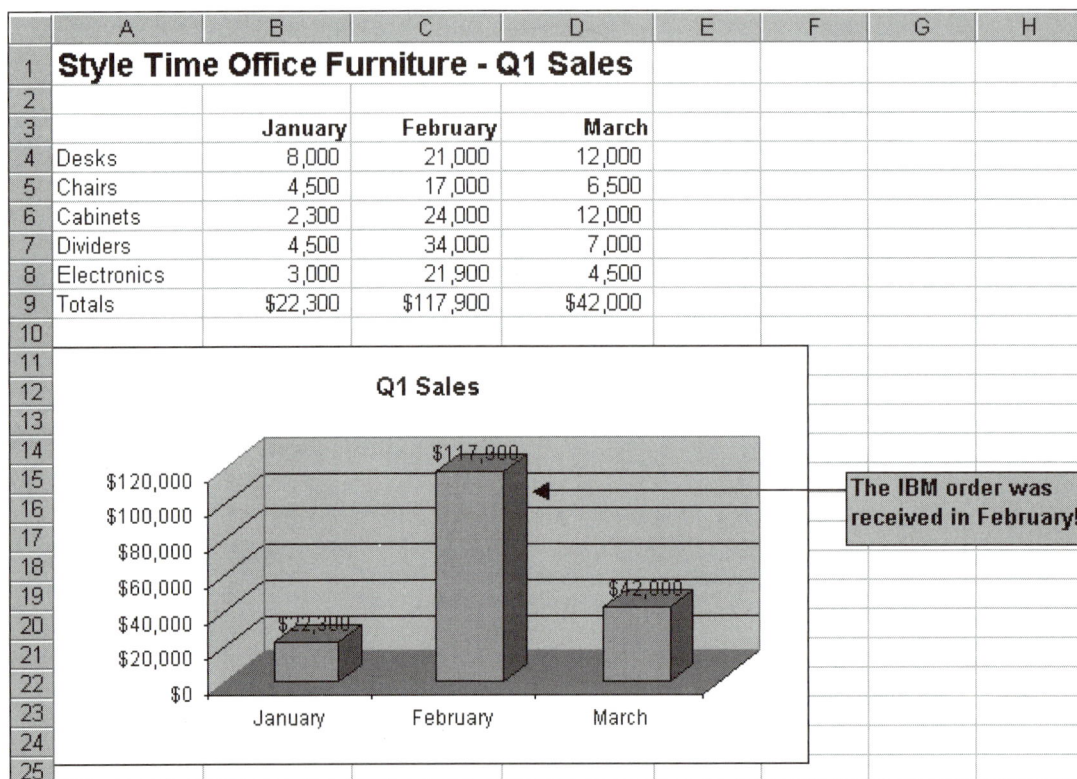

	A	B	C	D	E	F	G	H
1	**Style Time Office Furniture - Q1 Sales**							
2								
3		**January**	**February**	**March**				
4	Desks	8,000	21,000	12,000				
5	Chairs	4,500	17,000	6,500				
6	Cabinets	2,300	24,000	12,000				
7	Dividers	4,500	34,000	7,000				
8	Electronics	3,000	21,900	4,500				
9	Totals	$22,300	$117,900	$42,000				
10								

Q1 Sales

The IBM order was received in February!

Assessment 10.2 Create a Template with a Chart

In this assessment, you will create a template for the Redmont School District. Each school within the district will use the template to create a budget workbook and accompanying chart.

1. Create the following worksheet and embedded pie chart. Notice that the elevation has been increased on the chart, using the 3-D View option.

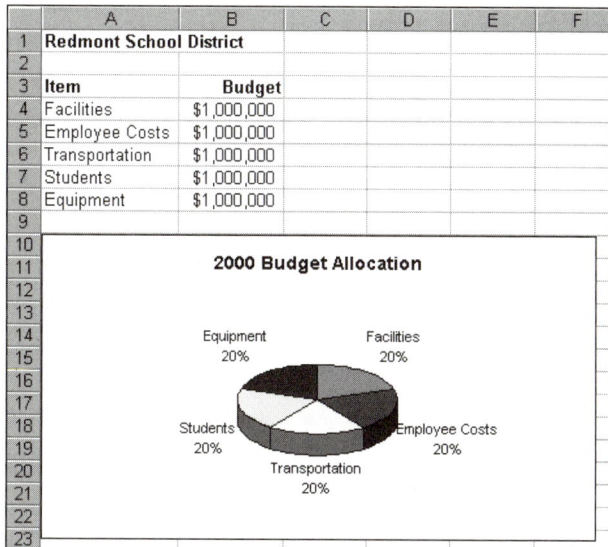

	A	B	C	D	E	F
1	Redmont School District					
2						
3	Item	Budget				
4	Facilities	$1,000,000				
5	Employee Costs	$1,000,000				
6	Transportation	$1,000,000				
7	Students	$1,000,000				
8	Equipment	$1,000,000				
9						

2000 Budget Allocation

Equipment 20%
Facilities 20%
Students 20%
Employee Costs 20%
Transportation 20%

2. Create a footer that displays only the filename in the center section of the footer.

3. Delete the dummy data in Cells B4:B8, and save the workbook to your exercise diskette as a template named **Redmont.**

4. Close the template, and then use My Computer to navigate to your exercise diskette, and create a new workbook that is based upon the template.

5. Add the phrase **(Barrett School)** to the end of the title in Cell A1, and enter the data in Cells B4:B8 as shown below. The chart in your new workbook should display the new percentages shown below.

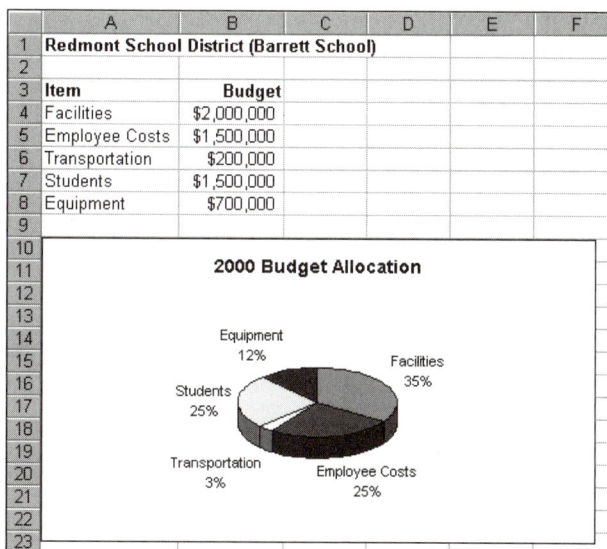

	A	B	C	D	E	F
1	Redmont School District (Barrett School)					
2						
3	Item	Budget				
4	Facilities	$2,000,000				
5	Employee Costs	$1,500,000				
6	Transportation	$200,000				
7	Students	$1,500,000				
8	Equipment	$700,000				
9						

2000 Budget Allocation

Equipment 12%
Facilities 35%
Students 25%
Transportation 3%
Employee Costs 25%

6. Save the new workbook with the name **Assessment 10.2,** and then close the workbook.

7. Close all open My Computer windows.

Critical Thinking

Critical Thinking 10.1 On Your Own

Jeff Adams is the sales manager for Performance Office Systems, a company that distributes high-end computer systems, monitors, printers, and copy machines. Jeff manages three sales people, each with a monthly quota of $100,000. He has asked you to set up a workbook template that can be distributed to each sales person. The template must include a row for each item (computers, monitors, printers, and copy machines). In addition, it should include the number of units sold for the current month, the dollar value of the units sold, the number of units forecasted for the next month, and the dollar value of the forecasted units to be sold. Save your completed workbook as a template with a descriptive name.

Critical Thinking 10.2 On Your Own

Cindy Chang is the founder and CEO of Web Research Services, which conducts research for companies on a contract basis. Recently, Cindy signed a contract with Jack Norton of Norton Travel Alternatives. Jack wants to put his travel company on the Web. However, before making such a move, he wants to know the growth potential of the online travel services industry for each of the next five years. This information is important because it will help Jack determine the budget for his new Web site and will give him some insight into the competition he may face. After conducting the necessary research, Cindy has crunched the numbers and come up with the following data.

Year	Estimated Revenues for Online Travel Services
FY 2000	$1.1 Billion
FY 2001	$2.5 Billion
FY 2002	$3.7 Billion
FY 2003	$6.2 Billion
FY 2004	$7.5 Billion

Using the data in the table above, set up a worksheet and embedded column chart that depicts the growth of the online travel services industry. Use the years FY 2000, FY 2001, etc. as the x-axis labels. Use the numbers 1.1, 2.5, 3.7, 6.2, and 7.5 as the values. Indicate in one of the chart titles that the numbers are in billions of dollars. Remove the legend from the chart.

Using the AutoShapes button, insert this callout that points to the last column in the chart: **This represents nearly 700% growth over a five year period.** Format the callout with an attractive color and apply a fill color to the callout. Save the workbook with a descriptive name when you have finished.

Critical Thinking 10.3 Web Research

Create a new workbook based on the template you created in Critical Thinking exercise 10.1. Use Internet Explorer and a search engine of your choice to locate Web sites of companies that sell personal computers, monitors, printers, and copy machines. Choose a typical top-of-the-line personal computer, a 600 dpi laser printer, a 17" monitor, and a copy machine, and record the model numbers and prices in the Critical Thinking 10.1 workbook. You can choose models that you desire. You only need to choose one computer, printer, monitor, and copy machine.

Include the name of each item in the item column of the Critical Thinking 10.1 exercise. For example, use Printers (HP LaserJet 6P) if you chose an HP LaserJet 6P. Insert a new column in the worksheet in front of the dollar volume column. Enter the prices of each item you researched into the new column, and label the column Unit Price.

Enter a formula in the Dollar Value column to calculate the dollar volume as the Units Sold multiplied by the Unit Price. Your dollar volume numbers will definitely increase or decrease depending upon the items you chose. Use formulas in the Forecasted Dollar Value column to calculate the Forecasted Dollar Volume as the Unit Price multiplied by the Units Forecasted. Save your workbook as a template with a descriptive name.

Critical Thinking 10.4 As a Group

Email the template you created in Critical Thinking 10.3 to three classmates. Instruct them to create a new workbook based on the template and to enter new Units Sold and Units Forecasted numbers in the worksheet. They can use any numbers they want. The formulas in the worksheet should automatically recalculate the dollar value and forecasted dollar value numbers. Also instruct them to include their name somewhere in the worksheet. Finally, instruct them to save the modified worksheets with descriptive names specified by you. You should choose names that will allow you to identify the worksheets and from whom they originated. Have your classmates email the workbooks back to you. Copy the worksheets from your classmates into a single workbook. Rename the worksheet tabs so that each worksheet is identified with a particular classmate. Save the workbook with a descriptive name.

The IF Function and Lookup Functions

Complex worksheets often require functions that make decisions based upon the values in other cells. Excel provides several functions that meet this need. The result returned by the IF function is dependent upon whether a logical condition is true or false. The HLOOKUP and VLOOKUP functions return values from lookup tables. In this lesson, you will use the IF function and VLOOKUP function.

In This Lesson

Case Study

Wanda Richardson is the Accounting Manager at a wholesale paper distributor named Paper Plus. Wanda needs to calculate monthly commissions for the Paper Plus sales force. The sales force is organized into a telemarketing group and a direct sales group. The commission rate of each sales person is dependent upon his or her total monthly sales. Wanda sets up a worksheet that uses the IF function to calculate commission rates for the telemarketing group. She uses the VLOOKUP function for the more complex calculations required for the direct sales group. The worksheet you will create in this lesson is shown below.

	A	B	C	D	E
1	**Paper Plus Monthly Commission Calculations**				
2	**November 1999 Report**				
3	*Prepared by Wanda Richardson*		*11/30/99*		
4					
5	**Telemarketing Sales**	**November Sales**	**Commission Rate**	**Total Commission**	**Above or Below Quota?**
6	Bill Evans	11,000	10%	1,100	Above Quota
7	Dorothy Simms	12,500	10%	1,250	Above Quota
8	Ted Long	8,000	5%	400	Below Quota
9	Elsie Green	4,500	5%	225	Below Quota
10					
11					
12	**Direct Sales**	**November Sales**	**Commission Rate**	**Total Commission**	**Above or Below Quota?**
13	Ned Greenfield	19,500	10%	1,950	Below Quota
14	Vincent Coleman	21,000	15%	3,150	Above Quota
15	Richard Medford	9,500	0%	-	Under Achiever
16	Donna Brownlow	52,000	25%	13,000	Over Achiever
17	Alonzo Cortez	24,500	15%	3,675	Above Quota
18	Bill Peterson	12,500	10%	1,250	Below Quota
19	Willie Wilson	4,000	0%	-	Under Achiever
20	Denise Barns	75,000	25%	18,750	Over Achiever
21					
22					
23			Sales Volume	Commission Rate	Message
24			-	0%	Under Achiever
25			10,000	10%	Below Quota
26			20,000	15%	Above Quota
27			30,000	20%	Above Quota
28			50,000	25%	Over Achiever

The IF Function

Excel's IF function uses a logical operator (such as > or <) to evaluate a condition. The result returned by the IF function depends upon whether the condition is true or false. The general syntax of the IF function is discussed below.

Syntax	Discussion
IF(Comparison,True,False)	The comparison statement typically compares a cell's content to a number or text string. The True and False parts of the argument are typically numbers, cell references, or text entries.

The following illustration provides a practical example of the IF function syntax. Take a few moments to carefully study this illustration.

This IF function is entered into Cell C2. The comparison statement, IF B2>=10000 is True because Cell B2 contains the number 11,000. The IF function returns the value 10% because 10% is in the True section of the function argument, as shown in the generic IF function syntax above.

C2	▼	=	=IF(B2>=10000,10%,5%)	
	A		B	C
1	Telemarketing Sales		November Sales	Commission Rate
2	Bill Evans		11,000	10%
3	Dorothy Simms		6,500	5%

This cell contains the same IF function except that it references Cell B3 instead of B2. The value 5% is returned because the value in Cell B3 is 6,500, which is less than 10000.

The following table defines the logical operators that can be used in IF functions.

Logical Operator	Description
=	Equal
<	Less than
>	Greater than
>=	Greater than or equal to
<=	Less than or equal to
<>	Not equal to

Hands-On 11.1 Use the IF Function

In this exercise, you will open a workbook on your exercise diskette. You will use an IF function to determine whether a telemarketing sales representative should receive a 5% or 10% commission rate for the month. The commission rate will be determined by the IF function after the function determines whether or not the sales rep achieved the monthly quota of $10,000.

Enter the IF Function

1. Open the workbook named Hands-On Lesson 11.

2. Click Cell C6.
   Take a moment to study the worksheet. Bill Evans (the sales person in Row 6) should have a commission rate of 10% if his sales are greater than or equal to $10,000, and 5% if his sales are less than $10,000. The IF function you are about to enter will return 5% because the value in Cell B6 is 6,500, which is less than $10,000.

3. Enter the function **=IF(B6>=10000,10%,5%)** in Cell C6; the result should be .05.

4. Format the cell with the Percent [%] style to display the number as 5%.

5. Take a few moments to study the function you just entered, and try to understand the logic.

6. Click Cell B6, and change the number to 11,000.
   Cell C6 should now display 10% because the sales rep exceeded the $10,000 quota.

Enter Another IF Function in Cell C7

7. Click Cell C7, and enter the formula **=IF(B7>=10000,10%,5%)**.
   The result should be 0.1.

8. Format Cell C7 with the Percent [%] style.

Copy the IF Function and Calculate the Commissions

9. Click Cell C7, and use the fill handle to copy the IF function down to Cells C8 and C9.

10. Click Cell D6, and enter the formula **=B6*C6**.
    *The result should be 1,100. The commission is equal to the Sales * Commission Rate.*

11. Use the fill handle to copy the formula in D6 down to Cells D7, D8, and D9.

12. Save the changes, and continue with the next topic.

Returning Text Entries with the IF Function

Thus far, you have used the IF function to return percentages. You can also return text entries with the IF function. For example, in the next exercise, the IF function will return the phrase Below Quota if sales are less than 10,000, or Above Quota if sales are greater than or equal to 10,000. You must enclose text in quotation marks if you use it as the True or False argument in an IF function. For example, the function you will enter in Cell E6 is =IF(B6>=10000,"Above Quota","Below Quota"). The text that is used for the True and False values is surrounded by quotation marks.

Returning Null Values with the IF Function

A null value is equivalent to an empty cell. A null value is not the same as entering zero in a cell. You may want the IF function to return a null value in some situations. For example, you may want the function to enter a phrase in a cell if the IF statement is true, and nothing if the statement is false. You specify a null value as an argument by typing an opening and closing parenthesis with nothing between them. The null value can be used in either the true or false arguments of the IF function.

Hands-On 11.2 Return Text with the IF Function

1. Click Cell E6, and enter the function **=IF(B6>=10000,"Above Quota","Below Quota")**.
   Make sure you type the formula exactly as shown. It is especially important that you type the commas, quotations, and parentheses correctly. The phrase Above Quota should be entered in Cell E6 because the sales were 11,000, which is greater than 10,000.

2. Use the fill handle to copy the IF function down to Cells E7, E8, and E9.

3. Right Align [≣] Cells E6 through E9 (the cells with the Above Quota and Below Quota text).

(Continued on the next page)

4. At this point, Rows 1 through 9 of your worksheet should match the example below.

	A	B	C	D	E
1	**Paper Plus Monthly Commission Calculations**				
2	**November 1999 Report**				
3	*Prepared by Wanda Richardson*		*11/30/99*		
4					
5	**Telemarketing Sales**	**November Sales**	**Commission Rate**	**Total Commission**	**Above or Below Quota?**
6	Bill Evans	11,000	10%	1,100	Above Quota
7	Dorothy Simms	12,500	10%	1,250	Above Quota
8	Ted Long	8,000	5%	400	Below Quota
9	Elsie Green	4,500	5%	225	Below Quota

5. Save the changes, and continue with the next topic.

Lookup Functions

Excel's VLOOKUP (Vertical Lookup) and HLOOKUP (Horizontal Lookup) functions look up values in tax tables, commission rate tables, and other types of lookup tables. The VLOOKUP function is used most often, so it is discussed in this lesson. The generic syntax of the VLOOKUP function and a discussion of its arguments appear below.

VLOOKUP(search argument, lookup table, column number)

The following table outlines the three arguments of the VLOOKUP function. The table refers to the illustration on the following page as an example. Also, you will notice that the table highlights the lookup table argument (the second argument in the function) before it highlights the search argument (the first argument). As you review the table and the illustration following the table, make sure you refer to the formula that is shown in the formula bar of the illustration (=VLOOKUP(B13,Comm_Table,2).

Argument	Discussion
lookup table	This is the name or range reference of a lookup table. In the following illustration, the lookup table is in the Range A17:C22, and it has been given the name Comm_Table.
search argument	The lookup function searches down the left column of the lookup table for the search argument. The search argument is usually a number or a reference to a cell that contains a number. In the following illustration, the function searches down the left column of the lookup table looking for the number 19500 (19500 is the search argument in Cell B13).
column number	After VLOOKUP locates the search argument in the left column of the lookup table, it moves across the table to the specified column number. In the following illustration, the number 2 is used in the VLOOKUP function, so the function moves to the second column in the lookup table.

The following illustration provides additional details on the VLOOKUP function.

This VLOOKUP function is in Cell C13.

The search argument is B13. VLOOKUP searches down the left column of the lookup table for the number 19500 (the number that is in Cell B13). VLOOKUP doesn't need to find an exact match in the table, it just needs to locate the range within which 19500 falls. It chooses Row 19. The reason for this is discussed below.

This is the lookup table. It has been given the range name Comm_Table. The range name identifies the table as occupying the Range A17:C22.

C13	▼	=	=VLOOKUP(B13,Comm_Table,2)	
	A	B	C	D
11				
12	**Direct Sales**	**November Sales**	**Commission Rate**	**Above or Below Quota?**
13	Ned Greenfield	19,500	10%	Below Quota
14				
15				
16				
17	Sales Volume	Commission Rate	Message	
18	-	0%	Under Achiever	
19	10,000	10%	Below Quota	
20	20,000	15%	Above Quota	
21	30,000	20%	Above Quota	
22	50,000	25%	Over Achiever	

The third argument in the function is 2. This instructs the lookup function to move across Row 19 to the second column in the table. This is Cell B19, which contains the value 10%. That value is returned and displayed in Cell C13.

Additional VLOOKUP Details

VLOOKUP searches down the left column of the lookup table for the search argument. In the preceding example, VLOOKUP would search for the number 19500. The function doesn't need to find the exact number 19500. As soon it locates a number that is greater than the search argument (19500), it stops and chooses the *previous* table row. In the preceding example, it stops when it finds 20000 and then chooses the previous row (Row 19). The function then goes to the column number in the lookup table specified in the third argument of the function. In the preceding example, the function goes to the second column in the lookup table. The cell value in the cell it goes to is then returned. In the preceding example, the function goes to Row 19 and the 2nd column of the lookup table. This is Cell B19, so the number 10% is returned.

Sorting Lookup Tables

The VLOOKUP function searches down the first column of the lookup table and stops when it finds the first value that is greater than or equal to the search argument. For this reason, the rows in the lookup table must be sorted in ascending order on the first column. This way, you can be assured that VLOOKUP will stop at the proper row and return the correct value.

Hands-On 11.3 Use VLOOKUP

Set Up the Lookup Table

1. If necessary, use the zoom control until you can see at least 25 rows in your worksheet.

2. Enter the phrase **Sales Volume** in Cell C20.

3. Complete the lookup table by entering the text and numbers shown below.
   Keep in mind that this illustration only shows Rows 19 through 25 of the worksheet. Rows 1 through 18 are not shown to conserve space in the illustration.

	A	B	C	D	E
19					
20			Sales Volume	Commission Rate	Message
21			0	5%	Below Quota
22			10,000	10%	Below Quota
23			20,000	15%	Above Quota
24			30,000	20%	Above Quota
25			50,000	25%	Over Achiever

4. Format the text and numbers in the lookup table as shown in the preceding illustration. The Sales Volume numbers are formatted as Comma style with zero decimals.

Assign a Range Name to the Table

In the next few steps, you will assign a range name to the table. You will use the range name in the VLOOKUP function to reference the table.

5. Follow these steps to create the range name.

Ⓐ *Select the table as shown below.*　　Ⓑ *Click in the **Name** box and type the name **Comm_Table**.*　　Ⓒ *Tap* (ENTER) *to complete the name.*

Comm_Table ▼　=　Sales Volume

	A	B	C	D	E	F
19						
20			Sales Volume	Commission Rate	Message	
21			-	5%	Below Quota	
22			10,000	10%	Below Quota	
23			20,000	15%	Above Quota	
24			30,000	20%	Above Quota	
25			50,000	25%	Over Achiever	
26						

6. Click any cell in the table to deselect the table.
   Notice that the range name is no longer displayed in the Name box. You must select all cells in the table (or any named range) in order for the range name to appear in the name box.

7. Select the entire table (the range C20:E25), and the name Comm_Table will appear in the Name box.

Use the VLOOKUP Function

You will use the VLOOKUP function to calculate the commission rates in Cells C13 through C18. These commission rates cannot be calculated with the IF function. This is because there are five different commission levels that the direct sales people can achieve depending upon their sales volume. The IF function can only handle two levels because of its True/False limitations.

8. Click Cell C13, and enter the function **=VLOOKUP(B13,Comm_Table,2)**.
   Excel should return the number .1 (10%).

9. Take a few moments to study the function you just entered and understand how it works.
   Keep in mind that you are trying to determine the commission rate that Ned Greenfield should be paid. The function looks for Ned's sales number, 19,500, in the left column of the lookup table. It stops when it gets to 20,000 (Cell C23) and then backs up one row because Ned's sales are between 10,000 and 20,000. The function then moves across Row 22 to the second column in the lookup table, which is Column D. This makes sense because Column D contains the commission rates. Cell D22 contains the 10% rate that Ned should be paid. The number .1 (10%) is then returned and displayed in Cell C13.

10. Click Cell C14, and enter the function **=VLOOKUP(B14,Comm_Table,2)**.
    The number .15 (15%) should be returned. Notice that all arguments were the same for this function, except that you told VLOOKUP to look up the number in Cell B14 instead of B13.

Copy the Function

11. Click Cell C14, and use the fill handle to copy the VLOOKUP function down to cells C15:C18.

12. Click Cell C15, and notice that the VLOOKUP function has been updated in the Formula bar.
    The relative cell reference B14 in the function is updated to B15, B16, etc. as the function is copied down the column. This is correct because you want the function to lookup the number to the left of the function.

Calculate the Commissions, and Copy Cell Formats

13. Click Cell D13, and enter the formula **=B13*C13**.
    The result should be 1,950.

14. Use the fill handle to copy the formula in Cell D13 down to Cells D14:D18.

15. Apply the Percent **%** style to Cells C13:C18.

Use VLOOKUP to Determine the Messages in Column E

16. Click Cell E13, and enter the function **=VLOOKUP(B13,Comm_Table,3)**.
    The message Below Quota should be returned. Notice you used the same arguments for this function as you did with the function in Cell C13, except the last argument is 3 instead of 2. This instructs VLOOKUP to return the value from Column 3 of the lookup table instead of Column 2.

17. Use the fill handle to copy the VLOOKUP function from Cell E13 down to Cells E14:E18.

18. Right Align ▤ Cells E13:E18 (the cells with the Above Quota and Below Quota results).

(Continued on the next page)

19. Rows 12 through 25 of the worksheet should match the following illustration.

	A	B	C	D	E
11					
12	**Direct Sales**	**November Sales**	**Commission Rate**	**Total Commission**	**Above or Below Quota?**
13	Ned Greenfield	19,500	10%	1,950	Below Quota
14	Vincent Coleman	21,000	15%	3,150	Above Quota
15	Richard Medford	9,500	5%	475	Below Quota
16	Donna Brownlow	52,000	25%	13,000	Over Achiever
17	Alonzo Cortez	24,500	15%	3,675	Above Quota
18	Bill Peterson	12,500	10%	1,250	Below Quota
19					
20			Sales Volume	Commission Rate	Message
21			-	5%	Below Quota
22			10,000	10%	Below Quota
23			20,000	15%	Above Quota
24			30,000	20%	Above Quota
25			50,000	25%	Over Achiever

20. Click Cell D21, and change the number in that cell to **0%**.
Cell C15 should have a rate of 0%, and the corresponding commission in Cell D15 will be null.

21. Click Cell E21, and change the message to **Under Achiever**.
The Under Achiever message will appear in Cell E15.

Move the Lookup Table and Add Two More Sales Reps

Suppose that two new sales reps are hired. The lookup table currently occupies Row 20. For this reason, you must move the table before adding the new sales reps. Moving the table is easy because you assigned the range name (Comm_Table) to the table. You can move a table with a range name and the VLOOKUP functions will continue to refer to the correct cells in the new table location.

22. Follow these steps to move the table down three rows.

Comm_Table ▼	=	Sales Volume			
	A	B	C	D	E	F
19						
20			Sales Volume	Commission Rate	Message	
21			-	0%	Under Achiever	
22			10,000	10%	Below Quota	
23			20,000	15%	Above Quota	
24			30,000	20%	Above Quota	
25			50,000	25%	Over Achiever	
26						
27						
28						
29				C23:E28		
30						

Ⓐ *Click the **Name** box drop-down button, and choose Comm_Table from the Name list. The lookup table will be selected.*

Ⓑ *Position the mouse pointer on the bottom edge of the selected table, and drag the table down three rows.*

23. Enter Rows 19 and 20 as shown below.

You will need to enter the data shown in Cells A19, B19, A20, and B20. You can copy the formulas from Row 18 down to the other cells in Rows 19 and 20. The completed workbook is shown below.

	A	B	C	D	E
1	**Paper Plus Monthly Commission Calculations**				
2	**November 1999 Report**				
3	*Prepared by Wanda Richardson*		*11/30/99*		
4					
5	**Telemarketing Sales**	**November Sales**	**Commission Rate**	**Total Commission**	**Above or Below Quota?**
6	Bill Evans	11,000	10%	1,100	Above Quota
7	Dorothy Simms	12,500	10%	1,250	Above Quota
8	Ted Long	8,000	5%	400	Below Quota
9	Elsie Green	4,500	5%	225	Below Quota
10					
11					
12	**Direct Sales**	**November Sales**	**Commission Rate**	**Total Commission**	**Above or Below Quota?**
13	Ned Greenfield	19,500	10%	1,950	Below Quota
14	Vincent Coleman	21,000	15%	3,150	Above Quota
15	Richard Medford	9,500	0%	-	Under Achiever
16	Donna Brownlow	52,000	25%	13,000	Over Achiever
17	Alonzo Cortez	24,500	15%	3,675	Above Quota
18	Bill Peterson	12,500	10%	1,250	Below Quota
19	Willie Wilson	4,000	0%	-	Under Achiever
20	Denise Barns	75,000	25%	18,750	Over Achiever
21					
22					
23			Sales Volume	Commission Rate	Message
24			-	0%	Under Achiever
25			10,000	10%	Below Quota
26			20,000	15%	Above Quota
27			30,000	20%	Above Quota
28			50,000	25%	Over Achiever

24. Save the changes to the workbook, and then close the workbook.

Concepts Review

True/False Questions

1. The IF function determines whether a comparison is true or false.　　TRUE　FALSE

2. The second argument in an IF function is the False argument.　　TRUE　FALSE

3. The VLOOKUP function searches down the left column of the lookup table.　　TRUE　FALSE

4. The VLOOKUP function stops searching when it finds a value that is less than the search argument.　　TRUE　FALSE

5. A lookup table cannot be moved once it has been created.　　TRUE　FALSE

6. The last argument in a VLOOKUP function specifies the column from which the entry or number should be chosen.　　TRUE　FALSE

7. The entries in the left column of the lookup table should be in descending order.　　TRUE　FALSE

8. The VLOOKUP function cannot return text entries.　　TRUE　FALSE

Multiple-Choice Questions

1. Which of the following IF functions has proper syntax?
   a. =IF(B2>10000,10%,5%)
   b. IF(B2+35,10%,5%)
   c. =IF(B2<>150,10%,5%)
   d. None of the above

2. Which of the following logical operators can be used in IF functions?
   a. >=
   b. <=
   c. =
   d. All of the above

3. If an IF statement is entered into Cell B5 and the condition evaluates to true, then which cell displays the number that is returned by the IF function?
   a. B5
   b. B6
   c. A5
   d. None of the above

4. Which characters must surround text if you want an IF function to enter the text in a cell?
   a. ( )
   b. " "
   c. [ ]
   d. None of the above

Skill Builders

Skill Builder 11.1 Use the IF Function with Absolute References

In this exercise, you will set up the commission analysis worksheet shown on the following page. You will use an IF function in the commission rate column. The IF function's arguments will reference the quota and commission rates in Cells C3, C4, and C5. You will use absolute values in the IF function to allow you to copy the function to other cells.

Set Up an IF Function and Copy It

1. Open the workbook named **Skill Builder 11.1.**

2. Click Cell C9, and enter the function **=IF(B9>=C3,C4,C5)**.
   The result should be .05. Take a moment to study the function you just entered. Notice that the IF statement compares the sales in Cell B9 to the quota in Cell C3. The $700,000 sales are not greater than or equal to the $725,000 quota, so the expression is false. The False part of the IF function references Cell C5, which contains the number 5% or .05. This is why .05 is entered into Cell C9.

3. Use the fill handle to copy the IF function down to Cells C10, C11, C12, and C13.
   Your objective is to have a commission rate of .05 or .1 entered into the cells. You will get the wrong results in all cells other than Cell C10. Can you figure out why you got incorrect results? The next few steps in this exercise will explain why this happened.

4. Click Cell C11.
   Look at the Formula bar. The formula should be =IF(B11>=C5,C6,C7). Notice that the B11 reference is referring to the correct cell. Are the C5, C6, and C7 references correct? The B11>=C5 argument should be comparing the sales in Cell B11 to the Quota in Cell C3. Likewise, the references to Cells C6 and C7 should actually be referring to the commission rates in Cells C4 and C5. The problem is that you should have used absolute cell references for the C3, C4, and C5 references in the original IF function in Cell C9. You want the IF functions in Cells C10, C11, C12, and C13 to continue to reference those cells. You will correct this in the next few steps.

5. Click Undo ⤺ to reverse the copy.

6. Click Cell C9.

7. Click in the Formula bar just in front of the C3 reference.

8. Tap the (F4) key, and Excel will insert dollar signs $ in front of the C and the 3.
   This converts the reference to absolute.

9. Click just in front of the C4 reference in the Formula bar, and tap (F4) again.

10. Convert the C5 reference to absolute, and complete the entry.
    The result should still be .05.

(Continued on the next page)

Copy the Formula Again

11. Use the fill handle to copy the formula down to Cells C10, C11, C12, and C13.
    This time the IF functions should return the correct percentages of .05 and .1.

12. Click any of the cells, and review the Formula in the formula bar.
    Try to understand how the IF function works and how the absolute values allowed you to copy the function.

13. Format Cells C9:C13 with the Percent **%** style.

14. Calculate the Commissions Paid in Column D.
    *The Commissions Paid = Sales * Commission Rate.*

15. Calculate the Total Commissions Paid in Cell D14.
    The completed worksheet should match the worksheet shown below.

Play What-if Analyses

In the next few steps, you will change the quota in Cell C3, and the commission rates in Cells C4 and C5. The IF functions and the Commissions Paid formulas will be recalculated. This will let you determine the impact that changing the quota and commission rates has on the Total Commissions Paid in Cell D14.

16. Click Cell C3, and change the quota to $500,000.
    Notice that all the sales reps are now paid 10%, and that the commissions paid increases substantially.

17. Change the Above Quota commission rate to 8%, and notice the impact this has on the Total Commission Paid.

18. Feel free to continue playing what-if analyses.

19. Save the changes, and close the workbook when you have finished.

	A	B	C	D
1	Commission Analysis Worksheet			
2				
3	Quota		$725,000	
4	Above Quota		10%	
5	Below Quota		5%	
6				
7				
8		May Sales	Commission Rate	Commissions Paid
9	Wellington	$700,000	5%	$35,000
10	Banks	$550,000	5%	$27,500
11	Burnett	$650,000	5%	$32,500
12	Johnson	$900,000	10%	$90,000
13	Curtin	$800,000	10%	$80,000
14	Total Commission Paid			$265,000

Skill Builder 11.2 **Use the IF Function with Absolute References**

In this exercise, you will use an IF function to determine whether or not sales reps should receive a bonus for their quarterly sales.

1. Open the workbook entitled **Skill Builder 11.2.**

2. Use AutoSum $\boxed{\Sigma}$ in Column E to calculate each sales rep's total sales for July, August, and September.
   The results should match the worksheet below.

3. Calculate the commissions in Column F.
   The Commissions are calculated as the Total Sales in Column E multiplied by the Commission Rate in Cell B4. There is no need to use an IF function because there is just one commission rate. However, you will need to use an absolute reference to Cell B4 if you want to copy the formula down the column.

4. Click Cell G7, and enter the function **=IF(E7>=70000,$B$3,0)**. The result should be 0.
   Take a moment to study the function you just entered. How much must the sales rep sell in order to receive a bonus? What amount is the bonus? What bonus is paid if the sales do not meet the objective specified in the IF function?

5. Copy the function down the column.

6. Calculate the Total Compensation in Column H as the Commission plus the Bonus.

7. Format the cells as shown below.

8. Save the changes to the workbook, and then close the workbook.

	A	B	C	D	E	F	G	H
1	Sales Rep Compensation Report							
2								
3	Bonus	2,000						
4	Commission Rate	16%						
5								
6		July	August	September	Total Sales	Commission	Bonus	Total Compensation
7	Sales Rep	$14,000	$23,000	$21,000	$58,000	$9,280	$0	$9,280
8	Larson	12,000	29,000	45,000	86,000	13,760	2,000	15,760
9	Jackson	10,000	21,000	54,000	85,000	13,600	2,000	15,600
10	Tate	23,000	12,000	34,000	69,000	11,040	-	11,040
11	Belum	32,000	32,000	21,000	85,000	13,600	2,000	15,600
12	Davidson	12,000	23,000	21,000	56,000	8,960	-	8,960
13	Winston	43,000	32,000	12,000	87,000	13,920	2,000	15,920

Skill Builder 11.3 **Perform Calculations within an IF Function**

In this exercise, you will create the worksheet shown below. You will use IF functions in Columns D and E to determine which items need to be reordered, and the quantity to reorder.

1. Start a New Workbook, and enter the data shown in Rows 1 through 3 and Columns A through C below.
   You will need to widen the columns as shown.

2. Click Cell D4.
   In the next step, you will enter an IF function in Cell D4. The IF function will display a Reorder message if the Current Inventory is less than the Reorder Point. The IF function will display a null value (leave the cell empty) if the Current Inventory is greater than the Reorder Point. You display a null value by entering open and closed quotation marks ("").

3. Enter the function **=IF(C4<B4,"Reorder","")**; the cell should appear empty.
   Type the function exactly as shown with the quotation marks in the correct positions. The Current Inventory is 40, which is greater than the Reorder Point, so there is no need to reorder.

4. Copy the function down the column and you should receive the results shown below.

5. Click Cell E4 enter the function **=IF(D4="Reorder",B4-C4+20,"")**.
   Notice that this function checks Cell D4 to see if the word Reorder has been entered in that cell. If Reorder has been entered in the cell, then the function subtracts the Current Inventory from the Reorder Point to determine the difference. It then adds 20 to that number and the resulting number becomes the Quantity to Reorder. In other words, you want to reorder up to the reorder point plus 20 additional products. If Column D does not contain the Reorder message, then the open and closed quotation marks ("") return a null value, and the cell remains empty. This function demonstrates that you can perform calculations as an argument within an IF function.

6. Copy the formula down the column to get the completed worksheet shown below.

7. Save the workbook with the name **Skill Builder 11.3,** and then close the workbook.

	A	B	C	D	E
1	Inventory Order Worksheet				
2					
3	Item	Reorder Point	Current Inventory	Reorder?	Reorder Quantity
4	Walton Dinnerware	25	40		
5	Sterling China	30	28	Reorder	22
6	Biltmore Tea Service	45	40	Reorder	25
7	Walthington Silverware	50	55		
8	Stewart Crystal	25	50		
9	Oakley Pots	80	65	Reorder	35
10	Barnsworth Skillets	120	85	Reorder	55

Skill Builder 11.4 VLOOKUP

In this exercise, you will use a lookup table and a VLOOKUP function to assign the letter grades A–F to students based upon their test scores. The completed worksheet will match the worksheet below.

Set Up the Worksheet and Lookup Table

1. Start a New Workbook, and enter the data shown below in Rows 1 through 3 and Columns A and B.
   In a moment, you will use a lookup function to determine the letter grades in Column C.

2. Type the data shown in the lookup table below into Columns E and F.

3. Select the data in the lookup table as shown to the right.

Test Scores	Letter Grade
0	F
65	D
70	C
80	B
90	A

4. Click in the Name box on the left end of the Formula bar, and type the name **Grade_Table**.

5. Tap (ENTER) to assign the name Grade_Table to the lookup table.
   Once again, you should always assign a name to a lookup table and reference that name in the VLOOKUP function.

Enter the VLOOKUP Functions

6. Click Cell C4, and enter the function **=VLOOKUP(B4,Grade_Table,2)**.
   The result should be B. Take a few moments to study this function and understand how it works. Once again, the VLOOKUP function will search down the left column of the lookup table for the search argument 87 (the value in Cell B4). It will stop at 90, which is the first number larger than 87, and it will move up to the previous row. It will then go to the second column in the lookup table and return the letter grade B that is in Cell F8.

7. Use the fill handle to copy the function down the column.
   The completed worksheet should match the worksheet shown below.

8. Save the workbook with the name **Skill Builder 11.4,** and then close the workbook.

	A	B	C	D	E	F
1	**Final Grade Calculations**					
2						
3	**Student**	**Test Scores**	**Letter Grade**		**Grade Table**	
4	Mildred Thomas	87	B		Test Scores	Letter Grade
5	Alicia Kim	95	A		0	F
6	Susan Savant	34	F		65	D
7	Ralph Reed	67	D		70	C
8	Bill Bickerson	82	B		80	B
9	Ruth Ashley	91	A		90	A
10	Tim Thompson	94	A			
11	Bernice Brown	78	C			

Skill Builder 11.5 VLOOKUP in a Financial Model

In this exercise, you will create a simple financial model that uses tax rates from a lookup table to calculate the Net Profit. The tax rate calculations in this model have been simplified to make the model easy to understand.

Calculate the Five-Year Growth Using Percentages

1. Open the workbook named Skill Builder 11.5.
   In the first part of this exercise, you will calculate five-year projections for Projected Sales, Employee Costs, Capital Expenditures, etc. by multiplying the numbers in Column B by percentages. These formulas will be inserted in Column C, and then copied across the rows.

2. Click Cell C4.
   The owner of King's bakery is projecting sales growth of 27% for each of the next five years. You will model this in Cell C4.

3. Enter the formula **=B4*1.27**.
   The result should be 508000. Multiplying by 1.27 is equivalent to adding 27% of 400000 to 400000. In the next step, you will copy this formula across the row. This will show growth of 27% for each year.

4. Use the fill handle to copy the formula in Cell C4 across the row.

5. Use the preceding steps to calculate the growth for the items in Rows 5 through 9. The growth rates are shown in the table below. Make sure you copy the formulas across the rows after you enter them, and make sure you add 1 to the growth rates. For example, the growth rate of employee costs is 15%, but you should use the number 1.15 in the formula.

Item	Growth Rate
Employee Costs	15%
Capital Expenditures	15%
Operating Costs	25%
Cost of Goods Sold	12%
Marketing and Advertising	20%

6. Format the cells with the Currency and Comma formats shown on the following page.
   Make sure that your numbers match the numbers on the following page.

Calculate the Gross Profit

The Gross Profit is equal to the Projected Sales in Row 4 minus the expenses in Rows 5 through 9. You will calculate the Gross Profit with a formula that uses the SUM function to sum the expenses, and then subtracts the result from the Projected Sales.

7. Click Cell B10, and enter the formula **=B4-SUM(B5:B9)**.
   The result should be $15,000. You can include functions like SUM or IF inside other formulas.

8. Use the fill handle to copy the formula across the row.

Calculate the Total Taxes Using the VLOOKUP Function

9. Click the Name list button on the left side of the Formula bar, and choose Tax_Table from the list.

The Tax Table at the bottom of the worksheet will become selected. This lookup table was assigned the name Tax_Table before the workbook was copied to your exercise diskette.

10. Click Cell B11, and enter the formula `=B10*VLOOKUP(B10,Tax_Table,2)`.

The result should be 1500. Once again, you can embed functions like VLOOKUP into formulas. In this example, the Total Taxes are calculated as the Gross Profit in Cell B10 multiplied by the Tax Rate that is returned by the VLOOKUP function.

11. Copy the formula across the row.

Calculate the Net Profit, and Format All Cells

12. Click Cell B12, and enter a formula to calculate the Net Profit as the Gross Profit – Total Taxes.

The result should be $13,500.

13. Copy the formula across the row.

14. Format all cells with the Currency and Comma formats shown below.

15. Apply bold formatting to Cells B10:F12.

Your completed worksheet should match the worksheet shown below.

16. Save the changes to the workbook, and then close the workbook.

	A	B	C	D	E	F
1	King's Bakery Five-Year Financial Projections (1999 - 2003)					
2						
3		1999	2000	2001	2002	2003
4	Projected Sales	$400,000	$508,000	$645,160	$819,353	$1,040,579
5	Exployee Costs	185,000	212,750	244,663	281,362	323,566
6	Capital Expenditures	30,000	34,500	39,675	45,626	52,470
7	Operating Costs	50,000	62,500	78,125	97,656	122,070
8	Cost Of Goods Sold	95,000	106,400	119,168	133,468	149,484
9	Marketing and Advertising	25,000	30,000	36,000	43,200	51,840
10	Gross Profit	**$15,000**	**$61,850**	**$127,530**	**$218,041**	**$341,148**
11	Total Taxes	**$1,500**	**$15,463**	**$47,186**	**$85,036**	**$133,048**
12	Net Profit	**$13,500**	**$46,388**	**$80,344**	**$133,005**	**$208,100**
13						
14						
15		Tax Table				
16		Income	Tax Rate			
17		-	0			
18		10,000	10%			
19		20,000	15%			
20		30,000	25%			
21		65,000	32%			
22		100,000	37%			
23		150,000	39%			

Assessments

Assessment 11.1 IF Functions

In this exercise, you will use two IF functions to create the worksheet shown below. The IF function in Column D will assign bonus points if a certain number of homework assignments have been turned in. The IF function in Column F will return a letter grade of A or B depending on the Total Points earned in Column E.

1. Start a new workbook, and enter the data shown in Rows 1 through 3 and Columns A through C below.

   You will need to use the ALT +ENTER *keystroke combination to create the double-line entries in Row 3. You will also need to widen the columns as shown.*

2. Use an IF function to calculate the Bonus Points in Column D.

   A bonus of 15 points is given if the Total Homework Assignments Turned In is greater than or equal to 12; otherwise, no bonus points are given. =IF(C4>=12,15,0)

3. Calculate the Total Points in Column E as the Total Test Points for Semester in Column B plus the Bonus Points in Column D.   =B4 + D4

4. Use an IF function to calculate the Final Grade in Column F.

   A grade of A is given if the value of Total Points is greater than or equal to 450; otherwise, a grade of B is given. Remember that the IF function will only return text arguments (such as A or B) if the argument is enclosed in quotation marks (" ") within the IF function. =IF(E4>=450,"A","B")

5. Your completed worksheet should match the worksheet shown below.

6. Save the workbook with the name **Assessment 11.1,** and then close the workbook.

	A	B	C	D	E	F
1	Final Grade Report					
2						
3	Student	Total Test Points for Semester	Total Homework Assignments Turned In	Bonus Points	Total Points	Final Grade
4	Cathy Wilson	425	10	0	425	B
5	Lisa Johnson	454	13	15	469	A
6	Steven Chang	410	8	0	410	B
7	Jill Downey	490	15	15	505	A
8	Carlos Martinez	475	15	15	490	A
9	Jermaine Green	495	15	15	510	A
10	Marty Austin	440	15	15	455	A

Assessment 11.2 VLOOKUP and IF Functions

In this exercise, you will use IF functions and VLOOKUP functions to create the worksheet below. The IF functions in Column C will determine if the customer qualifies for the Free Rental program. The VLOOKUP functions in Column D will determine how many free rentals the customer receives.

1. Start a New Workbook, and enter the data shown in Rows 1 through 3, and Columns A and B below.

2. Use IF functions in Column C to determine if a customer qualifies for the frequent renter program. Customers qualify if they have five or more frequent renter points in Column B. The IF function should return the message Free Rentals if they qualify and nothing if they don't qualify. =IF(B4>=5, "Free Rentals", "")

3. Set up the lookup table located at the bottom of the worksheet, and name it **Free_Rentals_Table**.

4. Use VLOOKUP functions in Column D to determine the number of free rentals each customer should receive. The function should use the Frequent Renter Points Earned in Column B as the search argument, and it should search the Free_Rentals_Table for the correct # of Free Rentals.

5. Your completed worksheet should match the worksheet shown below.

6. Save the workbook with the name **Assessment 11.2,** and then close the workbook.

	A	B	C	D
1	Julie's Videos Frequent Renter Awards			
2				
3	Customer	Frequent Renter Points Earned	Qualify for Free Rentals?	# of Free Rentals
4	Dale Smith	6	Free Rentals	1
5	Sue Jackson	17	Free Rentals	3
6	Liz Johnson	3		0
7	Al Chase	22	Free Rentals	4
8	Bruce Pique	11	Free Rentals	2
9	Benny Jones	4		0
10	Tim Taylor	14	Free Rentals	2
11				
12				
13				
14			Free Rentals Table	
15			Frequent Renter Points	Free Rentals
16			0	0
17			5	1
18			10	2
19			15	3
20			20	4
21			25	5

Critical Thinking

Critical Thinking 11.1 On Your Own

Leonard James is the owner of Quick and Easy Video Rentals. Leonard has asked you to create a worksheet that allows him to easily determine whether or not videos should be removed from the new-releases section. To make this decision, Leonard has you enter the number of days per month that each video has been rented. If a video has been rented more than 15 fifteen times, then it remains on the new-releases shelf. If it has been rented less than 15 times, then it is removed from the new-releases shelf. Leonard wants the worksheet to display the message New Release if the video is to remain on the new-releases shelf and Discount Shelf if it is to be removed from the new-releases shelf. Leonard provides you with the following data as a starting point for the worksheet.

Title	Number of Rentals
Hope Floats	27
The Matrix	23
The English Patient	7
Out of Africa	9
Saint	15

Set up a worksheet that automatically enters the phrases New Release and Discount Shelf in cells, depending on whether or not the titles listed above have been rented 15 or more times. Sort the rows in ascending order based upon the number of rentals. Save your workbook with a descriptive name. Leave the workbook open because you will continue to use it.

Critical Thinking 11.2 On Your Own

Leonard James has asked you to create another worksheet that allows him to easily determine the late charge for customers returning overdue videos. Leonard charges late fees as shown in the following table.

Days Late	Late Fee
One	$1.00
Two	$1.50
Three	$2.00
Four or more	$3.00

Leonard has given you the following customer account data as a starting point for the worksheet.

Customer Name	Title Rented	Due Date	Return Date
Jill Madison	Saint	2/1/2000	2/2/2000
Tina Thomas	Terminator	2/5/2000	2/9/2000
Ralph Wilson	The English Patient	2/6/2000	2/8/2000
Leslie Chang	Out of Africa	2/6/2000	2/7/2000
Wanda Richardson	Ghost	2/8/2000	2/15/2000

In the workbook that you used in the previous exercise, set up another worksheet that includes the data shown in the table above. Use a VLOOKUP function and a lookup table to calculate the late fees. You will need to add one or more new columns to the worksheet. Rename both of the worksheets with descriptive names. Save the changes to the workbook.

Critical Thinking 11.3 Web Research

Use Internet Explorer and a search engine of your choice to visit the Web sites of the universities listed in the table below. Determine the estimated tuition, fees, room and board, and expenses for a resident, undergraduate student at each university.

University of Illinois at Champaign-Urbana	Princeton
Purdue University	Duke University
University of Southern California	Cal State Hayward

Use the VLOOKUP function and a lookup table to categorize the cost of each university as follows:

Inexpensive <=$10,000
Average >$10,000 but <=$17,500
Expensive >$17,500

The lookup function should display the words Inexpensive, Average, or Expensive in a cell, depending upon the costs. Save the workbook with a descriptive name.

Financial Functions and Goal Seeking

Excel's built-in financial functions can be used for various types of financial analyses. In this lesson, you will use the PMT (Payment) function to determine the monthly payment for a new automobile. In addition, you will use the FV (Future Value) function to determine the future value of investments. Excel also provides tools to help you find solutions to financial questions. In this lesson, you will use the Goal Seeker and Solver to answer a variety of questions.

In This Lesson

Case Study

Jane Evans has often dreamed of owning a shiny new Chevrolet Corvette. Recently, she was promoted in her job and received a significant pay raise. She has also profited handsomely from the rising stock market. Jane decides it is time to explore the idea of making her dream come true by purchasing a new Corvette. Jane sets up an Excel worksheet that calculates the monthly payment on a car loan using a variety of input variables. She uses the PMT (Payment) function to calculate the monthly payment, and Excel's Goal Seeker and Solver tools to explore various financing scenarios.

	A	B	C	D	E
1	Car Loan Analysis for Jane Evans				
2					
3	Make and Model	99 Corvette Coupe			
4	Purchase Price	$38,850			
5	Down Payment	10,000			
6	Loan Amount	28,850			
7	Interest Rate	8%			
8	Number of Months	60			
9	Monthly Payment	$583.33			
10	Total Interest	$6,150.00			
11	Total Vehicle Cost	$45,000.00			
12					
13					
14		**Interest vs. Purchase Price**			
15					
16					
17			Purchase Price 86%		
18					
19					
20					
21		Total Interest 14%			
22					
23					
24					
25					

Financial Functions

Excel provides a variety of financial functions that calculate important financial numbers. For example, Excel has basic financial functions for determining monthly payments on loans, the total interest paid on loans, the future value of investments, and other such questions. Excel also has advanced financial functions for calculating depreciation of assets, internal rates of return, and other more advanced topics. In this lesson, you will use the PMT (Payment) and FV (Future Value) functions. These are the most useful financial functions for the average Excel user.

Syntax of Financial Functions

You can enter financial functions using the Paste Function ![fx] button on the Standard toolbar, or you can enter them with the keyboard. Like all functions, financial functions have a specific syntax you must follow. The generic syntax of the PMT and FV functions is shown in the following table.

Function	Syntax
PMT (Payment)	PMT(rate, periods, loan amount)
FV (Future Value)	FV(rate, periods, payment)

Working with Annuities

An annuity is a series of equal payments made over a period of time. For example, most car loans or fixed-rate mortgages are annuities because the payment amounts remain constant throughout the term of the loan. The PMT and FV functions are used with annuities where the payment amount remains constant. The various arguments in the PMT and FV functions are outlined in the following Quick Reference table.

Quick Reference

FINANCIAL FUNCTION ARGUMENTS	
Argument	**Description**
Periods	This is the number of periods in the annuity. Most annuities (such as loans) have a monthly payment period. For this reason, you should specify the number of months in the function, as opposed to the number of years. For example, you should use 60 as the number of periods for a five-year auto loan (5 years * 12 months per year).
Rate	This is the interest rate for each period in an annuity. Most annuities have a monthly period, so the monthly interest rate should be specified. For example, you should use 1% as the interest rate for a loan with a 12% annual rate (1% per month).
Payment	This is the payment amount for each period in the annuity. The payment must be the same for each period.
Loan amount	Opening balance or amount borrowed for a loan.

In this exercise, you will set up a loan worksheet that will calculate the monthly payment on a car loan. The payment will be calculated using the PMT function. You will set up the purchase price, down payment, and interest rate as variables. This way, you will be able to change these parameters and see the impact the changes have on the payment.

Set Up the Worksheet

1. Start a new workbook.

2. Enter the data shown below. Format the text and numbers, and widen Columns A and B as shown.

	A	B
1	Car Loan Analysis for Jane Evans	
2		
3	Make and Model	99 Corvette Coupe
4	Purchase Price	$37,000
5	Down Payment	10,000
6	Loan Amount	
7	Interest Rate	
8	Number of Months	
9	Monthly Payment	
10	Total Interest	
11	Total Vehicle Cost	

Calculate the Loan Amount

The Loan Amount is the Purchase Price minus the Down Payment. The PMT function will use the Loan Amount as one of its arguments.

3. Click Cell B6, and enter the formula **=B4-B5**.
   The result should be 27,000.

4. Click Cell B7, and enter the interest rate **12%**.

5. Click Cell B8, and enter **60** as the number of months.

Calculate the Monthly Payment with the PMT function

6. Click Cell B9, and enter the formula **=PMT(B7,B8,B6)**.
   The result should equal ($3,243.61). The generic PMT function syntax is =PMT(rate, periods, loan amount). Notice how the B7, B8, and B6 references used in the function refer to the interest rate, number of months, and loan amount in the worksheet.

   Notice that Excel formats the payment with the Currency format, and that the payment is colored red and surrounded in parenthesis. The red color and parenthesis indicate this is a negative number. Excel treats payments as debits (money you are paying), so they are assigned a negative number. This is a convention that bankers and other financial professionals use. You will convert this number to a positive number in the following steps.

   Finally, notice that $3,243.61 is a very large payment. This is because the interest rate in Cell B7 is an annual rate of 12%. These financial functions have monthly periods, so you are paying 12% interest per month! The interest rate must be divided by 12 (the number of months in a year) in order to use a monthly interest rate in the function. You will do this in the following steps.

(Continued on the next page)

7. Make sure the highlight is in Cell B9.

8. Click in the Formula bar and edit the formula as follows:

   - Insert a minus sign – between the equal sign = and function name (PMT).

   - Divide the B7 reference by 12. The completed formula is = – PMT(B7/12,B8,B6).

9. Complete the entry; the new payment should equal $600.60.
   This payment will certainly be more affordable. The minus sign converts the number to a positive, and the B7/12 argument establishes a 1% per month rate.

Calculate the Total Interest

The Total Interest can be calculated by first multiplying the Monthly Payment by the Number of Months to determine the total payments. The Loan Amount in Cell B6 can then be subtracted from the total payments to determine the Total Interest.

10. Click Cell B10, and enter the formula **=B9*B8–B6**.
    The Total Interest in Cell B10 should equal $9,036.01.

Calculate the Total Vehicle Cost

The Total Vehicle Cost is simply the total payments plus the down payment.

11. Click Cell B11, and enter the formula **=B9*B8+B5**.
    The result should equal $46,036.01. As you can see, the Purchase Price of $37,000 plus the Total Interest of $9,036.01 equal $46,036.01.

12. The completed worksheet is shown below (although the example below also shows selected data that will be used to create a chart in the next few steps).

	A	B
1	Car Loan Analysis for Jane Evans	
2		
3	Make and Model	99 Corvette Coupe
4	Purchase Price	$37,000
5	Down Payment	10,000
6	Loan Amount	27,000
7	Interest Rate	12%
8	Number of Months	60
9	Monthly Payment	$600.60
10	Total Interest	$9,036.01
11	Total Vehicle Cost	$46,036.01

Create a Pie Chart

13. Select Cells A4:B4 and A10:B10 as shown above (you must use the (CTRL) key).
    This selection will allow the pie chart to compare the Total Interest to the Purchase Price.

14. Click the Chart Wizard button.

15. Use the Chart Wizard to create the embedded pie chart shown to the right.

16. Save the workbook as **Hands-On Lesson 12,** and continue with the next topic.

Interest vs. Purchase Price

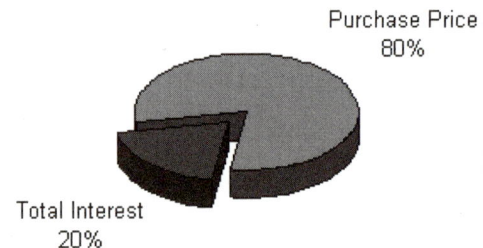

Purchase Price
80%

Total Interest
20%

Goal Seeking

Excel provides several tools to let you perform advanced what-if analysis. In this topic, you will use the Goal Seeker tool. The Goal Seeker lets you set a goal for a cell that contains a formula. For example, you will set a goal of $550 for the Monthly Payment in Cell B9. The Goal Seeker lets you choose another cell whose contents the Goal Seeker will change. The cell with the formula must be dependent on the second cell. For example, you will let the Goal Seeker adjust the Down Payment in order to achieve the $550 Monthly Payment.

Hands-On 12.2 Use the Goal Seeker

1. Click Cell B9.
   It is usually a good idea to click the cell you want to set a goal for prior to starting the goal seeker. This way, the first option in the Goal Seeker will already be set when you start it. Also, this will ensure you are setting a goal for the correct cell.

2. Choose **Tools→Goal Seek** from the menu bar.

3. Follow these steps to set the Goal Seek parameters.

   Ⓐ *This option should already be set to B9. This is the cell for which you are setting a goal.*

   Ⓑ *Click in this box, and type* **550**. *This is the monthly payment goal for Cell B9.*

   Ⓒ *Click in the* **By changing cell** *box, then click Cell B5 in the worksheet. Excel will insert the absolute reference $B$5 in the* **By changing cell** *box. Notice that you can type entries in the Goal Seeker or use point mode (as you just did).*

(Continued on the next page)

4. Click **OK,** and the Goal Seeker will indicate that it has found a solution to the goal.
   Notice that the Down Payment in the worksheet has been adjusted to 12,275.

5. Click **OK** on the Goal Seek Status dialog box to confirm the change to the Down Payment.
   As you can see, a larger down payment is required to achieve a $550 Monthly Payment.

Use the Goal Seeker to Adjust the Interest Rate

6. Click Undo 🔄 to reverse the change to the Down Payment.

7. Click Cell B9, and choose **Tools→Goal Seek** from the menu bar.

8. Type **550** in the To value box.

9. Click in the *By changing cell* box, then click Cell B7 in the worksheet (the Interest Rate cell).

10. Click **OK,** and the interest rate will be set to 8%.

11. Click **OK** again to confirm the change to the Interest Rate.
    Notice the impact this change has on the chart. The Total Interest (in the chart) has decreased to 14%.

Play What-if Analysis

You can also play what-if analysis by changing the Interest Rate, Down Payment, Purchase Price, and other values.

12. Click Cell B4, and change the Purchase Price to **$20,000**.
    What impact does this change have on the other variables, and the chart?

13. Feel free to experiment with the Goal Seeker.

14. Save the changes when you have finished, and continue with the next topic.

Solver

The Goal Seeker is easy to use, but it is somewhat limited. This is because it can only adjust one variable at a time. Excel's Solver tool can be used for solving problems where more than one variable requires adjustment. You display the Solver dialog box with the **Tools→Solver** command.

Solver Options

Solver gives you additional options for specifying the value of the target cell. You can specify a precise value, as with the Goal Seeker, or you can specify a Min or Max value. For example, you could set up a Solver scenario and specify a maximum monthly payment of $650. In addition, Solver lets you specify one or more **constraints.** Constraints give you additional control over the scenario by allowing you to specify a range of values that a particular cell or cells can have.

*The **Equal To** options are used to specify the target cell value. You can specify an exact value or a **Max** or **Min** value.*

Multiple variable cells are entered here. Solver will adjust all variables in order to find a solution.

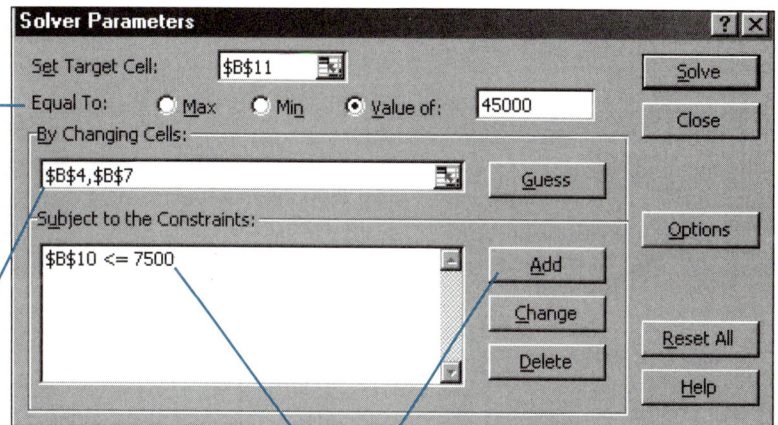

Solver Parameters

Set Target Cell: `$B$11`

Equal To: ○ Max ○ Min ● Value of: `45000`

By Changing Cells: `$B$4,$B$7`

Subject to the Constraints: `$B$10 <= 7500`

Solve | Close | Guess | Options | Add | Change | Delete | Reset All | Help

*One or more constraints can be specified. Constraints are added by clicking the **Add** button and filling in the options in the Add Constraint box.*

Installing Solver

Solver is not installed as part of the typical Office 2000 installation. Solver is an add-in program that will only appear on the Tools menu if a full installation of Excel was performed. If Solver does not appear on the Tools menu, you can choose **Tools→Add Ins** and then choose Solver Add-In from the Add-Ins Available box. Excel will instruct you to insert your Office 2000 CD ROM, and you can follow the steps to install Solver.

In this exercise, you will use Solver to determine the purchase price and interest rate required to achieve the Total Vehicle Purchase Price you specify.

NOTE! *In order to do this exercise, Solver must be installed using the procedure discussed in the preceding topic.*

1. Click Cell B11, and choose **Tools→Solver** from the menu bar.

2. Follow these steps to set the target cell value and to specify the variable cells.

A *Make sure the **Set Target Cell** box is set to B11.*

B *Choose the **Value of** option, click in this box, and type **45000**. Notice that you could set a **Max** or **Min** value if desired.*

C *Click in this box, and then click Cell B4 in the worksheet. The absolute reference $B$4 will be entered in this box.*

D *Type a comma, and then click Cell B7 in the worksheet.*

E *Click the **Add** button to display the Add Constraint box.*

3. Follow these steps to specify a constraint.

A *Click Cell B10 in the worksheet to enter the B10 reference in this box.*

B *Make sure this option is set to <=.*

C *Type **7500** in the **Constraint** box. This constraint will prevent the total interest from being set higher than 7500.*

D *Click **OK** to complete the constraint.*

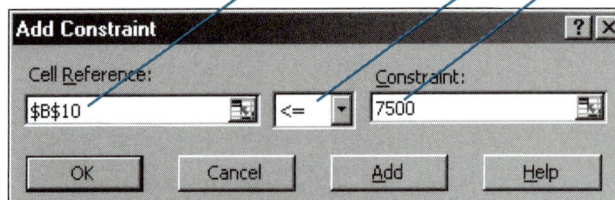

The constraint will appear in the constraint box of the Solver Parameters box.

4. Take a moment to review the parameters you have set prior to initiating Solver.

5. Click the **Solve** button, and the Solver will go to work. *When the Solver has completed, the Solver Results box should report that a solution has been found.*

6. Make sure the Keep Solver Solution option is chosen, and click **OK.**
The completed solution should match the example shown to the right.

7. Take a few minutes to experiment with Solver.

8. When you have finished, save the changes to the workbook, and then close the workbook.

	A	B
1	**Car Loan Analysis for Jane Evans**	
2		
3	Make and Model	99 Corvette Coupe
4	Purchase Price	$37,500
5	Down Payment	10,000
6	Loan Amount	27,500
7	Interest Rate	10%
8	Number of Months	60
9	Monthly Payment	$583.33
10	Total Interest	$7,500.00
11	Total Vehicle Cost	$45,000.00

Concepts Review

True/False Questions

1. The PMT function can only be used if the payment amount is the same for each payment period.   TRUE   FALSE

2. Most loans and other annuities have a yearly payment period.   TRUE   FALSE

3. The cell for which you are seeking a goal must contain a formula.   TRUE   FALSE

4. Solver can adjust more than one variable.   TRUE   FALSE

5. Solver is installed as part of the default Office 2000 installation.   TRUE   FALSE

Multiple-Choice Questions

1. Which command is used to initiate the Goal Seeker?
   a. Edit→Goal Seek
   b. Format→Goak Seek
   c. Tools→Goal Seek
   d. None of these

2. Which of the following PMT functions has the arguments in the correct positions?
   a. =PMT(rate, periods, loan amount)
   b. =PMT(rate, loan amount, periods)
   c. =PMT(periods, rate, loan amount)
   d. None of these

3. Which command is used to initiate Solver?
   a. Edit→Solver
   b. File→Solver
   c. Format→Solver
   d. None of these

4. Which tool are constraints used with?
   a. Solver
   b. Goal Seek
   c. PMT function
   d. FV funtion

Skill Builders

Skill Builder 12.1 Use PMT Function

In this exercise, you will use the PMT function to calculate mortgage payments on a 30-year fixed mortgage. You will multiply the 30 years by 12 within the PMT function to determine the total number of periods in the loan. The generic syntax of the PMT function is repeated below for your convenience.

Payment Function Syntax =PMT(rate, periods, loan amount)

Set Up the Worksheet

1. Start a New Workbook, and set up the worksheet shown to the right.
   Make sure you use a formula to calculate the Loan Amount in Cell B5 as the Purchase Price – Down Payment.

	A	B
1	**30-Year Mortgage Worksheet**	
2		
3	Purchase Price	260,000
4	Down Payment	25,000
5	Loan Amount	235,000
6	Interest Rate	9%
7	Number of Years	30
8	Monthly Payment	
9	Total Interest	
10	Total Cost of Home	

2. Click Cell B8, and enter the formula
   =-PMT(B6/12,B7*12,B5).
   The result should equal $1,890.86. Notice that the formula has a minus sign between the equal sign and the PMT function. Also, the first argument divides the Interest Rate in Cell B6 by 12 because the argument requires the monthly rate. Likewise, the second argument multiplies the Number of Years in Cell B7 by 12 because the argument requires the number of months. Excel also formats the result with the Currency style because you used the PMT function.

3. Click Cell B9, and use the formula **=B8*B7*12-B5** to calculate the Total Interest.
   The result should equal $445,710.73. Take a few moments to study the formula, and notice that it calculates the total payments over the term of the loan and subtracts the Loan Amount. Also notice that the number of months was determined by multiplying the number of years in Cell B7 by 12.

4. Click Cell B10, and use the formula **=B9+B3** to calculate the Total Cost of Home.

Create a Pie Chart

5. Select Cells A3:B3 and A9:B9, as shown to the right.
   This selection will allow the pie chart to compare the Total Interest to the Purchase Price.

	A	B
1	**30-Year Mortgage Worksheet**	
2		
3	Purchase Price	260,000
4	Down Payment	25,000
5	Loan Amount	235,000
6	Interest Rate	9%
7	Number of Years	30
8	Monthly Payment	$1,890.86
9	Total Interest	$445,710.73
10	Total Cost of Home	$705,710.73

(Continued on the next page)

6. Click the Chart Wizard 📊 button and create the embedded pie chart shown below.

Interest vs. Purchase Price

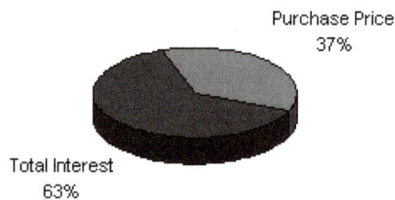

Purchase Price
37%

Total Interest
63%

Play What-if Analysis

7. Click Cell B6.
Notice that the Monthly Payment in Cell B8 is approximately 1,890.

8. Change the Interest Rate to 8%, and notice the impact it has on the Monthly Payment.

9. Experiment with various interest rates. Also, try changing the down payment, and note the impact it has on the Monthly Payment.

10. Save the workbook as **Skill Builder 12.1,** and then close the workbook.

Skill Builder 12.2 Use FV Function

In this exercise, you will use the Future Value (FV) function to determine the future value of a college fund. This could be important if you are planning on saving for a college education. This worksheet can be used to determine the future value of nearly any investment that has consistent contributions. The generic syntax of the FV function is repeated below for your convenience.

Future Value Function Syntax =FV(rate, periods, payment)

Set Up the Worksheet

1. Start a new workbook.

2. Use the **Format→Column Width** command to set the width of Column A to 19 and Column B to 14.

3. Enter the data shown in the worksheet to the right.

	A	B
1	**Ted's College Fund**	
2		
3	Interest Rate	8%
4	Number of years	18
5	Monthly Contribution	200
6	Future Value	

4. Click Cell B6, and enter the function **=FV(B3/12,B4*12,B5)**.

   The result should equal ($96,017.23). The FV function returns a negative number, as did the PMT function. Also, notice that the Interest Rate in Cell B3 is divided by 12 to give a monthly rate. The Number of Years in Cell B4 is multiplied by 12 to give the total number of monthly payments.

5. Click Cell B6, and then click in the Formula bar and insert a minus sign (–) between the equal (=) sign and the FV function name.

6. Complete the entry, and the result should be positive.

Use the Goal Seeker

7. Click Cell B5, and change the Monthly Contribution to **$300**.
   Notice that this increases the Future Value of the investment to approximately $144,000. In the next few steps, you will use the Goal Seeker to determine the interest rate necessary to have a Future Value of $200,000 with a Monthly Contribution of $300.

8. Click Cell B6, and choose **Tools→Goal Seek** from the menu bar.

9. Set the To Value option to **$200,000**.

10. Set the By changing cell option to **B3** (the Interest Rate cell).

11. Click **OK,** and notice that an 11% Interest Rate is required.

12. Click Cancel on the Goal Seek Results dialog box to cancel the change to the interest rate.

13. Use the Goal Seeker to determine the Interest Rate that is required to achieve a $275,000 Future Value with a $325 Monthly Contribution.

14. Save the workbook as **Skill Builder 12.2,** and then close the workbook.

Assessments

Assessment 12.1 Use FV Function

1. Create the worksheet below, using the FV function to calculate the future value in Cell B7.

	A	B
1	Investment Projections	
2		
3	Account	Utilities Mutual Fund
4	Projected Annual Rate of Return	11%
5	Number of Years	20
6	Monthly Contribution	$800
7	Future Value	$692,510

2. Format all cells as shown, and adjust the width of Columns A and B to 19.

3. Print the worksheet, save the workbook as **Assessment 12.1,** and then close the workbook.

Assessment 12.2 Use PMT Function

1. Create the worksheet below using the PMT function to calculate the monthly payment in Cell B7.

	A	B
1	Home Equity Loan Analysis	
2		
3	Lender	Wells Fargo
4	Interest Rate	10.50%
5	Number of Years	10
6	Loan Amount	$15,000
7	Monthly Payment	$202

2. Format all cells as shown, and adjust the width of Column A to 24 and Column B to 11.

3. Print the worksheet, save the workbook as **Assessment 12.2,** and then close the workbook.

Critical Thinking

Critical Thinking 12.1 On Your Own

Jane Sinclair is part of the new wave of independent investors who are taking control of their own investment portfolios. Jane recently discovered a corporate bond fund where she feels her principal will be quite safe. It pays an 8% annual return. Jane makes every investment decision with retirement in mind. She is 38 years old and plans to retire when she is 58. Jane plans on contributing $350 per month to the bond fund for the next 20 years. Set up a worksheet that uses the Future Value function to determine the future value of her bond fund investment. Save the workbook with a descriptive name, and leave it open because you will continue to use it.

Critical Thinking 12.2 On Your Own

After analyzing the future value of her potential bond fund investment, Jane realizes that her investment just won't be large enough after 20 years to give here the income she will need at retirement. Jane has other investments in stocks and real estate and she can count on social security; however, she expects a large part of her retirement income to come from the bond fund. Jane decides to explore other bond funds, and she considers increasing her monthly contributions. Use the Goal Seeker and the worksheet you set up in the previous exercise to answer the following questions. Write your answers in the space provided.

- If the annual rate of return is 11% and the number of years is 20, then what must be the monthly contribution in order to have a future value of $1,000,000? _____

- If the rate of return is 11% and the monthly contribution is $800, then what must be the number of years in order to have a future value of $1,000,000? _____

- If the number of years is 20 and the monthly contribution is $800, then what must be the rate of return in order to have a future value of $1,000,000? _____

Leave the workbook open; you will continue to use it.

Critical Thinking 12.3 On Your Own

Jane Sinclair purchased her home 15 years ago. Since that time, she has built up over $100,000 equity in her home. Recently, Jane's financial advisor recommended that she consider taking out a home equity loan to pay off some bills and consolidate the rest of her debts. Set up another sheet in the current workbook that uses the PMT function to determine monthly payments on a home equity loan. Assume an annual interest rate of 8%, a ten year term, and a loan amount of $15,000. Leave the workbook open.

Critical Thinking 12.4 On Your Own

Use the Goal Seeker and the payment worksheet you set up in the previous exercise to answer the following questions. Write your answers in the space provided.

- If the interest rate is 9% and the number of years is 10, then what must be the loan amount in order to have a monthly payment of $175? _____

- If the interest rate is 7% and the loan amount is $15,000, then what must be the number of years in order to have a monthly payment of $175? _____

- If the number of years is 10 and the loan amount is $15,000, then what must be the interest rate in order to have a monthly payment of $175? _____

Save the changes to the workbook, and close it.

Critical Thinking 12.5 Web Research

Carl Jenkins is considering the purchase of a new Chevrolet Corvette Coupe automobile. Carl has $15,000 for a down payment and figures he can afford $500 for the monthly payment plus an additional $100 per month for insurance. Use Internet Explorer and a search engine of your choice to help Carl determine whether or not he can afford the vehicle. First, you will need to locate a site where you can determine the cost of the Corvette. You may need to make decisions on vehicle options to help Carl meet his budget. Record all of the information in an Excel workbook. Next, locate one or more sites offering automobile loan information. If you are requested to enter personal and credit information then use the information for Carl below. Record all of the loan information in the workbook. You should include the URL of the Web site, interest rate, amount borrowed, term, and monthly payment.

Age: 37

Income: $42,000 per year

Monthly Mortgage Payment: $650

Other debts (including student loans and credit cards): $0

Location: Carl lives in Richmond, CA (zip code 94803)

Driving record: Perfect (before buying the Corvette)

Finally, locate several Web sites offering automobile insurance quotations. Use Carl's information above to obtain a rate quote. Also, choose a $500 deductible, full coverage, with $100,000/$300,000 liability limits. You may find that the rates vary considerably from one company to the next. Record all of your findings in the workbook, and determine whether or not Carl can afford the vehicle. Keep in mind that you have a $600 per month budget to work with. Carl doesn't mind if the payment is a little higher than $500 or if the insurance is less than $100—as long as the total monthly expenditure is $600 or less. Save your completed workbook with a descriptive name.

Web Integration: Posting an Online Workbook

Office 2000 is designed to make integration with the Web easier than ever before. For example, most Office 2000 application programs let you save your work in Web page (HTML) format. Posting information as a Web page makes it easier for others to access it whenever they need to. You can also bring together pieces of work created with several different programs into a single Office 2000 file. In this integration lesson, you will combine information from members of a project team into a single Excel workbook. Then you will post the workbook to the Web, where every project team member can access the information over the Internet.

In This Lesson

Case Study

Deion is a Print Production Manager in Los Angeles with the Acme Trading Company, an import-export firm. His primary role is to coordinate the efforts of his production team to get various publications ready for print. The production team members are scattered geographically. For example, there is a copy editor in Oregon and a graphic artist in Boston. Each team member is an expert, and they can all work smoothly together over the Internet. Deion is about mid-way through a project to produce Acme's annual report. He wants all of the production team members to know the status of the project. So he decides to assemble information about the production tasks and the schedule into an Excel workbook, then post the workbook to the Web so that everyone can review it.

From:	Terry Sanchez	Sent: Tue 9/21/99 12:23 PM
To:	Deion Anderson	
Cc:		
Subject:	Re: Status lists	

Here is the layout schedule. It is in the attached Word document.
Terry

📄 Layout Schedule.d...

Deion received data from one of his project team members in a Word document attached to an email message.

Acme Trading Company

Annual Report Layout Schedule

Chapter	Status	Start Date	Due Date
1—Introduction	☑	4-Sep	11-Sep
2—The Year in Review	☑	11-Sep	14-Sep
3—Status Report	☒	14-Sep	19-Sep
4—Stock Performance	☐	19-Sep	24-Sep
5—Dividend Performance	☐	24-Sep	30-Sep
6—Looking Ahead	☐	3-Oct	7-Oct
7—Charts and Tables	☐	7-Oct	10-Oct
Key	☑ Done		
	☒ In Progress		
	☐ Awaiting Manuscript		

Deion copied the company logo from their Web site then placed it at the top of each worksheet. He was also able to place a background image in his worksheets.

Deion was able to place the data from the Word document into an Excel worksheet. He was happy that he did not have to re-type the data himself.

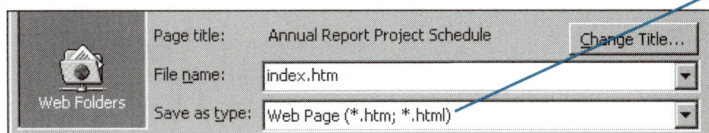

Page title:	Annual Report Project Schedule	Change Title...
File name:	index.htm	
Save as type:	Web Page (*.htm; *.html)	

Web Folders

Deion saved his Excel workbook into a Web Folder as a Web page. The Web folder immediately sent his workbook to the company Web server. Now all of Deion's project team members can view the project schedule over the Web.

Obtaining and Organizing the Information

It is always a good idea to set up one or more folders for special projects. This helps you find any files related to the project and prevents their being mixed in with other files. By creating a shortcut and Favorite to the project folder, you will save yourself time searching for it later. The following Hands-On exercise will give you additional practice with these tasks.

Creating a Folder from within Excel

The Create New Folder [icon] button lets you create new folders from Excel's Save As and Open dialog boxes. The button is on the dialog box toolbar. This button lets you create new folders when you need them, without leaving Excel.

Hands-On 13.1 Set Up a Project Folder

Before you begin: *You may want to review the topics on creating project folders, shortcuts on the Desktop, and Favorites to folders before you begin this exercise. They appear in Lesson 7* Internet Integration: Online Collaboration. *The following instructions will assume you are familiar with these tasks.*

In this exercise, you will use the Save As command to create a new folder, a shortcut on the desktop, and Favorite for the folder.

Create a New Folder from Within Excel

1. Start Excel; then choose **File→Save As** from the menu bar.

2. Choose the *3½ Floppy (A:)* drive in the Save in box at the top of the dialog box.

3. Click the Create New Folder [icon] button on the Save As dialog box toolbar.
   A dialog box will appear asking for the name of the new folder.

4. Type **Annual Report** as the new folder name; then tap the (ENTER) key.
   The new folder is created and Excel immediately displays the empty folder in the Save in box.

5. Click the Up [icon] button to navigate to the base (root) level of your floppy disk.
   Now the Annual Report folder is displayed in the file list. Next you will create a shortcut to this new folder.

6. *Right-click* on the Annual Report folder; then choose *Send to→Desktop (create shortcut)* from the pop-up menu.
   The new shortcut is sent to the Desktop. You will use it later in this lesson.

7. Follow these steps to create a Favorite for the Annual Report folder.

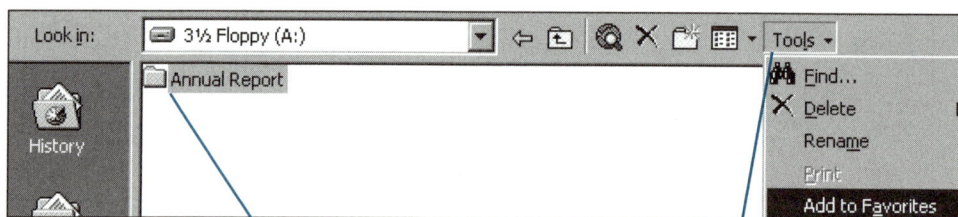

Ⓐ *Click to select the Annual Report folder.*

Ⓑ *Click the Tools button; and then choose Add to Favorites.*

8. Click the **Favorites** button on the left side of the dialog box. Scroll down the Favorites list if necessary until the **Annual Report** Favorite is visible.
   You may see some additional Annual Report Favorites with a number in parenthesis. These are additional Favorites to the Annual Report folder that were created by previous students. Since they are unnecessary, you may delete them in the next step.

9. If you see a Favorite named **Annual Report (2)** follow the steps below; otherwise skip to Step 11:

   ■ Click to select **Annual Report (2).**

   ■ Click the Delete ⊠ button on the dialog box to delete the Favorite. Click **Yes** if You are asked to confirm the deletion.

   ■ *Delete* any other **Annual Report Favorites** with a number in parentheses after the name.

10. Double-click on **Annual Report** in the Favorites list.
    The empty folder is displayed in the dialog box. As you can see, the Favorite lets you navigate to the folder quickly, without needing to work your way through the various disk drives and folders that a folder might lie within.

11. Enter **Status** as the new filename for the workbook; then tap (ENTER).

12. Minimize ⬛ the Excel window.

Saving Images on Web Pages

Sometimes you may come upon a Web page with an interesting image that you want to save. You can save images from Web pages as individual image files on your computer. You can also copy and paste images on a Web page into other programs. For example, you might want to use a photo from a travel Web site of the spot you've picked out for a vacation. You could copy the photo and paste it into a letter or an email message. There are two ways you can save Web images:

■ *Save* the image as a file on a hard drive or floppy disk by giving a *right-click*, and then choosing the **Save Picture As** command.

■ *Copy* the image to the clipboard, and then *paste* it into your work in another application program.

Copyright

Just because you can save parts or all of a Web page doesn't make it your property. You can make only limited use of what you copy from most Web sites. Here are a few tips on copyright and Web page content:

■ Never place the content on a commercial Web site without permission.

■ In general, what you copy from another Web site should be for your personal use, not for distribution.

NOTE!

Since Deion is going to copy an image from Acme's own Web site, he does not need to worry about copyright in this case.

SAVING A WEB IMAGE

Task	Procedure
Save an image from a Web page.	■ *Right-click* the image on the Web page; then select **Save Picture As** from the pop-up menu.
	■ You can also *drag* and *drop* an image from its Web page to a folder or disk displayed in a My Computer or Exploring window.
Copy and paste an image from a Web page.	■ *Right-click* on the image you wish to copy.
	■ Choose **Copy** from the pop-up menu.
	■ Activate the program into which you wish to paste the image.
	■ Click the insertion point where you wish to paste the image; then choose **Edit→Paste** from the menu bar.

Hands-On 13.2 Save a Logo from a Web Page

In this exercise, you will navigate to a page on Acme's Web site and save the logo on that page for later use in an Excel workbook.

1. Start **Internet Explorer** from its icon on the Desktop or the Quick Launch toolbar.

   Internet Explorer

2. Follow these steps to navigate to the Acme Trading Co. Web page.

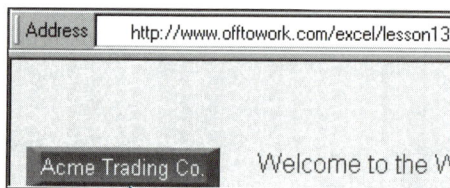

   | Address | http://www.offtowork.com/excel/lesson13 |

   A *Click in the Address bar, and type the following URL:* **www.offtowork.com/excel/lesson13** *then tap the* (ENTER) *key.*

   Acme Trading Co. | Welcome to the W

   B *Click the* Acme Trading Co. *button.*

   A simulated Acme Trading Company home page will be displayed.

3. Follow these steps to save the company logo on this page as a file:

Ⓐ Right-click *on this logo.*

Ⓑ *Choose* **Save Picture as** *from the pop-up menu.*

Ⓒ *Click the* **Save in** *drop-down list; then choose the 3½ Floppy (A:) drive.*

Ⓓ *Double-click to open the Annual Report folder.*

Ⓔ *Click the* **Save** *button to save the logo as a picture file on your floppy disk.*

Open Link
Open Link in New Window
Save Target As...
Print Target

Show Picture
Save Picture As...

Save in: 3½ Floppy (A:)
Annual Report

4. Click the **Background Tile Image** hyperlink at the bottom of the Welcome page.
The Internet Explorer window will display a small image that serves as the background to this page. By repeating this small image many times, Internet Explorer can display a colorful background without needing to use a large image. You will use this same image as the background of your worksheet pages later in this lesson.

5. *Right-click* anywhere on the image; choose **Save Picture As** from the menu bar; then click the **Save** button.
The tile image is saved to the Annual Report folder on your floppy disk.

6. Click the **Back** button on the Internet Explorer toolbar to return to the *Welcome* Web page; then click the **Back** button again to return to the *Lesson 13* Web page.

Back

7. Minimize ▬ the Internet Explorer window.

Saving Attachment Files

You learned how to save attachments to email messages in another lesson. Attachments can be any type of file. In the following exercise, you will save a Word document and a Notepad file from two different email messages.

Hands-On 13.3 **Save Email Attachments**

Before you begin, *if you do not have access to email in the computer lab, you should skip directly to the* Save Files Off the Web Page *section (Step 14) near the end of this exercise.*

Send an Email Message

1. Use **Start→Programs→Microsoft Outlook** to start the *Outlook 2000* application.

2. Click the **Inbox** button on the Outlook bar at the left side of the window to display the Inbox view.

3. Click the New Mail [New] button at the left side of the Outlook toolbar to create a new email message.

4. Taking care to separate them with a *semicolon* (;), type the following email addresses in the *To:* line: **terry@offtowork.com; jchan@offtowork.com**

5. Tap the (TAB) key until the insertion point is blinking on the **subject line.** Type the following subject: **Status lists**.

6. Tap the (TAB) key to jump to the body of the message; then type the following message:

```
Hello Terry and Jackie:

Please send me your latest project status list by
email. It should list the various chapters of the
annual report, the date work is scheduled to begin,
and the date each chapter is due. I will publish
your list on the Web so other production workers
can follow our schedule.

Regards,

[Your Name]
```

7. Click the **Send** button to send your message.

8. Click the Send/Receive [Send/Receive] button on the Outlook toolbar to check for responses to your message. Keep checking every minute until you have received a reply from both Terry and Jacqueline; then go on to the next step.

Save the Attachment Files

9. *Double-click* to open the message from **terry@offtowork.com.** Read over the message; then follow these steps to save the attachment in the *Annual Report* folder:

Ⓐ Right-click *on the attachment **icon** (not the filename) at the bottom of the message.*

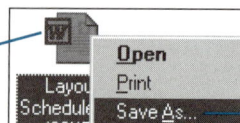

Ⓑ *Choose **Save As** from the pop-up menu.*

Ⓒ *Click the **Favorites** button on the lower-left side of the dialog box; then double-click to open the Annual Report Favorite. Notice how this folder opens immediately, saving you the time of navigating to the 3½ Floppy (A:) drive.*

Ⓓ *Click the **Save** button to save the attachment file.*

364 Lesson 13: Web Integration: Posting an Online Workbook

10. Close ⊠ the message from Terry; then double-click to open the message from **jchan@offtowork.com**.

Notice that the attachment at the bottom of this message has a different icon from the one you saw in the message from Terry. This is because Jacqueline sent you a file in a text *file format rather than a Word document.*

11. *Right-click* on the attachment file icon at the bottom of the message; then choose **Save As** from the pop-up menu. Click the **Save** button to save this file in the **Annual Report** folder.

12. Close ⊠ the message from Jacqueline.

13. Close ⊠ the Outlook window.

You can skip the next section of this exercise and continue reading the next topic.

Save the Files Off the Web Page

If you do not have access to email in the computer lab, you should use this alternative process to save the files from Terry Sanchez and Jacqueline Chan off of a Web page.

14. Restore the **Internet Explorer** window by clicking its button on the Windows Taskbar.

You should see the Lesson 13 *Web page that you left open in Hands-On Exercise 13.2.*

15. Follow these steps to save the first document file:

Ⓐ Right-click *on the* Annual Report Editing Schedule *hyperlink; then choose* **Save Target As** *from the pop-up menu.*

Ⓑ *Choose the 3½ Floppy (A:) drive in the* **Save in** *box.*

Ⓒ *Double-click to open the* Annual Report *folder.*

Ⓓ *Click the* **Save** *button.*

Internet Explorer will display a dialog box showing the progress of copying the file from the Web page to your floppy disk.

16. Click the **Close** button on the *Download Complete* dialog box.

17. Right-click on the **Annual Report Layout Schedule** hyperlink, and choose **Save Target As** from the pop-up menu; then save the file to the Annual Report folder on your floppy disk. Click the **Close** button on the *Download Complete* dialog box.

18. Minimize ▬ the Internet Explorer program.

Integrating Multiple Data Sources

You can bring data from other application programs into Excel. This is called *importing.* For example, if a co-worker writes up some information in Word, you can import this data directly onto an Excel worksheet. Excel can import a variety of data into your workbooks.

File Formats

A file format is a technique for storing data in a computer file. Most application programs use a specific file format to save anything you create in that program. For example, Word has its own *document* format, Excel has its own *workbook* format, and Web pages are saved in HTML format. The format an application program normally uses to save files is called its *native* file format.

Converters

A *converter* is a small program that lets an application program open and save files that are not in its native file format. The Office 2000 applications come with a variety of converters that are installed automatically. You can also install additional converters that may become available as new file formats are introduced. For example, when a new version of an application program is released, it usually introduces a new native file format.

Example

You decide to place an image on an Excel worksheet. You use the **Insert→Picture→From File** command. Excel displays any image files for which it has an installed converter. When you choose an image file to insert and click **OK,** Excel uses the appropriate converter to read the file and place it in the worksheet.

Project Data Sources

In this lesson, you will work with the following types of data sources:

- A Word document

- A Notepad text-only document

- Two images

- An Excel worksheet saved as a Web page

Hands-On 13.4 Import Data from Other Data Sources

In this exercise, you will insert the Acme Trading Company *logo at the top of each workbook page. Then you will insert text from the two documents into the workbook.*

Add the Logo to the Top of Each Worksheet Page

1. *Restore* the **Excel** window by clicking its button on the Windows Taskbar.

2. Click in Cell **A1** on the first worksheet; then choose **Insert→Picture→From File** from the menu bar.

3. Click the **Favorites** button on the left side of the dialog box; then double-click on the **Annual Report** Favorite.

4. Double-click to insert the **logo** (or **logo.jpg**) file.
   The logo is immediately placed at the top-left corner of the worksheet.

5. Click the Copy 📋 button on the toolbar.

6. Click the **Sheet 2** tab at the bottom of the workbook window.

7. Make sure the highlight is in Cell **A1**; then click the Paste 📋 button on the toolbar.
   As you may recall from an earlier lesson, the clipboard will retain the most recently copied or cut item until you copy or cut a new item. Thus, you can paste the logo onto multiple pages after you give the Copy command.

8. Click the **Sheet 3** tab, and paste the logo into Cell **A1** of that worksheet.

Rename the Worksheets

Deion renames the worksheets to make the workbook easier to navigate. He also deletes any surplus worksheets that are not needed.

9. Double-click the **Sheet 1** tab, and change the name to `Editing Schedule`, and tap (ENTER).

   ▪ Change the **Sheet 2** tab to `Layout Schedule`, and tap (ENTER).

   ▪ Change the **Sheet 3** tab to `Production Schedule`, and tap (ENTER).

10. Save 💾 the workbook.

Importing Data from Text Files

Some programs can save data in a text-only format that is easy for Excel to import. For example, the simple Notepad applet that comes with Windows can save text-only files. Three methods you can use to import data onto an Excel worksheet are listed below.

   ▪ **Import the text file as data**—You import text files onto a worksheet as data with the *Data→Get External Data→Import Text File* command.

   ▪ **Drag-and-Drop**—You can open the text file data in another application program, then drag-and-drop the data onto an Excel worksheet.

   ▪ **Copy and Paste**—You can use standard copy and paste commands to bring text file data onto a worksheet.

Types of Text Files

Two types of text files are used most often in conjunction with Excel.

   ▪ **Tab-delimited**—A tab-delimited file uses a tab character to separate the data on each column. In the example of a tab-delimited file below, each small arrow represents a tab character. When the file is imported, Excel will place each data item following a tab character in a new column.

```
First      →    Last     →    Phone      →    City
Deion      →    Anderson →    213-638-1234 →  Los·Angeles
Jacqueline →    Chan     →    541-321-8989 →  Ashland
Terry      →    Sanchez  →    617-540-2220 →  Boston
```

- **Comma-delimited**—A comma delimited text file has a comma between each column of data. An example of the same data in a comma-delimited file appears below. When the file is imported, Excel will place each data item following a comma in a new column.

```
First,Last,Phone,City
Deion,Anderson,213-638-1234,Los Angeles
Jacqueline,Chan,541-321-8989,Ashland
Terry,Sanchez,617-540-2220,Boston
```

The Import Text File Command

You can import a text file onto an Excel worksheet as data. When you import a text file, Excel examines the file to determine if the formatting in the file will help lay out the data neatly into rows and columns. For example, if the text file is tab-delimited, Excel can import the data into the proper columns. The Import Text File command can also help you deal with certain formatting problems you may encounter with tab-delimited or comma-delimited text files.

Importing Text File Data with Drag-and-Drop

You can drag-and-drop data between other applications and an Excel workbook. For example you can drag-and-drop a table or text from a Word document onto an Excel worksheet. You simply select the data to be imported, then drag-and-drop it onto the desired worksheet. When you use the drag-and-drop technique, the data is deleted (cut) from the source file. However, if you do not *save* the changes to the source file when you close it, the data you dragged and dropped will be retained.

NOTE!

Since Notepad does not support the drag-and-drop technique, the next exercise will use copy-and-paste. However, you will use the drag-and-drop technique with a Microsoft Word document in a later exercise. You can also use this technique with any text file you open in Word, or other programs that support drag-and-drop.

Quick Reference

IMPORTING DATA FROM TEXT FILES

Task	Procedure
Import a text file onto an Excel worksheet.	■ Display the worksheet upon which you wish to import the text file data.
	■ Choose Data→Get External Data→Import Text File from the menu bar.
	■ Navigate to the location of the text file on your hard drive or floppy disk; then select the text file and click Import.
	■ Follow the instructions in the Text Import Wizard; then click Finish.
	■ Click the cell where you wish to begin the data import; then click OK.
Import text data with drag and drop.	■ Open the Excel window and an application window displaying the text data side-by-side.
	■ Display the worksheet onto which you wish to import the text data.
	■ Drag to select the text data in the other program; then drag-and-drop it onto the Excel worksheet.

Hands-On 13.5 Import Data from a Text File

Jacqueline uses a very basic program to create short documents. There is no formatting in the document she sent. In this exercise, you will import data from the project editor's text file using the copy-and-paste technique. Then you will use the Import Text File command to import the same data

Copy and Paste the Text Data

1. Minimize ▬ the Excel window.

2. *Double-click* the **Annual Report** shortcut.
   A My Computer window will appear to display the contents of your Annual Report folder. Shortcuts like this can save you time navigating through the disk drives to locate a specific folder.

3. Double-click on the **editing** (or **editing.txt**) file.
   Windows will probably open the file in the Notepad applet. Notepad is a simple text editor that comes with Windows. Notice that the columns are neatly aligned in this document.

4. Choose **Edit→Select All** from the menu bar; then use (CTRL)+C to copy the document to the clipboard.

5. Close ☒ the Notepad window. Click **No** if you are asked if you wish to save the document.
   Even though you have closed the Notepad window, everything you copied in Step 4 is still on the Windows clipboard.

6. **Restore** the Excel window by clicking its button on the Windows Taskbar.

7. Click the tab for the **Editing Schedule** Worksheet; then click on Cell **A7,** and use (CTRL)+V to *Paste* the text data onto the worksheet.
   Notice that the once-neat columns on the right are now crooked. This is because Jacqueline used the (TAB) key to align her columns. But if an item did not align, she pressed (TAB) again to move it over. When you placed the text into Excel, each tab character in the document shifted the text over one column on the worksheet. You could use drag and drop to align these cells manually. However, the Import Text File method can help you tackle this problem more efficiently, as you will see in a moment.

8. Click Undo ↰ on the toolbar to undo your recent drag-and-drop command.
   Now you will use a different command to accomplish the same end—importing the text file data onto a worksheet.

(Continued on the next page)

Use the Import Text File Command

9. Choose **Data→Get External Data→Import Text File** from the menu bar.

A dialog box appears to display the available text files in the current folder. Notice that your workbook, the Word file, and the two image files are not displayed in this list, since they are not text files.

10. Click the *editing* file; then click **Import.**

The Import Text Wizard dialog box will appear. This Wizard will guide you through the steps of importing the text file data. At the top of the dialog box, notice that the Wizard indicates the editing file is a delimited file. The Wizard always analyzes text files to determine if they are a specific type of file that can aid the import process.

There is also a preview of the text file in the lower portion of the dialog box. The preview shows the tab codes as small boxes rather than arrows. Notice that you can change the setting of the first row to be imported. For example, if you wanted to leave out the heading, you could start the import process with row three. Since the default settings are correct, you can proceed to the next step.

11. Click **Next.**

Step 2 of the Wizard displays the next set of options. Since the editing file was determined to be tab-delimited, this option has already been selected for you. Notice in the Data Preview section how the columns are not lined up. You saw this problem earlier when you dragged and dropped the data. There are too many tab codes. The Wizard has an option that will help you correct this.

12. Follow these steps to continue with Step 2 of the Wizard.

A *Right-click on the* Treat Consecutive delimiters as one *option to view a description; then choose* What's This? *from the pop-up menu to view a description. This option will solve the problem of Jacqueline using the* TAB *key more than once in some rows. After you have read the description, click the pop-up* Help *box to make it disappear.*

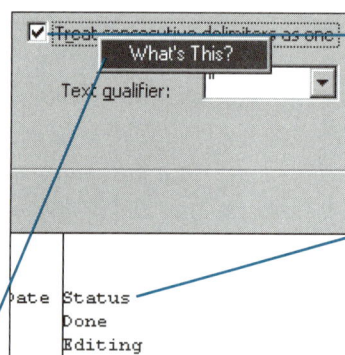

B *Check the* Treat Consecutive delimiters as one option.

C *Notice that the data columns are now neatly aligned in the* Data Preview.

13. Click **Next** to continue with Step 3 of the Wizard.

This step lets you adjust the date format of columns. You can even exclude selected columns from the import command.

14. Follow these steps to set the date column format for the Due Date column.

Ⓐ *Click the column heading to select the* Due Date *column.*

Ⓑ *Choose* DMY *from the Date selection list. This tells Excel to import the dates in a Day-Month-Year format.*

Ⓒ *Notice that the data columns are now neatly aligned in the* Data Preview.

15. Click **Finish** to execute the *Import Text File* command.
The Wizard will ask you to specify a range for the import command. You can simply specify the top-left cell for the range instead.

16. If necessary, click Cell **A7;** then click **OK**.
The text file data appears on the worksheet. Notice that unlike your previous Copy-and-Paste command, now the columns are aligned neatly. Notice also that the dates are listed in day/month format, but there is no year. Apparently Jacqueline did not type out the year in her original file, so the Import command did not include the year in the conversion.

17. Add bold formatting to the headings in Row **9** and the heading in Cell **A7**. Format the column headings so that they stand out. Add any other formatting you think will make the table more readable.

18. Save ⊞ the Workbook.
It's always a good idea to issue the Save command after you have completed five or ten minutes worth of work. If the computer should halt unexpectedly (crash) all of your work up to the most recent Save command is safely stored on the floppy disk.

Importing Data from Other Applications with Copy-and-Paste

You can copy and paste data between other applications and an Excel workbook. For example you can copy and paste a table or text from a Word document onto an Excel worksheet. You simply select the data to be imported, then cut or copy the data and paste it onto the desired worksheet. You can also use the Paste Special command to paste data into Excel in a specific format (See Lesson 7).

Tiled Backgrounds on Worksheets

Excel lets you place an image in the background of any worksheet. If the image is smaller than the viewable area of the worksheet, it will be tiled (repeated) to fill the entire worksheet window. In the next Hands-On exercise, you will tile the small background image you saved from the Acme home page earlier in this lesson.

Quick Reference

HOW TO ASSIGN A BACKGROUND IMAGE TO A WORKSHEET	
Task	**Procedure**
Place a tiled background image on a worksheet.	■ Display the worksheet you wish to assign a background image.
	■ Choose **Format→Sheet→Background** from the menu bar.
	■ Choose a background image; then click **Insert**.

Repeating Your Most Recent Command

From the Keyboard

F4 to repeat your most recent command.

There may be times when you need to apply the same command at several places in a workbook. For example, you may give a format cell command that you wish to repeat on cells in a different worksheet. Excel lets you repeat your most recent command by tapping the **F4** function key on the keyboard. Just as you can paste the same item from the clipboard repeatedly, you can continue using the **F4** function key to repeat the same command until you issue a different command.

Hands-On 13.6 Import Data with Drag and Drop

In this exercise, you will open a Word file and then drag and drop data from the file onto an Excel worksheet. You will also drag-and-drop data from a Web page.

Add Word Text to a Worksheet

Terry used Word to compose her status list. You will copy and paste from her Word document into her page in the workbook.

1. *Restore* the **A:\Annual Report** window by clicking its button on the Windows Taskbar.

2. Double-click on the **layout** (or **layout.doc**) file in the *Annual Report* folder.
   Windows will start Microsoft Word to display the document. Before copying this information, you will need to minimize the My Computer window.

3. Follow these steps to minimize the My Computer window.

Ⓐ *Right-click on the* **A:\Annual Report** *button on the Windows Taskbar.*

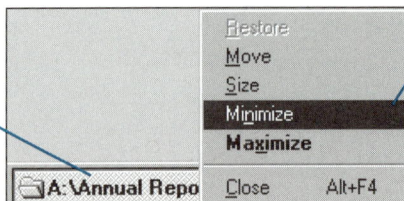

| Restore |
| Move |
| Size |
| Minimize |
| Maximize |
| Close   Alt+F4 |

🗗 A:\Annual Repo

Ⓑ *Choose* **Minimize** *from the pop-up menu.*

4. Follow these steps to display the Word and Excel windows side-by-side.

Ⓐ Right-click *on a clear portion of the Windows Taskbar. (Do not right-click on a button.) The best spot to locate a clear area is toward the right side of the Taskbar.*

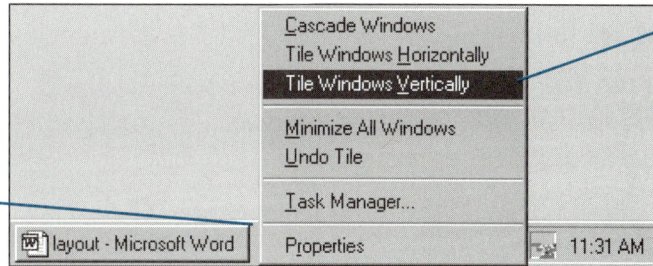

| Cascade Windows |
| Tile Windows Horizontally |
| **Tile Windows Vertically** |
| Minimize All Windows |
| Undo Tile |
| Task Manager... |
| Properties |

layout - Microsoft Word · · · · 11:31 AM

Ⓑ *Choose* Tile Windows Vertically *from the pop-up menu.*

Now the two program windows are side-by-side. This will make it easy to drag and drop the data from Word into Excel.

5. Click the tab for the **Layout Schedule** worksheet at the bottom of the Workbook window; then click Cell **A7.**
Terry used Word's table feature to create a well-formatted table. Let's see if this formatting gets copied into Excel.

6. Follow these steps to drag and drop the layout schedule from the Word document onto the Excel worksheet.

Ⓐ *Position the mouse pointer to the left of the Annual Report Layout Schedule heading, and a* **right-pointing arrow** *will appear, as shown here.*

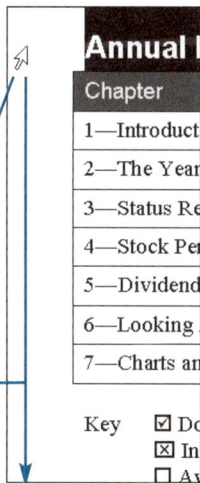

Annual

| Chapter |
| 1—Introduct |
| 2—The Year |
| 3—Status R |
| 4—Stock Per |
| 5—Dividend |
| 6—Looking |
| 7—Charts an |

Key ☑ Dc
☒ In
☐ Av

Ⓑ Drag *straight down to select the entire content of the page, including the* **Key** *lines at the bottom of the document.*

Ⓒ *Release the mouse button, and point at any part of the selection; then drag toward the* **A7** *cell in the worksheet window.*

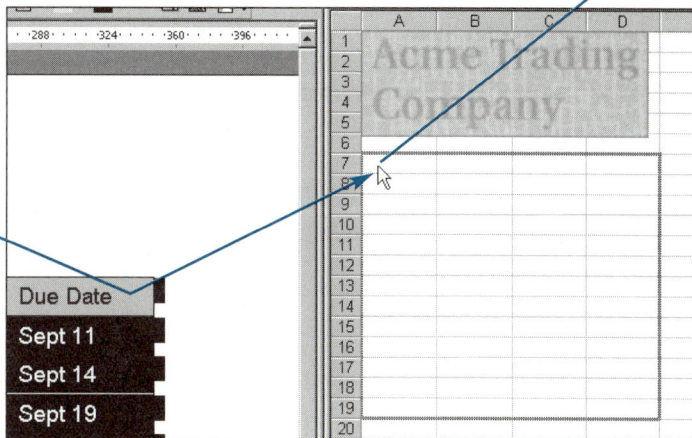

Ⓓ *Release the mouse button over the* **A7** *cell. You will be able to see the outline of the cells that will receive the content that you are dragging.*

Ⓔ *Click on any cell outside of the content you just dragged and dropped. This will remove the selection from this content.*

	A	B	C	D	E
1					
2	Acme Trading				
3					
4	Company				
5					
...	...	...	...	...	...

Due Date

Sept 11

Sept 14

Sept 19

The selected content from the Word document is pasted onto the worksheet. Notice that this content has disappeared from the Word document.

(Continued on the next page)

7. Close ☒ the *Word* window. Click **No** when you are asked to save changes to the document.
This will prevent the loss of the content that you just dragged and dropped. The next time you open this document, all of the content will reappear.

8. Maximize ☐ the *Excel* window.
Thanks to Excel's Word filter, the formatting was essentially carried over into the Excel worksheet. However, the column widths did not fare as well. Let's fix that.

9. Follow these steps to clean up the Word table:

Ⓐ *Double-click this column boundary to AutoFit Column A. Notice that the column expands too wide due to the heading in Cell* **A7**.

Ⓑ *Drag to adjust Column A to fit the text in the body of the table as shown here.*

	A	B	C	D	E
7	**Annual Report Layout Schedule**				
8	Chapter	Status	Start Date	Due Date	
9	1—Introduction	☑	4-Sep	11-Sep	
	2—The Year in Review	☑	11-Sep	14-Sep	

Ⓒ *Drag to adjust the remaining columns to fit the data in each column as shown here.*

10. Drag on the *headings* to select Columns **C** and **D** as shown at right.

B	C	D

11. Click the Align Right ☰ button on the toolbar.
Now the columns look good, and the height of the rows has been adjusted as well.

12. Save ☐ the Workbook.

Copy HTML Data with Drag and Drop

Now you will add Deion's worksheet to the workbook. Deion had already saved his production schedule worksheet as a Web page. (You will learn how to do this later in this lesson.) Drag and Drop is one technique you can use to copy data from Web pages (HTML documents) onto Excel worksheets.

13. Click the **Production Schedule** worksheet tab; then click on Cell **A7.**

14. Restore the **Internet Explorer** window by clicking its button on the Windows Taskbar.

15. Click the **Non-Interactive** button on the **Lesson 13** window.
This page displays an Excel worksheet that has been saved as a Web page without any interactive features. You will learn more about the interactive option later in this lesson.

16. *Right-click* on a clear area of the Windows Taskbar; then choose **Tile Windows Vertically** from the pop-up menu.

17. Follow these steps to drag and drop data from the Internet Explorer window onto the Excel worksheet.

Ⓐ Drag *down and to the right to select the table in the Internet Explorer window.*

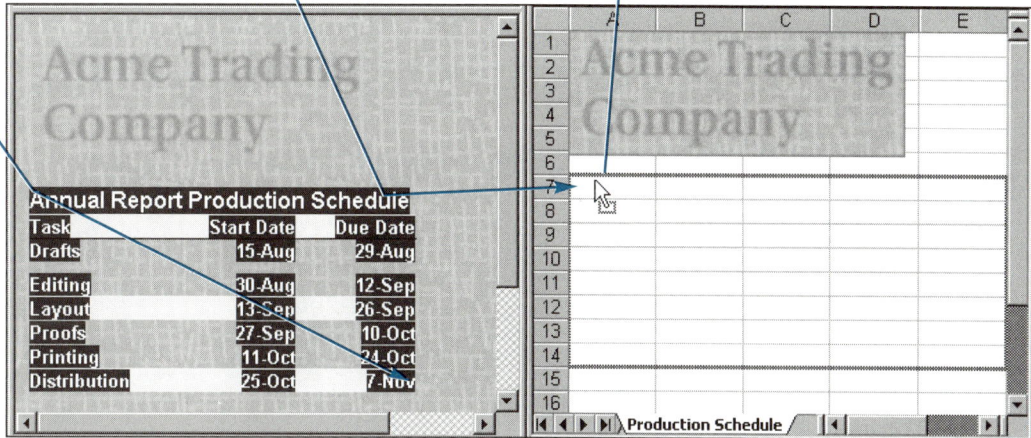

Ⓑ Point *at any part of the selection, then* drag *toward Cell **A7** in the Excel window.*

Ⓒ *Release the mouse button when the insertion point is over Cell **A7** and you will see a **rectangle** that represents the content being dragged, as shown here.*

18. Close ☒ the *Internet Explorer* window; then Maximize ☐ the *Excel* window.

19. Adjust the row and column widths until the table is similar to the example shown below. Adjust the formatting of the labels and shading if you like.

20. Save 🖫 the Workbook.

Add a Background Image

When you save the worksheet as a Web page, it will look more attractive if there is some color on the page. You will now add the background image you copied from the Web page earlier in the lesson to the background of each worksheet.

21. Choose **Format→Sheet→Background** from the menu bar.

22. Double-click to choose the **tile** (or **tile.jpg**) file as the background image.
Just as you saw on the Web page in an earlier exercise, the tile image is repeated to cover the entire Excel worksheet.

(Continued on the next page)

23. Click the **Layout Schedule** tab at the bottom of the workbook window; then tap the (F4) function key to repeat the previous command.

The background is set for Sheet 2. Excel will keep repeating your most recent command each time you tap the (F4) function key.

24. Click the **Editing Schedule** tab; then tap the (F4) function key.

25. Save 🖫 the workbook.

Leave the Workbook open; you will continue to use it.

Converting Workbooks to Other File Formats

In the previous topic, you learned that the native file format is how an application normally saves files. But what if you want to save a file in a different (non-native) file format? This is called *exporting*. In order to export your work to a different file format, Excel must use a conversion filter to convert the workbook file into the new format.

Limitations of File Formats

Some file formats will not be able to save all of the information in the workbook file. For example, a *tab delimited* file won't be able to save data on multiple worksheets or any text formatting. Excel will warn you about any features, formatting, or data you might lose in the new file format. If you save to a non-Excel file format, your original workbook file is always kept intact. The converted workbook is saved to different file.

The Save As Command

The *Save As* command is very similar to the Save command—it saves your work. However, the Save As command lets you perform several additional tasks as listed below.

- **Save the file with a different file format (export)**—The Save As command lets you change the file format of a workbook file. For example, you can save a worksheet in the workbook in a tab-delimited format so other application programs can read the data.

- **Save a file with a different name**—The Save As command lets you save a copy of an existing workbook with a new name. The old version of the workbook remains on your hard drive or floppy disk.

- **Save a file to a new location on the computer system**—The Save As command lets you save a workbook to a different disk drive or folder. You can save the workbook to the new location with the same name or a different name.

- **Manage files**—You can also rename files displayed in the Save As dialog box, create new folders, and even delete unwanted files.

TIP!

The first time you give the Save *command with a new workbook, Excel automatically displays the* Save As *dialog box.*

Task	Procedure
Save a copy of a file with a new name.	■ Open the workbook in Excel; then choose *File→Save As* from the menu bar.
	■ Type the new name in the Filename box; then click Save.
Rename and delete files from within Excel.	■ Choose *File→Save As* from the menu bar; then navigate to the folder where you wish to manage files.
	■ Right-click on any file(s) you wish to manage; then choose the desired command from the pop-up menu.

Exporting to Other Applications

One reason to convert a workbook to another file format is to make it available to other applications that cannot read workbook files. For example, you can convert a database file into a comma-delimited format that can be read by many other types of database application program such as Microsoft Access. Or you may wish place an Excel worksheet inside a Word document. Listed below are three useful methods for exporting Excel workbook data to other application programs.

- **Copy→Paste Special**—You can copy a range on a worksheet, then use the Paste Special command in the target application program to paste the data in a useful format.

- **Convert (export) the worksheet or workbook**—You save the workbook and/or worksheets in a file format that the other application program can read and convert (import). However, many of these file formats will only allow you to save one worksheet at a time. So you might have to give several Save As commands to save the individual worksheets in certain file formats.

- **The Insert→Object command**—you can choose to insert an Excel chart or worksheet into an application that supports *Object Linking and Embedding* (OLE).

Example

You have a co-worker who still uses an older version of Lotus 1-2-3 as her spreadsheet program. You want to send her information from an Excel workbook. You open the workbook normally in Excel and use the Save As command to choose a different file format (export) and save it. Then you send the exported file to your co-worker. You end up with two different copies of the workbook, each in a different format.

Task	Procedure
Export a Workbook to a different file format.	■ Open the workbook in Excel; then choose **File→Save As** from the menu bar.
	■ Click on the **Save As Type** box; choose the desired file format; then click **Save**.
	■ Read any warnings Excel displays about the potential for lost formatting and/or worksheets in the new file; then click **OK** or **Cancel**.

In this exercise, you will use the Save As command to save a copy of the workbook with another name, and another copy to a new location. You will also use the Save As command to Export the workbook to another file format for use with other application programs.

Save Copies of the Workbook with Save As

1. Choose **File→Save As** from the menu bar.
   Notice that the current filename is already selected, ready for you to change it.

2. Tap the (END) key on the keyboard; then tap the (SPACE BAR) and add **(backup copy)** to the end of the filename. Click **Save** to complete the command.
   You have created a new copy of the file with a new name. The old version of the file remains on your floppy disk. Notice that the name of the copy is displayed on the top-left corner of the Title bar. This is the currently opened file. The Status file has been closed.

3. Choose **File→Save As** from the menu bar.
   Notice that the Annual Report folder is currently displayed in the Save In box. This is the current location of the workbook. Now you will navigate to a new location on your floppy disk and save the workbook there.

4. Click the Up 🔼 button on the dialog box toolbar to navigate to the base (root) level of your floppy disk.
   Notice that the 3½ Floppy (A:) drive is now displayed in the Save in box near the top of the dialog box. This is the new location where the file will be saved.

5. Click **Save.**
   The workbook is saved in the new location. The file now exists at the root level of the floppy disk and in the Annual Report folder.

6. Choose **File→Close** to close the workbook.

Delete a File from within Excel

7. Click the Open 📂 button on the Excel toolbar.

8. Scroll down the file list until the *Status (backup copy)* workbook is visible. *Right-click* on the *Status (backup copy)* workbook file; then choose **Delete** from the pop-up menu. Click **Yes** if you are asked to confirm the deletion.
   You can delete and rename files from within Excel's Save As and Open dialog boxes.

9. Double-click the *Annual Report* folder; then double-click to open the **Status** workbook.

Use Save As to Export the Workbook to a New File Format

Now you will save the workbook in a tab-delimited format. This format places a tab character between the values in each column of the worksheet you are exporting. As you will see, this format also deletes all of the formatting from the worksheet.

10. Click the **Production Schedule** worksheet tab.

11. Click the Help [?] button on the Excel toolbar if you do not see the *Office Assistant*. The animated Office Assistant on your computer may appear different from the example shown here.

12. Choose **File→Save As** from the menu bar.

13. Follow these steps to save the file with a different file format.

A *Click at the end of the **File name** box; then add* **(tab delimited)** *to the end of the filename, as shown here.*

B *Click the **Save as type** drop-down list button. Scroll up and down the list to review the available file formats. Every format type in this list has a corresponding converter that was installed along with Excel. It is possible to install additional converters later if they are needed.*

| File name: | Status (tab delimited) |
| Save as type: | Microsoft Excel Workbook |

Microsoft Excel Workbook
Web Page
Template
Text (Tab delimited)
Unicode Text
Microsoft Excel 5.0/95 Workbook

C *Choose the **Text (Tab Delimited)** format near the top of the list.*

D *Click the **Save** button to complete the command.*

Excel will warn you that the Text file format cannot save data on multiple worksheets. For this example, that's OK. However, if you needed to save all of the data in this workbook, you would either place all of the data onto a single worksheet before you save the workbook, or you would have to save each worksheet individually. For now, you will save just the data on the Production Schedule worksheet.

14. Click **OK** to accept the fact that only the currently active worksheet will be saved to the new file.
    Excel will prompt you that some data and/or formatting could be lost when you save to this file format. You are given the choice of preserving the features of the workbook, or aborting the save and saving the file in Excel's native file format.

15. Click **Help** near the bottom-left corner of the Office Assistant Speech Balloon.   [● Help]
    The primary Help window will appear to display information on file formatting that is not transferred when you convert a file.

16. If necessary, *scroll down* near the bottom of the Help window; then click the Text (Tab Delimited) (*.txt) hyperlink. Look over the first two paragraphs of information on converting a worksheet to this format.
    This Help information can aid you in choosing the correct file format, or in foreseeing the types of formatting that would be lost.

17. Close ☒ the **Help** window.

18. Click **Yes** on the Office Assistant speech balloon to accept saving to the newly selected file format and the loss of formatting.

19. Close ☒ the **Excel** window. Click **No** if you are asked to save changes to the Status (tab delimited) workbook.

View the Worksheet File in Its New Format

20. Click the **A:\Annual Report** button on the Taskbar to restore that window.

21. Double-click the **Status (tab delimited)** file.
    The file will be displayed in the Notepad applet. Notice that all of your formatting has been stripped away. Notice also that the columns no longer line up neatly. You would need to "clean up" the alignment of the columns in this Notepad file just as you had to clean up the Editing Schedule file that you copied into the Workbook earlier.

(Continued on the next page)

22. Close ☒ the **Notepad** window.

23. Make sure that the *Status (tab delimited)* file is selected in the My Computer window; then tap the (DELETE) key on the keyboard. Click **Yes** if you are asked to confirm the deletion.

Saving an Excel Workbook for the Web

Like most of the Office 2000 applications, Excel is designed to post information to the Web whenever you need this capability. You no longer need to send an individual file to each person participating in a project. Now you can simply post the workbook to the Web. When someone needs the information, they can save the Web page or copy and paste individual cells from the online workbook.

Publishing Compared to Saving as Web Page

When you save an Excel workbook for viewing on the Web you have two basic options. Each option has benefits and limitations.

- **Save as Web Page**—This save option lets you save the entire workbook in Web (HTML) format with a single command. *Save as Web Page* lets users navigate among the worksheets with the familiar tabs at the bottom of the window. However, a workbook saved as a Web page cannot offer any of the interactive features available with the other formats.

- **Publish**—This save option allows you to save only one worksheet (or a range of cells on one worksheet) at a time. You should use the *Publish* option when you want to offer *interactivity* features with a worksheet (see *Allowing Interactivity* on page 382. For example, users can enter new data into a worksheet, and then save it, or they can view a pivot table online.

Web Page Preview

In previous lessons you have used the Print Preview command to see how an Excel workbook will appear in print. Excel also makes it easy to see what the workbook will look like when you post it to the Web. The **File→Web Page Preview** command launches your Web browser and displays the workbook exactly as it will appear on the Web.

Quick Reference

HOW TO SAVE A WORKBOOK AS A WEB PAGE	
Task	**Procedure**
Save an entire workbook so that it may be viewed on the Web.	■ Open the Workbook in Excel.
	■ Choose **File→Save As Web Page** from the menu bar.
	■ If desired, click the **Change Title** button to type the title that will appear in the Web browser when the workbook is displayed over the Web.
	■ Choose a **destination** for the Web page. This can be a folder on a disk drive or a Web folder (see *Publishing with Web Folders* on page 384).
	■ Click **Save** to save the workbook in Web page format.
Preview a workbook in your Web browser.	■ Choose **File→Web Page Preview** from the menu bar.

Deion decides to publish the worksheets of his workbook to the Web. This will allow each project team member to view each other's schedules and keep abreast of any delays or rushes that may affect their own work.

Hands-On 13.8 Save the Workbook as a Web Page

In this exercise, you will use Web Page Preview, and then save the workbook as a Web page.

Preview the Workbook as a Web Page

1. Double-click the **Status** workbook file in the My Computer window.

2. Choose **File→Web Page Preview** from the menu bar.
   Excel will start Internet Explorer or your default Web browser program. The page is displayed just as it would appear if it were viewed over the Web. Notice that the worksheet tabs at the bottom of the browser window are similar to the tabs at the bottom of every Excel workbook window.

3. If necessary, Maximize ⬜ the Internet Explorer window.

4. Click each of the worksheet tabs at the bottom of the Internet Explorer window to view the three worksheets.
   There's really not much difference between viewing the workbook in a Web browser and viewing it in an Excel window. About the only things missing are the gridlines.

5. Close ❌ the **Internet Explorer** window.
   You are back to viewing the Excel window.

Save the Workbook as a Web Page

Now you will save the workbook as a Web page on your floppy disk. Later, you will learn how to save the workbook as a Web page on the World Wide Web.

6. Choose **File→Save As Web Page** from the menu bar.

7. Click the **Change Title** button near the lower-right corner of the dialog box; then type the title: **Annual Report Production**, and click **OK.**
   This command sets the title that displays when your workbook is viewed in a Web browser.

8. Click the Save 💾 button.
   There will be a pause as the workbook is converted to Web page (HTML) format and all of the necessary data is saved to your floppy disk.

(Continued on the next page)

Open the Web Page

9. Minimize ▬ the Excel window.
   The Annual Report window should now be active.

10. Choose **View→Large Icons** from the menu bar.

11. Choose **View→Arrange Icons→By Name** from the menu bar.
    Notice that there are now two files named Status; *one for each version of the file that you have saved as shown below.*

The Web page (HTML) version of the workbook ——— Status   Status ———*The native Excel format version of the workbook*

12. Double-click the **Status** icon for the **Web page** version of your workbook.
    Internet Explorer (or another browser program) will start to display the workbook.

13. Click each of the worksheet tabs at the bottom of the Internet Explorer window to verify that the workbook was successfully converted to Web page format.
    The worksheets should appear as they did when you viewed the workbook with the Web Page Preview *command earlier in this exercise. Leave the Internet Explorer window open.*

Allowing Interactivity

It is also possible to save an individual worksheet with interactive capabilities. This means that users viewing the worksheet in their Web browser can enter, format, and analyze data. So, formulas will take any applicable data entered and display new calculations.

TIP!

In order to view an interactive worksheet on a Web page, the viewer must be running Internet Explorer *version 4.01 or later and also have installed the* Microsoft Office Web Components.

Quick Reference

HOW TO SAVE AN INTERACTIVE WORKSHEET	
Task	**Procedure**
Save a Worksheet so that others can interact with its data in an Internet Explorer window.	■ Display the worksheet in the workbook window.
	■ Choose **File→Save as Web Page** from the menu bar.
	■ Click the **Selection: Sheet** option in the dialog box; then make sure that the *Add interactivity* box is checked.
	■ Make sure that the filename and Web Page title settings are correct; then click the **Save** button.

Lost Formatting on Interactive Worksheets

When you save an interactive worksheet as a Web page, not all of the features and formatting of the worksheet will be retained. For example, any *images, pattern fills*, and *comments* on worksheets are **not** saved when the workbook is saved as an interactive Web page. Some formatting, such as font settings and color fills, will still display correctly. Excel's online help lists the functionality that is lost or retained when you save your workbook as a Web page. You may also need to experiment and make sure all of the necessary elements of the workbook are visible in Web page format.

In this exercise, you will navigate to a worksheet that has been saved to support interactivity. The worksheet uses formulas to calculate dates. You will change the date in a cell and observe the new dates on the Web worksheet.

1. Type the Web address of the lesson Web page in the Address box of the Internet Explorer toolbar: **www.offtowork.com/excel/lesson13**.

2. Click the **Interactive** button.
   This page displays the part of the production schedule worksheet that contains data. You can save an interactive worksheet that only contains selected cells. Notice that the graphics are missing from this worksheet. This is one limitation of interactive worksheets.

3. Follow these steps to enter new data into the worksheet.

   Ⓐ Double-click *in Cell* **C3**. *Notice that the formula in this cell is displayed.*

   Ⓑ *Click once on Cell* **C4**. *Notice that the formula is no longer displayed.*

   Ⓒ Double-click *in other cells to view their formulas or values.*

   Ⓓ *Click once in Cell* **C5**; *then type* **9-30** *and tap* (ENTER). *Notice the new date that appears in the cell.*

   Ⓔ *Notice that the cells below this cell have changed to reflect the new date.*

	A	B	C
1	Annual Report Production Schedule		
2	Task	Start Date	Due Date
3	Drafts	15-Aug	=B3+14
4	Editing	30-Aug	13-Sep
5	Layout	14-Sep	28-Sep
6	Proofs	29-Sep	13-Oct
7	Printing	14-Oct	28-Oct
8	Distribution	29-Oct	12-Nov

4. In Cell **C6**, type **10-16** as the new date for this cell and tap the (ENTER) key.
   Cells in rows 7 and 8 will change to reflect the new date.

5. Close ☒ the Internet Explorer window.

Thus far, your workbook has been saved as a Web page, but by itself this does not make the page available over the Internet. In order for others to view the workbook over the Internet, you must *publish* the page to a *Web server*. You will learn how to do this in the next topic.

Publishing with Web Folders

In order for others to view your Web pages over the Internet or an intranet, the pages must be *hosted* on a Web server. The act of placing your Web pages into a folder on a Web server is called *publishing* the pages. Most *Internet service providers* (ISPs) provide their subscribers with at least a megabyte or more of free Web space. Many ISPs offer a variety of hosting plans and services to meet the needs of individuals, small businesses, and large corporations.

Publishing Methods

You can choose from several methods to publish your Web pages to a Web server. The method you choose depends on the capabilities of the ISP or corporate network system that hosts the Web site. Some of the easiest methods are listed in the following table.

Method	When to Use It
Web folders	Use this method if your operating system supports Web folders. Windows 95, 98, NT 4.0, and Windows 2000 all support the use of Web folders to publish Web pages.
Via FTP (File Transfer Protocol)	Use this method when there is no automated method to publish the pages. An FTP utility allows you to manually send your pages to the folder/directory in the hosting service system that will serve your pages.
ISP-provided utilities	Use this method when the ISP that hosts the Web site provides a special utility for publishing your Web pages.

Naming Web Pages

When you create your own Web pages, you should pay careful attention to their names. Many Web servers run on an operating system called UNIX, which has rules for naming files that differ from Windows. The following points will help you name the workbook files that you publish to the Web so that they are compatible with most Web server systems:

- **Never use spaces in the filenames of Web pages and graphics**—UNIX systems do not allow spaces in filenames.

- **Give the primary page on your Web site the name *index.htm*—**If someone browses to your folder with the URL, but does not type a filename, most Web servers will display the index.htm page automatically. If you do not have an index.htm page on your Web site, someone browsing your site may get an error message.

- **Try not to use uppercase letters in filenames**—Web page filenames are case-sensitive. On UNIX servers for example, *MyHomePage.htm* and *myhomepage.htm* represent different filenames. If you consistently use lowercase letters in the filenames for Web pages and graphics on your Web site, it is less likely that those browsing your site will receive an error message.

Linking the Workbook to a Web Page

When you post a workbook to the Web, you may want to include one or more hyperlinks to help users navigate to other Web pages. As is the case with other Office 2000 applications, Excel lets you insert hyperlinks wherever you need them.

HOW TO INSERT A HYPERLINK ONTO A WORKSHEET

Task	Procedure
Insert a hyperlink to another Web page onto a worksheet	■ Display the worksheet that will contain the hyperlink.
	■ Click in the cell that will contain the hyperlink.
	■ Click the Insert Hyperlink [icon] button on the toolbar.
	■ Fill in the dialog box, and click **OK**.

Hands-On 13.10 Insert Hyperlinks on Worksheets

In this exercise, you will insert a hyperlink to the Acme home page and then copy the hyperlink to the other worksheets in the workbook.

Insert the Hyperlink

1. *Rest*ore the **Excel** window by clicking its button on the Windows Taskbar.

2. Click the **Editing Schedule** worksheet tab.

3. Click Cell **A20;** then click the Insert Hyperlink [icon] button on the toolbar.
   The Insert Hyperlink dialog box will appear. This dialog box offers several different methods to place a hyperlink. You will use one of the easiest methods in this exercise.

4. Click the **Web Page** button on the right side of the dialog box.
   The Internet Explorer browser window will appear.

5. Follow these steps to navigate to the Acme Trading Co. Web page.

Address	http://www.offtowork.com/excel/lesson13

Ⓐ *Click in the **Address** bar, type the following URL:* **www.offtowork.com/excel/lesson13** *and then tap* (ENTER).

Ⓑ *Click the Acme Trading Co. button.*

Acme Trading Co.   Welcome to the W

   The simulated Acme Trading Company home page will be displayed. Notice the Web address (URL) in the address bar.

6. Click the **Excel** button on the Windows Taskbar to make it the active window.
   You are back to viewing the Insert Hyperlink dialog box.

(Continued on the next page)

7. Follow these steps to finish inserting the hyperlink.

A *Select the existing text in the* **Text to display** *box, then type* **Return to the Acme home page**.

B *Notice that the Web page address is now displayed in the dialog box.*

C *Click* **OK** *to insert the new hyperlink.*

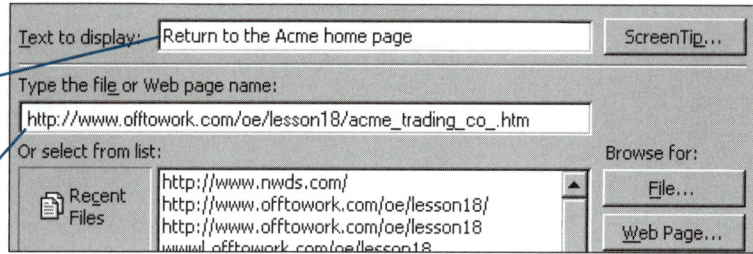

| Text to display: | Return to the Acme home page | ScreenTip... |

Type the file or Web page name:

http://www.offtowork.com/oe/lesson18/acme_trading_co_.htm

Or select from list: Browse for:

Recent Files
| http://www.nwds.com/ |
| http://www.offtowork.com/oe/lesson18/ |
| http://www.offtowork.com/oe/lesson18 |
| www.offtowork.com/oe/lesson18 |

File...

Web Page...

8. Point (don't click) over the new hyperlink you just created.
Notice how the mouse pointer changes to a small hand 🖑 *. This indicates that the cell is functioning as a hyperlink. Excel will also display a ScreenTip with the Web address (URL) of the linked Web page.*

Paste the Hyperlink

9. *Right-click* on the new hyperlink; then choose **Copy** from the pop-up menu as shown at right. If you give a normal click (left-click) by mistake, click the **Back** button on the left side of the toolbar, and you will return to the worksheet view.

Return to the Acme home
✂ Cut
📋 Copy

10. Click the **Layout Schedule** tab, click in Cell **A20,** and then click the Paste 📋 button on the toolbar.
The hyperlink you copied in Step 9 is pasted in the cell.

11. Click the **Production Schedule** tab, click in Cell **A16,** and then click the Paste 📋 button on the toolbar.

12. Save 💾 the Workbook.

Test the Hyperlink

13. Point on the hyperlink you just pasted until the pointer looks like a hand 🖑 ; then click.
An Internet Explorer window will appear to display the Acme home page. This may be a new window, or it may be a transformation of your Excel window.

14. Click the Back ⬅ button to return to the worksheet.
The Internet Explorer window transforms back into an Excel window. Leave the Excel window open.

Using Web Folders

Web Folders

Web folders allow you to publish Web pages and graphics with drag-and-drop ease. A Web folder is a folder on the computer that is directly associated with a folder on a Web server system. When you move or copy files to a Web folder, the files are automatically copied to the associated folder on the Web server system. Deleting files from a Web folder causes them to be deleted from their associated Web server folder.

SAVE A WORKBOOK TO A WEB FOLDER

Task	Procedure
Publish to a Web site with a Web folder.	■ Choose **File→Save as Web Page** from the menu bar.
	■ Click the **Web Folders** button on the left side of the dialog box, or click the *My Network Places* button if you are running Windows 2000.
	■ Double-click to open the desired Web folder.
	■ Complete the Save command normally.
Delete files from a Web site with a Web folder.	■ Open a *My Computer* or *Exploring* window; then open the *Web folders* folder or *My Network Places* if you are running Windows 2000.
	■ Open the Web folder from which you wish to delete files. Select any files you wish to delete; then click the **Delete** button on the toolbar.

Hands-On 13.11 Publish the Workbook

In this exercise, you will save your workbook in Web page format to a Web folder. You will then navigate to the URL (Web address) for the Web folder to view your files over the Internet or your school's intranet.

Before you begin, ask your instructor for the Web folder name, user name, and password you will use to access the appropriate Web folder. Complete these items of information on the lines below:

Web Folder Name: _____

User Name: _____ (optional)

Password: _____ (optional)

Publish to a Web Folder

1. Choose **File→Save as Web Page** from the menu bar.

2. Click the **Web Folders** button on the left side of the dialog box or click **My Network Places** if you are running *Windows 2000;* then follow these steps to save the workbook to a Web folder.

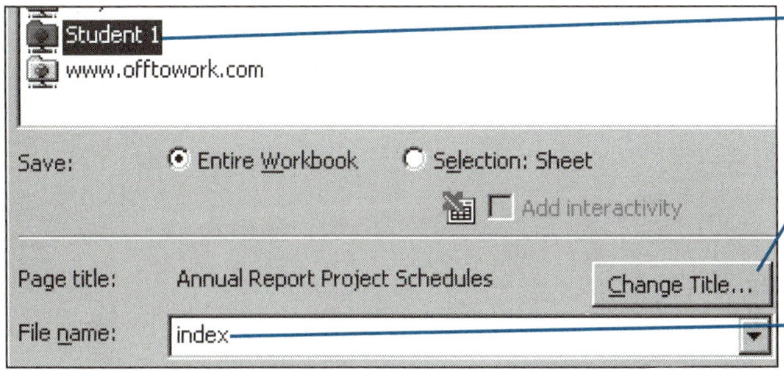

Ⓐ *Double-click on the Web folder you have been assigned for this lesson. Click* **OK** *if a dialog box appears asking you for a network password.*

Ⓑ *Click the* **Change Title** *button; then enter a title of:* **Annual Report Project Schedules** *and click* **OK**.

Ⓒ *Taking care to type in all* **lower-case** *letters, change the name of the workbook to* **index***, as shown here.*

Ⓓ *Click the* **Save** *button to convert the workbook to Web page format and save it to the Web folder. Click* **Yes** *if you are asked to replace an existing file.*

A Transferring File dialog box will appear to show the progress of the transfer as the workbook is transmitted to the associated Web server folder. Your workbook is now hosted on the Internet!

(Continued on the next page)

Display the Workbook Over the Internet

3. After the Transferring File window disappears, choose **File→Close** from the menu bar and Minimize ▬ the Excel window.

4. Open a My Computer window; then follow the instructions for your version of Windows as listed below:

   ■ **Windows 95, 98, NT 4.0**—If necessary, scroll down the My Computer window until the **Web Folders** icon is visible; then *double-click* to open Web Folders. If you do not see a Web Folders icon like the one at right toward the bottom of the My Computer window, then the Web folders feature is not installed on your computer. See your instructor for assistance.

   Web Folders

   ■ **Windows 2000**—Click the Up one Level button; then double-click on the *My Network Places* icon. You may see one or more Web folders along with other network resources.

   This window will display all of the available Web folders you may publish to. Depending on how your system is configured, there may be just one folder or several.

5. Double-click to open your assigned Web folder. Click **OK** if you are prompted to enter a user name and password, and the password is already filled in. Otherwise, fill in the user name and password you received earlier; then click **OK.**
   After a pause, the contents of the folder will be displayed. There may be some files displayed in this folder that belong to other students who have published their files.

6. After the contents of the folder are displayed, double-click the **index** file in the Web folder window.
   The Internet Explorer Web browser will start and display your workbook Web page over the Internet. Notice the URL in the Address bar *near the top of the Internet Explorer window. It should start with http://www.*

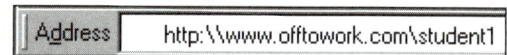

   | Address | http:\\www.offtowork.com\student1 |

7. Look over your workbook Web page. When you are done, leave the Internet Explorer window open.

TIP!

After you have completed this exercise, feel free to tell others the URL of your Web workbook. Your workbook will be displayed until another student uses this computer to perform a Hands-On exercise with this Web folder.

Importing from Web Pages (HTML Files)

Excel can import data from Web pages. Web pages are programmed and saved in a file format called HTML. A Web page can contain one or more data tables. In addition to the drag-and-drop and cut-and-paste techniques, you can also import tables from Web pages with a Web Query. A Web Query tells Excel to analyze the selected Web page and transfer all the data on the page, or just data from tables on the Web page. The data is transferred to cells on the desired worksheet in your workbook.

IMPORTING TABLES FROM WEB PAGES	
Task	**Procedure**
Import a table from an HTML file (Web page) onto an Excel worksheet.	■ Display the worksheet upon which you wish to import the table.
	■ Choose *Data→Get External Data→New Web Query* from the menu bar.
	■ Enter the filename of the HTML file; or click *Browse Web* to display the desired Web page from the Web with Internet Explorer and click the *Excel* button on the Windows taskbar to return to the Excel window.
	■ Choose the import options you wish to use; then click *OK*.
	■ Click the cell where you wish to import the data; then click *OK*.

Round Trips

When you save a workbook to the Web in a *non-interactive* Web page format, some features of the workbook are not available. For example, the formulas in the workbook will not work from within the Web browser window. However, all of the data in your workbook (including formulas and comments) are still stored in the Web page version. If you load the Web page version of the workbook back into Excel, you can restore the file to the native Excel format. Once this has been done, the formulas and other interactive features of the workbook are available again. The process of taking an Excel workbook from workbook (native) format to Web page (HTML) format then back again to workbook format is called a *round trip*. This process is shown in the diagram below.

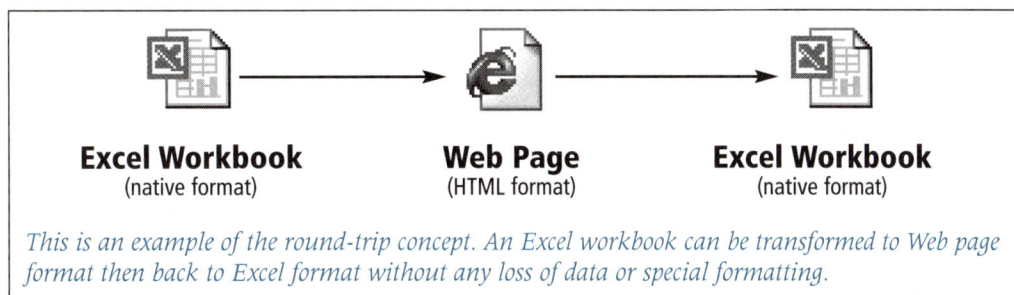

Excel Workbook
(native format)
→
Web Page
(HTML format)
→
Excel Workbook
(native format)

This is an example of the round-trip concept. An Excel workbook can be transformed to Web page format then back to Excel format without any loss of data or special formatting.

CONVERT A WEB FORMAT WORKBOOK BACK TO NATIVE FORMAT

Task	Procedure
Save an Excel workbook that is posted on the Web.	■ Open the workbook in Internet Explorer. ■ Click the **Edit** button on the Internet Explorer toolbar; then choose *Microsoft Excel* from the drop-down list. ■ Click **OK** if you are asked for a network password. ■ After the file has loaded in Excel, choose **File→Save As** from the menu bar. ■ Change the Save as type to *Microsoft Excel Workbook* format and click **OK**.

Hands-On 13.12 Perform a Round Trip with an Excel Workbook

In this exercise, you will load the Web page version of your workbook into Excel; then save it as a normal Excel workbook.

1. Make sure that the Web page version of your workbook is still displayed in the Internet Explorer window.

NOTE!

If you were unable to perform Hands-On Exercise 13.10, double-click the shortcut on the Desktop to your Annual Report *folder; then follow* Steps 10–12 of Hands-On Exercise 13.7 on page 378 *to open the Web page version of your workbook.*

2. Follow these steps to load the Web page version workbook into Excel.

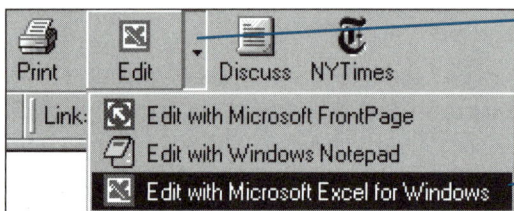

A *Click the **drop-down list** portion of the **Edit** button.*

B *Choose **Microsoft Excel** from the drop-down menu.*

You may receive a prompt that some files for this Web page are not in the expected location. This is a security feature to help you avoid files that might contain a computer virus. Since you created this file yourself, there is no need to worry.

3. Click **Yes** if you receive a notification that some files on this Web page are not in the expected location.

4. Click **OK** if you receive a prompt to enter a Web folder .

5. Click the various worksheet tabs to confirm that the Web page was loaded successfully from the Web site.

6. Choose **File→Save As** from the menu bar.

7. Follow these steps to finish saving the workbook in Excel format.

Ⓐ *Click the* **Favorites** *button on the dialog box; then double-click to open the* Annual Report *folder.*

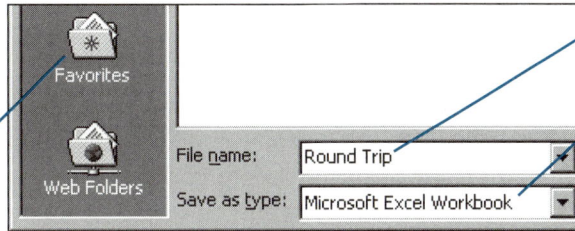

Favorites

Web Folders

File name: ⌊Round Trip⌋

Save as type: ⌊Microsoft Excel Workbook⌋

Ⓑ *Enter a new file name:* **Round Trip**.

Ⓒ *Click the* **Save as type** *box; then choose* **Microsoft Excel Workbook** *as shown here.*

Ⓓ *Click the* **Save** *button.*

8. Choose **File→Save As** from the menu bar.
Notice that the Save as type *box now reads* Microsoft Excel Workbook. *This indicates that you have successfully converted the workbook from the Web page format to the native Excel format (a round trip).*

9. Click the **Cancel** button to close the dialog box.

10. Close ☒ the Excel, Internet Explorer, and any open My Computer windows.

11. Drag the **Annual Report** shortcut to the *Recycle Bin* on the Desktop. Click **Yes** if you are asked to confirm the deletion.

Concepts Review

True/False Questions

1. Importing is the process of bringing in data from a non-native file format. TRUE FALSE

2. Exporting is the process of saving data in a non-native file format. TRUE FALSE

3. You can place an image in the background of a worksheet. TRUE FALSE

4. An attachment file can only contain a Web page. TRUE FALSE

5. You can always use any picture you save from the Web for any type of project. TRUE FALSE

6. A file format is a technique for saving data. TRUE FALSE

7. All of the features of a worksheet can be saved in Web page format. TRUE FALSE

8. You publish a workbook by saving it to the hard drive. TRUE FALSE

9. Publishing and saving a workbook are identical processes. TRUE FALSE

10. Interactivity lets users modify a worksheet while viewing it in Internet Explorer. TRUE FALSE

Multiple-Choice Questions

1. Which statement best describes an attachment to email?
   a. An attachment is really an email message.
   b. An attachment is a file that arrives as part of an email message.
   c. An attachment is an Excel file that may be viewed over the Internet.
   d. None of the above

2. Which of the following represent an export of a workbook?
   a. A workbook that has been saved as a series of tab-delimited text files—one for each worksheet
   b. A workbook that has been sent to a user in another country
   c. A workbook with several worksheets that has been saved as a single tab-delimited text file.
   d. All of the above

3. Which of the following statements best describes a Web folder?
   a. A Web folder copies any files you drag into it to a Web server.
   b. A Web folder is the name for any folder on a Web site.
   c. A Web folder is created automatically when you subscribe to an Internet Service Provider (ISP).
   d. All of the above

4. Which of the statements below best describes a round trip?
   a. You convert an Excel workbook that was in Web page format back to its native format.
   b. You send an Excel workbook to someone as an attachment to email and then receive it back with revisions.
   c. You copy and paste data into an Excel workbook from a text file and then convert the workbook into a text (tab delimited) format.
   d. None of the above

Macros and VBA

Many Excel workbooks are used on a recurring basis. Some examples include monthly expense accounts, sales forecasts, and databases of various types. Often, the same tasks are performed in these workbooks over and over. Excel allows you to create macros to automate repetitive tasks. In addition, Excel lets you assign macros to shortcut keys, custom toolbar buttons, and custom buttons in a worksheet. Excel and the other Office 2000 applications also let you use the Visual Basic for Applications (VBA) programming language to edit recorded macros and customize Excel. In this lesson, you will use macros, custom buttons, and VBA to automate procedures in an Excel worksheet.

In This Lesson

Case Study

The West County Vocational Training center is one of the most successful job training centers in its area. The administrators of the training center consider training the staff to be just as important as training the students who attend the center. Tina Johnson, the Administrative Secretary, has become a MOUS certified Excel user at the expert level. Tina is responsible for maintaining a roster of enrolled students, which she has set up in Excel. Tina decides to use macros to sort the roster in various ways. In addition, Tina adds custom buttons to the worksheet and attaches her macros to the buttons. Now with the click of a button, Tina can sort her roster as desired.

	A	B	C	D	E	F	G
1	**West County Vocational Training**						
2							
3	Instructor	Student	Section	Starting Date			
4	Allison	Ames, Alice	2	1/4/99			
5	Allison	Ames, Donna	1	1/8/99			
6	Allison	Ames, Jason	1	1/1/99			
7	Allison	Leno, Jane	1	10/23/99			
8	Allison	Turner, Ted	2	6/6/99			
9	Allison	Williams, Cora-Lee	1	3/6/99			
10	Allison	Yee, Donese	3	3/3/99			
11	Allison	Zobe, Wayne	2	10/10/99			
12	Dawes	Almore, Brian	3	10/11/99			
13	Dawes	Brown, Carl	3	2/10/99			
14	Dawes	Brown, Lisa	1	6/8/99			
15	Dawes	Carlson, Michael	2	10/20/99			
16	Dawes	Davis, Ted	2	3/11/99			
17	Dawes	Jackson, Mary	1	8/9/99			
18	Dawes	Jones, Al	2	3/4/99			
19	Smith	Ames, Donald	2	8/9/99			
20	Smith	Carey, Harry	3	6/6/99			
21	Smith	Carey, Mary	3	5/5/99	Sort by Section		
22	Smith	Ellsworth, Sid	3	3/17/99			
23	Smith	Norman, Will	2	3/2/99	Sort by Instructor		
24	Smith	Sorrell, Barbara	1	9/12/99			
25	Smith	Tomei, Mel	2	2/23/99			
26	Smith	Wilson, Wanda	1	10/22/99			

Macros

A macro is a set of instructions that can be played back at any time. Macros are useful for automating routine tasks, especially if those tasks are lengthy.

Recording Macros

Excel's macro recording feature can record your keystrokes and the commands you issue. You can then play back a recorded macro at a later time. This is similar to the automatic redial feature on telephones. The redial feature allows you to record frequently used phone numbers that can subsequently be redialed by pressing one or two keys. Similarly, macros can easily play back recorded keystrokes and commands.

Assigning Macros

Macros should be designed to save time and help you become more productive. In order for this to occur, macros must be easy to run, especially if you use the same macro repeatedly. Excel lets you assign macros to shortcut keystrokes and to various objects, including toolbar buttons, menus, and custom buttons within a worksheet. You can run a macro by issuing a shortcut keystroke or clicking the object to which the macro is assigned.

Creating Macros for the Current Workbook Only

Macros are only available in the workbook you create them in unless you assign them to the **Personal Macro Workbook.** The Personal Macro Workbook makes macros available in all workbooks on your computer system. This is useful if the macro can be used in various workbooks. For example, you may want a macro to format headings with a format you are particularly fond of. You could create a macro to accomplish this and then make the macro available to all workbooks. You will assign macros to the Personal Macro Workbook later in this lesson. Some macros, however, are useful only in a particular workbook. For example, in the first few Hands-On exercises, you will develop a macro to sort worksheet rows in a specific manner. The macro will only be useful in the workbook in which it is created.

Quick Reference

RECORDING A MACRO

- Develop the worksheet, and prepare to record the macro.
- Choose Tools→Macro→Record New Macro from the menu bar.
- Type a descriptive name in the Macro Name box. Do not use spaces in the name, because spaces are not allowed in macro names.
- Click **OK** to begin recording.
- Execute the commands and procedures you want the macro to record.
- Click the Stop ■ button on the Macro toolbar when you have finished recording.

1. Open the workbook named **Hands-On Lesson 14.**

2. If necessary, use the Zoom Control until you can see 25 rows in the worksheet.
   Take a moment to review the worksheet. Notice that it contains a list of students. Each student has been assigned to an instructor. Also notice that the list isn't sorted in any particular order. The goal of the next few exercises is to be able to add new students to the bottom of the list. The list will then be sorted, and the new students will move to the appropriate locations in the list. You will record macros to automate the sorting process.

   Keep in mind that it is usually best to practice the procedure you wish to automate before you actually record the macro. This will help you avoid mistakes during the recording process. In this exercise, you will skip the practice steps because you will be guided step-by-step through the recording process.

3. Choose **Tools→Macro→Record New Macro** form the menu bar.
   The Record Macro dialog box appears.

4. Follow these steps to name the macro and begin the recording process.

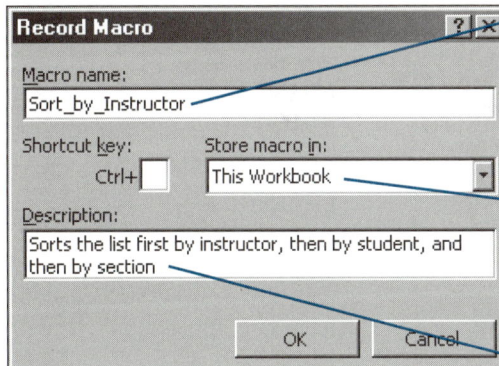

A *Type* **Sort_by_Instructor** *here. Use the underscore character between words instead of spaces. Spaces are not allowed in macro names.*

B *Make sure this option is set to* This Workbook. *The macro would be available in all workbooks if* Personal Macro Workbook *were chosen.*

C *Type the description shown here.*

5. Click **OK,** and the macro will begin recording your actions.
   The Stop Recording button and toolbar should appear somewhere in the worksheet. If it doesn't appear, then display it with the View→Toolbars→Stop Recording command.

6. Click Cell A5.
   The purpose of this action is to position the highlight somewhere in the list. You learned in an earlier lesson that Excel selects all rows in a list when you use the Sort command. By positioning the highlight in Cell A5, you can be certain that Excel will select the list prior to sorting it. This action has been recorded by the macro, and the highlight will move to Cell A5 when the macro is run.

7. Choose **Data→Sort** from the menu bar.
   The macro won't actually record this action until the Sort command is completed.

(Continued on the next page)

8. Follow these steps to set the Sort parameters.

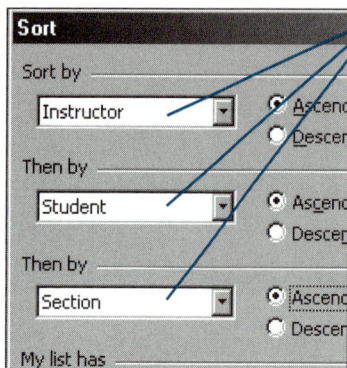

Ⓐ *Set the three sort keys as shown here. You will need to click the drop-down button on each list.*

Ⓑ *Click **OK**.*

The list should be sorted as shown below. Keep in mind that the macro recorded this sort sequence.

	A	B	C	D
1	West County Vocational Training Student Roster			
2				
3	Instructor	Student	Section	Starting Date
4	Allison	Ames, Alice	2	1/4/99
5	Allison	Ames, Donna	1	1/8/99
6	Allison	Ames, Jason	1	1/1/99
7	Allison	Turner, Ted	2	6/6/99
8	Allison	Williams, Cora-Lee	1	3/6/99
9	Allison	Yee, Donese	3	3/3/99
10	Dawes	Brown, Carl	3	2/10/99
11	Dawes	Brown, Lisa	1	6/8/99
12	Dawes	Davis, Ted	2	3/11/99
13	Dawes	Jackson, Mary	1	8/9/99
14	Dawes	Jones, Al	2	3/4/99
15	Smith	Ames, Donald	2	8/9/99
16	Smith	Carey, Harry	3	6/6/99
17	Smith	Carey, Mary	3	5/5/99
18	Smith	Ellsworth, Sid	3	3/17/99
19	Smith	Norman, Will	2	3/2/99
20	Smith	Sorrell, Barbara	1	9/12/99
21	Smith	Tomei, Mel	2	2/23/99

9. Click the Stop Recording ■ button to stop the recording process.
The macro is now ready to be played back.

Running Macros

Macros can be run in a variety of ways. The method used to run a macro depends upon how the macro was assigned during the recording process. In the previous exercise, you created a macro without assigning it to a button, toolbar, or shortcut key. For this reason, you must run the macro with the standard procedure shown in the following Quick Reference table. This procedure can be used to run any macro recorded in the current workbook, even if the macro was assigned to a button, toolbar, or shortcut key.

Quick Reference

RUNNING MACROS IN THE CURRENT WORKBOOK

■ Choose Tools→Macro→Macros from the menu bar.

■ Choose the desired macro from the Macro Name list.

■ Click the Run button.

Hands-On 14.2 Add New Students, and Run the Macro

1. Click Cell A22.
   Students will always be added to the end of this list.

2. Add this student to the list.

   | 22 | Allison | Zobe, Wayne | 2 | 10/10/99 |

3. Choose **Tools→Macro→Macros** from the menu bar.
   The Sort_by_Instructor macro should be the only macro on the list. However, there may be one or more macros that are preceded by the phrase PERSONAL.XLS. If you see a personal macro, then there are personal workbook macros on your system. Personal workbook macros are available to all workbooks. You will work with personal workbook macros later in this lesson.

4. Choose Sort_by_Instructor, and click the **Run** button.
   The list should be sorted, and Zobe, Wayne should move to Row 10 and become the last of Instructor Allison's students.

5. Click Cell A23, and add this student to the list.

   | 23 | Dawes | Almore, Brian | 3 | 10/11/99 |

6. Use Steps 3 and 4 above to run the macro.
   Keep in mind that you can have the highlight anywhere in the worksheet when you run the macro. This is because the first step in the macro moves the highlight to Cell A5. The list is then sorted properly because Cell A5 is within the list.

7. Save the changes to the workbook, and continue with the next topic.
   The macro is saved with the workbook. If you were to close the workbook, the macro would be available the next time you opened the workbook.

Using Custom Buttons in Worksheets

Excel has a Forms toolbar with buttons to assist you in creating online forms. Online forms can have various types of controls to assist users in data entry, decision making, and other tasks.

The Button ⬚ control lets you insert custom buttons in worksheets. You can assign macros to custom buttons. A macro assigned to a custom button is run whenever the button is clicked. You can position custom buttons anywhere in a worksheet. A custom button can also have descriptive text to help identify its function or the macro that is assigned to it.

Quick Reference

ASSIGN A MACRO TO A CUSTOM BUTTON

■ Record the macro.

■ Create a button by clicking Button ⬚ on the Forms toolbar and then clicking in the worksheet. The Forms toolbar is displayed with the View→Toolbars→Forms command.

■ Choose the desired macro from the Assign Macro dialog box, and click OK.

■ Select the button text and type the desired replacement text.

■ If necessary, resize the button, and drag it to the desired worksheet location.

Hands-On 14.3 Assign Macros to Buttons

Create a Button

1. Choose **View→Toolbars→Forms** from the menu bar.
   This will display the Forms toolbar.

2. Click the Button ⬚ button.

3. Click the mouse pointer in an open part of the worksheet.
   A button will be created, and the Assign Macro dialog box will appear.

4. Choose Sort_by_Instructor from the list, and click **OK.**

Widen the Button, and Move It

5. Follow this step to widen the button.

   A *Drag a side-sizing handle until the button is approximately this wide.*

6. Follow these steps to move the button.

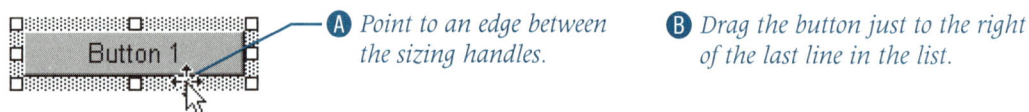

   A *Point to an edge between the sizing handles.*   **B** *Drag the button just to the right of the last line in the list.*

Edit the Button

7. Drag the mouse pointer over the Button 1 text, and it will become selected, as shown to the right.

8. Type the phrase **Sort by Instructor**, and it will replace the Button 1 text.

9. Click outside the button, and it should have the appearance shown to the right.

Sort by Instructor

10. Right-click the button, and choose **Edit Text** from the pop-up menu.
    The insertion point will be positioned within the button text. At this point, you can edit the text, drag a sizing handle, or move the button. Make any adjustments to the button until it matches the example shown in the preceding illustration.

11. Click outside the button to deselect it.

Add Students, and Run the Macro by Clicking the Button

12. Add this student in Row 24.

| 24 | Dawes | Carlson, Michael | 2 | 10/20/99 |

13. Click the **Sort by Instructor** button to run the macro.
    The new record should be sorted into the list.

14. Add these two students to the bottom of the list.

| 25 | Smith | Wilson, Wanda | 1 | 10/22/99 |
| 26 | Allison | Leno, Jane | 1 | 10/23/99 |

15. Click the **Sort by Instructor** button to run the macro.

Record Another Macro

16. Choose **Tools→Macro→Record New Macro** from the menu bar.

17. Type **Sort_by_Section** in the Macro name box.
    There is no need to type a description for this macro.

18. Click **OK** to begin the recording process.

19. Click Cell A5 to position the highlight within the list.

20. Choose **Data→Sort** from the menu bar.

21. Set the first two sort fields as shown to the right, and set the third sort field to (none).

22. Click **OK** to complete the sort.

23. Click the Stop Recording ■ button to stop the recording process.
    Take a few moments to make sure the worksheet is sorted correctly. The rows should be sorted first by section, and then each section should be sorted by instructor.

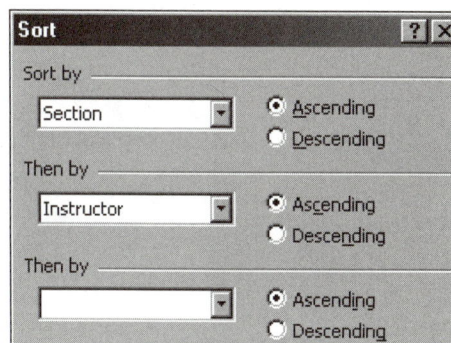

Assign the Macro to a Button

24. Click Button 🔲 on the Forms toolbar, and click in the worksheet to create a button.

25. Choose **Sort_by_Section** from the Assign Macro box, and click **OK.**

26. Drag the button to a position just above the **Sort by Instructor** button.

27. Widen the button until it is the same width as the **Sort by Instructor** button.

28. Select the Button 2 text, and type the phrase **Sort by Section**.

(Continued on the next page)

Create Another Sort Macro and Button

29. Use the techniques you have just learned to create another macro named Sort_by_Start_Date that sorts the list first by the Starting Date and then by the Section. Make sure you click somewhere in the list as the first step in the recording process.

30. Assign the macro to a new button.

31. Position the new button above the **Sort by Section** button.

32. Widen the button until it is the same width as the other two buttons.

33. Change the button text to **Sort by Start Date**.

Run the Macros

34. Click any of the buttons to change the way the list is sorted.

35. Click each button several times to make sure the macros are functioning correctly.
Keep in mind that the macros in this worksheet will probably be useful only in this worksheet. You can use macros to automate any routine task (like sorting). However, macros like those you just created are only useful if the worksheet is used on an ongoing basis. In the following sections, you will create macros that can be used with a variety of workbooks.

36. Save the changes to your workbook, and continue with the next topic.

The Personal Macro Workbook

Macros are only available in the workbook they are created in unless you assign them to the Personal Macro Workbook. Macros in the Personal Macro Workbook are available to all workbooks on your computer system. This workbook is normally hidden from view. Later in this lesson, you will learn to unhide the Personal Macro Workbook to enable you to delete macros from it.

Quick Reference

ASSIGN A MACRO TO THE PERSONAL MACRO WORKBOOK

■ Choose Tools→Macro→Record New Macro from the menu bar.

■ Click the *Store macro* in drop-down button and choose Personal Macro Workbook.

■ Name the macro, and record the macro as you would any other macro.

In this exercise, you will create a macro that formats text. This macro will be available in all workbooks because you will assign it to the Personal Macro Workbook. Formatting macros are good candidates for the Personal Macro Workbook because they can help ensure consistent and rapid formatting across workbooks.

Begin Recording

1. Click Cell A1.

2. Choose **Tools→Macro→Record New Macro** from the menu bar.

3. Type **FormatTitle** as the macro name.

4. Choose *Personal Macro Workbook* from the *Store macro in* list.

5. Click **OK** to begin recording. You will need to click **Yes** to replace the macro if Excel tells you it already exists.

Format the Title While the Macro Records

6. Set the font size to 14, and click the Bold **B** button.

7. Use the Font Color **A** button to choose any color.

8. Click the Stop Recording button.

Use the Macro in Another Workbook

9. Click the New button to start a new workbook.
Notice that a new button appears on the Windows Taskbar at the bottom of the screen. Excel 2000 displays a separate button for each open workbook.

10. Enter the phrase **This is a test heading** in Cell A1.

11. Make sure the highlight is in Cell A1; then choose **Tools→Macro→Macros** form the menu bar.

12. Take a few moments to study the names in the Macro Name list.
Notice that the macros you recorded in the other workbook have a Hands-On Lesson 14 prefix. These macros are only available in the Hands-On Lesson 14 workbook because they were not assigned to the Personal Macro Workbook. Also notice the macro named PERSONAL.XLS!FormatTitle. Personal Macro Workbook macros are always preceded by the PERSONAL.XLS! prefix, and they can be used in all workbooks.

13. Choose PERSONAL.XLS!FormatTitle, and click the **Run** button.
The heading should be formatted exactly as in the other workbook.

14. Leave the workbook open because you will continue to use it.

Shortcut Keys

Excel lets you assign macros to shortcut keys. You can run a macro assigned to a shortcut key by pressing the shortcut key combination. This technique is useful for running Personal Workbook Macros in any workbook. You must use the (CTRL) key or (CTRL)+(SHIFT) as part of the shortcut key combination.

> **ASSIGNING MACROS TO SHORTCUT KEYS**
>
> ■ Choose Tools→Macro→Record New Macro from the menu bar.
>
> ■ Click the Shortcut Key box and enter the desired keystroke.
>
> ■ Record the macro.

Hands-On 14.5 Assign a Macro to a Shortcut Key

In this exercise, you will create another macro that formats the list headings. You will assign the macro to the Personal Macro Workbook, and you will assign it a shortcut key.

Record the Macro

1. Click the **Hands-On Lesson 14** button on the Windows Taskbar.
   The Hands-On Lesson 14 workbook should be displayed.

2. Select the list headings in Row 3.

3	Instructor	Student		Section	Starting Date

3. Choose **Tools→Macro→Record New Macro** from the menu bar.

4. Type **FormatHeadings** as the Macro Name.
   Notice that the Store macro in option is set to Personal Macro Workbook. The most recent Store macro in setting remains in effect until it is changed again.

5. Follow these steps to assign the shortcut key.

   Ⓐ *Click in the Shortcut key box, and type a lower case k. This assigns the Shortcut key (CTRL)+k to the macro. You could also press the (SHIFT) key while typing the k to assign the (CTRL)+(SHIFT)+k keystroke combination.*

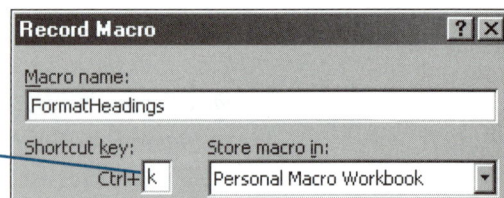

   Ⓑ *Make sure the Store macro in option is set to Personal Macro Workbook.*

6. Click **OK** to begin recording the macro. If Excel warns you that another macro is already using the (CTRL)+k shortcut key, then click **OK** and enter a different letter in the shortcut key box.

Format the Headings

7. Click the Bold **B** button.

8. Click the Font Color **A** button to apply the most recently used font color.

9. Use the Fill Color button to apply a fill color to the cells.
   If you chose a poor color combination, feel free to choose another. The macro will record (and later play back) all these actions, but the end result will be the desired combination.

10. Click the Stop Recording ▪ button to turn off the recording process.

This macro will now be available in all workbooks on your computer system.

Use the Macro

11. Click the **Book2** button on the Windows Taskbar.

This will switch you to the new workbook that you started in the previous exercise.

12. Type the headings shown to the right in Row 3.

3	Date	Name	Payment

13. Select the headings you just typed.

14. Press the (CTRL) key while you tap the letter **k** on your keyboard.

The macro will format the headings with the same formatting you applied in the other workbook. You can now use this macro to format headings in any workbook. Notice how the shortcut keys were fast and easy to use; however, they must be memorized. A shortcut key works well if you use the macro often and you can memorize the shortcut key. In the next topic, you will assign a macro to a toolbar button that will also be available to all workbooks.

15. Choose **File→Close**, and choose **No** when Excel asks if you want to save the workbook.

This will close the new workbook and return you to the Hands-On Lesson 14 workbook. Leave the Hands-On Lesson 14 workbook open because you will continue to use it.

Customizing Toolbars

Earlier in this lesson, you assigned macros to buttons within a worksheet. Unfortunately, worksheet buttons are only available in the worksheet in which they were created. You can overcome this shortcoming by assigning macros to toolbar buttons. Excel allows you to add new custom buttons to toolbars. You can even create your own custom toolbars. Toolbars are available in all workbooks, so you can use custom toolbar buttons to run Personal Workbook Macros. Assigning macros to toolbars is convenient because there is no need to remember shortcut keystrokes.

Quick Reference

CUSTOMIZING TOOLBARS

To assign a macro to a toolbar button:

- ■ Right-click any toolbar, and choose Customize from the pop-up menu.
- ■ Click the Commands tab.
- ■ Scroll through the Categories list, and choose Macros.
- ■ Drag the smiley face custom button from the dialog box to any toolbar.
- ■ Click the Modify Selection button in the Customize dialog box, and choose Assign Macro from the pop-up menu.
- ■ Choose the desired macro, and click OK.

In a previous exercise, you created the FormatTitle macro. In this exercise, you will assign this Personal Workbook Macro to a custom toolbar button.

1. Follow these steps to display the Customize dialog box.

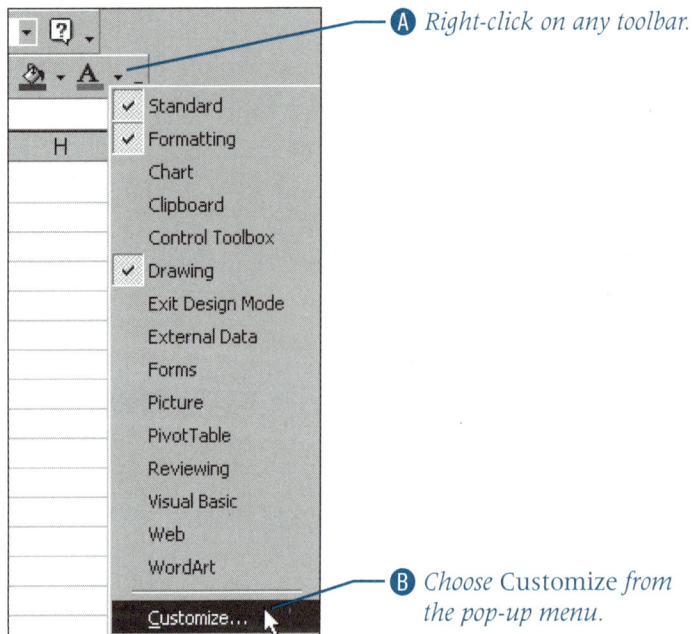

Ⓐ *Right-click on any toolbar.*

Standard ✓
Formatting ✓
Chart
Clipboard
Control Toolbox
Drawing ✓
Exit Design Mode
External Data
Forms
Picture
PivotTable
Reviewing
Visual Basic
Web
WordArt
Customize...

Ⓑ *Choose* Customize *from the pop-up menu.*

2. Click the Commands tab in the Customize dialog box.

3. Scroll through the Categories list, and choose Macros.
   The custom button smiley face will appear on the Commands list.

4. Follow these steps to add a button to the Formatting toolbar.

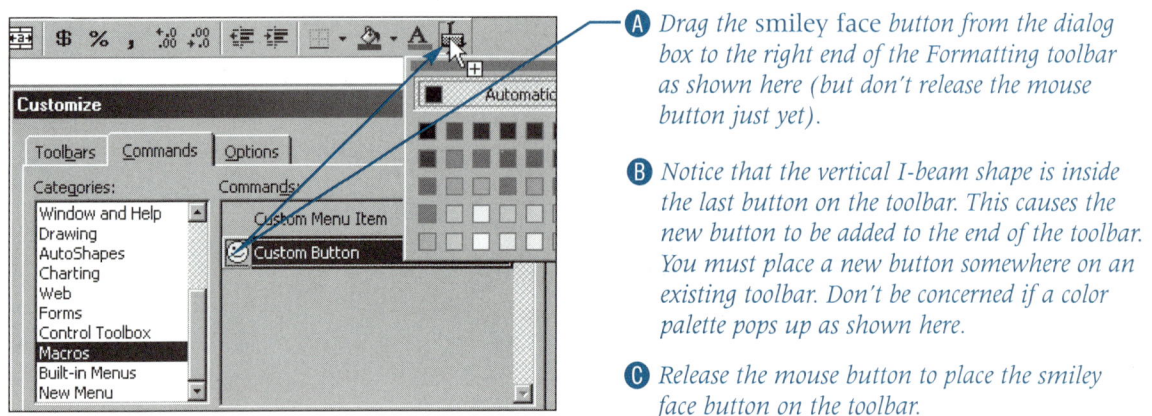

Customize

Toolbars | Commands | Options

Categories:
Window and Help
Drawing
AutoShapes
Charting
Web
Forms
Control Toolbox
Macros
Built-in Menus
New Menu

Commands:
Custom Menu Item
Custom Button

Automatic

Ⓐ *Drag the* smiley face *button from the dialog box to the right end of the Formatting toolbar as shown here (but don't release the mouse button just yet).*

Ⓑ *Notice that the vertical I-beam shape is inside the last button on the toolbar. This causes the new button to be added to the end of the toolbar. You must place a new button somewhere on an existing toolbar. Don't be concerned if a color palette pops up as shown here.*

Ⓒ *Release the mouse button to place the smiley face button on the toolbar.*

5. Click the **Modify Selection** button in the Customize dialog box, and choose Assign Macro from the bottom of the pop-up menu.

6. Choose the PERSONAL.XLS!FormatTitle macro, and click **OK.**
   The macro has been assigned to the button. Leave the Customize dialog box open because you will continue to use it in the next exercise.

Using Descriptive Text on Custom Buttons

Excel allows you to use descriptive text (such as a macro name) on a custom button. This makes it easy to identify the macro assigned to a button. In the following exercise, you will use this technique to replace the smiley face with descriptive text.

ADD DESCRIPTIVE TEXT TO A CUSTOM BUTTON

- Right-click any toolbar, and choose Customize from the shortcut menu.
- Click the button that you wish to customize.
- Click the Modify Selection button in the Customize dialog box.
- Type the desired text in the Name box of the shortcut menu.
- Choose *Text only (Always)* from the shortcut menu, and close the Customize box.

Hands-On 14.7 Add Descriptive Text to the Custom Button

The Customize dialog box should still be open from the previous exercise.

1. Follow these steps to add text to the button.

Ⓐ *Click the **Modify Selection** button.*

Ⓑ *Type the text* **FormatTitle** *in the **Name** box.*

Ⓒ *Choose **Text Only (Always)**. The button should now have the FormatTitle text on it as shown on the toolbar at the top of this illustration.*

2. Click the **Close** button on the Customize dialog box.

(Continued on the next page)

Use the Button in a New Workbook

3. Click the New [ ] button.

4. Enter the phrase **This is a test** in Cell A1.

5. Make sure the highlight is in Cell A1, and then click the FormatTitle button on the toolbar.
   The macro should run and format Cell A1 with the formatting options set earlier in this lesson. Once again, this toolbar button and the corresponding macro are now available to all workbooks on this computer system.

6. Choose **File→Close,** and then choose **No** to close the workbook without saving the changes.
   Leave the Hands-On Lesson 14 workbook open because you will continue to use it.

Deleting Macros and Buttons

You can delete macros using the procedure outlined in the following Quick Reference steps. However, any shortcut keys or buttons that have been assigned the macros will no longer function. You can delete a custom worksheet button by right-clicking the button and choosing Cut from the pop-up menu. A custom toolbar button can be deleted by displaying the Customize dialog box and dragging the desired button from the toolbar into the dialog box. You can drop the button anywhere in the Customize dialog box.

DELETE A WORKBOOK MACRO

- Open the workbook that contains the macro.
- Choose Tools→Macro→Macros from the menu bar.
- Choose the macro from the Macro Name list, click Delete, and confirm the deletion.

Deleting Macros from the Personal Macro Workbook

Excel stores Personal Workbook Macros in the Personal Macro Workbook. The Personal Macro Workbook is always open; however, it is normally hidden from view. In order to delete macros from the Personal Macro Workbook, you must first unhide the workbook. The macros can then be deleted using the procedure in the preceding Quick Reference table. When you are finished, you should hide the Personal Macro Workbook. Hiding and unhiding workbooks is discussed in the next topic.

Hands-On 14.8 Delete a Workbook Macro and Button

Delete the Sort by Start Date Macro

1. Choose **Tools→Macro→Macros** from the menu bar.

2. Choose the Sort_by_Start_Date macro.

3. Click the **Delete** button, and then click **Yes** to confirm the deletion.

Delete the Sort by Start Date Button

4. Right-click on the **Sort by Start Date** button in the worksheet, and the shortcut menu will appear.

5. Choose **Cut** to delete the button.

Hiding and Unhiding Worksheets and Workbooks

Excel lets you hide worksheets and entire workbooks from view. This is done for a variety of reasons. For example, you may want to hide an important sheet in a workbook to prevent inexperienced users from damaging it. Also, you must unhide the Personal Macro Workbook if you want to delete Personal Workbook macros. The following Quick Reference table describes how to hide and unhide worksheets and workbooks.

HIDING AND UNHIDING WORKSHEETS AND WORKBOOKS

Hide and Unhide Worksheets

- ■ Choose Format→Sheet from the menu bar, and choose Hide or Unhide.

Unhide a Workbook

- ■ Choose Window→Unhide from the menu bar.
- ■ Choose the desired workbook from the Unhide box, and click OK.

Hide a Workbook

- ■ Open the workbook, or switch to the workbook if it is already open.
- ■ Choose Window→Hide from the menu bar.

Hands-On 14.9 Delete a Personal Workbook Macro and Toolbar Button

Unhide the Personal Macro Workbook

1. Choose **Window→Unhide** from the menu bar.
   The Unhide dialog box lists all hidden workbooks. The Personal workbook will usually be the only workbook displayed in this dialog box.

2. Choose Personal, and click **OK.**
   Excel will display the Personal Macro Workbook, although it will appear to be empty. Even though the Personal Macro Workbook appears to be empty, you must still have it open if you want to delete macros from it.

Delete the FormatHeadings macro

3. Choose **Tools→Macro→Macros** from the menu bar.

4. Choose the FormatHeadings macro.

5. Click the **Delete** button, and then click **Yes** to confirm the deletion.
   Keep in mind that you could not have deleted this macro if you had displayed the Macro dialog box from the Hands-On Lesson 14 workbook. The macro would have been displayed in the Macro dialog box, but Excel would not have let you delete it. You can only delete Personal Macro Workbook macros by first unhiding the Personal Macro Workbook.

6. Choose **Window→Hide** to hide the Personal Macro Workbook.
   You should always hide the Personal Macro Workbook after deleting macros from it.

(Continued on the next page)

7. Right-click the FormatTitle button on the toolbar, and choose Customize from the pop-up menu.

8. Drag the FormatTitle button from the toolbar into the dialog box.

9. Drop the button anywhere in the dialog box, and it will vanish.

10. Close the Customize dialog box.

11. Save the changes to your workbook, and continue with the next topic.

Visual Basic for Applications

Visual Basic for Applications is a programming language that runs within Office 2000 applications. Visual Basic can be used to automate processes within applications and to customize applications. When you record a macro in Excel, you are creating a Visual Basic module that contains programming instructions. Excel's macro recorder constructs a sequence of Visual Basic statements that are executed when the macro is run. The remainder of this lesson will introduce you to Visual Basic. However, a complete discussion of Visual Basic is beyond the scope of this course.

Using Modules to Edit Macros

A module is an Excel sheet where Visual Basic code is entered during the recording of a macro. Modules are normally hidden from view. You can edit a recorded macro by displaying the macro's Visual Basic module and deleting or modifying the Visual Basic code. You can also add new code to a module. To display a module, you choose **Tools→Macro→Macros** from the menu bar, choose the desired macro, and click the **Edit** button. This command sequence starts the Visual Basic Editor, and the module appears in the Visual Basic Editor window. The Visual Basic Editor is a program independent of Excel. The Visual Basic Editor has its own menus, toolbars, and commands that allow you to develop, edit, and test Visual Basic applications. The illustration on the next page shows the Visual Basic Editor window. The programming code shown in the right side of the window is the code from a macro that you will record in the next Hands-On exercise.

```
Microsoft Visual Basic - Hands-On Lesson 14.xls - [Module2 [Code]]
File  Edit  View  Insert  Format  Debug  Run  Tools  Add-Ins  Window  Help
                                                                    Ln 2, Col 2

Project - VBAProject                    (General)              InsertSchoolName

  VBAProject (Hands-On Lesson 14.xls)     Sub InsertSchoolName()
    Microsoft Excel Objects               '|
      Sheet1 (Sheet1)                     ' InsertSchoolName Macro
      Sheet2 (Sheet2)                     ' Macro recorded 7/31/1999 by Brian
      Sheet3 (Sheet3)                     '
      ThisWorkbook
    Modules                               '
      Module1
      Module2                                 Range("A1").Select
  VBAProject (PERSONAL.XLS)                   ActiveCell.FormulaR1C1 = "West County Training"
                                              With Selection.Font
                                                  .Name = "Arial"
                                                  .Size = 12
                                                  .Strikethrough = False
Properties - Module2                              .Superscript = False
Module2 Module                                    .Subscript = False
                                                  .OutlineFont = False
Alphabetic  Categorized                           .Shadow = False
(Name)  Module2                                   .Underline = xlUnderlineStyleNone
                                                  .ColorIndex = xlAutomatic
                                              End With
                                              Selection.Font.Bold = True
                                              Selection.Font.ColorIndex = 3
                                          End Sub
```

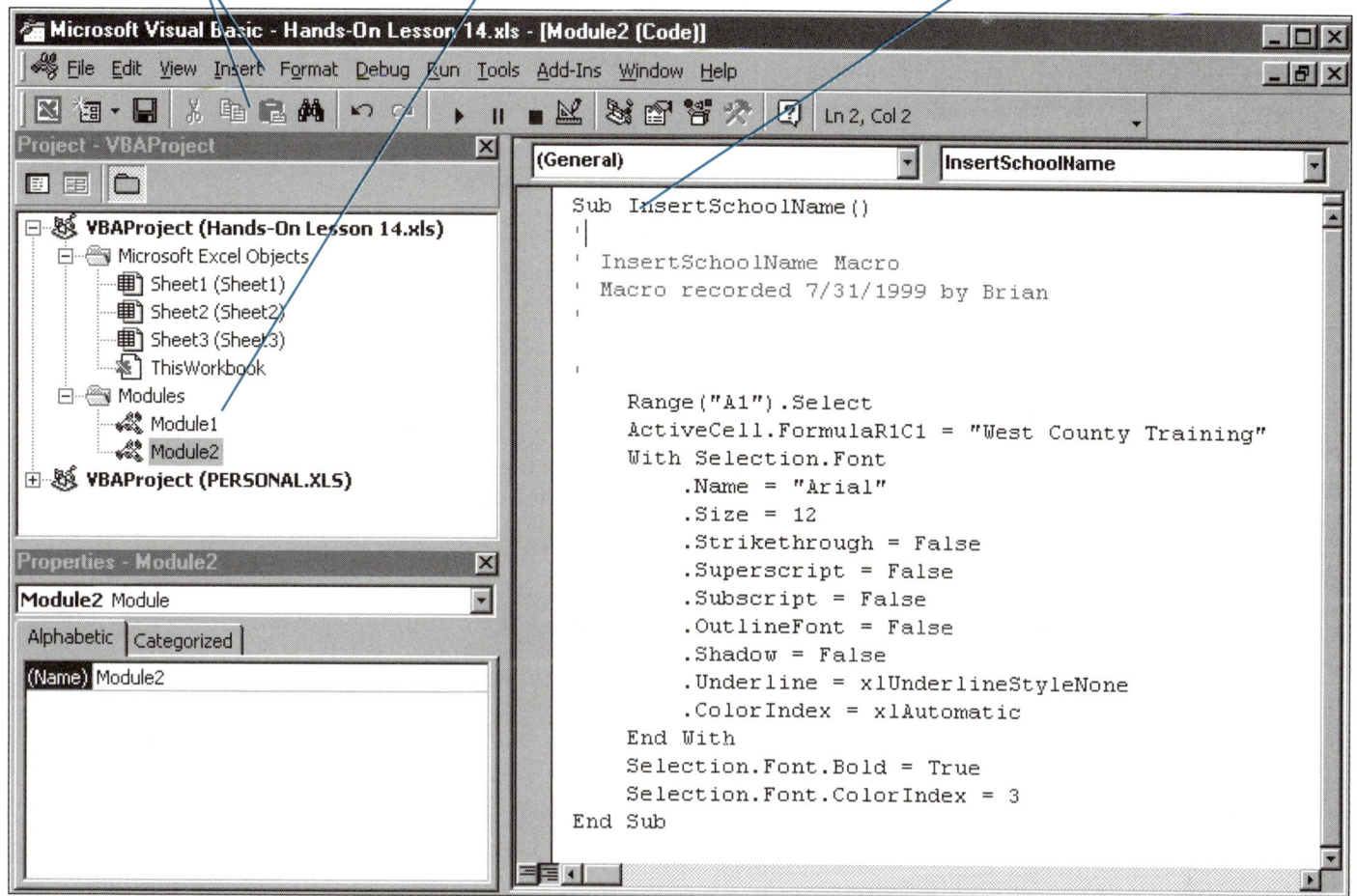

Hands-On 14.10 Record a Macro, and Display the Module

In this exercise, you will record a new macro in the Hands-On Lesson 14 workbook that inserts and formats a title. You will also display the Visual Basic Editor to view the macro code.

Clean Up the Title Cell

1. Click any blank cell in the worksheet, and then click the Format Painter ⟨brush icon⟩.

2. Click Cell A1 to copy the formats to the title.
   This will remove all formats from the title.

3. Tap (DELETE) to remove the title.

Record the Macro

4. Choose **Tools→Macro→Record New Macro** from the menu bar.

5. Type the name **InsertSchoolName** in the Macro name box.

6. Set the *Store macro in* option to This Workbook, and click **OK** to begin recording.

7. Click Cell A1 (even if the highlight is already in the cell).
   The macro will record your mouse click as a selection command.

(Continued on the next page)

8. Type the name **West County Training** in Cell A1, and click the Enter ☑ button on the Formula bar to complete the entry.
Using the Enter button will keep the highlight in Cell A1.

9. Set the font size to 12, and click the Bold **B** button.

10. Use the Font Color **A▾** button to choose any color.

11. Click the Stop Recording **■** button.

Test the Macro

12. Click any blank cell in the worksheet, and then click the Format Painter **🖌**.

13. Click Cell A1 to copy the formats to the title.

14. Tap (DELETE) to remove the title.

15. Choose **Tools→Macro→Macros** from the menu bar.

16. Choose the InsertSchoolName macro, and click the **Run** button.

Display the Module Window

17. Choose **Tools→Macro→Macros** from the menu bar.

18. Choose InsertSchoolName from the Macro name list, and click the **Edit** button.
The Microsoft Visual Basic editor will open in a separate program window. The InsertSchoolName macro code will be displayed in the right pane of the window.

19. Follow these steps to explore the modules list in the left pane of the window.

Ⓐ *Notice the* Modules *folder in the left pane. Module 3 is highlighted, so its code is displayed in the right pane.*

Ⓑ *Double-click another module to display its code in the right pane.*

Ⓒ *Now double-click the module with the macro code* InsertSchoolName *(Module 3 in this illustration).*

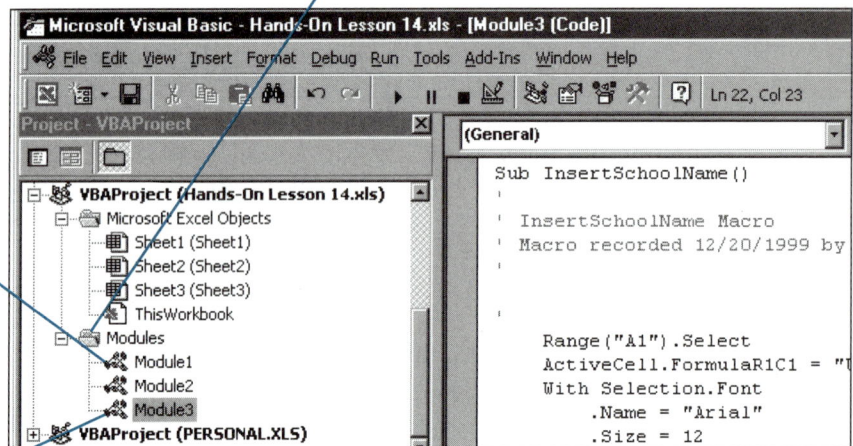

Objects, Methods, and Properties

Visual Basic recognizes all Excel items as objects. Some examples of objects include an entire worksheet, a chart, and a range. Object names form an important part of the syntax of many Visual Basic statements. For example, the first significant statement in the macro you just recorded is:

Range ("A1") .Select

This Visual Basic statement specifies an **object** (the Range A1) and an action to be performed upon that object (Select). The Select action is known as a **method.** Visual Basic objects (like the range object) can have many methods or actions performed upon them. The Visual Basic statement described above simply instructs Excel to select the Range A1. This instruction was inserted in the module when you clicked Cell A1 during the recording process.

Properties are another important part of Visual Basic syntax. Many objects can have one or more properties associated with them. For example, one of the statements in your macro is:

Selection.Font.Size = 12

This statement specifies that the selection should be assigned a font size of 12. In this statement, 12 is the property, Selection is the object, and Font.Size is the method.

Modifying Code In Visual Basic Modules

Once the Visual Basic Editor window is open, you can modify the code within the module window. For example, in the InsertSchoolName macro you may want to change the font size property from 12 to 14, or perhaps you would like to change the text that is inserted in Cell A1. You can make these changes directly in the module window and then close the Visual Basic Editor when finished. The modified macro will play back the next time you run the macro.

Hands-On 14.11 Edit the Macro

The Visual Basic Editor window should be displayed from the previous exercise. The InsertSchoolName module should be displayed on the right side of the window.

Edit the Macro

1. Follow these steps to modify the macro code.

```
(General)                                InsertSchoolName

Sub InsertSchoolName()
'
'  InsertSchoolName Macro
'  Macro recorded 7/31/1999 by Brian
'
'
    Range("A1").Select
    ActiveCell.FormulaR1C1 = "West County Vocational Training"
    With Selection.Font
        .Name = "Arial"
        .Size = 14
        .Strikethrough = False
        .Superscript = False
        .Subscript = False
        .OutlineFont = False
        .Shadow = False
        .Underline = xlUnderlineStyleNone
        .ColorIndex = xlAutomatic
    End With
    Selection.Font.Bold = True
    Selection.Font.ColorIndex = 5
End Sub
```

A *Notice the Sub and End Sub statements at the beginning and end of the module. Your macro routine is enclosed within these statements.*

B *Click to the right of the word County, and insert the word* **Vocational***, as shown here. This statement instructs Excel to insert the indicated phrase in Cell A1.*

C *Change the font size property from 12 to* **14***.*

D *Change the color assigned to the entry to* **5***, which is the property setting for the color blue.*

2. Take a few moments to review the code in the module window.
   Try to understand the objects, methods, and properties associated with the various statements.

3. When you have finished reviewing the code, click the Close ☒ button at the top right corner of the Visual Basic Editor window.

Run the Edited Macro

4. Click Cell G4.

5. Choose **Tools→Macro→Macros** from the menu bar.

6. Choose the InsertSchoolName macro, and click the **Run** button.
   Notice that the title in Cell A1 is now formatted with a 14-point blue font, and the word Vocational has been included in the title. Also, the macro inserted the modified title in Cell A1 even though the highlight was in Cell G4 when you ran the macro. This is because the Range statement at the start of the macro selected Cell A1.

7. Feel free to customize your macros using the techniques you have learned in this section.

8. When you have finished, save the changes to your workbook, and then close the workbook.

Concepts Review

True/False Questions

1. Personal Workbook Macros are only available in the workbook in which they were created.   TRUE   FALSE

2. Excel lets you create macros by recording your keystrokes and commands.   TRUE   FALSE

3. Macro names cannot contain spaces.   TRUE   FALSE

4. The Tools→Macro→Macros command is used to record a new macro.   TRUE   FALSE

5. The Personal Macro Workbook is always open, but it is normally hidden from view.   TRUE   FALSE

6. Macros can be assigned to shortcut keys.   TRUE   FALSE

7. The Customize dialog box is used to assign a macro to a customized toolbar button.   TRUE   FALSE

8. You can edit Visual Basic code using the Visual Basic Editor window.   TRUE   FALSE

Multiple-Choice Questions

1. Which of the following commands is used to record a new macro?
   a. Tools→Record New Macro
   b. Tools→Macro→Macros
   c. Tools→Macro→Record New Macro
   d. None of these

2. Which of the following commands can be used to run a macro?
   a. Tools→Macro→Run Macro
   b. Tools→Macro→Macros
   c. Tools→Record Macro→Run
   d. None of these

3. Which command is used to unhide the Personal Macro Workbook?
   a. Tools→Macro→Unhide
   b. Window→Unhide
   c. Format→Workbook→Unhide
   d. None of these

4. Where is the Visual Basic code for a macro stored?
   a. Module
   b. Object
   c. Property
   d. Method

Skill Builders

Skill Builder 14.1 Create a Personal Workbook Macro

In this exercise, you will create a macro that selects an entire worksheet, widens the columns, and formats all cells with bold. You will assign the macro to the Personal Macro Workbook.

Begin Recording the Macro

1. Start a new workbook and choose **Tools→Macro→Record New Macro** from the menu bar.

2. Type the macro name **FormatSheet** in the Record Macro dialog box.

3. Set the *Store macro in* option to Personal Macro Workbook.

4. Click **OK** (replace the macro if it already exists) to begin the recording process.

Set the Desired Formats

5. Click the Select All [ ] button at the top left corner of the worksheet.

6. Click Bold **B** to bold all cells.

7. Choose **Format→Column→Width** from the menu bar.

8. Type **12** in the Column Width box, and click **OK.**

9. Click the Stop Recording [■] button.

Run the Macro

10. Choose **File→Close,** and choose **No** when Excel asks if you want to save the workbook.

11. Start a new workbook, and choose **Tools→Macro→Macros** to display the Macro dialog box.

12. Choose the PERSONAL.XLS!FormatSheet macro, and click the **Run** button.
    The column and text formats will be set. Keep in mind that you can apply virtually any cell, column, text, or number format with a macro. Only your needs and creativity limit you.

Delete the Macro from the Personal Macro Workbook

13. Choose **Window→Unhide** from the menu bar.

14. Choose Personal from the Unhide box and click **OK.**
    The Personal Macro Workbook will appear.

15. Choose **Tools→Macro→Macros** from the menu bar.

16. Choose the FormatSheet macro from the list.

17. Click the **Delete** button, and then click **Yes** to confirm the deletion.

18. Choose **Window→Hide** to hide the Personal Macro Workbook.
    In this exercise, you deleted the macro to keep the computer system "clean." Normally, you would leave Personal Macro Workbook macros on the system, so they could be used in all workbooks.

19. Close the empty workbook without saving it.

Skill Builder 14.2 **Create a Print macro**

In this exercise, you will create a print macro that maximizes the print area by switching the orientation to Landscape and reducing the margins. The macro will also change the default footer. You will store the macro in the Personal Macro Workbook to make it available to all workbooks.

Begin Recording

1. Start a new workbook, and choose **Tools→Macro→Record New Macro.**

2. Type the macro name **Maximize_Print_Area** in the Record Macro dialog box.

3. Set the *Store macro in* option to Personal Macro Workbook.

4. Click **OK** (replace the macro if it already exists) to begin the recording process.

Set the Desired Page Setup Options

5. Choose **File→Page Setup** from the menu bar.

6. Click the Page tab, and click the Landscape orientation button.

7. Click the Margins tab, and set all four margins to **.5**.

8. Click the Header/Footer tab.

9. Choose a Footer that will print just the filename.
   The filename footer option will be listed as Book1 or Book2, etc. depending upon the name of the current workbook.

10. Click **OK** to complete the Page Setup options.

11. Click the Stop Recording ▣ button.

12. Close the workbook without saving it.

Run the Macro

13. Start a New Workbook, and enter the phrase **This is a test** into Cell A1.

14. Choose **Tools→Macro→Macros** from the menu bar.

15. Choose the PERSONAL.XLS!Maximize_Print_Area macro, and click the **Run** button.
   Your screen will probably flash while the macro sets up the page. This will take a few moments.

16. Click the Print Preview 🔍 button. The page should have the landscape orientation and other Page Setup options you recorded in the macro.
   Keep in mind that you could assign this (and any other Personal Macro Workbook macro) to a shortcut key or to a customized toolbar button.

17. Close Print Preview; then close the workbook without saving it.

Skill Builder 14.3 Create a Formatting Macro

In this exercise, you will create a macro that formats numbers with a floating currency format. Many Excel users prefer this format to the fixed dollar sign format that is applied by the Currency button on the Formatting toolbar. The floating format is a good candidate for a macro. This is because you normally have to apply this format with the Format Cells dialog box, which can be time-consuming and cumbersome.

Begin Recording the Macro

1. Start a new workbook, and enter the number **100000** in Cell A1.
   You will format this number while recording the macro. This way, you can be certain the proper format has been applied to the number.

2. Make sure the highlight is in Cell A1; then choose **Tools→Macro→Record** New Macro.

3. Type the name **Floating_Currency_Format**.

4. Make sure the *Store macro in* option is set to Personal Macro Workbook.

5. Click the Shortcut key check box, and type a lowercase **c** in the box.
   This will set the shortcut key to (CTRL)+*c.*

6. Click **OK** (replace the macro if it already exists) to begin the recording process.

Set the Currency Format

7. Choose **Format→Cells** from the menu bar, and click the Number tab.

8. Choose Currency from the Category list, and set the Decimal Places to 0.

9. Make sure the Symbol box is set to dollar sign $.

10. Leave the Negative Numbers format as it is, and click **OK.**
    The number should be formatted with the floating currency format, $100,000.

11. Click the Stop Recording ■ button.

Use the Macro in a Worksheet

12. Close the workbook without saving the changes.

13. Open the workbook named Skill Builder 14.3.

14. Select Cells B6:E6 in Row 6.

15. Press (CTRL)+C, and the floating currency format should be applied to the cells.
    (CTRL)+C was the shortcut keystroke you assigned to your macro.

16. Use your macro to apply the floating currency format to the subtotals in Rows 10 and 14 and the totals in Row 16. You will need to select the cells first and then press (CTRL)+c. Once again, this macro can be used in any workbook because you assigned it to the Personal Macro Workbook.

17. Save the changes to the workbook, and then close the workbook.

Skill Builder 14.4 Assign a Macro to a Button

In this exercise, you will open a workbook from your diskette. You will create a macro that deletes rows from the workbook. You will copy one of the existing buttons in the worksheet and then assign the macro to the new button.

Begin Recording

1. Open the workbook named **Skill Builder 14.4,** and Excel will display a message box indicating that the workbook contains macros that may have viruses.
This is a warning message to protect you against macro viruses.

2. Click the **Enable Macros** button to open the workbook.
Notice that this workbook is a duplicate of the Hands-On Lesson 14 workbook you used throughout the Hands-On exercises in this lesson. Now you will add a button that deletes students from the list.

3. Click Cell A8.
You will delete Ted Turner from the list and have the macro record this action.

4. Choose **Tools→Macro→Record New Macro** from the menu bar.

5. Type the name **Delete_Students**.

6. Set the *Store macro in* option to This Workbook.
This macro will only be used in this workbook.

7. Click **OK** to begin the recording process.

Delete Row 8

8. Choose **Edit→Delete** from the menu bar.

9. Choose the Entire Row option, and click **OK** to delete the row.

10. Click the Stop Recording ▣ button.

Copy a Button, and Assign a New Macro to the Copied Button

11. Right-click the **Sort by Section** button, and choose **Copy** from the shortcut menu.

12. Click anywhere in the worksheet, right-click the button again, and choose **Paste** from the shortcut menu.
Excel will paste a copy of the button slightly off of the original button.

13. Drag the copied button up, and drop it just above the **Sort by Section** button.

14. Select the text on the copied button, and change it to **Delete Students**.

15. Click outside the button to deselect it.

16. Right-click the Delete Students button again, and choose Assign Macro from the menu.

17. Choose the Delete_Students macro, and click **OK.**

(Continued on the next page)

Move the Buttons to the Top of the Worksheet

In the next few steps, you will move the buttons to the top of the worksheet. The buttons are currently in the rows you will delete. They would be deleted with the rows if you were to leave them there. For this reason, you will move them to the top of the worksheet.

18. Click Cell A2, and choose **Insert→Rows** from the menu bar.
    You will position the buttons in Rows 2 and 3 between the title and headings.

19. Right-click the Delete Students button to select it.
    The button must be selected in order to move it.

20. Drag the button to the top of the worksheet just below the title.
    The button should be somewhere in Rows 2 and 3.

21. Drag the other buttons to the locations shown below.

	A	B	C	D	E	F
1	**West County Vocational Training**					
2	Delete Students		Sort by Section		Sort by Instructor	
3						
4	Instructor Student		Section Starting Date			

Freeze the Header Rows

In the next two steps, you will freeze Rows 1–4 with the Window→Freeze Panes command. This way, the heading row and the buttons will always be visible.

22. Click Cell A5.

23. Choose **Window→Freeze Panes** from the menu bar.

Use the Button to Delete Several Rows

24. Click Cell A18.
    The Al Jones row needs to be deleted.

25. Click the **Delete Students** button, and the row should be deleted.

26. Use your new button to delete Row 20 (the Mary Carey row).
    You will need to click in the row first and then click the Delete Students button.

27. Select Rows 5 and 6 by dragging the mouse pointer over the row headings at the left end of the rows.

28. Click the **Delete Students** button.
    Both Alice Ames and Donna Ames should be deleted.

29. Feel free to delete additional Rows or add students to the bottom of the list. Use the **Sort by Section** and **Sort by Instructor** buttons to sort the list. These buttons have the same sorting macros assigned to them as you created earlier in this lesson.

30. Save the changes, and then close the workbook.

Assessments

Assessment 14.1 Create a Macro that Inserts the Date

In this assessment, you will create a macro that inserts the phrase "Today's Date" in Cell A1 and the TODAY() function in Cell A2. The macro will also format the two cells. You will assign the macro to the current workbook only.

Record the Macro

1. Start a new workbook, and begin recording a new macro. Give the macro the name **Assessment_14_1**, set the *Store macro in* option to This Workbook, and assign the shortcut keystroke (CTRL)+d to the macro. Your macro should record all of the actions in Steps 2–7 below.

2. Enter the phrase **Today's Date** into Cell A1.

3. Format Cell A1 with an Arial 16 Bold Italic font, and use the Font Color ⬛ button to apply a color to the text.

4. Enter the **=TODAY()** function in Cell A2.
   This function should insert the current date in the cell.

5. Left Align ⬛ the date in Cell A2.

6. Format Cell A2 with an Arial 12 Bold Italic font, and use the Font Color ⬛ button to apply the same color you used in Cell A1.

7. Set the width of Column A to 20.

8. Stop the macro recording.

Undo the Changes, and Test the Macro

9. Use Undo ⬛ to undo all the actions the macro recorded.
   The worksheet should be back in the original state it was in prior to recording the macro. However, the macro has been saved and can be used to restore the changes at any time.

10. Run the macro.
    If your macro does not insert and format the text and widen Column A as discussed above, then you will need to record it again or edit it.

11. Once your macro is functioning properly, delete the contents of Cells A1 and A2, and restore their formatting to the default settings. You can use the Format Painter to copy the formats from any empty cell to Cells A1 and A2.

12. Set the width of Column A to **8.43** (the default width).
    Your worksheet should look like a new worksheet.

13. Save the workbook as **Assessment 14.1.**

Demonstrate the Macro

14. Demonstrate the macro to your instructor by using the (CTRL)+D keystroke combination.

15. After demonstrating the macro, save the changes to your workbook, and then close it.
    This will preserve the data entry, formatting, and column width adjustments the macro has made.

Assessment 14.2 Create Macros and Assign them to Buttons

1. Open the workbook named **Assessment 14.2.**

2. Create three macros for use in this workbook only, and assign them to buttons as shown in the following table. The table describes the button text, macro names, and macro function for each button. Position the buttons as shown in the completed worksheet on the following page.

Button text	Macro name	Macro function
Sort by Patron	Sort_by_Patron	Sort the list in ascending order based upon the patron names in Column A.
Sort by Details	Sort_by_Details	Sort the list in ascending order based upon the details in Column C.
Currency Format	Currency_Format	Format the current cell (or selected cells) with a floating currency format with 0 decimals. The floating currency format must be set with the Format Cells dialog box. This macro will be used to format the detail entries in Column C.

3. Test your macros until they function correctly.

4. Remove the Currency format from all entries in Column C in preparation for demonstrating the macros to your instructor.

Demonstrate the Macros

5. Demonstrate the sort buttons to your instructor.

6. Use **Sort by Details** as the final sort demonstration.

7. Demonstrate the **Currency Format** button by formatting all number entries in Column C with the Floating Currency format.

8. When you have finished demonstrating, your worksheet should have the appearance shown on the next page.

9. Close the workbook, and save the changes.

	A	B	C	D	E
1	**Annual Holiday Donation Drive**				
2					
3	**Patron**	**Type of Donation**	**Details**		
4	Sato, Michael	Money	$5		
5	Turner, Jane	Money	$10		
6	Townsend, Brian	Money	$25		
7	Bixby, Bill	Money	$50		
8	Sinhg, Ricky	Money	$65	Sort by Patron	
9	Carlson, Wanda	Money	$100		
10	Leonard, Leroy	Food	Canned Goods	Sort by Details	
11	Williams, Bernice	Food	Canned Goods		
12	Kester, Glenn	Food	Dried Goods	Currency Format	
13	Williams, John	Food	Turkey		

Critical Thinking

Critical Thinking 14.1 On Your Own

Ted is a student intern working in the accounting department of a food and beverage distribution company. As a student intern, Ted is constantly given assignments that require him to organize information in Excel worksheets. He prepares the worksheets and then provides the accountants in the department with the completed worksheets. Most of the accountants are interested primarily in the subtotal and total rows. Ted has been instructed to format the subtotals and totals with a consistent format for use throughout the department. Help Ted set up two Personal Workbook Macros. The first macro will be used to format subtotal rows that allow them to stand out in worksheets. You can use bold face type, colors, or fill patterns. The second macro will be used to format total rows in the same fashion. Try to create some consistency between the formats you use for the subtotal and total rows. The formats and macros should be designed so that they can be used in a wide range of worksheets. Also, assign the macros to shortcut keys that are easy to remember. This will make it easy to run the macros.

Critical Thinking 14.2 On Your Own

Cindy Clements is Ted's immediate supervisor in the accounting department. Cindy needs to prepare a report on the dollar value of returned items for the prior quarter. She gives Ted all of the returned-items reports for the prior quarter and instructs Ted to organize them in a single Excel worksheet. She provides Ted with the following information.

Category / Subcategory	Q1	Q2	Q3
Food Items			
Packaged Goods	$1,250	$1,350	$2,250
Breads and Grains	$750	$550	$800
Fruits and Vegetables	$450	$230	$475
Household Items			
Cleaners	$545	$655	$345
Utensils	$345	$785	$215
Beverages			
Alcoholic	$2,345	$1,345	$2,800
Soft Drinks	$1,235	$2,445	$935
Bottled Water	$350	$450	$540
Pet Items			
Food	$345	$225	$645
Toys	$120	$340	$520
Health	$235	$215	$135

Set up a worksheet with subtotal rows for each category. You should have subtotal rows for Food Items, Household Items, Beverages, and Pet Items. Add a total row that totals the categories for each quarter. Use the formatting macros that you set up in Critical Thinking 14.1 to format the subtotal and total rows. Save the completed workbook with a descriptive name.

Critical Thinking 14.3 Web Research

Use Internet Explorer to visit the Web site of Microsoft Corporation at www.microsoft.com. Microsoft's home page has a search box where you can search for Web pages and articles relating to the search text you enter. Conduct a search for VBA. This will display numerous pages and articles relating to Visual Basic for Applications. Browse through the various articles and pages searching for any that may be of interest. If you are interested in learning more about Visual Basic for Applications, Microsoft's Web site is a great place to begin searching for information. You will find links to many good books and examples of VBA code written by professional programmers.

Critical Thinking 14.4 As a Group

Set up a contact list in a new workbook. Include the firstname, lastname, company, street address, city, state, zip code, and phone number in separate columns. Include at least six contacts. You can fabricate all of the contact information or use friends, family, or business associates as the contacts. Format the contact list as desired, and then copy the contact list to two other sheets in the workbook.

Choose three classmates to whom you will email the workbook. Name the worksheet tabs using the names of your three classmates. Email the workbook to the first of your classmates. Instruct your classmate to create a macro for only the current workbook that sorts the contact list on the lastname field. Instruct your classmate to attach the macro to a button in the first worksheet. Instruct your classmate to forward the workbook to the classmate listed on the second worksheet tab when he or she has finished. Have the second classmate create a macro that sorts the list on the company field. Have the classmate insert a button in the second worksheet and attach the macro to the button. Repeat this process for the third classmate, instructing that classmate to create a macro that sorts on the zip code field. Finally, instruct the third classmate to send the workbook back to you.

Databases

Excel is often used to store organized lists of information or databases. Excel worksheets provide the perfect structure for organizing such data. In addition, Excel provides several tools to help you enter, view, and analyze data stored in a database structure. In this lesson, you will set up a database and use Excel's Data Form tool to enter data into the database. In addition, you will use subtotals to analyze data and filters to view data in various ways.

In This Lesson

Case Study

National Computing Solutions is a nationwide provider of customized hardware and software solutions for businesses. Donna Boyer, the National Sales Manager, wants to track and analyze the sales performance of her sales representatives. Donna wants the sales data separated by hardware and software sales. In addition, she wants to organize the sales representatives by region and position. You will develop a database that lets Donna organize the data and analyze it using subtotals and filters. The database you will create is shown below, subtotaled on the Region field.

	A	B	C	D	E	F	G
1	National Computing Solutions						
2	1999 Sales Database						
3							
4	Name	Years Employed	Position	Region	State	SW Sales	HW Sales
5	Wilson, Bernie	1	Sales Rep	Central	IL	120,000	170,000
6	Thomas, Will	2	Sales Rep	Central	IL	230,000	120,000
7	Cain, Mary	5	Senior Sales Rep	Central	IL	234,000	560,000
8				**Central Total**		584,000	850,000
9	Hubbs, Daniel	4	Telemarketer	Eastern	FL	340,000	230,000
10	Smith, Michael	5	Telemarketer	Eastern	MA	123,000	230,000
11	Watson, Tom	8	Sales Rep	Eastern	MA	230,000	340,000
12	Williams, Michael	3	Sales Rep	Eastern	FL	120,000	340,000
13	Martinez, Carlos	4	Senior Sales Rep	Eastern	FL	450,000	450,000
14				**Eastern Total**		1,263,000	1,590,000
15	Smith, Bob	3	Sales Rep	Western	CA	200,000	180,000
16	Zain, Beth	7	Senior Sales Rep	Western	CA	340,000	800,000
17	Alvizo, Alex	7	Senior Sales Rep	Western	CA	450,000	340,000
18	Brown, Bill	3	Telemarketer	Western	CA	546,000	120,000
19	Richards, Paul	4	Telemarketer	Western	WA	234,000	546,000
20	Cray, Zip	6	Telemarketer	Western	WA	900,000	780,000
21				**Western Total**		2,670,000	2,766,000
22				**Grand Total**		4,517,000	5,206,000

Excel Databases

Databases let you store and manage sets of related data. For example, in this lesson, you will create a database that holds sales data for sales representatives. The database will store all of the information for the sales representatives. The database will also let you analyze the sales data with automatic subtotaling and filters.

Records

Databases are composed of records, and each record contains the same type of data. For example, your sales representative database will have one record for each sales representative. In Excel, each row in the database is a record.

Fields

Each record in a database is divided into fields. Records can have many fields. For example, your sales representative database will have fields for the sales representative's name, position, length of employment, and sales results. In Excel, each column in the database is a field.

Database Tools

Excel provides a number of features that are designed specifically to work with databases. For example, Excel can display a data entry form to make it easy to enter records into a database. You can easily sort databases, find records, create subtotals, and analyze data.

Setting Up a New Database

You create a database as you would create any other worksheet. However, there are three rules you should follow when setting up a new database. These rules are described in the following illustration.

Rule 1: Always give the database the name Database *as shown here. Many of Excel's tools will identify a range named* Database *as a database.*

	A	B	C	D	E	F	G
1	National Computing Solutions						
2	1999 Sales Database						
3							
4	Name	Years Employed	Position	Region	State	SW Sales	HW Sales
5							
6							

Rule 2: Always use column headings for the first row in the database. These column headings become the field names that identify the fields in the database.

Rule 3: Always select the column headings and one blank row when naming the database. The blank row lets you use the data form to enter new records into the database.

Hands-On 15.1 Set Up the Database

Adjust Column Widths, and Enter the Data

1. Start Excel to display a new workbook.
2. Make sure the highlight is somewhere in Column A, and choose **Format→Column→Width** from the menu bar.
3. Set the width to **17**, and click **OK.**
4. Adjust the other column widths as shown in the following table.

Columns	Use this width
B and C	15
D and E	Leave as is
F and G	11

5. Enter the data shown below.

	A	B	C	D	E	F	G
1	National Computing Solutions						
2	1999 Sales Database						
3							
4	Name	Years Employed	Position	Region	State	SW Sales	HW Sales

Name the Database

6. Follow these steps to name the database.

(A) Select the range A4:G5 as shown below. Make sure you select the empty cells in Row 5 as shown. Also, select only the cells shown (not the entire rows).

Database = Name

	A	B	C	D	E	F	G
1	National Computing Solutions						
2	1999 Sales Database						
3							
4	Name	Years Employed	Position	Region	State	SW Sales	HW Sales
5							
6							

*(B) Click in the **Name** box, type* **Database**, *and tap* (ENTER).

You should always name a database using the technique above. Including the blank cells in the selection allows Excel's Data Form tool to identify the location where new rows are to be added. It is also important to use the name Database. *The data form tool easily identifies this name, as do many of Excel's other database tools.*

(Continued on the next page)

Format the Cells and Numbers

7. Follow these steps to format several cells.

Ⓐ *Use the Center Align [icon] button to center the Years Employed heading and the blank cell below it.*

Ⓑ *Use the Right Align [icon] button to right align Cells F4 and G4.*

4	Name	Years Employed	Position	Region	State	SW Sales	HW Sales
5							

8. Follow these steps to format two blank cells.

Ⓐ *Select Cells F5 and G5.*

4	Name	Years Employed	Position	Region	State	SW Sales	HW Sales
5							

Ⓑ *Click the Comma Style [icon] button.*

Ⓒ *Click the Decrease Decimal [icon] button twice.*

You won't be able to see the Comma Style in Cells F5 and G5 until you enter numbers in those cells. All the formats you just set will be carried to each new record you add to the database.

9. Save the workbook as **Hands-On Lesson 15.**

Data Forms

The **Data→Form** command displays the Data Form dialog box. Data forms make it easy to enter, edit, and locate records in a database. When you issue the **Data→Form** command, Excel automatically identifies a database that has been given the name Database and displays a record in the data form.

Hands-On 15.2 Use the Data Form to Enter Records

1. Choose **Data→Form** from the menu bar.
   Excel will identify your database (because you named it Database) and display the data form.

2. Follow these steps to enter the first record.

A Notice that Excel uses the field names from your database as labels for the boxes in the data form.

B Type the name **Smith, Bob** in the **Name** box, then tap the [TAB] key on the keyboard to move to the **Years Employed** field.

C Enter the data in the rest of the form as shown here. Use [TAB] to complete each entry and move to the next field.

D When you have finished entering the data in this record, click the **New** button to insert the record in the database and to prepare to enter another record.

3. If necessary, drag the Data Form dialog box slightly until you can see your database.
Notice that the record has been inserted below the heading row. The data form was able to insert the record in this location because you included a blank row in the selection when you named the database in the previous exercise. Also notice that the numbers in Cells F5 and G5 have the Comma Style you set in the previous exercise.

4. Enter the following 13 records into the database.
You will need to click the New button after typing the data for each record. Make sure you enter all the records, because you will need the data throughout this lesson. Also, there is no need to type the comma in the SW Sales and HW Sales numbers. Excel will format the numbers with the Comma format as they are entered in the database.

Name	Years Employed	Position	Region	State	SW Sales	HW Sales
Hubbs, Daniel	4	Telemarketer	Eastern	FL	340,000	230,000
Smith, Michael	5	Telemarketer	Eastern	MA	123,000	230,000
Watson, Tom	8	Sales Rep	Eastern	MA	230,000	340,000
Williams, Michael	3	Sales Rep	Eastern	FL	120,000	340,000
Martinez, Carlos	4	Senior Sales Rep	Eastern	FL	450,000	450,000
Wilson, Bernie	1	Sales Rep	Central	IL	120,000	170,000
Thomas, Will	2	Sales Rep	Central	IL	230,000	120,000
Cain, Mary	5	Senior Sales Rep	Central	IL	234,000	560,000
Zain, Beth	7	Senior Sales Rep	Western	CA	340,000	800,000
Alvizo, Alex	9	Senior Sales Rep	Western	CA	450,000	340,000
Brown, Bill	3	Telemarketer	Western	CA	546,000	120,000
Richards, Paul	4	Telemarketer	Western	WA	234,000	546,000
Cray, Zip	6	Telemarketer	Western	WA	900,000	780,000

(Continued on the next page)

5. Make sure you click the **New** button after entering the last record.
   This button inserts the record into the database. This step is necessary because you will use the form to browse through and edit the records in the next few steps. You would lose the last record if you browsed prior to using the New button.

6. Click the **Find Previous** button until the Alvizo, Alex record is displayed.

7. Click in the Years Employed field, and change the 9 to a **7**.

8. Use the vertical scroll bar in the data form dialog box to scroll through the records.

9. Try dragging the scroll box [ ] up or down, and notice that the record number is displayed at the top right corner of the data form box.

10. Move to record 4; then move to record 10.

11. Notice the **Delete** and **Restore** buttons on the data form.
    The Delete button permanently deletes a record, and Restore lets you reverse your last action such as an editing change. However, Restore will not let you recover a deleted record.

12. Click the **Close** button to return to the database.

13. Save the changes to your workbook, and continue with the next topic.

Using Criteria to Find Records in a Data Form

The Data Form has a **Criteria** button that lets you locate records by specifying logical search criteria. For example, you may want to find a record where the Name = Smith, Bob or you may want to find the next record where SW Sales >700000. You can use the same logical operators (< > =) with search criteria as you can use with IF and other logical functions. You can also use the asterisk * wildcard character with search criteria. This character is convenient if you know only the first part of the name or word for which you are searching. For example, you could search for Smith* in the Name field, and Excel would locate the first record beginning with Smith. Search criteria are most useful in large databases that have many records.

Hands-On 15.3 Use Criteria to Locate Records

1. Choose **Data→Form** to display the data form.

2. Click the **Criteria** button, and all of the field boxes will appear empty.

3. Click in the Name box, and type **=Watson, Tom**.

4. Click the **Find Next** button or tap (ENTER), and the Watson, Tom record will appear.

5. Click the **Criteria** button, and type **=Brown***.

6. Click the **Find Next** button, and the Brown, Bill record will appear.

7. Take five minutes to practice locating records using various criteria. Try entering criteria in other boxes, but make sure you click the **Criteria** button before entering each search criteria. Also, Excel may "beep" when you try to locate a record. If this happens, you will need to search in the opposite direction. For example, if you use the **Find Next** button and Excel "beeps," then try using the **Find Prev** button.

8. Close the data form when you have finished.

Displaying Automatic Subtotals

You can use Excel's Subtotal tool to display subtotals and grand totals for numeric fields in a list. You can rapidly display subtotals to analyze your data and then remove them just as easily. The following illustration shows the Hands-On Lesson 15 database with subtotals displayed.

Excel displays an Outline bar to let you increase or decrease the amount of information displayed in the subtotaled list.

In this example, the database is sorted on the State field, and SW Sales and HW Sales subtotals are inserted each time the State field changes. Excel automatically inserts the subtotals and Grand Total, and formats the worksheet as shown.

		A	B	C	D	E	F	G
	1	National Computing Solutions						
	2	1999 Sales Database						
	3							
	4	Name	Years Employed	Position	Region	State	SW Sales	HW Sales
	5	Smith, Bob	3	Sales Rep	Western	CA	200,000	180,000
	6	Zain, Beth	7	Senior Sales Rep	Western	CA	340,000	800,000
	7	Alvizo, Alex	7	Senior Sales Rep	Western	CA	450,000	340,000
	8	Brown, Bill	3	Telemarketer	Western	CA	546,000	120,000
	9					CA Total	1,536,000	1,440,000
	10	Williams, Michael	3	Sales Rep	Eastern	FL	120,000	340,000
	11	Martinez, Carlos	4	Senior Sales Rep	Eastern	FL	450,000	450,000
	12	Hubbs, Daniel	4	Telemarketer	Eastern	FL	340,000	230,000
	13					FL Total	910,000	1,020,000
	14	Wilson, Bernie	1	Sales Rep	Central	IL	120,000	170,000
	15	Thomas, Will	2	Sales Rep	Central	IL	230,000	120,000
	16	Cain, Mary	5	Senior Sales Rep	Central	IL	234,000	560,000
	17					IL Total	584,000	850,000
	18	Watson, Tom	8	Sales Rep	Eastern	MA	230,000	340,000
	19	Smith, Michael	5	Telemarketer	Eastern	MA	123,000	230,000
	20					MA Total	353,000	570,000
	21	Richards, Paul	4	Telemarketer	Western	WA	234,000	546,000
	22	Cray, Zip	6	Telemarketer	Western	WA	900,000	780,000
	23					WA Total	1,134,000	1,326,000
	24					Grand Total	4,517,000	5,206,000

Sorting the List

The most important step in the subtotaling process is to first sort the list. You must sort the list on the field that you want to base the subtotals upon. For example, sort on the State field if you want subtotals to appear each time the state field changes. When the Subtotal command is issued, Excel will group all rows with the same state and calculate subtotals for the group.

The Subtotal Dialog Box

The **Data→Subtotals** command displays the Subtotal dialog box. The Subtotal dialog box lets you determine the fields for which subtotals are calculated and the function used in the calculations. The following illustration discusses the options in the Subtotal dialog box.

This field must be set to the same field you used when sorting the database.

You can choose Sum, Average, Min, Max, *and other functions from this list. The function you choose is used to calculate the subtotals for each group.*

A subtotal is calculated for each field checked in this list.

This button removes all subtotals.

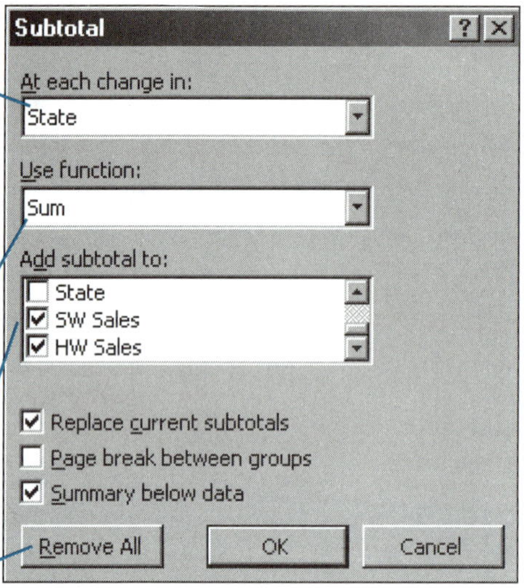

Quick Reference

DISPLAYING AND REMOVING SUBTOTALS

To display subtotals:

- Sort the database on the field that you want subtotals to be based upon.
- Choose Data→Subtotals from the menu bar.
- Set the *At Each Change In* field to the same field you sorted on.
- Choose the desired function from the Use Function box.
- Choose the numeric fields you want subtotaled in the Add Subtotal box, and click OK.

To remove subtotals:

- Choose Data→Subtotals from the menu bar.
- Click the Remove All button.

Hands-On 15.4 Experiment with Subtotals

Sort the Database

1. Click Cell E5.

2. Click the Sort Ascending ![A/Z] button to sort the database based upon the state field in Column E.
   All CA records will appear first followed by FL, etc. When you issue the Subtotals *command, Excel will create subtotals for the CA group, the FL group, etc.*

Display Subtotals

3. Choose **Data→Subtotals** from the menu bar.

4. Follow these steps to set the subtotal options.

Ⓐ *Set this option to* State. *A subtotal will appear each time the* State *field changes.*

Ⓑ *Leave this option set to* Sum. *You can use a variety of functions for subtotals, but* Sum *is used most often.*

Ⓒ *Scroll through this list of field names, and check* SW Sales *and* HW Sales. *These fields will be subtotaled each time the* State *field changes.*

Ⓓ *Click* **OK** *to display the subtotals.*

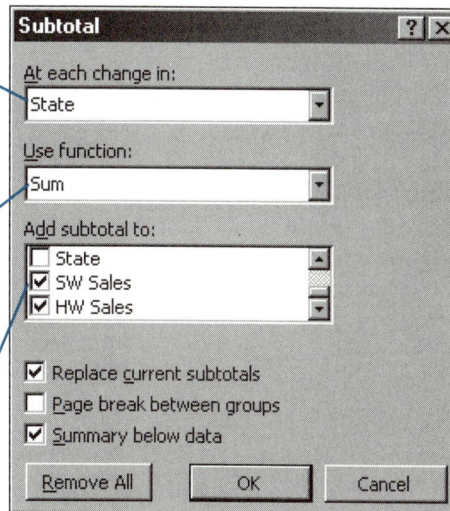

Subtotal [?][X]

At each change in:
[State ▼]

Use function:
[Sum ▼]

Add subtotal to:
[ ] State
[✓] SW Sales
[✓] HW Sales

[✓] Replace current subtotals
[ ] Page break between groups
[✓] Summary below data

[Remove All] [OK] [Cancel]

Take a few moments to review the subtotals before continuing.

Use the Outline Bar

5. Follow these steps to experiment with the Outline bar on the left side of the worksheet.

Ⓐ *Click the **1** button and only the Grand Total will be displayed.*

Ⓑ *Click the **2** button to display the Subtotals and Grand Total.*

Ⓒ *Click the **3** button to display the complete database again, including the subtotals and Grand Total.*

Ⓓ *Experiment with these buttons. They will display or hide one set of detail records at a time, such as the CA or FL records.*

[1][2][3]

1
2
3
4
5
6
7
8
9
10
11
12
13
14

Remove the Subtotals

6. Make sure the highlight is somewhere in the database, and choose **Data→Subtotals** from the menu bar.

7. Click the **Remove All** button.

As you can see, subtotals are easy to display and remove. The key to subtotals is to sort the database on the field that the subtotals will be based upon. In this example, the control field was State, *so subtotals were displayed each time the* State *field changed.*

Filtering Lists

Excel's filtering options let you temporarily hide rows in a list or database that meet the criteria you specify. You can use the AutoFilter command for basic filtering or the Advanced Filter for more complex filtering.

AutoFilter

The **Data→Filter→AutoFilter** command displays a drop-down button next to the column heading of each field in a list. You can rapidly filter the list by clicking the drop-down button and choosing a value from the drop-down menu. The following illustration shows the Hands-On Lesson 15 database filtered on the State field. Only records where the state is equal to CA are displayed.

Drop-down buttons appear next to each column heading.

Clicking a drop-down button displays a menu with every unique value for that field.

When you choose a value from the menu, only records containing that value are displayed in the list.

	A	B	C	D	E	F	G
1	National Computing Solutions						
2	1999 Sales Database						
3							
4	Name ▼	Years Employe ▼	Position ▼	Region ▼	State ▼	SW Sale ▼	HW Sale ▼
5	Smith, Bob	3	Sales Rep	Weste	(All)	200,000	180,000
6	Zain, Beth	7	Senior Sales Rep	Weste	(Top 10...)	340,000	800,000
7	Alvizo, Alex	7	Senior Sales Rep	Weste	(Custom...)	450,000	340,000
8	Brown, Bill	3	Telemarketer	Weste	CA	546,000	120,000
19					FL		
20					IL		
21					MA		
					WA		

Using AutoFilter on More Than One Column

You can use AutoFilter to filter on more than one column. For example, suppose you want to only see records where the state is equal to CA and the position is Senior Sales Rep. You can accomplish this by first filtering on the State column and then filtering on the Position column. Subsequent filters choose records from the subset of records displayed by the previous filter.

The Custom AutoFilter Option

A Custom option appears on the drop-down menu when you click an **AutoFilter** button. The Custom option displays the Custom AutoFilter dialog box. You can use the Custom AutoFilter dialog box to specify AND and OR filtering criteria for a single field. In addition, you can specify logical operators such as greater than >, less than <, greater than or equal to >=, etc. The example shown in the illustration on the next page would display all records where the state equals CA or FL.

You can choose And *or* Or *and specify a criteria on the second row to establish a logical AND or OR condition.*

You choose logical operators using these buttons.

You choose the desired value using these buttons.

Custom AutoFilter	? X

Show rows where:
State

| equals ▼ | CA ▼ |

○ And   ⦿ Or

| equals ▼ | FL ▼ |

Use ? to represent any single character
Use * to represent any series of characters

| OK | Cancel |

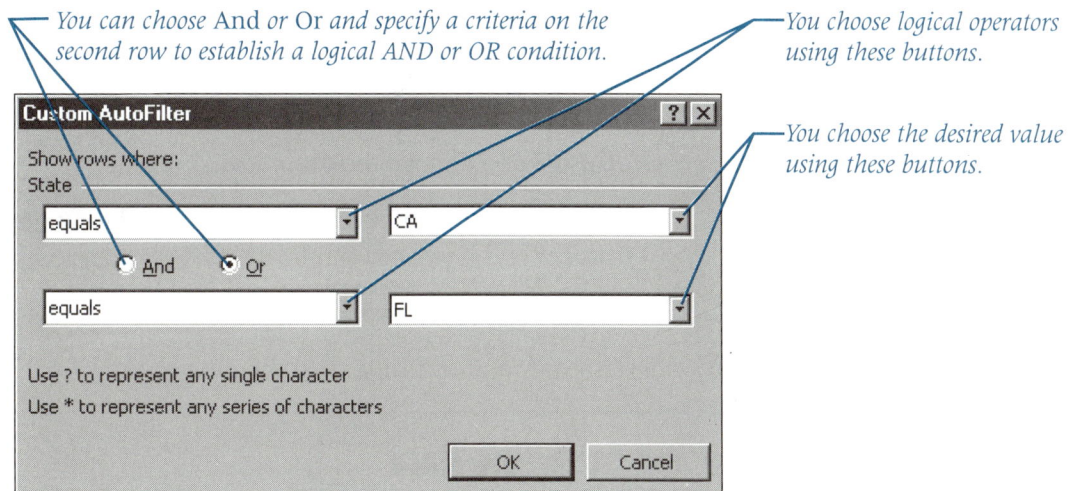

USING BASIC AUTOFILTERING

Apply an AutoFilter

- ■ Click anywhere in the list and choose Data→Filter→AutoFilter.

- ■ Click the drop-down arrow next to the field you want to filter on, and choose the desired value from the list. Repeat this step if you want to filter on two or more fields.

Remove AutoFilter

- ■ Choose Data→Filter→Show All to display all records and leave the AutoFilter buttons displayed. Choose Data→Filter→AutoFilter to display all records, and remove the AutoFilter buttons.

Hands-On 15.5 Use AutoFilter

Use Basic AutoFiltering

1. Click anywhere in the database, and choose **Data→Filter→AutoFilter.**

2. Click the button ▼ to the right of the State field, and choose CA from the list.
   Only the CA records should be displayed. The other records are still in the database, but they are not displayed at the moment.

3. Click the button ▼ to the right of the Position field, and choose Senior Sales Rep from the list.
   Only records with a State field equal to CA and a Position field equal to Senior Sales Rep will be displayed. There should only be two records displayed. As you can see, the second AutoFilter choice created a subset of the first choice.

Use Custom AutoFiltering

4. Click the State AutoFilter button ▼, and choose Custom from the drop-down menu.

5. Set the Custom AutoFiltering settings as shown in the illustration to the right and click **OK.**
   Only records where the state is CA or FL should be displayed.

Custom AutoFilter	? X

Show rows where:
State

| equals ▼ | CA ▼ |

○ And   ⦿ Or

| equals ▼ | FL ▼ |

(Continued on the next page)

6. Choose **Data→Filter→Show All** from the menu bar.
   Notice that all records are displayed, and the drop-down buttons remain.

7. Choose **Data→Filter→AutoFilter** to remove the drop-down buttons.

8. Take a few minutes to experiment with AutoFilter and subtotals. Try to understand the differences between these two features and how they can be used.

9. Remove all AutoFiltering and subtotals when you have finished experimenting.

10. Save the changes to your database, and continue with the next topic.

Advanced Filtering and Extracting Data

The **Data→Filter→Advanced Filter** command displays the Advanced Filter dialog box. You can use advanced filtering to filter data in ways not available with AutoFiltering. The most common uses of advanced filters are to specify an OR condition between two columns and to **extract** filtered data to another worksheet location. To set up an advanced filter, you must specify a criteria range above the list where filtering criteria are entered. The criteria range must include one or more column headings from the list and one or more filtering criteria. The following illustration discusses these concepts.

Rows have been inserted above the list, and the criteria are entered in this criteria range.

The SW Sales and HW Sales headings used for Columns F and G are copied to the criteria range.

	A	B	C	D	E	F	G
1	National Computing Solutions						
2	1999 Sales Database						
3							
4	SW Sales	HW Sales					
5	>300000						
6		>300000					
7							
8	Name	Years Employed	Position	Region	State	SW Sales	HW Sales
10	Zain, Beth	7	Senior Sales Rep	Western	CA	340,000	800,000
11	Alvizo, Alex	7	Senior Sales Rep	Western	CA	450,000	340,000
12	Brown, Bill	3	Telemarketer	Western	CA	546,000	120,000
13	Hubbs, Daniel	4	Telemarketer	Eastern	FL	340,000	230,000
14	Williams, Michael	3	Sales Rep	Eastern	FL	120,000	340,000
15	Martinez, Carlos	4	Senior Sales Rep	Eastern	FL	450,000	450,000
19	Cain, Mary	5	Senior Sales Rep	Central	IL	234,000	560,000
20	Watson, Tom	8	Sales Rep	Eastern	MA	230,000	340,000
21	Richards, Paul	4	Telemarketer	Western	WA	234,000	546,000
22	Cray, Zip	6	Telemarketer	Western	WA	900,000	780,000

The two >300000 criteria are entered on separate rows. This creates a logical OR condition. If they were both entered on Row 5, then a logical AND condition would be created.

Only records where the SW Sales are >300000 OR the HW Sales are >300000 are chosen.

Hands-On 15.6 Use Advanced Filtering and Data Extraction

Filter and Extract the Data

1. Position the mouse pointer on the Row 4 row heading, and drag down to select Rows 4–7.

2. Choose **Insert→Rows** to insert four blank rows.

3. Enter the criteria shown in the illustration on the previous page into the range A4:B6. Make sure you enter the SW Sales and HW Sales headings exactly as shown. Also, enter the numbers 300000 (five zeros), not 30000 (four zeros).

4. Choose **Data→Filter→Advanced Filter** from the menu bar.
   Excel should automatically identify the list because you named it Database. The flashing marquee will surround the list.

5. Follow these steps to filter the list.

A *Click the Copy to another location button. In a moment, you will use this option to extract the filtered data.*

B *Click in the Criteria range box, and then select the criteria range A4:B6 in the worksheet. The range reference will be entered in the box.*

C *Click in the Copy to another location box, and then click Cell A25 in the worksheet.*

D *Click OK, and the filtered data will be extracted (copied) to the range beginning at Cell A25.*

Notice that Excel has copied the filtered data to the range beginning in Cell A25. This is known as extracting the data. Extracting can be useful in large databases where you want to extract just certain records. You can also extract to another worksheet in the workbook. You can do this by simply clicking the desired worksheet tab in the workbook when entering the Copy to range in the Advanced Filter dialog box.

6. Feel free to experiment with advanced filtering.

7. When you have finished, save the changes to the workbook, and then close the workbook.

Querying Databases

Microsoft Query is a tool that can be used to import data from external data sources into Excel. External data sources include database programs such as Microsoft Access and Microsoft SQL Server. You can also use Query to extract data from an Excel list or database. Query lets you choose the fields to include in the extracted data, and it also lets you specify criteria to select only those records you wish to include in the extracted data. You can save queries and then run them at any time.

Setting Up Queries

Use the **Data→Get External Data→New Database Query** command to set up a new query. Query is not installed as part of the typical Office 2000 installation, so Excel will prompt you to install Query if it is your first time using it. The Choose Data Source box is displayed and lets you choose the data source from which the query will extract data.

The Query Wizard

The Choose Data Source dialog box has a check box that initiates the Query Wizard. The Query Wizard guides you step-by-step through the process of setting up and running a query. It also lets you choose the fields (columns) to include in the query, specify criteria (filters), and sort the resulting worksheet data. The following sequence of screens shows a query being set up in the Hands-On Lesson 15 database using the Query Wizard. The extracted worksheet data is also shown.

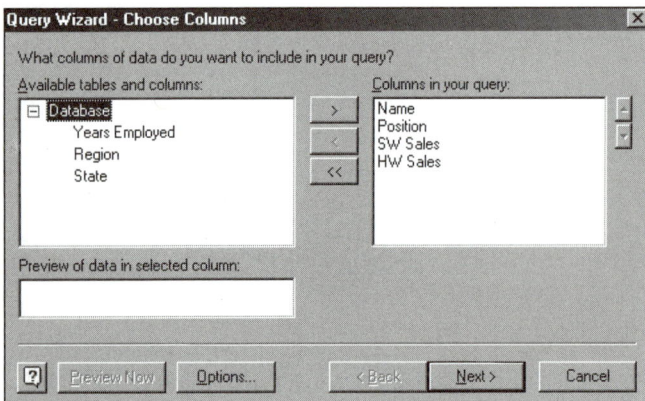

Query fields are specified.

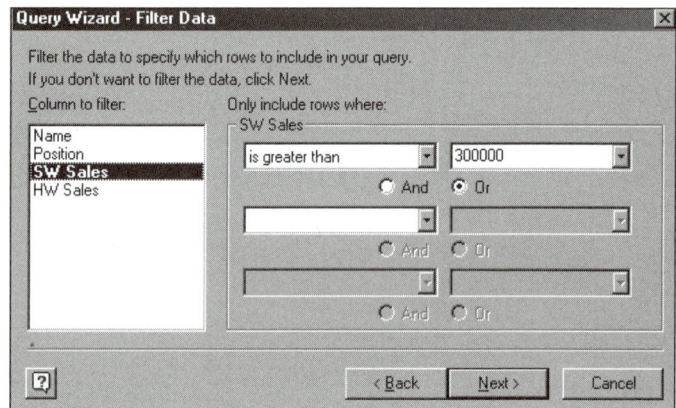

Criteria are set.

	A	B	C	D
1	Name	Position	SW Sales	HW Sales
2	Alvizo, Alex	Senior Sales Rep	450,000	340,000
3	Brown, Bill	Telemarketer	546,000	120,000
4	Cray, Zip	Telemarketer	900,000	780,000
5	Hubbs, Daniel	Telemarketer	340,000	230,000
6	Martinez, Carlos	Senior Sales Rep	450,000	450,000
7	Zain, Beth	Senior Sales Rep	340,000	800,000

Extracted Worksheet data

For further information on Microsoft Query, use the Office Assistant to get online assistance. There is no hands-on exercise to accompany this topic, since Query is an add-in that may not be installed on your computer system.

Concepts Review

True/False Questions

1. Database records are composed of fields.   TRUE   FALSE

2. You should always give the name Database to a database.   TRUE   FALSE

3. A data form can be used to filter data in a database.   TRUE   FALSE

4. You can use the =, <, and > operators in search criteria.   TRUE   FALSE

5. You should click in the field you wish to sort, prior to sorting a database.   TRUE   FALSE

6. Databases can only be sorted in ascending order.   TRUE   FALSE

7. AutoFilter inserts both subtotals and totals for the control field you specify.   TRUE   FALSE

8. Clicking OK on the Subtotal dialog box automatically sorts the database on the subtotal field.   TRUE   FALSE

Multiple-Choice Questions

1. Which command is used to display the Data Form dialog box?
   a. Format→Form
   b. Data→Form
   c. Tools→Form
   d. None of these

2. Which button(s) can be used on the data form to locate records?
   a. Find Prev
   b. Find Next
   c. Criteria
   d. All of these

3. Which command is used to display subtotals?
   a. Format→Subtotals
   b. Tools→Subtotals
   c. Tools→Database Subtotals
   d. None of these

4. Which command is used to remove subtotals?
   a. Data→Subtotals
   b. Tools→Subtotals
   c. Format→Subtotals
   d. None of these

Skill Builders

Skill Builder 15.1 Use Subtotals

In this exercise, you will experiment with subtotals and totals in the Hands-On Lesson 15 database.

1. Open the Hands-On Lesson 15 database.

2. Click Cell C9, and then click the Sort Ascending [↑] button.
   Remember you must always sort on the field you want to base the subtotals upon.

3. Choose **Data**→**Subtotals** from the menu bar.

4. Set the *At each change in* field to Position.

5. Make sure both SW Sales and HW Sales are checked in the *Add subtotal to* list.

6. Click **OK** to complete the subtotals.
   You should have a subtotal for each group of positions (Sales Rep, Senior Sales Rep, and Telemarketer).

7. Now remove all subtotals from the database.
   Leave the database open because you will continue to use it.

Skill Builder 15.2 Use AutoFilter

In this exercise, you will use AutoFilter to display only the records where the Position is equal to Sales Rep and the Years Employed is greater than 2.

1. Choose **Data**→**Filter**→**AutoFilter** from the menu bar.

2. Click the button [▼] to the right of the Position field, and choose Sales Rep from the list.
   Only the records where the Position *is equal to* Sales Rep *will be displayed.*

3. Click the button [▼] to the right of the Years Employed field, and choose (Custom . . .).

4. Follow these steps to set the Custom AutoFilter parameters.

Ⓐ *Choose* is greater than *from this list.*

Ⓑ *Type* **2** *in this box (or choose 2 from the drop-down list), and click* **OK**. *This instructs Excel to display only records where the* **Years Employed** *is greater than 2.*

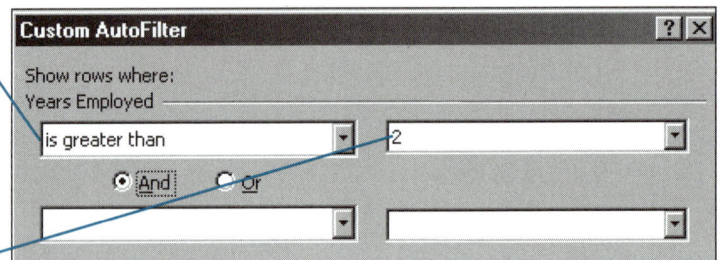

Excel should only display records where the Position = Sales Rep *and the* Years Employed *is greater than 2. The second AutoFilter setting (Years Employed is greater than 2) created a subset of the first setting (Position = Sales Rep). Notice you have combined a Custom AutoFilter setting with a regular AutoFilter setting.*

5. Choose **Data**→**Filter**→**AutoFilter** to remove the filtering.

6. Take five minutes to filter the database in various ways.

7. Remove filtering when you have finished experimenting.

8. Save the changes to the workbook, and then close the workbook.

Skill Builder 15.3 Set Up a Database

In this Skill Builder, you will set up a new database that tracks supporter information for a political campaign. You will enter data using a data form.

1. Start a new workbook, and set up the database structure shown below. Select the Range A4:F5 as shown below, and assign the name **Database** to the range.

	A	B	C	D	E	F
1	Jake Reynolds for City Council					
2	Supporters Database					
3						
4	Name	Contact Type	Organization	Contribution 1	Contribution 2	Last Election Contribution
5						

2. Format the blank Cells D5:F5 as Comma style with 0 decimals.

3. Use the **Data→Form** command to display the data form.

4. Use the data form to enter the data shown in the completed database below.

	A	B	C	D	E	F
1	Jake Reynolds for City Council					
2	Supporters Database					
3						
4	Name	Contact Type	Organization	Contribution 1	Contribution 2	Last Election Contribution
5	Alex Gardner	Business Owner	Symtron	1,000	230	-
6	Betty Post	Business Owner	Café Ritz	300	350	100
7	Bill Evans	Union Member	Teamsters	1,000	1,250	2,000
8	Bill Jones	Private Individual	Homeowner	25	-	25
9	Dawn Newell	Union Member	UAW	750	250	1,000
10	Ed Watkins	Business Owner	Ron's Deli	450	450	200
11	Jason Lopez	Business Owner	PC Solutions	1,300	500	1,500
12	Jimmy Peters	Business Owner	Cablespace	250	200	250
13	Martha Adams	Private Individual	Homeowner	250	100	100
14	Sam Bond	Private Individual	Homeowner	85	100	100
15	Steven Rogers	Business Owner	Steve's Auto Care	350	250	500
16	Sylvia Porter	Union Member	AFLCIO	1,500	900	1,200
17	Ted Thomas	Union Member	UAW	800	1,000	1,000
18	Tom Carter	Private Individual	Homeowner	75	25	100
19	Wanda Wilson	Union Member	Teamsters	750	450	1,000

5. Save the database as **Skill Builder 15.3.**

You will continue to use the database in the next two exercises.

Skill Builder 15.4 Use Subtotals

1. Use Excel's subtotaling tool to subtotal the database as shown below. You will need to sort the database on the Contact Type field before subtotaling.

	A	B	C	D	E	F
1	Jake Reynolds for City Council					
2	Supporters Database					
3						
4	Name	Contact Type	Organization	Contribution 1	Contribution 2	Last Election Contribution
5	Alex Gardner	Business Owner	Symtron	1,000	230	-
6	Betty Post	Business Owner	Café Ritz	300	350	100
7	Ed Watkins	Business Owner	Ron's Deli	450	450	200
8	Jason Lopez	Business Owner	PC Solutions	1,300	500	1,500
9	Jimmy Peters	Business Owner	Cablespace	250	200	250
10	Steven Rogers	Business Owner	Steve's Auto Care	350	250	500
11		**Business Owner Total**		**3,650**	**1,980**	**2,550**
12	Bill Jones	Private Individual	Homeowner	25	-	25
13	Martha Adams	Private Individual	Homeowner	250	100	100
14	Sam Bond	Private Individual	Homeowner	85	100	100
15	Tom Carter	Private Individual	Homeowner	75	25	100
16		**Private Individual Total**		**435**	**225**	**325**
17	Bill Evans	Union Member	Teamsters	1,000	1,250	2,000
18	Dawn Newell	Union Member	UAW	750	250	1,000
19	Sylvia Porter	Union Member	AFLCIO	1,500	900	1,200
20	Ted Thomas	Union Member	UAW	800	1,000	1,000
21	Wanda Wilson	Union Member	Teamsters	750	450	1,000
22		**Union Member Total**		**4,800**	**3,850**	**6,200**
23		**Grand Total**		**8,885**	**6,055**	**9,075**

2. Now subtotal the database as shown below. The only difference between these subtotals and those in the previous step is that the Average function was chosen in the Subtotal dialog box instead of the Sum function.

	A	B	C	D	E	F
1	Jake Reynolds for City Council					
2	Supporters Database					
3						
4	Name	Contact Type	Organization	Contribution 1	Contribution 2	Last Election Contribution
5	Alex Gardner	Business Owner	Symtron	1,000	230	-
6	Betty Post	Business Owner	Café Ritz	300	350	100
7	Ed Watkins	Business Owner	Ron's Deli	450	450	200
8	Jason Lopez	Business Owner	PC Solutions	1,300	500	1,500
9	Jimmy Peters	Business Owner	Cablespace	250	200	250
10	Steven Rogers	Business Owner	Steve's Auto Care	350	250	500
11		**Business Owner Average**		608	330	425
12	Bill Jones	Private Individual	Homeowner	25	-	25
13	Martha Adams	Private Individual	Homeowner	250	100	100
14	Sam Bond	Private Individual	Homeowner	85	100	100
15	Tom Carter	Private Individual	Homeowner	75	25	100
16		**Private Individual Average**		109	56	81
17	Bill Evans	Union Member	Teamsters	1,000	1,250	2,000
18	Dawn Newell	Union Member	UAW	750	250	1,000
19	Sylvia Porter	Union Member	AFLCIO	1,500	900	1,200
20	Ted Thomas	Union Member	UAW	800	1,000	1,000
21	Wanda Wilson	Union Member	Teamsters	750	450	1,000
22		**Union Member Average**		960	770	1,240
23		**Grand Average**		592	404	605

3. Save the changes to your workbook, and continue with the next exercise.

Skill Builder 15.5 Add a Sheet, and Use Filtering

1. Double-click the Sheet1 worksheet tab, and rename it as **Subtotals**.

2. Use the Select All button, and the Copy and Paste buttons to copy the entire database to Sheet2.
   Keep in mind that you would not normally make a copy of a database. You are doing this so that you can practice your filtering skills without having to remove the subtotals.

3. Rename Sheet2 as **Filtering**.

4. Click the drop-down button on the Name box on the left end of the formula bar.
   The range name Database is still assigned to the database in the Subtotals sheet. A range name can only be assigned to one range, so your new Filtering list has no name assigned to it.

5. Click anywhere in the list in the Filtering worksheet, and remove all subtotals.

6. Use the **Data→Filter→AutoFilter** command to display the filtering arrows.

(Continued on the next page)

7. Filter the list as shown below. You will need to examine the following illustration to determine which field to filter on.

	A	B	C	D	E	F
1	Jake Reynolds for City Council					
2	Supporters Database					
3						
4	Name	Contact Type	Organization	Contribution	Contribution	Last Election Contributic
5	Alex Gardner	Business Owner	Symtron	1,000	230	-
6	Betty Post	Business Owner	Café Ritz	300	350	100
7	Ed Watkins	Business Owner	Ron's Deli	450	450	200
8	Jason Lopez	Business Owner	PC Solutions	1,300	500	1,500
9	Jimmy Peters	Business Owner	Cablespace	250	200	250
10	Steven Rogers	Business Owner	Steve's Auto Care	350	250	500

8. Now use the AutoFilter Custom option to filter the list as shown below. You will need to filter on the same field that you filtered on in the previous step, although you will use an OR condition in the Custom AutoFilter dialog box.

	A	B	C	D	E	F
1	Jake Reynolds for City Council					
2	Supporters Database					
3						
4	Name	Contact Type	Organization	Contribution	Contribution	Last Election Contributic
5	Alex Gardner	Business Owner	Symtron	1,000	230	-
6	Betty Post	Business Owner	Café Ritz	300	350	100
7	Ed Watkins	Business Owner	Ron's Deli	450	450	200
8	Jason Lopez	Business Owner	PC Solutions	1,300	500	1,500
9	Jimmy Peters	Business Owner	Cablespace	250	200	250
10	Steven Rogers	Business Owner	Steve's Auto Care	350	250	500
15	Bill Evans	Union Member	Teamsters	1,000	1,250	2,000
16	Dawn Newell	Union Member	UAW	750	250	1,000
17	Sylvia Porter	Union Member	AFLCIO	1,500	900	1,200
18	Ted Thomas	Union Member	UAW	800	1,000	1,000
19	Wanda Wilson	Union Member	Teamsters	750	450	1,000

9. Save the changes to your workbook, and then close the workbook.

Assessments

Assessment 15.1 Set Up a Database

1. Follow these guidelines to create the database shown below.

   ■ Enter the data in the same cells as shown.

   ■ Format the titles and column headings as shown. You will need to use the (ALT)+(ENTER) keystroke combination to create the multiline entries in Cells C4 and D4.

   ■ Format the numbers in Columns C and D with the Comma style shown.

   ■ Assign the range name **Database** to the range A4:D17.

2. Save the database as **Assessment 15.1.**

3. Leave the workbook open because you will continue to use it.

	A	B	C	D
1	**Westside Electric Supplies**			
2	*Employee Compensation Database*			
3				
4	**Name**	**Category**	**1999 Compensation**	**1999 Retirement Plan Contributions**
5	Jackson, Samuel	Salaried	45,000	4,700
6	Ellison, Linda	Salaried	32,000	2,500
7	Monroe, James	Hourly	34,000	4,250
8	Wilson, Larry	Salaried	89,000	21,890
9	Hughes, Ralph	Hourly	23,000	-
10	Peterson, Lisa	Hourly	31,000	2,300
11	Watson, Bill	Hourly	27,000	1,600
12	Templeton, James	Salaried	45,000	1,900
13	Barton, Lisa	Salaried	51,000	6,000
14	Erickson, Brian	Hourly	38,000	4,500
15	Thomas, Lynn	Salaried	34,000	2,700
16	Chin, Raymond	Salaried	56,000	3,450
17	Zurlow, Jack	Hourly	30,000	3,450

Assessment 15.2 Use Subtotals

1. Copy the database in the Assessment 15.1 worksheet to Sheet2.

2. Rename Sheet2 as **Subtotals**, and rename Sheet1 as **Database**.

3. Subtotal the list in the Subtotals sheet as shown below. Notice that the subtotals use the AVERAGE function.

	A	B	C	D
1	**Westside Electric Supplies**			
2	*Employee Compensation Database*			
3				
4	**Name**	**Category**	**1999 Compensation**	**1999 Retirement Plan Contributions**
5	Monroe, James	Hourly	34,000	4,250
6	Hughes, Ralph	Hourly	23,000	-
7	Peterson, Lisa	Hourly	31,000	2,300
8	Watson, Bill	Hourly	27,000	1,600
9	Erickson, Brian	Hourly	38,000	4,500
10	Zurlow, Jack	Hourly	30,000	3,450
11	**Hourly Average**		30,500	2,683
12	Jackson, Samuel	Salaried	45,000	4,700
13	Ellison, Linda	Salaried	32,000	2,500
14	Wilson, Larry	Salaried	89,000	21,890
15	Templeton, James	Salaried	45,000	1,900
16	Barton, Lisa	Salaried	51,000	6,000
17	Thomas, Lynn	Salaried	34,000	2,700
18	Chin, Raymond	Salaried	56,000	3,450
19	**Salaried Average**		50,286	6,163
20	**Grand Average**		41,154	4,557

4. Save the changes to the workbook, and then close the workbook.

Critical Thinking

Critical Thinking 15.1 On Your Own

Linda Johnson is the owner of Linda's Home and Garden Supply. Linda's suppliers deliver products to her each Friday. She has asked you to set up an Excel worksheet that records the incoming supplies from the various suppliers. Currently, Linda receives supplies from Bay Area Garden Supply, Bright Flowers Supplies, and Home and Garden Warehouse. Set up a worksheet that lists the supplier name, product name, category ID, wholesale price, and retail price of each product. The retail price should be calculated as the wholesale price multiplied by three. Assign the name database to the list. Use the data form tool to enter the data shown below into the database.

Supplier	Product	Category ID	Wholesale Price, $
Bay Area Garden Supply	Shovels	Garden	12.95
Bay Area Garden Supply	Rakes	Garden	11.95
Bright Flowers Supplies	Orchids	Home	1.95
Bright Flowers Supplies	Potting Soil	Home	3.95
Home and Garden Warehouse	Pots	Home	2.35
Bright Flowers Supplies	Fertilizer	Home	2.35
Bay Area Garden Supply	Seeds	Garden	0.25
Home and Garden Warehouse	Bricks	Home	0.75
Home and Garden Warehouse	Stones	Home	2.35
Bay Area Garden Supply	Stakes	Garden	0.15
Bright Flowers Supplies	Planters	Home	7.95
Bright Flowers Supplies	Watering Buckets	Home	2.10
Bay Area Garden Supply	RotoTiller	Garden	545.00
Home and Garden Warehouse	Hoses	Home	4.50
Bay Area Garden Supply	Spades	Home	1.25
Home and Garden Warehouse	Miracle Grow	Home	2.65
Bright Flowers Supplies	Azaleas	Home	0.69
Bright Flowers Supplies	Ferns	Home	0.35
Bright Flowers Supplies	Fake Plants	Home	13.95
Home and Garden Warehouse	Books	Home	2.95

Save your workbook with a descriptive name, and leave it open for continued use.

Critical Thinking 15.2 On Your Own

Linda Johnson wants the incoming supplies database subtotaled and filtered in several ways. Copy the entire worksheet to the other two worksheets. Name the first worksheet Subtotals, the second worksheet Home, and the third worksheet Garden. Subtotal the list in the first worksheet on the Category ID field, adding subtotals to both the wholesale price and retail price fields. Use AutoFilter to filter the list in the second worksheet so that only products with a Home Category ID are displayed. Filter the list in the third worksheet so that only products with a Garden Category ID are displayed. Save the changes to your workbook when you have finished.

Critical Thinking 15.3 On Your Own

Ned Armstrong is the returns manager for Parker Book Publishers, Inc. Ned has asked you to set up an Excel database to track and analyze customer returns. The database should have fields for the return authorization code, customer name, return date, title, book category, quantity returned, unit price, and refund amount. The refund amount is calculated as the quantity returned multiplied by the purchase price. Set up the database and enter the data shown below.

Return Auth Code	Customer	Return Date	Title	Category	Quantity	Unit Price
1122	Nita Wilson	2/3/00	Take Charge of Your Life	Self Improvement	1	21.00
1122	Nita Wilson	3/5/00	Walking for Your Heart	Fitness	1	9.95
1123	Ray Barker	3/5/00	Swim for Your Life	Fitness	1	15.00
1124	Bill Simms	3/6/00	Meals for Working Moms	Cooking	2	21.50
1125	Julia Wilson	3/7/00	Attitude is Everything	Self Improvement	1	22.95
1125	Julia Wilson	3/7/00	Soil Conservation Guide	Gardening	1	13.45
1125	Julia Wilson	3/7/00	The Fish Book	Cooking	1	22.00
1126	Alex Evans	3/7/00	You're Number One	Self Improvement	1	12.50
1127	Alexia Wilson	3/8/00	Walking for Your Heart	Fitness	2	9.95
1128	Betty Bird	3/9/00	Beefing Up	Cooking	3	16.55
1128	Betty Bird	3/9/00	Perfect Orchids	Gardening	1	12.95
1129	Carl Biltmore	3/9/00	Weight Training Guide	Fitness	3	11.95
1130	Billy Baskins	3/10/00	Healthy Relationships	Self Improvement	2	12.95
1131	Bobby Johnson	3/11/00	Steak Well Done	Cooking	4	21.25
1132	Rita Lane	3/11/00	Eating Right	Fitness	1	23.45
1132	Rita Lane	3/11/00	Organic Gardening	Gardening	3	18.50
1132	Rita Lane	3/11/00	Tomatoes and Potatoes	Gardening	2	12.50
1133	Cynthia Vincent	3/12/00	Weight Training Guide	Fitness	1	11.95
1134	Bill Brown	3/12/00	Healthy Relationships	Self Improvement	1	12.95
1135	Sheryl Barnett	3/13/00	Soil Conservation Guide	Gardening	1	13.45

Make sure you add a Refund Amount column, and calculate the refund amount as the quantity multiplied by the unit price. Subtotal the database on the category field using the sum function on the unit price field. Save the database with a descriptive name when you have finished.

LESSON 16

PivotTables, Styles and Outlines

Excel has many features to help you perform sophisticated data analyses. Some of the most powerful data analysis tools in Excel are the PivotTable and PivotChart. PivotTables let you summarize worksheet data dynamically to view the data in various ways. With simple drag-and-drop commands, you can arrange your data and Excel creates summary formulas in the rows and columns automatically. PivotCharts offer the same power and flexibility for charting data. Excel's Styles feature lets you give a name to cell formatting and then apply it with ease. Styles can help you format your worksheets more quickly and with greater consistency. Outlines and grouping let you selectively hide detail data with a single mouse click, so that it doesn't clutter your view of summary data.

In This Lesson

Case Study

Allen is the assistant to the national sales manager at the Acme Net Works. As part of his monthly routine, Allen gathers and presents sales data to the sales manager. Allen is expected to create various views of data that help the sales manager perceive trends and track the efficiency of the sales staff.

Allen knew the basics of working with values and formulas when he started his job, but he's always looking for ways to make his work easier. When he started his position, Allen would create workbooks with several views of the sales data. But this rather static view doesn't really allow him to analyze the data very efficiently. Allen hears about Excel's PivotTable feature at a one-day seminar for administrative assistants. He learns that PivotTables let you look at data in a variety of ways without the tedium of sorting and laying out the data manually.

Sum of SW Sales		Position			
Region	Name	Sales Rep	Senior Sales Rep	Telemarketer	Grand Total
Central	Cain, Mary		234,000		234,000
	Thomas, Will	230,000			230,000
	Wilson, Bernie	120,000			120,000
Central Total		350,000	234,000		584,000
Eastern	Hubbs, Daniel			340,000	340,000
	Martinez, Carlos		450,000		450,000
	Smith, Michael			123,000	123,000
	Watson, Tom	230,000			230,000
	Williams, Michael	120,000			120,000
Eastern Total		350,000	450,000	463,000	1,263,000
Western	Alvizo, Alex		450,000		450,000
	Brown, Bill			546,000	546,000
	Cray, Zip			900,000	900,000
	Richards, Paul			234,000	234,000
	Smith, Bob	200,000			200,000
	Zain, Beth		340,000		340,000
Western Total		200,000	790,000	1,680,000	2,670,000
Grand Total		$ 900,000	$ 1,474,000	$ 2,143,000	$ 4,517,000

Allen is also expected to post data for the sales force to review. Rather than sending it out with email messages, Allen posts worksheets to the Web. He formats and organizes the data to enhance its readability and usefulness. Excel's styles and grouping features are very useful tools for this task.

Styles let Allen apply consistent formatting to worksheets very quickly.

The grouping and outline features let him create workbooks that can expand and collapse the view of detail data.

	A	E	F	G	H
1	National Computing Solutions				
2	Sales by Region				
3					
4	Name	State	SW Sales	HW Sales	Total Sales
8	Central Region Subtotal		584,000	850,000	1,434,000
14	Eastern Region Subtotal		1,263,000	1,590,000	2,853,000
21	Western Region Subtotal		2,670,000	2,766,000	5,436,000
22	Totals		4,517,000	5,206,000	9,723,000

Working with PivotTables

PivotTables are a powerful data analysis tool in Excel. PivotTables let you view the data in various ways, and change the view instantly to a new one. Compared to performing similar data analysis on a standard worksheet, PivotTables offer tremendous speed and flexibility. You create PivotTables from data on an Excel worksheet that is organized into a database. You learned how to create an Excel database in Lesson 15.

How PivotTables Work

PivotTables organize the data in an Excel database into several different areas. Each area of the PivotTable plays a role in the organization of your data. The areas of the PivotTable are displayed in the figure below. You define a PivotTable by dragging and dropping various fields from the Excel database onto the PivotTable outline. Where you place fields into the outline determines how the PivotTable summarizes the data.

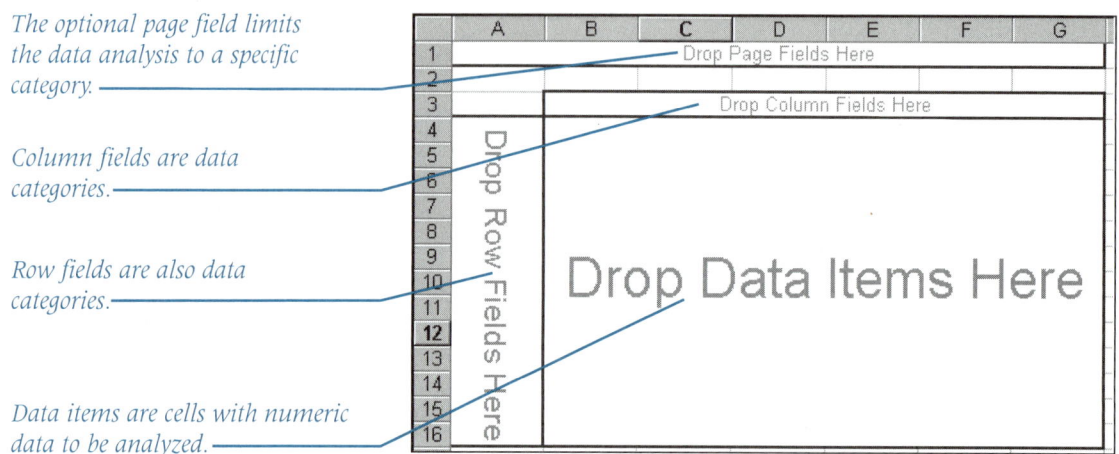

The optional page field limits the data analysis to a specific category.

Column fields are data categories.

Row fields are also data categories.

Data items are cells with numeric data to be analyzed.

After you drag and drop data fields into the PivotTable outline, Excel summarizes the data for you automatically. You can also drag fields out of the PivotTable, or into new locations in the outline.

3	Region ▾	Data ▾	Total
4	Central	Sum of SW Sales	584000
5		Sum of HW Sales	850000
6	Eastern	Sum of SW Sales	1263000
7		Sum of HW Sales	1590000
8	Western	Sum of SW Sales	2670000
9		Sum of HW Sales	2766000
10	Total Sum of SW Sales		4517000
11	Total Sum of HW Sales		5206000

The Region field was dropped into the Row area.

The HW Sales and SW Sales fields were dropped into the Data area.

The PivotTable automatically calculates summaries of the Data area fields.

In this example, a PivotTable summarizes the breakdown of Hardware and Software sales by Region.

Hands-On 16.1 Create a New PivotTable

The best way to understand the dynamic capabilities of a PivotTable is to create one. In this exercise, you will review the database and a worksheet-based method of analysis; then you will create a new PivotTable from the database data.

Review the Data

1. Open the **Hands-On Lesson 16.1** workbook on your exercise diskette.

2. Set the zoom level so that all of the data on the worksheet is visible.
   The first worksheet contains the Excel database you will use to create a PivotTable. Look over the data fields in the column headings and the various records in the rows. Each record contains data for a specific salesperson.

   Notice that the only numeric *data in the database is contained in the* HW Sales *and* SW Sales *columns. This means that you will want to use these fields in the* Data *area of the PivotTable later in this exercise. All of the other fields contain text values.*

3. Click the *Sales by Region* worksheet tab. Set the zoom level if necessary so that all of the data is visible.
   This layout summarizes the hardware and software sales by region. To create this summary, the database had to be sorted by region. Then additional rows were added for the subtotal rows and total row.

4. Click the *Sales by Position* worksheet tab. Set the zoom level if necessary so that all of the data is visible.
   This layout summarizes the hardware and software sales by the type of position each salesperson holds. To create this summary, the database had to be sorted by position and region. Then additional rows were added for the subtotal rows and total row. As you can imagine, it took some time and manual work to create these two worksheets to perform a specific type of analysis. A PivotTable can lay out the data for this type of analysis with much greater flexibility.

(Continued on the next page)

Create a PivotTable

Now you will create a PivotTable that summarizes HW and SW sales by region. This table will perform a function similar to the Sales by Region worksheet you viewed a moment ago.

5. Click the Sales Database tab; then click on Cell **A4**.
   You should select a cell within the database before you create the PivotTable.

6. Choose **Data→PivotTable and PivotChart Report** from the menu bar.
   The PivotTable and PivotChart Wizard dialog box will appear to display Step 1.

7. Leave the default choices at *Microsoft Excel list or database* and *PivotTable* in Step 1 of the Wizard; then click **Next**.

8. Leave the default choice at *Database* in Step 2 of the Wizard; then click **Next**.

9. Leave the default choice at *New worksheet;* then click **Finish.**
   A new worksheet will appear with the PivotTable outline. The PivotTable toolbar is also displayed.

10. Double-click the *Sheet 1* worksheet tab; then rename the worksheet **PivotTable**, and tap the
    (ENTER) key.

11. If necessary, drag the PivotTable toolbar so that it does not cover any part of the PivotTable outline areas.
    Notice that the bottom portion of the PivotTable toolbar contains a list of all the data fields in the database, such as Name, HW Sales, SW Sales, *etc.*

12. Click Cell **A18,** which is outside the boundary of the PivotTable outline.
    Notice that the field names disappear from the PivotTable toolbar and that most of the buttons on the toolbar are grayed out. You must select a cell within the PivotTable outline to display the available field names and toolbar buttons.

13. Click on Cell **A4,** within the PivotTable outline, to restore the fields on the PivotTable toolbar.

14. Follow these steps to define the PivotTable.

Ⓐ *Drag and drop the Region field into the Row fields area.*

Ⓑ *Drag and drop the SW Sales field into the Data area. Notice how the Data area has shrunk to just the column necessary to hold the SW Sales summary.*

Ⓒ *Drag and drop the HW Sales field into the Data area of the PivotTable. The Data area will enlarge to hold the new summary data.*

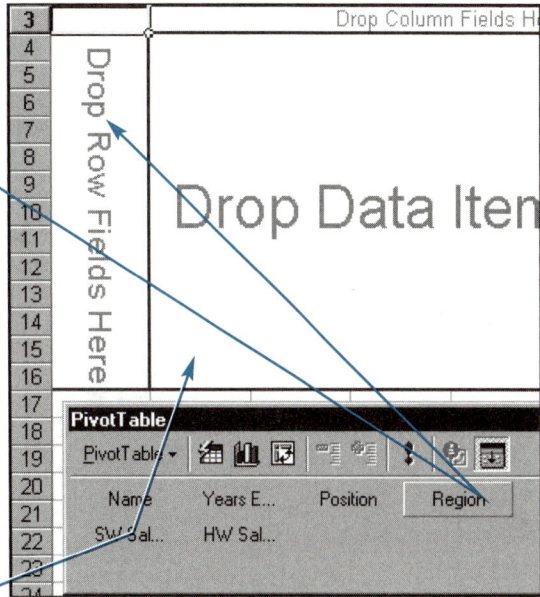

3	Sum of SW Sales	
4	Region ▼	Total
5	Central	584000
6	Eastern	1263000
7	Western	2670000
8	Grand Total	4517000

You have defined a PivotTable that summarizes HW and SW sales by region. The summary calculations are created for you automatically.

15. Examine the total SW and HW sales figures for the *Central* region, and keep the figures in mind.

16. Click the *Sales by Region* worksheet tab. Compare the totals from the PivotTable with the Central region totals on this worksheet. They should be identical.

17. Click the *PivotTable* worksheet tab to display the PivotTable again.

Manipulating Fields on a PivotTable

You can add and subtract fields on a PivotTable by simply dragging and dropping. The PivotTable will automatically reconfigure to display the new data. One of the most powerful ways to manipulate data is to move a field from the Row area to the Column area or vice versa. This is called *pivoting* the field (thus the name *PivotTable*). You can also change the order of fields within the Row and Column areas. This rotates the display of the data field to give you an entirely different view of your data. An example is shown below.

You pivot the field by dragging from the Row area to the Column area, and vice versa.

			Position ▼		
Region ▼	Name ▼	Data ▼	Sales Rep	Senior Sales Rep	Telemarketer
Central	Cain, Mary	Sum of SW Sales		234,000	
		Sum of HW Sales		560,000	
	Thomas, Will	Sum of SW Sales	230,000		
		Sum of HW Sales	120,000		
	Wilson, Bernie	Sum of SW Sales	120,000		
		Sum of HW Sales	170,000		
Central Sum of SW Sales			350,000	234,000	
Central Sum of HW Sales			290,000	560,000	
Eastern	Hubbs, Daniel	Sum of SW Sales			340,000
		Sum of HW Sales			230,000
	Martinez, Carlos	Sum of SW Sales		450,000	
		Sum of HW Sales		450,000	
	Smith, Michael	Sum of SW Sales			123,000
		Sum of HW Sales			230,000
	Watson, Tom	Sum of SW Sales	230,000		
		Sum of HW Sales	340,000		
	Williams, Michael	Sum of SW Sales	120,000		
		Sum of HW Sales	340,000		
Eastern Sum of SW Sales			350,000	450,000	463,000
Eastern Sum of HW Sales			680,000	450,000	460,000
Western	Alvizo, Alex	Sum of SW Sales		450,000	
		Sum of HW Sales		340,000	
	Brown, Bill	Sum of SW Sales			546,000
		Sum of HW Sales			120,000
	Cray, Zip	Sum of SW Sales			900,000
		Sum of HW Sales			780,000
	Richards, Paul	Sum of SW Sales			234,000
		Sum of HW Sales			546,000
	Smith, Bob	Sum of SW Sales	200,000		
		Sum of HW Sales	180,000		
	Zain, Beth	Sum of SW Sales		340,000	
		Sum of HW Sales		800,000	
Western Sum of SW Sales			200,000	790,000	1,680,000
Western Sum of HW Sales			180,000	1,140,000	1,446,000

Before pivoting: The SW and HW sales data is summarized in the rows. This makes it easy to compare the software to hardware sales by each salesperson. After pivoting is shown below.

		Data ▼ Sum of SW Sales			Position ▼ Sum of HW Sales		
Region ▼	Name ▼	Sales Rep	Senior Sales Rep	Telemarketer	Sales Rep	Senior Sales Rep	Telemarketer
Central	Cain, Mary		234,000			560,000	
	Thomas, Will	230,000			120,000		
	Wilson, Bernie	120,000			170,000		
Central Total		350,000	234,000		290,000	560,000	
Eastern	Hubbs, Daniel			340,000			230,000
	Martinez, Carlos		450,000			450,000	
	Smith, Michael			123,000			230,000
	Watson, Tom	230,000			340,000		
	Williams, Michael	120,000			340,000		
Eastern Total		350,000	450,000	463,000	680,000	450,000	460,000
Western	Alvizo, Alex		450,000			340,000	
	Brown, Bill			546,000			120,000
	Cray, Zip			900,000			780,000
	Richards, Paul			234,000			546,000
	Smith, Bob	200,000			180,000		
	Zain, Beth		340,000			800,000	
Western Total		200,000	790,000	1,680,000	180,000	1,140,000	1,446,000

Suppressing the Display of Data Items

You can set the PivotTable to exclude specific items from the data summaries. Each field on the PivotTable has a drop-down list button. You can uncheck items in the drop-down list to suppress their display in the PivotTable. An example is shown below.

3	Region ▼	Data ▼
4	☑ Central	W Sales
5	☐ Eastern	W Sales
6	☑ Western	W Sales

In this example, the display of Eastern Region *data will be suppressed from the PivotTable summaries.*

Page Fields on a PivotTable

The Page field area is at the very top of the PivotTable outline. When you drop a field into this area, you can choose to display all of the items in this field, or select a single type of item for display. For example, you could choose to display only a specific type of sales position in the PivotTable data summaries. The Page field area lets you control the display of data without adding additional columns to the PivotTable.

Position	(All) ▼
	··· (All)
State ▼	··· Sales Rep
CA	··· Senior Sales Rep
	Telemarketer

In this example, Allen chooses to display only Telemarketer *sales data in the body of the PivotTable.*

🖱 Hands-On 16.2 Manipulate Fields on the PivotTable

Now you will redefine the PivotTable to create a different view of the data. The first change will be to summarize the data by State.

Add Fields to the PivotTable

1. Follow these steps to add the *State* field to the *Row* data area.

Ⓐ *Start to drag the State field over the* Region *column.*

Ⓑ *Release the mouse button when you see the vertical gray bar along the right side of the* Region *column.*

3	Region ▼	Data
4	Central	Sum of
5		Sum of
6	Eastern	Sum of
7		Sum of
8	Western	Sum of
9		Sum of
10	Total Sum of SW Sales	
11	Total Sum of HW Sales	
12		

Region   State

The PivotTable automatically creates new rows and summaries for the State data. Imagine what you would have to do to create these summaries in a standard worksheet!

(Continued on the next page)

2. Taking care to see that the gray bar is displayed as shown below, drag and drop the *Name* field between the Region and State fields.

Notice how the data is now summarized by Region, Name, then by State. This looks rather awkward, since each Salesperson only operates in one state. It would be more useful to view the data by Region, then by State, then by Name. Let's reconfigure the PivotTable to do just that.

3. Follow these steps to move the Name field.

Ⓐ *Drag the Name field directly to the right, toward the column boundary of the State and Data fields.*

Ⓑ *Release the mouse button when you see the gray bar between the State and Data fields as shown here.*

This PivotTable configuration displays the data much more logically.

Suppress the Display of Items in a PivotTable

4. Follow these steps to suppress the display of data for the *Eastern* Region.

Ⓐ *Click the drop-down list button for the Region field.*

Ⓑ *Click to uncheck the Eastern data item.*

Ⓒ *Click OK to close the drop-down item list.*

Notice that no data is displayed for the Eastern region. You can use this method to switch the display of individual data items on and off for any field.

5. Click the drop-down list button for the *Region* field again; then click to *check* the *Eastern* check box, and click **OK.**

6. Drag the *Position* field from the PivotTable toolbar into the *Drop Page Fields Here* area at the top of the PivotTable.
Notice that the body of the table does not change, since the Position field is set to display (All).

7. Follow these steps to display only data for telemarketer positions.

Ⓐ *Click the drop-down list button for the Position field.*

Ⓑ *Click on Telemarketer in the list, then click OK.*

Now only the names and data for telemarketers is displayed. Without the Page field area, you would have needed to insert the Position column into the body of the table; then switch off the display of the other two types of positions.

8. Click the Position field drop-down list button; then choose *Senior Sales Rep* from the list, and click **OK.**

Now only data for senior sales reps is displayed.

Remove a Field from the PivotTable

9. Follow these steps to remove the *Region* field from the PivotTable.

Ⓐ *Point at the* Region *heading until you see the four-pointed arrow; then start to drag the* Region *field off of the PivotTable.*

Region	State	Name	Data	Total
Central	IL	Cain, Mary	Sum of HW Sales	560000
			Sum of SW Sales	234000
		Thomas, Will	Sum of HW Sales	120000

Ⓑ *Release the mouse button when the field is outside the boundary of the PivotTable. You will see a delete symbol under the mouse pointer when the field is outside the PivotTable.*

The Region-level summary items are removed from the table. Now the data is organized by State and then by Name, but only displays the data for Senior Sales reps.

10. Drag the *State* field off the PivotTable.

11. Drag the gray *Position* field heading (not its drop-down list) from the top of the PivotTable to the left side of the table as shown at right.

Now the data is organized by Position, then by Name. Now all of the data for the three types of positions is displayed again.

	A	
1	Position	(A
2		
3		D
4	Name	S
5	Alvizo, Alex	
6	Brown, Bill	

12. Follow these steps to pivot the *Data* field from the Rows area to the Columns area.

Now the SW Sales and HW Sales are arrayed in columns rather than in rows. This makes the data more readable.

Ⓐ *Start to drag the* Data *field immediately to the right, over the* Total *cell.*

	Data	Total
	Sum of SW Sales	200000
	Sum of HW Sales	180000

Ⓑ *Release the mouse button when you see the gray highlight around the border of the* Total *cell as shown here.*

13. Follow these steps to pivot the *Position* field from the Rows area to the Columns area.

Now you see the Position data arrayed in columns rather than by rows. The Name field is automatically sorted alphabetically. The ability to pivot the position of a field is one of the most dynamic features of PivotTables.

Ⓐ *Start to drag the Position field immediately under the Data field.*

		Data		
Position	Name		Sum of SW Sales	Sum of HW Sales
Senior Sales Rep	Alvizo, Alex		450000	340000

Ⓑ *Release the mouse button when you see the gray bar beneath the Data field as shown here.*

14. Save ▣ the workbook.

PivotTable AutoFormat

You can use normal formatting commands to format the cells of a PivotTable. There is also a special *PivotTable AutoFormat* command that works similar to the AutoFormat command for worksheets. Excel provides over twenty different AutoFormat styles that you can apply to a PivotTable.

Hands-On 16.3 AutoFormat the PivotTable

1. Make sure you have selected at least one cell in the PivotTable; then choose **Format→AutoFormat** from the menu bar.
   The AutoFormat dialog box displays formats designed especially for PivotTables.

2. Scroll up and down to review the available AutoFormats; then choose the *Table 10* format near the bottom of the list, and click **OK**.

3. Click on Cell **B6** to clear the selection so you can view the results of the AutoFormat more easily.
   This format highlights the column headings and totals for greater readability.

4. Click the AutoFormat button on the PivotTable toolbar; then choose *Report 6* in the dialog box, and click **OK**.
   Notice that this AutoFormat pivoted the Position *field back into the* Rows *field area at the left side of the PivotTable. An AutoFormat command can pivot fields to conform to the selected AutoFormat design.*

   Leave the PivotTable worksheet page open; you will use it again in a moment.

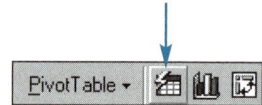

Working with PivotCharts

A PivotChart lets you summarize data in a chart with the same methods you use in a PivotTable. To create a PivotChart, you can either chart a PivotTable directly, or you can create the PivotChart from scratch with the same Wizard that helps you create a PivotTable. Once you have created a PivotChart, you can use the same techniques to position and pivot fields that you learned to use on the PivotTable.

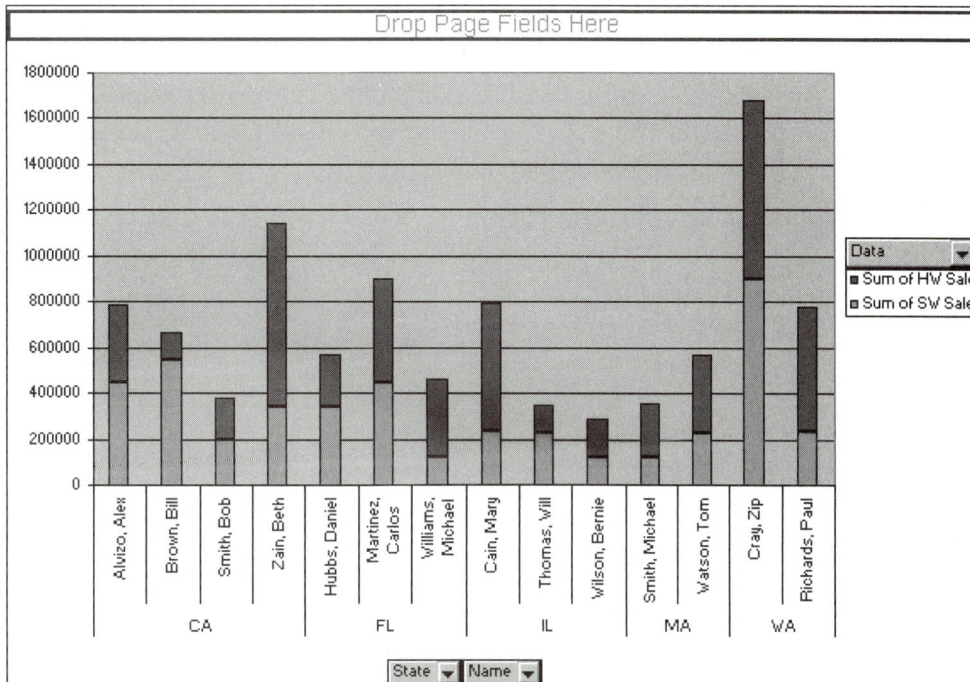

This PivotChart lets you use PivotTable techniques to organize the chart data. Notice how the Names field items are arranged by State.

Formatting PivotCharts

You use the same commands and Wizards to format PivotCharts that you use with normal Excel charts. You can choose from the same variety of chart styles such as bar, column, and line. You can format chart objects just as you would on a normal Excel chart.

Quick Reference

HOW TO CREATE A PIVOTCHART	
Task	**Procedure**
Create a PivotChart from an Excel database.	■ Click on any cell of the database.
	■ Choose *Data→PivotTable and PivotChart* Report from the menu bar.
	■ Choose the *Microsoft Excel list or database* and *PivotChart* in Step 1 of the Wizard; then click *Next*.
	■ Choose *Database* in Step 2 of the Wizard; then click *Next*.
	■ Choose whether to create the PivotChart on a *New* or *Existing work sheet;* then click *Finish*.
Create a PivotChart from an existing PivotTable.	■ Click on any cell in the PivotTable.
	■ Click the *Chart Wizard* button on the PivotTable toolbar.

In this exercise, you will create a PivotChart from your PivotTable. In the Skill Builder 16.2 exercise, you will create a PivotChart from a database.

1. Click on any cell within the PivotTable; then click the *Chart Wizard* button on the PivotTable toolbar.
   A new bar chart worksheet is created immediately from your present PivotTable data. Notice that the Names data is arranged by Position, just as it was in the PivotTable.

2. Double-click the *Chart 1* worksheet tab, rename the tab **PivotChart**, and tap (ENTER).
   Once you have created the PivotChart, you can add and delete fields just as you did with the PivotTable. You can also pivot fields between the lower (Rows) area and the right (columns) area.

3. Follow these steps to add a new field to the PivotChart.

   Ⓐ *Start dragging the Region field down by the* Position *field heading.*

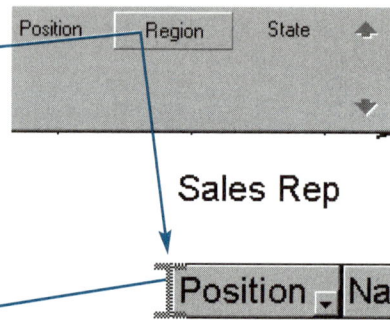

   Ⓑ *Release the mouse button when you see the gray bar to the left of the* Position *field.*

   Now the bar chart is further arranged by Region. This enables you to visually analyze the productivity of sales staff within each region

4. Drag the *Position* field directly to the left so that it lies to the left of the *Region* field as shown here.
   Now you can compare the performance of sales staff between the various regions.

5. Click the *Chart Wizard* button on the PivotTable toolbar. Choose the *Line* chart type; then choose any specific *subtype*, and click **Finish.**
   The chart is reconfigured to the new chart type. You can use normal chart formatting commands as you learned in Lesson 6.

6. Save the workbook.

Interactive PivotTables on the Web

You can save a PivotTable as a Web page just as you can with normal Excel worksheets. You can also publish the PivotTable as an *interactive* Web page. Interactivity allows users to manipulate and pivot the fields when viewing the PivotTable in their Web browser. Fields can be added, moved, and removed in the Web browser just as they can on a normal PivotTable worksheet. You can also save the PivotTable without interactivity. This option displays the PivotTable with a static view that users cannot manipulate in their Web browser.

NOTE!

Remember that various types of formatting may be lost when you save a worksheet as an interactive *Web page. See* Lost Formatting on Interactive Worksheets *in Lesson 13 for details.*

Quick Reference

SAVE A PIVOTTABLE AS A WEB PAGE WITH INTERACTIVITY

Task	Procedure
Save a PivotTable as a Web page with interactivity.	■ Display the worksheet with the PivotTable. Make sure that the PivotTable fields are configured as you wish them to display in a Web browser.
	■ Choose *File→Save as Web Page* from the menu bar.
	■ Click the *Publish: Sheet* option. Make sure that the *Add Interactivity* checkbox is checked; then click *Publish*.
	■ Click the *Add interactivity with* checkbox under viewing options; then choose *PivotTable functionality* from the drop-down list.
	■ If desired, change the page title and/or filename; then click *Publish*.

Hands-On 16.5 Publish an Interactive PivotTable Web Page

In this exercise, you will save the PivotTable as a Web page with interactivity. Then you will test the functionality of the Interactive Worksheet Web page in the Internet Explorer Web browser.

Preview the PivotTable as a Web Page

1. Click the *PivotTable* worksheet tab.

2. Choose **File→Web Page Preview** from the menu bar.
   Excel will start the Internet Explorer browser to display your PivotTable as a Web page. This displays how the PivotTable will appear if the workbook is saved as a standard (non-interactive) Web page.

3. Close ⊠ the Internet Explorer window.

Save the PivotTable as an Interactive Web Page

4. Choose **File→Save as Web Page** from the menu bar.

5. Follow these steps to begin saving the Web page.

   Ⓐ *Click* Selection: Sheet *to save just the PivotTable worksheet.*

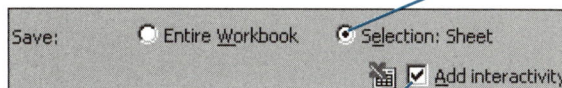

Save:	○ Entire Workbook	⦿ Selection: Sheet
		☒ ☑ Add interactivity

   Ⓑ *Click to check the* Add Interactivity *checkbox.* ──── Ⓒ *Click the* **Publish** *button.*

(Continued on the next page)

6. Follow these steps to finish publishing the interactive PivotTable.

Ⓐ *Click to choose PivotTable as the item to publish.*

Ⓑ *Make sure that this box is set to PivotTable functionality.*

Ⓒ *Make sure that the Open published web page in web browser checkbox is checked.*

Ⓓ *Click* **Change***, then type* **Interactive PivotTable***, as shown here, and click* **OK***.*

Ⓔ *Click* **Browse***, then choose the 3½ Floppy (A:) drive in the Save in box. Taking care to use only lowercase letters, change the name in the file-name box to pivottable, then click* **OK***.*

Ⓕ *Click Publish to complete the command.*

Item to publish
Choose: | Items on Sheet1

| Sheet | All contents of Sheet1 |
| PivotTable | PivotTable2 ($A$3:$E$37) |

Viewing options
☑ Add interactivity with: | PivotTable functionality

▨ Pivot, filter, and sort data in Microsoft Internet Explorer 4.01 or greater.

Publish as
Title: Interactive PivotTable
File name: A:\pivottable.htm

Change...
Browse...

☑ Open published web page in browser   Publish   Cancel

Internet Explorer will start and display your newly published interactive PivotTable. Notice that the formatting for the PivotTable has been lost. This did not happen when you executed the Web page preview earlier in this exercise. Many formatting features are lost when you publish a worksheet as a Web page with interactivity.

Try Some Interactivity Features

7. Click the drop-down list button for the *Position* field; then click to *uncheck* the *Telemarketer* item, and click **OK**.

| Position ▼ |

Display of this item is suppressed, just as it was in the PivotTable worksheet, only this time you are giving the command inside your Web browser

8. Follow these steps to pivot the *Region* field.

Ⓐ *Start to drag the* Region *field to the* Column Fields *area of the PivotTable.*

Ⓑ *Release the mouse button when you see a blue highlight around the edges of the Column Fields area.*

		Drop Column Fields Here	
▼ Region ▼	Name ▼	Sum of SW Sales	Sum of
⊟ Central	⊞ Thomas, Will	230000	
	⊞ Wilson, Bernie	120000	

The PivotTable pivots the Region field and reconfigures the rows and columns.

9. Feel free to try pivoting other fields and dragging fields off of the PivotTable.
These manipulations will work as they did in previous exercises. You can also add fields to an interactive PivotTable, which is explained in the next topic.

10. Close ☒ the Internet Explorer window.

Publish the Web Page to Your Web Folder (Optional)

If the computers in your lab have Web folders, you can publish your interactive PivotTable and browse it over the Internet.

NOTE! *If your computer does not have a Web folder, you should skip the rest of this exercise.*

11. Minimize ⬛ the Excel window.

12. Open a My Computer window; then navigate to the *3½ Floppy (A:) drive.*

13. Hold down the ⟨CTRL⟩ key; then click to select the *pivottable* file and the *pivottable_files* folder. Release the ⟨CTRL⟩ key.
    Excel created the pivottable_files *folder when you saved your interactive PivotTable Web page. This folder contains additional data required to display the PivotTable properly in the Web browser.*

14. Click the Copy 📋 button on the toolbar, or choose **Edit→Copy** from the menu bar.

15. Click the Up one Level 📁 or Back ⬅ button to return to the *My Computer* level.

16. Follow the instructions for your version of Windows as listed below:

    ▪ **Windows 95, 98, NT 4.0**—If necessary, scroll down the My Computer window until the **Web Folders** icon is visible; then *double-click* to open Web Folders. If you do not see a Web Folders icon like the one at right then the Web folders feature is not installed on your computer. See your instructor for assistance.

    Web Folders

    ▪ **Windows 2000**—Click the Up one Level 📁 button; then double-click on the **My Network Places** icon. You may see one or more Web folders along with other network resources.

    This window will display all of the available Web folders to which you may publish. Depending on how your system is configured, there may be just one folder or several.

17. Double-click to open your assigned Web folder. Click **OK** if you are prompted to enter a user name and password, and the password is already filled in. Otherwise, fill in the user name and password you received in Lesson 13; then click **OK.**
    After a pause, the contents of the folder will be displayed. There may be some files displayed in this folder that belong to other students who have published their files.

18. Click the Paste 📋 button on the toolbar, or choose **Edit→Paste** from the menu bar. Click **Yes to All** if you are prompted to overwrite any of the files in the folder.
    Your files will be copied into the Web folder. After a pause, you will also see a window displaying your files being copied to the Web server. *Depending on the speed of your Internet connection, this process may take a few seconds or over a minute.*

19. After the file transfer is completed, double-click the *pivottable* file in the Web folder window.
    The Internet Explorer Web browser will start and display your interactive PivotTable Web page over the Internet. Notice the URL in the Address bar near the top of the Internet Explorer window. It should start with http://www.

20. Try manipulating some of the fields on the PivotTable.

21. When you are done, close ❌ the Internet Explorer window.

22. Close ❌ the Web folder window; then restore the Excel window to the Desktop.

Adding Fields to an Interactive PivotTable Web Page

There is a Field List ⊞ button on the interactive Web page toolbar, which displays a list of all the fields in the PivotTable database. You can drag and drop to add any field from the list onto the PivotTable. The Field List window also cont.ins an **Add** button that you can use to add fields to the PivotTable. An example of a field list and its components is described below.

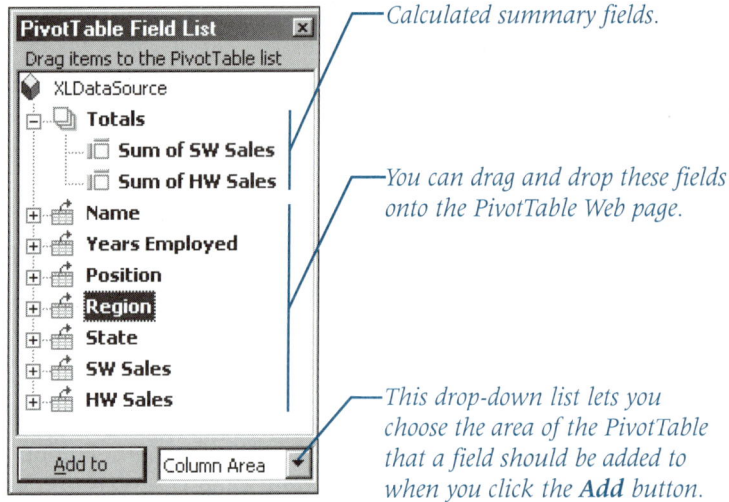

—Calculated summary fields.

—You can drag and drop these fields onto the PivotTable Web page.

*—This drop-down list lets you choose the area of the PivotTable that a field should be added to when you click the **Add** button.*

Working with Styles

A *style* is cell formatting to which you give a name. Once you have defined a style, you can apply its formatting to any cell with just a couple of mouse clicks. Some styles may be very simple, such as changing the color of a cell's contents. Other styles may combine changes in the font, number format, borders, and shading. To apply a style, you select the range of cell(s) to be formatted; then choose a style from the style box on the toolbar, or use *Format→Style* to choose a style from a dialog box.

The Benefits of Styles

Using styles offers two tremendous advantages compared to manual formatting methods:

■ **Styles make your formatting more consistent**—When you use a style, you no longer need to remember the format settings used for specific types of cells, such as headings and subtotals. You simply apply the appropriate style. If you change your mind later, you can edit the style and the changes will be applied to every cell in the workbook to which the style was applied previously.

■ **Styles are more convenient**—Especially when you must make several format changes in a cell, applying a style is a faster method than manual methods. It is even faster than using the format painter. Using styles can spare you the tedium of repeatedly giving the same formatting commands in various cells.

Creating Styles

When you want to create a style, you have two methods to choose from:

- **Create by Example**—With this method, you manually apply all of the formatting commands to a cell; then assign a style name to the formatting. This is probably the easiest method for creating new styles.

- **Create by Definition**—With this method, you open the Style dialog box and choose the format settings you wish to assign to the style.

The Style Box

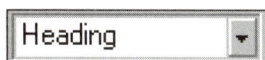

Excel's toolbar can contain a style box that lists all of the available styles. The style box is very useful if you like to define styles by example. Unfortunately, Excel's default Formatting toolbar does not contain the Style box, but it is easy to add it to the toolbar yourself. The first part of the next Hands-On Exercise will show you how to do this.

The Style List

Every workbook has its own style list. The list includes styles in the template from which you created the workbook, and any additional styles you create in that workbook. The styles you edit or create in one workbook will not appear in other workbooks. However, you can *Merge* (i.e., copy) styles into a workbook from other open workbooks with the Merge button in the Style dialog box.

TIP!

If you often need create the same new styles in many of your workbooks, consider creating a workbook template file that contains the styles, or modify the standard workbook template. The styles defined a template are added to every workbook you create from that template. See Creating Your Own Templates *in Lesson 10.*

Quick Reference

DEFINING STYLES BY EXAMPLE	
Task	**Procedure**
Create a new style by example.	■ Select a cell in the workbook.
	■ Apply any custom formatting to the cell that you wish to incorporate in the new style.
	■ Click in the Style box on the toolbar; then type a name for the style, and tap (ENTER). Or you can choose *Format→Style* from the menu bar; then type the new style name in the dialog box, and click *OK*.
Edit a style by example.	■ Click a cell on the worksheet to which you have already applied the style you wish to edit.
	■ Manually format the cell with the desired changes for the style.
	■ Click the drop-down list ▾ button (not the style name) on the Style box; then choose the same style name.
	■ Click *Yes* when Excel asks if you wish to redefine the style based upon your selection.

Hands-On 16.6 Define and Edit Styles by Example

Make Sure That the Styles Box Is on the Formatting Toolbar

Having the Style box on the Excel toolbar makes defining styles by example much more convenient. Since the Style box is not part of Excel's default Formatting toolbar, you may need to add it.

1. Click the Sales Database worksheet tab; then click on Cell **A4.**

2. Examine the Formatting toolbar. If you see a box on the toolbar with the name *Normal* inside it, the Style box is already installed on the toolbar, and you can skip to *Step 6.*

3. Right-click on any toolbar; then choose **Customize** from the pop-up menu.

4. Follow these steps to add the Style box to the Formatting toolbar.

Ⓐ *Click the* Commands *tab near the top of the dialog box.*

Ⓑ *Click the* Format *category.*

Ⓒ *Start to drag the* Style *box up to the very left side of the* Formatting *toolbar.*

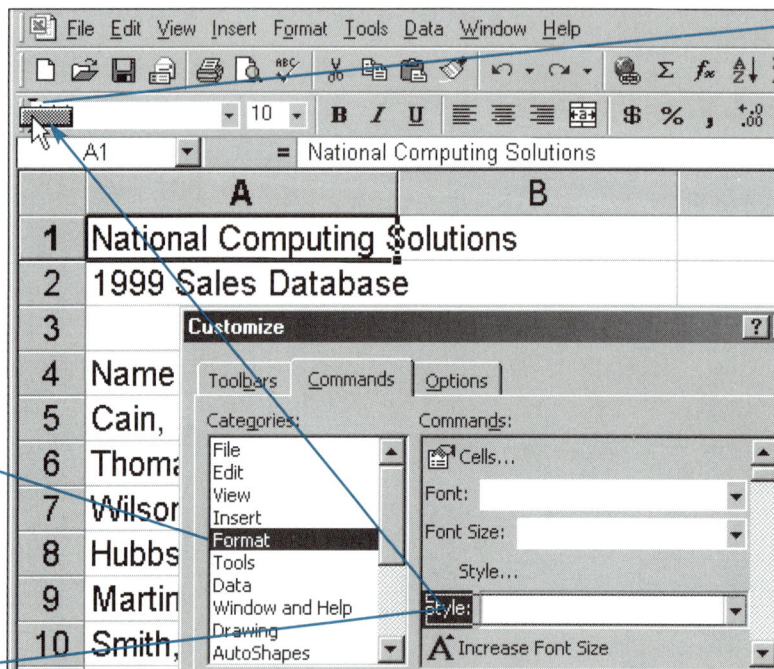

Ⓓ *Release the mouse button when the* Style *box is positioned over the* Formatting *toolbar as shown here.*

5. Close the Customize dialog box.

Define a Style by Example

Now you will define a style for use with column headings.

6. Make sure that the highlight is still in Cell **A4.**

7. Set the *Font Color* to a light shade of yellow; then set the *Fill Color* to a dark shade of blue.
   These formats will define your style. Now you will use these formats to define a style named Heading.

8. Click in the Style box on the toolbar; then type **Heading** as the name for the new style, and tap (ENTER).
   That's all there is to it! You have created a new style by example. Now let's apply the style to other cells.

9. Drag to select Cells **B4:G4**. Click the Style box drop-down list button; then choose Heading from the list.
   The formatting of your new style is immediately applied to the cells.

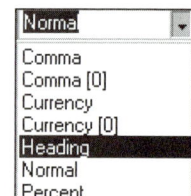

10. Click the *Sales by Region* worksheet tab; then drag to select Cells **A4:H4**.

11. Click the drop-down list ▾ button on the Style box; then choose *Heading*.
   Once you have defined a style, it is available to use on any worksheet in the workbook.

Edit a Style by Example

You will now edit the style by example and review the results.

12. Click to select Cell **A4**.
   When you edit a style by example, you must always begin by selecting a cell to which the style has already been applied.

13. Set the *Font Color* to a dark shade of green; then set the *Fill Color* to a light shade of green.

14. Choose *Heading* from the *Style* list.
   Excel will ask if you wish to redefine the Heading style to match the changes you made in Cell A4.

15. Click **Yes** to redefine the style by example.
   Notice that all of the cells with the Heading style have now changed to match the new style definition. Styles can save you a lot of time when you need to change a worksheet's formatting.

16. Click the *Sales Database* worksheet tab.
   Perhaps you saw this coming! Your new style definition has been applied to this worksheet as well. Styles are a very powerful formatting tool.

The Styles Dialog Box

The Styles dialog box contains a list of all available styles and command buttons to add, modify, and delete styles. For example, you use the **Delete** button in the Styles dialog box to delete unneeded styles. You can also use the Styles dialog box to copy styles from one open workbook to another. The Styles dialog box also gives you the option to include or exclude various types of formatting from a style definition. A portion of a typical Style dialog box is displayed below.

Only formats that are checked are applied by the style. In this example, cell Alignment *is not checked, so the current cell alignment is retained when the style is applied.*

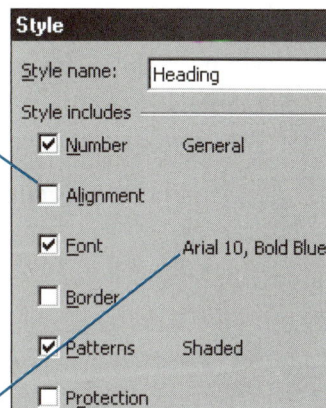

Each active format setting has a brief description.

Style		
Style name:	Heading	
Style includes		
☑ Number	General	
☐ Alignment		
☑ Font	Arial 10, Bold Blue	
☐ Border		
☑ Patterns	Shaded	
☐ Protection		

Overriding a Style

You can always change the formatting of a cell that has had a style applied to it. This is called *overriding* the style. When you override a style, the change will remain, even if the style is redefined later.

TIP!

To end an override, you must re-apply the style to the cell(s); then click No when you are asked if you wish to redefine the style.

Quick Reference

WORKING WITH STYLES

Task	Procedure
Create or edit a style by definition.	■ Click a cell in the workbook. The formatting of this cell will serve as the basis for the new style.
	■ Choose *Format→Style* from the menu bar; then type the new style name in the dialog box, and click *Add*.
	■ Click the *Modify* button; then make the desired settings in the *Format Cells* dialog box for the style, and click *OK*.
	■ Click *OK* to close the Styles dialog box when you are finished.
Delete a style.	■ Choose *Format→Style* from the menu bar.
	■ Choose the style to be deleted from the style list; then click *Delete*. *Note:* You can never delete the *Normal* style.

Hands-On 16.7 Edit a Style by Definition

Most of the time you will define styles by example. However, you can also accomplish the same tasks with the Styles dialog box. In this exercise, you will edit a style for numeric values and override the style setting in a range of cells.

1. Click on Cell **F5** on the *Sales Database* worksheet.

2. Choose **Format→Style** from the menu bar.
   Notice that this cell already has a style assigned to it (Comma). At present, this style only has number formatting assigned to it. The Comma style is a default style that is created in new workbooks.

3. If necessary, click the *Font* and *Patterns* checkboxes to place a check in the boxes.
   The present setting for these types of formatting appear to the right of the check boxes. These checked format types are now part of the style definition.

4. Click the **Modify** button.
   The Formatting dialog box appears. It is just like the one displayed when you choose Format→Cells from the menu bar.

5. Make sure that the Font tab is selected; then set the font color to *dark blue* and the font style to *bold*.

6. Click the *Patterns* tab in the dialog box; then choose a shade of *light blue* for the cell shading.

7. Click **OK** to close the Format Cells dialog box. Examine the descriptions beside the Font and Patterns format settings that you just changed.
   The descriptions now match the new settings.

8. Click **OK** to close the Styles dialog box.
   Since most of the cells in the SW and HW Sales columns use the Comma style, the formatting immediately changes to reflect to reflect the new style definition. This change to the Comma style will only affect this workbook. It will not affect other workbooks, nor new workbooks that you create later.

Override a Style

9. Click the *Sales by Region* worksheet tab.
   The style change was applied to this worksheet as well.

10. Select Cells F8 to H8; then use the Fill Color button on the toolbar to set the fill for these cells to a shade of yellow.
    The fill color for the Comma style has been overridden in cells F4–G4.

11. Click Cell **G5.** Set the fill color for this cell to a light shade of green.

12. Choose *Comma* in the Style box. Click **Yes** when you are asked to confirm that you wish to redefine the style.
    Notice that Cells F8:H8 where you overrode the style were not affected by the style change. Your formatting override will stay in effect until the style is applied to these cells again. Let's do that now.

13. Select Cells **F8:H8;** then choose *Comma* in the Style box.
    Excel will ask again if you wish to redefine the style based upon the example. In this case, you don't want to redefine the style—you want to re-apply the style to these cells and remove the override.

14. Click **No** to reapply the style to the selected cells.
    The override is canceled, and these cells will conform to the Comma style whenever it is changed in the future.

15. Save 🖫 the workbook.

Working with Outlines and Grouping

Excel's Outline feature lets you control the display of detail data in worksheets. This helps you see the big picture, while still being able to view the details when necessary. If your worksheet contains SUM formulas to summarize data, Excel can apply an outline to the data automatically. For detail areas without summary formulas, you can manually group rows and columns of cells.

How Outlines Work

When you create an outline for a worksheet, Excel groups the data into detail rows and columns. This structure is displayed visually along the top and left border of the worksheet. The outline area also contains plus and minus symbols you can click to expand and collapse your view of the data. An example of an outlined worksheet is displayed below.

These buttons let you expand and collapse the outline to a specific level.

Columns B and C contain two items of detail data about the sales personnel that has been grouped. You can use the minus sign button to hide the detail data.

You can use this plus sign button to expand the display of hidden detail Columns F and G.

The detail data rows for the Sales Reps are displayed.

The detail data rows for these Senior Sales Reps and Telemarketers are hidden.

	A	B	C	D	E	H
1	National Computing Solutions					
2	Sales by Position					
3						
4	Name	Years Employed	Position	Region	State	Total Sales
5	Thomas, Will	2	Sales Rep	Central	IL	350,000
6	Wilson, Bernie	1	Sales Rep	Central	IL	290,000
7	Watson, Tom	8	Sales Rep	Eastern	MA	570,000
8	Williams, Michael	3	Sales Rep	Eastern	FL	460,000
9	Smith, Bob	3	Sales Rep	Western	CA	380,000
10	Sales Rep Subtotal					2,050,000
15	Senior Sales Rep Subtotal					3,624,000
21	Telemarketer Subtotal					4,049,000
22	Totals					9,723,000

Auto Outline

Excel can analyze and apply an outline to most worksheets automatically. The key to smooth automatic outlining is to arrange the detail and summary data consistently. For example, if the data is laid out in columns, make sure that all of the detail data lies to the right or left of the summary formulas. The more hierarchical your layout, the more effective the resulting outline will be. Excel will try to outline all data related to summary formulas in the worksheet. If you are not satisfied with the results of the Auto Outline command, you can still group rows and columns manually.

AUTO OUTLINING A WORKSHEET

Task	Procedure
Apply an automatic outline to a worksheet.	■ To be Auto Outlined, the detail rows or columns should be located immediately to the left of or above cells with formulas that summarize the detail data.

Tip: You can adjust the relative position of summary formulas to detail data with the Data→Group and Outline→Settings command.

	■ Select the portion of the worksheet to be outlined, or click in a single cell to outline the entire worksheet.
	■ Choose *Data→Group and Outline→Auto Outline* from the menu bar.
Clear the outline from a worksheet.	■ Choose *Data→Group and Outline→Clear Outline* from the menu bar.

Hands-On 16.8 **Automatically Outline a Worksheet**

In this exercise you will use the Auto Outline command to outline a worksheet; then you will try expanding and collapsing the outline.

1. Click the *Sales by Position* worksheet tab.

2. Choose **Data→Group and Outline→Auto Outline** from the menu bar.
   Excel will automatically group the rows and columns of the table. Notice that the rows are divided into three groups at Level 2 and one larger group at Level 1. There is just one group formed for the columns. Excel reviewed the formulas on the worksheet to arrive at these groupings

3. Follow these steps to collapse the display of detail data.

   Ⓐ *Click the* Level 1 *button for the column group. Notice how the* SW *and* HW *sales columns have collapsed, leaving only the* Total Sales *summary column in view.*

   Ⓑ *Click the* Level 1 *button for the row groups. This leaves only a single figure for the grand total sales.*

   Ⓒ *Click the* Level 2 *button for the row groups. Now you can see subtotals for the three types of sales positions.*

*Notice the plus (+) and minus (−) buttons in the outline area. An outline with a **Minus** button is currently displaying its detail data. An outline with a **Plus** button has details that are not displayed.*

(Continued on the next page)

4. Follow these steps to collapse and expand the *row* detail data.

Ⓐ *Click the plus button for the* Sales Rep *Subtotal row.*
This expands the detail display of individual sales reps.

4	Name	Years
10	Sales Rep Subtotal	
15	Senior Sales Rep Subtotal	
21	Telemarketer Subtotal	
22	Totals	

Ⓑ *Click the plus button for the* Telemarketer *Subtotal*
row. Now the details for this group are displayed.

5. Click the **Level 2** button for the row groups.
   The expanded Level 3 rows for the Level 2 groups are immediately
   collapsed again. Now only the Level 2 rows are visible.

6. Click the **Level 3** button for the row groups.
   This command reveals all of the detail rows that were grouped at the lowest level
   of the outline. You can independently expand and collapse individual groups with
   the **Plus** *and* **Minus** *buttons. The Level 1, 2, 3 buttons save you the time of*
   clicking the **Plus** *and* **Minus** *buttons for the individual groups at each level.*

Creating Groups Manually

When you have non-numeric detail data, or when Excel simply does not outline the worksheet as you desire, you can group rows and columns manually. You simply select the rows or columns to be grouped; then choose *Data→Group and Outline→Group* from the menu bar. The selected rows or columns will be grouped together in the outline or added to an existing adjacent group. You use a similar procedure to manually ungroup rows and columns. If desired, you can even ungroup rows or columns that were originally grouped by Excel's *Auto Outline* command.

Quick Reference

MANUALLY SETTING GROUPS

Task	Procedure
Manually group rows or columns.	■ Select the *detail* row(s) or column(s) to be grouped.
	■ Choose *Data→Group and Outline→Group* from the menu bar.
Manually ungroup rows or columns.	■ Select the rows or columns to be ungrouped.
	■ Choose *Data→Group and Outline→Ungroup* from the menu bar.

Hands-On 16.9 Create Groups Manually

In this exercise, you will create a new group manually. This group was not created by the Auto Outline command because there were no summary formulas for the detail data.

Add a Group to the Auto Outline

1. Follow these steps to create a group for the detail sales staff data.

   A *Select Columns B and C by dragging the column headings.*

   B *Choose* **Data→Group and Outline→Group** *from the menu bar.*

	A	B	C	D
1	National Computing	Solutions		
2	Sales by Position			
3				
4	Name	Years Employed	Position	Region
5	Thomas, Will	2	Sales Rep	Central
6	Wilson, Bernie	1	Sales Rep	Central

   C *Click the new Group's* **Minus** *button to collapse the detail columns. Now the* Years Employed *and* Position *details about the salespersons is hidden from view, allowing you to concentrate on the data in other columns.*

Clear the Outline

2. Click the **Level 2** button to expand the *column* groups. Columns B, C, F, and G should now be visible.
   In the next step, you will clear the auto outline. It is always a good idea to display all of the hidden detail rows and columns before you clear an outline.

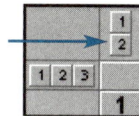

3. Click Cell **A1.**
   If you have selected a range of cells, the Clear Outline command will only affect outline levels that lie within the selected cells. Any cells outside the selection would not be ungrouped.

4. Choose **Data→Group and Outline→Clear Outline** from the menu bar.
   All of the outline groups on the worksheet are cleared, even the group you created manually in Step 1.

Create an Outline Manually

5. Select Columns B–E.

6. Choose **Data→Group and Outline→Group** from the menu bar.
   The new group is created. Although the Auto Outline is handy for certain types of worksheets with summary formulas, it is also easy to create groups manually.

7. Click the **Minus** button for the newly created group to collapse its data.

8. Select Rows 5–9 by dragging the mouse over the row headings at the left edge of the worksheet.
   These are the detail rows for the Sales Rep subtotal. Now you will create a group out of these detail rows that you can collapse and expand.

9. Choose **Data→Group and Outline→Group** from the menu bar; then click the **Minus** button to collapse the new group.

(Continued on the next page)

Use the Ungroup Command

10. Click the **Plus** button for both groups to expand the detail rows and columns.
    *You could also have clicked the **Level 2** buttons for the row and column groups at the top-left corner of the worksheet.*

11. If necessary, select Rows 5 through 9; then choose **Data→Group and Outline→Ungroup** from the menu bar.
    The selected rows are ungrouped manually.

12. Click on any cell in the worksheet to deselect Rows 5 through 9; then choose **Data→Group and Outline→Clear Outline** from the menu bar.
    The column group is removed as well. This command can remove both auto outline groups and manually created groups.

13. Save 🖫 the workbook; then close ⊠ the Excel window.

Concepts Review

True/False Questions

1. A PivotTable automatically creates summary formulas for your data.   TRUE   FALSE

2. Changing the order of the fields in the Row or Column areas of a PivotTable does not affect the display of data.   TRUE   FALSE

3. A PivotChart does not allow you to rearrange the data fields.   TRUE   FALSE

4. A style is created automatically whenever you change the formatting of a cell.   TRUE   FALSE

5. Styles help you to format worksheets consistently.   TRUE   FALSE

6. You cannot outline a worksheet manually.   TRUE   FALSE

7. The Auto Outline command only groups cells with label data.   TRUE   FALSE

8. The Clear Outline command only removes groups that were created with the *Data→Group and Outline→Auto Outline* command.   TRUE   FALSE

Multiple-Choice Questions

1. What happens on a PivotTable when you *pivot* a field from the Rows to the Columns area?
   a. Nothing happens. Only numeric data fields can be placed in the Row and Columns areas.
   b. The field exchanges positions with a field that is already positioned in the Columns area.
   c. The data for the field is summarized in columns rather than in rows.
   d. You cannot pivot a field directly between Rows and Columns; you must remove it from the PivotTable first, then add the field to the Column fields area.

2. How do you change the chart type of a PivotChart?
   a. You can only use the chart types designed specifically for PivotCharts.
   b. You use the same chart type commands that you would use for normal Excel charts.
   c. You arrange the fields on the PivotTable; then give the PivotChart command.
   d. You cannot change the chart type of a PivotChart. You must use the default format assigned by Excel.

3. To create a style by example, which procedure works best?
   a. Use the *Format→Styles* command; then define the style and click OK.
   b. Type a new name for the style in the Style box on the toolbar; then assign formatting for the style.
   c. Click the style name in the Style box; then click Yes to redefine the style.
   d. Manually format a cell; then type a name for the style in the Style box on the toolbar.
   e. None of the above

4. What happens when you give the Auto Outline command?
   a. Only rows and columns with summary formulas are grouped.
   b. Excel creates groups for all types of detail data on the worksheet.
   c. You must select the rows or columns to be grouped; then give the Group command.
   d. Excel creates an outline based upon your entries in a dialog box.

Skill Builders

Skill Builder 16.1 Create a PivotTable

In this exercise, you will create a PivotTable from another database. You will practice placing and pivoting fields to change your view of the data.

1. Start Excel; then open the *Skill Builder 16.1* workbook on the exercise diskette.
   This workbook displays one month's activity at Acme Auto Sales. Before you create a PivotTable, it is always a good idea to take a moment and look over the layout of the data fields and records. For example, there is just one field for numeric data in this database. Therefore, you will want to place the Price *field in the Data area of the PivotTable.*

2. Click on Cell **A4**.
   This tells Excel that it should use the database fields when you create the PivotTable.

3. Choose **Data→PivotTable and PivotChart Report** from the menu bar; then click **Finish** to use the default settings in the Wizard.

4. Double-click the *Sheet 1* worksheet tab, and rename it **PivotTable**.

5. Drag the *Sold By* field into the *Row Fields* area along the left side of the PivotTable.
   Since there is no data to display for the field yet, the PivotTable just shows the location of this field.

6. Drag the *Price* field into the *Data* area of the PivotTable.
   The PivotTable displays the total sales for each salesperson. Next, you might want to know which type of car each salesperson sold this month, so you will place a new field in the Row Fields area.

7. Follow these steps to add the *Type* field to the *Row Fields* area of the PivotTable.

   Ⓐ *Start to drag the* Type *field over the* Row Fields *area of the PivotTable.*

Drop Page Fields Here	
Sum of Price	
Sold By ▾	Total
Bob	122620
Kelly	154675
Sam	120470
Grand Total	397765

   PivotTable
   PivotTable ▾ | Sold By | Type

   Ⓑ *Release the mouse button when you see the gray bar just to the right of the* Sold By *field.*

   The PivotTable expands to display the sales of the various types of vehicle sold by each salesperson. However, it would also be interesting to summarize how the revenue at the dealership breaks down by vehicle type. So in the next step you will pivot the Type field from the Row Fields area to the Column Fields area.

8. Drag the *Type* field to the *Column Fields* area (where you see the word *Total*) as shown at right.
   Now the Grand Total line at the bottom of the PivotTable displays the revenue for each type of car.

Sum of Price		
Sold By ▾	Type ▾	Total
Bob	Sedan	55445

9. Drag the *New/Used* field into the left side of the *Row Fields* area of the PivotTable (just to the left of where the *Sold By* field is located now).

10. Pivot the *New/Used* field into the *Column Fields* area of the PivotTable (where the *Type* field is located now).

Set the PivotTable Options

There is an Options dialog box for the PivotTable. This lets you control several aspects of the way your PivotTable displays data.

11. Click the **PivotTable** button on the PivotTable toolbar; then choose **Table Options** from the drop-down menu.

12. Uncheck the *Grand totals for columns* and *Grand totals for rows* options; then click **OK.**
    The grand totals on the bottom row and right column are removed from the table.

13. Click the Undo button on the Excel toolbar to restore the grand totals.

14. Try experimenting with other fields on the PivotTable, and practice pivoting fields between the *Row* and *Column* Field areas. You can also remove fields from the PivotTable.

15. When you are done, save the workbook.

Skill Builder 16.2 Create a PivotChart

In this exercise, you will create a PivotChart to display the same data you used in Skill Builder 16.1. You will practice placing and pivoting fields to change the PivotChart's display of this data.

1. Click the *January Sales* worksheet tab; then click on any cell of the database.
   This tells Excel that it should use the database fields when you create the PivotChart.

2. Choose **Data→PivotTable and PivotChart Report** from the menu bar.
   The PivotTable and PivotChart Wizard will display Step 1.

3. Change the report type to *PivotChart;* then click **Next.**

4. Click **Next** again to accept the database as the data range for the PivotChart.
   If you performed Skill Builder 16.1, Excel will now ask if you wish to base this PivotChart on the existing PivotTable report. Since the reports ought to reflect the same data anyway, it makes sense to answer yes.

5. Click **Yes** if you were asked to use the same source data and reduce the size of the workbook file.

6. Click **Next** to accept the existing PivotTable as the data source.

7. Choose the *New worksheet* option; then click **Finish.**

8. Drag and drop the *Sold By* field into the *Category fields* area at the bottom of the chart.

(Continued on the next page)

9. Drag and drop the *Price* field into the *Data Items* area at the center of the chart.
   The PivotChart will display a summary of the total sales for each salesperson.

10. Drag and drop the *New/Used* field into the *Series fields* area on the right side of the chart.
    It looks like Bob brought in the highest used car revenue, while Kelly was the leader in overall revenue.

11. Drag and drop the *Type* field into the *Series* area on the right side of the chart.
    This produces a confusing array of data. Let's pivot a field and see if that helps

12. Drag the *New/Used* field just to the **left** of the *Sold By* | New/Used ▼ | Sold By ▼ |
    field in the *Categories* area at the bottom of the chart.
    This makes a more informative display. Now you can see the breakdown of vehicle types more clearly.
    You can also compare the sales of new and used cars.

13. Now drag the *New/Used* field to the **right** of the *Sold By* field. | Sold By ▼ | New/Used ▼ |
    Now you can very easily compare the performance of the individual salespersons. The ability to pivot the data in the various areas is a key feature of PivotCharts.

14. Try experimenting with other fields on the PivotChart, and practice pivoting fields between the *Row* and *Column* Field areas. You can also remove fields from the PivotChart.

15. When you are done, save 💾 the workbook.

Skill Builder 16.3 Create and Apply Styles

In this exercise, you will create styles by example for numeric fields and dates.

1. Click the *January Sales* worksheet tab.

Create and Edit a Style for Numeric Values

2. Click Cell **E5;** then click the Currency 🔲$ button on the toolbar.
   Excel formats the cell with the dollar sign ($) and adds two decimal places. Notice that the Currency *style is displayed in the* Style *box. This is a built-in style that came from the standard Excel workbook template. Rather than alter this built-in style, you will create a new style.*

3. Click in the *Style* box on the toolbar; then type **Price** as the new style name, and tap (ENTER).
   The new style name is now displayed in the Style box.

4. Select Cells **E6** through **E27;** then choose *Price* in the Style box.
   Now all of the cells have the dollar sign and decimal places. Since you don't really need the decimals, let's edit the style by example to remove them.

5. Click Cell **E27;** then click the Decrease Decimal [.00→.0] button twice to eliminate the unnecessary decimal places.

6. Choose *Price* again from the Style list.
   Excel will ask if you want to redefine the Price style to match the formatting in the selection.

7. Click **Yes** to redefine the style by example.
   Notice how all of the other cells formatted with the Price style immediately lost their decimals. Using styles helps you create consistent formatting throughout a workbook. Styles also can save time by allowing you to easily update the formats of cells to which the styles have been applied.

Create and Use a Style for Dates

8. Click Cell **F5.**

9. Choose **Format→Cells** from the menu bar. Click the *Number* tab; then choose the *3/14* date style from the top of the *Type* list, and click **OK.**

10. Click in the *Style* box on the toolbar; then type **Date** as the new style name, and tap (ENTER).

11. Select the range **F6:F24;** then choose *Date* from the Style box.
    The date format in the selected cells immediately changes to the new style.

12. Click on one of the date cells; then choose **Format→Cells** from the menu bar. Change the date format of the cell; then redefine the Date style by example.
    All of the date cells should change to reflect the style change.

13. Feel free to practice creating a style for other cells on the worksheet. For example, you might want to create a style for the column headings, including bold type, font color, and cell border settings.

14. When you are done, save ⊞ the workbook.

Skill Builder 16.4 Outline a Worksheet

In this exercise, you will use the Auto Outline command; then manually group and ungroup columns.

1. If necessary, start Excel; then open the *Skill Builder 16.1* workbook on the exercise diskette.

2. If it is not already displayed, click the *January Sales* worksheet tab.

Auto Outline the Worksheet

3. Click Cell **E26.** Examine the formula in this cell.
   This cell contains the only summary formula in the worksheet.

4. Choose **Data→Group and Outline→Auto Outline** from the menu bar.
   Excel automatically outlines the detail rows of the worksheet, above the Total Sales row. None of the columns were outlined because there are no summary formulas to summarize column data.

5. Click the **Level 1** button near the upper-left corner of the worksheet to collapse the display of the detail data rows.
   Now only the summary data is visible.

6. Click the **Plus** button on the left side of the worksheet to expand the view of the detail rows.

(Continued on the next page)

Manually Group Columns

The columns contain detail data, but it is not numeric. In this case, you can group the columns manually.

7. Drag on the column headings to select columns **C** through **E;** then choose **Data→Group and Outline→Group** from the menu bar.

8. Click the **Minus** button near the top of the worksheet to collapse the detail data columns. Then click the **Plus** button to expand the detail data columns.

9. Click the *Column B* heading to select the column; then choose **Data→Group and Outline→Group** from the menu bar.

10. Click the **Plus** button on the top of the worksheet window.
    Notice how Column B *has been added to the group you created in Step 7. If a column lies directly to the left of a group, Excel will add it to the existing group. The same thing happens if you select a row that is immediately above an existing group.*

11. Choose **Data→Group and Outline→Settings** from the menu bar.
    The Settings dialog box displays options for the placement of summary rows and columns. As you can see, the default for columns is summary columns positioned to the right of detail columns. If your worksheet is laid out differently, you can adjust these options so that the Auto Outline and Group commands will function differently.

12. Click **Cancel** to close the Settings dialog box.

Ungroup the Worksheet

13. Drag on the column headings to select Columns **B** through **E;** then choose **Data→Group and Outline→Ungroup** from the menu bar.
    The group is removed. You can manually ungroup columns and rows, including groups created by the Auto Outline command.

14. Click the Undo ⟲ button on the Excel toolbar to restore the group.

15. Click on any cell in the worksheet to de-select the columns.

16. Choose **Data→Group and Outline→Clear Outline** from the menu bar.

17. Feel free to experiment with manually grouping rows and columns.

18. When you are done, save 🖫 the workbook; then close it.

Assessments

Assessment 16.1 **Create a PivotTable**

1. Open the Assessment 16.1 workbook on your exercise diskette.
   This database records expenses at the Capitol City Animal Shelter.

2. Examine the *March Expense Report* worksheet. Look over the data before you create the PivotTable. Be sure to identify the data fields in the database.

3. Create a PivotTable on a new worksheet.

4. Drag fields onto the PivotTable to display the data as described below:

   ■ The data should summarize the total cost of care and shelter.

   ■ The columns should compare the cost of caring for Healthy and Sick animals.

   ■ The rows should summarize the data by Cats/Dogs; then by Age.

5. Leave the workbook open, as you will continue to use it.

		Healthy	Sick	Grand Total
Cat	Adult	$205.00		$ 205.00
	Pup/Kitten	$ 67.75	$102.00	$ 169.75
Cat Total		$272.75	$102.00	$ 374.75
Dog	Adult	$369.75	$ 55.25	$ 425.00
	Pup/Kitten	$146.50	$282.00	$ 428.50
Dog Total		$516.25	$337.25	$ 853.50
Grand Total		$789.00	$439.25	$ 1,228.25

When you finish, your PivotTable should look like this figure. Note that the Field buttons have been removed from the figure.

Assessment 16.2 **Create a Pivot Chart**

1. Examine the *March Expense Report* worksheet in the Assessment 16.1 workbook. Look over the data before you create the PivotChart. Be sure to identify the data fields in the database.

2. Create a PivotChart on a new worksheet.

3. Drag fields onto the PivotChart to display the data as described below:

   ■ The data bars should summarize the total cost of care and shelter.

   ■ The data bars should display the costs of care for sick and healthy animals.

   ■ The data should be broken down by the costs for cats and dogs, and compare the costs between kittens/pups, and adults.

(Continued on the next page)

4. Leave the workbook open as you will continue to use it.

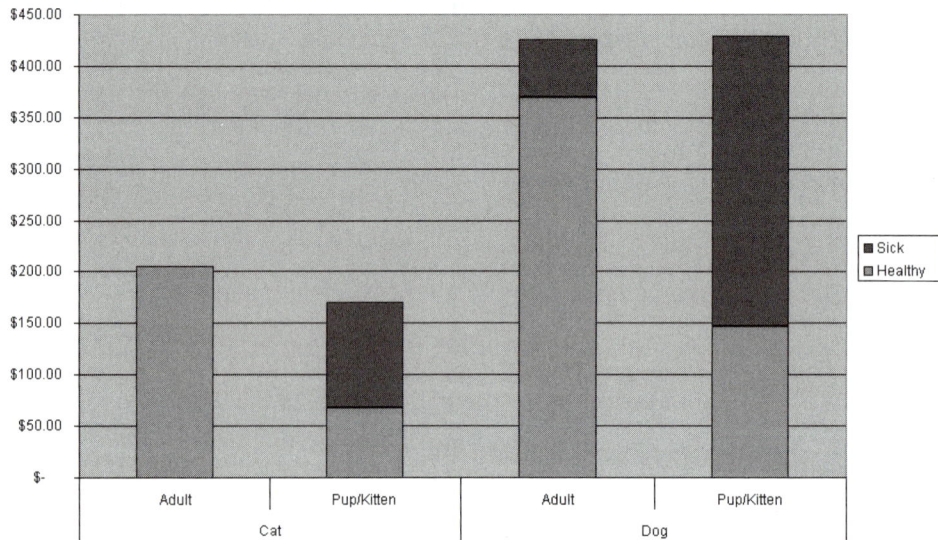

When you finish, your PivotTable should look like the figure above. Note that the Field buttons have been removed from the figure.

Assessment 16.3 Apply Styles to a Worksheet

1. Display the *March Expense Summary* worksheet in the Assessment 16.1 workbook.

2. Create a style for the column headings according to the specifications below:

- The style name should be **column head**.

- The font style should be bold, with the font color set to a shade of blue.

- There should be a border on the bottom of the cell.

3. Apply the column head style to all of the column headings.

4. Create a style for the subtotal rows named according to the specifications below:

- The style name should be **subtotals**.

- The font style should be bold, with the font color set to a shade of red.

- There should be a light fill color on the cell that makes the font easy to read.

5. Apply the subtotals style to all of the subtotal rows.

6. Edit the subtotal style to feature a dark fill color and a light text color.

7. Leave the workbook open as you will continue to use it.

Assessment 16.4 Outline a Worksheet

1. Display the *March Expense Summary* worksheet in the Assessment 16.1 workbook.

2. Use any methods you choose to group the worksheet according to the description below:

   ◼ The details of shelter cost and veterinary care should be grouped.
   You may need to ungroup the Date Arrived column.

   ◼ The details of Age and Health should be grouped.

   ◼ The detail rows for all subtotals should be grouped.

   ◼ The subtotal rows should be grouped.

TIP!

	A	B	C	D	E	F	G
1	**Capitol City Animal Shelter**						
2	March Expense Summary						
3							
4	Animal	Age	Health	Date Arrived	Shelter Cost	Veterinary Care	Total Costs
5	Cat	Adult	Healthy	1-Mar	$ 82.50	$ 10.00	$ 92.50
6	Cat	Adult	Healthy	9-Mar	$ 60.50	$ 10.00	$ 70.50
7	Cat	Adult	Healthy	24-Mar	$ 19.25	$ 10.00	$ 29.25
8	Cat	Adult	Healthy	30-Mar	$ 2.75	$ 10.00	$ 12.75
9	Cat Subtotal				$ 165.00	$ 40.00	$ 205.00
10	Cat	Pup/Kitten	Sick	3-Mar	$ 77.00	$ 25.00	$ 102.00
11	Cat	Pup/Kitten	Healthy	10-Mar	$ 57.75	$ 10.00	$ 67.75
12	Kitten Subtotal				$ 134.75	$ 35.00	$ 169.75
13	Dog	Adult	Healthy	2-Mar	$ 79.75	$ 10.00	$ 89.75
14	Dog	Adult	Healthy	8-Mar	$ 63.25	$ 10.00	$ 73.25
15	Dog	Adult	Healthy	9-Mar	$ 60.50	$ 10.00	$ 70.50
16	Dog	Adult	Healthy	11-Mar	$ 55.00	$ 10.00	$ 65.00
17	Dog	Adult	Sick	20-Mar	$ 30.25	$ 25.00	$ 55.25
18	Dog	Adult	Healthy	20-Mar	$ 30.25	$ 10.00	$ 40.25
19	Dog	Adult	Healthy	28-Mar	$ 8.25	$ 10.00	$ 18.25
20	Dog	Adult	Healthy	30-Mar	$ 2.75	$ 10.00	$ 12.75
21	Dog Subtotal				$ 330.00	$ 95.00	$ 425.00
22	Dog	Pup/Kitten	Sick	3-Mar	$ 77.00	$ 75.00	$ 152.00
23	Dog	Pup/Kitten	Healthy	3-Mar	$ 77.00	$ 10.00	$ 87.00
24	Dog	Pup/Kitten	Healthy	13-Mar	$ 49.50	$ 10.00	$ 59.50
25	Dog	Pup/Kitten	Sick	15-Mar	$ 44.00	$ 25.00	$ 69.00
26	Dog	Pup/Kitten	Sick	27-Mar	$ 11.00	$ 50.00	$ 61.00
27	Pup Subtotal				$ 258.50	$ 170.00	$ 428.50
28	Total Costs				$ 888.25	$ 340.00	$ 1,228.25

When you finish, your PivotChart should look like this figure.

Critical Thinking

Critical Thinking 16.1 On Your Own

Linda Johnson decides to use the database you developed in Critical Thinking exercise 15.1 to keep track of her new purchases for the month. She asks you to add new columns to the Subtotals worksheet that calculate the quantity of each product ordered and the wholesale price paid for the purchases.

- Add a column to the database named **Quantity.**

- Add a second column to the database named: **Wholesale Value.** The rows in this column should calculate the **Wholesale price** multiplied by the **Quantity.**

- Use the data form tool to insert the quantities of each product to be ordered according to the table below.

Product	Quantity
Rakes	12
Roto Tiller	4
Seeds	144
Shovels	12
Stakes	144
Azalias	48
Books	12
Bricks	200
Fake Plants	6
Ferns	48
Fertilizer	36
Hoses	24
Miracle Grow	48
Orchids	48
Planters	72
Pots	72
Potting Soil	24
Spades	12
Stones	24
Watering Buckets	18

Critical Thinking 16.2 Groups of Two

Linda Johnson was pleased with the database you developed in Critical Thinking 15.1 and the summary worksheets you designed in 15.2. She wants to know if PivotTables can display these summaries too. Like many Excel users, Linda would rather have someone show her how to use a technique, rather than learn it on her own. She tells you to design a PivotTable and a PivotChart from the database. Later that morning, she wants you to teach her how to create the PivotTable and PivotChart herself.

In this exercise, you will pair-up with a classmate. There are three tasks. One of you will perform Task A and the other will perform Task B. Then you will take turns undertaking Task C.

Task A: Create a PivotTable

■ You have 10 to 15 minutes to complete Task A.

■ Create a PivotTable on a new worksheet from the database on the Subtotals worksheet.

TIP!

Before you can create a PivotTable or PivotChart from the database in Critical Thinking 15.1, you must remove the subtotals from the database.

■ Add fields to the PivotTable to display a summary of the Wholesale Value of each product ordered, organized by Category ID.

■ Add a field to the PivotTable that displays the summary broken down by Supplier.

■ Edit the PivotTable so that the Garden category is excluded from the summary. When you are done, your PivotTable should look similar to the example below.

			Total
Home	Bay Area Garden Supply	Spades	$ 15.00
	Bay Area Garden Supply Total		$ 15.00
	Bright Flowers Supplies	Azalias	$ 33.12
		Fake Plants	$ 83.70
		Ferns	$ 16.80
		Fertilizer	$ 84.60
		Orchids	$ 93.60
		Planters	$ 572.40
		Potting Soil	$ 94.80
		Watering Buckets	$ 37.80
	Bright Flowers Supplies Total		$1,016.82
	Home and Garden Warehouse	Books	$ 35.40
		Bricks	$ 150.00
		Hoses	$ 108.00
		Miracle Grow	$ 127.20
		Pots	$ 169.20
		Stones	$ 56.40
	Home and Garden Warehouse Total		$ 646.20
Home Total			$1,678.02
Grand Total			$1,678.02

(Continued on the next page)

■ Take a few minutes to try other configurations of the PivotTable. See if there are any other useful ways to display the data.

■ When you are done with this task, save the workbook and see if your classmate is also done with Task B. Then go on to Task C.

Task B: Create a PivotChart

■ You have 10 to 15 minutes to complete Task B.

■ Create a PivotChart on a new worksheet from the database on the Subtotals worksheet.

TIP!

Before you can create a PivotTable or PivotChart from the database in Critical Thinking 15.1, you must remove the subtotals from the database.

■ Add fields to the PivotChart to display summary of the wholesale value of products purchased, broken down by Category ID.

■ Add a field to the PivotChart to display the summary broken down by Supplier.

■ Add a field to the PivotChart to display the summary broken down by Product. When you are done, your PivotTable should look similar to the example below.

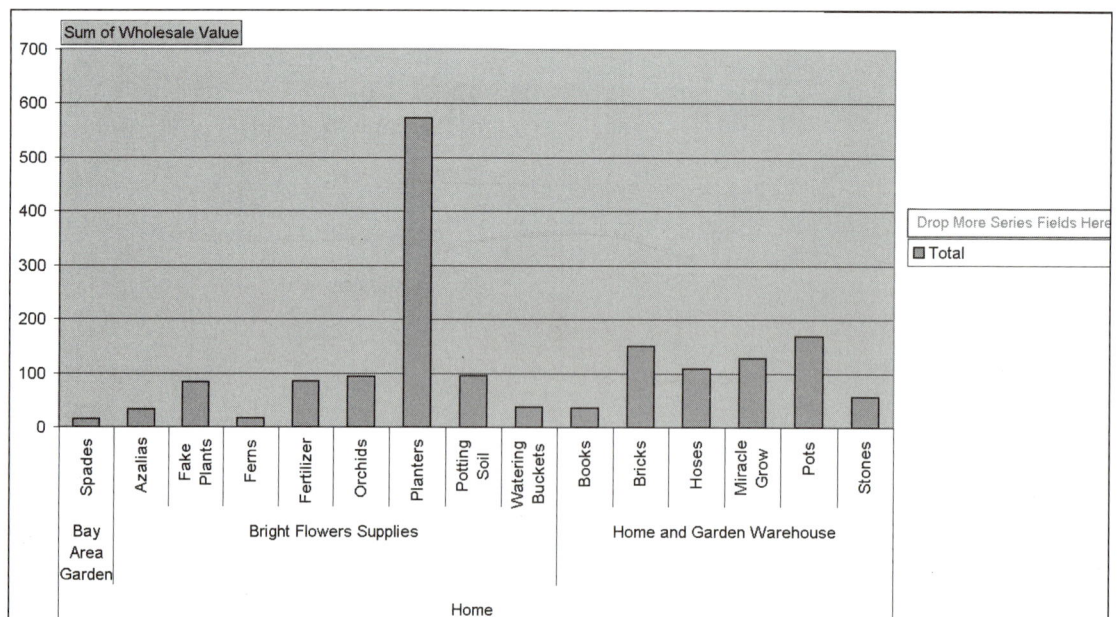

■ When you are done with this task, save the workbook and see if your classmate is also done with Task A. Then go on to Task C.

Task C: Tutor Your Classmate On How to Accomplish Your Task

TIP!

When you are the "tutor" in this task, do your best to let your classmate control the computer. Do not touch the mouse unless absolutely necessary.

- If you performed Task A, talk your classmate through the steps of creating the PivotTable. At your classmate's workstation, go through the steps of Task A together. Let your classmate control the computer and mouse as you indicate what to do. At the end of the session, your classmate should have completed his or her own version of the PivotTable.

- If you performed Task B, talk your classmate through the steps of creating the PivotChart. At your classmate's workstation, go through the steps of Task B together. Let your classmate control the computer and mouse as you indicate what to do. At the end of the session, your classmate should have completed his or her own version of the PivotChart.

Critical Thinking 16.3 On Your Own

Ned Armstrong is happy with the database you created in Critical Thinking exercise 15.3 to analyze book returns. He returns the workbook to you and asks if you can streamline the look of the worksheet. Sometimes there is more data visible than he needs Ned ask you to set up the worksheet so he can focus only on the **Return Date, Title,** and **Refund Amount** columns. Group the worksheet so that Ned can suppress the display of the other columns on the worksheet at will.

Advanced Formatting and Analysis Tools

Many Excel workbooks are designed by experienced Excel users but are used by individuals with little Excel experience. Excel's Data Validation tool can assist users with data entry by forcing values to fall within a specified range. Excel's Conditional Formatting tool can be used to format values that fall within an acceptable range, thus drawing attention to those values. Excel also provides data tables and the Scenario Manager for advanced data analysis. The Scenario Manager is a powerful tool that can let you analyze scenarios with up to 32 input variables.

In This Lesson

Case Study

Bob Johnson is the Sales Manager of Seminar Solutions. Part of Bob's compensation package is a quarterly bonus that is based upon the sales and expenditures of the regions he manages. Bob is rewarded for maximizing sales and minimizing expenses. Bob needs a workbook to help him maximize his quarterly bonus. The workbook will store detailed information in separate sheets and will use Excel's consolidation feature to summarize the data into a master sheet. In addition, he will use conditional formatting, data validation, Scenario Manager, and other tools to format the workbook and analyze the data. The following illustrations show the master worksheet and a report from the Scenario Manager.

	A	B	C	D	E
1	Bonus Analysis				
2					
3					
4	**Sales**	Q1	Q2	Q3	Q4
5	Gross Sales	3,320,000	3,310,000	4,380,000	4,590,000
6	Returns	166,000	94,000	185,000	124,000
7	Net Sales	$3,154,000	$3,216,000	$4,195,000	$4,466,000
8					
9					
10	**Expenses**	Q1	Q2	Q3	Q4
11	Sample Costs	50,700	24,000	97,890	44,450
12	Trade Shows	107,490	6,700	122,000	96,000
13	Automobile	18,000	18,500	15,000	14,600
14	Cell Phones	10,800	12,900	11,140	11,100
15	Entertainment	17,900	20,100	11,700	10,200
16	Total Expenses	$ 204,890	$ 82,200	$ 257,730	$ 176,350
17					
18	*Expenses vs Net Sales*	6.50%	2.56%	6.14%	3.95%

Scenario Summary

	Current Values:	Scenario 1	Scenario 2	Scenario 3	Scenario 4
Changing Cells:					
Net_Sales	1,000,000	1,000,000	1,000,000	2,000,000	2,000,000
Sample_Costs	10,000	10,000	10,000	17,000	20,000
Trade_Shows	10,000	10,000	20,000	12,500	20,000
Automobile	10,000	10,000	7,000	14,000	10,000
Cell_Phones	10,000	10,000	4,000	5,000	7,500
Entertainment	10,000	10,000	10,000	85,000	35,000
Result Cells:					
Expenses_vs._Net_Sales	5.00%	5.00%	5.10%	6.68%	4.63%

Notes: Current Values column represents values of changing cells at time Scenario Summary Report was created. Changing cells for each scenario are highlighted in gray.

Validating Data Entry

Excel data validation tool lets you restrict data entry in cells. You can restrict both the type and range of acceptable values. For example, you may want to restrict data entry to whole numbers between 0 and 100,000. You can also create both input messages and error alert messages. Input messages are displayed whenever the highlight is in a restricted cell. Error messages are displayed whenever data entry is attempted and the data is not of the correct type or within the accepted range.

Quick Reference

VALIDATING DATA ENTRY

- Select the desired cells.

- Choose **Data→Validation.**

- Choose the type of data to be allowed in the cells.

- If desired, set an acceptable range, input message, and output message.

Hands-On 17.1 Set Up Data Validation

In this exercise, you will explore the structure of the master and supporting worksheets in the Seminar Solutions workbook. You will assign names to ranges and set up data validation for the named ranges.

Explore the Workbook

1. Open the workbook named **Hands-On Lesson 17.**
   Take a few moments to study the workbook. Notice there is a Master sheet and sheets for three regions. Notice that the ranges B5:E6 and B11:E15 in the Master sheet are empty. Later in this lesson, these cells will receive data from the Region1–Region3 sheets through the Data Consolidation command.

2. Click the Region1 sheet tab and notice that this worksheet has the same structure as the Master sheet.
   The data consolidation technique is especially useful in workbooks with a uniform structure such as this. Also notice that the Region2 and Region3 sheets have the same structure.

Assign Range Names

In the next few steps, you will assign names to the ranges B5:E6 and B11:E15 in all four worksheets. These names will be useful as you develop the workbook.

3. Click the Master sheet tab.

4. Follow these steps to select the desired cells.

Ⓐ *Select the range B5:E6.*

Ⓑ *Press the (CTRL) key while you select the range B11:E15. Both ranges will be selected as shown here.*

5. Click in the Name box on the left end of the Formula bar.

6. Type the name **Consolidation_Data**, and tap (ENTER) to assign the name to the range.

7. Click the Region1 tab.

8. Select the ranges B5:E6 and B11:E15 using the (CTRL) key technique as in the previous steps.

9. Assign the name **Region1_Data** to the range.

10. Assign the names **Region2_Data** and **Region3_Data** to the same ranges in the Region2 and Region3 sheets.

Turn on Data Validation

11. Click the Name box drop-down button, and choose Region1_Data as shown to the right.
The range B5:E6 and B11:E15 should become selected in the Region1 sheet.

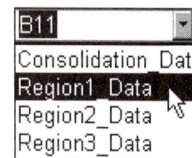

12. Choose **Data→Validation** from the menu bar.

(Continued on the next page)

13. Follow these steps to set the data entry restrictions.

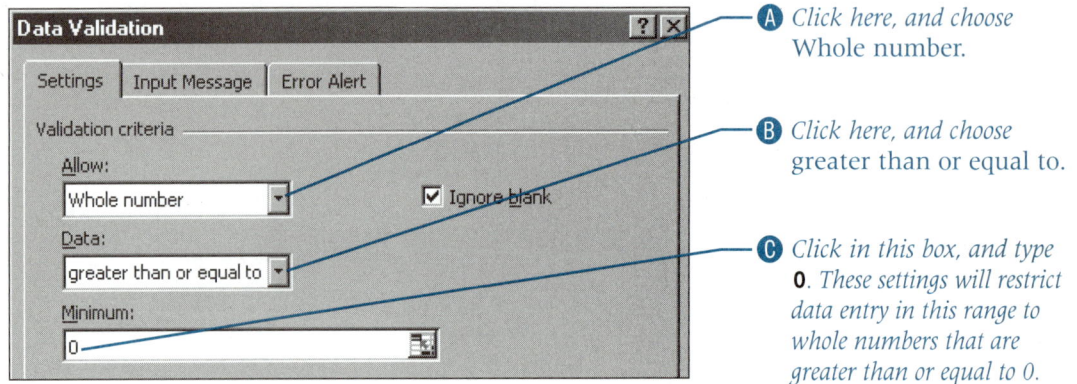

Data Validation dialog box:

Settings | Input Message | Error Alert

Validation criteria

Allow:
Whole number   ☑ Ignore blank

Data:
greater than or equal to

Minimum:
0

Ⓐ *Click here, and choose* Whole number.

Ⓑ *Click here, and choose* greater than or equal to.

Ⓒ *Click in this box, and type* **0**. *These settings will restrict data entry in this range to whole numbers that are greater than or equal to 0.*

14. Click the Input Message tab on the dialog box.
Notice that you can create an input message that appears whenever the highlight is in a restricted cell. You will not use this option in this exercise. You will use an error alert message instead.

15. Click the Error Alert tab.

16. Follow these steps to set an error alert message.

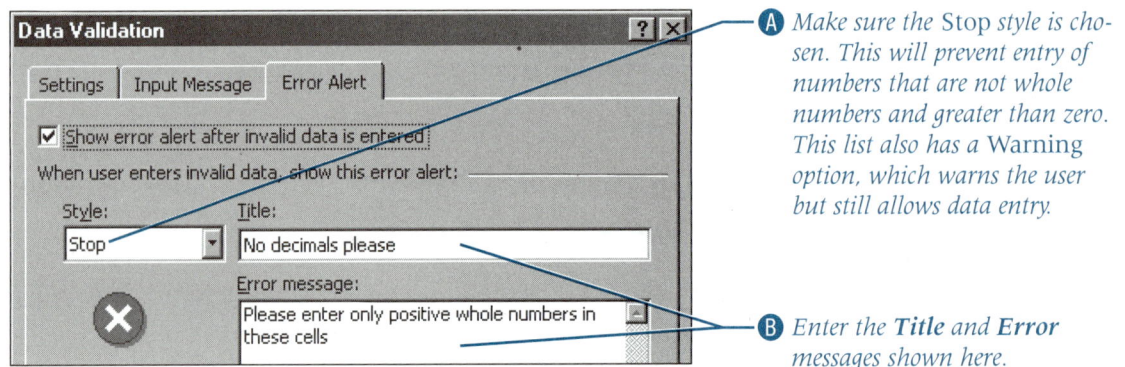

Data Validation dialog box:

Settings | Input Message | Error Alert

☑ Show error alert after invalid data is entered

When user enters invalid data, show this error alert:

Style:
Stop

Title:
No decimals please

Error message:
Please enter only positive whole numbers in these cells

Ⓐ *Make sure the Stop style is chosen. This will prevent entry of numbers that are not whole numbers and greater than zero. This list also has a Warning option, which warns the user but still allows data entry.*

Ⓑ *Enter the* **Title** *and* **Error** *messages shown here.*

17. Click **OK** to complete the data validation steps.

Test the Data Validation

18. Click Cell B5 in the Region1 sheet.

19. Type the number **–1000**, and tap ⏎ ENTER.
The error alert message should appear. The data restrictions only allow you to enter positive whole numbers in this cell.

20. Click the Retry button.

21. Type the number **1000.50**, and tap ⏎ ENTER.
Once again, this is not a whole number, so it won't be accepted.

22. Click the **Retry** button, and enter the original number, **890000**.

23. Now apply the same data validation restrictions and error alert message to the ranges Region2_Data and Region3_Data.
You can easily select the desired ranges by choosing the range names from the Name box.

24. Save the changes, and continue with the next topic.

Consolidating Worksheet Data

Excel's consolidation options combine values from source worksheets into a destination sheet. For example, in the Hands-On Lesson 17 workbook, you will consolidate cells in the range B5:E6. The consolidation will add the values in Cells B5:E6 of the Region1–Region3 sheets. The results will be displayed in Cells B5:E6 of the Master sheet. The following illustration shows the consolidation of values in Cell B6 of the Hands-On Lesson 17 workbook.

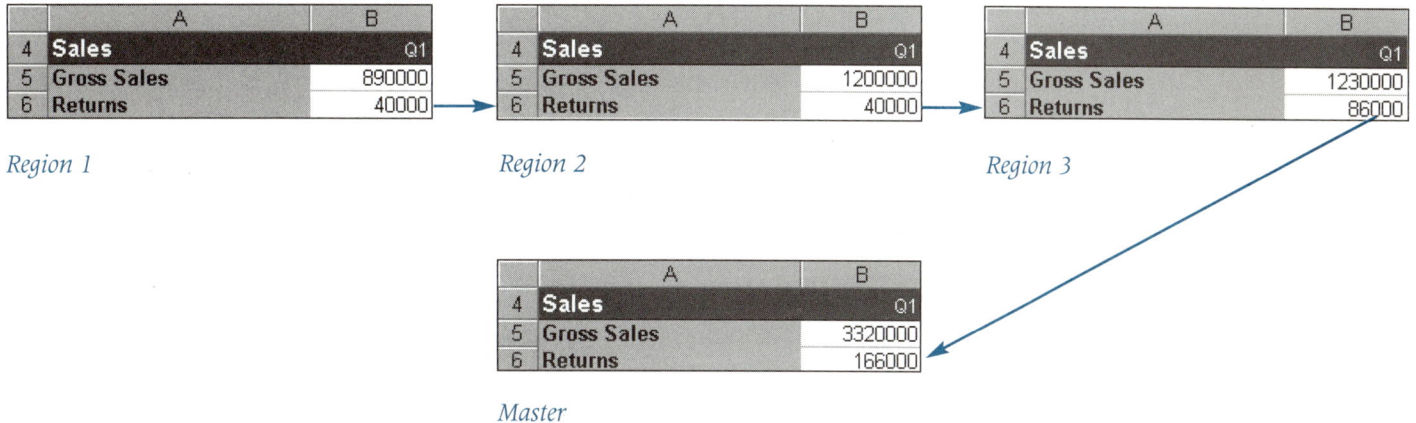

	A	B
4	Sales	Q1
5	Gross Sales	890000
6	Returns	40000

Region 1

	A	B
4	Sales	Q1
5	Gross Sales	1200000
6	Returns	40000

Region 2

	A	B
4	Sales	Q1
5	Gross Sales	1230000
6	Returns	86000

Region 3

	A	B
4	Sales	Q1
5	Gross Sales	3320000
6	Returns	166000

Master

NOTE! *The values in Cell B6 of each Region sheet are consolidated. The result appears in Cell B6 of the Master sheet. In this example, the consolidation function was SUM, so the values were summed.*

Consolidation Functions

The SUM function is the most widely used consolidation function. SUM was used in the preceding illustration to obtain the sum of the region numbers. However, you can also use functions such as AVERAGE, MIN, and MAX when consolidating. The desired function is chosen in the Consolidate dialog box when the consolidation is set up.

Types of Consolidation

You can consolidate data using three different methods as described in the following table.

Consolidation type	Description
3-D referencing	Uses a function such as SUM to reference cells in multiple worksheets. This is known as 3-D referencing. For example, a SUM function in Cell B6 of the Master sheet can be used to sum the values in Cell B6 of each region sheet. This, in effect, consolidates the values into the Master sheet.
By position	Consolidating by position is useful if all worksheets have an identical layout. When consolidating by position, you specify the same range in all work sheets, and Excel applies the consolidation function to each cell in the range.
By category	Consolidating by category is useful if the supporting worksheets have different layouts. Excel uses the row and column headings to determine how the data should be consolidated. The consolidation produces one row or column in the master sheet for each unique row or column encountered in the supporting sheets.

CONSOLIDATING DATA

Consolidate Using 3-D Referencing

- Click the cell in the destination sheet where the consolidated data is to be placed.
- Click AutoSum Σ, or begin typing another function, such as AVERAGE.
- Press the (SHIFT) key while you click the sheet tabs of each source sheet that you want to include in the consolidation.
- Click the cell (in any sheet) that contains the data you wish to consolidate.
- Click Enter ✓ to complete the entry. You can repeat this process for other destination cells, or you can copy the formula in the destination sheet to other cells.

Consolidate by Position

- Select the range in the destination sheet where the consolidated data will be placed. This range will not include column or row labels—just the cells where the consolidated values will be placed.
- Choose Data→Consolidation from the menu bar.
- Choose a consolidation function (this will usually be SUM).
- Uncheck the *Use labels in* boxes.
- Click in the Reference box, click the sheet tab of the first source sheet you wish to include in the consolidation, and then select the data in the source sheet. When consolidating by position, the data will include the same cells that are in the destination range, except they will be in the source sheet.
- Click the **Add** button to add the range to the All references list.
- Continue to select data in the source sheets and add the ranges to the All references list.
- Click the **OK** button to complete the consolidation.

Consolidate by Category

- Click a cell in the destination sheet to be used as the starting point for the consolidated data.
- Choose Data→Consolidation from the menu bar.
- Choose a consolidation function (this will usually be SUM).
- Click in the Reference box, click the sheet tab of the first source sheet you wish to include in the consolidation, and then select the data in the source sheet. The data you select must include either row or column labels. Excel will use the labels to determine which rows or columns to consolidate with the other consolidation ranges you specify.
- Click the **Add** button to add the range to the All references list.
- Continue to select data in the source sheets and add the ranges to the All references list. You must include either row or column labels in each selected range.
- Check either the *Top row* or *Left* column check boxes in the Use labels in area. Check *Top row* if you included column labels in your selections and *Left column* if you included row labels.
- Click **OK** to complete the consolidation.

Hands-On 17.2 Consolidate Data

In this exercise, you will use the SUM function with 3-D references to consolidate all cells in the range B5:E6 of the Master sheet. You will also consolidate data by position.

Consolidate Using 3-D References

1. Click the Master sheet tab, and then click Cell B5.

2. Click AutoSum $\boxed{\Sigma}$.

   In the next few steps, you will build the SUM function by selecting the Region1–Region 3 sheets and clicking Cell B5. When you have finished, your SUM function will reference Cell B5 in each of the region sheets. This is known as 3-D referencing.

3. Click the Region1 tab.
   Notice the Region1 sheet name is displayed in the SUM function in the Formula bar.

4. Press the (SHIFT) key while you click the Region2 and Region3 tabs.

5. Now click Cell B5 in the Region1 sheet, and the expression =SUM('Region1:Region3'!B5) should appear in the Formula bar.
   Take a moment to study this expression and try to understand how it functions. You could also have built this expression by clicking the sheet tabs individually and then clicking Cell B5 in each sheet.

6. Click the Enter $\boxed{\checkmark}$ button on the Formula bar to complete the entry.
   The result should equal 3320000.

Consolidate Another Cell

7. Click Cell B6 in the Master sheet, and then click AutoSum $\boxed{\Sigma}$.

8. Click the Region1 tab.

9. Press the (SHIFT) key while you click the Region2 and Region3 tabs.

10. Click Cell B6 in the Region1 sheet, and complete $\boxed{\checkmark}$ the entry.
    The result should equal 166000.

Copy the Formulas

11. Select Cells B5 and B6 in the Master sheet.

12. Use the fill handle to copy the formulas across the rows.
    Rows 5 and 6 of the Master sheet should now match the example shown to the right.

	A	B	C	D	E
1	Bonus Analysis				
2					
3					
4	Sales	Q1	Q2	Q3	Q4
5	Gross Sales	3320000	3310000	4380000	4590000
6	Returns	166000	94000	185000	124000
7	Net Sales				

Consolidate by Position

In the remainder of this exercise, you will use the Consolidation command to consolidate the range B11:E15 by position. This is possible because all worksheets have the same layout.

13. Select the range B11:E15 in the Master sheet.
You begin a consolidation by position by selecting the consolidation range in the master sheet.

14. Choose **Data→Consolidate** from the menu bar.

15. Follow these steps to explore the Consolidate dialog box.

A *Click this box, and notice the various consolidation functions. Make sure that* Sum *is chosen.*

B *Click in the Reference box. This box lets you specify the references you wish to consolidate from other worksheets. You will use this box in a moment.*

C *Notice these options (but don't choose them). The labels options are used when consolidating by category but not when consolidating by position. The create links box creates links between data in the master and supporting sheets. This way, the master sheet is updated when data in the supporting sheets changes.*

16. If necessary, move the Consolidate dialog box until you can see the range B11:E15 in the Master sheet and the sheet tabs at the bottom of the Excel window.

17. Click the Region1 sheet tab.
The expression Region1! will appear in the Reference *box within the* Consolidate *box.*

18. Select the range B11:E15 in the Region1 sheet.
The expression will now become Region1!$B$11:$E$15. This is the reference of the range B11:B15 in the Region1 sheet.

19. Click the **Add** button on the right side of the dialog box.
This adds the reference to the All references list. You build a consolidation range by adding references to the All references list.

20. Click the Region2 sheet tab.
Notice the flashing marquee on the range B11:E15. Also, notice the reference Region2!$B$11:$E$15 appears in the Reference box within the Consolidate dialog box. Excel correctly assumes that you want to consolidate the same range that you used in the Region1 sheet.

21. Click the **Add** button to add that range to the All references list.

22. Now click the Region3 sheet tab, and click the Add button to add the range B11:E15 from Region3 to the All references list.

23. Click **OK,** and Excel will consolidate the data into the Master sheet.

Your Master sheet should have the consolidated numbers shown below.

	A	B	C	D	E
1	Bonus Analysis				
2					
3					
4	**Sales**	Q1	Q2	Q3	Q4
5	Gross Sales	3320000	3310000	4380000	4590000
6	Returns	166000	94000	185000	124000
7	Net Sales				
8					
9					
10	**Expenses**	Q1	Q2	Q3	Q4
11	Sample Costs	50700	24000	97890	44450
12	Trade Shows	107490	6700	122000	96000
13	Automobile	18000	18500	15000	14600
14	Cell Phones	10800	12900	11140	11100
15	Entertainment	17900	20100	11700	10200
16	Total Expenses				

Examine the Results

24. Click any cell in the range B11:E15 in the Master sheet.

Look at the Formula bar and notice that a number is displayed. The Consolidation command sums the values in the selected ranges and enters the results in the master sheet. These numbers will not change if the data in the supporting worksheets changes (because they are not linked).

25. Click any cell in the range B5:E6.

You created these 3-D SUM functions in an earlier exercise. These functions are linked to the supporting worksheets. The numbers in the Master sheet will change if the numbers in the supporting worksheets change.

26. Choose **Data→Consolidate** from the menu bar.

Notice that the references you created are still displayed on the All references list. These references will remain on the list even after you close and save the workbook. This is convenient because you may want to add another worksheet at a later time. You could include the range B11:E5 from the new worksheet in the consolidation by adding it to the list. Also notice the Browse button on the dialog box. This button lets you specify the location of workbooks on the computer system. This option is used when you are trying to consolidate data from other workbooks. You can consolidate from within a workbook (as in this exercise) or from other workbooks.

27. Close the Consolidate dialog box.

28. Save the changes and continue with the next topic.

You will receive additional practice with consolidation in the end of lesson exercises.

Natural Language Formulas

Excel 2000 lets you use row and column headings in formulas instead of cell references. This lets you create formulas using natural language expressions. For example, in the next exercise, you will create a formula in Cell B7 of the Master sheet. The formula will calculate the Net Sales as Gross Sales – Returns. Until now, you would have been instructed to enter this formula as =B5–B6. With Excel 2000, however, you can type the formula exactly as it is written: =Gross Sales–Returns.

Hands-On 17.3 Use Natural Language Formulas

Calculate the Net Sales

1. Click the Master sheet tab, and then click Cell B7.

2. Type the formula **=Gross Sales-Returns**, and use the Enter ☑ button to complete the entry.
   The result should equal 3154000. At this point, you might be wondering why you have been instructed to use cell references in formulas throughout this course. This is because you may need to use an older version of Excel or perhaps a different spreadsheet program. The cell reference techniques you have learned thus far can be used with all versions of Excel (and other programs). Natural language formulas were introduced in Excel 97. Also, there are limitations on the use of natural language formulas.

3. Use the fill handle to copy the formula across the row.

4. Click Cell C7, and notice that the natural language formula has been copied to that cell.

Use AutoSum to Calculate the Total Expenses

5. Select the range B16:E16, and click AutoSum Σ .
   The Total Expenses in Row 16 should be calculated. You could have used a natural language formula such as =SUM(Q1) and then copied it across the row. However, it is much easier to use AutoSum in this situation. Also, natural language formulas can be a little unpredictable when used with functions such as SUM.

Calculate the Expenses vs. Net Sales

6. Click Cell B18, and then enter the formula **=Total Expenses/Net Sales**.
   The result should equal .06496195.

7. Use the fill handle to copy the formula across the row.
   At this point, Rows 4–18 of your Master worksheet should match the example below.

	A	B	C	D	E
4	**Sales**	Q1	Q2	Q3	Q4
5	**Gross Sales**	3320000	3310000	4380000	4590000
6	**Returns**	166000	94000	185000	124000
7	**Net Sales**	3154000	3216000	4195000	4466000
8					
9					
10	**Expenses**	Q1	Q2	Q3	Q4
11	**Sample Costs**	50700	24000	97890	44450
12	**Trade Shows**	107490	6700	122000	96000
13	**Automobile**	18000	18500	15000	14600
14	**Cell Phones**	10800	12900	11140	11100
15	**Entertainment**	17900	20100	11700	10200
16	**Total Expenses**	204890	82200	257730	176350
17					
18	*Expenses vs Net Sales*	0.06496195	0.0255597	0.06143743	0.03948724

Copy the Formulas Using 3-D Selections

In the next few steps, you will copy the formulas from the Master sheet to the Region1–Region3 sheets. You will copy and paste each formula just once using 3-D referencing.

8. Select the Net Sales totals in Cells B7:E7.

9. Click the Copy [icon] button.

10. Click the Region1 sheet tab.

11. Select the range B7:E7.

12. Press (CTRL) while you click the Region2 and Region3 tabs.
    This selects the same cells in all three worksheets.

13. Click the Paste [icon] button.

14. Click the Region1, Region2, and Region3 tabs, and notice that the formulas have been copied.

15. Now copy the Total Expenses and Expenses vs. Net Sales formulas from the Master sheet to Regions 1–3.
    Feel free to browse through the Regions 1–3 sheets and review the results.

Format the Cells

16. Click the Name box drop-down button, and choose Consolidation_Data as shown to the right.
    You created this name earlier in this lesson. The ranges B5:E6 and B11:E15 should be selected.

17. Press (SHIFT), and click the Region3 sheet tab.
    This will select all four sheets. Excel selects all sheets between the Master sheet and Region3.

18. Format the numbers as Comma [icon] style with no decimals.

19. Click the various sheet tabs, and notice that the range is formatted in all sheets.

20. Click the Master sheet tab.

21. Select both the Net Sales and Total Expenses numbers in the ranges B7:E7 and B16:E16.

22. Press (SHIFT), and click the Region3 tab.

23. Format the numbers as Currency [icon] style with no decimals.
    Notice that all four sheet tabs are still active. Any range you select now will be selected in all four sheets. Formatting commands will affect all active sheets as long as they remain active.

24. Select the Expenses vs. Net Sales numbers in the range B18:E18.

25. Format them as Percent [icon] style with two decimals.

26. Click the various sheet tabs, and notice that the numbers have been formatted in all sheets.

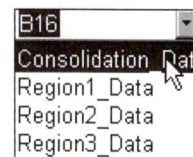

Conditional Formatting

Excel lets you assign conditional formats to cells. Conditional formats are activated only when the conditions you specify are met. For example, in the next exercise, you will apply a conditional format to the Expenses vs. Net Sales percentages in Row 18 of the Master sheet. The conditional format will assign a red color to a cell if the percentage is greater than 6%. Conditional formats are often used as alarms. They let you draw attention to values that fall outside an acceptable range. You use the **Format→Conditional Formatting** command to specify conditional formats. The following illustration discusses the Conditional Formatting dialog box.

This option will almost always be set to Cell Value Is.

A comparison operator is chosen from this list.

Specify the comparison value here.

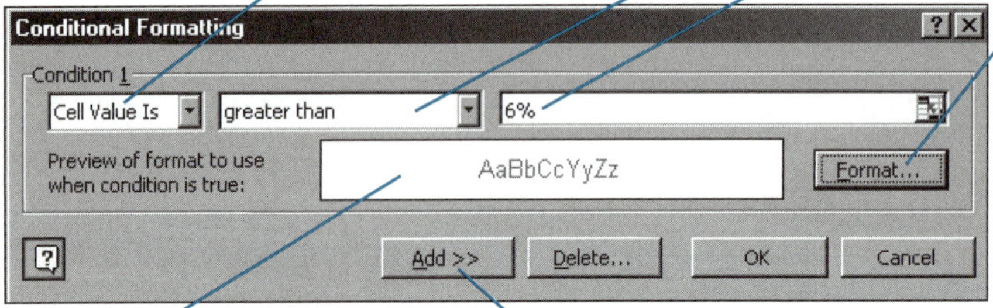

The **Format** *button displays the Format Cells dialog box, allowing you to specify font formats, borders, and shading to be applied if the condition is met.*

A preview of the formatted text appears here.

This button lets you specify additional conditions for the cell(s). You can specify up to three conditions for a cell.

Hands-On 17.4 Apply Conditional Formatting

1. Deselect the sheet tabs by clicking one of the Region tabs.

2. Select the range B18:E18 in the Master sheet.

3. Choose **Format→Conditional Formatting** from the menu bar.

4. Follow these steps to apply the conditional format.

Ⓐ *Set this option to* greater than.

Ⓑ *Type* **6%** *here.*

Ⓒ *Click the* **Format** *button, and notice that you can set font, border, and pattern formats.*

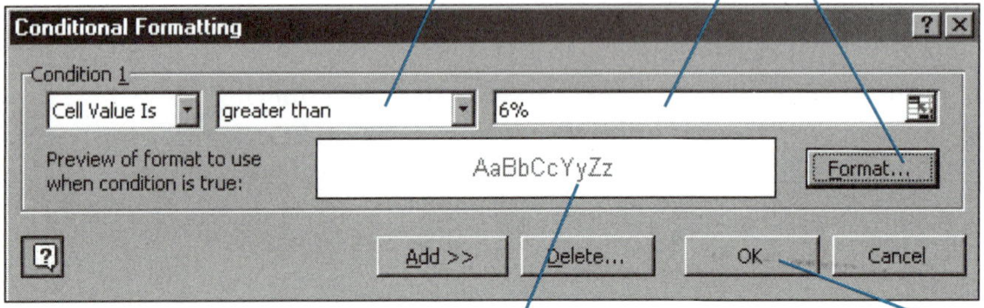

Ⓓ *Choose a red font color, and click* **OK** *on the* Format Cells *dialog box.*

Ⓔ *Notice that a preview of the format appears here.*

Ⓕ *Click* **OK** *to apply the conditional formats.*

5. Click anywhere in the Master sheet to deselect the range.
   The conditional format should have been applied to Cells B18 and D18.

6. Now click the Region1 tab, and select the range B18:E18.

7. Press (SHIFT), and click the Region3 tab.

8. Apply the same conditional format to these ranges.
   Once again, you can apply any format to 3-D selections.

Data Tables

Data tables let you see the affect changing variables have on a formula. For example, Bob Johnson's quarterly bonus is calculated as a function of two variables: Net Sales and the Expenses vs. Net Sales ratio. You will use a two-variable data table to determine how these variables affect Bob's bonus. Excel supports both one-variable and two-variable data tables. You will work with a two-variable table in this section.

Setting Up a Two-Variable Data Table

The following illustration discusses the layout and set up of a typical two-variable data table. Take a few moments to review this illustration carefully.

*In this example, Cells A2 and B1 are the input cells. Input cells are always empty in a data table. When you issue the **Data Table** command, Excel will substitute the Net Sales and Expenses vs. Net Sales variables into the input cells.*

This formula is entered in Cell B2. This rather complex formula is used to calculate Bob's bonus. Also notice the input Cells A2 and B1 are referenced in the formula.

B2   =A2*1%*(1-10*B1)

	A	B	C	D	E	F	G
1			Expenses vs net Sales				
2		0	1%	2%	4%	6%	8%
3	Net Sales	$ 1,000,000	9000	8000	6000	4000	2000
4		$ 2,000,000	18000	16000	12000	8000	4000
5		$ 3,000,000	27000	24000	18000	12000	6000
6		$ 4,000,000	36000	32000	24000	16000	8000
7		$ 5,000,000	45000	40000	30000	20000	10000

Various Expenses vs. Net Sales ratio percentages are used as the row variables. These percentages can be adjusted at any time, and the data table will be recalculated.

Various Net Sales numbers are used as the column variables. These can also be adjusted to see the affect they have on the data table.

*The **Data→Table** command is issued and produces these results. The command substitutes one pair of variables at a time into the input cells. The formula in Cell B2 then calculates the result and inserts it into the table. This process continues for each variable pair until all the results are calculated.*

A Specific Example

A good way to understand data tables is to use a specific example. Look at the preceding illustration and notice that the variable in Cell C2 is 1%, and the variable in Cell B3 is $1,000,000. The result in Cell C3 is 9000. When the **Data→Table** command is issued, 1% is substituted into Cell B1, and $1,000,000 is substituted into Cell A2. The formula then calculates the result (9000) and inserts it in Cell C3 (the intersection of the input variable cells). This process continues for all variable combinations in the table.

Quick Reference

SETTING UP A TWO-VARIABLE DATA TABLE

■ Set up a worksheet with various row and column input variables. Leave one blank column to the left of the column variables and one blank row above the row variables.

■ Insert a formula in the blank cell located above the column variables and to the left of the row variables. The formula will use the pairs of input variables to perform the calculation you desire.

■ Select the data table, including the cell with the formula, all input variables, and the cells that will hold the calculated results.

■ Choose Data→Table from the menu bar.

■ Specify the Row input cell and Column input cell. The Row input cell is the blank cell above the formula. The Column input cell is the blank cell to the left of the formula.

■ Click OK to calculate the table.

Hands-On 17.5 Create a Two-Variable Data Table

Set Up the Table

1. Click the Master sheet tab and choose **Insert→Worksheet** from the menu bar.

2. Rename the new sheet as **Bonus Analysis**.

3. Enter the data shown to the right into the new sheet, and format the numbers as shown.

	A	B	C	D	E	F	G
1			Expenses vs. Net Sales				
2			1%	2%	4%	6%	8%
3	Net Sales	$ 1,000,000					
4		$ 2,000,000					
5		$ 3,000,000					
6		$ 4,000,000					
7		$ 5,000,000					

4. Click Cell B2.
   You will enter a formula in this cell. You always set up a two-variable data table in this manner. One set of variables is placed immediately to the right of the formula (the percentages in this example). The other set of variables is placed immediately below the formula (the dollars in this example). The Net Sales and Expenses vs. Net Sales labels can be placed anywhere as long as they do not interfere with the table.

5. Enter the formula **=A2*1%*(1-10*B1)** in Cell B2.
   *The result should equal 0. This formula calculates Bob's quarterly bonus as 1% of Net Sales multiplied by a percentage. The percentage is calculated by the (1–10*B1) part of the formula. This component penalizes Bob as the Expenses vs. Net Sales ratio increases. In other words, if Bob's regions spend too much compared to what they sell, then Bob gets penalized. Take a few moments to understand the way this formula works.*

Complete the Data Table

The final steps in creating the data table are to select the table and use the Data→Table command.

6. Select the range B2:G7 as shown to the right.

When selecting the data prior to creating a data table, you must include the formula, variables and table cells in the selection.

	A	B	C	D	E	F	G
1			Expenses vs. Net Sales				
2		0	1%	2%	4%	6%	8%
3	Net Sales	$ 1,000,000					
4		$ 2,000,000					
5		$ 3,000,000					
6		$ 4,000,000					
7		$ 5,000,000					

7. Choose **Data→Table** from the menu bar.

8. Follow these steps to choose the input cells.

Table

Row input cell: `B1`

Column input cell: `A2`

OK   Cancel

Ⓐ *Enter **B1** as the row input and **A2** as the column input.*

Ⓑ *Click **OK**.*

The data table will be completed as shown below. The Row input cell is the cell that you want the row variables (Expenses vs. Net Sales) to be substituted into. Likewise, the Column input cell is where the column variables (Net Sales) will be substituted. If you look at the formula in Cell B2, you will see that these substitutions make sense.

	A	B	C	D	E	F	G
1			Expenses vs. Net Sales				
2		0	1%	2%	4%	6%	8%
3	Net Sales	$ 1,000,000	9000	8000	6000	4000	2000
4		$ 2,000,000	18000	16000	12000	8000	4000
5		$ 3,000,000	27000	24000	18000	12000	6000
6		$ 4,000,000	36000	32000	24000	16000	8000
7		$ 5,000,000	45000	40000	30000	20000	10000

Apply Conditional Formatting to the Table

Bob has a "bottom line" when it comes to his quarterly bonus. He is unwilling to accept a bonus that is less than $20,000. For this reason, you will format the cells in the data table using a conditional format. Cells where the bonus is greater than or equal to $20,000 will be formatted with a blue color. This will let Bob instantly see the combinations of Net Sales and Expenses vs. Net Sales that are acceptable.

9. Select the range C3:G7.

10. Choose **Format→Conditional Formatting** from the menu bar.

(Continued on the next page)

11. Follow these steps to set the condition.

Ⓐ *Set this option to* greater than or equal to.

Ⓑ *Type* **20000** *here.*

Ⓒ *Click the* **Format** *button, choose a blue font color, and click* **OK** *in the* Format Cells *dialog box.*

Ⓓ *Click* **OK** *in the Conditional Formatting box.*

Conditional Formatting	? ✕
⌐Condition 1	
Cell Value Is ▾ greater than or equal to ▾ 20000 ▤	
Preview of format to use when condition is true: AaBbCcYyZz Format...	

Only values greater than or equal to 20000 should appear in blue. As you can see, this data table and conditional formatting clearly show which Net Sales and Expenses vs. Net Sales ratio combinations are required to achieve a $20,000 (or greater) bonus.

12. Feel free to experiment with your data table. For example, try changing the Net Sales variables in Column B and the Expenses vs. Net Sales variables in Row 2.
    The data table will be recalculated each time you change a variable.

13. Save the changes when you have finished, and continue with the next topic.

Scenario Manager

Data tables let you see the impact that changing variables have on a formula. However, data tables are limited to just two variables. Excel provides the Scenario Manager for what-if models requiring more than two variables. In fact, the Scenario Manager can be used with up to 32 variables! This allows you to model virtually any what-if scenario.

What Is a Scenario?

A scenario is a combination of values assigned to variables in a what-if model. The model calculates results based upon the values used in the scenario. Scenarios are given names to identify them, and they are saved and organized using the Scenario Manager.

Managing Scenarios

The Scenario Manager lets you create and manage a large number of scenarios. This way, you can compare the various scenarios and the results they achieve. The Scenario Manager also lets you display and print out the results of multiple scenarios.

Adding Scenarios

You use the **Tools→Scenarios** command to display the Scenario Manager dialog box. The Scenario Manager has an **Add** button to allow you to add new scenarios. You assign a name to new scenarios and then specify scenario values. Scenario values are the values you assign to one or more variables in your workbook. The combination of values you specify constitutes the scenario. The following illustration shows the Scenario Values dialog box with values assigned to variables in the Hands-On Lesson 17 workbook.

	Scenario Values			
	Enter values for each of the changing cells.		OK	
1:	Net_Sales	1000000	Cancel	
2:	Sample_Costs	10000	Add	
3:	Trade_Shows	10000		
4:	Automobile	10000		
5:	Cell_Phones	10000		

The values shown are applied to cells in the worksheet, thus forming a scenario.

Hands-On 17.6 Use the Scenario Manager

In this exercise, you will help Bob Johnson set up a model to further analyze expenses. Bob's data table has shown him that reducing expenses will increase his bonus. For this reason, Bob wants to take a closer look at each component of the expenses. You will set up a model that calculates the Expenses vs. Net Sales ratio using Net Sales and the expense components in Rows 11–15 as variables. The Scenario Manager will be used to set up and manage multiple scenarios.

Set Up the Model

1. Click the Bonus Analysis sheet tab, and then click Cell B10.

2. Enter the data shown to the right.
   You will need to widen Column B as shown. Also, notice that Cell C18 is empty at this point.

3. Click Cell C18 and enter the formula **=SUM(C13:C17)/C12**.
   The result should equal .05. Notice that this formula sums the expenses and divides by the Net Sales.

4. Format the range C12:C17 as Comma style with no decimals and Cell C18 as Percent style with two decimals.
   The completed model should match the example shown to the right. This model will form the starting point from which you will create scenarios.

	A	B	C
9			
10		Expenses vs. Net Sales Model	
11			
12		Net Sales	1000000
13		Sample Costs	10000
14		Trade Shows	10000
15		Automobile	10000
16		Cell Phones	10000
17		Entertainment	10000
18		Expenses vs. Net Sales	

	A	B	C
9			
10		Expenses vs. Net Sales Model	
11			
12		Net Sales	1,000,000
13		Sample Costs	10,000
14		Trade Shows	10,000
15		Automobile	10,000
16		Cell Phones	10,000
17		Entertainment	10,000
18		Expenses vs. Net Sales	5.00%

Name the Variable Cells

*In the next few steps, you will name the variable cells in the model using the **Insert→Name→Create** command. Naming the variable cells is beneficial because the names will appear in the Scenario Manager dialog box.*

	A	B	C
9			
10		Expenses vs. Net Sales Model	
11			
12		Net Sales	1,000,000
13		Sample Costs	10,000
14		Trade Shows	10,000
15		Automobile	10,000
16		Cell Phones	10,000
17		Entertainment	10,000
18		Expenses vs. Net Sales	5.00%

5. Select the range B12:C18 as shown to the right.

6. Choose **Insert→Name→Create** from the menu bar.

7. Make sure the Left column box is checked, and click **OK.**

8. Click Cell C12, and notice that the name Net_Sales appears in the Name box.
All other variable cells have also been assigned names.

Create the First Scenario

9. Select the range C12:C17 as shown to the right (don't select Cell C18).
Only the variables will be adjusted in the Scenario Manager.

	A	B	C
9			
10		Expenses vs. Net Sales Model	
11			
12		Net Sales	1,000,000
13		Sample Costs	10,000
14		Trade Shows	10,000
15		Automobile	10,000
16		Cell Phones	10,000
17		Entertainment	10,000
18		Expenses vs. Net Sales	5.00%

10. Choose **Tools→Scenarios** from the menu bar.
The dialog box should indicate that no scenarios are currently defined.

11. Click the **Add** button to add a new scenario.

12. Type the name `Scenario 1` in the Scenario name box.

13. Notice the Changing cells box.
This box determines which variable cells will be changed to create the scenario. This option should be set to C12:C17. This is because you selected those cells prior to starting the Scenario Manager. It is usually best to select the variable cells prior to starting the Scenario Manager (although you can always select them once the Add Scenario box is displayed).

14. Click **OK,** and the Scenario Values box will appear.

15. Follow these steps to explore the Scenario Values box.

Ⓐ *Notice that the cell names are displayed to the left of the variable boxes. This is because you named the cells.*

Ⓑ *Notice that the variable boxes contain values. You create scenarios by entering values or formulas in the boxes.*

Ⓒ *Scroll down until the Entertainment variable is visible. You can have up to 32 variables in a scenario.*

Ⓓ *Click OK to close the dialog box. Scenario 1 will use these values.*

The Scenario Manager dialog box will remain open. This scenario will serve as a starting point for other scenarios. The other scenarios you create will be compared to this one.

Add Another Scenario

16. Click the **Add** button.

17. Type the name **Scenario 2**, and click **OK.**

18. Enter the variables shown to the right (there is no need to change the Entertainment variable).

19. Click **OK** on the Scenario Values box.
Scenario 1 and Scenario 2 will now appear in the Scenario Manager dialog box.

Scenario Values		? ☒
Enter values for each of the changing cells.		
1: Net_Sales	1000000	OK
2: Sample_Costs	10000	Cancel
3: Trade_Shows	20000	Add
4: Automobile	7000	
5: Cell_Phones	4000	

Show the Results

20. Make sure Scenario 2 is chosen, and click the **Show** button.
Excel will substitute the scenario values into the model, and the formula in Cell C18 will calculate the result. The result should equal 5.10%.

21. Choose Scenario 1, and click the **Show** button.
As you can see, the Scenario Manager lets you rapidly see the results of various scenarios.

22. Now add two new scenarios, using the data in the following table.

Scenario Name	Variable	Set to
Scenario 3	Net Sales	2000000
	Sample Costs	17000
	Trade Shows	35000
	Automobile	14000
	Cell Phones	5000
	Entertainment	85000
Scenario 4	Net Sales	2000000
	Sample Costs	20000
	Trade Shows	20000
	Automobile	10000
	Cell Phones	7500
	Entertainment	35000

23. Use the **Show** button to show the results of each scenario.

Edit a Scenario

24. Choose Scenario 3, and click the **Show** button.
The Expenses vs. Net Sales should equal 7.80%. The data table you created earlier shows that Bob's bonus will be around $4,000 for this scenario. Bob will not be happy with this! Fortunately, the Scenario Manager lets you adjust scenario values until a desired result is achieved.

25. Make sure Scenario 3 is chosen, and click the **Edit** button.

26. Click **OK** on the Edit Scenario box.

(Continued on the next page)

27. Change the Trade_Shows number to **12500**, and click **OK.**

28. Click the **Show** button again, and the result should equal 6.68%.
    Bob can use these scenarios to determine which expense items to trim.

Display a Summary of All Scenarios

29. Click the **Summary** button.
    Notice that you can display a scenario summary and a scenario PivotTable. You will display a summary in the next few steps.

30. Choose the Scenario summary option, and click **OK.**
    Excel will insert the summary on a new worksheet. Review the summary carefully. You can print a summary as you print any other worksheet. You can also delete a summary by deleting the summary worksheet.

The Report Manager

Excel's Report Manager is an add-in program that lets you manage reports. A report can be a workbook, a custom view created with Excel's View Manager, or a scenario. The Report Manager is particularly useful if you have to generate more than one printed report from a workbook on a recurring basis. The Report Manager helps you manage the various reports and print them as needed.

Installing the Report Manager

The Report Manager is not installed as part of the Office 2000 typical installation. To install the Report Manager, you choose **Tools→Add-ins** and select Report Manager from the add-in list. The Office 2000 installer will prompt you to insert your Office 2000 CD ROM to complete the installation.

Using the Report Manager

You display the Report Manager dialog box with the **View→Report Manager** command. The Report Manager dialog box lets you add, print, edit, and delete reports. The Add option displays the Add Report dialog box where you define your report. For further information on the Report Manager, use the Office Assistant to get online assistance. There is no hands-on exercise to accompany this topic since the Report Manager is an add-in that may not be installed on your computer system.

Concepts Review

True/False Questions

1. Data validation cannot be used in cells that contain numbers.   TRUE   FALSE

2. Data validation can provide error alert messages, but it can't prevent a user from entering unacceptable data.   TRUE   FALSE

3. Consolidation can only be used in worksheets that have an identical layout.   TRUE   FALSE

4. Other functions besides SUM can be used when consolidating worksheets.   TRUE   FALSE

5. All worksheets must have an identical layout when consolidating by position.   TRUE   FALSE

6. Conditional formats can apply colors to cells.   TRUE   FALSE

7. You can use up to four variables in a data table.   TRUE   FALSE

8. You can use up to 32 variables with Scenario Manager.   TRUE   FALSE

Multiple-Choice Questions

1. Which command is used to turn on data validation?
   a. Tools→Validation
   b. Format→Validation
   c. Data→Validation
   d. None of these

2. Which command is used to set conditional formats?
   a. Format→Conditional Formatting
   b. Tools→Conditional Formatting
   c. Insert→Conditional Formatting
   d. None of these

3. Which of the following format categories can be applied with conditional formats?
   a. Fonts
   b. Borders
   c. Patterns
   d. All of these

4. Which of the following statements is true?
   a. You can apply conditional formats using 3-D selecting.
   b. You cannot apply conditional formats using 3-D selecting.
   c. You can apply number formats using 3-D selecting.
   d. Both a and c

Skill Builders

Skill Builder 17.1 Consolidate Data by Category

In this exercise, you will open a workbook that tracks compensation paid to independent contractors. Independent contractors are issued 1099 statements (similar to W2s) at the end of the year. The workbook has a Year-to-date sheet and sheets for each month. You will use the consolidate by category option to consolidate the months in the Year-to-date sheet.

1. Open the workbook named **Skill Builder 17.1.**
   Notice that the Year-to-date sheet has column headings in Row 3, but there is no data. The data will be inserted by the consolidation command.

2. Click the January sheet tab.
   Notice that there are six 1099 recipients listed with the number of hours and compensation of each recipient. This recipient list is different for each month. This is because these temporary contractors come-and-go on a regular basis.

3. Click Cell C4.
   Notice that the compensation is calculated as the hours multiplied by $21.35. The consolidation command will consolidate the hours and compensation from the monthly sheets. You can consolidate cells with values or formulas (as in this example).

4. Click the February sheet tab.
   Notice that there are seven recipients for February. Several of the recipients are different from those in the January sheet.

5. Click the March sheet tab, and notice once again that the recipient list has changed.
   *In the next few steps, you will use the **Consolidate by Category** command in the Year-to-date sheet. You cannot consolidate by position (as you did in the Hands-On Lesson 17 workbook), because the monthly sheets have different layouts (different recipients).*

6. Click the Year-to-date sheet tab, and then click Cell A4.
   Cell A4 will form the starting point for the consolidated data. When consolidating by category, it is best to click the starting point of the consolidated data prior to issuing the Consolidate command.

7. Choose **Data→Consolidate** from the menu bar.
   In the next few steps, you will specify the range references you wish to consolidate. You will do this by selecting the ranges in the various sheets and adding them to the All references list.

8. Make sure the insertion point is the Reference box, and click the January sheet tab.
   You may need to move the dialog box out of the way.

9. Follow these steps to select the desired range.

Ⓐ *Select the range A4:C9 as shown here.*

	A	B	C	D	E	F
1	January Compensation					
2						
3	Name	Hours	Compensation			
4	Ben Johnson	15	320.25			
5	Robin Parson	12	256.20			
6	Scott Williams	23	491.05			
7	Eddie Richardson	34	725.90			
8	Bill Jones	21	448.35			
9	Wanda Thomas	18	384.30			
10						

Ⓑ *The dialog box will temporarily shrink as you select the data.*

Consolidate - Reference: 6R x 3C   ? ✕

January!$A$4:$C$9

Notice that the row labels in Column A were included in the selection. This is necessary because there are no row labels in the year-to-date sheet. The consolidate by category command will use these labels to determine which rows to consolidate from the monthly sheets.

Add Additional Ranges

10. Click the **Add** button.

11. Click the February sheet tab.
Notice that Excel inserts the reference February!$A$4:$C$9 into the Reference box and the marquee surrounds the reference in the worksheet. Excel assumes you want to reference the same cells as in the January sheet. This is an incorrect assumption. You will override Excel's proposal by selecting the correct cells in the next step.

12. Select the range A4:C10, and click the **Add** button.

13. Click the March sheet tab, and select the range A4:C11.

14. Click the **Add** button to complete the selection of references.

Consolidate the Data

15. Click the Left column check box.
This instructs Excel to consolidate the data based upon the names in the left column of the selected ranges. Excel will create one consolidated row in the Year-to-date sheet for each name. For example, the name Ben Johnson appears in two sheets. Excel will create one Ben Johnson row in the Year-to-date sheet. This row will contain the consolidated numbers for Ben Johnson.

(Continued on the next page)

16. Click **OK** to complete the consolidation as shown to the right.

Notice that each name appears just once in the consolidated list. Feel free to browse through the monthly sheets. You will notice that the consolidated numbers are the summation of the numbers for the individual months.

	A	B	C
1	1099 Recipient Compensation		
2			
3	Name	Hours	Compensation
4	Ben Johnson	27	576.45
5	Cheryl Lake	77	1,643.95
6	Robin Parson	67	1,430.45
7	Scott Williams	35	747.25
8	Eddie Richardson	46	982.10
9	Bill Jones	51	1,088.85
10	Wanda Thomas	65	1,387.75
11	Leslie Wilson	38	811.30
12	Ted Simpson	12	256.20
13	Ellen Ellis	10	213.50
14	Stewart Williams	8	170.80

Add Another Worksheet

One of the benefits of consolidation is that it makes it easy to add data and worksheets at a later time. You can easily consolidate the data again by adding an additional consolidation range. In the next few steps, you will add an April sheet and reconsolidate the data.

17. Insert a new worksheet, and change the name to **April**.

18. Drag the sheet tab until it is positioned to the right of the March sheet.

19. Click the March sheet tab, and use the Select All ⬜ button to select the entire sheet.

20. Copy 📋 the sheet, and click the April sheet tab.

21. Make sure the highlight is in Cell A1, and click the Paste 📋 button.

22. Select Rows 6 and 7 and use the **Edit→Delete** command to remove them.
Scott Williams and Eddie Richardson did not receive compensation in April.

23. Add the recipients shown to the right to Rows 10 and 11.
Excel should automatically calculate the compensation in Cells C10 and C11.

10	Pete Sanchez	23
11	Doness Yee	21

Consolidate Again

24. Click the Year-to-date sheet tab.

25. Select all the consolidated data in the range A4:C14, and delete it by tapping the (DELETE) key.
It is best to delete the data before consolidating. This is because the new consolidation will overwrite the existing data. If the new consolidation has fewer rows than the original consolidation, then there will be leftover (and incorrect) rows at the bottom of the consolidated data.

26. Click Cell A4, and choose **Data→Consolidate** from the menu bar.
Notice that the consolidation ranges you chose before are still on the All references list. This is convenient because now you only need to add the April range.

27. Make sure that the insertion point is in the References box, and click the April sheet tab.

28. Select the range A4:C11, and click the **Add** button.

29. Click **OK** to complete the consolidation.
You should now have 13 unique rows of consolidated data.

30. Now add a May sheet (use whichever data you desire), and consolidate the data again.

31. Feel free to experiment further with this workbook.

32. Save the changes to the workbook, and then close the workbook.

Skill Builder 17.2 Construct a Loan Payment Data Table

In this exercise, you will create a two-variable data table. The data table will calculate monthly payments on an automobile loan using various interest rates and terms.

1. Start a new workbook, and enter the data shown to the right.
   Make sure the numbers in Column B are formatted with percentage symbols as shown.

	A	B	C	D	E	F	G
1	Automobile Loan Analysis						
2							
3			Months				
4			36	42	48	54	60
5	Rate	8.00%					
6		9.00%					
7		10.00%					
8		11.00%					
9		12.00%					
10		13.00%					
11		14.00%					
12		15.00%					

2. Click Cell B4.
   In the next step, you will enter a formula that uses the PMT function. The PMT function calculates payments using an interest rate, number of payments, and opening balance as arguments.

3. Enter the function **=PMT(A4/12,B3,22000)**, and complete the entry.
   The result should equal #DIV/0! This message appears because Cells A4 and B3 are empty. These are the input cells for the data table. The formula is interpreted as follows.

   - The A4/12 reference is the interest rate argument. The A4 reference is divided by 12 because the PMT function requires a monthly rate, and the rates in Column B are annual rates. The formula references Cell A4 because it is the input cell for the data table. The interest rates in Column B will be substituted into Cell A4 when the data Table command is issued.

   - The B3 reference refers to input Cell B3. The months in Row 4 will be substituted into this cell when the Data Table command is issued.

   - The 22000 constant is the loan amount.

4. Select the range B4:G12, and choose **Data→Table** from the menu bar.

5. Enter **B3** as the Row input cell and **A4** as the Column input cell.

6. Click **OK,** and the table should be calculated.
   The numbers in the table will be negative. The PMT function always returns a negative number. You will change this in the next few steps.

7. Click Cell B4.

8. Click in the formula bar and insert a minus sign between the equal sign and PMT function.

9. Complete the entry, and the numbers should be positive.

(Continued on the next page)

10. Now select the range C5:G12.

11. Format the numbers in the range C5:G12 as Comma style with no decimals.

12. Apply a conditional format that changes the font color to blue when the value is less than or equal to 550.
We will assume you are trying to keep the monthly payment under $550.

13. Your completed worksheet should match the worksheet shown to the right.

	A	B	C	D	E	F	G
1	Automobile Loan Analysis						
2							
3			Months				
4		#DIV/0!	36	42	48	54	60
5	Rate	8.00%	689	602	537	486	446
6		9.00%	700	613	547	497	457
7		10.00%	710	623	558	508	467
8		11.00%	720	633	569	518	478
9		12.00%	731	644	579	529	489
10		13.00%	741	655	590	540	501
11		14.00%	752	666	601	551	512
12		15.00%	763	676	612	563	523

Adjust the Loan Amount

Now imagine that you want to see the same analysis for a different loan amount. This is easily accomplished by changing the loan amount within the PMT function.

14. Click Cell B4.

15. Click in the formula bar, and change the 22000 number to **25000** in the PMT function.

16. Complete the entry, and the data table will be recalculated.
The conditional formatting will also adjust to highlight only cells with a monthly payment of $550 or less.

17. Feel free to experiment by changing the loan amount, interest rates, and months.

18. Save the workbook as **Skill Builder 17.2,** and then close the workbook.

Skill Builder 17.3 Use Scenario Manager

In this exercise, you will use the Scenario Manager to project the profit for a new children's toy manufacturer named KidCraft. Donna Williams, the founder of KidCraft, needs to set up the model as part of her business plan. She is trying to raise funds, and a business plan and financial model are a crucial part of this process.

1. Start a new workbook, and follow these guidelines to create the worksheet shown to the right.

   ■ Enter the labels in Column A and the values in the range B3:B8.

   ■ Use a SUM function in Cell B9 to calculate the expenses in the range B5:B8.

   ■ Calculate the Gross Profit in Cell B11 as the Forecasted Revenue – Total Costs.

   ■ Calculate the Net Profit in Cell B12 as the Gross Profit * 70%.

   ■ Format the values with the comma and currency formats shown.

	A	B
1	KidCraft 2000 Projected Income	
2		
3	Forecasted Revenue	$ 345,000
4		
5	Employee Costs	62,000
6	Capital Expenditures	75,900
7	Manufacturing	58,650
8	Marketing & Sales	55,200
9	Total Costs	$ 251,750
10		
11	Gross Profit	$ 93,250
12	Net Profit	$ 65,275

Name the Cells

2. Select the range A3:B8.

3. Choose **Insert→Name→Create** from the menu bar.

4. Make sure the Left column box is checked, and click **OK.**
   This will assign names to the cells in Column B. This will be helpful when using the Scenario Manager.

Create the First Scenario

5. Click Cell B3.

6. Press the (CTRL) key while you select the range B5:B8.
   This technique is necessary because Cell B4 should not be included in the selection. You will create scenarios by changing the selected cells.

7. Choose **Tools→Scenarios** from the menu bar.

8. Click the **Add** button.

9. Type the name **Scenario 1**, and click **OK.**

10. Click **OK** on the Scenario Values box to choose the values displayed in the boxes.

Add Other Scenarios

11. Click the **Add** button.

12. Type the name **Scenario 2**, and click **OK.**

13. Change only the Forecasted Revenue number to **500000**, and click **OK.**

14. Now add two new scenarios using the data in the following table.

Scenario name	Variable	Set to
Scenario 3	Forecasted Revenue	700,000
	Employee Costs	80,000
	Capital Expenditures	35,000
	Manufacturing	98,000
	Marketing & Sales	85,000
Scenario 4	Forecasted Revenue	700,000
	Employee Costs	80,000
	Capital Expenditures	42,000
	Manufacturing	85,000
	Marketing & Sales	70,000

15. Use the **Show** button on the Scenario Manager dialog box to show the results of each scenario.

(Continued on the next page)

Display a Summary of All Scenarios

16. Click the Summary button.

17. Choose the *Scenario summary* option, and click **OK.**

    Excel will insert the summary on a new worksheet. The summary is shown below. Notice that the Scenario Manager assumed Cell B12 as the Result Cell. This happens to be the correct assumption because it is the Net Profit in Cell B12 that we are interested in seeing.

Scenario Summary		Current Values:	Scenario 1	Scenario 2	Scenario 3	Scenario 4
Changing Cells:						
	Forecasted_Revenue	$ 700,000	$ 345,000	$ 500,000	$ 700,000	$ 700,000
	Employee_Costs	80,000	62,000	62,000	80,000	80,000
	Capital_Expenditures	42,000	75,900	75,900	35,000	42,000
	Manufacturing	85,000	58,650	58,650	98,000	85,000
	Marketing__Sales	70,000	55,200	55,200	85,000	70,000
Result Cells:						
	$B$12	$ 296,100	$ 65,275	$ 173,775	$ 281,400	$ 296,100

Notes: Current Values column represents values of changing cells at time Scenario Summary Report was created. Changing cells for each scenario are highlighted in gray.

18. Feel free to create additional scenarios.

19. Save the workbook as **Skill Builder 17.3,** and then close the workbook.

Assessments

Assessment 17.1 Consolidate Data by Position

1. Follow these guidelines to create a new workbook with the sheets shown below and on the following page.

   - Make sure you enter the data in the correct cells. This is necessary because you will consolidate the data by position later in this assessment.

   - Make sure the column widths and cell formats are the same in all worksheets. You can accomplish this by setting up one sheet and copying it to the others.

   - Use the sheet names shown in the illustrations.

   - The cells with hyphens should contain zeros. The hyphens appear because all values are formatted as Comma style with two decimal places.

	A	B	C	D	E	F
1	1999 Credit Card Transaction Summary					
2						
3	Card Name	Purchases	Cash Advances	Interest	Payment	Credits
4	American Express					
5	National Bank Visa					
6	Western Visa					
7	Discover					
8	Norfolk Master Card					
9						
10						

Year-to-date / January / February / March /

	A	B	C	D	E	F
1	January Transactions					
2						
3	Card Name	Purchases	Cash Advances	Interest	Payment	Credits
4	American Express	125.00	200.00	25.78	100.00	-
5	National Bank Visa	500.00	-	35.00	250.00	50.00
6	Western Visa	-	-	-	-	-
7	Discover	450.00	125.00	125.65	200.00	35.98
8	Norfolk Master Card	25.00	-	-	60.00	-
9						
10						

Year-to-date \ **January** / February / March /

	A	B	C	D	E	F
1	February Transactions					
2						
3	Card Name	Purchases	Cash Advances	Interest	Payment	Credits
4	American Express	679.56	-	30.23	350.00	85.89
5	National Bank Visa	345.00	900.00	38.90	200.00	-
6	Western Visa	400.00	-	-	-	-
7	Discover	345.00	-	130.35	500.00	-
8	Norfolk Master Card	-	-		25.00	-
9						
10						

Year-to-date / January \ **February** / March /

(Continued on the next page)

	A	B	C	D	E	F
1	March Transactions					
2						
3	Card Name	Purchases	Cash Advances	Interest	Payment	Credits
4	American Express	-	-	28.50	300.00	-
5	National Bank Visa	-	-	44.50	1,000.00	-
6	Western Visa	-	-	-	400.00	-
7	Discover	-	-	127.90	2,000.00	-
8	Norfolk Master Card	-	-	-	25.00	-
9						
10						

Year-to-date / January / February / **March** /

2. Use the consolidation by position command to consolidate the three monthly sheets into the Year-to-date sheet.

The consolidated Year-to-date sheet should match the following example.

	A	B	C	D	E	F
1	1999 Credit Card Transaction Summary					
2						
3	Card Name	Purchases	Cash Advances	Interest	Payment	Credits
4	American Express	804.56	200.00	84.51	750.00	85.89
5	National Bank Visa	845.00	900.00	118.40	1,450.00	50.00
6	Western Visa	400.00	-	-	400.00	-
7	Discover	795.00	125.00	383.90	2,700.00	35.98
8	Norfolk Master Card	25.00	-	-	110.00	-
9						
10						

Year-to-date / January / February / March /

3. Save the workbook as **Assessment 17.1,** and then close the workbook.

Assessment 17.2 Create a Data Table

In this assessment, you will create the data table shown below. This table calculates monthly payments for a home mortgage using various interest rates and terms.

1. Follow these guidelines to create the data table.

   ▪ Enter the interest rates in Column B and the months in Row 2 as shown.

   ▪ Use the PMT function to create the formula in Cell B2. You used the PMT function in Skill Builder 17.2. Assume the mortgage will be $200,000.

   ▪ Do not enter the numbers shown in the range C3:F8. Excel will calculate these numbers when you issue the data table command.

   ▪ Format the values in the range C3:F8 as Comma style with no decimals.

   ▪ Apply a conditional format that changes the font color to blue when the value is less than or equal to 1,650.

	A	B	C	D	E	F
1			Months			
2		#DIV/0!	180	240	300	360
3	Rate	6.00%	1,688	1,433	1,289	1,199
4		6.50%	1,742	1,491	1,350	1,264
5		7.00%	1,798	1,551	1,414	1,331
6		7.50%	1,854	1,611	1,478	1,398
7		8.00%	1,911	1,673	1,544	1,468
8		8.50%	1,969	1,736	1,610	1,538

2. When you have finished, save the workbook as **Assessment 17.2,** and then close the workbook.

Critical Thinking

Critical Thinking 17.1

Martha Richardson is considering investing in an IRA (Individual Retirement Account). Martha is 35 years old and wants to retire at age 60. For this reason, she plans on making uniform, monthly IRA contributions for the next 25 years. Federal regulations restrict IRA contributions to a $2,000 maximum per year, so Martha's maximum monthly contribution is limited to approximately $166 per month. Set up a data table that uses the FV (Future Value) function to calculate the future value of Martha's IRA contributions assuming she makes uniform monthly contributions for 25 years. Use interest rates as one of the variables in the data table. Use the rates 5%, 7%, 9%, 12%, and 15% to represent the potential returns Martha could realize from various investment vehicles. Use the monthly contributions $50, $75, $100, $125, and $166 as the other variable in the data table. Generate the data table results, and save the workbook with a descriptive name.

Critical Thinking 17.2

Jim McDaniel is the fund raising director at his church. Jim has proposed the idea of publishing and selling a calendar featuring artwork from children who attend the church. Jim has asked you to set up a financial model that will help him determine whether or not the project will be profitable. Jim has already done a lot of research and has come up with the following assumptions.

Revenue

- The base-selling price is $5. Jim is quite confident he can sell 4,200 calendars at the $5 price.

- Jim figures he will sell 500 less calendars for each $1 increase in the selling price. However, he will print a minimum of 4,200 calendars.

- Jim estimates that, at most, he will be able to sell 6,500 calendars

Production cost is a one time fixed cost of $500.

The base marketing cost will be $2,500. Jim figures he can sell an additional 250 calendars for each additional $1,000 spent on marketing and advertising. If Jim decides to increase his marketing budget above $2,500, then he will print additional calendars to meet the estimated increase in sales attributable to the increased marketing expenditures.

Print Cost

- Cost to print 1,000 calendars is $7,500

- Cost to print each additional calendar is $1.95

Create a model that calculates the potential profitability of the project. Set up the model so that only two variables need to be adjusted: Selling Price and Marketing Expenditures. The model should automatically recalculate the units sold, revenue, print cost, and profit or loss when the selling price and/or marketing expenditures are adjusted. This will require a lot of thought and creativity on your part.

Apply conditional formatting to the profit or loss cell. Format the cell with a blue color if the project is profitable and a red color if it is not profitable. Use the Scenario Manager to create four or five scenarios for your model. The scenarios will use only the selling price and marketing cost as variables. Display a scenario summary for various selling price and marketing expenditure combinations. Save your completed workbook with a descriptive name.

Critical Thinking 17.3 Web Research

Use Internet Explorer and a search engine of your choice to locate an investment Web site that publishes information on IRA's, Roth IRA's, and SEP IRA's. Set up sections in the worksheet where information for all three types of IRA's can be stored. Record the annual contribution limitations for each type of IRA. Also, record information on the tax advantages of each type of IRA. Feel free to set up models that show the future value of the various IRA's using contribution amounts, investment returns, investment terms, and other options that you desire.

Workgroup Collaboration

Excel has many features to support workgroup collaboration. Each can help facilitate the smooth exchange of information. Workbook property settings let you record information about how a workbook relates to your work or a specific project. One of Excel's most powerful collaboration features is the ability to create shared workbooks. You can set up a workbook that several other users can access simultaneously. Excel's change history tracking can help you avoid and resolve potential conflicts when data is edited by multiple users. You can also distribute the same workbook and then merge all of the changes automatically into one workbook. You can also link cells in a source workbook with cells in other workbooks. When you change the cells in the source workbook, the cells change in linked workbooks automatically.

In This Lesson

Case Study

Grace continues to run the Connections project that was the subject of Lesson 7. She uses Excel for several of the project activities. Grace must coordinate the project budget and information from various levels at the college. She interacts with faculty and staff at Columbia State College to keep their financial reports up-to-date. Early in the project, Grace did all of the work on the Excel workbooks herself. But she grew tired of cutting and pasting other people's input, sometimes cell-by-cell. Grace has set up a system that allows her to share workbooks with others and then review and combine the data with much greater efficiency.

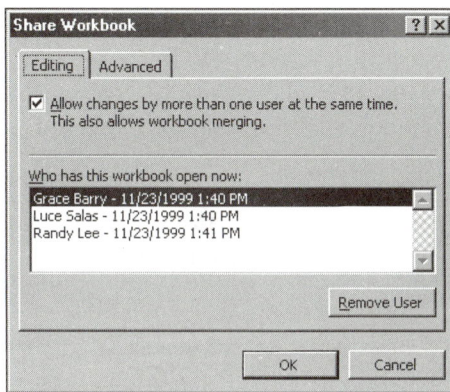

*The **Share Workbook** command lets several users access and edit the same workbook simultaneously. In this example, three users are currently working on this shared workbook.*

Grace also sets up workbooks that she can share with her project assistant. If the project assistant makes changes to the workbook, Grace can review and accept or reject each change with ease. This makes it easier for Grace to delegate research and data gathering activities. Also, both she and her assistant always have access to the same workbook data.

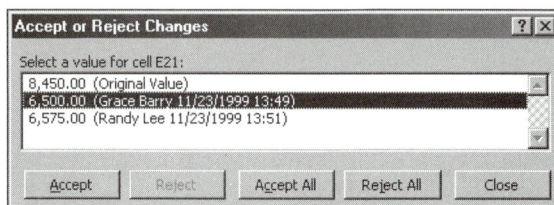

In this example, Grace and a co-worker both edited the same cell. Excel's Accept or Reject Changes dialog box helps Grace review the changes, displaying who changed what and when, and lets her decide which changes to keep.

Grace works with several others at the college who access the grant project data in a project workbook. Everyone has equal access to the data. As the project manager, however, Grace also adds a file password to the workbook so that data cannot be altered or viewed by staff who are not authorized to work on the project.

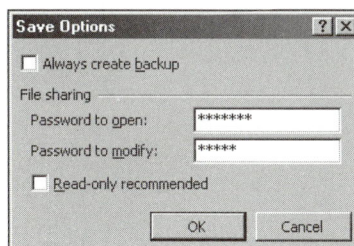

The Save Options dialog box lets you assign different passwords to open and modify the workbook.

Setting Workbook Properties

Workbook properties can help you keep track of a workbook's history and use. Excel handles many of these properties automatically. Other properties can be edited and customized by users. You can view the properties of a workbook before you open it in the Open File dialog box, and in a My Computer or Exploring window by giving a right-click on the file and then choosing *Properties*.

Property Types

The five types of properties are described in the table below:

Property Type	Description
General	Gives details related to the location of the file, when it was created, and when it was last modified.
Summary	A user-modified area to record basic information about the workbook, such as Title, Author, Category, Comments, and other details.
Statistics	This property records the creation, modification, and access information. It can also track the revisions and editing time spent on the workbook.
Contents	This property lists all of the worksheets and charts in the workbook.
Custom	A user-modified area where you can enter just about any type of information. There are many predefined properties you can enter, such as Department, Checked by, and Status. You can also add your own custom properties at any time.

Summary Properties

The Summary properties tab lists data items that help identify the workbook. For example, you can assign keywords that may help you search for the workbook later. Some summary properties are set automatically. For example, when you create a new workbook, Excel automatically enters the current user name into the Author box of the Summary properties tab and a Company name.

Title:	Connections Grant project
Subject:	Information Technology program development
Author:	Grace Barry
Manager:	
Company:	Columbia State College
Category:	grants, curriculum development
Keywords:	connections grant

The Summary properties tab is a good place to identify the activities and persons that the workbook data supports. You can create searches on the data in the Summary tab to help locate a hard-to-find workbook.

Quick Reference

VIEW WORKBOOK PROPERTIES

Task	**Procedure**
View and edit workbook properties.	■ Choose *File→Properties* from the menu bar.
	■ Click the tabs to view the various properties.

Hands-On 18.1 View and Edit the Workbook Properties

In this exercise, you will view and set several summary and custom properties.

Edit the Summary Properties

1. Open the **Hands-On Lesson 18** workbook on your exercise diskette.
   This workbook contains another version of the Connections Grant workbook you used back in Lesson 7.

2. Choose **File→Properties** from the menu bar.
   The most recently used property tab is displayed.

3. If necessary, click the *General* tab.
   The General tab tells you when the workbook was created, modified, and most recently accessed (opened).

4. Click the **Statistics** tab.
   This tab contains information similar to what you saw on the General tab. Notice the items that record the number of revisions and the total editing time.

5. Click the **Contents** tab.
   This tab displays the names assigned to the worksheets, PivotTables, and charts in the workbook. Like the other two tabs you just viewed, you cannot edit the contents of this tab.

6. Click the **Summary** tab.
   This tab contains several boxes that you can edit. Notice that the author name and Company name are already entered.

7. Click in the *Title* box; then type **December Quarterly Report**.

8. Click in the Keywords box; then type **Connections grant**.
   These keywords can help you search for the workbook, as you will see in a moment.

9. Click the *Save preview picture* box near the bottom of the dialog box to place a check mark.
   This option creates a preview of the workbook that you can display in the Open File dialog box. This option increases the size of the workbook file somewhat.

10. Click **OK** to close the Properties dialog box; then Save ▦ the workbook.

Search for a Workbook

11. Click the Open 📂 button on the toolbar. If necessary, choose the your exercise diskette in the *Look in* box.

12. Scroll down the file list, and click the *Hands-on Lesson 18* file.

13. Click the View ▦▾ button drop-down list on the toolbar; then choose **Properties.**
    A view of the summary properties will appear in the right half of the dialog box.

14. Click the View ▦ button to cycle to the **Preview** mode.
    A preview of the worksheet will appear. Excel made a preview of the worksheet that was displayed when you checked the preview option on the Summary tab in Step 9.

(Continued on the next page)

15. Click the [Tools ▾] button on the toolbar; then choose **Find**.

   A Find dialog box will appear. You can define sophisticated searches for Office files with a variety of search conditions. In this example, you will create a search for one of the keywords you entered in the Summary tab.

16. Follow these steps to search for a keyword.

   A *Click the* Property *box drop-down list button; then tap the K key and choose the* Keyword *property.*

   B *Click in the* Value *box; then type* **Connections***.*

   C *Click* **Add to List** *to add this condition to your search.*

   D *Click the Search subfolders box to place a check mark. This option includes all files in any subfolders within the drive or folder you choose in the next step.*

   ┌─ Define more criteria ──┐
   │   [Add to List]│
   │ ◉ And   Property: Condition: Value: │
   │ ○ Or   [Keywords   ▾] [includes words ▾] [Connections   ]│
   │   │
   │ Look in: [A:\   ▾] ☑ Search subfolders │
   │   │
   │ [Find Now]   [Cancel]   [Save Search...] [Open Search...]│
   └──┘

   E *Click the Look in box drop-down list button; then choose the 3½ Floppy (A:) drive.*

   This is an example of how you would set up a search for a keyword in the Summary properties. Unfortunately, it takes about 4-5 minutes to run a search on your floppy disk. (It would take just a few seconds on a hard drive.) Let's use your time for other things.

17. Click **Cancel** to close the Find dialog box

18. Right-click on the *Hands-on Lesson 18* file; then choose **Properties** from the pop-up menu.
   The Properties dialog box appears to display the Summary tab with your recent additions. Notice that the boxes are grayed out. You cannot edit the file properties from the Open dialog box.

19. Click **Cancel** to close the *Properties* dialog box; then click **Cancel** again to close the *Open* dialog box.

Custom Properties

The Custom properties tab can contain just about any type of information you wish to record in the workbook. The Name box has a list of predefined properties you can choose, such as *Checked by, Project,* and *Telephone number.* You can also manually create any type of property you might need. For example, you might want to add a property for the name of an *auditor* or the date the workbook was distributed for review.

Properties:	Name	Value	Type
	Department	Grants Office	Text
🔗	Total Grant Funding	300000	Number
	Report Deadline	1/15/2000	Date

The Custom properties tab lets you define and list a wide variety of data for the workbook. Notice the different data types used here.

Linked Data in Custom Properties

If you name cells in the workbook, you can link these data items to properties in the Custom properties. For example, you could name a grand total cell, then display the current grand total on the Custom properties tab. A links symbol appears beside each linked property. When the data in the cell is changed, the value displayed in Custom properties changes as well.

🔗 Total Grant Funding

Saving Properties in a Workbook Template

You can build in values for Summary and Custom properties in a workbook template. When a new workbook is based on the template, the template properties settings are transferred to the new workbook. For example, you might set up a template for a special project that includes the project name, project manager, and department in the properties of every new worksheet you create.

Quick Reference

CREATE CUSTOM PROPERTIES

Task	Procedure
Create a custom property.	■ Choose *File→Properties* from the menu bar; then click the *Custom* tab.
	■ Choose a name from the list beneath the *Name* box, or type a new name for the custom property in the *Name* box.
	■ Choose the type of data for this custom property in the *Type* box.
	■ Type the data for the custom property in the *Value* box.
	■ Click the *Add* button.
Create a custom property linked to a cell in the workbook.	■ Insert a *name* for the cell to which the data will be linked.
	■ Choose *File→Properties* from the menu bar; then click the *Custom* tab.
	■ Type a new name for the custom property in the *Name* box.
	■ Click to check the *Link to content* check box.
	■ Choose the desired cell name in the *Source* box.
	■ Click the *Add* button.

Before you open the Properties dialog box, you will name a cell to use later in the exercise.

1. Click Cell **B26**; then click in the Name box on the left end of the formula bar, type **GrantFunds**, and tap ⟨ENTER⟩.

2. Choose **File→Properties** from the menu bar; then click the *Custom* tab.
   This tab can contain a wide variety of data items. Notice the Name *list, which contains many predefined custom properties.*

3. Follow these steps to add a predefined custom property.

Ⓐ *Click* Department *in the* Name *list.*

Ⓑ *Type* **Grants Office** *in the* Value *box as shown here.*

Ⓒ *Click* **Add** *to add the custom property.*

Ⓓ *If necessary, adjust the column widths so you can view the property details.*

The predefined Names include many useful categories to hold additional details about the workbook and any projects or activities it supports. However, it is also easy to create new property names, as you will see in the next step.

4. Follow these steps to define a new custom property.

Ⓐ *Type* **Report Deadline** *in the* Name *box. You can always define a new property name by typing it here rather than choosing a predefined name from the list.*

Ⓑ *Choose* Date *from the* Type *box. The value you enter for this property must always match this data type.*

Ⓒ *Type* **1/15/[current year]** *in the* Value *box.*

Ⓓ *Click* **Add** *to add the custom property.*

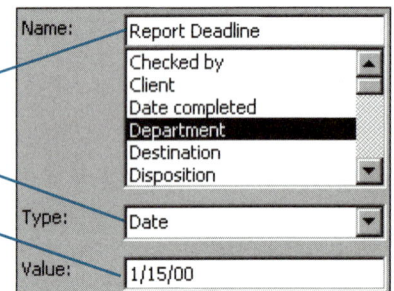

Custom properties allow you to include almost any type of data in the properties dialog box. When you set a type for the property, make sure that it will work with the sort of values you intend to store. When in doubt, set the property type to Text.

Create a Linked Custom Property

This custom property will link to the cell you named in Step 1. Linked custom properties are a convenient way to record details that may change over time.

5. Follow these steps to add the linked custom property.

Ⓐ *Type* **Total Grant Funding** *in the* Name *box.*

Ⓑ *Click the* Link to content *box. Notice that the* Value *box has changed to* Source.

Ⓒ *Choose* GrantFunds *in the Source box.*

Ⓓ *Click Add.*

A special link symbol to the left of the property name indicates that this is a linked property. Notice that the value of the cell is displayed. Now if the total funding of the grant changes, it is reflected in the value of this property automatically. The next three steps will demonstrate this.

6. Click **OK** to close the dialog box.

7. Click Cell B11; then enter a new value of **55000**.
   Notice that the total in Cell B26 (GrantFunds) has changed to 300,000.

8. Choose **File→Properties** from the menu bar; then examine the *Total Grant Funds* property in the lower portion of the dialog box.
   The value of this linked property has changed to reflect the new total on the worksheet. You can set a linked property for any cell that you name on a worksheet.

9. Click the Report Deadline property in the Properties list; then click the **Delete** button.
   The custom property is removed from the Properties list. You can add and subtract items from the Custom properties at any time.

10. Click **OK** to close the dialog box.

Working with File Passwords

In Lesson 9, you learned about using passwords to protect worksheets and workbooks. File passwords are another level of password protection you can apply to a workbook. File passwords control the ability of other users to open or modify a workbook. You set, edit, and remove File passwords from the Tools menu in the Save As dialog box.

TIP!

File passwords are completely independent of the worksheet and workbook passwords you learned about in Lesson 9. You can use all three types of passwords in the same workbook.

Functions of File Passwords

File passwords serve two primary functions:

- **Prevent opening a workbook**—You can set a file password to prevent unauthorized users from opening the workbook.

- **Prevent modifying a workbook**—You can set a file password that lets other users open the workbook but prevents unauthorized users from modifying any its cells, worksheets, charts, and properties.

TIP!

Some users rely on just one or two passwords for all of their workbooks and documents. This reduces the number of passwords they need to memorize.

About Passwords

When you set file passwords, there are a few facts that you should keep in mind.

- **Passwords are case-sensitive**—File passwords are case-sensitive. This means that if you use capital letters in the password, these must be typed exactly when entering the password to open the workbook. For example, the passwords *OffToWork* and *offtowork* are not identical.

- **Don't forget the password**—If you set a file password, then later forget it, there is no way to open the file again. When you create a new password, it is a good idea to write it down and keep it in a secure, easy-to-find place.

- **Don't use obvious passwords**—the name of a spouse, a birthday, and other items that may be common knowledge are not good choices for passwords. The most effective passwords usually include one or more numbers as well as letters.

TIP!

The Read-only recommended option can be switched on and off without assigning a password.

The Read-Only Recommended Option

The same dialog box you use to set a password also has a check box for the *Read-only recommended* option. When this option is checked, Excel will display a recommendation to open the workbook as a read-only file whenever it is opened. The only way to save changes to a read-only file is to save it with a new name. This option may be useful for workbooks that contain archival data that should normally not be modified.

Quick Reference

SETTING A WORKBOOK PASSWORD	
Task	**Procedure**
Set a file password for a workbook.	■ Choose *File→Save As* from the menu bar.
	■ Click *Tools→General Options* from the Save As dialog box.
	■ Enter a password(s) to open and/or modify the workbook.
	■ If desired, check the *Read-Only recommended* check box.
	■ Re-enter the password(s) when Excel prompts you for confirmation.
	■ Click *Yes* if Excel asks if you wish to replace the existing file.(This will happen if you save the file with the same filename.)

In this exercise, you will set a file password for the Connections Grant workbook; then close the file so that you can open it with the new passwords.

1. Choose **File→Save As** from the menu bar.

2. Click the Tools ▾ button on the toolbar; then choose **General Options.**
    The Save Options dialog box displays the password settings.

3. Follow these steps to assign passwords to the workbook file.
    As you type the passwords, notice how Excel places asterisks in the boxes. This prevents passers-by from reading the passwords as you type.

    Ⓐ *Type, exactly as shown here,* **4GrantS** *as the password to open the file.*

    Ⓑ *Type, exactly as shown here, the password* **connect** *as the password to modify the file.*

    Ⓒ *Click the* Read-only recommended *option to place a check mark.*

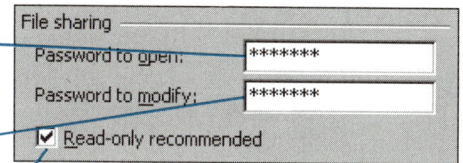

    > File sharing
    > Password to open: *******
    > Password to modify: *******
    > ☑ Read-only recommended

    A user who wants to modify this file will need both passwords.

4. Click **OK** to close the dialog box.
    A Confirm Password dialog box will appear. Excel asks you to retype the password to proceed (i.e., open the workbook). This double-entry of passwords helps avoid typographic errors when a password is defined.

5. Taking care to properly type the uppercase letters, enter **4GrantS** in the password box; then tap (ENTER).
    Now you are asked to confirm the password to modify the workbook. Notice the stringent warning against losing or forgetting the password.

6. Type **connect** in the password box; then tap (ENTER).
    You are back to the Save As dialog box. Now you will finish saving the file to save the new passwords.

7. Click **Save;** then click **Yes** to confirm replacement of the existing version of the workbook.

8. Click the lower of the two *close window* sizing buttons to close the workbook (not the Excel) window.

Open the File Password-Protected Workbook

In the next step, you will learn a convenient shortcut to open the most recently closed workbook file. This technique works with many other programs as well.

9. Use (ALT)+F to open the file menu; then tap 1 (one) on the keyboard to open the *Hands-On Lesson 18* workbook.
    You will be prompted that the file is protected and asked to supply a password. In the next step, you will deliberately type the password incorrectly, without uppercase letters.

10. Taking care to use only lowercase letters, enter **4grants**; then tap (ENTER).
    You are prompted that the password is incorrect. Excel suggests one reason you might not have entered the password correctly.

(Continued on the next page)

11. Click **OK** to close the dialog box.

12. Use (ALT)+F; then tap 1 to open the workbook again.

13. Now enter the correct password, **4GrantS**, and tap (ENTER).
A new password dialog box opens. This time you must enter the password to modify the file, or click the Read-Only button to open the file in a form you cannot save with the same file name.

14. Click the **Read Only** button.
The workbook opens. At this point you can view any worksheets in the workbook that do not have worksheet protection set. Protected worksheets may have a different password and could still be off-limits.

15. Click the *Columbia State College* workbook tab. Click Cell **C11**; then type **5844**, and tap (ENTER).
Now that you have edited a cell in this read-only workbook file, let's see what happens when you try to save it.

16. Save 🖫 the workbook.
A prompt warns you that this is a read-only file.

17. Click **OK;** then click **Cancel** to close the Save As dialog box.
Although you could have saved the file with a new name, in this case you will abandon the change and enter the password required to modify the file instead.

18. Close the workbook window; then click **No** when you are asked if you wish to save the file.

Open the File Again

19. Use (ALT)+F; then tap 1 to open the workbook again.

20. Enter the *open file* password **4GrantS**; then tap (ENTER).

21. Enter the **modify file** password **connect**, then tap (ENTER).
Excel will prompt you that this file should be opened as read-only. This is due to the Read-only recommended option that you checked when you set up the passwords. This time, you will not open the file as read-only.

22. Click **No** to open the workbook as a normal file to which you can save changes.

23. Click the *Columbia State College* worksheet tab. Click Cell **C11**; then type **5844** and tap (ENTER).

24. Save 🖫 the workbook.
Now the workbook file saves normally.

Editing and Removing Passwords

You edit and/or remove passwords in the same dialog box you used to enter them. You can change either or both passwords with the same command. You can also remove one password while keeping the other.

Quick Reference

REMOVING A WORKBOOK PASSWORD

Task	Procedure
Remove a file password from a workbook.	■ Choose *File→Save As* from the menu bar.
	■ Click *Tools→General Options* from the Save As dialog box.
	■ Delete the password(s) to open and/or modify the workbook from the desired boxes.
	■ Click *Yes* if Excel asks if you wish to replace the existing file. (This will happen if you save the file with the same filename.)

Hands-On 18.4 Remove a Workbook Password

In this exercise, you will remove the modify password and switch off the read-only recommended option. The password required to open the workbook file will remain.

1. Choose **File→Save As** from the menu bar.

2. Click the Tools ▾ button on the toolbar; then choose **General Options.**

3. Select and delete the password in the *Password to modify* box.

4. Uncheck the *Read-only recommended* box; then click **OK**

5. Click **Save;** then click **Yes** to overwrite the existing copy of the file.

6. Close the workbook window; then use ALT+F and tap 1 to open the workbook.

7. Enter the **4GrantS** password to open the file.
   The file is opened and ready for you to edit and save any changes.

Tracking Changes to Workbooks

When several persons use a workbook, there may be situations where one person should review and approve each change. Excel can maintain a *change history* that tracks each change to the workbook. The change history displays the user name of the person who made each change along with the original and new value for each cell. The change history lets you review each change and accept or reject it. Excel's track changes feature is also required to share and merge workbooks, as you will see later in this lesson. You activate tracking changes with the *Tools→Track Changes→Highlight Changes* command.

Example

Grace gives a workbook file to her assistant and asks him to contact several faculty members for information on any expenditure that may have been missed. Grace turns on the Track Changes feature so that she can quickly see and review all changes that have been made.

TRACKING CHANGES TO A WORKBOOK

Task	Procedure
Switch on Track Changes for a workbook.	■ Choose *Tools→Track Changes→Highlight Changes* from the menu bar.
	■ Check the *Track changes while editing* option.
	■ Choose the options for the changes that should be highlighted, such as *When*, *Who*, and *Where*.
	■ Set whether you wish the changed cells to be highlighted on the screen; then click *OK*.
	■ Click *Save*, then click *Yes* when you are prompted to save the workbook. The workbook must be saved in order to activate the Track Changes command.

Hands-On 18.5 Track Changes to the Workbook

In this exercise, you will switch on the Track Changes feature; then edit several workbook cells. As you work, the Track Changes feature will record your edits for later review.

Switch-On Track Changes

Because change tracking records the name of each user who edits the workbook, you will check the user name and change it to your own name if necessary.

1. Choose **Tools→Options** from the menu bar; then click the *General* tab.

2. If necessary, type **your name** in the *User name* box; then click **OK.**

3. Choose **Tools→Track Changes→Highlight Changes** from the menu bar.

4. Follow these steps to set up the Track Changes feature.

Ⓐ *Check the* Track changes *option.*

Ⓑ *Make sure that the* When *option is checked and set to* All.

Ⓒ *Make sure that the* Who *option is checked and set to* Everyone.

Ⓓ *Click the Question Mark button.*

Ⓔ *Click on the label for the* Highlight *option to view its description; then click on the description to dismiss it.*

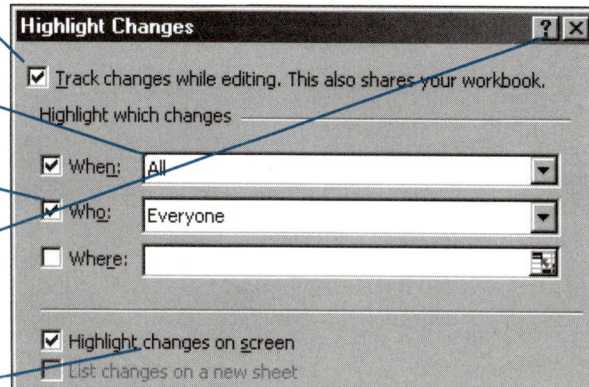

Highlight Changes   [?][X]

☑ Track changes while editing. This also shares your workbook.

Highlight which changes

☑ When: | All |

☑ Who: | Everyone |

☐ Where: | |

☑ Highlight changes on screen
☐ List changes on a new sheet

5. Click **OK** to close the dialog box; then click **Save** to save the workbook. Click **Yes** when you are asked if you wish to replace the existing file.
   You must save the file in order to activate the track changes feature. Now Excel is set up to record every change you make to the workbook.

Edit the Workbook

6. Click the *Columbia State College* worksheet tab; then click Cell **E21;** then enter a value of **1725.**
   Notice the border around the cell and the small triangle in the upper-left corner. This mark tells you that the cell has been edited since Track Changes was activated.

7. Right-click on Cell **E21;** then choose insert Comment from the pop-up menu. Type a comment for the cell: **Network server had to be replaced.**

NOTE!   *If the comment box remains visible after you click Cell G16 in the next step, check View→Comments, and make sure that the display comments option is not switched on.*

8. Click Cell **G16;** then enter a value of **725.**

9. Click Cell **G11;** then enter a value of **5844.**

10. Save 💾 the workbook.
    You are done editing the workbook. Now read on to see how Grace reviews the edits.

Reviewing Tracked Changes

You can review changes to a workbook that has the Track Changes feature switched on. When you review changes, Excel can jump you from one change to the next and gives you the opportunity to accept or reject each change. After you have reviewed a change, Excel still keeps a record of the change until you deactivate the Track Changes feature. The list below describes each of your review options.

- **Accept**—An accepted change is kept in the cell. The change history records the old value that was replaced.

- **Reject**—A rejected change is replaced in the cell by the old value. The change history records the new value that was rejected.

- **Accept All or Reject All**—All of the changes that have not yet been reviewed can be rejected or accepted with a single command.

The Change History

After you have reviewed changes to a worksheet, the change history retains a copy of the reviewed cells, including their old and new values and any rejected values. Thus, even after you accept a change, you could refer to the change history and manually reinstate an old or rejected value.

REVIEWING TRACKED CHANGES

Task	Procedure
Review and approve changes to a workbook.	■ Choose *Tools→Track Changes→Accept or Reject Changes* from the menu bar.
	■ Choose the categories of changes that you wish to review; then click *OK*.
	■ Use the buttons in the dialog box to navigate through the changes and accept or reject changes as desired.
View the change history for a workbook.	■ Choose *Tools→Track Changes→Highlight Changes* from the menu bar.
	■ Click to check the *List changes on a new sheet* option; then click *OK*.
	■ The worksheet will remain visible until you give the *Save* command.

Hands-On 18.6 Review the Changes

In this exercise, you will take on the role of Grace reviewing the changes.

1. Choose **Tools→Options** from the menu bar. Type **Grace Barry** in the User name box; then click **OK**.
   Notice how the borders around the changed cells have changed color. This alerts you that the cells were changed by someone besides the present user.

2. Choose **Tools→Track Changes→Accept or Reject Changes** from the menu bar.
   A dialog box appears in which you can select the changes to accept or reject.

3. Follow these steps to examine your choices.

   Ⓐ *Click the When list; then choose Not yet reviewed.*

   Ⓑ *Click the Who list. Notice that your name and Grace's appear in the list, along with other choices. Choose Everyone; then click OK.*

   Ⓒ *Click the Question Mark button; then click on the Where box. Read the description of this option; then click on the description to dismiss it.*

   Ⓓ *Click OK to continue.*

   The Accept or Reject Changes dialog box will appear. This will take you from one changed cell to the next.

4. If necessary, move the *Accept or Reject Changes* dialog box so that Cell **E21** is visible.
   Notice that the first cell you changed already has a marquee.

5. Point (don't click) over Cell E21. Notice that you cannot view the comment.
   Before reviewing a changed worksheet, you may want to display or review the comments first.

6. Click **Accept** to accept this change to the workbook.
   Notice that there is no longer a change box around Cell E21, since the change has been reviewed.

   The marquee moves on to the next changed cell. Grace recognizes this figure as advance payment for travel by a faculty member to a training seminar. She decides to reject this change, since she knows this expense should not be recorded until next quarter, when the training actually takes place.

7. Click **Reject.**
   Cell G16 reverts to its old value of blank.

8. Click **Accept** for Cell **G11.**
   Notice that the change boxes have returned to Cells E21 and G11, where you accepted the change. These cells will remain marked until you switch off the Track Changes command.

9. Point at Cell **E21.**
   Notice that the entry from the change history appears for this cell. It tells you the name of the person who changed the cell, the old and new values, and who entered the comment.

10. Save 🖫 the workbook.

View the Change History

11. Choose **Tools→Track Changes→Highlight Changes** from the menu bar.

12. Click the **List changes on a new sheet** option near the bottom of the dialog box to place a check mark; then click **OK.**
    The History worksheet will appear. The History worksheet maintains a complete record of every change to the workbook. Notice that the last line even describes how Cell G16 reverted to blank as a result of a rejected change.

13. Save 🖫 the workbook.
    Notice that the History worksheet disappears after you save the workbook.

Switch Off Track Changes

14. Choose **Tools→Track Changes→Highlight Changes** from the menu bar.

15. Uncheck the *Track changes while editing* option; then click **OK.**
    Excel displays a warning that the change history will be erased. Track Changes is a feature used with the shared workbook feature you will learn about in the next topic, and this warning relates to that feature as well.

16. Click **Yes** to confirm deactivating the Track Changes feature.
    The workbook is saved as the change history data is deleted. Notice that there are no longer borders around the changed cells.

Sharing Workbooks

In a workgroup environment, there may be times when several team members need to access the same workbook simultaneously. For example, they may be independently checking data, or adding data to a project workbook. Excel's shared workbook feature lets you set a workbook for sharing and can automatically record a history of changes to the workbook. Then you can review the change history and correct any conflicts between entries to the same cells.

Characteristics of Shared Workbooks

When you set up a workbook for sharing, several features work together to coordinate the use of the workbook.

- **Change History**—The change history is activated automatically whenever you create a shared workbook. This feature must be active throughout the period that the workbook is shared.

- **Resolve Conflicts**—When you save changes to a shared workbook, and there are conflicts between what you and another user have entered, Excel displays a dialog box to help you review and resolve the conflicts.

Simultaneous Access to Shared Workbooks

When you share a workbook, several users can access and even change the workbook simultaneously. As additional users save their work, it is saved to the change history for later review. When the last user to have the shared workbook open gives the save command, Excel analyzes the change history and alerts the last user to review cells that two users have tried to change simultaneously.

NOTE!

If more than one person tries to open a standard Excel workbook, the second person to open the workbook will receive a warning message, and must open a read-only copy if he or she wishes to view the file.

Shared Workbooks May Disable Some Excel Features

There are several Excel features that are disabled when a workbook is shared. For example, you cannot delete rows and columns from a worksheet in a shared workbook or add charts. Nor can you change passwords to protect worksheets—although password protection applied *before* the workbook is shared will remain in effect. For further details, check the *Limitations of Shared Workbooks* topic in Excel's online Help.

Quick Reference

SHARING A WORKBOOK

Task	Procedure
Set up the workbook to be shared.	■ Choose *Tools→Share Workbook* from the menu bar; then click the *Editing* tab.
	■ Check the *Allow changes by more than one user at the same time* box, and then click **OK**.
	■ Click *OK* to confirm saving the workbook. If necessary, create additional copies of the workbook to transmit to others.
Share a workbook over a network.	■ Switch on workbook sharing as described in the task above.
	■ Copy the workbook to a network folder or other location where the entire workgroup has access to it.

In this exercise, you will set up a shared workbook. Then you will open the workbook in two different Excel windows simultaneously to simulate multiple users working on a shared workbook.

Set Up the Shared Workbook

1. Choose **Tools→Share Workbook** from the menu bar.

2. On the *Editing* tab, check the box for *Allow changes by more than one user at the same time.*

3. Choose the *Advanced* tab. Make sure that the *Ask me which changes win* option is chosen near the bottom of the dialog box.
   This option ensures that you can review and accept or reject any conflicting changes to cells whenever you save the workbook.

4. Click **OK.** Then click **OK** again to confirm saving the workbook.
   Notice that the word [Shared] appears on the title bar, beside the file name. This tells you that sharing has been enabled for this workbook.

5. Choose **Tools→Track Changes→Highlight Changes** from the menu bar.
   Notice that the Track Changes option is checked. Track Changes was switched on automatically when you gave the command to share the workbook.

6. Check the *Who* checkbox and make sure that *Everyone* is chosen in the Who list.
   This will set the change history to display change boxes around the changes that everyone makes in the workbook, not just users besides Grace. Remember that Grace Barry is still the user name set in the Options dialog box, so Excel considers her to have created this shared workbook.

7. Click **OK** to close the dialog box. Click **OK** again if you see a dialog box informing you that *No changes were found with the specified properties.*

Edit the Shared Workbook

8. Make sure that the *Columbia State College* worksheet is displayed.

9. Click Cell **C15;** then enter **2000** as the new value for the cell.

10. Click Cell **H18;** then enter **700** as the new value for the cell.

11. Click Cell **G15;** then enter **1450** as the new value for the cell.

Open a Second Copy of the Workbook

NOTE!

This new window will be referred to as the Second Excel *window for the remainder of this exercise and the following Hands-On Exercise.*

Now you will work as if you were a second person accessing the workbook simultaneously with Grace.

12. Choose **Start→Programs→Microsoft Excel** to open a second Excel window. Click the **Read Only** button if you see a dialog box titled *File in Use* that tells you the *Personal.xls* workbook is locked for editing.

(Continued on the next page)

13. Choose **Tools→Options** from the menu bar. Choose the *General* tab; then enter **[Your Name]** in the *User name* box; then click **OK.**
   Now when you open the workbook, Excel will recognize you as a different user making changes to the workbook.

14. Open the *Hands-On Lesson 18* workbook on your exercise diskette.
   A password dialog box will prompt you to enter the open file password. This password is still active in the shared workbook.

15. Enter the password **4GrantS**; then tap ⟮ENTER⟯.
   Notice again that the word [Shared] appears just to the right of the file name on the title bar. You now have this file open in two Excel program windows at once. This would not be possible with a standard Excel workbook, only on a shared workbook.

16. Click the *Columbia State College* worksheet tab; then click Cell **C15;** then enter **3250** as the new value for the cell.
   This new value will conflict with the 2000 that you entered in Step 9. However, as you will see later, Excel will help you catch conflicts like this. Notice also that this second open copy of the shared workbook does not display change boxes like the first one. However, the changes are being saved to the change history, and will be displayed later in the exercise when you review the changes.

17. Click Cell **G16;** then enter **350** as the new value for the cell.
   This value does not conflict with any other values entered by Grace.

18. Save 🖫 the workbook.
   The changes to this second open copy of the workbook have been saved to the change history. Excel will use the change history to enter the data into Grace's copy of the workbook in the First Excel window, and to resolve the conflict in Cell C15.

19. Minimize ▬ the *Second* Excel window; then make the *First* Excel window active.

Resolve Conflicts

You are back to viewing Grace's work in the first Excel window. Notice that the changes you made in the First Excel window are not visible yet. They are in the change history. The changes won't be visible until Grace gives the Save command on her open copy of the workbook.

20. Save 🖫 the workbook in the first Excel window.
   A Resolve Conflicts dialog box appears. This alerts Grace that her change conflicts with a change you made in the second Excel window a few moments ago. Notice how the name, time and other details of the two changes are displayed. Based upon her knowledge of the project, Grace recognizes that the higher figure is correct.

21. Click the **Accept Other** button on the right side of the dialog box.
   Excel displays a message that the workbook has been updated with the various changes. Notice that the change made in Cell G16 of the second Excel window has been entered.

22. Click **OK** to acknowledge the *saved successfully* message.

Review Changes to the Shared Workbook

Now you will look over the change boxes on the worksheet and review the change history worksheet.

23. Choose **Tools→Track Changes→Highlight Changes** from the menu bar.

24. Follow these steps to review the change history.

Ⓐ *Choose* All *from the* When *list.*

Ⓑ *Check the* List changes on a new sheet *option.*

Ⓒ *Click* **OK** *to close the dialog box.*

The History worksheet is displayed again. As you would expect, all of the changes are recorded here. Notice however, that there is nothing recorded for the 2000 that you entered into Cell C15 in the First Excel window. That was the cell with the conflicting changes. Since you dismissed the 2000 value for the 3,250 value, the change history does not record the conflict, just the resolution.

25. Click the *Columbia State College* worksheet.
Notice that change boxes have appeared around all of the cells that were changed earlier in this exercise. Notice also that there is no change box around Cell G11, which you changed in Hands-On Exercise 18.5. This cell is no longer marked because the previous change history was erased when you turned off the Track Changes command in at the end of Hands-On Exercise 18.6.

26. Save 🖫 the workbook.
Notice how the History worksheet disappears after the save. However, you can still see the change boxes.

Switching Off Sharing

When you switch off sharing, the change history is erased and any unsaved changes by other users are lost. You should not turn off sharing to a workbook unless you are satisfied that everyone's data has been saved and that any conflicts have been resolved satisfactorily. Once you disable the sharing feature for a workbook, there is no turning back.

WARNING!

When you turn off sharing, make sure that all other users have saved their changes and closed the workbook. Otherwise, their changes will be lost.

Quick Reference

DISABLING WORKBOOK SHARING	
Task	**Procedure**
Disable workbook sharing.	■ Choose *Tools→Share Workbook* from the menu bar; then click the *Editing* tab.
	■ Uncheck the *Allow changes by more than one user at the same time* check box, and then click OK.
	■ Click *Yes* when you are warned that the change history will be erased and that other users will not be able to save their work.

In this exercise, you will disable sharing for the workbook. This command will also erase the change history and deactivate the track changes feature.

1. Choose **Tools→Share Workbook** from the menu bar; then choose the **Editing** tab.
   Notice that the Who has this workbook open now *list on the dialog box displays both of the Excel windows. You should see your own name on the second line along with the time that you opened the workbook in the second window. Although you could use the* Remove User *button near the bottom of the dialog box to close the other window, it is much more polite to contact the user and make sure that he or she has had an opportunity to save the workbook. Otherwise, the unsaved changes will be lost.*

2. Click **Cancel** to close the dialog box.

3. Close ☒ the *First* Excel window you are currently viewing.

4. Click the **Microsoft Excel** button on the Windows taskbar to restore the window.

5. Choose **Tools→Share Workbook** from the menu bar.
   The Who has this workbook open now *list now shows just the one open copy of the shared workbook. Now it is safe to turn off sharing this workbook.*

6. Uncheck the *Allow changes by more than one user at the same time* option; then click **OK.**
   Excel displays a warning that removing the workbook from shared use will make it impossible for other users to save their changes. You are also warned that the change history will be erased. Notice that anyone can give this command to the shared workbook.

7. Click **Yes** to confirm removing the workbook from shared use.
   The workbook is saved. Now it can only be opened by one user at a time.

8. Click **OK** to acknowledge the successful save message.

Merging Multiple Workbooks

When you share a workbook, you also have the capability to merge multiple copies of the workbook into a single workbook. This saves you the tedium of opening each workbook individually; then selecting, copying, and pasting the necessary cells into the primary workbook.

TIP!

You can only merge workbooks with a shared workbook. The Merge command is grayed out for normal Excel workbooks.

Example

Grace creates a shared workbook. She saves several copies of the shared workbook and sends the copies to people by email, requesting that they fill-in data on specific sections. As the workbook copies are returned Grace merges them into her original shared workbook. Grace will not have to look for, copy, then paste the data. The merge command will place the data from the other workbooks automatically.

Merged Cells Compared to Merged Workbooks

Do not confuse the *merge workbook* command with *merged* cells, which you learned about in Lesson 2. Merged cells let you combine a range of cells and center a label across the cells. You cannot merge cells in a shared workbook. You must either merge cells before sharing the workbook, or turn off sharing.

What Happens When You Merge Workbooks

Excel performs several operations when you merge workbooks. The details are described in the table below:

Change	Description
Data is merged into the currently active workbook.	Whichever copy of the shared workbook you have open when you give the merge command is the one that receives the merged data. The copies of the workbook you are merging *from* do not receive merged data.
Merged data replaces original data.	Data merged from other workbook(s) will replace any data already existing in the same cells of the workbook you are merging into.
A change history is recorded.	Excel records all of the changes that occur during the merge command, including where the data came from and who made the change.

Quick Reference

MERGING SHARED WORKBOOKS

Task	Procedure
Merge multiple copies of a shared workbook.	■ Set up the workbook to be shared. Distribute copies of the shared workbook to others that will contribute data. ■ Make sure that all workbooks to be merged are closed. ■ Choose *Tools→Merge Workbooks* from the menu bar. ■ Select the workbook(s) to be merged; then click *OK*.
Review merged changes to a workbook.	■ Choose *Tools→Track Changes→Accept or Reject Changes* from the menu bar. ■ Choose the types of changes you wish to review; then click *OK*. ■ Use the buttons in the dialog box to navigate through the changes and accept or reject changes as desired.

Password Protection for a Shared Workbook

You can set a password that prevents other users from switching off the change history feature from an individual copy of a shared workbook. The *Track Changes* option in the Highlight Changes dialog box will be grayed out. This password is distinct from any passwords set to protect cells or worksheets, or any open or modified password that has already been assigned to the workbook.

TIP!

When you activate password protection for a shared workbook, the shared workbook is automatically created and the track changes feature activated. Thus, there is no need to execute the Tools→Share Workbook *command separately.*

Quick Reference

PASSWORD PROTECTION FOR WORKBOOK SHARING

Task	Procedure
Password-protect the change tracking for a shared workbook.	■ Choose *Tools→Protection→Protect Shared Workbook* from the menu bar.
	■ Click to check the *Sharing with track changes* option.
	■ Type the password; then click *OK*.
	■ Enter the password again when prompted, and click *OK*.
	■ Click *OK* again to confirm saving the shared workbook.
Disable sharing a workbook with password protection for the change history.	■ Choose *Tools→Protection→Unprotect Shared Workbook* from the menu bar.
	■ Enter the password; then click *OK*.
	■ Click *Yes* to confirm removing the workbook from shared use.

Hands-On 18.9 Merge Two Workbooks

In this exercise, you will merge changes from a copy of a shared workbook into the original shared workbook.

Create a Shared Workbook with Password Protection

In this part of the exercise, you will create a password-protected shared workbook. You will then create a second copy of the workbook with a different name.

1. Choose **Tools→Protection→Protect and Share Workbook** from the menu bar.

2. Follow these steps to assign a password to the shared workbook.

Ⓐ *Check the* Sharing with track changes *option.*

Ⓑ *. Type the password* **connect**; *then tap* (ENTER).

3. Enter the password again when prompted, and tap (ENTER).

4. Click **OK** to confirm saving the shared workbook.
   Now that you have created the shared workbook, you will save a second copy with a different name. You can do this to create as many copies of the shared workbook as you need. Excel will still recognize these variously named workbooks as being shared with the original workbook.

5. Choose **File→Save As** from the menu bar. Enter **Southern College** as a new name for the workbook; then click **Save.**

Enter Data into the Shared Workbook

When you merge data into a workbook, the new data in a cell being merged always replaces any data that may already be in the cell. Let's place a new value in one of the cells and see if Excel helps us catch any potential problems.

6. Click Cell **C15;** then enter **6000** as the new value. Change the font to **Bold** for this cell so that it stands out.

7. Click the *Southern College* worksheet tab.
   Now you will open a workbook file identical to one you used earlier in Lesson 7. You will use the Paste Special command to paste data into the shared workbook.

8. Click the Open 📂 button; then open the *Hands-On Lesson 18b* workbook file.

9. Select Cells **C11:H22;** then click the Copy 📋 button on the toolbar.

10. Choose **Window→Southern College** to display the shared workbook.

11. Click Cell **C11;** then choose **Edit→Paste Special** from the menu bar.
    The Paste Special dialog box displays the various ways you can paste the data you copied from the other workbook. In this case, you just want to paste the values, not any of the formatting.

12. Choose *Values* as the paste mode and click **OK.**

13. Close ☒ the *Southern College* workbook. Click **Yes** when you are asked to save the changes.
    You cannot merge from an open workbook.

14. Close ☒ the *Hands-on Lesson 18b* workbook as well. Click **No** if you are asked to save the contents of the clipboard.

Merge the Workbooks

Now that the Southern College workbook is edited, let's merge the changes into the Hands-On Lesson 18 workbook.

15. Open the **Hands-On Lesson 18** workbook. Enter the password **4GrantS** when prompted; then tap (ENTER).

16. Click the *Southern College* worksheet tab.

17. Choose **Tools→Merge Workbooks** from the menu bar; then click **OK** to approve saving the workbook.
    A dialog box will open from which you can select one or more files to merge. To select more than one file from the list, hold down the (CTRL) key as you make your selections.

(Continued on the next page)

18. Scroll to the end of the file list; then double-click the *Southern College* workbook to merge it into your open workbook.

Your Hands-on Lesson 18 workbook is saved again as the merge is processed.

All of the data for the Southern College worksheet has been merged into place.

19. Click the Columbia State College worksheet tab.

Notice that the newly merged 6000 that you entered into the Southern College workbook has replaced the old figure. New data merging into a workbook always replaces the old data. However, you still have the chance to review the changes and reject incorrect merge results.

Visually Review the Changes

You will use two methods to survey the results. First, you will perform a visual review of highlighted changes. Then you will use the Accept or Reject Changes command to review the change.

20. Choose **Tools→Track Changes→Highlight Changes** from the menu bar.

21. Follow these steps to display the change history worksheet.

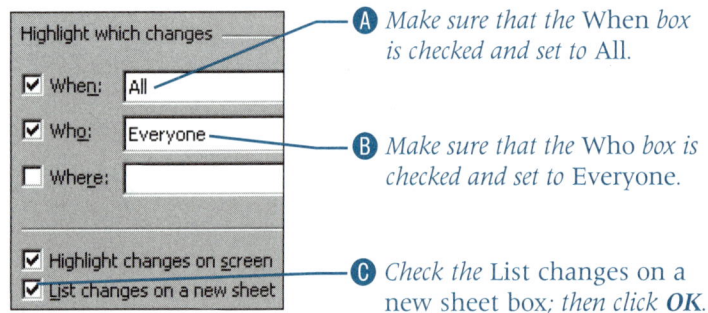

> **A** *Make sure that the* When *box is checked and set to* All.
>
> **B** *Make sure that the* Who *box is checked and set to* Everyone.
>
> **C** *Check the* List changes on a new sheet *box; then click* OK.

22. Examine column **F** of the History worksheet. This column displays all of the worksheets on which changes were recorded.

Notice that Cell F2 is the only cell that displays Columbia State College. *All of the other changes are on the* Southern College *worksheet. This tips you off on the potential problem.*

23. Click the *Columbia State College* worksheet tab.

Notice that there is a change box around the changed cell-another visual indication that a change you might not want has taken place. You could manually change this cell if necessary. However, let's use the Accept or Reject Changes *command instead.*

24. Click the *Southern College* worksheet tab.

All of the values you merged to this worksheet have change boxes.

Accept and Reject Changes

25. Choose **Tools→Track Changes→Accept and Reject Changes** from the menu bar. Make sure that that the dialog box is set as shown at right; then click **OK.**

The first change is displayed. In fact it's the only one we need to worry about.

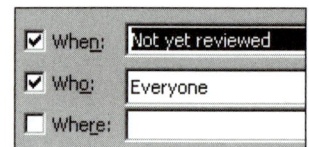

26. Click **Reject** to replace 6000 with the old value.

Now you see the first change on the Southern College worksheet. You know that all of these values are good. It would be tedious to click Accept through all of these changes one-by-one. Fortunately, you can simply accept them all.

27. Click **Accept All** to accept all of the remaining changes.

That was easy! Now let's turn off sharing on this password-protected workbook.

28. Choose *Tools→Protection→Unprotect Shared Workbook* from the menu bar.

29. Enter the password **connect**; then tap (ENTER). Click **Yes** to confirm that the workbook should no longer be shared.

Now that the workbook is no longer shared, you cannot perform any additional merge commands. You would need to share the workbook again; then create additional copies in order to merge with this workbook. Notice that the change boxes are no longer visible, since the change history has also been deactivated.

Creating Workspaces

A workspace is a special file that tells Excel how to open several workbooks at once. There may be some projects in which you often work on several workbooks simultaneously. For example, one workbook may contain sensitive data, and another workbook may contain a subset of that data. You may often need to edit both workbooks at the same time. A workspace file makes it easy to open a set of workbooks with a single command. The settings a workspace contains are listed below:

- **The filenames**—You can specify the names of multiple workbook files to be opened in the workspace.

- **The file locations**—You can open multiple workbooks located in different folders.

- **The window size**—You can position workspace files anywhere in the Excel window. When you open the workspace, each workbook opens in the specified location.

Quick Reference

HOW TO CREATE A WORKSPACE FILE

Task	Procedure
Create a workspace file.	■ Open the desired workbooks, and configure their windows in the Excel window.
	■ Choose *File→Save Workspace* from the menu bar.
	■ Enter a name for the workspace, and click *OK*.
Open a workspace.	■ Open the workspace file with the *File→Open* command from the Excel menu bar, or you can double-click the workspace file in a My Computer or Exploring window.
	■ All of the workbooks in the workspace will be opened and their windows configured as specified.

Hands-On 18.10 Create an Excel Workspace

In this exercise, you will open three workbooks simultaneously and then create a workspace for these files.

1. Click the lower restore button to restore the *workbook* window.
   Now you will shape and position this window; then open and position two other windows. When you finish, the Excel window should look similar to the figure below. However, you do not need to match the illustration exactly.

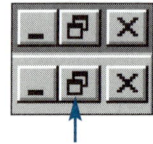

Hands-on Lesson 18				Hands-on Lesson 18b				
	A	B	C	D	A	B	C	D	E
1	**Connections Grant**				**Connections Grant**				
2	Quarterly Report for 1st Quarter 2000				Southern College				
3									
4		Authorized	October	October	No	Authorized	Apr-99	Apr-99	May-9
5		Budget	grant	match		Budget	grant	match	grant
6									
7	INCOME	290,000			INCOME				
8									
9	EXPENSES				EXPENSES				
10	PROJECT STAFF				PROJECT STAFF				
11	Salaries	45,000	4,223	1,400	Salaries		1,462	600	1,2
12	Benefits	9,000	1,135	280	Benefits		284	120	19

Quarterly Budget Report / Columbia State College / South   Southern College

2. Drag on the borders of the window to make it cover the left side of the Excel window.

3. Click the Open button; then open the *Hands-On Lesson 18b* workbook file. Drag on the window borders to make it cover the right side of the Excel window.

4. Choose **File→Save Workspace** from the menu bar.

5. Name the workspace **connections grant;** then click **Save.**

6. Close both workbooks.

7. Click the Open button; then open the Connections Grant workspace file.
   Excel will prompt you for the password of the Hands-On Lesson 18 *workbook. Even though this workbook is part of a workspace, you still need to provide the password.*

8. Enter **4GrantS** in the password box, and click **OK.**
   Both workbooks are open with their windows configured exactly as they were when you saved the workspace.

9. Close the *Hands-on Lesson 18b* workbook. Click **No** if you are asked to save any changes to the workbook.
   You can always close a workbook in a workspace independently.

10. Maximize the *Hands-On Lesson 18* workbook window.

Linking Workbooks

It is possible to link data in a workbook so that it appears in a different workbook. The linked data is dynamically updated, so that if you change the data in a source workbook the change will automatically appear in the linked workbook. Once the cells from the source workbook are linked, you can treat their data like that of any other cell. For example, you can define formulas that work with the linked data cells.

Quick Reference

HOW TO LINK DATA IN ONE WORKBOOK TO ANOTHER WORKBOOK

Task	Procedure
Link cells from one workbook to another.	■ In the *source* workbook, select the cell(s) to be linked; then give the *Copy* command.
	■ In the *linked* workbook, select the cell(s) where the linked data is to be pasted; then choose *Edit→Paste Special* from the menu bar, and click the *Paste Link* button.
Unlink cells on two workbooks.	■ In the *source* workbook, select the linked cell(s), and then give the *Copy* command.
	■ In the *linked* workbook, select the linked cell(s), and then give the Paste command (that is, a normal Paste command).

Hands-On 18.11 Create a Link Between Two Workbooks

In this exercise, you will create a source version of a workbook and then link cells in that workbook to a second workbook. Finally, you will edit the cells in the source workbook and see how the linked cells update in the linked workbook.

Create the Source Workbook

1. Click the **Quarterly Budget Report** worksheet tab.

2. Choose **File→Save-as** from the menu bar. Enter **Source 18** as the new name for the workbook; then click **Save.**

3. Select Cells **A7:B23** on the worksheet; then click the Copy button on the toolbar.

4. Click the Open button, then open the *Hands-On Lesson 18* workbook file. Enter **4Grants** in the password box; then tap (ENTER).

5. Click Cell **A7;** then choose **Edit→Paste Special** from the menu bar, and click the **Paste Link** button near the bottom of the dialog box.
   The data from the Source workbook is pasted and linked into the cells. There's no change to the Lesson 18 *workbook yet, since both files were based upon the same data.*

6. Examine the Formula bar for Cell **A7.**
   Notice that the formula bar now lists the Source 18 *workbook and gives a reference to the cell from that workbook from which the data is linked. Now let's edit the Source workbook and see what happens to the linked cells.*

7. Choose **Window→Source 18** from the menu bar.

(Continued on the next page)

8. Click Cell **A16;** then enter **Faculty Training** as the new label for the cell. Change the font in the cell to **Bold.**

9. Click Cell **B16;** then enter **34500** as the new value for the cell.

10. Choose **Window→Hands-on Lesson 18** from the menu bar; then examine Cells A16:B16.
Notice that your edits are already displayed in the linked cells. You didn't even have to save the Source 18 workbook to cause the linked data to change. Notice also that the Bold formatting you applied to Cell A16 in the Source workbook did not link over to the Lesson 18 workbook. Formatting does not link, only data, formulas and labels can link.

Check the Link

11. Choose **Window→Source 18** from the menu bar; then close ☒ the *Source 18* workbook. Click **Yes** when you are asked to save the changes.
Now the Hands-on Lesson 18 file should be active.

12. Choose **Edit→Links** from the menu bar.
The Links dialog box displays all of the links in the workbook. Right now there is just one range of cells linked, but you could easily add more. Notice that the filename of the linked workbook is displayed in the Source file list. Notice also that the Manual option is grayed out in the lower portion of the dialog box. You cannot choose manual link updating for linked workbook data. You may be able to choose the manual option when you link to data from other types of files, such as a Word document.

13. Click the **Open Source** button on the right side of the dialog box. Enter the password **4GrantS** when prompted.
The Source 18 workbook is immediately opened. Now you will unlink the cells.

Unlink the Workbooks

14. Select Cells **A7:B23** on the worksheet; then click the Copy 🖺 button on the toolbar.

15. Choose **Window→Hands-on Lesson 18** from the menu bar.

16. Click Cell A7; then click the Paste 🖺 button.
This normal paste command replaces the links with the actual contents of the cells in the Source 18 workbook. Notice that the Formula Bar no longer refers to the linked file and cells.

17. Close ☒ the Excel window. Click **No** when you are asked to save changes.

Concepts Review

True/False Questions

1. Workbook properties can only be displayed while the workbook is open in Excel.   TRUE   FALSE

2. You can only select Custom properties from the list of predefined items on the Custom tab.   TRUE   FALSE

3. If a file password is set as **GoForIt**, you can still enter the password as **goforit**.   TRUE   FALSE

4. A workbook can have a file password, a protect worksheet password, and a protect workbook password simultaneously.   TRUE   FALSE

5. The change history is a permanent part of a workbook.   TRUE   FALSE

6. When you review tracked changes, Excel displays a change box around each cell that has been changed since the Track Changes feature was activated.   TRUE   FALSE

7. If a workbook is set up for sharing, several users can open it simultaneously.   TRUE   FALSE

8. You can perform the **Merge** command with standard (unshared) Excel workbooks.   TRUE   FALSE

9. An Excel workspace lets you open several workbooks with a single command.   TRUE   FALSE

10. To link cells between workbooks, you must use the **Paste→Special** command.   TRUE   FALSE

Multiple-Choice Questions

1. Which features require that *track changes* be active?
   a. Shared workbooks
   b. Linked workbooks
   c. Merging workbooks
   d. Workspaces
   e. Both a and c

2. Which statements about shared workbooks are true?
   a. Only one user at a time can open a shared workbook.
   b. A shared workbook can only have one file name.
   c. A shared workbook cannot have a file password.
   d. Some Excel features may not work on a shared workbook.
   e. All of the above

3. What can you do if you forget an *open file* pass word?
   a. Send the file to Microsoft for decoding.
   b. Use the *protect workbook* password.
   c. Run a shareware program on the file to list the password.
   d. Nothing. You cannot open the workbook.
   e. None of the above

4. When you merge data into a workbook, what happens when the new data being merged conflicts with old data that is already in a cell?
   a. The conflicting new data is excluded from the merge, and all other new data merges into empty cells.
   b. The new data replaces the existing data.
   c. Excel displays a Conflict Resolution dialog box so that you can review the conflicts.
   d. The merge is aborted.
   e. None of the above

Skill Builders

Skill Builder 18.1 Set Workbook Properties

In this exercise, you will set and edit various workbook properties.

Name Cells

In order to use the linked custom properties feature, you will name four cells in the workbook.

1. Open the **Skill Builder 18.1** file on your exercise diskette.

2. Name the cells listed in the table below:

TIP!   *Remember that you cannot have a space character in a cell name.*

Worksheet	Cell	Name
Sales Summary	B9	**TotalSales**
Bob's Sales	E20	**BobTotal**
Kelly's Sales	E20	**KellyTotal**
Sam's Sales	E20	**SamTotal**

Edit Workbook Properties

3. Choose **File→Properties** from the menu bar; then click the Summary tab.

4. Enter information into the *Summary* properties as listed in the table below:

Property	Setting
Title	**January Sales Summary**
Author	**[blank]**
Manager	**Randy Young**
Company	**Acme Auto Sales**
Keywords	**sales January**

5. Click the *Custom* tab.

6. Follow these steps to add a new custom property.

   ■ Click *Date Completed* in the Name list.

   ■ Set the *Type* for this custom property to *Date*.

   ■ Enter [**today's date**] as the *Value*.

   ■ Click the *Add* button to add the new custom property.

In the next step, you will create a new custom property name. You can always create new names for custom properties. You are not limited to the names listed below the Name box.

7. Follow these steps to add another custom property.

   ■ Enter **Instructor Name** in the Name box.

   ■ Set the *Type* for this custom property to *Text*.

   ■ Enter your instructor's name in the Value box.

   ■ Click the **Add** button to add the new custom property.

   Now you will add a custom property linked to the content of a named cell in the workbook. The value for this property will display the current value in the cell.

8. Enter **Monthly Sales** in the Name box.

9. Click the *Link to content* checkbox; then scroll down the *Source* list, choose *TotalSales* and click **Add.**

   This property is linked to the total in the named cell. Right now the total should read zero (0). However, this will change as you add data to this workbook.

10. Add custom properties for the various sales people according to the table below.

Linked Custom Property	Named Cell
Bob	BobTotal
Kelly	KellyTotal
Sam	SamTotal

11. Click **OK** to close the Properties dialog box.

12. Save ▣ the workbook.

Skill Builder 18.2 Set File Passwords

In this exercise, you will set a password to prevent opening the workbook.

Create a File Password

1. The **Skill Builder 18.1** workbook should be open.

2. Choose **File→Save As** from the menu bar.

3. Click the **Tools** button on the toolbar, then choose **General Options.**

4. Taking care to capitalize the letters exactly as shown here, enter **AcmeSales** in the *Password to open* box; then click **OK.**

   A Confirm Password dialog box will appear. This helps ensure that you did not have a typographic error when you originally entered the password.

(Continued on the next page)

5. Taking care to use capitol letters as you did in the previous step, re-type the password in the confirmation box and click **OK.** If you receive a message that the confirmation password is not identical, go back to Step 4.

6. Click **Save;** then click **Yes** when asked if you wish to overwrite the existing workbook file.

7. Close ☒ the workbook (but not the Excel window).
   Now you will use a keyboard shortcut to quickly re-open the file. Excel always lets you access the most recently closed file from the File menu by tapping 1.

8. Use [ALT]+F then 1 to open the workbook file that you just closed.

9. Enter the password; then tap [ENTER]. If you are told that the password is not correct, repeat Step 8; then be sure to use capital letters in the password.

Remove a File Password

10. Choose **File→Save As** from the menu bar.

11. Click the **Tools** button on the toolbar; then choose **General Options.**

12. Tap the [DELETE] key to delete the current *Password to open;* then click **OK.**

13. Click **Save;** then click **Yes** when asked if you wish to overwrite the existing workbook file.
    The password will no longer be needed to open this file.

Skill Builder 18.3 Track Changes to a Workbook

In this exercise, you will set up the workbook to track changes. Then you will add some data to the workbook.

Turn on Track Changes

1. The **Skill Builder 18.1** workbook should be open.

2. Choose **Tools→Track Changes→Highlight Changes** from the menu bar.

3. Set the Highlight changes options as shown in the figure below.

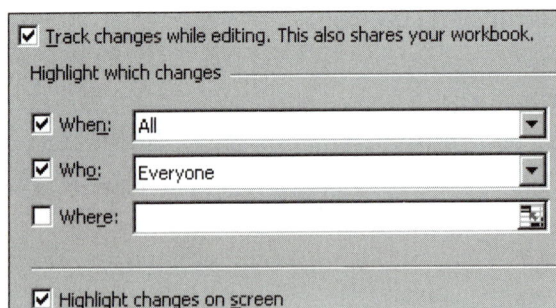

4. Click **OK;** then click **OK** again to confirm saving the workbook.

Edit the Worksheet

5. Click the *Bob's Sales* worksheet tab; then click Cell **E20.**

6. Click the AutoSum Σ button; then set the range to Cells **E5:E19** and click the AutoSum button again.
   Notice the change box that appears where you inserted the new formula.

7. Click the Copy button; then Paste the formula into Cell **E20** of the *Kelly's Sales* and *Sam's Sales* worksheets.

Review the Changes

8. Choose **Tools→Track Changes→Accept or Reject Changes** from the menu bar; click **OK** to approve saving the workbook.
   Now you can select the changes you wish to review.

9. Set the *Who* list to display [your user name]; then click **OK.**
   This will cause Excel to review only the changes you made. If someone else had made changes to this workbook, their changes would not be part of this review. Notice that the Bob's Sales worksheet is now displayed, since that is where you made the first change.

10. Click **Accept** to accept the edit.
    Notice that now the Kelly's Sales worksheet is displayed. Excel jumps you to the next change after each edit is accepted or rejected.

11. Click **Accept** for the other two changes.
    When you have reviewed all of the changes, the dialog box will disappear. Notice that the change boxes are still displayed, however. They will remain until you switch off the Track Changes feature.

Display the Change History

Excel can display the change history of the workbook. This can be useful for reviewing edits.

12. Choose **Tools→Track Changes→Highlight Changes** from the menu bar.

13. Check the *List changes on a new sheet* option at the bottom of the dialog box; then click **OK.**
    A History worksheet will appear to list all of the changes you made to the workbook.

Stop Tracking Changes

14. Choose **Tools→Track Changes→Highlight Changes** from the menu bar.

15. Uncheck the *Track changes while editing* box; then click **OK.**
    Excel will ask you to approve removing the workbook from shared use. Any time you switch on the Track Changes feature, the workbook is automatically set up to be shared.

16. Click **Yes** to approve removing the workbook from shared use.

Skill Builder 18.4 **Share a Workbook**

In this exercise, you will create a shared workbook; then you will create a copy of the workbook to send to another user.

1. The **Skill Builder 18.1** workbook should be open.

2. Choose **Tools→Share Workbook** from the menu bar.

3. Check the *Allow changes* checkbox.

4. Click the *Advanced* tab; then make sure the settings match the figure below.

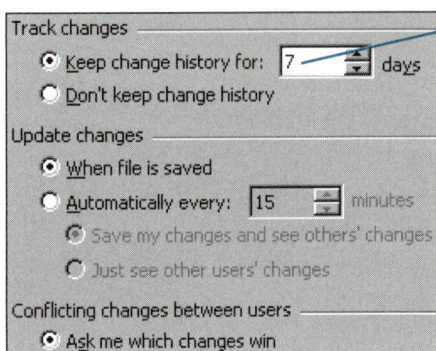

Track changes
- Keep change history for: 7 days
- Don't keep change history

Update changes
- When file is saved
- Automatically every: 15 minutes
  - Save my changes and see others' changes
  - Just see other users' changes

Conflicting changes between users
- Ask me which changes win

(A) *Set the* Keep change history for 7 *days to reduce the potential size of the file. The longer changes are kept, and the more changes that are tracked, the larger the workbook file will become.*

5. Click **OK;** then click **OK** again to approve saving the workbook.
The workbook is now ready for shared use. Look at the Title bar at the top of the Excel window. Notice the [Shared] *label to the right of the filename.*

6. Choose **Tools→Track Changes→Highlight Changes** from the menu bar.
Notice that the Track Changes feature has been switched on. This was done automatically when you set the workbook for sharing. Notice also that the When *setting is* Since I last saved. *This causes the highlight to disappear each time the workbook has been saved. However, all changes will still be listed in the Change History.*

7. Click **Cancel.**

Create a Copy of the Shared Workbook

8. Choose **File→Save As** from the menu bar.

9. Name the file **Bob's January Sales Figures** and click **Save.**
You could now send this file to Bob as an email attachment or on a floppy disk. After Bob enters his sales data, you could merge it onto the original copy of the shared workbook. You could actually make several copies of this workbook, then merge all the changes to a common copy of the shared workbook.

10. Close ⊠ the workbook.

Skill Builder 18.5 Merge Workbooks

In this exercise, you will merge data from three copies of a shared workbook. Each copy was created from the original shared workbook.

Merge Data Into the Shared Workbook

1. Open the **Skill Builder 18.2** workbook on your exercise diskette.
   Look at the title bar at the top-left corner of the Excel window. Notice that this is a shared workbook.

2. Choose **Tools→Merge Workbooks** from the menu bar; then click **OK** approve saving the workbook during the merge.
   A dialog box will appear, from which you can select the workbook files to be merged. Remember that you can only merge copies of workbooks made from the original shared workbook. The files on your exercise diskette have already been created and edited from the Skill Builder 18.2 file you are sharing.

3. Click the **Skill Builder 18.3** workbook in the file list; then hold down (CTRL) as you click to select the **Skill Builder 18.4** and **Skill Builder 18.5** workbooks.
   You have selected three workbooks to be merged with a single command.

   During the next step, watch the Status bar at the bottom of the Excel window to monitor the progress of the command. From time to time, also notice that the total for each salesperson appears in the Sales Summary as the data is merged.

4. Click **OK** to start the merge.

5. Display the worksheet for each salesperson to confirm the merged data.
   Since each salesperson entered data for his or her worksheet in their copy of the shared workbook, there were no conflicts during the merge operation.

Turn Off Sharing

6. Choose **Tools→Share Workbook** from the menu bar.

7. Click the *Editing* tab; then uncheck the *Allow changes* box and click **OK.**
   Excel asks if you really want to remove the workbook from shared use. Notice that the change history is erased if the workbook is no longer shared. Also, you can not perform a merge after the workbook is no longer shared.

8. Click **Yes** to approve removing the workbook from shared use.
   The [Shared] *label next to the filename disappears.*

Skill Builder 18.6 **Link Workbooks**

In this exercise, you will link cells in one workbook to data in cells from another workbook. Then you will edit some of the linked data and observe how it is immediately copied into the linked workbook.

1. The **Skill Builder 18.2** workbook should be open.

2. Click the *Sales Summary* tab.

3. Open the **Skill Builder 18.6** workbook file on your exercise diskette.
   This workbook contains sales quota and other personal data for the sales force.

4. Select Cells **B4:B7;** then click the Copy 🖺 button.

5. Choose **Window→Skill Builder 18.2** from the menu bar.

6. Click Cell **C4;** then choose **Edit→Paste Special** from the menu bar.
   The Paste Special dialog box displays the various ways you can paste the data.

7. Click the **Paste Link** button.
   The data is pasted into the cells. Notice that the formatting of the cells was not copied/linked, however.

8. Select Cells **B4:B7,** click the Format Painter 🖌 button on the toolbar; then select Cells **C4:C7** to format the newly linked cells.

Edit the Linked Data

Now you will edit the data in the source workbook and observe how it changes in the linked workbook.

9. Choose **Window→Skill Builder 18.6** from the menu bar.

10. Click Cell **B7;** then enter **125000** as the new quota and tap (ENTER).

11. Choose **Window→Skill Builder 18.2** from the menu bar.
    Notice that the quota for Sam in Cell C7 has changed.

12. Close ☒ the **Skill Builder 18.2** workbook file. Click **Yes** when you are asked to save the changes.
    Now you will change the data in the source workbook while the linked workbook is closed. Then you will open the linked workbook.

13. Click Cell **B6;** then enter **225000** as the new quota and tap (ENTER).

14. Close ☒ the **Skill Builder 18.6** workbook file. Click **Yes** when you are asked to save the changes.

Open the Linked Workbook

15. Open the **Skill Builder 18.2** workbook file.

    Excel will prompt you that the file is linked to another workbook and ask if you wish to update the linked data.

16. Click **Yes** to approve updating the linked data.

    Notice that the quota for Kelly in Cell C6 has changed. So, linked data is updated even when the linked workbook is closed when the source data is edited.

17. Close ☒ the Excel window. Click **Yes** when you are asked to save changes to the **Skill Builder 18.2** workbook file.

    Although you did not edit any cells yourself, it is a good idea to save the updated link data. However, if you did not save it, the data would still be updated the next time you open the workbook.

Assessments

Assessment 18.1 Set Workbook Properties

In this exercise, you will set several summary properties and create two custom properties for a workbook.

1. Open the **Assessment 18.1** workbook on your exercise diskette.

2. Set the workbook properties according to the table below:

Property Tab	Type	Setting/Value
Summary	Title	`Lesson 18 Assessment`
Summary	Company	`[Name of School/College]`
Summary	Keywords	`Shared Track Changes`
Custom	Course Number	`[Course Number]`
Custom	Checked by	`[Instructor Name]`
Custom	Total Costs	`[Linked to Cell B7]`
		Note: At the moment there is no value in this cell.

3. Save ⊞ the workbook.

Assessment 18.2 Set File Passwords

In this exercise, you will set a password to prevent unauthorized users from opening the workbook.

1. Open the **Assessment 18.1** workbook on your exercise diskette.

2. Assign the following passwords to the workbook.

Password Type	Password
To Open the Workbook	Sesame
To Modify the Workbook	Not2Change

3. When you are done assigning the passwords and testing them, close the workbook.

4. Have your instructor or a lab assistant open the workbook and initial _____ that the passwords were successfully assigned.

5. Remove the passwords; then close the workbook.

6. Have your instructor or a lab assistant open the workbook and initial _____ that the passwords were successfully removed.

Assessment 18.3 Track Changes to a Workbook

In this exercise, you will set the workbook to track changes, then make several edits on a worksheet. You will then review the edits and turn off the Track Changes feature.

1. Open the **Assessment 18.1** workbook on your exercise diskette.

2. Set the workbook to highlight and track changes.

3. Edit the Expense Report worksheet according to the instructions below.

   - Cell **B5** should equal the value of Cell **E9** on the *Cats* worksheet.

   - Cell **B6** should equal the value of Cell **E9** on the *Dogs* worksheet.

   - Cell **B7** should sum Cells **B5:B6**.

4. Save the workbook.

5. Display the *Change History* for the workbook; then print the Change History worksheet.

6. Give the command to *Accept or Reject Changes;* then approve all of the changes you made to the workbook.

7. Turn off the *Track Changes* feature.

8. Save the workbook.

Assessment 18.4 Share a Workbook

In this exercise, you will share a workbook file; then create two copies of it to merge in the next exercise.

1. Open the **Assessment 18.1** workbook on your exercise diskette.

2. Share the workbook.

3. Create two copies of the shared workbook named: **Assessment 18.2** and **Assessment 18.3**.

4. Close the **Assessment 18.3** workbook.

Assessment 18.5 Merge Workbooks

In this exercise, you will edit the two copies of the shared workbook you created in Assessment 18.4. Then you will merge the contents of the edited workbooks into the Assessment 18.1 workbook.

1. Open the **Assessment 18.2** workbook on your exercise diskette.

2. Edit the **Cats** worksheet to match the data items shaded in gray in the figure below.

Animal	Age	Health	Date Arrived	Shelter Cost
Cat	Adult	Healthy	1-May	$ 82.50
Cat	Adult	Healthy	9-May	$ 60.50
Cat	Kitten	Healthy	10-May	$ 57.75
Cat	Adult	Healthy	30-May	$ 2.75

3. Close the **Assessment 18.2** workbook.

4. Open the **Assessment 18.3** workbook on your exercise diskette.

5. Edit the **Dogs** worksheet to match the data items shaded in gray in the figure below.

Animal	Age	Health	Date Arrived	Shelter Cost
Dog	Adult	Healthy	2-May	$ 79.75
Dog	Adult	Healthy	8-May	$ 63.25
Dog	Pup	Sick	15-May	$ 44.00
Dog	Adult	Healthy	20-May	$ 30.25

6. Close the **Assessment 18.3** workbook.

7. Open the **Assessment 18.1** workbook.

8. Merge the contents of the **Assessment 18.2** and **Assessment 18.**3 workbooks into the **Assessment 18.1** workbook.

9. Save the **Assessment 18.1** workbook.

Assessment 18.6 Link Workbooks

In this exercise, you will link data from the Assessment 18.1 workbook into cells on the Assessment 18.4 workbook.

1. Open the **Assessment 18.1** and **Assessment 18.4** workbooks on your exercise diskette.

2. Create links between cells on the *Expense Report* worksheet of **Assessment 18.1** to cells on **Assessment 18.4** as listed below.

The data in this cell of Assessment 18.1 . . .	links to this cell in Assessment 18.4.
B5	B9
B6	C9

3. Close the **Assessment 18.1** workbook.

4. Save and close the **Assessment 18.4** workbook.

Critical Thinking

Critical Thinking 18.1 On Your Own

Graceilla is a member of a study group for her biology class. The members want to set up a schedule of when to meet each week. They also want to know about open times to meet just before exams. Graciella suggests that they each submit their weekly schedule. The schedules can be compared to see what time slots are open for all of the study group members. Graciella knows more about Excel than any of the other study group members, so she offers to create a workbook to help them work out their study schedule.

- Create a study schedule sheet that lets each student mark the times they have a class or work. The schedule should have a column for each day of the week, except Sunday. The schedule should have a time slot for every hour of the day from 8:00 am to 10:00 pm. Name this first worksheet **Master Schedule.**

- After you create the Master schedule worksheet, copy it to four other worksheets. Leave a row open at the top of each worksheet to list the student name for each schedule. There should now be five worksheets on the workbook. Save the workbook as **Critical Thinking 18.1.**

Critical Thinking 18.2 Groups of 3 to 4

Graciella wants to bring the schedule of each study team member into one master worksheet. She creates a shared copy of the master schedule workbook for each study team member; then tells them how to edit their worksheet to indicate their weekly schedules. After all of the schedules are entered, Graciella merges them into one of the shared workbook files and creates a formula to calculate which hours of time each week will be free for the study group members to meet.

Task A: Create a Shared Workbook

- Form a group of three to four students. Assign each student one of the non-master worksheets. Name one worksheet for each student, and place their name at the top of the worksheet as well.

- Set **Critical Thinking 18.1** to be a shared workbook. Create a copy of the shared workbook for each student in the group. Each group member should place their copy of the shared workbook on their own floppy disk.

Task B: Each Student Marks His or Her Schedule

■ Each student should mark their own schedule worksheet on their copy of the shared workbook. Place the numeral "1" in each cell for a day and hour that the student is unavailable to meet.

Tom	Mon	Tue	Wed	Thu	Fri	Sat
8:00 AM						
9:00 AM	1		1			
10:00 AM	1		1			
11:00 AM	1		1			
12:00 PM			1			
1:00 PM			1			
2:00 PM			1			
3:00 PM						
4:00 PM	1					
5:00 PM	1					
6:00 PM	1					
7:00 PM			1			
8:00 PM			1			
9:00 PM			1			
10:00 PM						

An example of one study team member's schedule.

Task C: Merge the Shared Workbooks

■ After all of the students have marked their schedules on their copies of the shared workbook, merge their changes into the **Critical Thinking 18.1** copy of the shared workbook.

■ Review the *Critical Thinking 18.1* workbook to confirm that each student's schedule was merged successfully.

(Continued on the next page)

Task D: Analyze the Schedules

■ Create the following formula in the first **8:00 AM** cell of the Master Schedule worksheet: Sum the values in Cell **B4** of all the student schedule worksheets. You will need to create a drill-down formula to do this. For example, the formula might read like this: **=SUM(Tom:Grace!B4)**.

■ Create a *conditional format* for the same cell that creates a desired background color whenever the value in the Cell's formula is less than one. This makes it easy to see which hours are available for the study group to meet.

■ Copy the first **8:00 AM** cell you just formatted to all of the other time schedule cells in the workbook. All cells with a sum of zero (0) should now be marked by the conditional format color. These are days and times when all of the study group members are available to meet.

■ Save the workbook as **Critical Thinking 18.2.** Give a copy of this new workbook to all of the students in the group.

Master Schedule						
	Mon	Tue	Wed	Thu	Fri	Sat
8:00 AM	0	0	0	0	0	0
9:00 AM	1	0	1	0	1	0
10:00 AM	2	1	2	1	2	0
11:00 AM	2	1	2	1	2	0
12:00 PM	0	1	2	1	1	0
1:00 PM	0	1	2	1	1	0
2:00 PM	1	1	2	1	1	0
3:00 PM	1	1	1	1	1	0
4:00 PM	1	1	1	1	2	0
5:00 PM	2	0	0	0	1	0
6:00 PM	3	1	1	1	1	0
7:00 PM	1	1	2	1	0	0
8:00 PM	2	1	2	1	0	0
9:00 PM	2	1	2	1	0	0
10:00 PM	0	0	0	0	0	0

When you are finished with Task D, the master schedule worksheet will look similar to the example above. Notice how the numbers also indicate how many study team members have scheduled time for each time block. For example, three study team members have other commitments at 6:00 PM on Mondays.

Critical Thinking 18.3 On Your Own

Graciella wants everyone in her study group to have access to the new group availability schedule. She converts the Master Schedule worksheet into a Web page, then uses a Web folder to post the Web page on the Internet. Graciella then sends all of the study group members the URL of the Web page in an email message.

- Save the **Master Schedule** worksheet as a non-interactive Web page.

- If your computer is equipped with a Web folder, use it to publish the Master Schedule Web page so others can view it over the Internet. Save the Web page with the name **schedule**.

- If you have an email account, compose an email message addressed to yourself that announces the posting of the schedule and gives the **URL** others can use to display the schedule Web page. An example of a URL is:
  www.offtowork.net/sfcc/student10/schedule.htm

- After you receive the message you sent yourself in the previous step, double-click on the URL in the message to open your Web browser, and view the schedule Web page.

Index

P

Page Break Preview, 152–153

page breaks for printing, 150–153

parentheses in formulas, 44

passwords
    for shared workbook, 544
    for workbook protection settings, 272–273
    for workbooks, 533–537
    See also protecting workbooks

Paste commands
    Cut, Copy, and Paste commands, 81–83
    Paste Special command, 215–217
    See also copying

payment argument, for financial functions, 342

Payment (PMT) function, 342–344

Percent number format, 47

percent operator, 44

periods argument, for financial functions, 342

Personal Macro Workbook, 402–403

pie charts, 173–174
    exploding slices, 179
    rotation and elevation of, 180

PivotCharts, 463–464

PivotTables, 454–462
    AutoFormat, 462
    creating, 455–457
    field manipulation, 458–461
    interactive PivotTables on the Web, 465–468

PMT function, 342–344

point mode
    for entering formulas, 44–45
    for entering functions, 79–81

Print button, 24–25

printing charts, 169–170

printing comments, 214–215

printing multiple-sheet workbooks, 276–277

printing worksheets
    header/footer options, 145–147
    margin options, 144–145
    Page Break Preview, 152–153
    page breaks, 150–151

    Page options, 142–143
    print area, 239–240
    Report Manager, 512
    selection of cells, 239
    Sheet options, 148–150

Print Preview button, 24

project organization, 196–202
    Favorites for folders, 199–202
    project folders, 196–197, 360–361
    shortcuts to folders, 198, 201

properties for workbooks, 528–533

protecting workbooks, 272–275
    unlocking cells, 274–275
    See also passwords

publishing with Web folders, 384–388

Q

querying databases, 440

Query Wizard, 440

R

range of cells, selecting, 18–20

range references
    in formulas, 43
    names for, 265–272

rate argument, for financial functions, 342

recording macros, 397–398

records in databases, 428

Redo button, 10

references. *See* cell references

relative references, 228

rename worksheet, 164

repeat a number series automatically, 42

Repeat command, 10

repeat most recent command, 372

replacing entries, 9

Report Manager, 512

Reviewing toolbar, for comments, 210–211

truncated text, 9
two-variable data table, 505–506

U

underscore (_), custom number format, 235
Undo button, 10
unhide
    rows and columns, 92–93
    worksheets and workbooks, 409–410
    See also displaying/hiding
unlocking cells, 274–275
user name for comments, 211

V

validating data entry, 494–496
value axis, 166
variables
    data tables and, 505–506
    Scenario Manager for, 508–512
VBA for macros, 410–414
vertical alignment, 111–112
viruses and email attachments, 207
Visual Basic for Applications, 410–414
VLOOKUP function, 322–327

W

Web folders
    publishing, 384–388
    save a workbook to, 386–388
Web Page Preview command, 380
Web pages
    importing from, 389–391
    interactive PivotTables, 465–468
    interactive worksheets, 382–383
    naming conventions, 384
    publishing with Web folders, 384–388
    Save As Web Page command, 380–382

save image from, 361–363
    See also online collaboration
what-if analyses, 238
    absolute references and, 228–233
    Goal Seeker tool, 345–346
    Scenario Manager for, 508–512
window panes, splitting, 139–140
WordArt, 295–296
workbooks
    convert to other formats, 376–380
    defined, 6
    emailing, 220–223
    hide/unhide, 409–410
    multiple-sheet workbooks, 257–277
    passwords for, 533–537
    properties for, 528–533
    protecting, 272–275
workgroup collaboration
    linking workbooks, 553–554
    merging multiple workbooks, 546–551
    passwords for workbooks, 533–537
    properties for workbooks, 528–533
    sharing workbooks, 542–546
    track changes to workbooks, 538–541
    workspaces, 551–552
worksheets
    copying, 261–262
    defined, 6
    hide/unhide, 409–410
    large worksheets, working with, 135–153
    managing, 164–166
    navigating, 6
    tiled backgrounds on, 372
workspaces, 551–552
Wrap Text option, 109

Z

zero symbol, custom number format, 235
Zoom Control, 91